Being tech-savvy is essential to success in college. You probably already have most of the skills you need but if you don't, it's important to make an effort to become fluent in the following:

- ✔ Composing in word-processing programs such as *Microsoft Word* or *Google Drive*
- ✔ Sending emails and attaching files to them
- ✔ Using the Internet and evaluating websites **(See Chapter 3, Chapter 13, and Chapter 21)**
- ✔ Using your library's electronic resources **(See Chapter 12)**
- ✔ Scanning and inserting documents that contain images as well as text
- ✔ Using technology to enhance a project—for example, learning how to use *PowerPoint* or *Keynote* for a presentation **(See Chapter 33)** or *Google Sheets* to make a table **(See Chapter 23)**
- ✔ Syncing information among various devices (phone, computer, tablet, etc.)
- ✔ Knowing when to use technology —and when not to **(See Chapters 22–23)**

FIGURE 10 Sample notes on a journal article in the *ZotPad* app.

Notetaking apps like *ZotPad* can be useful both in and out of the classroom.

Be aware of the online services your school offers.

Many campuses rely on customizable information-management systems called **portals**. You can use your user ID (or school email) and password to access services such as locating and contacting your advisor and viewing your class schedule and grades. Portals may also be connected to individual course websites.

9 Make contacts.

Classmates

Be sure you have the phone numbers and email addresses of at least two students in each of your classes. These will come in handy if you miss class, need help understanding notes, or want to form a study group.

FIGURE 11 Student talking with instructor.

Friends from Activities or Work-Study Jobs

Build relationships with students who participate in college activities with you. They are likely to share your goals and interests, and you may want to discuss decisions like choosing a major, considering further education, and making career choices.

Instructors

Develop a relationship with your instructors, particularly those in the areas of study that interest you most.

One of the things cited most often in studies of successful students is the importance of **mentors**, experienced academic and professional individuals whose advice you trust. Long after you leave college, you will find these contacts useful.

10 Be a lifelong learner.

✔ Get in the habit of reading local and national newspapers.
✔ Make connections outside the college community to keep in touch with the larger world.
✔ Attend plays and concerts sponsored by your school or community.
✔ Go to lectures offered at your local library or bookstore.

FIGURE 12 Students at a performance.

Never miss an opportunity to learn.

Think about the life you will lead after college. Think about who you want to be and what you have to do to get there. This is what successful students do.

The Brief Cengage Handbook

KIRSZNER
& MANDELL

Eighth Edition
2016 MLA Update Edition

Laurie G. Kirszner
University of the Sciences, Emeritus

Stephen R. Mandell
Drexel University

CENGAGE
Learning·

Australia • Brazil • Mexico • Singapore • United Kingdom • United States

CENGAGE
Learning®

The Brief Cengage Handbook, Eighth Edition 2016 MLA Update Edition
Laurie G. Kirszner,
Stephen R. Mandell

Product Director: Monica Eckman

Product Team Manager: Nicole Morinon

Product Manager: Laura Ross

Senior Content Developer: Leslie Taggart

Content Developer: Karen Mauk

Associate Content Developer: Karolina Kiwak

Associate Content Developer: Rachel Smith

Product Assistant: Claire Branman

Senior Managing Content Developer: Cara Douglass-Graff

Senior Marketing Manager: Erin Parkins

Senior Content Project Manager: Jennifer K. Feltri-George

Senior Art Director: Marissa Falco

Manufacturing Planner: Betsy Donaghey

IP Analyst: Ann Hoffman

IP Project Manager: Farah Fard

Production Service and Compositor: Karen Stocz, Cenveo® Publisher Services

Text and Cover Designer: Cenveo

Cover Image: James Weinberg

For product information and technology assistance, contact us at **Cengage Learning Customer & Sales Support, 1-800-354-9706.**

For permission to use material from this text or product, submit all requests online at **www.cengage.com/permissions**. Further permissions questions can be emailed to **permissionrequest@cengage.com**.

Library of Congress Control Number: On file.

ISBN: 978-1-337-28098-3

Loose-leaf Edition:
ISBN: 978-1-337-27989-5

Cengage Learning
20 Channel Center Street
Boston, MA 02210
USA

Cengage Learning is a leading provider of customized learning solutions with employees residing in nearly 40 different countries and sales in more than 125 countries around the world. Find your local representative at **www.cengage.com**.

Cengage Learning products are represented in Canada by Nelson Education, Ltd.

To learn more about Cengage Learning Solutions, visit **www.cengage.com**.

Purchase any of our products at your local college store or at our preferred online store **www.cengagebrain.com**.

Printed in China
Print Number: 02   Print Year: 2017

How to Use This Book

We would like to introduce you to the eighth edition of *The Brief Cengage Handbook*, a compact, easy-to-use reference guide for college students that comes out of our years of experience as full-time teachers of writing. This handbook offers concise yet complete coverage of the writing process, critical thinking, argumentation, common sentence errors, grammar and style, word choice, punctuation and mechanics, English for speakers of other languages, and college survival skills. In addition, it includes the most up-to-date information on composing in digital environments; MLA, APA, Chicago, and CSE documentation styles; writing in the disciplines; and document design.

Throughout, we balance what is new with practical advice from our years in the classroom. For this reason, despite its compact size, *The Brief Cengage Handbook* is more than just a quick reference; it is a comprehensive guide for writing in college and beyond. Most of all, it is a book that writers can depend on not only for sound, sensible advice about grammar and usage but also for up-to-date information about composing in various digital environments.

What's New in the Eighth Edition?

In this new edition, we kept what students and instructors told us worked well, and we fine-tuned what we thought could work better. In addition, we expanded our coverage to include the material students need to function in today's classrooms—and in today's world.

- **Updated and expanded coverage of the rhetorical situation** in Chapter 1, "Understanding the Rhetorical Situation," helps students make informed choices about content, emphasis, organization, format, style, and tone.
- **Three new chapters** (Chapter 9, "Writing Proposals"; Chapter 21, "Understanding, Exploring, and Developing Multimodal Texts"; and Chapter 25, "Composing a Rhetorical Analysis") guide students through the process of developing and delivering various texts in a range of genres.
- **Two thoroughly revised research chapters** (Chapter 12, "Finding Information," and Chapter 13, "Evaluating Sources") reflect the way students conduct research and address the issues they're likely to encounter.
- **Chapter 17, "MLA Documentation Style,"** includes the updated documentation guidelines put forth in the eighth edition of the *MLA Handbook* (2016).

- **Updated and expanded coverage of APA, Chicago, and CSE documentation styles** in Chapters 18–20 includes numerous model citations that help students correctly apply the latest documentation guidelines when writing in various disciplines.
- **New planning guides** throughout the text help students plan and organize a range of documents in various formats.
- **New exercises** throughout the text allow students to practice at each stage of the writing, revising, and editing processes.
- **A new "Ten Habits of Successful Students" foldout** illustrates and helps students apply the strategies of successful students both in and out of college.

Features of *The Brief Cengage Handbook*

Throughout the eighth edition of *The Brief Cengage Handbook*, we have focused on making the text clear, inviting, and easy to navigate. The book's many innovative pedagogical features, listed below, have helped us achieve these goals.

- **Frequently Asked Questions (FAQs)** appear at the beginning of each part, on the back of the tabbed dividers. Corresponding marginal FAQ icons appear in the chapters beside each answer.
- **Collaborative writing icons** appear alongside sections and exercises that emphasize peer review and other collaborative work.
- **Numerous checklists** summarize key information.
- **Close-up boxes** provide an in-depth look at some of the more challenging writing-related issues students will encounter.
- **Part 5** includes the most up-to-date documentation and format guidelines from the Modern Language Association, the American Psychological Association, the University of Chicago Press, and the Council of Science Editors. Specially designed documentation directories make it easy to locate models for various kinds of sources, including those found in online databases such as *Academic Search Premier* and *LexisNexis*. In addition, annotated diagrams of sample works-cited entries clearly illustrate the elements of proper citations.
- **Marginal cross-references** throughout the book enable students to flip directly to other sections that treat topics in more detail.
- **Marginal multilingual cross-references** (designated by **ml**) throughout the book direct students to appropriate sections of Part 13, "Composing for Multilingual Writers," where concepts are presented as they apply specifically to multilingual writers.
- **Multilingual tips** woven throughout the text explain concepts in relation to the unique experiences of multilingual students.

Acknowledgments

We would like to take this opportunity to thank Anne Stameshkin for her work on the new proposals and rhetorical analysis chapters, on the new exercises, on the new "Ten Habits of Successful Students" foldout, and on the documentation updates; Kelly Cannon, Muhlenberg College, for his research advice; and Sherry Rankins-Robertson, University of Arkansas at Little Rock, for her digital writing advice.

We also wish to thank the following reviewers for their advice, which helped us develop the eighth edition:

Negussie Abebe, *Lone Star College, University Park*
Christine Barr, *Lone Star College, University Park*
Christina Bisirri, *Seminole State College of Florida*
Woodward Bousquet, *Shenandoah University*
William Carney, *Cameron University*
James Crooks, *Shasta College*
Michael Duffy, *Moorpark College*
Christopher Ervin, *Western Kentucky University*
Daniel Fitzstephens, *University of Colorado Boulder*
Ginger Fray, *Lone Star College, Greenspoint Center*
Hillary Gallego, *North Lake College*
Andrew Green, *University of Miami*
Rebecca Hoff, *West Virginia University Parkersburg*
John Hyman, *American University*
Parmita Kapadia, *Northern Kentucky University*
Laura Knight, *Mercer County Community College*
Bobby Kuechenmeister, *University of Toledo*
Laura La Flair, *Belmont Abbey College*
Angela Laflen, *Marist College*
Meredith Love-Steinmetz, *Francis Marion University*
Walter Lowe, *Green River Community College*
Cassie Plott, *Rowan-Cabarrus Community College*
Chrishawn Speller, *Seminole State College of Florida*
Mary Tripp, *University of Central Florida*
Isera Tyson-Miller, *State College of Florida*
Martha Vertreace-Doody, *Kennedy-King College*
Alex Vuilleumier, *Portland Community College*
Ann Westrick, *Bowling Green State University*
Karen Wilson, *Lakeland Community College*

At Cengage, we are grateful to Nicole Morinon, Product Team Manager; Laura Ross, Product Manager; Leslie Taggart, Senior Content Developer; Rachel Smith, Associate Content Developer; and Claire Branman, Product Assistant, for keeping the project moving along; and to Rosemary Winfield, Senior Content Project Manager, for her careful attention to detail. Our biggest thanks go to Karen Mauk, our wonderful Content Developer; as always, it has been a pleasure to work with her.

The staff of Cenveo did its usual stellar job, led by our talented Project Manager and Copyeditor Karen Stocz. James Weinberg's cover design is the icing on the cake.

We would also like to thank our families for being there when we needed them. And, finally, we each thank the person on the other side of the ampersand for making our collaboration work one more time.

Laurie Kirszner
Steve Mandell
January 2016

Teaching and Learning Resources

Online Instructor's Manual and Answer Key

The Online Instructor's Manual and Answer Key contains an abundance of instructor materials, including sample syllabi, activities, and answers to the book's exercises. To download or print the manual, log on to login.cengage.com with your faculty account.

MindTap

MindTap® English for Kirszner and Mandell's *The Brief Cengage Handbook*, eighth edition, engages your students to become better thinkers, communicators, and writers by blending your course materials with content that supports every aspect of the writing process.

- Interactive activities on grammar and mechanics promote application in student writing
- Easy-to-use paper management system helps prevent plagiarism and allows for electronic submission, grading, and peer review
- A vast database of scholarly sources with video tutorials and examples supports every step of the research process
- Professional tutoring guides students from rough drafts to polished writing
- Visual analytics track student progress and engagement
- Seamless integration into your campus learning management system keeps all your course materials in one place

MindTap lets you compose your course, your way.

Approaching Texts

Approaching Texts

? Frequently Asked Questions

CHAPTER 1

Understanding the Rhetorical Situation

Everyone who sets out to write confronts a series of choices. In the academic, public, and private writing that you do in school, on the job, and in your personal life, your understanding of the rhetorical situation is essential—influencing the choices you make about content, emphasis, organization, format, style, and tone.

Note: Like written texts, <u>visual texts</u>—fine art, charts and graphs, photographs, infographics, maps, advertisements, and so on—are also created in response to specific rhetorical situations.

See 9c

Before you begin to write, you should try to answer the following questions:

- What is my **rhetorical situation**, or context for writing?
- What is my **purpose** for writing?
- Who is my **audience**?
- What **genre** should I use in this situation?

1a Considering the Rhetorical Situation

Begin by considering the <u>rhetorical situation</u>, the set of conventions that are associated with a particular writing assignment. By keeping this rhetorical situation in mind throughout the writing process, you make sure that your writing keeps its focus.

See 9c

In college, the rhetorical situation is often identified by your assignment. For example, if your assignment asks you to write about an event, such as a family tradition, you will need to identify a specific occurrence, such as a family beach trip, to focus on. In personal, civic, and professional writing, the rhetorical situation is often determined by a particular event, interest, or concern that creates the need for this writing. For example, you may write a proposal to your boss to request funding for a project or to suggest a better way of performing a particular task.

EXERCISE 1.1

A. Focus on a book that you liked or disliked very much. How would you write about the book in each of the following rhetorical situations? Consider how each situation would affect your choice of content, style, organization, format, tone, and emphasis.

- A post on your composition class's course site reflecting on your impressions of the book
- An exam question that asks you to summarize the book's ideas
- A book review for a composition class in which you evaluate the book's strengths and weaknesses
- An email in which you try to convince your local school board that the book should (or should not) be purchased for a public high school's library
- An editorial for your school newspaper in which you try to persuade other students that the book is (or is not) worth reading
- A text to a friend recommending (or criticizing) the book

B. Write responses for two of the rhetorical situations listed in Part A of this exercise.

1b   Determining Your Purpose

In simple terms, your **purpose** for writing is what you want to accomplish. For instance, your purpose may be to **reflect**, to express feelings or look back on your thinking. Sometimes your purpose may be to **inform**, to convey factual information as accurately and as logically as possible. At other times, your purpose may be to **persuade**, to convince your readers. Finally, your purpose may be to **evaluate**, to make a judgment about something, as in a book or film review, a recommendation report, or a comparative analysis.

1 Writing to Reflect

In journals, writers are often introspective, exploring ideas and feelings to make sense of their experiences; in autobiographical memoirs and personal blog posts, writers communicate their emotions and reactions to others. Another type of reflective writing is **metacognitive writing**, in which writers explain what they have learned and consider the decisions made throughout the writing process.

At the age of five, six, well past the time when most other children no longer easily notice the difference between sounds uttered at home and words spoken in public, I had a different experience. I lived in a world magically compounded of sounds. I remained a child longer than most; I lingered too long, poised at the edge of language—often frightened by the sounds of *los gringos*, delighted by the sounds of Spanish at home. I shared with my family a language that was startlingly different from that used in the great city around us. (Richard Rodriguez, *Aria: Memoir of a Bilingual Childhood*)

2 Writing to Inform

In news articles, writers report information, communicating factual details to readers; in reference books, instruction manuals, textbooks, and websites sponsored by nonprofit and government agencies, writers provide definitions and explain concepts or processes, trying to help readers see relationships and understand ideas.

> Most tarantulas live in the tropics, but several species occur in the temperate zone and a few are common in the southern U.S. Some varieties are large and have powerful fangs with which they can inflict a deep wound. These formidable-looking spiders do not, however, attack man; you can hold one in your hand, if you are gentle, without being bitten. Their bite is dangerous only to insects and small mammals such as mice; for man it is no worse than a hornet's sting. (Alexander Petrunkevitch, "The Spider and the Wasp")

Note: In your personal writing, you may convey information informally in *Facebook* updates, tweets, instant messages, and text messages.

3 Writing to Persuade

In proposals and editorials, as well as in political blogs and in advertising, writers try to convince readers to accept their positions on various issues.

> America must make sure the melting pot continues to melt: immigrants must become Americans. Seymour Martin Lipset, professor of political science and sociology at the Hoover Institution, Stanford University, observes: "The history of bilingual and bicultural societies that do not assimilate are histories of turmoil, tension and tragedy. Canada, Belgium, Malaysia, Lebanon— all face crises of national existence in which minorities press for autonomy, if not independence. Pakistan and Cyprus have divided. Nigeria suppressed an ethnic rebellion. France faces difficulties with its Basques, Bretons and Corsicans." (Richard D. Lamm, "English Comes First")

4 Writing to Evaluate

In reviews of books, films, or performances and in reports, critiques, and program evaluations, writers assess the validity, accuracy, and quality of information, ideas, techniques, products, procedures, or services, perhaps assessing the relative merits of two or more things.

Review of *A Dance with Dragons* by George R. R. Martin. Random House, 2011. May 16, 2015.

> I am a fan of the HBO series *Game of Thrones*, so I was looking forward to the release of *A Dance with Dragons*, the fifth book in the series *A Song of Ice and Fire*. Although I found the fourth book in the series slightly disappointing,

A Dance with Dragons is a great read. Westeros, the world created by George R. R. Martin, has a complex history that stretches back thousands of years. The characters who inhabit Westeros are interesting and believable. Their various motives, flaws, and morals drive their actions in compelling ways with surprising and far-reaching consequences. It was easy to get lost in this faraway world and wrapped up in its people and history. I'm looking forward to seeing how this latest volume comes to life on the screen in *Game of Thrones*.

Although writers write to reflect, to inform, to persuade, and to evaluate, these purposes are not mutually exclusive, and writers may have other purposes as well. The checklist below lists some specific purposes for writing.

CHECKLIST

Determining Your Purpose

Before you begin to write, you need to determine why you are writing. Your purposes can include any of the following:

❑ to reflect	❑ to draw comparisons	❑ to take a stand
❑ to inform	❑ to make an analogy	❑ to identify problems
❑ to persuade	❑ to define	❑ to suggest solutions
❑ to evaluate	❑ to criticize	❑ to identify causes
❑ to explain	❑ to motivate	❑ to predict effects
❑ to amuse or entertain	❑ to satirize	❑ to interpret
❑ to discover	❑ to speculate	❑ to instruct
❑ to analyze	❑ to warn	❑ to inspire
❑ to debunk	❑ to reassure	

As you begin to write, determining your purpose for writing is critical. As you consider the requirements of your assignment, your rhetorical situation and purpose work together. Later, identifying and considering the needs of your audience will help you shape the content, organization, tone, and style of your writing.

EXERCISE 1.2

The two student paragraphs that follow treat the same general subject, but their purposes are different. What do you see as the primary purpose of each paragraph? What other purposes might each writer have had in mind?

1. Answer to an essay exam question: "Identify the Boston Massacre."

The Boston Massacre refers to a 1770 confrontation between British soldiers and a crowd of colonists. Encouraged by Samuel Adams, the citizens had become more and more upset over issues such as the British government's stationing troops and customs commissioners in Boston. When angry colonists attacked a customhouse sentry on March 5, 1770, a fight broke out. Soldiers fired into the crowd, and five civilians were killed. Although the soldiers were found guilty only of manslaughter and given only a token punishment, Samuel Adams's propaganda created the idea of a "massacre" in the minds of many Americans.

2. Excerpt from "The Ohio Massacre: 1770 Revisited" (student essay):

> In two incidents that occurred exactly two hundred years apart, civilian demonstrators were shot and killed by armed troops. Although civilians were certainly inciting the British troops, starting scuffles and even brawls, these actions should not have led the Redcoats to fire blindly into the crowd. Similarly, the Ohio National Guard should not have allowed themselves to be provoked by students who were calling names, shoving, or throwing objects, and Governor Rhodes should not have authorized the troops to fire their weapons. The deaths—five civilians in Boston, Massachusetts, in 1770, and four students in Kent, Ohio, in 1970—were all unnecessary.

1c Identifying Your Audience

When you are in the early stages of a writing project and staring at a blank screen, it is easy to forget that you are writing for an audience. However, most of the writing you compose is directed at a specific **audience**, a particular reader or group of readers. Sometimes your audience is indicated by your assignment; at other times, you must decide for yourself who your readers are.

1 Writing for an Audience

At different times, in different roles, you address a variety of audiences. Before you write, you should think about the characteristics of the audience (or audiences) that you will be addressing.

- **In your personal life**, you may send notes, emails, or text messages to friends and family members. You may find yourself writing on social media and for special occasions in a variety of formats or genres.

See 1d

- **In your public life**, as a citizen, a consumer, or a member of a community, you may respond to social, economic, or political issues by writing letters or emails to newspapers, public officials, or representatives of special interest groups. You might also be called on to write media releases, brochures, flyers, or newsletters for civic, political, or religious organizations.

See Ch. 31

- **As an employee**, you may write emails, memos, proposals, and reports to your superiors, to staff members you supervise, or to coworkers; you may also be asked to address customers or critics, board members or stockholders, funding agencies or the general public.

See
Pt. 7

- **As a student**, you will likely write reflective statements and responses as well as essays, reports, and exams in various academic disciplines. You may also participate in peer review sessions, writing evaluations of classmates' drafts as well as responses to classmates' comments about your own work-in-progress.

As you write, you shape your writing according to what you think your audience needs and expects. Your assessment of your readers' interests, educational level, biases, and expectations determines not only the information you include, but also what you emphasize and how you arrange your material.

2 The College Writer's Audience

As a student, you may be asked to write for a specific audience, or you may be asked to select an audience. Often, college writers assume they are writing for an audience of one: the instructor who assigns the essay; however, this is not always the case because many instructors want students to address real-life rhetorical situations.

When writing for your instructors, you need to demonstrate your knowledge of the subject; instructors want to see whether you can express your ideas clearly and accurately. They assign written work to encourage you to think critically, so the way you organize and express your ideas can be as important as the ideas themselves.

See
Ch. 7

Instructors expect accurate information, standard grammar and correct spelling, logically presented ideas, and a reasonable degree of stylistic sophistication. They also expect you to define your terms and to support your generalizations with specific examples. Finally, instructors expect you to draw your own conclusions and to provide full and accurate documentation for ideas that are not your own.

See
Pt. 5

If you are writing in an instructor's academic field, you can omit long overviews and basic definitions. Remember, however, that outside their areas of expertise, most instructors are simply general readers. If you think you may know more about a subject than your instructor does, be sure to provide background and to supply the definitions, examples, and analogies that will make your ideas clear.

Even though all academic fields of study—or **disciplines**—share certain values, instructors in different disciplines emphasize different aspects of writing. For example, they expect your writing to conform to discipline-specific formats, conventions, and citation systems. Often, their requirements will be different from those you will learn in your composition classes. (**Part 7** of this text highlights the key features of writing in other disciplines and includes examples of assignments from disciplines in the humanities, the social sciences, and the natural and applied sciences.)

3 Writing for Other Students

Before you submit an essay to an instructor, you may have an opportunity to participate in **peer review**, sharing your work with your fellow students and responding in writing to their work. When you participate in peer review, it is helpful to think of your classmates as an audience whose needs you should take into account.

MULTILINGUAL TIP

Instructors are available outside of class during office hours, which are typically listed on your course syllabi. Keep in mind that instructors are available throughout the semester to help you succeed in your courses. It is a good idea to contact your instructors during the first week of school to introduce yourself and to explain what you hope to learn in your courses. You can email them to set up appointments or stop by during office hours.

- **Writing Drafts** If you know that other students will read a draft of your essay, consider how they might react to your ideas. For example, are they likely to disagree with you? To be confused, or even mystified, by any of your references? To be shocked or offended by your essay's language or content? You should not assume that your fellow students will automatically share your values, political opinions, or cultural frame of reference. For this reason, it is important to maintain a neutral tone and use moderate language in your essay and to explain any historical, geographical, or cultural references that you think might be unfamiliar to your audience.

See 6c2

- **Making Comments** When you respond to another student's writing, you should take into account how he or she will react to your comments. Your tone is important. You want to be as encouraging (and as polite) as possible. In addition, keep in mind that your purpose is to offer insightful comments that can help your classmate write a stronger essay. (Your instructor may have specific response prompts that you should use to provide feedback.) Remember, when you respond to another student's essay, your goal is to be constructive, not critical or negative.

CHECKLIST
Writing for an Academic Audience

Before you respond to an assignment in your college courses, you need to identify the audience you are writing for. The following questions can help you understand what your audience expects:

- ❑ What discipline are you writing for?
- ❑ What kinds of assignments are typical of this discipline?
- ❑ What expectations do instructors in this discipline have?
- ❑ What style considerations are important in this discipline?
- ❑ What writing conventions are used in this discipline?
- ❑ What formats are used in this discipline?
- ❑ What research sources are used in this discipline?
- ❑ What documentation style is used in this discipline?

1d   Selecting a Genre

In your college courses, you will compose many different kinds of texts—for example, academic essays, book reviews, research reports, proposals, lab reports, and case studies. These different types of texts—with their distinctive characteristics and conventions—are referred to as **genres**. In simple terms, a genre is a way of classifying a text according to its style, structure, and format.

A writer's choice of the genre, structure, and medium for writing is based on the message he or she wants to send and the audience he or she intends to reach. For example, if a writer seeks to inform an audience about an upcoming sales event, an *Instagram* post might be appropriate for college students, but a newspaper advertisement might be better for a more mature audience.

Most college writing assignments specify a particular genre. For example, your composition instructor might ask you to write an essay about a personal experience, to evaluate a novel or a film, or to take a position on an issue that you feel strongly about. In these cases, your familiarity with the conventions of the narrative essay, the book or film review, and argumentative writing, respectively, would help you decide how to approach and develop the assignment. Your knowledge of the requirements and features of a specific genre would also be essential if you were going to complete a literature review for your psychology class, a lab report for your chemistry class, or a business proposal for your management class. (For detailed discussions of the genres most frequently used in various disciplines, **see Pts. 7 and 8.**)

CHAPTER **2**

Reading and Interpreting Texts

Reading is an essential part of learning. Before you can become an effective writer and a successful student, you need to know how to get the most out of the texts you read.

Central to developing effective reading skills is learning the techniques of **active reading**. Being an active reader means being actively involved with the text: marking the text in order to identify parallels, question ambiguities, distinguish important points from not-so-important ones, and connect causes with effects and generalizations with specific examples.

The understanding you gain from active reading prepares you to think (and write) critically about a text.

MULTILINGUAL TIP

When you read a text for the first time, don't worry about understanding every word. Instead, just try to get a general idea of what the text is about and how it is organized. Later on, you can use a dictionary to look up any unfamiliar words.

2a   Previewing a Text

Before you begin reading a text, you should preview it—that is, skim it to get a sense of the writer's subject and emphasis.

When you preview a **periodical article**, skim the introductory and concluding paragraphs for summaries of the writer's main points. (Journal articles in the sciences and social sciences often begin with summaries called **abstracts**.) Thesis statements, topic sentences, repeated key terms, transitional words and phrases, and transitional paragraphs can also help you to identify the key points a writer is making. In addition, look for the **visual cues**—such as headings and lists—that writers use to emphasize ideas.

See 23b-c

When you preview a **book**, start by looking at its table of contents; then, turn to its index. A quick glance at the index will reveal the amount of coverage the book gives to subjects that may be important to you. As you leaf through the chapters, look at pictures, graphs, or tables and the captions that appear with them.

Close-Up   VISUAL CUES

When you preview a text, don't forget to note the use of color and of various typographical elements—typeface and type size, boldface and italics—to emphasize ideas.

CHECKLIST
Previewing a Text
When you preview a text, try to answer these questions:

❏ What is the text's general subject?

❏ What are the writer's main points?

❏ How much space does the writer devote to topics relevant to your interests or research?

continued

Previewing a Text *(continued)*

- ❏ What other topics are covered?
- ❏ Who is the author of the text? What do you know about this writer?
- ❏ Is the text current? Is its information up to date?
- ❏ Does the text strike you as interesting, accessible, and useful?

2b　Highlighting a Text

When you have finished previewing a work, photocopy relevant sections of books and articles, and print out useful material from online sources. Then, **highlight** the pages using a system of graphic symbols and underlining to identify the writer's key points and their relationships to one another.

CHECKLIST

Using Highlighting Symbols

When you read a text, use strategies such as the following to help you understand the material:

- ❏ Underline to indicate information you should read again.
- ❏ Box or circle key words or important phrases.
- ❏ Put question marks next to confusing passages, unclear points, or words you need to look up.
- ❏ Draw lines or arrows to show connections between ideas.
- ❏ Number points that are discussed in sequence.
- ❏ Draw a vertical line in the margin to set off an important section.
- ❏ Star especially important ideas.

2c　Annotating a Text

After you have read through your material once, read it again—this time, more critically. At this stage, you should **annotate** the content, recording your responses to what you read. This process of recording notes in the margins or between the lines will help you to better understand the writer's ideas and your own reactions to those ideas.

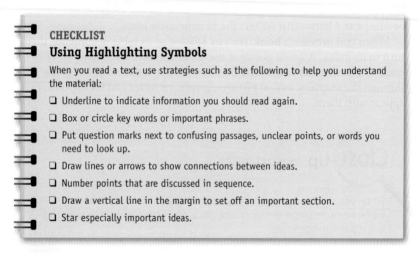

MULTILINGUAL TIP

You may find it useful to use your native language when you annotate a text.

Some of your annotations may be relatively straightforward. For example, you may define new words, identify unfamiliar references, or jot down brief summaries. Other annotations may reflect your personal reactions to the text. For example, you may identify a parallel between your own experience and one described in the text, or you may note your opinion of the writer's position.

As you start to **think critically** about a text, your annotations may identify points that confirm (or dispute) your own ideas, question the appropriateness or accuracy of the writer's support, uncover the writer's biases, or even question (or challenge) the writer's conclusion.

See Ch. 7

The following passage illustrates a student's highlighting and annotations of a passage from Michael Pollan's book *The Omnivore's Dilemma.*

People drank 5x as much as they do today

In the early years of the nineteenth century, Americans began drinking more than they ever had before or since, embarking on a collective bender that confronted the young republic with its first major public health crisis—the obesity epidemic of its day. Corn whiskey, suddenly superabundant and cheap, became the drink of choice, and in 1820 the typical American was putting away half a pint of the stuff every day. That comes to more than five gallons of spirits a year for every man, woman, and child in America. The figure today is less than one.

!!

As the historian W. J. Rorabaugh tells the story in *The Alcoholic Republic*, we drank the hard stuff at breakfast, lunch, and dinner, before work and after and very often during. Employers were expected to supply spirits over the course of the workday; in fact, the modern coffee break began as a late-morning whiskey break called "the elevenses." (Just to pronounce it makes you sound tipsy.) Except for a brief respite Sunday morning in church, Americans simply did not gather—whether for a barn raising or quilting bee, corn husking or political rally—without passing the whiskey jug. Visitors from Europe—hardly models of sobriety themselves—marveled at the free flow of American spirits.

?

"Come on then, if you love toping," the journalist William Cobbett wrote his fellow Englishmen in a dispatch from America. "For here you may drink yourself blind at the price of sixpence."

*

Did the gov't take action?

The results of all this toping were entirely predictable: a rising tide of public drunkenness, violence, and family abandonment, and a spike in alcohol-related diseases. Several of the Founding Fathers—including George Washington, Thomas Jefferson, and John Adams—denounced the excesses of "the Alcoholic Republic," inaugurating an American quarrel over drinking that would culminate a century later in Prohibition.

why?

*

But the outcome of our national drinking binge is not nearly as relevant to our own situation as its underlying cause. Which, put simply, was this: American farmers were producing far too much corn. This was

Examples from contemporary US farming?

?

This is his point

particularly true in the newly settled regions west of the Appalachians, where fertile, virgin soils yielded one bumper crop after another. A mountain of surplus corn piled up in the Ohio River Valley. <u>Much as today, the astounding productivity of American farmers proved to be their own worst enemy, as well as a threat to public health.</u> For when yields rise, the market is flooded with grain, and its price collapses. What happens next? The excess (biomass) works like a vacuum in reverse: <u>Sooner or later, clever marketers will figure out a way to induce the human omnivore to consume the surfeit of cheap calories.</u>

2d Reading Electronic Texts

Even when electronic documents physically resemble print documents (as they do in online newspaper articles), the way they present information can be very different. Print documents are **linear**; that is, readers move in a straight line from the beginning of a document to the end. Print documents are also self-contained, including all the background information, explanations, supporting details, and visuals necessary to make their point.

Electronic documents, however, are usually not linear. They often include advertising, marginal commentary, and graphics, and they may also include sound and video. In addition, links embedded in the text encourage readers to go to other sites for facts, statistical data, visuals, or additional articles that supplement the discussion. For example, readers of the electronic discussion of gun control pictured in Figure 2.1 could link to FBI data about the connection between "concealed carry laws" and violent crime. Once they access this material, they can choose to read it carefully, skim it, or ignore it.

The format of electronic texts presents challenges to readers. First, because links to other material interrupt the document's flow, it may be hard for readers to focus on a writer's main idea and key points or to follow an argument's logic. In addition, pages may be very busy, crowded with distracting marginalia, visuals, and advertisements. For these reasons, it makes sense to use a slightly different process when you apply active reading strategies to an electronic text.

Previewing During the previewing stage, you will probably want to skim the text online, doing your best to ignore visuals, marginal commentary, advertising, and links. If the text looks like something you will want to read more closely, you should print it out (taking care to print the "printer-friendly" version, which will usually omit the distracting material and enable you to focus on the text's content).

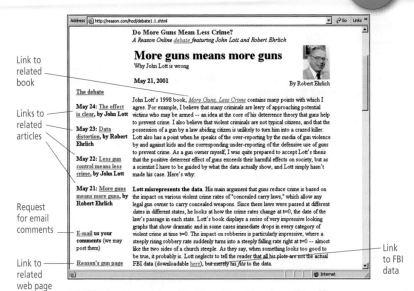

Link to related book

Links to related articles

Request for email comments

Link to related web page

Link to FBI data

FIGURE 2.1 Excerpt from "Do More Guns Mean Less Crime?" A *Reason Online* Debate. Reprinted by permission of Reason.

Highlighting and Annotating   Once you have hard copy of an electronic text, you can proceed to highlight and annotate it just as you would a print text. Reading on hard copy will enable you to follow the writer's main idea instead of clicking on every link. However, you should be sure to circle any links that look promising so you can explore them later on.

Note: You can also highlight and annotate web-based texts by using a program such as *Diigo*, which makes it possible for you to highlight and write self-stick notes on electronic documents.

EXERCISE 2.1

Find an article that interests you in a print or online newspaper or magazine. Read it carefully, highlighting it as you read. When you have finished, annotate the article. Then, answer the following questions:

- What is the writer's general subject?
- What are the writer's main points?
- What examples and details does the writer use to support these main points?
- What questions do you have about the writer's ideas?

2e Writing a Critical Response

Once you have previewed, highlighted, and annotated a text, you should have the understanding (and the material) you need to write a **critical response** that *summarizes, analyzes,* and *interprets* the text's key ideas and perhaps *evaluates* them as well. It can also *synthesize* the ideas in the text with ideas in other texts.

The following is a student's critical response to the passage from *The Omnivore's Dilemma* on pages 13–14.

Author and title identified — In an excerpt from his book *The Omnivore's Dilemma*, Michael Pollan discusses the drinking habits of nineteenth-century Americans and makes a connection between the cause of this "national drinking binge" and

Summary — the factors behind our twenty-first-century unhealthy diets. In both cases, he blames the overproduction of grain by American farmers. He links nineteenth-century overproduction of corn with "a rising tide of public drunkenness, violence, and family abandonment, and a spike in

Analysis and interpretation — alcohol-related deaths," and he also links the current overproduction of grain with a "threat to public health." Although there are certainly other causes of our current problems with obesity, particularly among young

Evaluation — children, Pollan's analogy makes sense. As long as farmers need to sell their overabundant crops, consumers will be presented with a "surfeit of cheap calories"—with potentially disastrous results.

EXERCISE 2.2

Write a critical response that reacts to the article you highlighted and annotated in Exercise 2.1.

CHECKLIST

Analyzing Texts

As you first read a text, keep the following questions in mind:

❑ Does the text provide any information about the writer's background? If so, how does this information affect your reading of the text?

❑ What is the writer's purpose? How can you tell?

❑ What audience is the text aimed at? How can you tell?

❑ What is the text's most important idea? What support does the writer provide for that idea?

Then, as you look more closely at the text, think about these questions:

❑ What information can you learn from the text's introduction and conclusion?

❑ What information can you learn from the thesis statement and topic sentences?

❑ Does the writer make any statements that suggest a particular bias?

❑ How would you characterize the writer's tone?

See
7c

❑ Are there parallels between the writer's experiences and your own?

❑ Where do you agree with the writer? Where do you disagree?

CHAPTER **3**

Reading and Interpreting Visuals

The texts you read in college courses—books, newspapers, and periodical articles, in print or online—are often accompanied by visual images. For example, textbooks often include illustrations to make complex information more accessible, newspapers use photographs to break up columns of written text, and websites use graphics of all kinds to add visual appeal.

Close-Up KINDS OF VISUALS

Visuals are used to convey information to supplement written text; they may also be used to persuade as well as to amuse.

Fine Art

Liliya Kulianionak/Shutterstock

Profile of a Woman Wearing a Jabot (pastel on paper) by Mary Stevenson Cassatt (1844–1926).

Photographs

Julian W/Shutterstock.com

Chinese traditional opera actor.

Maps

MAPS.com/Corbis

Map of Dublin, Ireland.

Cartoons

Stan Eales/CartoonStock.com

Cartoon by Stan Eales.

Scientific Diagrams

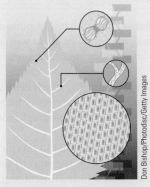

Plant engineering diagram.

Advertisements

Mini Cooper ad.

Infographics

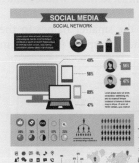

Social media infographic.

Bar Graphs

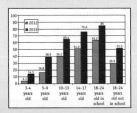

Bar graph from student essay.

Tables

Table 1

Relationship between Sleep Deprivation and Academic Performance

Grade Totals	Sleep Deprived	Not Sleep Deprived	Usually Sleep Deprived	Improved	Harmed	Continue Sleep Deprivation?
A = 10	4	6	1	4	0	4
B = 20	9	11	8	8	1	8
C = 10	10	0	6	5	4	7
D = 10	8	2	2	1	3	2
Total	31	19	17	18	8	21

Table from student essay.

3a   Analyzing and Interpreting Visuals

Because the global audience is becoming increasingly visual, it is important for you to acquire the skills needed to read and interpret visuals as well as to use them in your own written work. (For information on incorporating visuals into your own writing, **see 6b2**.)

The powerful newspaper photograph shown in Figure 3.1, which depicts a Marine in front of the Vietnam Veterans Memorial, uses a variety of techniques to convey its message. To **analyze and interpret** this photograph, you need to determine what strategies it uses to achieve its effect.

You might notice right away that contrasts are very important in this picture. In the background is the list of soldiers who died in the war; in the foreground, a lone member of a Marine honor guard stands in silent vigil, seemingly as static as the names carved in granite. Still, viewers know that the Marine is motionless only in the picture; when the photographer puts the camera down, the Marine will live on, in contrast to those whose names are listed behind him.

The large image of the Marine set against the smaller names in the background also suggests that the photographer's purpose is at least in

The whole world is watching.

Bryan Grigsby

Member of Marine honor guard passes the Vietnam memorial on which names of casualties of the war are inscribed.

FIGURE 3.1 Newspaper photograph taken at the Vietnam Veterans Memorial.

part to capture the contrast between the past and the present, the dead and the living. Thus, the photograph has a persuasive purpose: it suggests, as its title states, that "the whole world is watching" (and, in fact, *should* be watching) this scene in order to remember the past and honor the dead.

To convey their ideas, visuals often rely on contrasting light and shadow and on the size and placement of individual images (as well as on the spatial relationship of these images to one another and to the whole). In addition, visuals often use some words (captions, slogans, explanatory text), and they may also include color, animation, audio narration, and even musical soundtracks. Given the complexity of most visuals and the number of individual elements each one uses to convey its message, analyzing (or "reading") visual texts can be challenging. This task will be easier, however, if you follow the same **active reading** process you use when you read a written text.

3b Previewing a Visual

Just as with a written text, the first step in analyzing a visual text is to **preview** it, skimming it to get a sense of its subject, purpose, and emphasis. It is a good idea to begin thinking about who the audience might be and what techniques are being used to attract that audience's attention. At this stage, you may notice little more than the visual's major features: its central image, its dominant colors, its use of white space, and the most prominent words or lines of written text. Each of these elements sends a message about the product to the audience. Still, even these elements can give you a general idea of what the focus of the visual is and what purpose it might have.

For example, the New Balance ad shown in Figure 3.2 includes two large images—a foot and a shoe—both with the distinctive New Balance "N" logo. This logo also appears in the slogan "N is for fit," which has a prominent central position. The slogan is placed in the center of the advertisement, dividing the two images, with the text that explains the visual message appearing in much smaller type at the bottom of the advertisement. Yellow is used to highlight the logo, the shoe's tread, and the word *fit*.

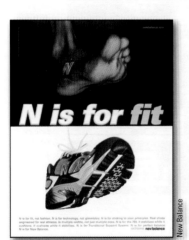

FIGURE 3.2 Magazine ad for New Balance sneakers.

3c　Highlighting and Annotating a Visual

When you **highlight** a visual text, you mark it to help you identify key images and their relationship to one another. You might, for example, use arrows to point to important images, or you might circle key words or details. When you **annotate** a visual text, you record your reactions to the images and words you see. (If a visual's background is dark, or if you are not permitted to write directly on it, you can do your highlighting and annotating on small self-stick notes.)

A student in a composition class was asked to analyze the advertisement for Mini Cooper automobiles shown in Figure 3.3. When she visited the company website, she saw that Mini Cooper was appealing to consumers who value affordability and reliability as well as the company's commitment to "minimalism" and fuel efficiency. However, the website was also appealing to those looking for features such as high performance, sporty design, and creativity—for example, the opportunity to "build your own" car by choosing features and colors. The student's highlighting and annotating

FIGURE 3.3 Mini Cooper ad.

focus on how the ad's written text and visuals work together to present the company's message: that the Mini Cooper is not just a practical choice but also one that offers possibilities for excitement and adventure.

CHECKLIST

Analyzing Visuals

❑ Who created the visual? Was the entire image created by one person, or is someone's work being used by another person for a particular purpose?

❑ For what purpose was the visual created? For example, does it seem to be primarily intended to be a work of art? Was it designed primarily to inform? To persuade? To entertain or amuse?

❑ Where did you access the visual? Where did it originally appear? What is the target audience for this publication?

❑ What scene does the visual depict? What message does this scene convey?

❑ What individual images are shown in the visual? What associations do you think these images have for the visual's intended audience?

❑ Does the visual include a lot of blank space?

❑ How large are the various elements (words and images)?

❑ Is the background light or dark? Clear or blurred? What individual elements stand out most clearly against this background?

❑ What general mood is suggested by the visual's use of color and shadow?

❑ Does the visual include any written text? What is its purpose? How are text and images juxtaposed?

❑ In general terms, what is the visual's message? How do its individual elements help to communicate this message?

❑ How would the visual's message or impact be different if something were added? If something were deleted?

Note: For information on analyzing a visual, **see 24b4**. For information on using visuals (such as editorial cartoons, photos, charts, and graphs) to support an argument, **see 10a**.

EXERCISE 3.1

Use the checklist above to help you write a paragraph in response to each of the following assignments:

1. On your way to campus or work, locate a billboard or a prominent sign (for example, on a train platform or bus shelter). What product or service does it promote? To what audience is it directed? How do you know? What does the image seem to assume about its intended audience (age, class, gender, and so on)?

2. Compare and contrast two magazine, television, or Internet advertisements for the same type of product (an automobile or cologne, for instance) that are aimed at two different audiences. How are the two ads different? How does each ad aim to reach its audience? What elements contribute to the persuasive message of each ad?

3. Select a website related to one of your courses. What visual elements of the site—images, typeface and type size, color, and so on—contribute to its usefulness as an information resource? How might the site benefit from additional (or fewer) visual features?

4. Select a chapter from one of your textbooks, and examine the way in which content is arranged on the pages. What visual elements (headings, lists, charts, tables, photographs, and so on) can you identify? How do these elements highlight important information?

EXERCISE 3.2

Write a paragraph in which you analyze the ad shown in Figure 3.4. Working with one or more classmates, consider the following questions:

- What audience is being addressed?
- What is the ad's primary purpose?
- What message is being conveyed?
- How do the various visual elements work together to appeal to the ad's target audience?

FIGURE 3.4 Ad warning against texting while driving.

PART **2**

Developing Essay Projects

Developing Essay Projects

? Frequently Asked Questions

CHAPTER 4

Planning

4a Understanding the Writing Process

Writing is a constant process of decision making—of selecting, reconsidering, deleting, and rearranging material as you plan, shape, draft and revise, and edit and proofread your work.

The Writing Process

The writing process includes the following stages:

Planning: Consider the rhetorical situation; choose your topic; discover ideas to write about.

Shaping: Decide how to organize your material.

Drafting: Write your first draft.

Revising: "Re-see" what you have written; write additional drafts.

Editing: Check grammar, spelling, punctuation, and mechanics.

Proofreading: Reread every word, checking for any remaining errors.

Of course, the neatly defined stages listed above do not communicate the reality of the writing process. In practice, this process is neither a linear series of steps nor an isolated activity. (In fact, in a digital environment, a significant part of the writing process can take place in full view of an online audience.) Writing is also often interactive: the writing process can be interrupted (and supplemented) by emailing, blogging, chat room discussions, or exploring the Internet.

Moreover, the stages of the writing process actually overlap: as you look for ideas, you begin to shape your material; as you shape your material, you begin to compose; as you develop a draft, you reorganize your ideas; as you revise, you continue to discover new material. These stages may be repeated again and again throughout the writing process. In this sense, the writing process is cyclical. During your college years and in the years that follow, you will develop your own version of the writing process and use it whenever you write, adapting it to the audience, purpose, and writing situation at hand.

Close-Up   COLLABORATIVE WRITING PROJECTS

In school—and particularly in the workplace—you will find that writing is increasingly a collaborative effort. On a regular basis, you will work with others to plan projects, do research, draft different sections of a single document (or different components of a larger project), and offer suggestions for revision. Software such as *Google Drive* allows users to compose documents synchronously and, with the History feature, to view changes made in a file or revert to an earlier version of the file.

EXERCISE 4.1

Write a paragraph in which you describe your own writing process. If you prefer, you may draw a diagram that represents your process. What do you do first? What steps do you return to again and again? Which stages do you find most satisfying? Which do you find most frustrating? Compare your paragraph with the paragraph written by another student in your class. How are your processes alike and different?

4b   Computers and the Writing Process

See
Ch. 32

See
33d2

Computers are essential for writing and communicating in both academic and workplace settings. In addition to using word-processing applications for typical writing tasks, writers may rely on programs such as *PowerPoint*® or *Prezi* for giving presentations; *Publisher*® or an Adobe application, such as *Photoshop*, *Illustrator*, or *InDesign*, for creating customized résumés or brochures; and web-page authoring software such as *Dreamweaver*® or Web 2.0 technologies, such as *Wix*, *Weebly*, or *Word-Press*, for creating Internet-accessible documents that include images, movies, and a wide range of visual effects.

With the prominent role of the Internet in professional, academic, and personal communication, it is increasingly likely that the feedback you receive on your writing will be electronic. For example, if your instructor uses course management software such as *Blackboard*™ or *Canvas*, you may receive an email from your instructor about a draft that you have submitted to a digital drop box. Or, you may use discussion boards for attaching or sharing your documents with other students. Chat room and Net meeting software also allow you to discuss ideas collaboratively and to offer and receive feedback on drafts.

Although the specific tools you use may be course- or workplace-specific, you will still have to develop an efficient writing process. **Chapter 22** provides more comprehensive information on the options available to you as you compose in digital environments.

4c Understanding Your Assignment

Planning your essay—thinking about what you want to say and how you want to say it—begins well before you actually start recording your thoughts in any organized way. This planning is as important a part of the writing process as the writing itself. During this planning stage, you determine your **purpose** for writing and identify your **audience**. Then, you go on to focus on your assignment, choose and narrow your topic, and gather ideas.

Before you start to write, be sure you understand the exact requirements of your **assignment**. Ask questions if necessary, and be sure you understand the answers.

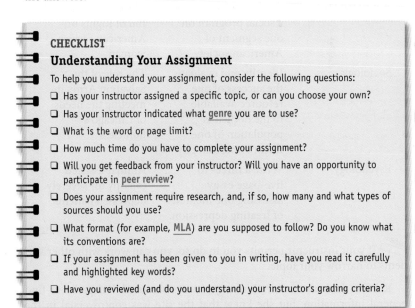

CHECKLIST

Understanding Your Assignment

To help you understand your assignment, consider the following questions:

- ❑ Has your instructor assigned a specific topic, or can you choose your own?
- ❑ Has your instructor indicated what genre you are to use?   See 1d
- ❑ What is the word or page limit?
- ❑ How much time do you have to complete your assignment?
- ❑ Will you get feedback from your instructor? Will you have an opportunity to participate in peer review?   See 6c2
- ❑ Does your assignment require research, and, if so, how many and what types of sources should you use?
- ❑ What format (for example, MLA) are you supposed to follow? Do you know what its conventions are?   See Ch. 17
- ❑ If your assignment has been given to you in writing, have you read it carefully and highlighted key words?
- ❑ Have you reviewed (and do you understand) your instructor's grading criteria?

Rebecca James, a first-year composition student, was given the following assignment prompt.

> *Wikipedia* has become a common starting point for students seeking information on a research topic. Because anyone can alter articles in this database, the reliability of *Wikipedia* as a valid source of information has been criticized by members of the academic community. In an essay of about three to five pages, evaluate the benefits and drawbacks of using *Wikipedia* in college research. To support your assessment, focus on a *Wikipedia* entry related to one of your courses.

The class was given three weeks to complete the assignment. Students were expected to do some research and to have the instructor and other students read and comment on at least one draft.

4d   Finding a Topic

Sometimes your instructor will assign a specific topic, but most of the time you will be given a general, structured assignment, which you will have to narrow to a **topic** that suits your purpose and audience.

From Assignment to Topic

Course	Assignment	Topic
American History	Analyze the effects of a social program on one segment of American society.	The effects of the GI Bill of Rights on American service-women
Sociology	Identify and evaluate the success of one resource available to the homeless population of one major American city.	The role of the Salvation Army in meeting the needs of Chicago's homeless
Psychology	Write a three- to five-page essay assessing one method of treating depression.	Animal-assisted therapy for severely depressed patients

& **Note:** If your instructor permits you to do so, you can work with other students to narrow your topic.

Rebecca had no trouble thinking of ways she used *Wikipedia* to find general information, but she knew that the site was controversial in the academic community because several of her instructors discouraged her from using it as a research source. As she composed her essay, she knew she would have to find a balance between the usefulness of *Wikipedia* on the one hand and its lack of reliability on the other.

Because her assignment was so specific, Rebecca was easily able to restate it in the form of a topic.

Topic: *Wikipedia* and college research

EXERCISE 4.2

College campuses across the United States are working to achieve sustainability, making an effort to be more sensitive to environmental concerns and to become "greener." With this exercise, you will begin the process of writing a three- to five-page essay in which you consider how your school is working toward this goal, what more it needs to do in the future, and how your suggestions for improvement will benefit your school.

Begin by researching *sustainability* online. Think about this issue as it applies to your school, and (with your instructor's permission) talk to your friends and classmates about it. When you think you understand what is being done (and what is not being done) to make your campus greener, list five specific environmental issues you could write about. Then, choose one of these areas of concern as the topic for your essay, and write a few sentences explaining why you selected this topic.

Your purpose in this essay will be to make recommendations for changes that could be adopted at your school. Your audience will be your composition instructor, members of your peer review group, and, possibly, a wider campus audience—for example, readers of your campus newspaper.

4e Finding Something to Say

Once you have a topic, you can begin to collect ideas for your essay, using one (or several) of the strategies discussed in the following pages.

1 Reading and Observing

As you read textbooks, magazines, and newspapers and explore the Internet, be on the lookout for ideas that relate to your topic. Films, television programs, interviews, letters, emails, and questionnaires can also provide material. But be sure your instructor permits such research—and remember to **document** ideas that are not your own. If you do not, you will be committing plagiarism.

See Ch. 16

When students in Rebecca's composition class were assigned to read *Wikipedia*'s policy statement, "Researching with *Wikipedia*," in preparation

MULTILINGUAL TIP
Don't use all your time making sure you are writing grammatically correct sentences. Remember, the purpose of writing is to communicate ideas. If you want to write an interesting, well-developed essay, you will need to devote plenty of time to the activities described in this section. You can then edit your work once you have determined and refined your ideas.

for their essay assignment, Rebecca learned about the problems of using *Wikipedia* in college-level research. This reading assignment gave her a wider perspective on her topic and encouraged her to look beyond her own experience with *Wikipedia*.

2 Keeping a Journal

Many professional writers keep print or electronic **journals** (sometimes in the form of blogs), writing in them regularly whether or not they have a specific project in mind. Journals, unlike diaries, do more than simply record personal experiences and reactions. In a journal, you explore ideas, ask questions, reflect on your thinking and the information you are processing, and draw conclusions. You might, for example, analyze your position on a political issue, try to solve an ethical problem, or trace the evolution of your ideas about an academic assignment.

One of Rebecca's journal entries appears below.

Journal Entry

> I use *Wikipedia* all the time, whenever something comes up that I want to know more about. Once my roommate and I were talking about graffiti art, and I started wondering how and where it began. I went to *Wikipedia* and found a long article about graffiti's origins and development as an art form. Some of my instructors say not to use *Wikipedia* as a research source, so I try to avoid going to the site for essay assignments. Still, it can be really helpful when I'm trying to find basic information. A lot of business and financial terms come up in my accounting class, and I can usually find simple explanations on *Wikipedia* of things I don't understand.

3 Freewriting

When you **freewrite**, you write nonstop about anything that comes to mind, moving as quickly as you can. Give yourself a set period of time—say, five minutes—and don't stop to worry about punctuation, spelling, or grammar, or about where your freewriting takes you. This strategy encourages your mind to make free associations; thus, it helps you to discover ideas you probably aren't even aware you have. When your time is up, look over what you have written, and underline, circle, bracket, star, boldface, or otherwise highlight the most promising ideas. You can then use one or more of these ideas as the center of a focused freewriting exercise.

When you do **focused freewriting**, you zero in on your topic. Here, too, you write without stopping to reconsider or reread, so you have no time to be self-conscious about style or form, to worry about the relevance of your ideas, or to count how many words you have (and panic about how many more you think you need). At its best, focused freewriting can suggest new details, a new approach to your topic, or even a more interesting topic.

Excerpts from Rebecca's freewriting and focused freewriting exercises appear below.

Freewriting (Excerpt)

I'm just going to list a bunch of things from my accounting class notes that I've recently looked up in *Wikipedia*: shareholder, stakeholder, strategic management, core competency, certified public accountant, certified management accountant, financial accounting, profit and loss. Not really sure which entry to focus on for this assignment. All the entries have strengths and weaknesses. I guess that's the point, but some *Wikipedia* articles are better than others. Maybe I'll choose an article that's sort of in the middle—one that provides some good basic info but could also be improved in some ways.

Focused Freewriting (Excerpt)

I think I'm going to use the "Financial Accounting" article as my focus for this essay. It explains this accounting field pretty clearly and concisely, which is good. However, it does have some problems, which are identified at the top of the article: specifically, a lack of cited sources. This article seems to represent a good balance of *Wikipedia*'s benefits and drawbacks. I hope I can think of enough things to say about the article in my essay. I could start off with some background info on *Wikipedia* and then lead into the financial accounting example. That way, I can use the financial accounting article to support my points about *Wikipedia* in general.

4 Brainstorming

One of the most useful ways to collect ideas is by brainstorming (either on your own or in a group). This strategy enables you to recall bits of information and to see connections among them.

When you **brainstorm**, you list all the points you can think of that seem pertinent to your topic, recording ideas—comments, questions, single words, symbols, or diagrams—without considering their relevance or trying to understand their significance.

An excerpt from Rebecca's brainstorming notes appears below.

Brainstorming Notes (Excerpt)

Topic: <u>Wikipedia</u> and College Research

What are <u>Wikipedia</u>'s benefits?

What are <u>Wikipedia</u>'s drawbacks?

→Head/Eisenberg article

→Reliability problems

Availability of info

→Financial accounting example

<u>Wikipedia</u> = a good starting point
for research

Close-Up COLLABORATIVE BRAINSTORMING

In addition to brainstorming on your own, you can also try **collaborative brainstorming**, working with other students to think of ideas to write about. If you and your classmates are working with similar but not identical topics—which is often the case—you will have the basic knowledge to help one another, and you can share your ideas without concern that you will all wind up focusing on the same few points.

Typically, collaborative brainstorming is an informal process. It can take place in person (in class or outside of class), on the phone, in a chat room, or on a class discussion board. Some instructors lead class brainstorming sessions; others arrange small-group brainstorming discussions in class.

Whatever the format, the exchange of ideas is likely to produce a lot of material that is not useful (and some that is irrelevant), but it will very likely also produce some ideas you will want to explore further. (Be sure you get your instructor's permission before you brainstorm with other students.)

5 Clustering

Clustering—sometimes called *webbing* or *mapping*—is similar to brainstorming. However, clustering encourages you to explore your topic in a more systematic (and more visual) manner.

Begin your cluster diagram by writing your topic in the center of a sheet of paper. Then, surround your topic with related ideas as they occur to you, moving outward from the general topic in the center and writing down increasingly specific ideas and details as you move toward the edges of the page. Following the path of one idea at a time, draw lines to create a diagram (often lopsided rather than symmetrical) that arranges ideas on spokes or branches radiating out from the center (your topic).

Rebecca's cluster diagram appears below.

Cluster Diagram

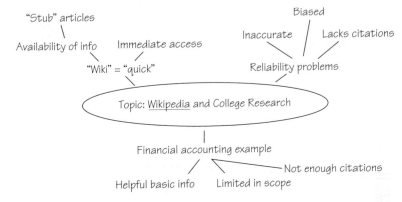

6 Asking Journalistic Questions

Journalists ask the **questions** *Who? What? Why? Where? When?* and *How?* to ensure that they have explored all angles of a story, and you can use these questions to make sure you have considered all aspects of your topic. Asking these basic questions is an orderly, systematic strategy for finding material to write about.

Rebecca's list of journalistic questions appears below.

Questions

- <u>Who</u> uses *Wikipedia*, and for what purposes?
- <u>What</u> is a wiki? <u>What</u> are *Wikipedia*'s benefits? <u>What</u> are its drawbacks?
- <u>When</u> was *Wikipedia* created? <u>When</u> did it become so popular among college students?
- <u>Where</u> do people go for more information after reading a *Wikipedia* article?
- <u>Why</u> are people drawn to *Wikipedia*? <u>Why</u> do some instructors discourage students from using it as a research source?
- <u>How</u> can *Wikipedia* be used responsibly? <u>How</u> can *Wikipedia* be improved?

> **MULTILINGUAL TIP**
>
> Using your native language for planning activities has both advantages and disadvantages. On the one hand, if you do not have the pressure of trying to think in English, you may be able to come up with better ideas. Also, using your native language may help you record your ideas more quickly and keep you from losing your train of thought. On the other hand, using your native language while planning may make it more difficult for you to move from the planning stages of your writing to drafting. After all, you will eventually have to write your essay in English.

7 Asking Journalistic Questions

If you have time, you can search for ideas to write about by asking a series of more focused questions about your topic. These **in-depth questions** can give you a great deal of information, and they can also suggest ways for you to eventually shape your ideas into paragraphs and essays.

In-Depth Questions

What happened? When did it happen? Where did it happen?	Questions suggest **narration** (an account of your first day of school; a summary of Emily Dickinson's life)
What does it look like? What does it sound like, smell like, taste like, or feel like?	Questions suggest **description** (of the Parthenon; of the electron microscope; of a website)
What are some typical cases or examples of it?	Question suggests **exemplification** (three infant day-care facilities; four popular fad diets)
How did it happen? What makes it work? How is it made?	Questions suggest **process** (how to apply for financial aid; how a bill becomes a law)
Why did it happen? What caused it? What does it cause? What are its effects?	Questions suggest **cause and effect** (the events leading to the Iraq War; the results of global warming; the impact of a new math curriculum)
How is it like other things? How is it different from other things?	Questions suggest **comparison and contrast** (of the popular music of the 1980s and 1990s; of two paintings)
What are its parts or types? Can they be separated or grouped? Do they fall into a logical order? Can they be categorized?	Questions suggest **division and classification** (components of the catalytic converter; kinds of occupational therapy; kinds of dietary supplements)
What is it? How does it resemble other members of its class? How does it differ from other members of its class?	Questions suggest **definition** (What is Marxism? What is photosynthesis? What is a wiki?)

An excerpt from Rebecca's list of in-depth questions appears below.

In-Depth Questions (Excerpt)

What are the elements of a helpful *Wikipedia* article? Comprehensive abstracts, internal links, external links, coverage of current and obscure topics.

What are the elements of an unreliable *Wikipedia* article? Factual inaccuracy, bias, vandalism, lack of citations.

Note: Many college assignments require research. **See Part 4** for information on composing with sources.

CHAPTER **5**

Shaping

Now it is time to start sifting through your ideas to choose those you can use. As you do this, you begin to **shape** your material into a thesis-and-support essay.

5a Understanding Thesis and Support

Your **thesis** is the main idea of your essay, the central point or claim that your ideas support. The concept of **thesis and support**—stating the thesis and then supplying information that explains and develops it—is central to much of the writing you will do in college and beyond.

PLANNING GUIDE

THESIS-AND-SUPPORT ESSAY

Your **assignment** will ask you to write an essay that supports a thesis.
Your **purpose** will be to present ideas and support them with specific reasons, examples, and so on.
Your **audience** will usually be your instructor or other students in your class.

continued

PLANNING GUIDE: Thesis-and-Support Essay *(continued)*

INTRODUCTION

Thesis statement templates:
- Although…, …
- Because…, it seems likely that…
- Many people believe…; however,…

- Begin by introducing readers to your subject.
- Use a specific introductory strategy to create interest.
- State your essay's thesis.

BODY PARAGRAPHS

Topic sentence templates:
- The first (second, third) cause is…
- One (another, the final) example is…

Templates for introducing support:
- For example,…
- As…points out,…
- According to…,…

- Begin each paragraph with a topic sentence that states the paragraph's main idea.
- In each paragraph, support the topic sentence with facts, details, reasons, examples, and so on.
- Arrange material in each paragraph according to a specific pattern of development: narration, cause and effect, comparison and contrast, and so on.
- Include transitional words and phrases to connect ideas within and between paragraphs.

CONCLUSION

Closing sentence templates:
- All in all,…
- All things considered,…
- For all these reasons,…

- Begin with a restatement of your thesis (in different words) or a review of your essay's main points.
- Use a specific concluding strategy to sum up your ideas.
- Try to close with a memorable sentence.

5b Developing a Thesis Statement

An effective **thesis statement** has four characteristics:

1. **An effective thesis statement clearly communicates your essay's main idea.** It tells readers what your essay's topic is and suggests what you will say about it. Thus, your thesis statement reflects your essay's purpose.

2. **An effective thesis statement is more than a general subject, a statement of fact, or an announcement of your intent.**

Subject	Statement of Fact	Announcement
The Military Draft	The United States currently has no military draft.	In this essay, I will reconsider our country's need for a draft.

Thesis Statement: Although an all-volunteer force has replaced the draft, a draft may eventually be necessary if the US is to remain secure.

3. **An effective thesis statement is carefully worded.** Because it communicates your essay's main idea, your thesis statement should be clearly and accurately worded. Your thesis statement—usually expressed in a single concise sentence—should be direct and straightforward. It should not include abstract language, overly complex terminology, or unnecessary details that might confuse or mislead readers.

Be particularly careful to avoid vague, wordy phrases—*centers on, deals with, involves, revolves around, has a lot to do with, is primarily concerned with*, and so on.

The real problem in our schools ~~does~~ not _{is} ~~revolve around~~ the absence of nationwide goals and standards; the problem is ~~primarily concerned with~~ the absence of resources.

Finally, an effective thesis statement should not include words or phrases such as "Personally," "I believe," "I hope to demonstrate," and "It seems to me," which weaken your credibility by suggesting that your conclusions are tentative or are based solely on opinion rather than on reading, observation, and experience.

4. **An effective thesis statement suggests your essay's direction, emphasis, and scope.** Your thesis statement should not make promises that your essay will not fulfill. It should suggest where you will place your emphasis and indicate in what order your major points will be discussed, as the following thesis statement does.

Effective Thesis Statement
Widely ridiculed as escape reading, romance novels are important as a proving ground for many never-before-published writers and, more significantly, as a showcase for strong heroines.

This thesis statement is effective because it tells readers that the essay to follow will focus on two major roles of the romance novel: providing markets for new writers and (more important) presenting strong female characters. It also suggests that the essay will briefly treat the role of the romance novel as escapist fiction. As the following diagram shows, this effective thesis statement also indicates the order in which the various ideas will be discussed.

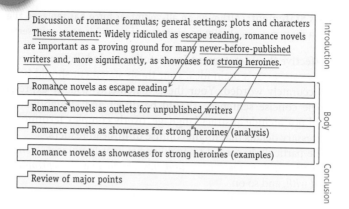

As she tried to decide on a thesis statement for her essay about *Wikipedia* and college research, Rebecca James reviewed her freewriting, brainstorming, and other prewriting material and also talked with friends, most of whom shared her own positive opinion of *Wikipedia*. To stress the value of *Wikipedia* in college research yet still acknowledge the drawbacks her instructors had pointed out, Rebecca drafted the following thesis statement.

Thesis Statement: Despite its limitations, *Wikipedia* can be a valuable tool for locating reliable research sources.

EXERCISE 5.1

Working in a group of three or four students, analyze each of the following items, and explain why none of them qualifies as an effective thesis statement.

1. In this essay, I will examine the environmental effects of residential and commercial development on the coastal regions of the United States.
2. Residential and commercial development in the coastal regions of the United States
3. How to avoid coastal overdevelopment
4. Coastal Development: Pro and Con
5. Residential and commercial development of America's coastal regions benefits some people, but it has a number of disadvantages.
6. The environmentalists' position on coastal development
7. More and more coastal regions in the United States are being overdeveloped.
8. Residential and commercial development guidelines need to be developed for coastal regions of the United States.
9. Coastal development is causing beach erosion.
10. At one time, I enjoyed walking on the beach, but commercial and residential development ruined the experience for me.

EXERCISE 5.2

Draft thesis statements for three of the following topics.

1. A local or national event that changed your life
2. Consequences of cheating in college
3. US immigration laws
4. Women in combat
5. Private versus public education
6. Birth control services provided by college health clinics
7. Government surveillance of phone and email conversations
8. What individuals can do to save the planet
9. The portrayal of an ethnic group in film or on television
10. Texting while driving

5c Revising Your Thesis Statement

At this point, your thesis statement is only **tentative**. As you write and re-write, you will think of new ideas and see new connections. As a result, you may change your essay's direction, emphasis, and scope, and if you do so, you must reword your thesis statement to reflect these modifications.

As Rebecca revised her essay, her thesis statement changed. Compare her tentative thesis above with her revised thesis statement in her essay's final draft in **6e**.

5d Constructing a Scratch Outline

Once you have a tentative thesis statement, you may want to construct a scratch outline to guide you as you write. A **scratch outline** is a brief, informal organizational plan that arranges your essay's main points (and perhaps its major supporting ideas) in an orderly way.

Rebecca's scratch outline appears below.

Scratch Outline

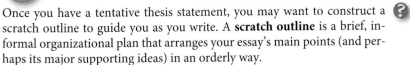

Thesis statement: Despite its limitations, *Wikipedia* can be a valuable tool for locating reliable research sources.

- Definition of *wiki* and explanation of *Wikipedia*
- *Wikipedia's* benefits
  - Links
  - Comprehensive abstracts
  - Current and popular culture topics
  - "Stub" articles

- *Wikipedia*'s potential
- *Wikipedia*'s drawbacks
  - Not accurate
  - Bias
  - Vandalism
  - Not enough citations
- Financial accounting example: benefits
- Financial accounting example: drawbacks

At this stage of the writing process, Rebecca decided that her scratch outline was all she needed to guide her as she wrote a first draft. (Later on, she might decide to construct a more formal outline to check her essay's logic and organization.)

Although you may be used to constructing outlines for your written work by hand, a number of software applications and formatting features can help in this process, including the outlining feature in some desktop publishing and word-processing programs (such as *Microsoft Word*). Another useful tool for outlining (particularly for **presentations**) is *Microsoft PowerPoint*, presentation software that enables you to format information on individual slides with major headings, subheadings, and bulleted lists.

See 33d2

Close-Up   FORMAL OUTLINES

Sometimes—particularly when you are writing (or revising) a long or complex essay—a scratch outline is not enough to guide you. In these cases, you will need to construct a **formal outline**, which indicates both the exact order and the relative importance of all the ideas you will explore. A formal outline can be either a sentence outline or a topic outline. (For information on how to construct a formal outline and for an example of a complete **sentence outline, see 6c4**. For an example of an excerpt from another sentence outline, **see 11k1**. For an example of a formal **topic outline, see 11i**.)

CHAPTER 6

Drafting and Revising

6a Writing a Rough Draft

Once you are able to see a clear order for your ideas, you are ready to write a rough draft of your essay. A **rough draft** usually includes false starts, irrelevant information, and unrelated details. At this stage, though, the absence of focus and order is not a problem. You write your rough draft simply to get your ideas down so that you can react to them. You should expect to add or delete words, reword sentences, rethink ideas, and reorder paragraphs as you write. You should also expect to discover some new ideas—or even to take an unexpected detour.

CHECKLIST
Drafting Strategies

The following suggestions can help you as you draft and revise:

❑ **Prepare your work area.** Once you begin to write, you should not have to stop because you need better lighting, important notes, or anything else.

❑ **Fight writer's block.** An inability to start (or continue) writing, writer's block is usually caused by fear that you will not write well or that you have nothing to say. If you really don't feel ready to start drafting, take a short break. If you decide that you really don't have enough ideas to get you started, use one of the strategies for finding something to say.

See 4e

❑ **Get your ideas down on paper as quickly as you can.** Don't worry about sentence structure, spelling and punctuation, or finding exactly the right word—just write. Writing quickly helps you uncover new ideas and new connections between ideas. You may find that following a scratch outline enables you to move smoothly from one point to the next, but if you find this structure too confining, go ahead and write without consulting your outline.

See 5d

❑ **Write notes to yourself.** As you type your drafts, get into the habit of including bracketed, boldfaced notes to yourself. These comments, suggestions, and questions can help you when you write subsequent drafts.

continued

Drafting Strategies *(continued)*

❏ **Take regular breaks as you write.** Try writing one section of your essay at a time. When you have completed a section—for example, one paragraph—take a break. Your mind will continue to focus on your assignment while you do other things. When you return to your essay, writing will be easier.

❏ **Leave yourself enough time to revise.** All writing benefits from revision, so be sure you have time to reconsider your work and to write as many drafts as you need.

MULTILINGUAL TIP

Using your native language occasionally as you draft your essay may keep you from losing your train of thought. However, writing most or all of your draft in your native language and then translating it into English is generally not a good idea. This process will take a long time, and the translation into English may sound awkward, especially if it comes from a translation tool located online or in your word-processing program.

When you write your rough draft, concentrate on the body of your essay, and don't waste time mapping out an introduction and conclusion. (These paragraphs are likely to change substantially in subsequent drafts.) For now, focus on drafting the support paragraphs of your essay.

Using her scratch outline to guide her, Rebecca James wrote the following rough draft. Notice that she included boldfaced and bracketed notes to remind herself to add or check information when she revised her draft.

Rough Draft

Wikipedia and College Research

When given an assignment, students often turn first to *Wikipedia,* the popular free online encyclopedia that currently includes over 26,000,000 articles. Despite its limitations, *Wikipedia* can be a valuable tool for locating reliable research sources. **[Add more here]**

A wiki is an open-source website that allows users to edit or alter its content. Derived from a Hawaiian word meaning "quick," the term *wiki* conveys the swiftness and ease with which users can access information on such sites. **[Do I need to document this? Definition from *Encyclopaedia Britannica*]** *Wikipedia* is the most popular wiki. It includes a range of topics, such as . . . . **[Include a couple of examples here]** *Wikipedia's* editing tools make it easy for users to add new entries or edit existing ones.

The site offers numerous benefits to its users. One benefit of *Wikipedia* over traditional print encyclopedias is its "wikilinks," or internal links to other content within *Wikipedia*. **[Use info from Head and Eisenberg article]** *Wikipedia* articles also often include external links to other sources as well as comprehensive abstracts. *Wikipedia* articles are constantly being updated and provide unmatched coverage of popular culture topics and current events. **[Make sure this is correct]** Finally, the site includes "stub" articles, which provide basic information that may be expanded by users.

Wikipedia claims that its articles "are never considered complete and may be continually edited and improved. Over time, this generally results in an upward trend of quality and a growing consensus over a neutral representation of information." **["About" page—need full citation]** *Wikipedia* ranks its articles according to the criteria of accuracy, neutrality, completeness, and style, letting users know which articles are among the site's best. In fact, some of *Wikipedia*'s best articles are comparable to those found in professionally edited online encyclopedias, such as *Encyclopaedia Britannica*. **[Check on this to make sure]** Although there's no professional editorial board to oversee the development of content within *Wikipedia,* experienced users may become editors, and this role allows them to monitor the process by which content is added and updated. Users may also use the "Talk" page to discuss an article's content and make suggestions for improvement.

Wikipedia's popularity has also stimulated emergent technologies. For example, the free open-source software *MediaWiki* runs numerous wiki websites. Other companies are also trying to capitalize on *Wikipedia*'s success by enhancing users' experience of the site. The online service *Pediaphon,* for instance, converts *Wikipedia* articles into MP3 audio files.

Wikipedia concedes "not everything in *Wikipedia* is accurate, comprehensive, or unbiased." **["Researching with *Wikipedia*" page—need full citation]** Because anyone can create or edit *Wikipedia* articles, they can be factually inaccurate, biased, and even vandalized. Many *Wikipedia* articles also lack citations to the sources that support their claims, revealing a lack of reliability. **[Need more here]**

Personally, I have benefited from using *Wikipedia* in learning more for my accounting class. For example, the *Wikipedia* article "Financial Accounting" defines the field in relation to basic accounting concepts. The article contains several internal links to related *Wikipedia* articles and some external links to additional resources and references. **[Compare this article to similar articles on sites like *Encyclopaedia Britannica*]**

Although the *Wikipedia* article on financial accounting provides helpful, general information on this accounting field, it is limited in terms of reliability and scope. **[Explain more here. Add a visual?]** The limitations of the financial accounting article suggest possible problems with *Wikipedia*.

Wikipedia articles are a good starting point for research and link to more in-depth sources. *Wikipedia* users should understand the current shortcomings of this popular online tool. **[Add more!]**

6b Moving from Rough Draft to Final Draft

As you revise successive drafts of your essay, you should narrow your focus from larger elements, such as overall structure and content, to increasingly smaller elements, such as sentence structure and word choice.

1 Revising Your Drafts

After you have developed a rough draft, set it aside for a day or two if you can. When you return to it, focus on only a few areas at a time. As you review this first draft, begin by evaluating your essay's thesis-and-support structure and general organization. Once you feel satisfied that your thesis statement says what you want it to say and that your essay's content supports this thesis and is logically arranged, you can turn your attention to other matters. For example, you can make sure that you have included all the <u>transitional words and phrases</u> that readers will need to follow your discussion.

See 34b2

As you review your drafts, you may want to look at the questions in the "Revising Your Essay" checklists on pages 58–59. If you have the opportunity for <u>peer review</u> with classmates or a visit to the writing center, consider your readers' comments carefully. At this stage of the process, you should also try to arrange a <u>conference</u> with your instructor.

See 6c2, 6c3

Because it can be more difficult to read text on the computer screen than on hard copy, you may want to print out your draft. This will enable you to make revisions by hand on printed pages and then return to the computer to type these changes into your document. (As you type your draft, you may want to leave extra space between lines. This will make any errors or inconsistencies more obvious and at the same time give you plenty of room to write questions and add new material.)

If you write your revisions by hand on hard copy, you may find it helpful to develop a system of symbols. For instance, you can circle individual words or box groups of words (or even entire paragraphs) that you want to relocate, using an arrow to indicate the new location. You can also use numbers or letters to indicate the order in which you want to rearrange ideas. When you want to add words, use a caret like *this*.

An excerpt from Rebecca's rough draft, with her handwritten revisions, appears below.

Draft with Handwritten Revisions (Excerpt)

The article contains several internal links to related *Wikipedia* articles and some external links to additional resources and references. In comparison, the wiki Citizendium doesn't contain an article on financial accounting, and the "Financial Accounting" article in the professionally edited Encyclopaedia Britannica consists only of a link to a related EB article.

2 Adding Visuals

As you write and revise, you should consider whether one or more **visuals** might strengthen your essay by providing support for the points you are making. Sometimes you may want to use a visual that appears in one of your sources; at other times, you may be able to create a visual (for example, a

Close-Up MANAGING FILES

As you revise, it is important to manage your files carefully, following these guidelines:

- First, be sure to save your drafts. Using the Save option in your word processor's file menu saves only your most recent draft. If you prefer to save every draft you write (so you can return to an earlier draft to locate a different version of a sentence or to reconsider a section you have deleted), use the Save As option instead.
- Also, be sure to label your files. To help you keep track of different versions of your essay, label every file in your project folder by content and date (for example, **First Draft, Nov 5**).
- Finally, be very careful not to delete material that you may need later; instead, move this material to the end of your document so that you can assess its usefulness later on and retrieve it if necessary.

photograph or a chart) yourself; at still other times, you may need to search *Google Images* or another image database to find an appropriate visual.

> **CHECKLIST**
>
> **Adding Visuals to Your Essay**
>
> To add a visual to your essay, follow these steps:
>
> ❑ Find an appropriate visual.
> ❑ Place the image in a suitable location in your essay.
> ❑ Format the image, and make sure it is clearly set off from the written text.
> ❑ Introduce the visual with a sentence (or refer to it in the text).
> ❑ Label the visual.
> ❑ Always document a borrowed visual.

Once you have decided to add a particular visual to your essay, the next step is to determine where to insert it. (In general, you should place the visual in the part of the essay where it will have the greatest impact in terms of conveying information or persuading your audience.) Then, you need to format the visual. (Within *Microsoft Word*, you can double-click on an image to call up a picture-editing menu that allows you to alter the size, color, and position of the image within your essay— and even enables you to wrap text around the image.) Next, you should make sure that the visual stands out in your essay: surround it with white space, add ruled lines, or enclose it in a box.

After you have inserted the visual where you want it, you need to integrate it into your text. You can include a sentence that introduces the visual (**The following table illustrates the similarities between the two health plans**), or you can refer to it in your text (**Figure 1 shows Kennedy as a young man**) to give it some context and explain why you are using it. You should also identify the visual by labeling it (**Fig. 1. Photo of John F. Kennedy, 1937**). In addition, if the visual is not one you have created yourself, you must document it. In most academic disciplines, this means including full source information directly below the image and sometimes in the list of references as well. (To see how Rebecca James integrated a visual into her essay, **see 6e**.)

See
Pt. 5

EXERCISE 6.1

Take a closer look at a rough draft you are working on for this or any other course. Follow the general guidelines outlined in **6b** to begin revising. As you continue working on your draft, focus on the specific revision strategies explained in **6c**.

6c Using Specific Revision Strategies

Everyone revises differently, and every writing task calls for a slightly different process of revision. Five strategies in particular can help you revise at any stage of the writing process.

1 Using Word-Processing Tools

Your word-processing program includes a variety of tools designed to make the revision process easier. For example, *Microsoft Word*'s **Track Changes** allows you to make changes to a draft electronically and to see the original version of the draft and the changes simultaneously. Changes appear in color as underlined or crossed-out text (or as balloons in the margin), and you can view the changes on the screen or in print. This feature also allows you to accept or reject all changes or just specific changes.

Another useful tool is **Compare Documents**. Whereas Track Changes allows you to keep track of changes to a single document, Compare Documents allows you to analyze the changes in two completely separate versions of a document, usually an original and its most recent update. Changes appear in color as highlighted text.

Rebecca used Track Changes as she revised her rough draft. An excerpt from her draft, along with her changes, appears below.

Draft with Track Changes (Excerpt)

A wiki is an open-source website that allows users to edit ~~or alter~~and add to its content. Derived from a Hawaiian word meaning "quick," the term *wiki* conveys the swiftness and ease with which users can access information on such sites. as well as contribute content ("Wiki"). Since its creation in 2001 by Jimmy Wales, *Wikipedia* has grown into a huge database of articles on ~~is the most popular wiki. It includes a range of~~ topics, ~~such as . . . .~~ ranging from contemporary rock bands to obscure scientific and technical concepts. In accordance with the site's policies, users can edit existing articles and add new articles using *Wikipedia*'s editing tools, which do not require specialized programming knowledge or expertise. ~~make it easy for users to add new entries or edit existing ones.~~

Close-Up   TRACK CHANGES VS. COMPARE DOCUMENTS

Where you are in the writing process can help you decide whether to track your changes or to compare one complete version of your document with another. **Track Changes** is especially useful in helping you follow sentence-level changes as you draft and revise; it can also be helpful later on, when you edit words and phrases. **Compare Documents** is most helpful when you are comparing global changes, such as paragraph unity and thesis-and-support structure, between one draft and another.

2 Participating in Peer Review

Peer review—a collaborative revision strategy that enables you to get feedback from your classmates—is another useful activity. With peer review, instead of trying to imagine an audience for your essay, you address a real audience, exchanging drafts with classmates and commenting on their writing. Such collaborative work can be formal or informal, conducted in person or electronically. For example, you and a classmate may email drafts back and forth, using *Word*'s Comment tool (see page 51), or your instructor may conduct the class as a workshop, assigning students to work in groups to critique each other's essays. Students can also comment on classmates' drafts posted on a course discussion board or listserv.

CHECKLIST

Guidelines for Peer-Review Participants

To get the most out of a peer-review session, keep the following guidelines in mind:

❑ **Know the material.** To be sure you understand what the student writer needs and expects from your comments, read the essay several times before you begin writing your response.

❑ **Focus on the big picture.** Try not to get bogged down in minor problems with punctuation or mechanics or become distracted by an essay's proofreading errors.

❑ **Look for a positive feature.** Try to zero in on what you think is the essay's greatest strength.

❑ **Be positive throughout.** Try to avoid words such as *weak, poor,* and *bad;* instead, try using a compliment before delivering the "bad news": "Paragraph 2 is very well developed; can you add this kind of support in paragraph 4?"

❑ **Show respect.** It is perfectly acceptable to tell a student that something is confusing or inaccurate, but don't go on the attack.

❑ **Be specific.** Avoid generalizations such as "needs more examples" or "could be more interesting"; instead, try to offer helpful, focused suggestions: "You could add an example after the second sentence in paragraph 2"; "Explaining how this process operates would make your discussion more interesting."

❑ **Don't give orders.** Ask questions, and make suggestions.

❑ **Include a few words of encouragement.** In your summary, try to emphasize the essay's strong points.

Close-Up ELECTRONIC PEER REVIEW

Some software is particularly useful for peer-review groups. For example, *Word*'s **Comment** tool allows several readers to insert comments at any point or to highlight a particular portion of the text they would like to comment on and then insert annotations. Comments are identified by the initials of the reviewer and by a color assigned to the reviewer.

Other online programs also facilitate the peer-review process. For example, *InSite* is a web-based application that allows students to respond to each other's drafts with a set of peer-review questions, as shown below.

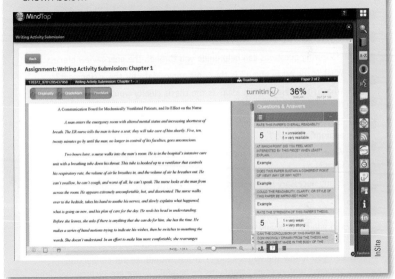

An excerpt from Rebecca's rough draft with peer reviewers' comments appears below. (Note that her classmates used *Word*'s Comment tool to insert comments.)

Draft with Peer Reviewers' Comments (Excerpt)

Personally, I have benefited from using *Wikipedia* in learning more for my accounting class. For example, the *Wikipedia* article "Financial

Comment [KL1]: It's also helpful for other classes outside my major.

Accounting" defines this field in relation to basic accounting concepts. The article contains several internal links to related *Wikipedia* articles and some external links to additional resources and references. In comparison, the wiki *Citizendium* doesn't contain an article on financial accounting, and the "Financial Accounting" article in the professionally edited *Encyclopaedia Britannica* consists only of a link to a related *EB* article.

Comment [KL2]: Why is this imp.? Maybe explain more??

Comment [BR3]: Yes! This is one of my fav. features of *Wikipedia*. ☺

Comment [CB4]: But sometimes these links don't lead to the best sources either . . .

CHECKLIST
Questions for Peer Review

The following questions can help guide you through the peer-review process:

❑ What is the essay about? Is the topic appropriate for the assignment?

❑ What is the essay's main idea? Is the thesis clearly worded? If not, how can the wording be improved?

❑ Is the essay arranged logically? Do the body paragraphs appear in an appropriate order?

❑ What ideas support the thesis? Does each body paragraph develop one of these ideas?

❑ Is any necessary information missing? Identify any areas that seem to need further development. Is any information irrelevant? If so, suggest possible deletions.

❑ Can you think of any ideas or examples from your own reading, experience, or observations that would strengthen the writer's essay?

❑ Can you follow the writer's logic? If not, would clearer connections between sentences or paragraphs be helpful? Where are such connections needed?

❑ Is the introductory paragraph interesting to you? Would another opening strategy be more effective?

❑ Does the conclusion leave you with a sense of closure? Would another concluding strategy be more effective?

❑ Is anything unclear or confusing?

❑ What is the essay's greatest strength?

❑ What is the essay's greatest weakness?

For information on audience concerns for peer-review participants, **see 1c3**.

3 Using Instructors' Comments

Instructors' comments—in conjunction with correction symbols, in marginal comments, or in conferences—can also help you revise.

Correction Symbols   If your draft is ready for editing, your instructor may indicate concerns about style, grammar, mechanics, or punctuation by using the correction symbols listed on the inside back cover of this book. Instead of correcting a problem, the instructor will simply identify it and supply the number of the section in this handbook that deals with the error. After reading the appropriate pages, you should be able to make the necessary corrections on your own. For example, the symbol and number noted within the following sentence referred a student to **39f2**, the section in this handbook that discusses sexist language.

> **Instructor's Comment:** Equal access to jobs is a desirable goal for all
> *Sxt—see 39f2*
> (mankind.)

After reading the appropriate section in the handbook, the student made the following change.

> **Revised:** Equal access to jobs is a desirable goal for everyone.

Marginal Comments   Instructors frequently write marginal comments on your essays to suggest changes in content or structure. These comments may ask you to add supporting information or to arrange paragraphs differently within the essay, or they may recommend stylistic changes, such as more varied sentences. Marginal comments may also question your logic, suggest a more explicit thesis statement, ask for clearer transitions, or propose a new direction for a discussion. In some cases, you can consider these comments to be suggestions rather than corrections. You may decide to incorporate these ideas into a revised draft of your essay, or you may not. In all instances, however, you should take your instructor's comments seriously.

An excerpt from Rebecca's rough draft, along with her instructor's comments, follows. (Note that her instructor used *Microsoft Word*'s Comment tool to insert comments.)

Draft with Instructor's Comments (Excerpt)

Personally, I have benefited from using *Wikipedia* in learning more for my accounting class. For example, the *Wikipedia* article "Financial Accounting" defines this field in relation to basic accounting concepts. The article contains several internal links to related *Wikipedia* articles and some external links to additional resources and references.

> Comment [JB5]: Revise to eliminate use of "personally" and the first person ("I") in this essay. Use this ¶ to talk about *Wikipedia*'s benefits to college students, using the accounting article as an example.

In comparison, the wiki *Citizendium* doesn't contain an article on financial accounting, and the "Financial Accounting" article in the professionally edited *Encyclopaedia Britannica* consists only of a link to a related *EB* article.

> Comment [JB6]: In your final draft, edit out all contractions. (Contractions are too informal for most college writing.) See **51b1**.

Conferences   Many instructors require or encourage one-on-one conferences, and you should certainly schedule a conference if you can. During a conference, you can respond to your instructor's questions and ask for clarification of marginal comments. If a certain section of your essay presents a problem, use your conference time to focus on it, perhaps asking for help in sharpening your thesis or choosing more accurate words.

CHECKLIST

Getting the Most Out of a Conference

To make your conference time as productive as possible, follow these guidelines:

❑ **Make an appointment.** If you are unable to keep your appointment, be sure to call or email your instructor to reschedule.

❑ **Review your work carefully.** Before the conference, reread your notes and drafts, and go over all your instructor's comments and suggestions. Make all the changes you can on your draft.

❑ **Bring a list of questions.** Preparing a list in advance will enable you to get the most out of the conference in the allotted time.

❑ **Bring your work-in-progress.** If you have several drafts, you may want to bring them all, but be sure you bring any draft on which your instructor has commented.

❑ **Take notes.** As you discuss your essay, write down any suggestions that you think will be helpful so you won't forget them when you revise.

❑ **Participate actively.** A successful conference is not a monologue; it should be an open exchange of ideas.

Close-Up   WRITING CENTER CONFERENCES

If you are unable to meet with your instructor—and, in fact, even if you are—it is a good idea to make an appointment with a tutor in your school's writing center. A writing tutor (who may be either a professional or a student) is likely to know a good deal about what your instructor expects and is trained to help you produce an effective essay.

> What a writing tutor can do is help you find ideas to write about and develop a thesis statement, identify parts of your essay that need more support (and help you decide what kind of support to include), and coach you as you revise your essay. What a tutor will *not* do is write your essay for you or act as a copyeditor or a proofreader.
>
> When you meet with a tutor, follow the guidelines in the checklist above—and always bring a copy of your assignment as well as your latest draft (including any instructor comments).

Conferences can also take place online—most often, through email. If you send emails to your instructor, to your writing center tutor, or to members of your peer-review group, include a specific subject line that clearly identifies the message as coming from a student writer (for example, "question about assignment" or "comments on my essay"). This is especially important if your email address does not include your name. When you attach a document to an email and send it for comments, mention the attachment in your subject line (for example, "first draft—see attachment")—and be sure your name appears on the attachment itself, not just on the email.

Note: Your instructor may also require conferences through course management software or through collaborative software such as *Google Drive*.

Close-Up   COLLABORATION AND THE REVISION PROCESS

In a sense, the feedback you get from your instructor (or from a writing center tutor)—in conference, by email, or in written comments on a draft—opens a dialogue that is a form of collaboration. Like the comments you get from your classmates during peer review, these comments present ideas for you to react to, questions for you to answer, and answers to questions you may have. As you react to these comments, you engage in a collaboration that can help you revise your work.

4 Using a Formal Outline

Outlining can be helpful early in the revision process, when you are reworking the larger structural elements of your essay, or later on, when you are checking the logic of a completed draft. A formal outline reveals at once whether points are irrelevant or poorly placed—or, worse, missing. It also reveals the hierarchy of your ideas—which points are dominant and which are subordinate.

The Conventions of Outlining

Formal outlines conform to specific conventions of structure, content, and style. If you follow the conventions of outlining carefully, your formal outline can help you make sure that your essay presents all relevant ideas in an effective order, with appropriate emphasis.

Structure

- Outline format should be followed strictly.

  I. First major point of your essay
  - A. First subpoint
  - B. Next subpoint
    - 1. First supporting example
    - 2. Next supporting example
      - a. First specific detail
      - b. Next specific detail

  II. Second major point

- Headings should not overlap.
- No heading should have a single subheading. (A category cannot be subdivided into one part.)
- Each entry should be preceded by an appropriate letter or number, followed by a period.
- The first word of each entry should be capitalized.

Content

- The outline should include the essay's thesis statement.
- The outline should cover only the body of the essay, not the introductory or concluding paragraphs.
- Headings should be concise and specific.
- Headings should be descriptive, clearly related to the topic to which they refer.

Style

- Headings of the same rank should be grammatically parallel.
- A **sentence outline** should use complete sentences, with all verbs in the same tense.
- In a sentence outline, each entry should end with a period.
- A **topic outline** should use words or short phrases, with all headings of the same rank using the same parts of speech.
- In a topic outline, entries should not end with periods.

As part of her revision process, Rebecca made the following sentence outline of her rough draft (shown on pages 44–46) to help her check her essay's organization.

Sentence Outline

Thesis statement: Despite its limitations, *Wikipedia* can be a valuable tool for locating reliable research sources.

I. A wiki is an open-source website that allows users to edit or alter its content.
   A. *Wikipedia* is the most popular wiki.
   B. *Wikipedia* includes a range of topics.

II. *Wikipedia* offers numerous benefits to its users.
   A. Many *Wikipedia* articles contain internal links.
   B. Many *Wikipedia* articles contain external links.
   C. Many *Wikipedia* articles contain comprehensive abstracts.
   D. Many *Wikipedia* articles cover current and popular culture topics.
   E. Site includes "stub" articles.

III. *Wikipedia* is making efforts to improve the quality of its content.
   A. *Wikipedia* ranks its articles using the criteria of accuracy, neutrality, completeness, and style.
   B. Users may serve as editors of the site's content.
   C. Users may use the "Talk" page to make suggestions for improvement.

IV. *Wikipedia*'s popularity has stimulated emergent technologies.
   A. The free open-source software *MediaWiki* runs numerous wiki websites.
   B. The online service *Pediaphon* converts *Wikipedia* articles into MP3 audio files.

V. *Wikipedia* also has several drawbacks.
   A. *Wikipedia* articles may be factually inaccurate.
   B. *Wikipedia* articles may be biased.
   C. *Wikipedia* articles may be vandalized.
   D. Many *Wikipedia* articles lack citations.

VI. The *Wikipedia* article "Financial Accounting" offers certain benefits.

    A. It defines the field in relation to basic accounting concepts.

    B. It offers a visual breakdown of the key terms within the discipline.

    C. It provides internal and external links to additional resources and references.

VII. *Wikipedia*'s "Financial Accounting" article is limited in the information it offers.

    A. It is unreliable.

    B. It is limited in scope.

This outline revealed some problems in Rebecca's draft. For example, she saw that point IV was not relevant to her discussion, and she realized that she needed to develop the sections in which she discussed the benefits and drawbacks of the specific *Wikipedia* entry that she selected for this assignment. Thus, the outline helped her to revise her rough draft.

5 Using a Revision Checklist

The revision checklists below (and the editing checklists on page 61) are keyed to sections of this text. Moving from global to specific concerns, they parallel the actual revision process. As your understanding of the writing process increases and you become better able to assess the strengths and weaknesses of your writing, you may want to add items to (or delete items from) these checklists. You can also use your instructors' comments to tailor the checklists to your own needs.

CHECKLISTS FOR REVISING YOUR ESSAY

The Whole Essay

❑ Do you understand your essay's purpose? (**See 1b.**)

❑ Have you taken your audience's needs into account? (**See 1c.**)

❑ Are your thesis and support logically related, with each body paragraph supporting your thesis statement? (**See 5a.**)

❑ Is your thesis statement clearly and specifically worded? (**See 5b.**)

❑ Have you discussed everything promised in your thesis statement? (**See 5b.**)

❑ Have you presented your ideas in a logical sequence? Can you think of a different arrangement that might be more appropriate for your purpose? (**See 5d.**)

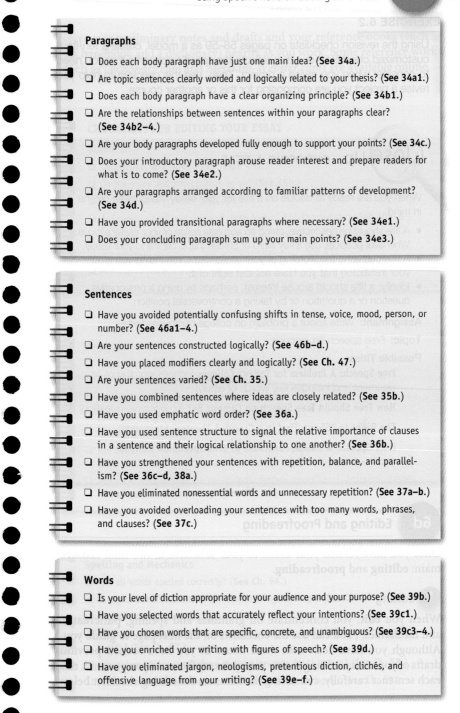

Paragraphs

☐ Does each body paragraph have just one main idea? (**See 34a.**)

☐ Are topic sentences clearly worded and logically related to your thesis? (**See 34a1.**)

☐ Does each body paragraph have a clear organizing principle? (**See 34b1.**)

☐ Are the relationships between sentences within your paragraphs clear? (**See 34b2–4.**)

☐ Are your body paragraphs developed fully enough to support your points? (**See 34c.**)

☐ Does your introductory paragraph arouse reader interest and prepare readers for what is to come? (**See 34e2.**)

☐ Are your paragraphs arranged according to familiar patterns of development? (**See 34d.**)

☐ Have you provided transitional paragraphs where necessary? (**See 34e1.**)

☐ Does your concluding paragraph sum up your main points? (**See 34e3.**)

Sentences

☐ Have you avoided potentially confusing shifts in tense, voice, mood, person, or number? (**See 46a1–4.**)

☐ Are your sentences constructed logically? (**See 46b–d.**)

☐ Have you placed modifiers clearly and logically? (**See Ch. 47.**)

☐ Are your sentences varied? (**See Ch. 35.**)

☐ Have you combined sentences where ideas are closely related? (**See 35b.**)

☐ Have you used emphatic word order? (**See 36a.**)

☐ Have you used sentence structure to signal the relative importance of clauses in a sentence and their logical relationship to one another? (**See 36b.**)

☐ Have you strengthened your sentences with repetition, balance, and parallelism? (**See 36c–d, 38a.**)

☐ Have you eliminated nonessential words and unnecessary repetition? (**See 37a–b.**)

☐ Have you avoided overloading your sentences with too many words, phrases, and clauses? (**See 37c.**)

Words

☐ Is your level of diction appropriate for your audience and your purpose? (**See 39b.**)

☐ Have you selected words that accurately reflect your intentions? (**See 39c1.**)

☐ Have you chosen words that are specific, concrete, and unambiguous? (**See 39c3–4.**)

☐ Have you enriched your writing with figures of speech? (**See 39d.**)

☐ Have you eliminated jargon, neologisms, pretentious diction, clichés, and offensive language from your writing? (**See 39e–f.**)

2 Proofreading

After you have completed your editing, print out a final draft and **proofread**, rereading every word carefully to make sure neither you nor your computer missed any typos or other errors.

Close-Up PROOFREADING STRATEGIES

To help you proofread more effectively, try using these strategies:

- Read your essay aloud, listening for places where you stumble or hesitate.
- Have a friend read your essay aloud to you.
- Read silently word by word, using your finger or a sheet of paper to help you keep your place.
- Read your essay's sentences in reverse order, beginning with the last sentence.

See
39f2

Use the Search or Find command to look for usage errors you commonly make—for instance, confusing *it's* with *its*, *lay* with *lie*, *effect* with *affect*, *their* with *there*, or *too* with *to*. You can also uncover sexist language by searching for words such as *he*, *his*, *him*, or *man*.

Keep in mind that neatness does not equal correctness. The clean text that your computer produces can mask flaws that might otherwise be apparent; for this reason, it is up to you to make sure no spelling errors or typos slip by.

When you have finished proofreading, check to make sure the final typed copy of your essay conforms to your instructor's format requirements.

Close-Up USING SPELL CHECKERS AND GRAMMAR CHECKERS

Although spell checkers and grammar checkers can make the process of editing and proofreading your work easier, they have limitations.

- **Spell Checkers** A spell checker simply identifies strings of letters it does not recognize; it does not distinguish between homophones or spot every typographical error. For example, it does not recognize *there* in "They forgot there books" as incorrect, nor does it identify a typo that produces a correctly spelled word, such as *word* for *work* or *thing* for *think*. Moreover, a spell checker may not recognize every technical term, proper noun, or foreign word you may use.

- **Grammar Checkers** A grammar checker scans documents for certain features (the number of words in a sentence, for example); however, it is not able to read a document to see if it makes sense. As a result, a grammar checker is not always accurate. For example, it may identify a long sentence as a run-on when it is, in fact, grammatically correct, and it generally advises against using passive voice—even in contexts where it is appropriate. Moreover, a grammar checker does not always supply answers; often, it asks questions—for example, whether *which* should be *that* or whether *which* should be preceded by a comma—that you must answer. In short, a grammar checker can guide your editing and proofreading, but you must be the one who decides when a sentence is (or is not) correct.

EXERCISE 6.3

Using the editing checklists on page 61 as a guide, edit an essay you have already revised for content, organization, and other larger issues. Be sure to proofread your essay carefully before you submit it.

6e Preparing a Final Draft

The annotated essay that follows is the final draft of Rebecca James's essay, which you first saw on pages 30–42. It incorporates the suggestions that her peer reviewers and her instructor made on her rough draft.

This final draft is very different from the rough draft of the essay. As she revised, Rebecca shifted her emphasis from her own largely positive view of *Wikipedia* to a more balanced, more critical view, and she revised her thesis statement accordingly. She also provided more examples, adding specific information from sources to support her points, and she included paren- See Ch. 17 thetical documentation and a works-cited list conforming to MLA documentation style. Finally, she added a **visual** (accompanied by a caption) to See 6b2 illustrate the specific shortcomings of the *Wikipedia* article she selected for the assignment.

James 3

be verifiable and must be based on documented, preexisting research. Although no professional editorial board oversees the development of content within *Wikipedia*, experienced users may become editors, and this role allows them to monitor the process by which content is added and updated. Users may also use the "Talk" page to discuss an article's content and make suggestions for improvement. With these control measures in place, some *Wikipedia* articles are comparable to articles in professionally edited online resources.

Limitations of *Wikipedia*

Despite its numerous benefits and its enormous potential, *Wikipedia* is not an authoritative research source. As the site's "Researching with *Wikipedia*" page concedes, "not everything in *Wikipedia* is accurate, comprehensive, or unbiased." Because anyone can create or edit *Wikipedia* articles, they can be factually inaccurate or biased—and they can even be vandalized. Many *Wikipedia* articles, especially those that are underdeveloped, do not supply citations to the sources that support their claims. This absence of source information should lead users to question the articles' reliability. Of course, many underdeveloped *Wikipedia* articles include labels to identify their particular shortcomings—for example, poor grammar or missing documentation. Still, users cannot always determine the legitimacy of information contained in the *Wikipedia* articles they consult.

Strengths of "Financial Accounting" *Wikipedia* article

For college students, *Wikipedia* can provide useful general information and links to helpful resources. For example, accounting students will find that the *Wikipedia* article "Financial Accounting" defines this field in relation to basic accounting concepts and offers a visual breakdown

James 4

of the key terms within the discipline. This article can help students in accounting classes to understand the basic differences between this and other types of accounting. The article contains several internal links to related *Wikipedia* articles and some external links to additional resources and references. In comparison, the wiki *Citizendium* does not contain an article on financial accounting, and the "Financial Accounting" article in the professionally edited *Encyclopaedia Britannica* consists only of a link to a related *EB* article.

Weaknesses of "Financial Accounting" *Wikipedia* article

Although the *Wikipedia* article on financial accounting provides helpful general information about this accounting field, it is limited in terms of its reliability and scope. The top of the article displays a warning label that identifies the article's shortcomings. As fig. 1 illustrates, the article's problems include a lack of cited sources. The limitations of the financial accounting article reinforce the sense that *Wikipedia* is best used not as a source but as a path to more reliable and comprehensive research sources.

 This article **needs additional citations for verification.** Please help improve this article by adding citations to reliable sources. Unsourced material may be challenged and removed. *(October 2007)*

Fig. 1. "Financial Accounting." *Wikipedia,* 14 Mar. 2016, 15:04, en.wikipedia.org/wiki/Financial_accounting.

Conclusion

Like other encyclopedia articles, *Wikipedia* articles should be used only as a starting point for research and as a link to more in-depth sources. Moreover, users should keep in mind that *Wikipedia* articles can include more factual errors, bias, and inconsistencies than professionally edited encyclopedia articles. Although future enhancements to the site may make it more reliable, *Wikipedia* users should understand the current shortcomings of this popular online tool.

James 5

Works Cited

"About *Wikipedia*." *Wikipedia,* 8 Mar. 2016, 15:07, en.wikipedia.
    org/wiki/Wikipedia:About.

Head, Alison J., and Michael B. Eisenberg. "How College
    Students Use the Web to Conduct Everyday Life
    Research." *First Monday,* vol. 16, no. 4, 2011. *Google
    Scholar,* papers.ssrn.com/sol3/papers.cfm?abstract_
    id=2281533.

"Researching with *Wikipedia*." *Wikipedia,* 8 Mar. 2016,
    15:25, en.wikipedia.org/wiki/Wikipedia:Researching_
    with_Wikipedia.

"Wiki." *Encyclopaedia Britannica,* 2014, www.britannica.com/
    topic/wiki.

PART 3

Developing Critical Thinking and Argumentation Skills

Developing Critical Thinking and Argumentation Skills

❓ Frequently Asked Questions

CHAPTER 7

Thinking Critically

As you read (and write) essays, you should carefully consider the strengths and weaknesses of the ideas they present. This is especially true in **argumentative essays**—those that take a stand on a debatable topic.

See Ch. 8

Although many writers try to be fair, others attempt to manipulate readers by using emotionally charged language, by unfairly emphasizing certain facts over others, and by intentionally using flawed logic. For this reason, it is important that you **think critically** when you read (and when you write). Specifically, you need to distinguish fact from opinion, evaluate supporting evidence, detect bias, evaluate visuals, and understand the basic principles of inductive and deductive reasoning.

7a Distinguishing Fact from Opinion

A **fact** is a verifiable statement that something is true or that something happened. An **opinion** is a personal judgment or belief that can never be substantiated beyond any doubt and is, therefore, debatable. In other words, a fact is something that is *known* to be true or have happened, and an opinion is something that is *believed* to be true or have happened.

Fact: Measles is a potentially deadly disease.

Opinion: All children should be vaccinated against measles.

An opinion may be supported or unsupported.

Unsupported Opinion: All children in Pennsylvania should be vaccinated against measles.

Supported Opinion: Despite the fact that an effective measles vaccine is widely available, several unvaccinated Pennsylvania children have died of measles each year since 1992. States that have instituted vaccination programs have had no deaths in the same time period. For this reason, all children in Pennsylvania should be vaccinated against measles.

Note: As the examples above show, supported opinion is much more convincing than unsupported opinion. Remember, however, that support can

71

only make a statement more convincing; it cannot turn an opinion into a fact.

Opinions can be supported with **examples**, **statistics**, or **expert opinion**.

Examples
The American Civil Liberties Union is an organization that has been unfairly characterized as left wing. It is true that it has opposed prayer in the public schools, defended conscientious objectors, and challenged police methods of conducting questioning and searches of suspects. However, it has also backed the antiabortion group Operation Rescue in a police brutality suit and presented a legal brief in support of a Republican politician accused of violating an ethics law.

Statistics
A recent National Institute of Mental Health study concluded that mentally ill people account for more than 30 percent of the homeless population (Young 27). Because so many homeless people have psychiatric disabilities, the federal government should expand the state mental hospital system.

Expert Opinion
No soldier ever really escapes the emotional consequences of war. As William Manchester, noted historian and World War II combat veteran, observes in his essay "Okinawa: The Bloodiest Battle of All," "the invisible wounds remain" (72).

Note: Remember that all words and ideas that you borrow from a source should be <u>documented</u>.

See
Pt. 5

EXERCISE 7.1

Some of the following statements are facts; others are opinions. Identify each fact with the letter *F* and each opinion with the letter *O*. Then, consider what kind of information, if any, could support each opinion.

1. The incidence of violent crime rose in the first six months of this year.
2. Expanded rights for gun owners and fewer police officers led to an increase in crime early in the year.
3. Affirmative action laws and policies have helped women and minority group members advance in the workplace.
4. Affirmative action policies need reform.
5. Women who work are better off today than they were twenty years ago.
6. The wage gap between men and women in similar jobs is smaller now than it was twenty years ago.

7. The Charles River and Boston Harbor are less polluted now than they were ten years ago.
8. We do not need to worry about environmental legislation anymore because we have made great advances in cleaning up our environment.

7b Evaluating Supporting Evidence

The examples, statistics, or expert opinion a writer uses to support a statement is called **evidence**. The more convincing the supporting evidence, the more likely readers will be to accept a statement.

Strong evidence convincingly supports a statement or assertion, while **weak evidence** does little to persuade readers that a point is worth considering. In general, evidence is strong if it is *accurate, sufficient, representative, relevant, authoritative*, and *documented*.

- Evidence is **accurate** if it meets commonly accepted standards of truth or correctness. Evidence is likely to be accurate if it comes from a reliable source. Such a source quotes exactly and does not present remarks out of context. It also presents examples, statistics, and expert testimony fairly, drawing them from other reliable sources.
- Evidence is **sufficient** if a writer presents enough information to justify a statement or conclusion. It is not enough, for instance, for a writer to cite just one example in an attempt to demonstrate that most poor women do not receive adequate prenatal care. Similarly, the opinions of just a single expert, no matter how reputable, are not enough to support this position.
- Evidence is **representative** if it reflects a fair range of viewpoints. Writers should not choose evidence that supports just their position and ignore evidence that does not.
- Evidence is **relevant** if it is on topic and specifically applies to the case being discussed. For example, a writer cannot support the position that increased airport security in Europe has discouraged terrorist attacks by citing examples from US airports.
- Evidence is **authoritative** if it comes from experts. In other words, evidence should come from books, periodicals, and websites written by people who are recognized as experts in a particular field. Personal experience can also serve as evidence if the writer has special insight into the issue or problem being discussed.
- Evidence is **documented** if it is accompanied by the information readers need to identify its source. By supplying this source information, writers help readers determine whether the evidence is valid and whether the writer is trustworthy. (**See Part 5** of this handbook for a discussion of different documentation formats.)

Americans are becoming more ecologically aware with each passing year, but their awareness may be limited. Most people know about the destruction of rainforests in South America, for example, or the vanishing African elephant, but few realize what is going on in their own backyards in the name of progress. Even people who are knowledgeable about such topics as the plight of the wild mustang, the dangers of toxic waste disposal, and acid rain frequently fail to realize either the existence or the importance of "smaller" ecological issues. The wetlands are a good case in point. In recent decades, more than 500,000 acres of wetlands a year have been filled, and it seems unlikely that the future will see any great change. What has happened in recent times is that US wetlands are filled in one area and "restored" in another area, a practice that is legal according to Section 404 of the Clean Water Act and one that does in fact result in "no net loss" of wetlands. Few see the problems with this. To most, wetlands are mere swamps, and getting rid of swamps is viewed as something positive. In addition, the wetlands typically contain few spectacular species—the sort of glamour animals, such as condors and grizzlies, that easily attract publicity and sympathy. Instead, they contain boring specimens of flora and fauna unlikely to generate great concern among the masses. Yet the delicate balance of the ecosystem is upset by the elimination or "rearrangement" of such marshy areas. True, cosmically speaking, it matters little if one organism (or many) is wiped out. But even obscure subspecies might provide some much-needed product or information in the future. We should not forget that penicillin was made from a lowly mold.

1. The loss of even a single species may be disastrous to the ecosystem of the wetlands.
2. Even though the wetlands are considered swamps, most people are very concerned about their fate.
3. Section 404 of the Clean Water Act is not sufficient to protect the wetlands.
4. Few Americans are concerned about environmental issues.
5. Most people would agree that the destruction of rainforests is worse than the destruction of the wetlands.

7e Understanding Deductive Reasoning

1 Moving from General to Specific

Deductive reasoning moves from a generalization believed to be true or self-evident to a more specific conclusion. Writers use deductive reasoning when they address an audience that is more likely to be influenced by logic than evidence. The process of deduction has traditionally been illustrated with a **syllogism**, a three-part set of statements or propositions that includes a **major premise**, a **minor premise**, and a **conclusion**.

Major Premise: All high-fat foods are unhealthy.

Minor Premise: French fries are a high-fat food.

Conclusion: Therefore, french fries are unhealthy.

The **major premise** of a syllogism makes a general statement that the writer believes to be true. The **minor premise** presents a specific example of the belief that is stated in the major premise. If the reasoning is sound, the **conclusion** should follow from the two premises. (Note that the conclusion contains no terms that have not already appeared in the major and minor premises.) The strength of a deductive argument is that if readers accept the premises, they must grant the conclusion.

Note: When you write an argumentative essay, you can use a syllogism during the planning stage (to test the validity of your points), or you can use it as a revision strategy (to test your logic). In either case, the syllogism enables you to express your deductive argument in its most basic form and to see whether it makes sense.

2 Constructing Sound Syllogisms

A syllogism is **valid** (or logical) when its conclusion follows from its premises. A syllogism is **true** when it makes accurate claims—that is, when the information it contains is consistent with the facts. To be **sound**, a syllogism must be both valid and true. However, a syllogism may be valid without being true or true without being valid. The following syllogism, for example, is valid but not true.

Major Premise: All politicians are male.

Minor Premise: Senator Mazie Hirono is a politician.

Conclusion: Therefore, Senator Mazie Hirono is male.

As odd as it may seem, this syllogism is valid. In the major premise, the phrase *all politicians* establishes that the entire class *politicians* is male. After Mazie Hirono is identified as a politician, the conclusion that she is male automatically follows—but, of course, she is not. Because the major premise of this syllogism is not true, no conclusion based on it can be true. Even though the logic of the syllogism is correct, its conclusion is not. Therefore, the syllogism is not sound.

3 Recognizing Enthymemes

An **enthymeme** is a syllogism in which one of the premises—often the major premise—is unstated. Enthymemes often occur as sentences containing words that signal conclusions—*therefore, consequently, for this reason, for, so, since,* or *because.*

Melissa is on the Dean's List; therefore, Melissa is a good student.

The preceding sentence contains the minor premise and the conclusion of a syllogism. The reader must fill in the missing major premise in order to complete the syllogism and see whether the reasoning is logical.

Major Premise: All those on the Dean's List are good students.

Minor Premise: Melissa is on the Dean's List.

Conclusion: Therefore, Melissa is a good student.

Note: Bumper stickers often take the form of enthymemes, stating just a conclusion ("Eating meat is murder") and leaving readers to supply the major and minor premises. Careful readers, however, are not so easily fooled. They supply the missing premise (or premises), and then determine if the resulting syllogism is sound.

7f　Recognizing Logical Fallacies

Fallacies are flawed arguments. A writer who inadvertently uses logical fallacies is not thinking clearly or logically; a writer who intentionally uses them is dishonest and trying to deceive readers. It is important that you learn to recognize fallacies so that you can challenge them when you read and avoid them when you write.

Logical Fallacies

- **Hasty Generalization** Drawing a conclusion based on too little evidence
  The person I voted for is not doing a good job in Congress. Therefore, voting is a waste of time. (One disappointing experience does not warrant the statement that you will never vote again.)

- **Sweeping Generalization** Making a generalization that cannot be supported no matter how much evidence is supplied
  Everyone should exercise. (Some people, for example those with severe heart conditions, might not benefit from exercise.)

- **Equivocation** Shifting the meaning of a key word or phrase during an argument

It is not in the public interest for the public to lose interest in politics. (Although clever, the shift in the meaning of the term *public interest* clouds the issue.)

- **Non Sequitur (Does Not Follow)** Arriving at a conclusion that does not logically follow from what comes before it
  Kim Williams is a good lawyer, so she will make a good senator. (Kim Williams may be a good lawyer, but it does not necessarily follow that she will make a good senator.)

- **Either/Or Fallacy** Treating a complex issue as if it has only two sides
  Either we institute universal health care, or the health of all Americans will be at risk. (Good health does not necessarily depend on universal health care.)

- **Post Hoc** Establishing an unjustified link between cause and effect
  The United States sells corn to China. This must be what caused the price of corn to rise. (Other factors, unrelated to the sale, could have caused the price of corn to rise.)

- **Begging the Question** (circular reasoning) Stating a debatable premise as if it were true
  Stem-cell research should be banned because nothing good can come from something so inherently evil. (Where is the evidence that stem-cell research is "inherently evil"?)

- **False Analogy** Assuming that because things are similar in some ways, they are similar in other ways
  When forced to live in crowded conditions, people act like rats. They turn on each other and act violently. (Both people and rats might dislike living in crowded conditions, but unlike rats, people do not necessarily resort to violence in this situation.)

- **Red Herring** Changing the subject to distract readers from the issue
  Our company may charge high prices, but we give a lot to charity each year. (What does charging high prices have to do with giving to charity?)

- **Argument to Ignorance** Saying that something is true because it cannot be proved false, or vice versa
  How can you tell me to send my child to a school where there is a child whose mother might have been exposed to Ebola? After all, doctors can't say for sure that my child won't catch Ebola, can they? (Just because a doctor cannot prove the speaker's claim to be false, it does not follow that the claim is true.)

(continued)

Logical Fallacies (*continued*)

- **Bandwagon** Trying to establish that something is true because everyone believes it is true

  Everyone knows that eating candy makes children hyperactive. (Where is the evidence to support this claim?)

- **Argument to the Person** (*Ad Hominem*) Attacking the person and not the issue

  Of course the former Vice President supports drilling for oil in the Arctic. He worked for an oil company. (By attacking his opponent, the speaker attempts to sidestep the issue.)

- **Slippery Slope** Suggesting, without justification, that one thing will inevitably lead to another, usually undesirable, thing

  We have to do something about tuition increases. This semester, my school increased tuition by 8 percent. Soon they'll be charging $100,000 a year. Where will it stop? (Tuition may be rising, but supposing such an extreme increase, without proof, is simply a scare tactic.)

CHECKLIST

Thinking Critically

- ❏ Are the writer's points supported primarily by fact or by opinion?
- ❏ Does the writer offer supporting evidence for his or her opinions?
- ❏ What kind of evidence is provided? How convincing is it?
- ❏ Is the evidence accurate? Sufficient? Representative? Relevant? Authoritative? Documented?
- ❏ Does the writer display any bias? If so, is the bias revealed through language, tone, or choice of evidence?
- ❏ Does the writer present a balanced picture of the issue?
- ❏ Are any alternative viewpoints overlooked?
- ❏ Does the writer omit pertinent examples?
- ❏ Does the writer use logical reasoning?
- ❏ Does the writer use any logical fallacies?
- ❏ Does the writer oversimplify complex ideas?
- ❏ Does the writer make reasonable inferences?
- ❏ Does the writer represent the ideas of others accurately? Fairly?

MULTILINGUAL TIP

In many cultures, people present arguments in order to persuade others to believe something. However, the rules for constructing such arguments are different in different cultures. In US academic settings, writers are discouraged from using the types of arguments outlined in section **7f** because they are not considered fair.

CHAPTER 8

Writing an Argumentative Essay

For many students, the true test of their critical thinking skills comes when they write an **argumentative essay**, one that takes a stand on an issue and uses logic and evidence to convince readers. When you write an argumentative essay, you follow the same process you use when you write any essay. However, because the purpose of an argument is to influence the way readers think, you need to use some additional strategies to present your ideas to your audience.

See
Chs.
4–6

8a Planning an Argumentative Essay

1 Choosing a Topic

As with any type of essay, choosing the right topic for your argumentative essay is important. First, you should choose a topic that you already know something about. The more you know about your topic, the easier it will be to gather the information you need to write about it. You should also choose a topic that interests and challenges you, one in which you have an emotional and intellectual stake.

It stands to reason that the more you care about a topic, the more enthusiastically you will pursue it. Still, you should be willing to consider other people's viewpoints—even those that contradict your own beliefs. If you find that you cannot be open-minded, you should choose another topic. Remember, in order to be persuasive, you will have to demonstrate to readers that your position is fair and that you have considered both the strengths and the weaknesses of opposing arguments.

Your topic should also be narrow enough so that you can write about it within the assigned page limit. If your topic is too broad, you will not be able to treat it in enough detail. Finally, your topic should be interesting to your readers. Keep in mind that some topics—such as "The Need for Gun Control" or "The Fairness of the Death Penalty"—have been discussed and written about so often that you may not be able to say anything new or interesting about them. Instead of relying on an overused topic, choose one that enables you to contribute something to the debate.

2 Developing a Thesis

See
5b
After you have chosen a topic, your next step is to take a stand—to state your position in the form of a **thesis statement**. Properly worded, this thesis statement lays the foundation for the rest of your argument. A thesis statement for an argumentative essay challenges readers to consider your points and to think in ways they may not have anticipated. It almost always raises questions that have no easy or pat answers. When you develop your thesis statement, make sure that it is *clearly stated* and that it is *debatable*.

> **CHECKLIST**
> ### Developing an Effective Thesis
> To make sure you have an effective thesis for your argumentative essay, ask the following questions:
> ❑ Does your thesis make clear to readers what position you are taking?
> ❑ Is your thesis one with which reasonable people might disagree?
> ❑ Can you formulate an antithesis?
> ❑ Can your thesis be supported by evidence?

A good thesis statement leaves no doubt in readers' minds about what you intend to discuss or what direction your argument will take. It is a good idea to write a preliminary draft of your thesis statement. If you write down this tentative thesis, you will be able to make sure that it says exactly what you want it to say and it is debatable.

For this reason, a **factual statement**—a verifiable assertion about which reasonable people do not disagree—is not suitable as a thesis statement for an argumentative essay.

Fact: First-year students are not required to purchase a meal plan from the university.

Thesis Statement: First-year students should not be required to purchase a meal plan from the university.

One way to make sure that your thesis statement actually is debatable is to formulate an **antithesis**, a statement that takes the opposite position. If you can state an antithesis, you can be certain that your thesis statement is debatable.

Thesis Statement: Term limits would improve government by bringing people with fresh ideas into office every few years.

Antithesis: Term limits would harm government because elected officials would always be inexperienced.

EXERCISE 8.1

& Working on your own or in a group, determine which of the following thesis statements are effective and which are not. Then, rewrite the ineffective thesis statements so that they are clear and debatable.

1. There are many different reasons for cheating.
2. Gun violence in the United States is on the rise.
3. The advantages of a flat tax clearly outweigh those of the current tax system.
4. In this essay, I am going to discuss the final book in the *Hunger Games* trilogy.
5. Although many people think buying counterfeit goods is acceptable, this activity harms the legitimate businesses whose merchandise is being copied.

3 Defining Your Terms

You should always define the most significant terms you use in your argument—especially any key terms you use in your thesis statement. After all, the soundness of an entire argument may hinge on the definition of a word that may mean one thing to one person and another thing to someone else. For example, in the United States, *democratic* elections involve the selection of government officials by popular vote; in other countries, the word *democratic* may be used to describe elections in which only one candidate is running or in which all candidates represent the same party. For this reason, if your argument hinges on a key term like *democratic*, you should make sure that your readers know exactly what you mean.

Close-Up USING PRECISE LANGUAGE

Be careful to use precise language in your thesis statement. Avoid vague and judgmental words, such as *wrong, bad, good, right*, and *immoral*.

Vague: Censorship of the Internet would be wrong.

Clearer: Censorship of the Internet would unfairly limit free speech.

---

4 Considering Your Audience

As you plan your essay, keep a specific **audience** in mind. Are your readers unbiased observers or people deeply concerned about the issue you plan to discuss? Can they be cast in a specific role—concerned parents, victims of discrimination, irate consumers—or are they so diverse that they cannot be categorized? If you cannot be certain who your readers are, direct your argument to a general audience.

Always assume a **skeptical audience**—one that is likely to question or even challenge your assumptions. Even sympathetic readers will need to

See 1c

be convinced that your argument is logical and that your evidence is solid. Skeptical readers will need reassurance that you understand their concerns and that you are willing to concede some of their points. However, no matter what you do, you may never be able to convince hostile readers that your conclusion is valid or even worth considering. The best you can hope for is that these readers will acknowledge the strengths of your argument even if they reject your conclusion.

5 Refuting Opposing Arguments

As you develop your argument, you should briefly summarize and then **refute**—that is, argue against—opposing arguments by showing that they are untrue, unfair, illogical, irrelevant, inaccurate, or misguided. In the following paragraph, a student refutes the argument that Sea World is justified in keeping whales in captivity.

> Of course, some will say that Sea World wants to capture only a few whales, as George Will points out in his commentary in *Newsweek*. Unfortunately, Will downplays the fact that Sea World wants to capture a hundred whales, not just "a few." And, after releasing ninety of these whales, Sea World intends to keep ten for "further work." At hearings in Seattle last week, several noted marine biologists went on record as condemning Sea World's research program.

Note: When you acknowledge an opposing view, be careful not to distort or oversimplify it. This tactic, known as creating a **straw man**, can seriously undermine your credibility. **See 7f** for coverage of logical fallacies.

EXERCISE 8.2

Choose one of the following five statements, and list the arguments in favor of it. Then, list the arguments against it. Finally, choose one position (pro or con), and write a paragraph or two supporting it. Be sure to refute the arguments against your position.

1. Public school students who participate in extracurricular activities should have to submit to random drug tests.
2. The federal government should limit the amount of violence shown on television.
3. A couple applying for a marriage license should be required to take STD tests.
4. Retirees making more than $100,000 a year should not be eligible for Social Security benefits.
5. Colleges and universities should provide free daycare for students' children.

8b   Using Evidence Effectively

1   Supporting Your Argument

Most arguments are built on **assertions**—statements that you make about your topic—backed by <u>evidence</u>—supporting information, in the form of examples, statistics, or expert opinion. Some of the most common sources of evidence are scholarly journals, magazines, newspapers, websites, and books. You may also get evidence from observations, interviews, surveys, and your own personal experience.

See 7b

Keep in mind that information—words and ideas—that you get from a source requires <u>documentation</u>. However, **common knowledge**—assertions that are **self-evident** ("All human beings are mortal"), **true by definition** ("2 + 2 = 4"), or **factual** ("The Atlantic Ocean separates Europe and the United States")—needs no documentation.

See Pt. 5

Even though you support your points with evidence from your sources, your argument should not be a patchwork of other people's ideas. In other words, *your* voice—not those of your sources—should dominate the discussion. Your sources are intended to add credibility to your argument, not do the job of the writer. You should present your points, introduce and interpret your evidence, and make sure that readers know how your ideas relate to one another and to your thesis. In this way, you let readers know that you are in control of the argument and that you have something to add to the discussion.

Note: Remember that you can never prove a thesis conclusively; if you could, there would be no argument. The best you can do is to provide enough evidence to establish a high probability that your thesis is reasonable or valid.

Close-Up   USING VISUALS AS EVIDENCE

A well-chosen visual can help support an argument—provided it conveys a clear message and is relevant to the discussion. For more on using visuals in your arguments, **see Chapter 10**.

---

2   Establishing Credibility

Clear reasoning, compelling evidence, and strong refutations are necessary components of an argument. But these elements in themselves are not sufficient to create a convincing argument. In order to convince readers, you have to satisfy them that you are someone they should listen to—in other words, that you have **credibility**.

Establishing Common Ground When you write an argument, it is tempting to go on the attack, emphasizing the differences between your position and those of your opponents. Writers of effective arguments, however, know they can gain a greater advantage by establishing common ground between their opponents and themselves.

One way to establish common ground is to use the techniques of **Rogerian argument**, based on the work of the psychologist Carl Rogers. According to Rogers, you should consider your readers colleagues with whom you must collaborate to find solutions to problems. Instead of verbally assaulting them, you should emphasize points of agreement. In this way, you establish common ground and work toward a resolution of the problem you are discussing.

Demonstrating Knowledge Including relevant personal experiences in your argumentative essay can show readers that you know a lot about your subject; demonstrating this kind of knowledge gives you authority.

You can also demonstrate knowledge by showing that you have done research into a subject. By referring to important and reliable sources of information and by providing accurate documentation, you show readers that you have done the necessary background reading.

Maintaining a Reasonable Tone Talk *to* your readers, not *at* them. If you lecture your readers or appear to talk down to them, you will alienate them. Remember that readers are more likely to respond to a writer who seems sensible than to one who is strident or insulting. For this reason, you should use moderate language, qualify your statements, and avoid words and phrases such as *never, all,* and *in every case,* which can make your claims seem exaggerated and unrealistic.

Presenting Yourself as Someone Worth Listening To Present your argument in positive terms, and don't apologize for your views. For example, do not rely on phrases—such as "In my opinion" and "It seems to me"—that undercut your credibility. Be consistent, and be careful not to contradict yourself. Finally, avoid using first person pronouns, such as *I,* as well as slang and colloquialisms.

❓ ③ Being Fair

Because argument promotes one point of view over another, it is seldom objective. However, college writing requires that you stay within the bounds of fairness and avoid <u>bias</u>. To be sure that the support for your argument is not misleading or distorted, you should take the following steps.

See
7c

Avoid Distorting Evidence Writers sometimes intentionally misrepresent their opponents' views by exaggerating them and then attacking this extreme position, but you should avoid this unfair tactic in your college writing.

Avoid Quoting Out of Context Be careful not to take someone's words out of their original setting and use them in another. When you select certain statements and ignore others, you can change the meaning of what someone has said or suggested.

Avoid Slanting Slanting occurs when you select only information that supports your case and ignore information that does not. Slanting also occurs when you use **inflammatory language**—language calculated to arouse strong emotions—to create bias.

Avoid Using Unfair Appeals Traditionally, writers of arguments try to influence readers by appealing to their sense of reason. Problems arise when writers attempt to influence readers unfairly. For example, writers can use fallacies to fool readers into thinking that a conclusion is logical when it is not. These unfair appeals are unacceptable in college writing.

See 7f

8c   Organizing an Argumentative Essay

In its simplest form, an argument consists of a thesis statement and supporting evidence. However, argumentative essays frequently use inductive and deductive reasoning and other strategies to win audience approval and overcome potential opposition.

See 7d–e

PLANNING GUIDE

ARGUMENTATIVE ESSAY

Your **assignment** will ask you to take a stand on an issue.
Your **purpose** will be to convince readers to accept your position on the issue.
Your **audience** will be your instructor or other students in your class or school.

INTRODUCTION

- Begin by presenting a brief overview of your subject.
- Show readers how your subject concerns them.
- State your thesis. (If your thesis is very controversial, you may want to delay stating it until later in the essay.)

Thesis statement templates:
- The idea that…is popular, but…
- Recent studies, however, suggest that…
- The following actions are necessary because…
- In my opinion,…

continued

PLANNING GUIDE: Argumentative Essay *(continued)*

BACKGROUND

Topic sentence templates:
- One (another) way is…
- The first (second, third) reason is…
- One advantage (another advantage) is…

- Briefly review the basic facts of the controversy.
- Provide definitions of key terms or an overview of others' opinions on the issue.

ARGUMENTS IN SUPPORT OF THE THESIS

Templates for introducing support:
- As…mentions in his/her article, "…"
- According to…,…
- In his/her book,…says, "…"

- Begin with your weakest argument and work up to the strongest.
- If your arguments are equally strong, begin with the one with which your readers are most familiar and most likely to accept.
- Support your arguments with evidence—facts, examples, and expert opinion.

REFUTATION OF OPPOSING ARGUMENTS

Refutation templates:
- Of course, not everyone agrees that…; however,…
- Although it is true that…, it is not necessarily true that…
- On the one hand,…; on the other hand,…

- Refute opposing arguments by demonstrating that they are untrue, unfair, illogical, or inaccurate.
- If an opposing argument is particularly strong, concede its strength, and point out its limitations.

CONCLUSION

Closing sentence templates:
- For these reasons,…
- The current situation can be improved by…
- Let us hope that…
- In conclusion,…

- Reinforce the stand you are taking.
- Remind readers of the weaknesses of opposing arguments, or underscore the logic of your position.
- End with a strong concluding statement, such as a memorable quotation or a call to action.

8d Writing and Revising an Argumentative Essay

The following student essay includes many of the elements discussed in this chapter. The student, Samantha Masterton, was asked to write an argumentative essay on a topic of her choice, drawing her supporting evidence from her own knowledge and experience as well as from other sources.

Masterton 1

Samantha Masterton

Professor Egler

English 102

14 April 2016

The Returning Student: Older Is Definitely Better

After graduating from high school, young people must decide what they want to do with the rest of their lives. Many graduates (often without much thought) decide to continue their education uninterrupted, and they go on to college. Introduction This group of teenagers makes up what many see as typical first-year college students. Recently, however, this stereotype has been challenged by an influx of older students, including myself, into American colleges and universities (Holland). Not only do these students make a valuable contribution to the schools they attend, but they also offer an alternative to young people who go to college simply because they do not know what else to do. A few years off between high school Thesis statement and college can give many students the life experience they need to appreciate the value of higher education and to gain more from it.

The college experience of an eighteen-year-old is quite Background different from that of an older "nontraditional" student. The typical high school graduate is often concerned with things other than studying—for example, going to parties, dating, and testing personal limits. However, older students—those who are twenty-five years of age or older—are serious about the idea of returning to college. Although many high school students do not think twice about whether or not to attend college, older students have much more to consider when they think about returning to college. For example, they must

Masterton 2

decide how much time they can spend getting their degree
and consider the impact that attending college will have on
their family and their finances.

Background (continued)

In the United States, the makeup of college students
is changing. According to the US Department of Education
report *Pathways to Success*, the percentage of students who
could be classified as "nontraditional" is continually increasing (2-3). So, despite the challenges that older students face
when they return to school, more and more are choosing to
make the effort.

Argument in support of thesis

Most older students return to school with clear goals.
Getting a college degree is often a requirement for professional advancement, and older students are therefore more
likely to take college seriously. In general, older students
enroll in college with a definite course of study in mind. For
older students, college is an extension of work rather than
a place to discover what they want to be when they graduate. An influential study by psychologists R. Eric Landrum,
Je T'aime Hood, and Jerry M. McAdams concluded, "Nontraditional students seemed to be more appreciative of their
opportunities, as indicated by their higher enjoyment of
school and appreciation of professors' efforts in the classroom" (744).

Argument in support of thesis

Older students also understand the actual benefits of
doing well in school; as a result, they take school seriously.
The older students I know rarely cut classes or put off
studying. This is because older students are often balancing
the demands of home and work and because they know how
important it is to do well. The difficulties of juggling school,
family, and work force older students to be disciplined and

Masterton 3

focused—especially concerning their schoolwork. This pays off: older students tend to spend more hours per week studying and tend to have a higher GPA than younger students do (Landrum et al. 742-43).

My observations of older students have convinced me that many students would benefit from delaying entry into college. Eighteen-year-olds are often immature and inexperienced. They cannot be expected to have formulated definite goals or developed firm ideas about themselves or about the world in which they live. In contrast, older students have generally had a variety of real-life experiences. Most have worked for several years, and many have started families. Their years in the "real world" have helped them become more focused and more responsible than they were when they graduated from high school. As a result, they are better prepared for college than they would have been when they were younger.

Of course, postponing college for a few years is not for everyone. Certainly some teenagers have a definite sense of purpose and these individuals would benefit from an early college experience. Charles Woodward, a law librarian, went to college directly after high school, and for him the experience was positive. "I was serious about learning, and I loved my subject," he said. "I felt fortunate that I knew what I wanted from college and from life." Many younger students, however, are not like Woodward; they graduate from high school without any clear sense of purpose. For this reason, it makes sense for them to postpone college until they are mature enough to benefit from the experience.

Granted, some older students have difficulties when they return to college. Because they have been out of school so long, these students may have problems studying and adapting

Argument in support of thesis

Refutation of opposing argument

Refutation of opposing argument

Masterton 4

to academic life. As I have seen, though, most of these problems disappear after a period of adjustment. Of course, it is true that many older students find it difficult to balance the needs of their family with college and to deal with the financial burden of tuition. However, this challenge is becoming easier with the growing number of online courses, the availability of distance education, and the introduction of governmental programs, such as educational tax credits (Agbo 164-65).

Conclusion

All things considered, higher education is often wasted on the young, who are either too immature or too unfocused to take advantage of it. Taking a few years off between high school and college would give these students the time they need to make the most of a college education. The increasing number of older students returning to college seems to indicate that many students are taking this path. According to a US Department of Education website, *Fast Facts*, eight million students enrolled in American colleges in 2012 were twenty-five years of age or older. Older students such as these have taken time off to serve in the military, to gain valuable work experience, or to raise a family. In short, they have taken the

Concluding statement

time to mature. By the time they get to college, these students have defined their goals and made a firm commitment to achieve them.

Masterton 5

Works Cited

Agbo, Seth. "The United States: Heterogeneity of the Student Body and the Meaning of 'Nontraditional' in U.S. Higher Education." *Higher Education and Lifelong Learners: International Perspectives on Change*, edited by Hans G. Schuetze and Maria Slowey, Routledge, 2000, pp. 149-69.

Holland, Kelley. "Back to School: Older Students on the Rise in College Classrooms." *NBCNews.com,* 28 Aug. 2014, www.nbcnews.com/business/business-news/back-school-older-students-rise-college-classrooms-n191246.

Landrum, R. Eric, et al. "Satisfaction with College by Traditional and Nontraditional College Students." *Psychological Reports,* vol. 89, no. 3, 2001, pp. 740-46.

United States, Department of Education, Institute of Educational Sciences. *Fast Facts.* National Center for Educational Statistics, 2014.

---. ---. *Pathways to Success: Integrating Learning with Life and Work to Increase National College Completion.* By the Advisory Committee on Student Financial Assistance, 2012.

Woodward, Charles B. Interview. 8 Mar. 2016.

Works-cited list begins on a new page

Two sets of three unspaced hyphens indicate that *United States and Dept. of Educ.* are repeated from the previous entry

CHECKLIST
Writing Argumentative Essays

☐ Does your essay have a debatable thesis?

☐ Have you adequately defined the terms you use in your argument?

☐ Have you considered the opinions, attitudes, and values of your audience?

☐ Have you supported your points with evidence?

☐ Have you summarized and refuted opposing arguments?

☐ Have you established your credibility?

☐ Have you been fair?

☐ Have you constructed your arguments logically?

☐ Have you avoided logical fallacies?

☐ Have you provided your readers with enough background information?

☐ Have you presented your points clearly and organized them logically?

☐ Have you written an interesting introduction and a strong conclusion?

☐ Have you documented all information that is not your own?

Using Transitions in Argumentative Essays

Argumentative essays should include transitional words and phrases to indicate which paragraphs are arguments in support of the thesis, which are refutations of arguments that oppose the thesis, and which are conclusions.

Arguments in Support of Thesis

accordingly	for instance	in general
because	generally	since
for example	given	

Refutations

admittedly	despite	naturally
although	granted	nonetheless
certainly	in all fairness	of course

Conclusions

all things considered	in conclusion	therefore
as a result	in summary	thus

CHAPTER 9

Writing Proposals

9a Determining Purpose and Audience

One common type of argumentative writing is the **proposal**, which attempts to convince readers to implement a solution to a problem. As with any writing project, you begin your proposal by determining the **rhetorical situation**.

See Ch. 1

1 Purpose

Unlike some arguments, proposals go beyond simply making a case for a position: they urge readers to take a specific action, and they support this position with reasons and examples. Proposals are often written to identify a specific problem or need and to propose a detailed, concrete plan for addressing it. Consider the following example:

> **Problem:** More than 10,000 students commute daily to X University, but the school only designates 4,000 on-campus spots for students. There is a shuttle from large off-campus lots, but it runs only a few times a day and not according to a schedule. As a result, there are not enough on-campus parking options for students.
>
> **Proposed Solution:** To better meet the needs of their commuter students, X University should provide a more regular shuttle service, one with a published schedule, from its off-campus lots. Also, the university should open 100 of the 300 spots in Faculty Lot B to students during specified times.

Note: The word *proposal* can also be used to describe the plan for a research project. **See 11b**.

2 Audience

The audience for a proposal should be someone who has the power to approve or enact the proposed solution or plan. This could be a single person (such as a landlord or dean), a smaller group of people (such as the tenants

95

of a building), or representatives of a larger organization (such as the registrar's office of your college or university).

When writing a proposal, consider what your readers already know about the situation, whether they consider it to be a problem, and, if they do, whether they will be open to your solution. Ask yourself if they are already planning to improve the situation with another strategy. If they are, why is your strategy better (cheaper, easier to implement, or more effective)? As with any argument, assume that your audience is skeptical but not hostile.

9b Planning and Writing a Proposal

Because a proposal is a type of argument, you should keep in mind the strategies that you use when writing an **argumentative essay**. Your goal is to persuade readers that your points are reasonable and worth considering. You do this by supplying evidence—details, examples, and the opinions of experts—and by refuting opposing arguments.

See Ch. 8

1 Planning a Proposal and Developing a Thesis

Begin planning your proposal by identifying a problem that you think is important and relevant—a situation, policy, or rule that you want to change. As with any argumentative essay, your topic should be narrow enough to treat within the page limits of your assignment. For instance, "The problem of high tuition" is too broad for a short proposal. However, "The confusing financial aid application process at X University" is more specific: a solution for this problem could be presented in a few pages.

Once you have defined your problem, consider its possible underlying causes. After listing them, brainstorm to come up with solutions. Even though you favor one solution, be sure to explore other possible solutions. You need to demonstrate to readers that you have considered all reasonable options and show why your solution is better than the others.

Finally, be sure that your thesis clearly states your position. An effective **thesis** for a proposal should leave no doubts in readers' minds about exactly what you intend to do. Remember, an argumentative thesis must be both reasonable and debatable.

See 5b

2 Writing and Organizing a Proposal

When you draft your proposal, keep the following guidelines in mind.

- **Provide context.** Early in the proposal, give as much background information as you think your readers need. If they are familiar with the situation, just supply a brief overview. If, however, they are unfamiliar with the situation, explain it in more depth—perhaps demonstrating to readers how the situation will affect them.

- **Define the problem.**   Clearly define the problem you are going to address. If your readers need to be convinced that a problem exists, devote several paragraphs to explaining the problem. If your readers already agree that a problem exists, focus on your shared concern about the need to address it. (Be sure to keep this part brief.)

- **Argue for the solution.**   Explain your solution in detail, emphasizing how it addresses the problem. Make sure that you supply enough evidence to support your points, using examples to show why the solution is needed and why it will work. If, for example, you are arguing for a change in the registration system at your school, provide the examples—possibly statistics, articles from the school newspaper, or your own personal experience—that will convince readers that your argument has merit.

- **List the benefits of your solution.**   Consider the advantages of your solution. Make sure your benefits relate to readers, not to yourself. For example, if you were writing a proposal to increase the number of online courses, list the benefits for the school (higher student retention and increased profit), not for yourself (you can sleep later and not have to commute).

- **Refute alternative solutions.**   Summarize and refute the most obvious alternatives to your solution. In the process, explain why your proposed solution is better. Remember to be reasonable and to avoid sarcasm and name-calling. After refuting opposing arguments, be sure to reinforce your solution and to emphasize its strengths.

- **Decide how to organize your proposal.**   One way to organize a proposal is to divide the problem into a series of smaller problems that you solve one at a time. Alternately, you can explain the entire problem and then discuss the different parts of the solution. The **patterns of paragraph development** you are likely to use in a proposal include description, narration, definition, cause and effect, division and classification, and process.

See
34d

PLANNING GUIDE

PROPOSAL

Your **assignment** will ask you to identify a problem and to suggest a solution.
Your **purpose** will be to convince readers that your solution is both practical
and reasonable.
Your **audience** will be your instructor, other students, and possibly an outside
audience.

INTRODUCTION

Thesis statement templates:
- The most effective way to solve... (problem) is by... (solution).
- Because of the problem of... presented by... (cause or causes), ... (we, you, the university, etc.) should take action by...
- To address the serious problem of..., (we, you, the university, etc.) must...
- ... has become a serious problem for... (those affected), as indicated by... (piece of credible evidence or reliable source); the best way to solve this is to... (solution).

- Present an overview of the situation.
- Briefly define the problem, establishing its importance.
- Consider using an appropriate introductory strategy, such as a brief narrative, to create interest.
- State your thesis.

BODY PARAGRAPHS

Topic sentence templates:
- The proposed solution of... would address... (specific aspect of problem) by... (specific part/ action of solution).
- The first step of... (solution) would be to...
- Other solutions that have been suggested include..., ..., and...
- Another solution, ..., involves ...; it offers... but is problematic because...
- Ultimately, ... is the best solution because it..., while the other options do not.

Templates for introducing support:
- One (another, the final) example is...
- For example, ...
- As... points out, ...
- According to..., ...

- Present a detailed explanation of the problem including related issues and concerns.
- Begin each paragraph with a topic sentence that states the paragraph's main idea.
- In each paragraph, include evidence to support the proposed solution.
- Include transitional words and phrases to connect ideas within and between paragraphs.
- Give specific examples or statistics to indicate the extent of the problem.
- Summarize your solution to the problem.
- Summarize possible objections to your solution. Refute these objections, explaining why they are unrealistic, unfeasible, or misguided.
- Explain why your solution makes more sense than others.

CONCLUSION

- Reemphasize the central point made by the proposal.
- Mention the importance of solving the problem and the effectiveness of your solution.
- Explicitly call for action.
- Use a specific concluding strategy to make a lasting impression.

Closing statement templates:
- If…(we, you, etc.) do not take action by…, the consequences will be severe:…(list consequences).
- For all these reasons, I/we urge you to address the problem of… by…
- In conclusion,…is the best approach to solving the problem of…; I/we thank you for considering this proposal and urge you to take action. We look forward to hearing how…will be implemented.

Conventions of Writing a Proposal

When you write a proposal, keep the following conventions in mind:

- Use boldfaced headings to help readers identify sections and locate information quickly within the proposal.
- Establish a reasonable tone. You may feel passionately about a problem or opportunity, but you should temper strong emotions in favor of a strong, balanced argument with reason as its foundation. Choose verbs over adjectives, and avoid words that sound desperate, accusatory, angry, overzealous, or that have negative connotations.
- Establish your authority by stating your ideas directly. Avoid subjective expressions such as "I feel," "I believe," and "In my opinion," which could weaken your argument.
- Avoid logical fallacies and be careful to focus on causation, not on similarity or sequence, when discussing problems and solutions.
- If your proposal refers to other sources, be sure to acknowledge them. Introduce the words or ideas of others with a phrase that introduces the source, and follow any borrowed material (paraphrase, summary, or quotation) with documentation. When quoting the exact words of a source, use quotation marks to distinguish those words from your own.

See
7f

See
Pt. 5

9c   Preparing a Final Draft

The following proposal was written in response to this assignment:

> Together with two or three classmates, determine a problem that affects students at this college. It should be a problem that all of you agree is important to solve and to which you think you could suggest a reasonable solution. Remember to consider other potential solutions to the problem (or other initiatives) and to show why yours is the best. Address your proposal to the audience that could best respond to—and consider enacting—your ideas.

Notice that the proposal contains headings to make it easier to read and to emphasize important points.

Sample Proposal: Financial Aid

To: Rayna Lombardo, Director of Financial Aid Services, East Marlboro County College

From: Keith Martell, Bianca Giocomo, Lourdes Martinez, and Rashmika Patel (composition students)

Date: November 13, 2015

Subject: Proposal for Student Collaboration to Improve Financial Aid Communication

Introduction

According to the *East Marlboro County College Factbook of 2013*, over 68 percent of our students receive financial aid. We rely on the services of this office to fund our education, and we appreciate your staff's hard work in helping us pay for college. However, there are problems of communication between the Office of Financial Aid Services (OFAS) and students. According to a survey we have conducted, long lines during registration periods, long waits on the phone, confusing emails, limited staff availability, and redundant paperwork have caused widespread student dissatisfaction. As the 687 signatures we have collected for our petition show, East Marlboro students want a change. We propose a collaboration between OFAS and students to improve the delivery of vital financial assistance.

Problem

In collaboration with the students of Dr. Shanelle Harris's section of Research Methods in Social Science, we have surveyed 236 students.

Overwhelmingly, the students cite long lines at the Financial Aid Office as their chief concern. In the days leading up to the start of each semester, the wait to speak to a registration counselor can be over three hours. Using the office's automated phone system is no better. Many students report being on hold for two hours, only to be told that the appropriate staff member is busy or that the information they want is not available. Of the survey respondents, 33 percent claim that they have at least once left the office line or hung up before speaking to a representative.

Most students visit the Financial Aid Office to inquire about the status of a grant or loan or to begin an application. However, 26 percent of respondents had to wait in line at the office because of one particular email regarding a consent form, which states that the student "is at risk of having financial aid suspended for this and future semesters if immediate action is not taken." Students were alarmed by the threatening tone of the email because they believed that the Free Application for Federal Student Aid (FAFSA) was the only form they needed to fill out. To add to students' frustration, the form itself was not attached to the email; it had to be picked up in person.

The *East Marlboro County College Factbook of 2013* states that 7 percent of East Marlboro students have taken advantage of the college's online course offerings by taking one or more semesters fully online. These students are full-time workers, parents, people with disabilities, and deployed military personnel. For them, a trip to campus is unreasonable, if not completely impossible. It does not make sense to implement online courses without also implementing matching online student services.

Proposed Solution

We propose a two-part solution to these problems. First, we propose the creation of a comprehensive and interactive website for OFAS. The site should contain clear instructions on how and when to apply for aid, downloadable or web-based forms, and opportunities for students to receive information in real time. The current site offers little more than some basic information and a link to the US government's FAFSA application site. We understand that both money and time are limited, so we suggest that the office collaborate with students in the Advanced Web Design course to create the website, potentially in the form of a class competition or final project.

Using free online tools such as *Google Chat* or *Skype* to connect with off-campus students can also cut costs.

Additionally, we propose that OFAS enlist the help of student advisors. We agree that only trained professionals should conduct official financial aid administration and advisement, but many routine communications do not require advanced training. For example, work-study students could answer phones, direct their peers during busy registration periods, and staff the aforementioned online chat programs. They could provide answers to frequently asked questions while leaving more time for staff to handle tougher cases. A student perspective would also be helpful in writing and editing mass emails, possibly avoiding the confusion that leads to long lines.

When OFAS representatives met with the authors of this proposal, they mentioned that the Financial Aid Office was exploring the option of extending hours until 7:00 p.m. two nights per week during periods of peak traffic. They added that extending hours would take funds from the department's thinly stretched budget. Although we applaud your commitment to providing additional services despite fiscal challenges, we feel strongly that extra hours alone will not solve the problem. Evening hours will not help the many students who have other obligations, and they are of no benefit to off-campus students. Our proposed changes would help everyone: student advisors could work flexible schedules during regular hours for little or no cost.

Conclusion

By joining efforts with students to update the Financial Aid Office website, OFAS could help students save precious time and resources, allowing them to focus on the most important aspect of college: their education. Student collaboration could offer cost-effective solutions while also addressing general dissatisfaction by fostering a sense of community among students and staff. Students would be able to apply their skills in tangible ways and learn new marketable skills. Please consider tapping into the wealth of enthusiasm and talent of those who care most deeply about East Marlboro County College: its students.

EXERCISE 9.1

Follow the assignment outlined in **9c** and write a proposal according to those instructions. As you work, refer to the Planning Guide on pages 98–99.

CHAPTER 10

Using Visuals as Evidence

10a Using Visuals

Because visual images can have such an immediate impact, they can make a good argumentative essay even more persuasive. In this sense, visuals can serve as **evidence**. For example, the addition of a photograph of a roadway work zone choked with traffic (Figure 10.1) could support your assertion that your township should provide more effective work zone strategies to reduce congestion. In addition, a graph or chart could easily establish the fact that traffic congestion has gotten considerably worse over the past thirty years (Figure 10.2).

FIGURE 10.1 Traffic jam in a roadway work zone.

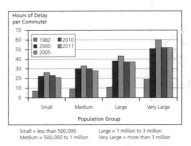

FIGURE 10.2 Chart showing the increase in traffic congestion.

To persuade readers, visuals rely on elements such as images, written text, white space, and color. Consider, for example, the editorial cartoon in Figure 10.3, which comments on the high cost of a college education. The structure of the cartoon is simple: graduating students are shown walking up a steep staircase that represents the challenges that they must meet in order to graduate. Once they receive their diplomas, however, they encounter two very large steps that represent the daunting challenges they face upon graduation. The use of written text is simple and direct. The person handing out diplomas congratulates the students and advises them to watch their step; the two large steps are labeled "cost of college" and "sour job market." (In addition, muted blue and grey colors reinforce the somber

CONGRATULATIONS.
PLEASE WATCH
YOUR STEP.

COST OF COLLEGE

SOUR JOB MARKET

2009 Jeff Parker, Florida Today/Cagle Cartoons, Inc.

FIGURE 10.3 Cartoon by Jeff Parker from *Florida Today*.

CHECKLIST
Selecting Visuals

❑ What point does the visual make?

❑ Does the visual clearly support your argument?

❑ How do the various elements of the visual reinforce your point?

❑ Is the visual aimed at a particular type of audience?

❑ Could your use of the visual confuse or distract your readers?

❑ Does the visual distort or misrepresent facts?

message of the cartoon.) Thus, with very few words, the visual forcefully makes the cartoonist's point: that in spite of the challenges graduating students have already overcome, they face ever greater—and perhaps insurmountable—challenges in the future. If you were writing an argument that took the same position, this cartoon could certainly help you make your point.

When you select visuals, it is important to remember your purpose and audience and the tone you wish to establish. Just as you would with any evidence in an argumentative essay, you should evaluate visuals to make sure that they are not taken out of context and that they do not make their points unfairly.

EXERCISE 10.1

Look carefully at the political cartoon in Figure 10.4. Using the questions in the checklist above as a guide, determine whether this visual would provide useful evidence to support each of the following argumentative thesis statements. Explain why it would or would not be an appropriate choice.

- Because public opinion seems to be turning against the death penalty, it should be abolished as soon as possible.
- If the death penalty is abolished, violent criminals will be more likely to commit violent crimes.
- Because the death penalty seems to be carried out in such an arbitrary way, it should be abolished as soon as possible.
- Until an exhaustive study of the death penalty can be carried out, state governors should declare a moratorium on capital punishment.
- Although many consider the death penalty to be "cruel and unusual punishment," it is still appropriate for particularly heinous crimes.

FIGURE 10.4 Cartoon by John Cole.

10b Evaluating Visuals

Just as you have to think critically about the ideas you read, you also have to think critically about the visuals that accompany these texts.

Almost all photographs that appear in print have been altered in some way. The most common changes involve **cropping** a picture to eliminate distracting background objects, **recoloring** a background to emphasize subjects in the foreground, and **altering the brightness and contrast** of an image to enhance its overall quality.

Problems arise, however, when an overly zealous editor, reporter, or photographer alters a photograph in order to support a particular point of view. Problems also occur when a researcher or reporter misrepresents experimental data in a graph or chart. Occasionally, this kind of error is caused by carelessness, but sometimes it is a deliberate attempt to mislead or deceive.

Close-Up   ALTERING IMAGES

Desktop digital imaging programs such as *Adobe Photoshop* give users access to a wide range of digital image editing techniques. Keep in mind, however, that you are only allowed to alter a person's **copyrighted work** under very specific circumstances that fall under the **fair use doctrine**. The fair use doctrine permits you to use copyrighted visual material (with proper acknowledgment) in a research paper, but it generally does not permit you to distort, misrepresent, or otherwise alter this material. If you use a copyrighted work in a publicly accessible document and you are unsure if it is an acceptable "fair use," you should obtain written permission from the copyright holder to use that work.

1 Recognizing Doctored Photographs

A photograph is **doctored** when it has been intentionally falsified or altered in some significant way. Consider the doctored photograph shown in Figure 10.5. Suppose a photographer for a travel agency had taken this picture to show the interior of a popular tourist site that was in the process of being refurbished. Notice that in addition to the building, the picture also shows homeless people who sleep inside it every night.

Sergemi/Shutterstock

FIGURE 10.5 Undoctored photograph of a popular tourist site.

Now suppose that soon after the picture was posted online, the owner of the travel agency began to get complaints. For example, a government official said that the picture is harming tourism. Eventually, the owner of the travel agency decided to take down the original picture and post the doctored picture shown in Figure 10.6. Viewers now have no idea that the homeless people were deleted to make the scene appear more inviting.

Sergemi/Shutterstock

FIGURE 10.6 Doctored photograph of a popular tourist site.

Unfortunately, the Internet is full of misleading and altered images. For this reason, you should be very careful when you select photographs from the Internet to support your arguments. If you suspect that a picture has been altered, research it to determine its validity, just as you would for a print source.

EXERCISE 10.2

Search online for "photo tampering throughout history" and examine three different doctored images. Then, working with two or three classmates, determine and describe what the person who doctored each photo was trying to accomplish.

2 Recognizing Staged Photographs

Another questionable tactic is the use of **staged photographs**, visual images that purport to be spontaneous when they are actually posed. Even the hint of staging can discredit a visual image.

One of the most famous debates about staged photographs concerns the flag-raising photograph at the battle of Iwo Jima during World War II (see Figure 10.7). Photographer Joe Rosenthal's Pulitzer Prize–winning image is perhaps the most famous war photograph ever taken. When it appeared in newspapers on February 25, 1945, it immediately captured the attention of the American public, so much so that it became the model for the Marine Corps monument in Washington, DC. Almost immediately, however, people began to question whether the photograph was staged. Rosenthal did not help matters when he seemed to admit to a correspondent that it was. Later, however, he said that he had been referring to a posed shot he took the same day (see Figure 10.8), not the famous flag-raising picture. Historians now agree that the flag-raising picture was not staged, but the charge that it was haunted Rosenthal his entire life and is still repeated by some as if it were fact.

FIGURE 10.7 Soldiers raise a flag at the battle of Iwo Jima, February 1945.

FIGURE 10.8 Soldiers pose before the camera at Iwo Jima, February 1945.

3 Recognizing Misleading Charts and Graphs

Charts and graphs are effective tools for showing relationships among statistical data in science, business, and other disciplines, where they are often used as supporting evidence. However, charts can skew results and mislead readers when their components (titles, labels, and so on) are manipulated—for example, to show just partial or mislabeled data. Whenever you encounter a chart or graph in a document, examine it carefully to be certain that visual information is labeled clearly and accurately and that data increments are large enough to be significant.

Consider, for example, the potentially misleading nature of the two salary charts below. At first glance, it appears as if the salaries in the "Salaries Up!" chart (Figure 10.9) rose dramatically while those in the "Salaries Stable!" chart (Figure 10.10) remained almost the same. A closer analysis of the two charts, however, reveals that the salaries in the two charts are nearly identical across the six-year period. The data in the two charts seem to differ dramatically because of the way each chart displays salary increases: in the first chart, salary increases are given in $500 increments; in the second

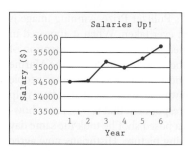

FIGURE 10.9 Salary chart 1 from the *CPIT Maths2Go* online tutorial.

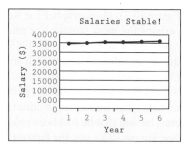

FIGURE 10.10 Salary chart 2 from the *CPIT Maths2Go* online tutorial.

chart, salary increases are given in $5,000 increments. For this reason, a $1,000 increase in the first chart registers quite visibly, whereas in the second chart it hardly shows at all.

Close-Up   INTEGRATING VISUALS

To make sure that your visuals are smoothly integrated into your argumentative essays, follow these guidelines:

- Place your visual as close as possible to the point in the essay where you discuss it.
- Include a specific reference to the visual—for example, *See Figure 3* or *See the figure below*.
- Explain the visual in the text of your essay so readers will understand what they are supposed to learn from it.
- Make sure the visual is large enough so readers can see its individual elements and read any words or numbers.
- If you take a visual from a source, be sure to document it.

Conducting Research

PART 4

Conducting Research

❓ Frequently Asked Questions

CHAPTER 11

Developing a Research Project

Research is the systematic investigation of a topic outside your own knowledge and experience. However, doing research means more than just reading other people's ideas. When you undertake a research project, you become involved in a process that requires you to **think critically**: to evaluate and interpret the ideas explored in your sources and to develop ideas of your own. Whether you are working with print sources (journals, magazines, books) or electronic sources (online catalogs or discovery services, databases, the Internet), in the library or on your own computer, your research will be most efficient if you follow a systematic process. (As an added benefit, such a process will help you avoid unintentional plagiarism.)

See Ch. 7

See Ch. 16

The Research Process

Activity	Date Due	Date Completed
Move from an Assignment to a Topic, **11a**	_____	_____
Do Exploratory Research and Formulate a Research Question, **11b**	_____	_____
Assemble a Working Bibliography, **11c**	_____	_____
Develop a Tentative Thesis, **11d**	_____	_____
Do Focused Research, **11e**	_____	_____
Manage Photocopies, Scans, and Downloaded Material, **11f**	_____	_____
Take Notes, **11g**	_____	_____

(continued)

The Research Process (*continued*)

Activity	Date Due	Date Completed
Fine-Tune Your Thesis, **11h**		
Construct an Outline, **11i**		
Write a Rough Draft, **11j**		
Revise Your Work, **11k**		
Prepare Your Final Draft, **11l**		

11a Moving from Assignment to Topic

1 Understanding Your Assignment

Every research project begins with an assignment. Before you can find a direction for your research, you must be sure you understand the exact requirements of the specific assignment.

CHECKLIST
Understanding Your Assignment

Asking yourself the following questions will help you focus on your research project:

❑ Has your instructor provided a list of possible topics, or are you expected to select a topic on your own?

❑ Is your purpose to explain? To persuade? Something else?

❑ Is your audience your instructor? Your fellow students? Both? Someone else?

❑ Can you assume that your audience knows a lot (or just a little) about your topic?

❑ When is the completed research project due?

❑ About how long should it be?

❑ Will you be given a specific schedule to follow, or are you expected to set your own schedule?

❑ Is peer review permitted? Is it encouraged? If so, at what stages of the writing process?

❑ Does your instructor expect you to prepare a formal outline?

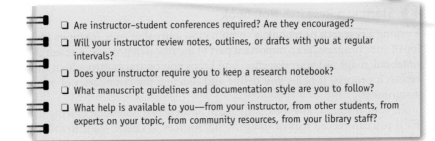

❏ Are instructor–student conferences required? Are they encouraged?

❏ Will your instructor review notes, outlines, or drafts with you at regular intervals?

❏ Does your instructor require you to keep a research notebook?

❏ What manuscript guidelines and documentation style are you to follow?

❏ What help is available to you—from your instructor, from other students, from experts on your topic, from community resources, from your library staff?

In **Chapters 4–6** of this text, you followed the writing process of Rebecca James as she planned, drafted, and revised a short essay for her first-semester composition course. In her second-semester composition class, Rebecca was given the following assignment prompt:

> Develop a ten- to fifteen-page research project that takes a position on any issue related to the Internet. Keep a research notebook that traces your progress.

Throughout this chapter, you will see examples of the work Rebecca did in response to this assignment.

❷ Finding a Topic

Once you understand the requirements and scope of your assignment, you need to decide on a topic. In many cases, your instructor will help you choose a topic, either by providing a list of suitable topics or by suggesting a general subject area—for example, a famous trial, an event that happened on the day you were born, a problem on college campuses, or an issue related to the Internet. Even in these cases, you will still need to choose one of the topics or narrow the subject area to a topic that you can write about: one trial, one event, one problem, or one issue.

If your instructor requires you to select a topic on your own, you should consider several possible topics and weigh both their suitability for research and your interest in them. You decide on a topic for your research project in much the same way you decide on a topic for a short essay: you read, brainstorm, talk to people, and ask questions. Specifically, you talk to friends and family, coworkers, and perhaps your instructor; attend a library orientation session with your class; read online magazines and news sources, blogs, and *Wikipedia* entries (*Wikipedia* can be a great resource for brainstorming, although it would not typically be referenced as a scholarly source in an academic research project); browse the library's online databases (especially those relevant to the discipline); take stock of your interests; and consider possible topics suggested by your other courses (historical events, scientific developments, and so on).

❸ Starting a Research Notebook

Keeping a **research notebook**, a combination journal of your reactions and log of your progress, is an important part of the research process. A research notebook maps out your direction and keeps you on track; throughout the research process, it helps you define and redefine the boundaries of your assignment.

In your research notebook (which can be an actual notebook or a digital file), you can record lists of things to do, sources to check, leads to follow up on, appointments, possible community contacts, questions to which you would like to find answers, stray ideas, possible thesis statements or titles, and so on. (Be sure to date your entries and to check off and date work you have completed.)

If you choose to use a digital file, you might consider one of the following options, each with distinct advantages:

1. *Microsoft Word* file plus electronic copies of documents in a folder on your hard drive or flash drive. Most users are very familiar with *Word*, so ease-of-use is a plus.
2. *Google Drive* document with electronic folder in which documents are stored. *Google Drive* has the distinct advantage of being "in the cloud" and so it follows you wherever you go. Also, there is no danger of losing documents if your hard drive crashes.
3. *Zotero* notes plus documents. *Zotero* is free citation software that easily and efficiently stores documents along with all notes and citation information. Also, *Zotero* is synced with your computer, smartphone, and the Internet, so you can work from any device. Consult the *Zotero* website and *Zotero* tutorials on *YouTube* for more information.

As she began her research, Rebecca James created a folder in *Google Drive* in which she planned to keep all the electronic documents for her paper. In a *Google* document that she labeled "Research Notebook," she outlined her schedule and explored some preliminary ideas.

Here is an entry from Rebecca's research notebook in which she discusses how she chose a topic for her research paper.

Excerpt from Research Notebook

Last semester, I wrote an essay for Professor Burks about using *Wikipedia* for college-level research. In class, we'd read *Wikipedia*'s policy statement, "Researching with *Wikipedia*," which helped me to understand *Wikipedia*'s specific limitations for college research. I used a sample *Wikipedia* entry related to my accounting class to support my points about the site's strengths and weaknesses. For my research project, which has to be about the Internet, I want to expand the essay I wrote for my first-semester comp course. This time, I want to talk more about the academic debate surrounding *Wikipedia*. (I asked Professor Burks if it would be OK for me to use this topic for her class this semester, and she said it would be fine. In fact, she really liked the idea.)

11b Doing Exploratory Research and Formulating a Research Question

During **exploratory research**, you develop an overview of your topic, searching the Internet and perhaps looking through the library's online reference collections, such as *Credo Reference* and the *Gale Virtual Reference Library*. Your goal at this stage is to formulate a **research question** that you want your research paper to answer. A research question helps you to decide which sources to seek out, which to examine first, which to examine in depth, and which to skip entirely. (The answer to your research question will be your paper's <u>thesis statement</u>.)

See
11d

When developing a list of keywords to help you focus your online searches, it is often helpful to see how others have framed questions about the same topic. You can gather a list of keywords and phrases (paying particular attention to specific words that appear together) from almost any information resource.

Rebecca began her exploratory research with a preliminary search on *Google* (see Figure 11.1). When she entered the keywords *Wikipedia and academia*, they generated millions of hits, but she wasn't overwhelmed. She had learned in her library orientation that the first ten to twenty items would be most useful to her because the results of a *Google* search are listed in order of relevance to the topic, with the most relevant sites listed first. After a quick review of these items, she moved on to a keyword search on *Questia*, a database to which her library subscribed (see Figure 11.2) and which offers two significant benefits over *Google* searches:

1. subject headings assigned to the database's articles from which she could acquire additional terms to incorporate into her searches and
2. access to what scholars wrote about her topic and the thesis statements they formulated in response to their own research questions—ones that could help her articulate her own research question.

When she finished her exploratory research, Rebecca was able to decide on a preliminary research question for her project.

Research Question: What effect has *Wikipedia* had on academic research?

She knew she would revise and clarify this question as she continued her research, but for now, it could help her focus.

11b Developing a Research Project

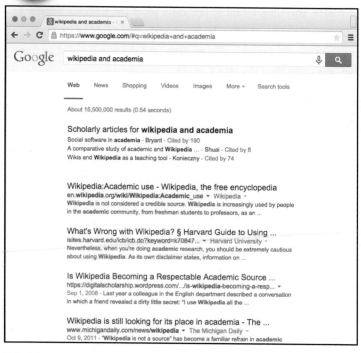

FIGURE 11.1 *Google* search results. © Google, Inc.

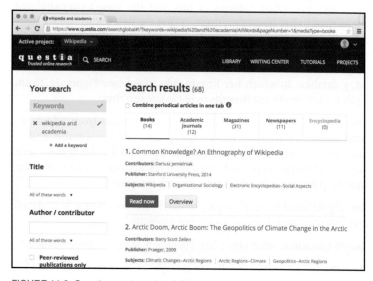

FIGURE 11.2 *Questia* search results. © Questia

11c Assembling a Working Bibliography

During your exploratory research, you begin to assemble a **working bibliography** of the sources you consult. This working bibliography will be the basis for your <u>works-cited list</u>, which will include all the sources you cite in your paper.

See 17a2

1 Keeping Track of Your Sources

As you consider each potential source, record full and accurate bibliographic information in your research notebook. Keep records of interviews (including telephone and email interviews), meetings, lectures, films, blogs, and websites as well as print and electronic articles and books. For each source, include basic identifying details—such as the date of an interview, the call number of a hard-copy library book, and the URL of an Internet source. (Make sure the URL is not unique to the search session. Some databases provide what is called a permalink. Such a durable or permanent URL is always preferable to the URL provided by a browser. One way to test the durability of a browser URL is to copy and paste the URL into a different browser and see if it still works.) Also, record the date you downloaded the source (and perhaps the search engine you used to find it as well), or the author of an article accessed from a database. Also write up a brief evaluation that includes your comments about the kind of information the source contains, the amount of information offered, its relevance to your topic, and its limitations.

Figure 11.3 shows two of the sources Rebecca found as she put together her working bibliography.

FIGURE 11.3 Sources for working bibliography. © First Monday

Following is an example of source information Rebecca kept for her working bibliography.

Information for Working Bibliography (in Research Notebook)

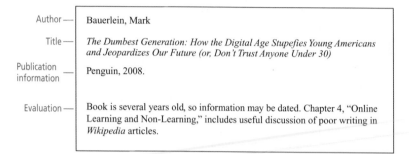

Author — Bauerlein, Mark

Title — *The Dumbest Generation: How the Digital Age Stupefies Young Americans and Jeopardizes Our Future (or, Don't Trust Anyone Under 30)*

Publication information — Penguin, 2008.

Evaluation — Book is several years old, so information may be dated. Chapter 4, "Online Learning and Non-Learning," includes useful discussion of poor writing in *Wikipedia* articles.

As you go about collecting sources and building your working bibliography, be careful to evaluate the quality and relevance of all the materials you examine. Making informed choices early in the research process will save you a lot of time in the long run. (For guidelines on evaluating sources, **see Chapter 13.**)

2 Preparing an Annotated Bibliography

Some instructors require an **annotated bibliography**, a list of all your sources accompanied by a brief summary and evaluation of each source. The following is an excerpt from Rebecca's annotated bibliography.

Annotated Bibliography (Excerpt)

Wilson, Jodi L. "Proceed with Extreme Caution: Citation to *Wikipedia* in Light of Contributor Demographics and Content Policies." *Vanderbilt Journal of Entertainment & Technology Law*, vol. 16, no. 4, 2014, pp. 857–908. *Academic Search Complete*, web.a.ebscohost.com.ezproxy.cul.columbia.edu/ ehost/detail/detail?vid=4&sid=14afe0c2-3351-4754-93dc-2371d2724d5d.

This academic journal article discusses the kinds of people who most commonly consult *Wikipedia*, considering factors such as age and education level. It includes charts that give percentages of *Wikipedia* users within these categories.

This article is a primary source that contains original research and has been peer-reviewed. It provides important data on *Wikipedia* users, arguing that, although the majority of *Wikipedia* users are educated adults, researchers should be careful to consider the credibility of the *Wikipedia* contributors to articles they use in their research.

11d Developing a Tentative Thesis

Your **tentative thesis** is a preliminary statement of the main point you think your research will support. This statement, which you will eventually refine into your paper's **thesis statement**, should answer your research question. Rebecca's progress from assignment to tentative thesis appears below.

See 11h

Tentative Thesis

Assignment	Topic	Research Question
Issue related to the Internet	Using *Wikipedia* for college-level research	What effect has *Wikipedia* had on academic research?

Tentative Thesis: The debate surrounding *Wikipedia* has helped people in the academic community to consider how college-level research has changed in recent years.

Because your tentative thesis suggests the specific direction your research will take as well as the scope and emphasis of your project, it can help you generate a list of the key points you plan to develop in your project. This list can help you narrow the focus of your research so you can zero in on a few specific areas to explore as you read and take notes.

Rebecca used her tentative thesis to help her generate the following list of points to explore further.

Points to Explore

Tentative thesis: The debate surrounding *Wikipedia* has helped people in the academic community to consider how college-level research has changed in recent years.

- Give background about *Wikipedia*; explain its benefits and drawbacks.
- Talk about who uses *Wikipedia* and for what purposes.
- Explain possible future enhancements to the site.
- Explain college instructors' resistance to *Wikipedia*.
- Talk about efforts made by librarians and others to incorporate *Wikipedia* into academic research.

11e Doing Focused Research

During exploratory research, you look at reference works to get an overview of your topic. During **focused research**, however, you dig deeper into your topic: you consult periodical articles, books, and other sources (in print and online) to find the specific information—facts, examples, statistics, definitions, quotations—you need to support your points. Once you have decided on a tentative thesis and have made a list of the points you plan to explore, you are ready to begin your focused research.

❶ Reading Sources

As you look for information, try to explore as many sources as possible. It makes sense to examine more sources than you actually intend to use so that you can proceed even if some of your sources turn out to be biased, outdated, unreliable, superficial, or irrelevant—in other words, not suitable.

As you explore various sources, quickly evaluate their potential usefulness. For example, if your source is a journal article, read the abstract; if your source is a book, skim the table of contents and the index. Then, if an article or a section of a book seems useful, photocopy it for future reference. As you explore sources online, you may find you have multiple windows open at once. If this is the case, be especially careful not to paste material you see onscreen directly into your paper. (This practice can lead to plagiarism.) Instead, send yourself the link (or print the pages you need) so you can evaluate the material further later on. (For information on evaluating electronic and print sources, **see Chapter 13.**)

See
Ch. 16

❷ Balancing Primary and Secondary Sources

During your focused research, you will encounter both **primary sources** (original documents and observations) and **secondary sources** (interpretations of original documents and observations).

Primary Source: United States Constitution, Amendment XIV (Ratified July 9, 1868). Section I.

All persons born or naturalized in the United States, and subject to the jurisdiction thereof, are citizens of the United States and the state wherein they reside. No state shall make or enforce any law which shall abridge the privileges or immunities of citizens of the United States; nor shall any state deprive any person of life, liberty, or property, without the process of law; nor deny to any person within its jurisdiction the equal protection of the laws.

Secondary Source: Paula S. Rothenberg, *Racism and Sexism: An Integrated Study.*

Congress passed the Fourteenth Amendment . . . in July 1868. This amendment, which continues to play a major role in contemporary legal battles over discrimination, includes a number of important provisions. It explicitly extends citizenship to all those born or naturalized in the United States and guarantees all citizens due process and "equal protection" of the law.

Close-Up DEFINING PRIMARY AND SECONDARY SOURCES

Academic research projects often combine primary and secondary sources. Before you begin any research project, it makes sense to consult with your instructor to see how he or she defines *primary* and *secondary* for your specific assignment. For Rebecca's project, for example, journal articles that report on studies in which people were interviewed or surveyed might be considered primary sources, as would Rebecca's own experiences with *Wikipedia* or with online research. A book on her subject or a literature review of several studies would be considered a secondary source.

For some research projects, primary sources are essential; however, most research projects in the humanities rely heavily on secondary sources, which provide scholars' insights and interpretations. Remember, though, that the further you get from the primary source, the more chances exist for inaccuracies caused by misinterpretations or distortions.

Primary and Secondary Sources	
Primary Source in the Humanities	**Secondary Source in the Humanities**
Novel, poem, play, film	Scholarly analysis and criticism
Diary, autobiography	Biography
Letter, historical document, speech, oral history	Review
Newspaper or magazine article from the time period being discussed	
Interview	
Primary Source in the Social Sciences and Sciences	**Secondary Source in the Social Sciences and Sciences**
Raw data from questionnaires or interviews	Literature review
Observation/experiment	
Scientific (empirical) article containing original research	
Case study	

11f   Managing Photocopies, Scans, and Downloaded Material

Much of the information you gather will be in the form of photocopies or scanned pages saved as PDFs (of articles, book pages, and so on) and material downloaded from the Internet or from a library database. Learning to manage this source information efficiently will save you a lot of time.

First, do not use the ease of copying and downloading as an excuse to postpone decisions about the usefulness of your sources. After all, you can easily accumulate so many pages that it will be almost impossible for you to keep track of all your information.

Also keep in mind that the sources you find are just raw material, not information that you have already interpreted and evaluated. Making copies of sources is only the first step in the process of taking thorough, careful notes. You still have to evaluate, paraphrase, and summarize your sources' ideas and make connections among them.

Moreover, photocopies, scans, and downloaded material do not give you much flexibility. For example, a single page of text may include information that should be earmarked for several different sections of your paper. This lack of flexibility makes it almost impossible for you to arrange source material into any meaningful order. Just as you would with any source, you will have to take notes on the information you read. These notes will give you the flexibility you need to write your paper.

Close-Up   AVOIDING PLAGIARISM

See Ch. 16

To avoid the possibility of accidental plagiarism, be sure to keep all downloaded material in a separate file—not in your Notes file. After you read this material and decide how to use it, you can move the information you plan to use into your Notes file (along with full source information).

CHECKLIST
Working with Photocopies, Scans, and Downloaded Material

To get the most out of photocopies, scans, and material downloaded from the Internet, follow these guidelines:

❏ Record full and accurate source information, including the inclusive page numbers, electronic address (URL), and any other relevant information, on the first page of each copy.

continued

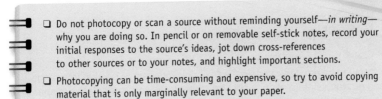

❑ Do not photocopy or scan a source without reminding yourself—*in writing*—why you are doing so. In pencil or on removable self-stick notes, record your initial responses to the source's ideas, jot down cross-references to other sources or to your notes, and highlight important sections.

❑ Photocopying can be time-consuming and expensive, so try to avoid copying material that is only marginally relevant to your paper.

❑ Keep photocopies in a separate file so you will be able to find them when you need them. Keep all electronic copies of source material together in one clearly labeled file.

11g Taking Notes

As you locate information, take notes to create a record of exactly what you found and where you found it. These notes will help you to fine-tune your thesis and decide how to develop your discussion.

See Ch. 14

Each piece of information you record in your notes (whether <u>sum-marized</u>, <u>paraphrased</u>, or <u>quoted</u> from your sources) should be accompanied by a short descriptive heading that indicates its relevance to one of the points you will develop in your paper. Because you will use these headings to guide you as you organize your notes, you should make them as specific as possible. For example, labeling every note for a paper on *Wikipedia* **Wikipedia** or **Internet** will not prove very helpful later on. More focused headings—for instance, ***Wikipedia*'s popularity** or **college instructors' objections**—will be much more useful.

Also include brief comments that make clear your reasons for recording the information. These comments (enclosed in brackets so you will know they are your own ideas, not those of your source) should establish the purpose of your note—what you think it can explain, support, clarify, describe, or contradict—and perhaps suggest its relationship to other notes or to other sources. Any questions you have about the information or its source can also be included in your comment.

Finally, each note should fully and accurately identify the source of the information you are recording. You do not have to write out the complete citation, but you do have to include enough information to identify your source. For example, **Wilson** would be enough to send you back to your working bibliography, where you would be able to find the complete documentation for the author's article.

MULTILINGUAL TIP

Taking notes in English (rather than in your native language) will make it easier for you to transfer the notes into a draft of your paper. However, you may find it faster and more effective to use your native language when writing your own comments about each note.

Close-Up TAKING NOTES

When you take notes, your goal is flexibility: you want to be able to arrange and rearrange information easily and efficiently as your paper takes shape.

Type each individual note (accompanied by source information) under a specific heading rather than listing all information from a single source under the same heading, and be sure to divide notes from one another with extra space or horizontal lines. (As you revise, you can move notes around so notes on the same topic are grouped together.)

CHECKLIST

Taking Notes

- ❏ **Identify the source of each piece of information,** including the page numbers for quotations from paginated sources.
- ❏ **Include everything now that you will need later** to understand your note—names, dates, places, connections with other notes—and to remember why you recorded it.
- ❏ **Distinguish quotations from paraphrases and summaries and your own ideas from those of your sources.** If you copy a source's words, place them in quotation marks (and boldface the quotation marks). If you record your own ideas, enclose them in brackets and boldface them as well. These techniques will help you avoid accidental plagiarism in your paper.

See Ch. 16

- ❏ **Put an author's ideas into your own words whenever possible,** summarizing and paraphrasing material as well as adding your own observations and analyses.
- ❏ **Copy quoted material accurately,** using the exact words, spelling, punctuation marks, and capitalization of the original.
- ❏ **Never paste information from a source directly into your paper.** This practice can lead to plagiarism.

Following is an example of the notes that Rebecca took.

Notes (in Research Notebook)

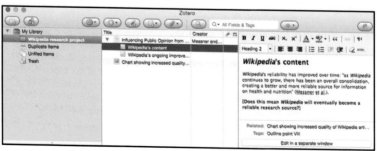

Note: Various note-taking programs, such as *Evernote* or *Note.ly* can help you to keep track of your notes.

11h Fine-Tuning Your Thesis

After you have finished your focused research and note-taking, you are ready to refine your tentative thesis into a carefully worded statement that expresses a conclusion your research can support. This **thesis statement** should be more precise than your tentative thesis, accurately conveying the direction, emphasis, and scope of your paper.

See 5a–b

Compare Rebecca's tentative thesis with her final thesis statement.

Thesis Statement

Tentative Thesis	Thesis Statement
The debate surrounding *Wikipedia* has helped people in the academic community to consider how college-level research has changed in recent years.	All in all, the debate over *Wikipedia* has been a positive development because it has led the academic community to confront the challenges of open, collaborative software on the web.

EXERCISE 11.1

Read the following passages. Assume that you are developing a research project on the influences that shaped young writers in the 1920s. What possible thesis statements could be supported by the information in each of these passages?

1. Yet in spite of their opportunities and their achievements the generation deserved for a long time the adjective ["lost"] that Gertrude Stein had applied to it. The reasons aren't hard to find. It was lost, first of all, because it was uprooted, schooled away and almost wrenched away from its attachment to any region or tradition. It was lost because its training had prepared it for another world than existed after the war and because the war prepared it only for travel and excitement. It was lost because it tried to live in exile. It was lost because it accepted no older guides to conduct and because it formed a false picture of society and the writer's place in it. The generation belonged to a period of transition from values already fixed to values that had to be created.

   (Malcolm Cowley, *Exile's Return*)

2. The 1920s were a time least likely to produce substantial support among intellectuals for any sound, rational, and logical program. Pre-war stability and convention were condemned because all evidences of stability seemed illusory and artificial. The very lively and active

interest in science was perhaps the decade's most substantial contribution to modern civilization. Yet in this case as well, achievement became a symbol of disorder and a source of disenchantment.

(Frederick J. Hoffman, *The 20's*)

3. Societies do not give up old ideals and attitudes easily; the conflicts between the representatives of the older elements of traditional American culture and the prophets of the new day were at times as bitter as they were extensive. Such matters as religion, marriage, and moral standards as well as the issues over race, prohibition, and immigration were at the heart of the conflict.

(Introduction to *The Twenties*, ed. George E. Mowry)

11i Constructing an Outline

See 5d Once you have a thesis statement, you are ready to construct an outline to guide you as you write your rough draft.

See 6c4 A formal outline is different from a **scratch outline**, which is a list of the key points you tentatively plan to develop in your paper. A **formal outline**—which may be either a **topic outline** or a **sentence outline**—includes all the ideas you will develop, indicating not only the exact order in which you will present these ideas but also the relationship between main points and supporting details. It may also be helpful to list sources by author name or by a brief description of where you plan to use them in your paper.

Note: The outline you construct at this stage is only a guide for you to follow as you write your rough draft. During the revision process, you may want to construct another outline to check the logic of your organization.

Rebecca James made the following topic outline to guide her as she wrote her rough draft.

Formal (Topic) Outline

Thesis statement: All in all, the debate over *Wikipedia* has been a positive development because it has led the academic community to confront the challenges of open, collaborative software on the web.

    I. Definition of wiki and explanation of *Wikipedia*

        A. Fast and easy

        B. Range of topics

    II. Introduction to *Wikipedia*'s drawbacks

        A. Warnings on "Researching with *Wikipedia*" page

        B. Criticisms in "Reliability of *Wikipedia*" article

        C. Criticisms by academics

1. Villanova University
2. Middlebury College history department

III. *Wikipedia*'s unreliability

    A. Lack of citations

    B. Factual inaccuracy and bias

    C. Vandalism

IV. *Wikipedia*'s poor writing

    A. *Wikipedia*'s coding system

    B. *Wikipedia*'s influence on students' writing (Bauerlein)

V. *Wikipedia*'s popularity and benefits

    A. Wilson's findings (charts)

    B. Comprehensive abstracts, links to other sources, and current and comprehensive bibliographies

VI. *Wikipedia*'s advantages over other online encyclopedias

    A. Very current information

    B. More coverage of popular culture topics

    C. "Stub" articles

VII. *Wikipedia*'s ongoing improvements

    A. Control measures

    B. Users as editors

    C. "Talk" page

VIII. *Wikipedia*'s content

    A. View of Messner et al.

    B. Chart showing increased quality of *Wikipedia* articles over time

IX. Academic community's reservations about *Wikipedia*

    A. Academics' failure to keep up with technology

    B. Academics' qualifications to improve *Wikipedia*

X. Instructors' and librarians' efforts to use and improve *Wikipedia*

    A. Snyder's and Power's support for *Wikipedia*

    B. Responsibility of academic community

XI. *Wikipedia* in the classroom

    A. *Wikipedia*'s education program

    B. Collaborative and critical thinking assignments

XII. Academics' changing view of *Wikipedia*

    A. Academics' increasing acceptance

    B. Academics' increasing involvement

    C. *Wikipedia*'s best practices

Close-Up　OUTLINING

Before you begin writing, create a separate file for each major section of your outline. Then, copy your notes into these files in the order in which you intend to use them.

Be sure to label the files clearly for later reference. Each file name should include a reference to the class and assignment for which it was written. For instance, Rebecca's file for the section of her English 102 essay on *Wikipedia*'s ongoing improvements is called "102 Wikipedia Ongoing Improvements." The individual files relating to this project are all collected in a folder titled "Eng 102 Wikipedia." By organizing your files in this way, you can use each file as a guide as you write.

11j　Writing a Rough Draft

See
6a

When you are ready to write your **rough draft**, check to be sure you have arranged your notes in the order in which you intend to use them. Follow your outline as you write, using your notes as needed. As you draft, write notes to yourself in brackets, jotting down questions and identifying points that need further clarification and areas that need more development. You can also use *Microsoft Word*'s Comment tool to add notes.

As you move along, leave space for material you plan to add, and identify phrases or whole sections that you think you may later decide to move or delete. In other words, lay the groundwork for revision.

As your draft takes shape, be sure to supply transitions between sentences and paragraphs to indicate how your points are related. Also be careful to copy source information fully and accurately in this and every subsequent draft, placing documentation as close as possible to the material it identifies.

Like any other essay, a research paper has an introduction, a body, and a conclusion. In your rough draft, as in your outline, you focus on the body of your paper. Don't spend too much time planning your introduction or conclusion at this stage; your ideas will change as you write, and you will need to revise and expand your opening and closing paragraphs later to reflect those changes.

PLANNING GUIDE

RESEARCH PROJECT

Your **assignment** will be to read a variety of sources to help you explore a subject that you want to learn more about.

Your **purpose** will be to interpret and evaluate your sources' ideas and to develop an original idea about your topic.

Your **audience** will usually be your instructor.

INTRODUCTION

- Begin by introducing readers to your subject and suggesting how you will approach it.
- Provide background to help readers understand the context for your discussion, perhaps briefly summarizing research already done on your topic.
- State your thesis, the position your research will support.

Thesis statement templates:
- Despite..., the evidence suggests that...
- Although many people believe..., it seems more likely that...is actually the case.

BODY PARAGRAPHS

- Begin each paragraph with a topic sentence that corresponds to a section of your outline.
- In each body paragraph, provide support for your thesis, synthesizing source information with ideas of your own.
- Use summary, paraphrase, and quoted material from your sources to support your statements.
- Use different patterns of development to shape the individual paragraphs of your essay.
- Connect sentences and paragraphs with clear transitions, including transitional paragraphs where necessary.
- Be careful to keep track of your sources and to avoid plagiarism.
- Consider including visuals where appropriate.
- Include parenthetical documentation where necessary.

Topic sentence templates:
- The first (second, final) point/example is...
- Another point that supports this position is...

Templates for introducing support:
- As many scholars observe,...
- Several sources make the case that...
- Another study demonstrates that...
- According to...,...

See 34d

See 34e1

CONCLUSION

- Restate your thesis (in different words).
- Summarize your key points.
- End with a strong concluding statement.

Concluding statement templates:
- As the ongoing debate around this issue suggests,...
- For all the reasons summarized above,...
- Given the supporting evidence outlined here, it seems likely that...

See
23b

See
14d

See
Ch. 3,
23d

Close-Up USING TOPIC SENTENCES AND HEADINGS

Clear, specific topic sentences will help readers follow your discussion.

> Without a professional editorial board to oversee its development, *Wikipedia* has several shortcomings that limit its trustworthiness.

You can also use headings if they are a convention of the discipline in which you are writing.

Wikipedia's Advantages

> *Wikipedia* has advantages over other online encyclopedias.

❶ Working Source Material into Your Paper

In the body of your paper, you evaluate and interpret your sources, comparing different ideas and assessing various points of view. As a writer, your job is to draw your own conclusions, blending information from various sources into a paper that coherently and forcefully presents your own original viewpoint.

Be sure to **integrate source material** smoothly into your discussion, clearly and accurately identifying the relationships among various sources (and between those sources' ideas and your own). If two sources present conflicting interpretations, you should be especially careful to use precise language and accurate transitions to make the contrast apparent (for instance, **Although some academics believe that** *Wikipedia* **should not be a part of college-level research, Snyder argues . . .**). When two sources agree, you should make this clear (for example, **Like Snyder, Power claims . . .** or **The findings of Messner et al. support Snyder's point**). Such phrasing will provide a context for your own comments and conclusions. If different sources present complementary information about a subject, blend details from the sources carefully, keeping track of which details come from which source.

❷ Integrating Visuals

Photographs, diagrams, graphs, and other visuals can enrich your discussion by providing additional support for the points you make. You can create a visual on your own (for example, by taking a photograph or creating a bar graph). You can also scan an appropriate visual from a book or magazine or access an image database. When you add a visual, be sure to provide a caption that identifies the name of the person who created it. This will enable readers to find full source information in your works-cited list.

Close-Up · CREATIVE COMMONS

Students who are developing projects for college classes generally do not have to be concerned about copyright issues ("fair use" protects most uses of copyrighted information in student work), but if a student planned to present his or her work at an undergraduate research conference, whose organizers might then publish the paper for wider distribution, any visuals used would be subject to copyright restrictions. To avoid the problem of having to request permission for the visuals used in their papers, Rebecca's instructor recommended that students use the *Creative Commons* website to find visuals whose creators had released their work from copyright restrictions.

When Rebecca searched *Google*'s image database via the *Creative Commons* website, she found a visual to include in her paper (see Figure 11.4).

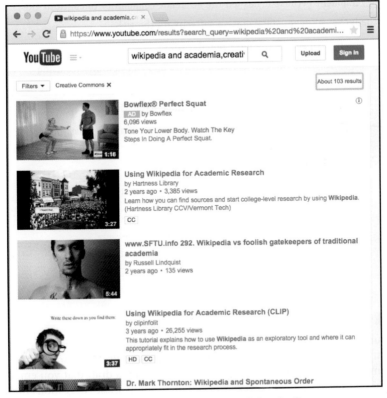

FIGURE 11.4 *Creative Commons* image search results. © Creative Commons

11k Revising Your Drafts

As you review your drafts, you follow the revision procedures that apply to any essay (**see 6b–c**). In addition, you should review the questions in the checklist on page 136, which apply specifically to research papers.

1 Outlining

See 6c4, 11i

A good way to begin revising is to make a formal <u>outline</u> of your draft to check the logic of its organization and the relationships among sections. When Rebecca began to revise, the first thing she did was construct a **sentence outline** to check the structure of her paper. An excerpt from her sentence outline is shown below.

Sentence Outline (Excerpt)

<u>Thesis statement:</u> All in all, the debate over *Wikipedia* has been a positive development because it has led the academic community to confront the challenges of open, collaborative software on the web.

    I. *Wikipedia* is the most popular wiki.

        A. Users can edit existing articles and add new articles using *Wikipedia*'s editing tools.

        B. *Wikipedia* has grown into a huge database.

    II. *Wikipedia* has several shortcomings that limit its trustworthiness.

        A. *Wikipedia*'s "Researching with *Wikipedia*" page acknowledges existing problems.

        B. *Wikipedia*'s "Reliability of *Wikipedia*" page presents criticisms.

        C. Academics have objections.

    III. *Wikipedia* is not always reliable or accurate.

        A. Many *Wikipedia* articles do not include citations.

        B. *Wikipedia* articles can be inaccurate or biased.

        C. *Wikipedia* articles can be targets for vandalism.

2 Instructor's Comments

Your instructor's suggestions for revisions can come in a conference or in comments on your paper. Your instructor can also use *Microsoft Word*'s Comment tool to make comments electronically on a draft that you email to him or her. When you revise, you can incorporate these suggestions into your revision, as Rebecca did.

Draft with Instructor's Comments (Excerpt)

Emory University English professor Mark Bauerlein
asserts that *Wikipedia* articles are written in a "flat,
featureless, factual style" (153). Even though *Wikipedia*
has instituted a coding system in which it labels the
shortcomings of its less-developed articles, a warning
about an article's poor writing style is likely to go unnoticed
by the typical user.

> Comment [JB1]: You need a transition sentence before this one to show that this ¶ is about a new idea. See 34b2.

> Comment [JB2]: Wordy. See 37a.

Revision Incorporating Instructor's Suggestions

Because they can be edited by anyone, *Wikipedia* articles are often
poorly written. Emory University English professor Mark Bauerlein asserts
that *Wikipedia* articles are written in a "flat, featureless, factual style"
(153). Even though *Wikipedia* has instituted a coding system to label the
shortcomings of its less-developed articles, a warning about an article's poor
writing style is likely to go unnoticed by the typical user.

③ Peer Review

Feedback you get from **peer review**—other students' comments, handwritten or electronic—can also help you revise. As you incorporate your classmates' suggestions, as well as your own changes and any suggested by your instructor, you can use *Microsoft Word*'s Track Changes tool to help you keep track of the revisions you make on your draft.

See 6c2

&

   Following are two versions of an excerpt from Rebecca's paper. The first
version includes comments (inserted with *Microsoft Word*'s Comment tool)
from three peer reviewers. The second uses the Track Changes tool to show
the revisions Rebecca made in response to these comments.

Draft with Peer Reviewers' Comments (Excerpt)

Because users can update articles in real time
from any location, *Wikipedia* offers up-to-the-minute
coverage of political and cultural events as well as
timely information on popular culture topics that
receive little or no attention in other reference
sources. In addition, because *Wikipedia* has such
a broad user base, more topics are covered in
Wikipedia than in other online resources. Even
when there is little information on a particular topic,

> Comment [RS1]: I think you need a better transition here.

> Comment [TG2]: I think an example here would really help.

> Comment [DL3]: I agree. Maybe talk about a useful *Wikipedia* article you found recently.

Wikipedia allows users to create "stub" articles, which provide minimal information that users can expand over time. Thus, *Wikipedia* can be a valuable first step in finding reliable research sources.

> Comment [RS4]: Why?

Revision with Track Changes

Wikipedia has advantages over other online encyclopedias. Because users can update articles in real time from any location, *Wikipedia* offers up-to-the-minute coverage of political and cultural events as well as timely information on popular culture topics that receive little or no attention in other reference sources. In addition, because *Wikipedia* has such a broad user base, more topics are covered in *Wikipedia* than in other online resources. For example, a student researching the history of video gaming would find *Wikipedia*'s "Wii U" article, with its numerous pages of information and nearly two hundred references, to be a valuable resource. *Encyclopaedia Britannica* does not contain a comparable article on this popular game console. Even when there is little information on a particular topic, *Wikipedia* allows users to create "stub" articles, which provide minimal information that users can expand over time. Thus, by offering immediate access to information on relatively obscure topics, *Wikipedia* can be a valuable first step in finding reliable research sources on such topics.

CHECKLIST

Revising a Research Paper

As you revise, consider the following questions:

❑ Should you do more research to find support for certain points?

❑ Do you need to reorder the major sections of your paper?

❑ Should you rearrange the order in which you present your points within sections?

❑ Do you need to add section headings? Transitional paragraphs?

See 14d

❑ Have you **integrated source material** smoothly into your paper?

❑ Have you chosen visuals carefully and integrated them smoothly into your paper?

❑ Are quotations blended with paraphrase, summary, and your own observations and reactions?

See Ch. 16

❑ Have you avoided **plagiarism** by carefully documenting all borrowed ideas?

❑ Have you analyzed and interpreted the ideas of others rather than simply stringing those ideas together?

❑ Do your own ideas—not those of your sources—define the focus of your discussion?

Note: You will probably take your paper through several drafts, changing different parts of it each time or working on one part over and over again. After revising each draft thoroughly, print out a corrected version, and label it *First Draft, Second Draft,* and so on. Then, make additional corrections by hand on that draft before typing in your changes to create the next draft. Be sure to save and clearly label every electronic draft so you can go back to a previous draft if necessary.

When you finish revising your paper, copy the file that contains your working bibliography and insert it at the end of your paper. Keep the original file for your working bibliography as a backup in case any data is lost in the process. Delete any irrelevant entries, and then create your works-cited list. (Make sure the format of the entries in your works-cited list conforms to the documentation style you are using.)

If you save multiple drafts of your works-cited list, be sure to name each file with the date or some other label so that it is readily identifiable. Keep all files pertaining to a single project in a folder dedicated to that paper or assignment.

Close-Up USING CITATION TOOLS

Use citation tools such as the following to create your bibliography and to make sure all the sources you used—and only those sources—appear in your works-cited list.

BibMe
- Free and easy to use: made for quick copying and pasting of citations anywhere; allows saving for later use
- Entirely web-based
- Supports MLA, APA, and Chicago documentation styles

EasyBib
- Free and easy to use: made for quick copying and pasting of citations anywhere; allows saving for later use
- Entirely web-based
- Supports MLA, APA, and Chicago documentation styles

EndNote
- Purchase required (consult with your college library or bookstore for free institutional access or student discounts; if you access through your institution's license, you may not be able to access your citations after graduation)

(continued)

USING CITATION TOOLS *(continued)*

- Easy to use: Allows you to collect citations and add notes with unlimited storage. Cite While You Write feature allows you to cite within a document. Compatible with *Microsoft Office*, *OpenOffice*, and *iWork Pages*.
- Works on both Mac and PC either offline or online, but more robust when used on a local computer. Syncs with *EndNote Basic* for web access.
- Supports MLA, APA, Chicago, CSE, and many other documentation styles

EndNote Basic/EndNote Web
- Free and easy to use: Allows sharing of citations with others, as in group projects. Compatible with *Microsoft Word*.
- Entirely web-based (Internet connection needed to access citations). Syncs with *EndNote* (on a local computer).

Mendeley
- Free (unless large-capacity online storage space is needed)
- Easy to use: Allows you to collect citations and add notes. Citations can be shared privately with up to two additional users or open to public viewing. Retains PDFs alongside citations with easy organization and retrieval. Compatible with *Microsoft Word*, *OpenOffice*, and *LaTeX*.
- Works on both Mac and PC either offline or online, but more robust when used on a local computer. Can be synced with multiple devices, allowing access to citations from anywhere.
- Supports MLA, APA, Chicago, and many other documentation styles

Qiqqa
- Free and easy to use: Allows you to collect citations and add notes. InCite feature allows you to cite within a document. Retains PDFs alongside citations with easy organization and retrieval.
- PC-compatible only
- Supports MLA, APA, Chicago, and many other documentation styles

RefWorks
- Purchase required (consult with your college library or bookstore for free institutional access or student discounts; if you access through your institution's license, you may not be able to access your citations after graduation)
- Easy to use: Allows you to collect citations and add notes. Write-N-Cite feature allows you to cite within a document. *RefShare* (a companion to *RefWorks*) allows you to share citations with others.
- Entirely web-based
- Supports MLA, APA, Chicago, CSE, and many other documentation styles

Zotero

- Free (unless large-capacity online syncing storage space is needed)
- Easy to use: Allows you to collect citations and add extensive review notes. Plug-in automatically inserts footnotes or parenthetical citations into a word-processing document. Quick Copy function allows you to drag and drop a citation in any text field in your document. "Scrapes" websites for citation information by taking a snapshot (some data may need to be added if *Zotero* cannot identify a particular field). Allows sharing of citations with others, as in group projects. Retains PDFs alongside citations with easy organization and retrieval. Compatible with *Microsoft Word*, *OpenOffice*, and *Google Drive*.
- Works on both Mac and PC either offline or online, but more robust when used on a local computer. Can be synced with multiple devices, allowing access to citations from anywhere. Prefers *Firefox* browser.
- Supports MLA, APA, Chicago, CSE, and many other documentation styles

11l   Preparing a Final Draft

Before you submit the final version of your paper, **edit and proofread** See 6d hard copy of both the paper itself and your works-cited list. Next, consider (or reconsider) your **title**. It should be descriptive enough to tell your readers what your paper is about, and it should create interest in your subject. Your title should also be consistent with your **purpose** and tone. See 1b (You would hardly want a humorous title for an essay about famine in Sub-Saharan Africa or inequities in the American judicial system.) Finally, your title should be engaging and to the point—and perhaps even provocative. Often, a quotation from one of your sources will suggest a likely title.

When you are satisfied with your title, read your paper one last time, proofreading for grammar, spelling, or typing errors you may have missed. Pay particular attention to parenthetical documentation and works-cited entries. (Remember that every error undermines your credibility.) Once you are satisfied that your paper is as accurate as you can make it, print out your final draft or email it to your instructor, following his or her guidelines. (For the final draft of Rebecca's research paper, along with her works-cited list, see **17c**.)

CHAPTER **12**

Finding Information

12a Finding Information in the Library

When it comes to finding trustworthy, high-quality, and authoritative sources, nothing beats your college library. A modern college library offers you resources that you cannot find anywhere else—even on the Internet.

> ## Close-Up WHY USE THE LIBRARY?
>
> - Many important publications are available only in print or through the library's databases.
> - The information in your college library is cataloged and classified.
> - Because the library's databases list only published sources, the information you access will always be available, unlike the information on the Internet.
> - Because librarians screen the resources in your college library, these resources are likely to meet academic standards of reliability. (Even so, you still have to <u>evaluate</u> any information before you use it in an essay.)
> - Bibliographic information for the documents in your college library is easy to determine, unlike that of documents on the Internet.
> - The library staff is available to answer your questions and to help you find material.

See
13a

1 Searching the Library's Online Catalog or Discovery Service

The best way to start your research is by visiting your college library's **website.** The website's home page is a gateway to a vast amount of information—for example, the library's catalog or discovery service, the databases the library makes available, special library services, and general information about the library. Figure 12.1 shows the home page of a library's website.

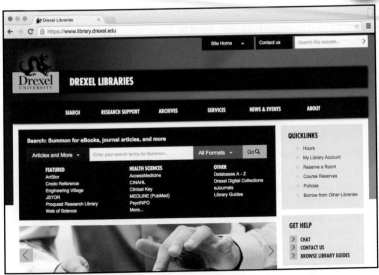

FIGURE 12.1 Home page of an academic library's website. © Drexel University.

Your next step is to search the library's **online catalog**, a database that lists the journal titles (but not the articles themselves), books, and multimedia held in the library's collections. When you search the online catalog or discovery service for information, you may do either a *keyword search* or a *subject search*.

Close-Up A DISCOVERY SERVICE

Many libraries have a **discovery service**, which includes not only the physical items held by a library but also e-books and journal articles, including those from electronic databases, as well as articles and books held at other libraries. These items may be obtained through interlibrary loan.

Doing a Keyword Search When you do a **keyword search**, you enter into the search box of the online catalog or discovery service a word (or words) associated with your topic. The computer then displays a list of entries (called **hits**) that contain these words. The more precise your keywords, the more specific and useful the information you retrieve will be. For example, *Civil War* will yield many thousands of hits; *The Wilderness Campaign* will yield far fewer.

Because vague or inaccurate keyword searching can yield an overwhelming number of irrelevant hits, you need to focus your search by using **search operators**, words or symbols that can narrow (or broaden) your query. One way to do this is to carry out a **Boolean search**, which combines keywords with the search operators *and*, *or*, or *not*.

CHECKLIST

Using Search Operators

When you do a keyword search, follow these guidelines:

- ❏ Use **quotation marks** to search for a specific phrase: *"Baltimore Economy."*
- ❏ Use an **asterisk** after a word to retrieve a root word with any ending: *photo** will yield *photograph, photographer, photojournalist, photoactive,* and so on.
- ❏ Use a **question mark** to replace a single character inside or at the end of a word: *wom?n* will yield *woman* and *women.*
- ❏ Use **and** to search for sites that contain both terms: *Baltimore* and *Economy.*
- ❏ Use **or** to search for sites that contain either term: *Baltimore* or *Philadelphia.*
- ❏ Use **not** to exclude the term that comes after the *not*: *Baltimore* and *Economy* not *Agriculture.*

Doing a Subject Search When you do a **subject search**, you enter a subject heading into the search box of the online catalog or discovery service. The resources in an academic library are classified under specific subject headings. Many online catalogs list these subject headings to help you identify the exact words that you need for your search. Figure 12.2 on page 143 shows the results of a subject search in a university library's discovery service.

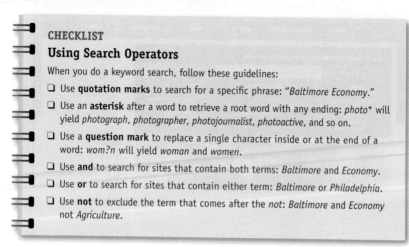

Close-Up KEYWORD SEARCHING VERSUS SUBJECT SEARCHING

When deciding whether to do a keyword search or a subject search, consider the strengths and weaknesses of each method.

Keyword Searching	Subject Searching
• Searches many subject areas	• Searches only a specific subject area
• Can use any significant word or phrase	• Can use only specific subject headings
• Retrieves a large number of items	• Retrieves a smaller number of items
• May retrieve many irrelevant items	• Retrieves few irrelevant items

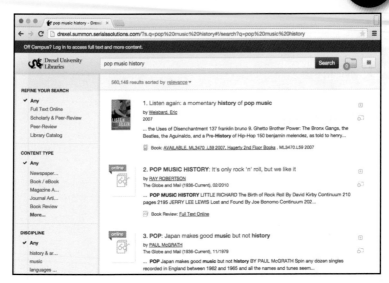

FIGURE 12.2 Discovery service search results for the subject heading *pop music history*. © Drexel University.

Note: *WorldCat* and *WorldCat Local* are "super" catalogs of millions of items. If your college library provides access to these resources, you can locate books, DVDs, music, photographs, and specialized databases from thousands of participating libraries around the world and in your community. Check with your reference librarian for information about these resources.

2 Searching the Library's Databases

Through your college library's website, you can also access a variety of databases to which the library subscribes. These **online databases** are collections of digital information—such as newspaper, magazine, and journal articles—arranged for easy access and retrieval. (You search these databases the same way you search the library's online catalog—by doing a keyword search or a subject search.)

See 12a1

One of the first things you should do is find out which databases your library subscribes to. You can usually access these databases through the library's website, and if necessary, you can ask a reference librarian for more information. Figure 12.3 shows a partial list of databases to which one library subscribes.

College libraries subscribe to information service companies, such as Gale Cengage Learning, which provide access to hundreds of databases not available for free on the Internet. These databases enable you to access

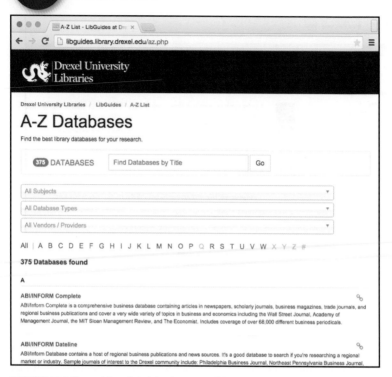

FIGURE 12.3 Excerpt from list of databases to which one academic library subscribes. © Drexel University.

current information from scholarly journals, abstracts, books, reports, case studies, government documents, magazines, and newspapers. Most libraries subscribe to databases that cover many subject areas (*Expanded Academic ASAP*, EBSCOhost's *Academic Search*, and *LexisNexis Academic Universe*, for example); others cover a single subject area in great detail (*PsycINFO* or *Sociological Abstracts*, for example).

Assuming that your library offers a variety of databases, how do you know which ones will be best for your research? First, you should determine the level of the periodical articles listed in the database. A **periodical** is a scholarly journal, magazine, newspaper, or other publication that appears at regular intervals (weekly, monthly, or quarterly, for example). **Scholarly journals** are often the most reliable sources you can find on a subject. They contain articles written by experts in a field, and because journals focus on a particular subject area, they usually provide in-depth analysis. However, because journal articles are aimed at experts, they can be difficult for general readers to understand. **Popular periodicals** are magazines and newspapers that publish articles aimed at general readers. These periodicals are more accessible, but they are less reliable than scholarly journals because they vary greatly in quality. Some articles might conform to academic standards of reliability, but others may be totally unsuitable as sources.

Close-Up CHOOSING A LIBRARY DATABASE

Consulting with a reference librarian is an excellent way to get connected to the best databases for your topic. You could also ask your instructor if your class will be visiting the library for a research session conducted by a reference librarian. These hands-on sessions will help guide you through the maze of resources to the best ones for your topic.

Next, you should look for a database that is suitable for your topic. Most libraries list databases alphabetically by title or arrange them by subject area. Some offer online **study guides** (also called research guides or subject guides) that were designed by reference librarians and that list databases (as well as other resources) that are appropriate for research in a given subject area. If you know what database you are looking for, you can find it in the alphabetical listing. If you don't, go to the subject list and locate your general subject area—*History, Nursing,* or *Linguistics,* for example. Then, review the databases that are listed under this heading.

You can begin with a multisubject **general database** such as *Expanded Academic ASAP* or EBSCOhost's *Academic Search* that includes thousands of full-text articles. Then, you can move on to more **specialized databases** that examine your specific subject in detail and that include a far greater number of discipline-specific sources than do general-interest databases.

Close-Up USING MULTI SEARCH

Check to see if your library uses EBSCO Discovery Service, which enables you to search many library databases at one time. Libraries often call it "One Search" or "Multi Search," and it typically appears as one search box on the home page, as in this example.

| Quick Search | Books & DVD's | Databases | Journals |

Search many online library resources at once

Search

University of Arkansas

Frequently Used General Databases

Database	Description
Academic OneFile	Articles from journals and reference sources in a number of disciplines
Credo Reference	A database of several hundred reference books
EBSCOhost's *Academic Search*	Thousands of periodical articles on many subjects
Expanded Academic ASAP	Articles from journals in the humanities, social sciences, and natural and applied sciences
JSTOR	Full-text articles from older issues (typically three to five years out) of hundreds of peer-reviewed journals spanning all disciplines from major academic presses, such as Stanford University and University of Chicago
LexisNexis Academic Universe	Full-text articles from national, international, and local news publications as well as legal and business publications
Opposing Viewpoints Resource Center	A library of debates on current topics
Project MUSE	Articles from dozens of major peer-reviewed journals with an emphasis on the humanities
ProQuest Research Library	An index of journal articles in various disciplines, many full text

Specialized Databases

HUMANITIES

Database	Description
Arts	
Art Abstracts	Articles in art magazines and journals
Communication	
Communication & Mass Media Complete	Index and abstracts for more than four hundred journals and coverage of two hundred more
History	
America: History and Life	Articles on North American history
Historical Abstracts	Articles on world history
History Reference Center	Full-text articles and other resources for the study of history

Literature

MLA International Bibliography	An index for books, articles, and websites focusing on literature, language, and film studies
Gale Literature Criticism Online	Full-text articles on literary criticism and analysis

Philosophy

Philosopher's Index	Index and abstracts from over five hundred fifty journals from forty countries

Religion

ATLA Religion	Articles in religion studies journals

SOCIAL SCIENCES

Database	Description

Business

ABI/INFORM Global	A ProQuest collection of over eighteen hundred journals and company profiles
Business Source Premier	Indexes more than seventy-eight hundred publications

Economics

EconLit	Offers a wide range of economics-related resources

Education

Education Research Complete	The world's largest collection of full-text education journals

Psychology

PsycINFO	Indexes books and journal articles in the psychological and behavioral sciences

Sociology and Social Work

Sociological Abstracts	An index of literature in sociology
Social Work Abstracts	An index of current research in social work

NATURAL AND APPLIED SCIENCES

Database	Description

Biology

Biological Sciences	Abstracts and citations from a wide range of biological research

Chemistry

American Chemical Society Publications	Articles from over thirty peer-reviewed journals

Computer Science

ACM Guide to Computing Literature	Over 750,000 citations and abstracts of literature about computing

Engineering

IEEE Xplore	Full-text access to all IEEE journals, magazines, and conference proceedings

continued

Specialized Databases *(continued)*

NATURAL AND APPLIED SCIENCES

Database	Description
Environmental Science	
Environmental Science Database	Information on environmental subjects
Nursing	
ProQuest Nursing & Allied Health Source	Resources for nursing and the allied health fields

CHECKLIST

Questions for Choosing the Right Database

Before you decide which database to use, ask the following questions:

❑ Is the database suited to your subject? Is it too general or too specialized?

❑ Does the database include scholarly journals, popular periodicals, or both?

❑ Does the database contain the full text of articles or just citations?

❑ Are you able to limit your search—for example, to just scholarly publications or to just peer-reviewed publications?

❑ How easy (or difficult) is the database to use?

❑ Does the database allow you to download and/or email documents?

❑ What years does the database cover?

3 Finding Books

The library's online catalog and discovery service also give you the information you need for locating specific books. Catalog entries for books include the author's name, the title, the subject, publication information, and a call number. A **call number** is like a book's address in the library: it tells you exactly where to find the book you are looking for. (Figure 12.4 shows the results of an author search in a university library's online catalog.)

Note: Do not limit yourself to your library's book collection. Ask your reference librarian about the interlibrary loan process. After you submit an interlibrary loan request, you will receive an email announcement that the book you requested can be picked up at your library's circulation desk.

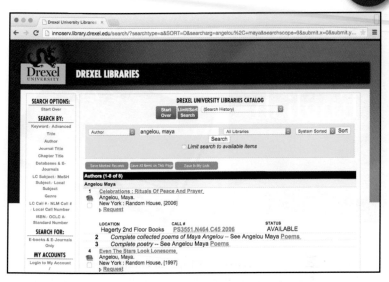

FIGURE 12.4 Online catalog search results for the author *Maya Angelou*.
© Drexel University.

CHECKLIST
Tracking Down a Missing Source

Problem	Possible solution
1. Book is checked out of library.	❏ Consult the person at the circulation desk.
2. Book is not in the library's collection.	❏ Ask your instructor if he or she owns a copy.
	❏ Arrange for an interlibrary loan (if time permits).
3. Periodical is not in the library's collection.	❏ See if the article is available in a full-text database.
	❏ Check *WorldCat* (worldcat.org) to see if other local libraries have what you need.
	❏ Arrange for an interlibrary loan (if time permits).
	❏ Ask a librarian if the article has been reprinted as part of a collection.

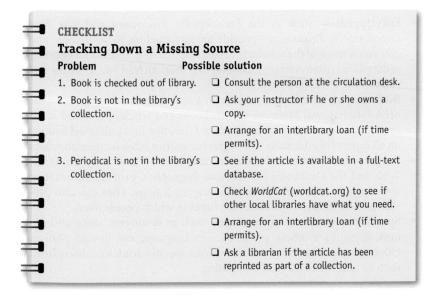

④ Consulting Reference Sources

Reference sources—online and print dictionaries, encyclopedias, almanacs, atlases, bibliographies, and so on—can provide an overview of your topic as well as essential background and factual information (see Figure 12.5).

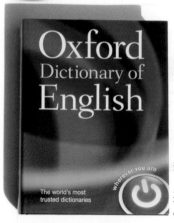

Ben Molyneux / Alamy

Helen Sessions / Alamy

FIGURE 12.5 Reference sources.

Even though they do not discuss your topic in enough depth to be used as research sources, the following reference works can be useful for gathering information and for focusing your research on the specific issues you want to explore in depth.

- **Encyclopedias**—such as the *Encyclopedia Americana* and *The New Encyclopaedia Britannica*—provide an introduction to your topic and give you a sense of the scholarly debates related to it. Individual encyclopedia entries often contain bibliographies that can lead you to works that you can use as research sources.
- **Bibliographies** are lists of sources on a specific topic. For example, the *MLA International Bibliography* lists books and articles published in literature, and the *Bibliographic Guide to Education* lists published sources on all aspects of education. Bibliographic entries often include abstracts.
- **Biographical reference books**—such as *Who's Who in America, Who's Who*, and the *Dictionary of American Biography*—provide information about people's lives as well as bibliographic listings. They can also provide general information about the times in which people lived.
- **Special dictionaries** focus on topics such as synonyms, slang and idioms, rhyming, symbols, proverbs, sign language, and foreign phrases. Other special dictionaries concentrate on specific academic disciplines, such as law, medicine, and computing.

EXERCISE 12.1

Which library sources would you consult to find the following information?

1. A review of the movie *Wild* (2014), based on Cheryl Strayed's memoir
2. A government publication about how to heat your home with solar energy

3. Biographical information about the American anthropologist Margaret Mead
4. Books about Margaret Mead and her work
5. Information about what is being done to prevent the killing of wolves in North America
6. Information about the theories of Albert Einstein
7. Current information about the gun lobby
8. The email address at which to contact Celeste Ng, an American writer
9. Whether your college library has *The Human Use of Human Beings* by Norbert Wiener
10. Current information about AmeriCorps

12b Finding Information on the Internet

The **web** (which is part of the Internet) is the research tool of choice for most college students. This strategy is not without its drawbacks, however. Because no one is responsible for checking web documents to make sure they are trustworthy, factually accurate, or current, you have to use them with care.

Of course, there are many trustworthy sources of information on the Internet. You can learn to use the search engine *Google* in ways to better find trustworthy materials, and *Google Scholar* provides links to scholarly and academic sources that can also be found in your college's online library databases. In addition, the *Directory of Open Access Journals* (doaj.org) lists almost ten thousand open-access scientific and scholarly journals—many of which are highly respected—in its directories.

Even though the Internet can be a valuable resource for research, you must be able to search effectively for, keep track of, and carefully evaluate materials you find. To carry out a web search, you need a **web browser**, an application—such as *Google Chrome*, *Mozilla Firefox*, *Microsoft Internet Explorer*, or *Safari*—that enables you to view information on the web.

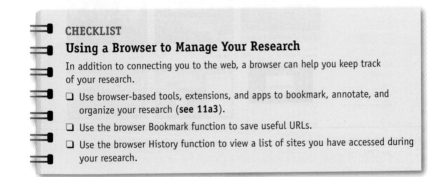

CHECKLIST

Using a Browser to Manage Your Research

In addition to connecting you to the web, a browser can help you keep track of your research.

❏ Use browser-based tools, extensions, and apps to bookmark, annotate, and organize your research (**see 11a3**).

❏ Use the browser Bookmark function to save useful URLs.

❏ Use the browser History function to view a list of sites you have accessed during your research.

You access information on the web by either entering a URL into your browser's search field or using your search engine to carry out a keyword search.

1 Pasting a URL

Every page and document on the web has an electronic address called a **URL** (uniform resource locator). When you paste a URL into your browser's location field and click Search, you will be connected to the website you want. (Figure 12.6 shows a location field.)

2 Doing a Keyword Search

Once you are connected to the web, use your browser to access a **search engine**, an application such as *Google* or *Google Scholar* that searches for and provides links to documents. You carry out a **keyword search** by entering a keyword (or keywords) into your search engine's search field. (Figure 12.7 shows a search engine's keyword search page.) The search engine will identify any site in its database on which the keyword (or keywords) you have typed appears. (These are called **hits**.)

You can develop a list of useful keywords by looking at your college library's online catalog or discovery service and using its headings as keywords. You can also find keywords by looking at the list of Library of Con-

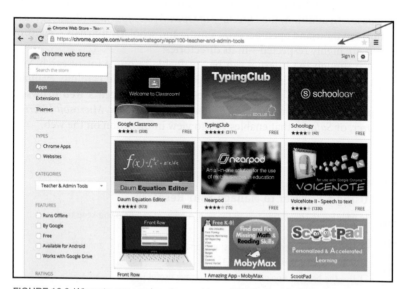

FIGURE 12.6 Where to copy and paste an address (URL) in *Google Chrome*.
© Google Chrome

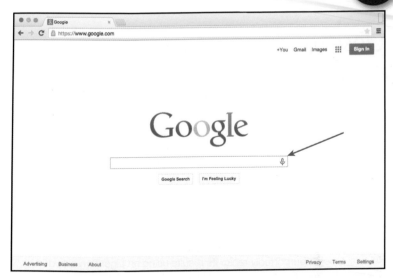

FIGURE 12.7 Google keyword search page. © Google

gress Subject Headings (id.loc.gov/authorities/subjects.html). Finally, you can access an online general encyclopedia, such as *Wikipedia*, and look at the category list that follows each article. These categories make excellent keywords that you can use as you search. (Keep in mind, however, that articles from general encyclopedias are typically not acceptable for including as sources in your writing for college-level research unless your assignment states otherwise.)

Many search engines have advanced options that enable you to limit the number of irrelevant results. For example, you can tailor your search so that it retrieves only documents from a particular type of site (.edu or .org, for example) or documents containing certain keywords in the title or URL. For more on Google search operators, see *googleguide.com/advanced_operators_reference.html*.

3 Choosing the Right Search Engine

General-Purpose Search Engines The most widely used search engines are **general-purpose search engines** that focus on a wide variety of topics. Some of these search engines are more user-friendly than others; some allow for more sophisticated searching functions; some are updated more frequently; and some are more comprehensive than others. As you try out various search engines, you will probably settle on a favorite that you will turn to first whenever you need to find information.

Close-Up   POPULAR GENERAL-PURPOSE
SEARCH ENGINES

Ask.com (ask.com): Allows you to narrow your search by asking questions, such as *Are dogs smarter than pigs?*

Bing (bing.com): Developed by Microsoft, *Bing* is a solid competitor to *Google*. *Bing* offers suggestions for follow-up searches, called "Also Try" and "Related Searches." *Bing* favors .edu, .gov, and .mil sites more than *Google*, paying close attention to top-level domain names, while *Google* pays more attention to PageRank (see the *Google* description below). *Bing* has excellent image and video functions.

Google (google.com): Arguably the best search engine available, it accesses a large database that includes both text and graphics. It is easy to navigate, and searches usually yield a high percentage of useful hits. *Google* purportedly ranks its results using an algorithm called PageRank, based on the number of times a page is linked to other sites. The more a page is linked, the higher it will rise to the top of the results list. (See pages 155–56 for more information about *Google* resources.)

Yahoo! (yahoo.com): *Yahoo!* relies heavily on the titles of pages. If your keywords appear in the title of a page, that page is likely to rise to the top of the results list. *Yahoo!* also favors more popular pages, measured by the number of times a page is clicked.

Because even the best search engines search only a fraction of the material available on the web, if you use only one search engine, you will most likely miss much valuable information. In addition, search engines vary widely in the way they rank results; this means that the results displayed on the first few pages of one search engine may be completely different from those displayed in another search engine. It is therefore a good idea to repeat each search with several different search engines or to use a **metasearch** or **metacrawler** engine that uses several search engines simultaneously.

Close-Up   METASEARCH ENGINES

Dogpile (dogpile.com)
Ixquick (ixquick.com)
Kartoo (kartoo.com)
Mamma (mamma.com)

SurfWax (surfwax.com)

Yippy (yippy.com)

Zoo (zoo.com)

Specialized Search Engines In addition to general-purpose search engines and metasearch engines, there are also **specialized search engines** devoted entirely to specific subject areas, such as literature, business, sports, and women's issues. Hundreds of specialized search engines are indexed at *listofsearchengines.info*.

Close-Up *GOOGLE* RESOURCES

Google is the most-used search engine on the Internet. Most people who use *Google*, however, do not actually know its full potential. Following are just a few of the resources that *Google* offers:

- *Blogger* (blogger.com)   A tool for creating and posting blogs online
- *Book Search* (books.google.com)   A database that allows users to access millions of books that they can either preview or read for free
- *Google Earth* (earth.google.com)   A downloadable, dynamic global map that enables users to see satellite views of almost any place on the planet
- *Finance* (google.com/finance)   Business information, news, and interactive charts
- *News* (news.google.com)   Enables users to search thousands of news stories
- *Patent Search* (google.com/patents)   Enables users to search the full text of US patents
- *Google Scholar* (scholar.google.com)   Searches scholarly literature, including peer-reviewed papers, books, and abstracts
- *Google Translate* (translate.google.com)   A free online language translation service that instantly translates text and web pages

Close-Up *GOOGLE SCHOLAR*

Google Scholar gives you access to some high-quality resources—such as full-text peer-reviewed articles, books, and abstracts—and ranks results according to relevance. It also has a "cited by" feature that links to

(continued)

GOOGLE SCHOLAR (continued)

articles in the *Google Scholar* database that have been cited in the article being viewed. Even so, it does have some drawbacks that users should be aware of:

- Because it does not clearly define *scholar*, you have to make sure that the material conforms to academic standards of reliability.
- Some articles are only abstracts, and others are pay-per-view. (Often, you can get the pay-per-view articles for free through your library's databases.)
- *Google Scholar* is uneven across disciplines and does not index many pre-1990 sources.
- The sources you find may not be current or comprehensive.
- Many important scholarly journals are not indexed in *Google Scholar*.

CHECKLIST

Tips for Effective Web Searches

☐ **Choose the right search engine.** No single all-purpose search engine exists. Review the list of search engines in the boxes on pages 154–55.

☐ **Choose your keywords carefully.** A search engine is only as good as the keywords you use.

☐ **Include enough terms.** If you are looking for information on housing, for example, search for several variations of your keyword: *housing, houses, home buyer, buying houses, residential real estate,* and so on.

☐ **Use more than one search engine.** Because different search engines index different sites, try several. If one does not yield results after a few tries, try another. Also, don't forget to try a metasearch engine such as *Zoo*.

☐ **Use the advanced search features of a search engine.** For example, *Google Advanced Search* (google.com/advanced_search) is a powerful search tool that makes Boolean operators unnecessary. It can limit your search to a specific date range and even limit by domain (such as .org, .edu, and harvard.edu).

☐ **Add useful sites to your Bookmark or Favorites list.** Whenever you find a particularly useful website, **bookmark** it by selecting this option on the menu bar of your browser (with some browsers, such as *Microsoft Internet Explorer,* this option is called Favorites).

EXERCISE 12.2

Choose a topic that interests you—for example, artificial intelligence or student loans. Then, choose two popular search engines (such as *Google, Bing,* or *Yahoo!*) and do a search of your topic on each. When you finish, compare the results, and answer the following questions:

1. How many results did you get from each search engine?
2. How useful were the results?
3. How easy is it to access visuals about your topic? Video? Blogs? News?
4. Which search engine seemed the most helpful? Why?
5. Which search features were similar, and which were different?

4 Using *Wikipedia* as a Research Source

Although no encyclopedia—electronic or print—should be used as a research source, *Wikipedia* requires an extra level of scrutiny.

Wikipedia is an open-source, online general encyclopedia created through the collaborative efforts of its users. Anyone (not necessarily experts) registered with the site can write an article, and in most cases, anyone who views the site can edit an article. The theory is that if enough people contribute, over time, entries will become more and more accurate. Many instructors point out, however, that the coverage in *Wikipedia* is uneven; some articles follow acceptable standards of academic research, but many others do not. Because some articles have little or no documentation, it is difficult to judge their merit. In addition, because *Wikipedia* does not have an editorial staff responsible for checking entries for accuracy, it is not necessarily a reliable source of information. Finally, critics point out that there is no foolproof way that *Wikipedia* can guard against **vandalism**—the purposeful addition of false or misleading information into an article.

Still, *Wikipedia* does have its strengths. Because its content is constantly being revised, *Wikipedia* can be more up to date than other reference sources. Also, many articles contain bibliographic citations that enable users to link to reliable sources of information. Still, even though you can use *Wikipedia* to get a general overview of your topic, most instructors do not consider it a trustworthy, let alone authoritative, research source.

12c Doing Field Research

In addition to using information you find in the library or on the Internet, you can find your own information by doing **field research**—making observations, conducting interviews, and conducting surveys.

1 Making Observations

Some writing assignments are based on your own **observations**. For example, an art history essay can include information gathered during a visit to a museum, and an education essay can include an account of a classroom visit.

CHECKLIST
Making Observations

- ☐ Decide what you want to observe and where you want to observe it.
- ☐ Determine in advance what you hope to gain from your observations.
- ☐ Bring a laptop or tablet so that you can record your observations.
- ☐ Make a record of the time, date, and place of your observations.

❷ Conducting Interviews

Interviews (conducted in person, by telephone, or by email) can provide material that you cannot find anywhere else—for example, a first-hand account of an event or an opinion of an expert.

CHECKLIST
Conducting Interviews

- ☐ Always make an appointment.
- ☐ Prepare a list of questions tailored to the subject matter.
- ☐ Do background reading about your topic. Do not ask for information that you can easily get elsewhere.
- ☐ Have a pen and paper or laptop with you. If you want to record the interview, get your subject's permission in advance.
- ☐ Send an email thanking the subject of the interview.

❸ Conducting Surveys

If your research project is about a contemporary social, political, or economic issue, a **survey** of attitudes or opinions can give you valuable information.

CHECKLIST
Conducting Surveys

- ☐ Determine what you want to know.
- ☐ Generate a list of questions.
- ☐ Decide how to distribute your survey. Will you email it? Post a questionnaire on *Facebook*? Use an online tool such as *SurveyMonkey* or *Google Forms*?
- ☐ Collect and analyze the responses.

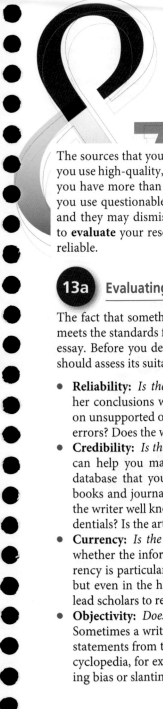

CHAPTER 13

Evaluating Sources

The sources that you use in your essays help you to establish credibility. If you use high-quality, reliable sources, your readers are likely to assume that you have more than a superficial knowledge of your subject. If, however, you use questionable sources, readers will begin to doubt your authority, and they may dismiss your ideas. For these reasons, it is very important to **evaluate** your research sources to make sure they are trustworthy and reliable.

13a Evaluating Library Sources

The fact that something is in the library does not necessarily mean that it meets the standards for academic research or that it is appropriate for your essay. Before you decide to use a library source (print or electronic), you should assess its suitability according to the following criteria:

- **Reliability:** *Is the source trustworthy?* Does the writer support his or her conclusions with facts and expert opinion, or does the source rely on unsupported opinion? Is the information accurate and free of factual errors? Does the writer include documentation and a bibliography?
- **Credibility:** *Is the source respected?* A contemporary review of a source can help you make this assessment. *UlrichsWeb* is a subject-specific database that your library may subscribe to that includes reviews of books and journals that have received attention in a particular field. Is the writer well known in his or her field? Can you check the writer's credentials? Is the article **refereed** (that is, chosen by experts in the field)?
- **Currency:** *Is the source up to date?* The date of publication tells you whether the information in a book or article is current. A source's currency is particularly important for scientific and technological subjects, but even in the humanities, new discoveries and new ways of thinking lead scholars to reevaluate and modify their ideas.
- **Objectivity:** *Does the writer strive to present a balanced discussion?* Sometimes a writer has a particular agenda to advance. Compare a few statements from the source with a neutral source—a textbook or an encyclopedia, for example—to see whether the writer seems to be exhibiting bias or slanting facts.

- **Scope of coverage:** *Does the source treat your topic in enough detail?* To be useful, a source should treat your topic comprehensively. For example, a book should include a section or chapter on your topic, not simply a brief reference or a note. To evaluate an article, either read the abstract or skim the entire article for key facts, looking closely at section headings, information set in boldface type, and topic sentences. An article should have your topic as its central subject (or at least one of its main concerns).

In general, **scholarly publications**—peer-reviewed books and journals aimed at an audience of expert readers—are more reliable than **popular publications**—books, magazines, and newspapers aimed at an audience of general readers. However, assuming they are current, written by reputable authors, and documented, articles from respected popular publications (such as *The Atlantic* and *Scientific American*) may be appropriate for your research. Check with your instructor to be sure.

Scholarly versus Popular Publications

FIGURE 13.1 Scholarly (left) and popular (right) publications.

Scholarly Publications	Popular Publications
Report the results of research	Entertain and inform
Are often published by a university press or have some connection with a university or other academic organization	Are published by commercial presses
Are usually peer reviewed—that is, reviewed by other experts in the author's field before they are published	Are usually not peer reviewed

Are usually written by someone who is a recognized authority in the field	May be written by experts in a particular field but more often are written by freelance or staff writers
Are written for a scholarly audience so often use technical vocabulary and include challenging content	Are written for general readers so tend to use an accessible vocabulary and do not include challenging content
Nearly always contain extensive documentation as well as a bibliography of works consulted	Rarely cite sources or use documentation
Are published primarily because they make a contribution to a particular field of study	Are published primarily to make a profit

Close-Up EVALUATING SOURCES

You can use the following ranking system (with the least authoritative source types listed last) to help determine the verifiability of sources.*

1. Academic peer-reviewed journal articles and academic peer-reviewed books
2. University-level textbooks
3. Books by respected publishing houses
4. Mainstream magazines respected in the field
5. Mainstream newspapers
6. Self-published blogs and opinion pieces
7. Non-published materials

*adapted from "*Wikipedia*: Verifiability"

EXERCISE 13.1

Find and evaluate three useful and reliable sources that would support this thesis:

> Winning the right to vote has (or has not) significantly changed the role of women in national politics.

13b Evaluating Internet Sources

Because anyone can post anything on the Internet, you can easily be overwhelmed by unreliable material. As you sort through and attempt to evaluate this information, the following general guidelines can help you distinguish between acceptable and unacceptable research sources.

Close-Up ACCEPTABLE VERSUS UNACCEPTABLE INTERNET SOURCES

Acceptable

- Websites sponsored and maintained by reliable organizations
- Articles in established online encyclopedias, such as (britannica.com)
- Websites sponsored by reputable newspapers and magazines
- Blogs by reputable authors

Unacceptable

- Information from anonymous sources
- Information found in chat rooms and on discussion boards
- Articles in e-zines and other questionable online publications
- Personal and commercial websites that post no standards for publication

---

Before you use an Internet source, you should evaluate it for *reliability, credibility, currency, objectivity,* and *scope of coverage.*

Reliability **Reliability** refers to the accuracy of the material itself and to its use of proper documentation.

Factual errors—especially errors in facts that are central to the main idea of the source—should cause you to question the reliability of the material you are reading. To evaluate a site's reliability, ask these questions:

- Is the text free of basic grammatical and mechanical errors?
- Does the site contain factual errors?
- Does the site provide a list of references?
- Are working links available to other sources?
- Can information be verified by print or other sources?

Credibility **Credibility** refers to the credentials of the person or organization responsible for the site.

Websites operated by well-known institutions (the Smithsonian or the Library of Congress, for example) have a high degree of credibility.

Those operated by individuals (personal web pages or blogs, for example) are often less reliable. To evaluate a site's credibility, ask these questions:

- Does the site list an author (or authors)? Are credentials (for example, professional or academic affiliations) provided for the author?
- Is the author a recognized authority in his or her field?
- Is the site **refereed**? That is, does an editorial board or a group of experts determine what material appears on the website?
- Can you determine how long the website has existed?

Currency **Currency** refers to how up to date the website is.

The easiest way to assess a site's currency is to see when it was last updated. Keep in mind, however, that even if the date on the site is current, the information that the site contains may not be. To evaluate a site's currency, ask these questions:

- Does the site indicate the date when it was last updated?
- Are all the links to other sites still functioning?
- Is the actual information on the page up to date?
- Does the site clearly identify the date it was created?

Objectivity **Objectivity** refers to the degree of bias that a website exhibits.

Some websites strive for objectivity, but others make no secret of their biases. They openly advocate a particular point of view or action, or they clearly try to sell something. Some websites may try to hide their biases. For example, a website may present itself as a source of factual information when it is actually advocating a political point of view. To evaluate a site's objectivity, ask these questions:

- Does advertising appear in the text?
- Does a business, a political organization, or a special interest group sponsor the site?
- Does the site express a particular viewpoint?
- Does the site contain links to other sites that express a particular viewpoint?

CHECKLIST

Determining the Legitimacy of an Anonymous or Questionable Web Source

When a web source is anonymous (or has an author whose name is not familiar to you), you have to take special measures to determine its legitimacy:

❏ **Follow the links.** Follow the hypertext links in a document to other documents. If the links take you to legitimate sources, you know that the author is aware of these sources of information.

continued

Determining the Legitimacy of an Anonymous or Questionable Web Source *(continued)*

❑ **Find out what web pages link to the site.** You can go to *alexa.com* to find information about a website. Type the website's URL into *Alexa's* search box, and you will be given the volume of traffic to the site, the ownership information for the site, and the other sites visited by people who visited the URL. You will also be given a link to the "Wayback Machine" (archive.org/web/web. php), an archive that shows what the page looked like in the past.

❑ **Do a keyword search.** Do a search using the name of the sponsoring organization or the author as keywords. Other documents (or citations in other works) may identify the author.

❑ **Verify the information.** Check the information you find against a reliable source—a textbook or a reputable website, for example. Also, see if you can find information that contradicts what you have found.

❑ **Check the quality of the writing.** Review the writing on the website to see if there are typos, misspellings, and errors in grammar or word choice. If the writer is careless about these things, he or she has probably not spent much time checking facts.

❑ **Look at the URL.** Although a website's URL is not a foolproof guide to the site's purpose, it does give you some useful information. The last part of a website's URL (immediately following the **domain name**) can often tell you whether the site is sponsored by a commercial entity (*.com*), a nonprofit organization (*.org*), an educational institution (*.edu*), the military (*.mil*), or a government agency (*.gov*). Knowing this information can help you assess its legitimacy.

Scope of Coverage **Scope of coverage** refers to the comprehensiveness of the information on a website.

More coverage is not necessarily better, but some sites may be incomplete. Others may provide information that is no more than common knowledge. Still others may present discussions that are not suitable for college-level research. To evaluate the scope of a site's coverage, ask these questions:

- Does the site provide in-depth coverage?
- Does the site provide information that is not available elsewhere?
- Does the site identify a target audience? Does this target audience suggest the site is appropriate for your research needs?

Close-Up EVALUATING MATERIAL FROM ONLINE FORUMS

Be especially careful with material posted on discussion boards, blogs, newsgroups, and other online forums. Unless you can adequately evaluate this material—for example, determine its accuracy and the credibility of the author or authors—you should not use it in your essay. In most cases, online forums are not good sources of high-quality information because they are published without formal review.

EXERCISE 13.2

Examine the home page of *National Geographic*'s website. Using the criteria discussed in **13b**, write a paragraph in which you evaluate the site's content in terms of reliability, credibility, currency, objectivity, and scope of coverage. Then, compare your paragraph with a classmate's.

See 11g

CHAPTER **14**

Summarizing, Paraphrasing, and Quoting Sources

Experienced researchers know that copying down the exact words of a source is the least efficient way of **taking notes**. A better approach is to take notes that combine summaries, paraphrases, and quotations. This strategy ensures that you understand your source material and see its relevance to your research.

14a Writing a Summary

A **summary** is a brief restatement of the main idea of a passage or an article. A summary is always much shorter than the original because it omits the examples, asides, analogies, and rhetorical strategies that writers use to add emphasis and interest.

When you summarize, *use your own words*, not the exact language or phrasing of your source. Remember that your summary should accurately represent the writer's ideas and should include only the ideas of your source, not your interpretations or opinions. Finally, be sure to document the summary.

Summaries

- **Summaries are original.** They should use your own language and phrasing, not the language and phrasing of your source.
- **Summaries are concise.** They should always be much shorter than the original.
- **Summaries are accurate.** They should precisely and accurately express the main idea of your source.
- **Summaries are objective.** They should not include your opinions.
- **Summaries are complete.** They should convey a sense of the entire passage, not just a part of it.

Compare the following three passages. The first is an original source; the second, an acceptable summary; and the third, an unacceptable summary.

Original Source

Today, the First Amendment faces challenges from groups who seek to limit expressions of racism and bigotry. A growing number of legislatures have passed rules against "hate speech"—[speech] that is offensive on the basis of race, ethnicity, gender, or sexual orientation. The rules are intended to promote respect for all people and protect the targets of hurtful words, gestures, or actions.

Legal experts fear these rules may wind up diminishing the rights of all citizens. "The bedrock principle [of our society] is that government may never suppress free speech simply because it goes against what the community would like to hear," says Nadine Strossen, president of the American Civil Liberties Union and professor of constitutional law at New York University Law School. In recent years, for example, the courts have upheld the right of neo-Nazis to march in Jewish neighborhoods; protected cross-burning as a form of free expression; and allowed protesters to burn the American flag. The offensive, ugly, distasteful, or repugnant nature of expression is not reason enough to ban it, courts have said.

But advocates of limits on hate speech note that certain kinds of expression fall outside of First Amendment protection. Courts have ruled that "fighting words"—words intended to provoke immediate violence—or speech that creates a clear and present danger are not protected forms of expression. As the classic argument goes, freedom of speech does not give you the right to yell "Fire!" in a crowded theater. (Sudo, Phil. "Freedom of Hate Speech?")

The following acceptable summary gives an accurate, objective overview of the original without using its exact language or phrasing.

Acceptable Summary: Some people think that stronger laws against the use of hate speech weaken the First Amendment, but others argue that some kinds of speech remain exempt from this protection (Sudo 17).

The following unacceptable summary uses words and phrases from the original without placing them in quotation marks. This use constitutes <u>plagiarism</u>. In addition, the unacceptable summary expresses the student writer's opinion (**Other people have the sense to realize . . .**).

See Ch. 16

Unacceptable Summary: Today, the First Amendment faces challenges from lots of people. Some of these people are legal experts who want to let Nazis march in Jewish neighborhoods. Other people have the sense to realize that some kinds of speech fall outside of First Amendment protection because they create a clear and present danger (Sudo 17).

PLANNING GUIDE

SUMMARY

- Reread the source until you understand it.
- Write a one-sentence restatement of the main idea.
- Write your summary, using the one-sentence restatement as your topic sentence.
- Use your own words and phrasing, not those of your source.
- Include quotation marks for all quoted material.
- Add appropriate documentation.
- Proofread to make sure that you have not inadvertently plagiarized.

EXERCISE 14.1

Choose a debatable issue from the following list:

- Undocumented immigrants' rights to medical care
- Undocumented immigrants' rights to work
- Helmet requirements for cyclists
- Community service requirements for college students
- Making English the official language of the United States
- Requiring every citizen to carry a national identification card
- A constitutional amendment prohibiting the defacing of the American flag

Write a one-sentence summary of your own position on the issue; then, interview a classmate and write a one-sentence summary of his or her position on the same issue. Be sure each sentence includes the reasons that support the position. Finally, write a single sentence that compares and contrasts the two positions.

14b Writing a Paraphrase

A summary conveys just the main idea of a source; a **paraphrase**, however, gives a *detailed* overview of a source's important ideas. It not only presents the source's main points, but it also reflects its tone and emphasis. For this reason, a paraphrase can sometimes be as long as—or even longer than— the source itself.

When you paraphrase, use your own words, except when you want to quote to give readers a sense of the original. Try not to look at the source as you write, use language and syntax that come naturally to you, and avoid duplicating the phrasing or sentence structure of the original. Whenever possible, use synonyms that accurately convey the meaning of the original word or phrase. If you cannot think of a synonym for an important term, quote it. Remember that your paraphrase should reflect the ideas of your source—not your analysis or interpretation of those ideas. Finally, be sure to document the paraphrase.

Paraphrases

- **Paraphrases are original.** They should use your original language and phrasing, not the phrasing and syntax of your source.
- **Paraphrases are accurate.** They should precisely convey both the key ideas and the emphasis of your source.
- **Paraphrases are objective.** They should not include your opinions.
- **Paraphrases are complete.** They should include all the important ideas in your source.

Compare the following three passages. The first is an original source, the second is an acceptable paraphrase, and the third is an unacceptable paraphrase.

Original Source

When you play a video game, you enter into the world of the programmers who made it. You have to do more than identify with a character on a screen. You must act for it. Identification through action has a special kind of hold. Like playing a sport, it puts people into a highly focused and highly charged state of mind. For many people, what is being pursued in the video game is not just a score, but an altered state.

The pilot of a race car does not dare to take . . . attention off the road. The imperative of total concentration is part of the high. Video games demand the same level of attention. They can give people the feeling of being close to the edge because, as in a dangerous situation, there is no time for rest and the consequences of wandering attention [are] dire. With pinball, a false move can be recuperated. The machine can be shaken, the ball repositioned. In a video game, the program has no tolerance for error, no margin for safety. Players experience their every movement as instantly translated into game action. The game is relentless in its demand that all other time stop and in its demand that the player take full responsibility for every act, a point that players often sum up [with] the phrase "One false move and you're dead." (Turkle, Sherry. *The Second Self: Computers and the Human Spirit.*)

The following acceptable paraphrase conveys the key ideas and emphasis of the source and maintains an objective tone. It quotes a key phrase, but its wording and sentence structure are very different from those of the source.

Acceptable Paraphrase: According to Turkle, the programmer defines the reality of the video game. The game forces a player to merge with the character who is part of the game. The character becomes an extension of the player, who determines how he or she will think and act. Like sports, video games put a player into a very intense "altered state" of mind that is the most important part of the activity (83).

For Turkle, the total involvement video games demand is what attracts many people to them. These games can simulate the thrill of participating in a dangerous activity without any of the risks. Players cannot stop to rest and there is no opportunity to correct errors of judgment. Unlike video games, pinball games are forgiving. A player can—within certain limits—manipulate a pinball game to correct minor mistakes. With video games, however, every move has immediate consequences. The game forces a player to adapt to its rules and to act carefully. One mistake can cause the "death" of the character on the screen and the end of the game (84).

The following unacceptable paraphrase mirrors the phrasing and syntax of the original, borrowing words and expressions without enclosing them in quotation marks. This constitutes <u>plagiarism</u>. In addition, the paraphrase gives the student writer's own opinions about the relative merits of pinball and video games (**That is why I like . . .**).

See Ch. 16

Unacceptable Paraphrase: Playing a video game, you enter into a new world—one the programmer of the game made. You can't just play a video game; you have to identify with it. You go to a new level, and you are put into a highly focused, highly charged state of mind.

Just as you would if you were driving a race car or piloting a plane, you must not let your mind wander. Video games demand complete attention. But the sense that at any time you could make one false move and lose is their attraction—at least for me. That is why I like video games more than pinball. Pinball is just too easy. You can always recover. By shaking the machine or quickly operating the flippers, you can save the ball. Video games, however, are not so easy to control. Usually, one slip and you're dead (Turkle 84).

PLANNING GUIDE

PARAPHRASE

- Reread the source until you understand it.
- Write your paraphrase, following the tone and emphasis of the original.
- Avoid using the words or phrasing of the original.
- Include quotation marks for all quoted material.
- Add appropriate documentation.
- Proofread to make sure that you have not inadvertently plagiarized.

14c Quoting Sources

Quote when you want to use a source's unique wording in your essay. When you **quote**, you copy a writer's statements exactly as they appear in a source, word for word and punctuation mark for punctuation mark, enclosing the borrowed material in quotation marks. As a rule, you should not quote extensively in a research paper. Numerous quotations interrupt the flow of your discussion and give readers the impression that your essay is just a collection of other people's ideas.

CHECKLIST

When to Quote

Quote a source only in the following situations:

❑ Quote when a source's wording or phrasing is so distinctive that a summary or paraphrase would diminish its impact.

- ❑ Quote when a source's words will lend authority to your discussion.
- ❑ Quote when a writer's words are so concise that paraphrasing would change the meaning of the original.
- ❑ Quote when you go on to disagree with a source. Using a source's exact words helps convince readers you are being fair.

Note: Remember to document all quotations that you use in your essay.

EXERCISE 14.2

Find a short online article about a current topic that interests you, and select a paragraph from the article to focus on. First, write a brief summary of the paragraph. Then, write a paraphrase of the paragraph, quoting only those words and phrases you consider especially distinctive.

14d Integrating Source Material into Your Writing

Weave quotations, paraphrases, and summaries smoothly into your discussion, adding your own analysis or explanation to increase coherence and to show the relevance of your source material to the points you are making.

Integrating Source Material into Your Writing

To make sure your sentences do not all sound the same, experiment with different methods of integrating source material into your essay:

- Vary the verbs you use to introduce a source's words or ideas (instead of repeating *says*).

acknowledges	concludes	implies	proposes
admits	concurs	indicates	reports
affirms	discloses	insists	speculates
believes	explains	notes	suggests
claims	finds	observes	summarizes
comments	illustrates	predicts	warns

- Vary the placement of the **identifying tag** (the phrase that identifies the source), putting it in the middle or at the end of the quoted material instead of always at the beginning.

(continued)

Integrating Source Material into Your Writing (*continued*)

Quotation with Identifying Tag in Middle: "A serious problem confronting Amish society from the viewpoint of the Amish themselves," observes Hostetler, "is the threat of absorption into mass society through the values promoted in the public school system" (193).

Paraphrase with Identifying Tag at End: The Amish are also concerned about their children's exposure to the public school system's values, notes Hostetler (193).

1 Integrating Quotations

Be sure to work quotations smoothly into your sentences. Quotations should never be awkwardly dropped into your essay, leaving the exact relationship between the quotation and your point unclear. Use brief introductory remarks to provide a context for the quotation, and quote only those words you need to make your point.

Acceptable: For the Amish, the public school system is a problem because it represents "the threat of absorption into mass society" (Hostetler 193).

Unacceptable: For the Amish, the public school system represents a problem. "A serious problem confronting Amish society from the viewpoint of the Amish themselves is the threat of absorption into mass society through the values promoted in the public school system" (Hostetler 193).

Whenever possible, use an identifying tag to introduce the source of the quotation.

Identifying Tag: As John Hostetler points out, the Amish see the public school system as a problem because it represents "the threat of absorption into mass society" (193).

Close-Up PUNCTUATING IDENTIFYING TAGS

Whether or not to use a comma with an identifying tag depends on where you place the tag in the sentence. If the identifying tag immediately precedes a quotation, use a comma.

As Hostetler points out, "The Amish are successful in maintaining group identity" (56).

If the identifying tag does not immediately precede a quotation, do not use a comma.

Hostetler points out that the Amish frequently "use severe sanctions to preserve their values" (56).

Note: Never use a comma after *that*: Hostetler says that, Amish society is "defined by religion" (76).

Substitutions or Additions within Quotations Indicate changes or additions that you make to a quotation by enclosing your changes in brackets.

Original Quotation: "Immediately after her wedding, she and her husband followed tradition and went to visit almost everyone who attended the wedding" (Hostetler 122).

Quotation Edited to Make Verb Tenses Consistent: Nowhere is the Amish dedication to tradition more obvious than in the events surrounding marriage. Right after the wedding celebration, the Amish bride and groom "visit almost everyone who [has] attended the wedding" (Hostetler 122).

Quotation Edited to Supply an Antecedent for a Pronoun: "Immediately after her wedding, [Sarah] and her husband followed tradition and went to visit almost everyone who attended the wedding" (Hostetler 122).

Quotation Edited to Change an Uppercase to a Lowercase Letter: The strength of the Amish community is illustrated by the fact that "[i]mmediately after her wedding, she and her husband followed tradition and went to visit almost everyone who attended the wedding" (Hostetler 122).

Omissions within Quotations When you delete unnecessary or irrelevant words, substitute an **ellipsis** (three spaced periods) for the deleted words.

See 53f1

Original Quotation: "Not only have the Amish built and staffed their own elementary and vocational schools, but they have gradually organized on local, state, and national levels to cope with the task of educating their children" (Hostetler 206).

Quotation Edited to Eliminate Unnecessary Words: "Not only have the Amish built and staffed their own elementary and vocational schools, but they have gradually organized . . . to cope with the task of educating their children" (Hostetler 206).

Close-Up OMISSIONS WITHIN QUOTATIONS

Be sure you do not misrepresent or distort the meaning of quoted material when you shorten it. For example, do not say, "the Amish have managed to maintain . . . their culture" when the original quotation is "the Amish have managed to maintain *parts of* their culture."

Note: If the passage you are quoting already contains ellipses, MLA style requires that you place brackets around any ellipses that you add.

See
52b
Long Quotations Set off a quotation of more than four typed lines of **prose** (or more than three lines of **poetry**) by indenting it one-half inch from the margin. Double-space, and do not use quotation marks.

If you are quoting a single paragraph, do not indent the first line. If you are quoting more than one paragraph, indent the first line of each complete paragraph an additional one-quarter inch. Integrate the quotation into your essay by introducing it with a complete sentence followed by a colon. Place parenthetical documentation one space after the end punctuation.

> According to Hostetler, the Amish were not always hostile to public education:
>
> > The one-room rural elementary school served the Amish community well in a number of ways. As long as it was a public school, it stood midway between the Amish community and the world. Its influence was tolerable, depending upon the degree of influence the Amish were able to bring to the situation. (196)

2 Integrating Paraphrases and Summaries

Introduce your paraphrases and summaries with identifying tags, and end them with appropriate documentation. By doing so, you enable your readers to differentiate your ideas from those of your sources.

Correct (Identifying Tag Differentiates Ideas of Source from Ideas of Writer): Art can be used to uncover many problems that children have at home, in school, or with their friends. For this reason, many therapists use art therapy extensively. According to William Alschuler in *Art and Self-Image,* children's views of themselves in society are often reflected by their art style. For example, a cramped, crowded art style using only a portion of the paper shows a child's limited role (260).

Misleading (Ideas of Source Blend with Ideas of Writer): Art can be used to uncover many problems that children have at home, in school, or with their friends. For this reason, many therapists use art therapy extensively. Children's views of themselves in society are often reflected by their art style. For example, a cramped, crowded art style using only a portion of the paper shows their limited role (Alschuler 260).

EXERCISE 14.3

Look back at the summary and paraphrase that you wrote for Exercise 14.2. Write three possible identifying tags for each, varying the verbs you use for attribution and the placement of the identifying tags. Be sure to include appropriate documentation at the end of each passage.

CHAPTER **15**

Synthesizing Sources

15a Understanding Synthesis

Summaries and paraphrases rephrase a source's main ideas, and quotations reproduce a source's exact language. **Synthesis** combines summary, paraphrase, and quotation to create a paragraph or essay that expresses your original viewpoint about a topic. An effective synthesis creates a context for your source material, showing the relevance of each source to your ideas. For this reason, knowing how to synthesize sources is an important skill.

The following synthesis from a student research paper uses summary, paraphrase, and quotation to define the term *outsider art.*

Sample Student Synthesis

Topic sentence states student's main point	Bill Traylor is one of America's leading outsider artists. According to *Raw Vision* magazine, Traylor is one of the foremost artists of the twentieth century (Karlins). Born on a cotton plantation as a slave in
Summary of online Karlins article	the 1850s and illiterate all his life, Traylor was self-taught and did not consider himself an artist. He created works for himself rather than for
Paraphrase from one-page Glueck article	the public (Glueck). The term *outsider art* refers to works of art created by individuals who are by definition outside society. Because of their economic condition, lack of education, criminal behavior, or physical handicaps, they are not part of mainstream society. According to Louis-
Quotation from introduction to exhibit pamphlet	Dreyfus, in the United States, "'Outsider Art' . . . refers to work done by the poor, illiterate, and self-taught African Americans whose artistic product is . . . [a reflection] of their untaught and impoverished social
Conclusion summarizes student writer's position	conditions" (iv). As a Southern African American man with few resources and little formal training, Traylor fits the definition of an outsider artist whose works are largely defined by the hardships he faced.

As this example demonstrates, an effective synthesis weaves information from different sources into the discussion, establishing the relationship between the sources and the writer's own ideas.

15b Planning a Synthesis

The first step in synthesizing material is to determine how your sources are alike and different, where they agree and disagree, and whether they reach the same conclusions. As you identify connections between one source and another or between a source and your own ideas, you will develop your own perspective on your subject. It is this viewpoint, summarized in a thesis statement (in the case of an entire essay) or in a topic sentence (in the case of a paragraph), that becomes the focus of your synthesis.

Close-Up QUESTIONS FOR MAKING CONNECTIONS BETWEEN AND AMONG SOURCES

As you plan your synthesis, ask yourself these questions:

- What positions do the sources take on the issue?
- What key terms do the sources identify and define?

- What background information do the sources provide?
- How do the sources address their audiences?
- How do the sources agree?
- How do the sources disagree?
- What evidence do the sources use to support their assertions?
- How do the sources address opposing points of view?
- How do the sources organize their main ideas?

PLANNING GUIDE

SYNTHESIS

- Analyze and interpret your source material.
- Begin with a statement that sums up the main idea you want your synthesis to convey.
- Blend sources carefully, identifying each source and naming its author(s) and title.
- Identify key similarities and differences among your sources.
- Use identifying tags and transitional words and phrases to help readers follow your discussion.
- Be sure to clearly differentiate your ideas from those of your sources.
- Document all paraphrased and summarized material as well as all quotations.
- Proofread to make sure that you have not inadvertently plagiarized.

15c Writing a Synthesis

In a first-semester composition class, Jay Gilman, a computer science major, was given the following assignment prompt.

> Choose an area related to your major that you think others would benefit from learning more about. Then, using three sources, write a synthesis that defines and explains this topic to an audience unfamiliar with the field. Use MLA (Modern Language Association) documentation style.

After carefully reading his sources and thinking critically about them, Jay wrote the following synthesis.

Effective Synthesis

> Computers carry out many of the tasks that make our way of
> life possible. For example, computer billing, with all its faults,

makes modern business possible, and without computers we would not have access to the cellular services and cable or satellite

Topic sentence states student's main point

television that we take for granted. But computers are more than just fast calculators; they are also equipped with artificial intelligence (AI), which has transformed fields such as medicine, agriculture, and manufacturing. One technology writer defines artificial intelligence

Quotation from Havenstein article

(AI) as "a field that attempts to provide machines with humanlike reasoning and language-processing capabilities" (Havenstein). Farming

Paraphrase of unsigned article's text and visual content

is an industry that is now using AI technology: with new, high-tech agricultural sprayers that treat crops precisely and accurately, farmers are able to improve the output and quality of their yield ("More Machine Intelligence"). AI has also made

Source

> There's no precise definition of AI, but broadly, it's a field that attempts to provide machines with humanlike reasoning and language-processing capabilities.

Source

Researchers at Oklahoma State University, meanwhile, have demonstrated the potential for adding machine intelligence to agricultural sprayers (photo). Enhanced with sensors and computers, the field sprayers dramatically increased the application efficiency by applying fertilizers and herbicides only where needed, reports John B. Solie, professor, power and machinery at Oklahoma State.

F. Schussler/PhotoLink/Getty Images

Summary of Howell article

possible numerous medical advances—for example, helping scientists

Conclusion summarizes student writer's position

to generate human tissue, bone, and organs for patients in need (Howell). Given the importance of AI technology, it seems certain that computers will change our lives even more in the future.

Source

Human 2.0
News that an artificial pancreas has been developed, which could help millions of diabetes patients, is only the tip of the iceberg as far as augmentation of the human body goes. We can already grow skin, cartilage, bone, ears and bladders.

This synthesis effectively defines the term *artificial intelligence (AI)* and uses information from three short articles to explain AI and briefly describe its use in various fields. The writer introduces his paragraph with a summary of computer applications familiar to his readers and then moves into a discussion of AI.

The sources selected for the above synthesis could have been used far less carefully and effectively. In the following ineffective synthesis, source material dominates the discussion, all but eliminating the writer's voice.

Ineffective Synthesis

Begins with out-of-context quotation from source, not student writer's own position

        Heather Havenstein defines artificial intelligence (AI) as "a field that attempts to provide machines with humanlike reasoning and language-processing capabilities." As reported in *IndustryWeek* magazine, the farming community is using

Source's exact words used without quotation marks, resulting in plagiarism

AI technology by adding machine intelligence to agricultural sprayers, dramatically increasing their application efficiency and improving the output and quality of crops ("More Machine Intelligence"). In the medical field, scientists have used AI to

Quotation used where paraphrase is more appropriate

"grow skin, cartilage, bone, ears and bladders" (Howell). AI technology has changed our lives in important ways, and it seems obvious that it will continue to do so in the future.

Vague conclusion

This example does not include a topic sentence that states the writer's position; it also lacks supporting examples and has a vague conclusion. Moreover, the paragraph **plagiarizes** its source's words.

See Ch. 16

EXERCISE 15.1

Examine a group of advertisements (in print, online, on television, or out in the world—on buildings, buses, billboards, or benches) that either target the same group of consumers (such as parents) or focus on a similar product (such as teeth whiteners or mobile service providers). Then, integrate information from at least three ads in a paragraph-length synthesis that explains the message the ads are trying to convey.

CHAPTER **16**

Using Sources Ethically

16a Defining Plagiarism

When you do a research project, you use information from your sources. It is your ethical responsibility to present this material fairly and to make sure that you document it appropriately.

Plagiarism occurs when a writer (intentionally or unintentionally) uses the words, ideas, or distinctive style of others without acknowledging the source. For example, you plagiarize when you submit someone else's work as your own or fail to document appropriately.

The harm plagiarism does extends beyond the act itself. Instructors assign research for a reason; they want students to become part of a community of scholars and to take part in the conversations that define this community. When you misappropriate the work of others, you deprive yourself of a unique opportunity to learn. Moreover, by plagiarizing, you devalue the work of other students who have acted ethically and responsibly. Finally, plagiarism (as well as other forms of academic dishonesty) compromises the academic mission of your school, weakens the intellectual foundation on which all colleges and universities rest, and undermines the climate of mutual trust and respect that must exist for learning to take place.

Most plagiarism is **unintentional plagiarism**—for example, a student might paste a quoted passage into a paper and forget to include the quotation marks and documentation. There is a difference, however, between an honest mistake and **intentional plagiarism**—for example, copying a passage word for word from a journal article or submitting a paper that someone else has written. The penalties for unintentional plagiarism may sometimes be severe, but intentional plagiarism is almost always dealt with harshly: students who intentionally plagiarize can receive a failing grade for the paper (or the course) and can even be expelled from school.

Close-Up DETECTING PLAGIARISM

The same technology that has made unintentional plagiarism more common has also made plagiarism easier to detect. By doing a *Google* search, an instructor can quickly find the source of a phrase that has been plagiarized from an Internet source. In addition, plagiarism detection services, such as *Turnitin.com*, can search scholarly databases and identify plagiarized passages in student essays.

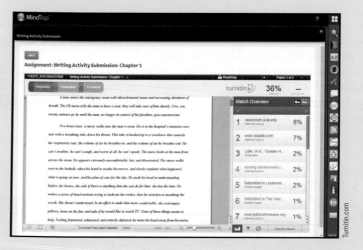

Turnitin.com

See 11c1

16b Avoiding Unintentional Plagiarism

The most common cause of unintentional plagiarism is sloppy research habits. To avoid this problem, start your research paper early. Do not cut and paste text from a website or full-text database directly into your essay. If you paraphrase, do so correctly by following the advice in **14b**.

In addition, make sure to **keep track of your sources**—especially those you scan, download, or otherwise save electronically—so that they do not overwhelm you. Unintentional plagiarism often occurs when students use source material thinking that it is their own.

MULTILINGUAL TIP

Plagiarism is a difficult concept for many multilingual students to grasp because it is not a concern in all countries. In cultures that value the group over the individual, including some Asian, African, and Latin American cultures, plagiarism is less of a concern because the group is thought to own the original work.

In places such as the United States, however, where the individual is valued over the group, plagiarism is considered stealing because the individual who originally developed the idea or work is considered to be its owner. Although you may be tempted to closely follow the syntax and word choice of your sources, be aware that this practice constitutes plagiarism.

See
Pt. 5
Another cause of unintentional plagiarism is failure to use proper <u>documentation</u>. In general, you must document the following information:

- Direct quotations, summaries, and paraphrases of material in sources (including web sources)
- Images that you borrow from a source (print or electronic)
- Facts and opinions that are another writer's original contributions
- Information that is the product of an author's original research
- Statistics, charts, graphs, or other compilations of data that are not yours

Material that is considered **common knowledge** (information most readers probably know) need not be documented. This includes facts available from a variety of reference sources, familiar sayings, and well-known quotations. Your own original research (interviews and surveys, for example) also does not require documentation.

So, although you do not have to document the fact that John F. Kennedy graduated from Harvard in 1940 or that he was elected president in 1960, you do have to document information from a historian's evaluation of his presidency. The best rule to follow is if you have doubts, document.

Close-Up   WHY DOCUMENT SOURCES?

There are a number of reasons to document sources:

- **To give credit**   By documenting your sources, you acknowledge the original work of others.
- **To become part of a conversation**   When you discuss the work of other scholars, you join an ongoing intellectual discussion.
- **To establish your credibility**   By indicating what sources you have consulted, you show readers that your conclusions should be taken seriously.
- **To differentiate your ideas from the ideas of your sources**   Documentation enables readers to identify the original ideas you have contributed to the discussion. Readers can then locate those cited sources if they wish to collect more information on the subject.

16c   Avoiding Intentional Plagiarism

When students plagiarize intentionally, they make a decision to misappropriate the ideas or words of others—and this is no small matter. Not only does intentional plagiarism deprive the student of a valuable educational experience (instructors assign research for a reason), it also subverts the educational goals of other students as well as of the institution as a whole. Because academic honesty is absolutely central to any college or university, intentional plagiarism is a very serious breach of trust.

So why do some students engage in this unethical (and risky) behavior? Research has shown that many students who intentionally plagiarize do so out of procrastination and fear. They put off working on their writing projects until they have no time to complete them. Or, they have trouble finding source materials. Some students find that as they do their research, their ideas change. As a result, they discover at the last minute that they have to shift the focus of their essays, and they panic. Finally, other students think that they are not up to the job of writing an essay that relies on research sources. The easiest way to deal with all these types of problems is to ask your instructor for help.

Of course, some students plagiarize out of laziness or because they mistakenly believe that buying an essay from an essay mill or paying someone to write an essay is "no big deal." Fortunately, these students are in the minority. Most, if not all, students realize that plagiarism is simply wrong.

16d   Avoiding Other Kinds of Plagiarism

When instructors assign a research paper, they expect it to be your original work. They also expect your essay to be written in response to specific assignments they give. For this reason, you should not submit an essay that you have written for another course. If you intend to substantially rework or expand the essay, however, you may be able to use it. Check with your instructor before doing so.

An essay prepared in collaboration with other students can also present challenges. It is not uncommon in some courses to do work as part of a team. This collaborative work is acceptable in the course for which it was assigned. Even so, each member of the group should clearly identify the sections on which he or she worked.

Finally, although your instructors may encourage you to go the writing center for help, they do not expect your essay to include passages written by a tutor. Passages written (or revised and edited) by a friend or a family member are also unacceptable. If you present material contributed by others as if it were your own, you are committing plagiarism.

16e   Revising to Eliminate Plagiarism

You can avoid plagiarism by using documentation wherever it is required and by following these guidelines.

1 Enclose Borrowed Words in Quotation Marks

Original: Historically, only a handful of families have dominated the fireworks industry in the West. Details such as chemical recipes and mixing procedures were cloaked in secrecy and passed down from one generation to the next. . . . One effect of familial secretiveness is that, until recent decades, basic pyrotechnic research was rarely performed, and even when it was, the results were not generally reported in scientific journals. (Conkling, John A. "Pyrotechnics.")

Plagiarism: John A. Conkling points out that until recently, little scientific research was done on the chemical properties of fireworks, and when it was, the results were not generally reported in scientific journals (96).

Even though the preceding example includes documentation, the student writer uses the source's exact words without placing them in quotation marks.

The writer can correct this problem either by putting the borrowed words in quotation marks or by paraphrasing them.

Correct (Borrowed Words in Quotation Marks): John A. Conkling points out that until recently, little scientific research was done on the chemical properties of fireworks, and when it was, "the results were not generally reported in scientific journals" (96).

Correct (Paraphrase): John A. Conkling points out that the little research conducted on the chemical composition of fireworks was seldom reported in the scientific literature (96).

Close-Up PLAGIARISM AND INTERNET SOURCES

Any time you download text from the Internet, you run the risk of committing unintentional plagiarism. To avoid the possibility of plagiarism, follow these guidelines:

- Download or otherwise collect information into individual files so that you can keep track of your sources.
- Do not cut and paste blocks of downloaded text directly into your essay; first summarize or paraphrase this material.
- If you record the exact words of your source, enclose them in quotation marks.
- Even if your information is from emails, online discussion groups, blogs, or websites, provide appropriate documentation.
- Always document figures, tables, charts, and graphs obtained from the Internet or from any other electronic source.

❷ Do Not Imitate a Source's Syntax and Phrasing

Original: If there is a garbage crisis, it is that we are treating garbage as an environmental threat and not what it is: a manageable—though admittedly complex—civic issue. (Patricia Poore, "America's 'Garbage Crisis'")

Plagiarism: If a garbage crisis does exist, it is that people see garbage as a menace to the environment and not what it actually is: a controllable—if obviously complicated—public problem (Poore 39).

Although this student does not use the exact words of her source, she closely follows the original's syntax and phrasing, simply substituting synonyms for the author's words.

Correct (Paraphrase in Writer's Own Words; One Distinctive Phrase Placed in Quotation Marks): Patricia Poore argues that America's "garbage crisis" is exaggerated; rather than viewing garbage as a serious environmental hazard, she says, we should look at garbage as a public problem that may be complicated but that can be solved (39).

❸ Document Statistics Obtained from a Source

Although many people assume that statistics are common knowledge, they are usually the result of original research and must, therefore, be documented. Moreover, providing the source of the statistics helps readers to assess their validity.

Correct: According to one study, male drivers between the ages of sixteen and twenty-four accounted for the majority of accidents. Of 303 accidents recorded almost one half took place before the drivers were legally allowed to drive at eighteen (Schuman et al. 1027).

❹ Differentiate Your Words and Ideas from Those of Your Source

Original: At some colleges and universities traditional survey courses of world and English literature . . . have been scrapped or diluted. At others they are in peril. At still others they will be. What replaces them is sometimes a mere option of electives, sometimes "multicultural" courses introducing material from Third World cultures and thinning out an already thin sampling of Western writings, and sometimes courses geared especially to issues of class, race, and gender. Given the notorious lethargy of academic decision-making, there has probably been more clamor than change; but if there's enough clamor, there will be change. (Howe, Irving. "The Value of the Canon.")

Plagiarism: Debates about expanding the literary canon take place at many colleges and universities across the United States. At many universities, the Western literature survey courses have been edged out by courses that emphasize minority concerns. These courses are "thinning out an already thin sampling of Western writings" in favor of courses geared especially to issues of "class, race, and gender" (Howe 40).

Because the student writer does not differentiate her ideas from those of her source, it appears that only the quotations in the last sentence are borrowed when, in fact, the second sentence also owes a debt to the original.

In the revised passage below, the writer clearly identifies the boundaries of the borrowed material by introducing it with an identifying tag and ending with documentation.

Correct: Debates about expanding the literary canon take place at many colleges and universities across the United States. According to critic Irving Howe, at many universities the Western literature survey courses have been edged out by courses that emphasize minority concerns. These courses, says Howe, are "thinning out an already thin sampling of Western writings" in favor of "courses geared especially to issues of class, race, and gender" (40).

CHECKLIST

Avoiding Plagiarism

❑ **Take careful notes.** Be sure you have recorded information from your sources carefully and accurately.

❑ **Keep track of your sources.** Place all source material, along with pertinent bibliographic information, in the appropriate files.

❑ **In your notes, clearly identify summaries, paraphrases, and quotations.** In handwritten notes, put all words borrowed from your sources inside circled quotation marks. In typed notes, boldface all quotation marks. Always enclose your own comments within brackets.

❑ **In your essay, differentiate your ideas from those of your sources** by clearly introducing borrowed material with an identifying tag and by following it with parenthetical documentation.

❑ **Enclose all direct quotations** used in your essay within quotation marks.

❑ **Review all paraphrases and summaries** in your essay to make certain that they use your own phrasing and syntax and that any distinctive words and phrases from a source are quoted.

❑ **Document all quoted material and all paraphrases and summaries** of your sources.

❑ **Document all information** that is not common knowledge.

- ❏ **Document all opinions, conclusions, figures, tables, statistics, graphs, and charts** taken from a source.
- ❏ **Never submit the work of another person as your own.** Do not buy an essay from a website or hand in an essay written by a friend. In addition, never include passages that have been written by a friend, relative, or writing tutor. If you run into trouble, get help.
- ❏ **Never use sources that you have not actually read (or invent sources that do not exist).**

EXERCISE 16.1

The following paragraph uses material from three sources, but its student author has neglected to cite them. After reading the paragraph and the three sources that follow it, identify the material that has been quoted directly from a source. Compare the wording to the original for accuracy, and insert quotation marks where necessary, making sure the quoted passages fit smoothly into the paragraph. Differentiate the ideas of the student from those of each of the three sources by using identifying tags to introduce any quotations. (If you think the student did not need to quote a passage, paraphrase it instead.) Finally, add parenthetical documentation for each piece of information that requires it.

Student Paragraph

Oral history is an important way of capturing certain aspects of the past that might otherwise be lost. While history books relate the stories of great men and great events, rarely do they include the experiences of ordinary people—slaves, concentration camp survivors, and the illiterate, for example. By providing information about the people and emotions of the past, oral history makes sense of the present and gives a glimpse of the likely future. But because any particular rendition of a life history relies heavily on personal memory, great care must be taken to evaluate and explain the context of an oral history. Like any other historical account, oral history is just one of many possible versions of an individual's past.

Source 1

Oral history relies heavily on memory, a notoriously malleable entity; people remake the past in light of present concerns and knowledge. Yet not all memories are false, and oral history gives us testimony that might otherwise be lost—stories of slaves, of concentration camp survivors, of the illiterate and the obscure, of the legion "ordinary people" who rarely find their way into the history books. Oral history gives us the human element, the thoughts and emotions and confusions that lie beneath the calm surface of written documents. Even when people remake the past because memories are faulty or unbearable, we can learn much about the ways in which the past affects the present. (Freedman, Jean R. "Never Underestimate the Power of a Bus: My Journey to Oral History." *Oral History Review*, vol. 29, no. 2, 2002, p. 30.)

Source 2

[There is a] widely held view that history belongs to great men and great events, not ordinary people or ordinary life. Yet we know that "ordinary" people in our local districts have important stories to tell. . . . Local histories tell us, on the one hand, that things were done differently in the past, but on the other hand, that in essence people and emotions were much the same. We need to learn from the past to make sense of the present, and get a glimpse of the likely future. (Gregg, Alison. "Planning and Managing an Oral History Collection." *Aplis*, vol. 13, no. 4, 2000, p. 174.)

Source 3

One aspect of oral history . . . concerns the way in which any particular rendition of a life history is a product of the personal present. It is well recognized that chronicles of the past are invariably a product of the present, so that different "presents" inspire different versions of the past. Just as all historical accounts—the very questions posed or the interpretive framework imposed—are informed by the historian's present, so, too, is a life history structured by both the interviewer's and the narrator's present. . . . [O]ral history cannot be treated as a source of some narrative truth, but rather as one of many possible versions of an individual's past . . . [and] the stories told in an oral history are not simply the source of explanation, but rather require explanation. (Honig, Emily. "Getting to the Source: Striking Lives: Oral History and the Politics of Memory." *Journal of Women's History*, vol. 9, no. 1, 1997, p. 139.)

16f Understanding Plagiarism in the Disciplines

Although plagiarism always involves the misappropriation of ideas, words, or research results, different disciplines have different conventions about what constitutes plagiarism. Becoming familiar with the conventions of the discipline in which you are writing will help you avoid the most common causes of plagiarism.

1 Plagiarism in the Humanities

In the humanities, plagiarism is often the result of inaccurate summarizing and paraphrasing, failure to use quotation marks where they are required, and confusion between your ideas and those of your sources. You can eliminate these problems by taking accurate notes, avoiding cutting and pasting sources directly into your papers, and documenting all words and ideas that are not your own.

❷ Plagiarism in the Social Sciences

In the social sciences, you can avoid plagiarism by correctly documenting paraphrases, summaries, and quotations as well as all statistics and visuals that are not your own. Keep in mind that the social sciences are bound by ethical considerations regarding the treatment of research subjects and the protection of privacy as well as the granting of credit to all individuals who contribute to a research project.

❸ Plagiarism in the Natural and Applied Sciences

In the natural and applied sciences, using the experimental results, computer codes, chemical formulas, graphs, images, or ideas or words of others without proper acknowledgment constitutes plagiarism. In addition, falsifying data, fabricating data, or publishing misleading information is considered scientific misconduct and can have serious consequences.

Documenting Sources

Documenting Sources

❓ Frequently Asked Questions

Directory of MLA Parenthetical References

Directory of MLA Works-Cited List Entries

Entries For Periodicals

Scholarly Journals

Magazines

Newspapers and News Services

Book Reviews, Newsletters, and Encyclopedias

Entries For Books

Authors

Parts of Books

Entries For Internet-Specific Sources

Entries For Other Sources

CHAPTER 17

MLA Documentation Style

Documentation is the formal acknowledgment of the sources you use in your essay. This chapter explains and illustrates the documentation style recommended by the Modern Language Association (MLA). Chapter 18 discusses the documentation style of the American Psychological Association (APA), Chapter 19 gives an overview of the format recommended by *The Chicago Manual of Style*, and Chapter 20 presents the format recommended by the Council of Science Editors (CSE) and the formats used by organizations in other disciplines.

Note: Note: **See 11k3** for a list and description of useful digital citation tools.

17a Using MLA Style

MLA style* is required by instructors of English and other languages as well as by many instructors in other humanities disciplines. MLA documentation has three parts: *parenthetical references in the body of the essay (also known as in-text citations), a works-cited list,* and *content notes.*

1 Parenthetical References

MLA documentation uses parenthetical references in the body of the essay keyed to a works-cited list at the end of the essay. A typical parenthetical reference consists of the author's last name and a page number.

> The colony appealed to many idealists in Europe (Kelley 132).

If you state the author's name or the title of the work in your discussion, do not also include it in the parenthetical reference.

> Penn's political motivation is discussed by Joseph J. Kelley in *Pennsylvania, The Colonial Years, 1681-1776* (44).

To distinguish two or more sources by the same author, include a shortened title after the author's name. When you shorten a title, begin with the word by which the work is alphabetized in the list of works cited.

> Penn emphasized his religious motivation (Kelley, *Pennsylvania* 116).

---

*MLA documentation style follows the guidelines set in the *MLA Handbook*, 8th ed. (MLA, 2016).

Close-Up PUNCTUATING WITH MLA PARENTHETICAL REFERENCES

Paraphrases and Summaries   Parenthetical references are placed *before* the sentence's end punctuation.

> Penn's writings epitomize seventeenth-century religious thought (Dengler and Curtis 72).

Quotations Run In with the Text   Parenthetical references are placed *after* the quotation but *before* the end punctuation.

> As Ross says, "Penn followed his conscience in all matters" (127).

> According to Williams, "Penn's utopian vision was informed by his Quaker beliefs . . ." (72).

See 52a3

Quotations Set Off from the Text   When you quote more than four lines of prose or more than three lines of poetry, parenthetical references are placed one space *after* the end punctuation.

> According to Arthur Smith, William Penn envisioned a state based on his religious principles:
>
> > Pennsylvania would be a commonwealth in which all individuals would follow God's truth and develop according to God's law. For Penn, this concept of government was self-evident. It would be a mistake to see Pennsylvania as anything but an expression of Penn's religious beliefs. (314)

Sample MLA Parenthetical References

1. A Work by a Single Author

Fairy tales reflect the emotions and fears of children (Bettelheim 23).

2. A Work by Two Authors

The historian's main job is to search for clues and solve mysteries (Davidson and Lytle 6).

3. A Work by Three or More Authors

List only the first author, followed by **et al.** ("and others").

Helping each family reach its goals for healthy child development and overall family well-being was the primary approach of Project EAGLE (Bartle et al. 35).

4. A Work in Multiple Volumes

If you list more than one volume of a multivolume work in your works-cited list, include the appropriate volume and page number (separated by a colon followed by a space) in the parenthetical citation.

> Gurney is incorrect when he says that a twelve-hour limit is negotiable (6: 128).

5. A Work without a Listed Author

Use the full title (if brief) or a shortened version of the title (if long), beginning with the word by which it is alphabetized in the works-cited list.

> The group later issued an apology ("Satire Lost" 22).

6. A Work That Is One Page Long

Do not include a page reference for a one-page article.

> Sixty percent of Arab Americans work in white-collar jobs (El-Badru).

7. An Indirect Source

If you use a statement by one author that is quoted in the work of another author, indicate that the material is from an indirect source with the abbreviation **qtd. in** ("quoted in").

> According to Valli and Lucas, "the form of the symbol is an icon or picture
>
> of some aspect of the thing or activity being symbolized" (qtd. in Wilcox 120).

8. More Than One Work

Cite each work as you normally would, separating one citation from another with a semicolon.

> The Brooklyn Bridge has been used as a subject by many American artists
>
> (McCullough 144; Tashjian 58).

Note: Long parenthetical references distract readers. Whenever possible, present them as <u>content notes</u>.

See 17a3

9. A Literary Work

When citing a work of **fiction**, it is often helpful to include more than the author's name and the page number in the parenthetical citation. Follow the page number with a semicolon, and then include any additional information that might be helpful.

> In *Moby-Dick*, Melville refers to a whaling expedition funded by Louis XIV of
>
> France (151; ch. 24).

Parenthetical references to **poetry** do not include page numbers. In parenthetical references to *long poems*, cite division and line numbers, separating them with a period.

> In the *Aeneid*, Virgil describes the ships as cleaving the "green woods re-
>
> flected in the calm water" (8.124).

(In this citation, the reference is to book 8, line 124, of the *Aeneid*.)

When citing *short poems*, identify the poet and the poem in the text of the essay, and use line numbers in the citation.

> In "My mistress' eyes are nothing like the sun," Shakespeare's speaker says, "I have seen roses damasked red and white, / But no such roses see I in her cheeks," (lines 5-6).

Note: When citing lines of a poem, include the word **line** (or **lines**) in the first parenthetical reference; use just the line numbers in subsequent references.

When citing a **play**, include the act, scene, and line numbers (in arabic numerals), separated by periods. Titles of classic literary works (such as Shakespeare's plays) are often abbreviated (**Mac. 2.2.14-16**).

10. Sacred Texts

When citing sacred texts, such as the Bible or the Qur'an, include the version (italicized) and the book (abbreviated if longer than four letters, but not italicized or enclosed in quotation marks), followed by the chapter and verse numbers (separated by a period).

> The cynicism of the speaker is apparent when he says, "All things are wearisome; no man can speak of them all" (*New English Bible*, Eccles. 1.8).

Note: The first time you cite a sacred text, include the version in your parenthetical reference; after that, include only the book. If you are using more than one version of a sacred text, however, include the version in each in-text citation.

11. An Entire Work

When citing an entire work, include the author's name and the work's title in the text of your essay rather than in a parenthetical reference.

> Lois Lowry's *Gathering Blue* is set in a technologically backward village.

12. Two or More Authors with the Same Last Name

To distinguish authors with the same last name, include their initials in your parenthetical references.

> Increases in crime have caused thousands of urban homeowners to install alarms (L. Cooper 115). Some of these alarms use sophisticated sensors that were developed by the army (D. Cooper 76).

13. A Government Document or a Corporate Author

Cite such works using the organization's name followed by the page number (**American Automobile Association 34**). You can avoid long parenthetical references by working the organization's name (not abbreviated) into your discussion.

According to the President's Commission for the Study of Ethical Problems
in Medicine and Biomedical and Behavioral Research, the issues relating to
euthanasia are complicated (76).

14. A Legal Source

Titles of acts or laws that appear in the text of your essay or in the works-
cited list should not be italicized or enclosed in quotation marks. In the
parenthetical reference, titles are usually abbreviated, and the act or law is
referred to by sections. Include the USC (United States Code) and the year
the act or law was passed (if relevant).

Such research should include investigations into the cause, diagnosis, early
detection, prevention, control, and treatment of autism (42 USC 284q, 2000).

Names of legal cases are usually abbreviated (**Roe v. Wade**). They are
italicized in the text of your essay but not in the works-cited list.

In *Goodridge v. Department of Public Health*, the court ruled that the
Commonwealth of Massachusetts had not adequately provided a reasonable constitutional cause for barring same-sex couples from civil marriages
(2003).

15. An Electronic Source

If a reference to an electronic source includes paragraph numbers rather
than page numbers, use the abbreviation **par.** or **pars.** followed by the paragraph number or numbers.

The earliest type of movie censorship came in the form of licensing fees, and
in Deer River, Minnesota, "a licensing fee of $200 was deemed not excessive
for a town of 1000" (Ernst, par. 20).

If the electronic source has no page or paragraph numbers, cite the work
in your discussion rather than in a parenthetical reference. By consulting
your works-cited list, readers will be able to determine that the source is
electronic and may therefore not have page numbers.

In her article "Limited Horizons," Lynne Cheney observes that schools do
best when students read literature not for practical information but for its
insights into the human condition.

2 Works-Cited List

The works-cited list, which appears at the end of your essay, is an alphabetical listing of all the research materials you cite. An effective works-cited entry
helps your readers locate its source, primarily by citing traits (like author,
title, and location) shared across most sources. These traits are referred to

as the nine *core elements*, and every source contains some combination (but not necessarily all) of them. Here is an overview of these elements.

1. Author

The person or people who wrote or otherwise created the source—or whose work on the source you are choosing to emphasize. This could mean an author, an editor (for a work with no author), a director, a composer, a director, a performer, or a narrator. It might be a full name or a Twitter handle.

- **One author:** Ng, Celeste.
- **Two authors:** Miller, Brenda, and Suzanne Paola.
- **Three or more authors:** Raabe, William A., et al.

2. Title of Source

The title of the specific source you are citing. This could be a whole book or a short poem within it, if your focus is on that poem. This could be a specific blog entry or an entire album. Shorter works or works that are part of a larger whole usually use quotation marks, while longer or stand-alone works use italics.

- **Essay:** "Once More to the Lake."
- **Television episode:** "Stolen Phone."
- **Play:** *The Tragedy of Hamlet, Prince of Denmark.*
- **Book:** *The Dirty Dust.*

3. Title of Container

A larger source containing the source you are citing. When citing a full, stand-alone source, element 3 = element 2. However, when citing an essay within a book or an episode of a television show, the container is the book or show. Italicize most containers.

- **Book:** *Frames of Mind: A Rhetorical Reader,*
- **Television show:** *Broad City,*
- **Website:** *The Toast,*

4. Other Contributors

Noteworthy contributors to the work not listed in element 1. These may include editors, translators, performers, etc. Introduce each name (or set of names) with a description of the role played. If listed after element 2, capitalize the description; if listed after element 3, do not.

- , adapted by Spike Lee,
- , performance by Octavia Spencer,
- , translated by Alan Titley,

5. Version

Description of a source that appears in more than one version. This appears most frequently for books that exist in multiple editions, whether these are numbered or indicated merely as "revised," "expanded," or similar. It may also apply to the "director's cut" of a film, a version of software, or similar.

- director's cut,
- 15th ed.,

6. Number

Number indicating source's place in a sequence. This could refer to a volume and/or issue number for journals, to volume numbers for books that appear in multiple volumes, or to season and episode numbers for shows.

- **Television episode:** season 2, episode 1,
- **Book:** vol. 6,
- **Journal Article:** vol. 119, no. 3,

7. Publisher

Organization that delivers the source to the public. Publishers should be listed for books, films, television shows, and similar, but *not* for periodicals, works published directly by authors or editors, Websites for which the publisher's name is the same as the title, or Websites that do not produce the works they house (examples: *YouTube, EccoHost,* or *WordPress*).

- U of Chicago P,
- Metropolitan Museum of Art,
- Lucasfilm,

8. Publication date

When the source was made available to the public. This could mean when a work was published or republished in print or online, or when it was released in theaters or on *iTunes,* broadcast on television, or performed live. It might be a year, a month, a specific date, or even a specific time.

- 2016,
- Spring 2016,
- 24 Mar. 2015,
- 10 Jan. 2016, 9:30 p.m.,

9. Location

Where to find the specific source. This could be a page number or range for print sources; a direct URL or DOI for online sources; or another type of identifier for specific source types. This is also the place to record the location of a lecture, live performance, or similar.

- pp. 30-36.
- www.newyorker.com/magazine/2015/07/20/the-really-big-one/.
- doi:10.1002/cplx.21590.
- Sheraton Hotel, New Orleans.

Not all sources contain all of the nine core elements, and some of them contain additional or optional elements, which you'll learn about in the sections that follow.

Containers within Containers

Some sources are housed in containers within larger containers. For instance, if you cite an article (source) from a journal (container #1) that you accessed through a service like *ProQuest* (container #2), or if you discuss an episode (source) of a television show (container #1) that you accessed on a service like *Netflix* (container #2), then you will need to include information about that larger container, too. This will help readers retrace your steps.

To create a works-cited entry for a source found in a container within a container, do the following:

- List core elements 1 (author) and 2 (title of source).
- List core elements 3-9 that provide information about the first container.
- List core elements 3-9 that provide information about the second container.

In the following example, a writer has identified and ordered source information for a television episode using the core elements. She used this process to create the works-cited entry that follows.

SOURCE

1. Author.   Dan Nowak.
2. Title of Source.   "Unraveling."
CONTAINER 1
3. Title of Container,   *The Killing*,
4. Other Contributors,   directed by Lodge Kerrigan,
5. Version,
6. Number,   season 4, episode 2,
7. Publisher,   AMC,
8. Publication date,   1 Aug. 2014.
9. Location.
CONTAINER 2
1. Title of Container,   *Netflix*,
2. Other Contributors,
3. Version,
4. Number,
5. Publisher,
6. Publication date,
7. Location.   www.netflix.com/watch/70306003.

WORKS-CITED ENTRY

Nowak, Dan. "Unraveling." *The Killing,* directed by Lodge Kerrigan, season 4, episode 2, AMC, 1 Aug. 2014. *Netflix,* www.netflix.com/watch/70306003.

The sections that follow will examine how to format these elements for specific source types. For every entry that is listed on your works-cited page, double-space within and between entries on the list, and indent the second and subsequent lines of each entry one-half inch. (**See 17b** for full manuscript guidelines.)

MLA Entries for Periodicals

Periodicals include scholarly journals, magazines, and newspapers. For each works-cited entry, include as many of the nine core elements (described at the beginning of this section) as possible. Figure 17.1 shows where you can

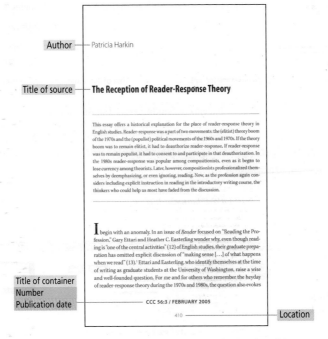

FIGURE 17.1 First page of a journal article showing the location of the information needed for documentation. © College Composition and Communication/National Council of Teachers of English.

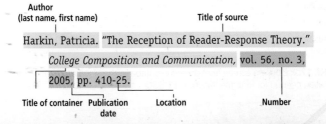

find this information in a print scholarly journal. Figure 17.2 shows where you can find the information in an online scholarly journal.

Scholarly Journals

1. An Article in a Scholarly Journal

When citing a print text, include the volume number (**vol.**) and issue number (**no.**) and be sure to include "**p.**" or "**pp.**" before page numbers.

> Harriss, M. Cooper. "One Blues Invisible: Civil Rights and Civil Religion in Ralph Ellison's Second Novel." *African American Review,* vol. 47, no. 2, 2014, pp. 247-66.

When citing an online text, include page numbers (if available) and be sure to include the full URL or DOI for the article, followed by a period.

> Maeseele, Thomas. "From Charity to Welfare Rights? A Study of Social Care Practices." *Social Work and Society: The International Online-Only Journal,* vol. 10, no. 1, 2010, www.socwork.net/sws/article/view/35/90.

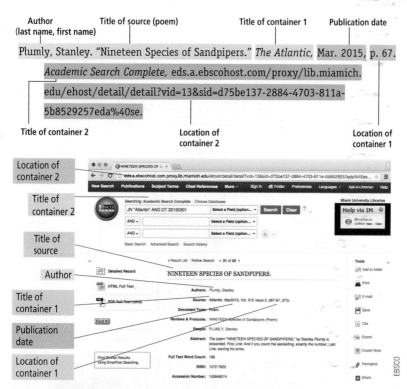

FIGURE 17.2 Opening screen from an online database showing the location of the information needed for documentation. © EBSCO.

2. An Article in a Scholarly Journal from an Online Database

Indicate the database you used to access the source and include the full URL or DOI, followed by a period.

> Kerness, Bonnie, et al. "Race and the Politics of Isolation in U.S. Prisons."
>
> > *Atlantic Journal of Communication,* vol. 22, no. 1, 2014, pp. 21-41.
> >
> > *Academic Search Complete,* doi:10.1080/15456870.2014.860146.

3. An Article with a Title within Its Title

If the article you are citing contains a title that is normally enclosed in quotation marks, use single quotation marks for the interior title.

> Zimmerman, Brett. "Frantic Forensic Oratory: Poe's 'The Tell-Tale Heart.'"
>
> > *Style,* vol. 35, 2001, pp. 34-50.

If the article you are citing contains a title that is normally italicized, use italics for the title in your works-cited entry.

> Zhang, Mingquan. "The Technological Diegesis in *The Great Gatsby.*" *English*
>
> > *Language Teaching,* vol. 1, no. 2, Dec. 2008, pp. 86-89. *ERIC,* files.eric.
> >
> > ed.gov/fulltext/EJ1082800.pdf.

Magazines

4. An Article in a Magazine

> "Ronald Reagan." *National Review,* 28 June 2004, pp. 14-17.
>
> Jackowe, David J. "Poison Gas Comes to America." *American History,* Dec.
>
> > 2014, www.historynet.com/poison-gas-comes-to-america.htm.

If the article begins on one page (say, page 186), but then skips to page 189, include the abbreviation "**pp.**" followed by the first page number and a plus sign.

> Di Giovanni, Janine. "The Shiites of Iraq." *National Geographic,* June 2004, pp. 1+.

5. An Article in a Magazine from an Online Database

For all periodical titles, include the initial article (usually "The") prior to the periodical title, as in the following example (***The*** before ***Atlantic***).

> Khazan, Olga. "The Bro Whisperer: Michael Kimmel's Quest to Turn College
>
> > Boys into Gentlemen—and Improve Sex on Campus." *The Atlantic,*
> >
> > Jan. 2015, pp. 20-21. *Academic OneFile,* connection.ebscohost.com/c/
> >
> > articles/99854172/bro-whisperer.

Newspapers and News Services

6. An Article in a Newspaper

Include the version of a text if there is more than one form for it (such as "**expanded ed.**" or "**2nd ed.**").

"Suicide Finding is Disputed." *The New York Times,* late ed., 11 Feb. 2015, p. B14.

Jones, Chris. "Don't Overlook the Need for Avant-Garde, Even in Chicago." *The*
Chicago Tribune, 11 Feb. 2015. www.chicagotribune.com/entertainment/
theater/ct-avante-garde-theater-tuta-column.html.

7. An Article in a Newspaper from an Online Database

Spiegel, Peter. "Third Time Lucky? The Latest Plan to Rescue Greece." *The*
Financial Times, 17 Sep. 2013, p. 17. *Academic OneFile,* go.galegroup.
com.eduproxy.tc-library.org:8080/ps/i.do?id=GALE%7CA343076709&sid=
summon&v=2.1&u=new30429&it=r&p=AONE&sw=w&asid=d9006f47ca3d73
b0a937c7b23f0636da.

8. A News Service

Ryan, Desmond. "Some Background on the Battle of Gettysburg."
Knight Ridder / Tribune Media Service, 7 Oct. 1993. *Academic*
OneFile, search.proquest.com.ezproxy.cul.columbia.edu/
docview/259995964.

"Russians Make Giant Snow Portrait of First Astronaut." *Reuters,* 11 Apr.
2016, www.reuters.com/article/us-russia-gagarin-
idUSKCN0X81PE?feedType=RSS&feedName=lifestyleMolt.

9. An Editorial or Letter to the Editor in a Newspaper

Insert a descriptor (such as "**Editorial**." or "**Letter**.") to stand in place of a
title (if none is given) or after a title. A descriptor designates a particular
section of a text.

"Lynching as Racial Terrorism." Editorial. *The New York Times,* late ed., 11
Feb. 2015, p. A26.

Rossi, Claire. Letter. *The New York Times,* 21 Mar. 2016, www.
nytimes.com/2016/03/21/opinion/women-in-science.
html?partner=rssnyt&emc=rss&_r=0.

Book Reviews, Newsletters, and Encyclopedias

10. A Book Review

DeSanctis, Maria. "Small Comforts." Review of *A Motor-Flight through France,*
by Edith Wharton. *Tin House,* vol. 16, no. 2, 2014.

Molzhan, Laura. Review of *The Incidents,* by Ayaka Kato. *The Chicago Tribune,*
8 June 2014, www.chicagotribune.com/entertainment/theater/dance/
chi-incidents-dance-review-20140608-story.html.

11. An Article in a Newsletter

Cappucci, Karen. "The Importance of Updated CORIs." *Glenwood News*, 8 Apr.
2016, p. 1.

"The Viking in Scandinavia." *HAAS Recycling Newsletter,* May 2014, www.
haas-recycling.com/tl_files/downloads/newsletter/en/HAAS-Newsletter-
Issue-No.8_04-2014.pdf.

12. An Article in an Encyclopedia

"Hawthorne, Nathaniel." *Encyclopaedia Britannica Online,* 20 Apr. 2015,
www.britannica.com/biography/Nathaniel-Hawthorne.

MLA Entries for Books

Books follow the same guidelines as periodicals. For each works-cited entry,
include as many of the nine core elements (described at the beginning of this
section) as possible. Figures 17.3 and 17.4 show where you can find this information in a print book.

Authors

13. A Book by One Author

Miller, Laura. *The Magician's Book: A Skeptic's Guide to Narnia.* Back Bay, 2009.

Douglass, Frederick. My Bondage and My Freedom, 1855. *Project Gutenberg,*
www.gutenberg.org/files/202/202-h/202-h.htm.

Close-Up PUBLISHERS' NAMES

MLA requires that you use abbreviated forms of publishers' names in the
works-cited list. In general, omit articles; abbreviations, such as *Inc.* and
Corp.; and words such as *Publishers, Books,* and *Press.* If the publisher's
name includes a person's name, use the last name only. Finally, use
standard abbreviations whenever you can—*UP* for University Press and
P for Press, for example.

Name	Abbreviation
Basic Books	Basic
Oxford University Press	Oxford UP
Alfred A. Knopf, Inc.	Knopf
Random House, Inc.	Random
University of Chicago Press	U of Chicago P

Author   Title of container
last name, first name

Kleiner, Fred S. *Gardner's Art through the Ages: A Global History.*

Enhanced 13th ed., Cengage, 2011.

Version   Publisher Publication
date

FIGURE 17.3 Title page from a book showing the location of the information needed for documentation. From KLEINER. *Gardner's Art through the Ages*, 13E. © 2011, Cengage Learning. Reproduced by permission. www.cengage.com/permissions

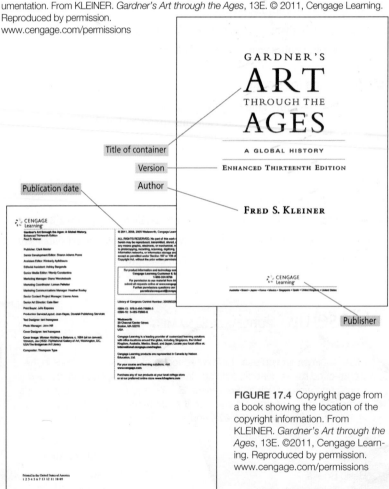

Title of container

Version

Publication date

Author

Publisher

FIGURE 17.4 Copyright page from a book showing the location of the copyright information. From KLEINER. *Gardner's Art through the Ages*, 13E. ©2011, Cengage Learning. Reproduced by permission. www.cengage.com/permissions

14. A Book by Two Authors

List the first author with last name first, followed by a comma and the word "**and**". Then list the second author with the first name first.

> Gulati, Varun, and Mythili Anoop. *Contemporary Women's Writing in India*.
>
> Lexington, 2014.

For books that are published by a university press (such as Cambridge University Press), use the abbreviation "**UP**."

> Slaughter, Sheila, and Gary Rhodes. *Academic Capitalism and the New Economy:*
>
> *Markets, State, and Higher Education*. Johns Hopkins UP, 2009, jhupbooks.
>
> press.jhu.edu/content/academic-capitalism-and-new-economy.

15. A Book by Three or More Authors

Include only the name of the first author (last name first), followed by a comma and **et al.** ("and others").

> Orr, Catherine M., et al. *Rethinking Women's and Gender Studies*. Routledge,
>
> 2011.

The following text is published by National Academies Press; the word "Press" is abbreviated with the letter "**P.**"

> Beatty, Alexandra S., et al. *Climate Change Education*. The National Academies
>
> P, 2014, www.nap.edu/read/18807/.

16. Two or More Books by the Same Author

List books by the same author in alphabetical order by title. After the first entry, use three unspaced hyphens followed by a period in place of the author's name.

> Ede, Lisa. *Situating Composition: Composition Studies and the Politics of*
>
> *Location*. Southern Illinois UP, 2004.
>
> ---. *Work in Progress*. 6th ed., Bedford, 2004.

17. A Book by a Corporate Author

If a text is both authored and published by the same organization, begin with the title of the text. If the corporate author is not the same as the publisher, begin with the name of the corporate author.

> *Grade Expectations: How Marks and Education Policies Shape Students'*
>
> *Ambitions*. Organisation for Economic Cooperation and Development,
>
> 2012, doi:10.1787/19963777.
>
> The Home Depot. *Home Improvement 1-2-3*. 2nd ed., Meredith Books, 2003.

18. An Edited Book

An edited book is a work prepared for publication by a person other than the author. If your focus is on the *author's* work, begin your citation with the author's name.

Twain, Mark. *The Adventures of Huckleberry Finn*. Edited by Michael Patrick

Hearn, Norton, 2001.

If your focus is on the *editor's* work, begin your citation with the editor's name, followed by a comma and the word "**editor.**" (For two editors, treat the entry as you would a book by two authors, but include the word "**editors**" after the second name. For three or more editors, include only the first editor's name (last name first), followed by a comma and the words "**et al., editors.**")

Hearn, Michael Patrick, editor. *The Adventures of Huckleberry Finn*. By Mark

Twain, Norton, 2001.

19. A Translation

If your focus is on the *translator's* work, place that name first in your citation, followed by the word "**translator.**" If your focus is on the *author's* work, follow the first entry under "An Edited Book."

Rabassa, Gregory, translator. *One Hundred Years of Solitude*. By Gabriel García

Márquez, Avon, 1991.

20. A Subsequent Edition of a Book

When citing an edition other than the first, include the edition number after the title of the book. The edition number usually appears on the work's cover and title page.

Yaghijian, Lucretia B. *Writing Theology Well: A Rhetoric for Theological and

Biblical Writers*. 2nd ed., Bloomsbury, 2015.

Miner, Dorothy, et al., editors. *Teaching Chemistry to Students with

Disabilities: A Manual for High Schools, Colleges, and Graduate Programs*.

4th ed., American Chemical Society, 2001. *ERIC*, files.eric.ed.gov/

fulltext/ED476798.pdf.

21. A Republished Book

Include the original publication date after the title of a republished book.

Wharton, Edith. *The House of Mirth*. 1905. Scribner's, 1975.

22. A Book in a Series

If the cover or title page indicates that the book is part of a series, include the series name, neither italicized nor enclosed in quotation marks, and the series number (if applicable) after the publication information.

Davis, Bertram H. *Thomas Percy*. Twayne, 1981. Twayne's English

Authors 313.

23. A Multivolume Work

When all volumes of a multivolume work have the same title, include the number of the volume you are using.

> *Writings of Charles S. Peirce: A Chronological Edition.* Vol. 4, edited by Max H.
>
> Fisch, Indiana UP, 2000.

If you use two or more volumes that have the same title, cite the entire work.

> *Writings of Charles S. Peirce: A Chronological Edition.* Edited by Max H. Fisch,
>
> Indiana UP, 2000. 6 vols.

24. An Illustrated Book or a Graphic Narrative

An illustrated book is a work in which illustrations accompany the text. If your focus is on the *author's* work, begin your citation with the author's name. After the title, include the words "**illustrated by**" followed by the illustrator's name and the publication information.

> Frost, Robert. *Stopping by Woods on a Snowy Evening,* illustrated by Susan
>
> Jeffers, Penguin, 2001.

If your focus is on the *illustrator's* work, begin your citation with the illustrator's name followed by a comma and the word "**illustator.**" After the title of the work, provide the author's name, preceded by the word "**By.**"

> Jeffers, Susan, illustrator. *Stopping by Woods on a Snowy Evening.* By Robert
>
> Frost, Penguin, 2001.

For a graphic novel, where the text and illustrations work together to tell a story, use the same citation you would for a book. If the author and illustrator are different people, cite them in one of the two ways described for an illustrated book.

> Bechdel, Alison. *Fun Home: A Family Tragicomic.* Houghton, 2006.

25. The Foreword, Preface, or Afterword of a Book

> Campbell, Richard. Preface. *Media and Culture: An Introduction to Mass*
>
> *Communication,* by Bettina Fabos, Bedford, 2005, pp. vi-xi.

26. A Book with a Title within Its Title

If the book you are citing contains a title that is normally italicized (a novel, play, or long poem, for example), do not italicize the interior title.

> Fulton, Joe B. *Mark Twain in the Margins: The Quarry Farm Marginalia and* A
>
> Connecticut Yankee in King Arthur's Court. U of Alabama P, 2000.

If the book you are citing contains a title that is normally enclosed in quotation marks (a short story or poem), keep the quotation marks.

Hawkins, Hunt, and Brian W. Shaffer, editors. *Approaches to Teaching Conrad's "Heart of Darkness" and "The Secret Sharer."* MLA, 2002.

27. Sacred Texts

The New English Bible with the Apocrypha. Oxford Study ed., Oxford UP, 1976.

Holy Qur'an. Translated by M. H. Shakir, Tahrike Tarsile Qur'an, 1999.

28. A Book Accessed through an E-reader

Sonnenberg, Brittani. *Home Leave: A Novel.* Kindle ed., Hachette, 2014.

Parts of Books

29. A Short Story, Play, or Poem in a Collection

Bukowski, Charles. "lonely hearts." *The Flash of Lightning behind the Mountain: New Poems,* Ecco, 2004, pp. 115-16.

30. An Essay in an Anthology or Edited Collection

Crevel, René. "From *Babylon.*" *Surrealist Painters and Poets: An Anthology,* edited by Mary Ann Caws. MIT P, 2001, pp. 175-77.

31. More than One Work from the Same Anthology

Provide a complete citation for the anthology, but list each work from that anthology separately (with a cross-reference to the entire anthology). Entries should appear in alphabetical order.

Agar, Eileen. "Am I a Surrealist?" Caws, *Surrealist Painters,* pp. 3-7.

Caws, Mary Ann, editor. *Surrealist Painters and Poets: An Anthology.* MIT P, 2001.

Crevel, René. "From *Babylon.*" Caws, *Surrealist Painters,* pp. 175-77.

32. A Scholarly Article Reprinted in a Collection

Booth, Wayne C. "Why Ethical Criticism Can Never Be Simple." *Style,* vol. 32, no. 2, 1998, pp. 351-64. Reprinted in *Mapping the Ethical Turn: A Reader in Ethics, Culture, and Literary Theory,* edited by Todd F. Davis and Kenneth Womack. UP of Virginia, 2001, pp. 16-29.

33. An Article in a Reference Book

For a signed article, begin with the author's name.

Birch, Dinah. "Expressionism." *The Oxford Companion to English Literature.* 7th ed., Oxford UP, 2009.

For an unsigned article, begin with the title.

"Cubism." *The Encyclopedia Americana.* 2012 ed.

MLA Entries for Internet-Specific Sources

When citing Websites, podcasts, *YouTube* videos, and blogs, include as many of the nine core elements (described at the beginning of this section) as possible. Figure 17.5 shows where you can find this information on a Website.

34. An Entire Website

When citing a Website, include the full URL for that site.

> Nelson, Cary, and Bartholomew Brinkman, editors. *Modern American Poetry*.
>
> Dept. of English, U of Illinois, Urbana-Champaign, 2014, www.english.
>
> illinois.edu/maps/poets.htm.

35. A Document within a Website

When citing a document or an article within a Website, include the full URL for the document or article.

> Nix, Elizabeth. "6 Viking Leaders You Should Know." *History.com,* A&E
>
> Television Networks, 6 Feb. 2014, www.history.com/news/history-
>
> lists/6-viking-leaders-you-should-know.

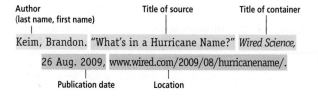

Author (last name, first name) — Title of source — Title of container

Keim, Brandon. "What's in a Hurricane Name?" *Wired Science,* 26 Aug. 2009, www.wired.com/2009/08/hurricanename/.

Publication date — Location

FIGURE 17.5 Part of an online article showing the location of the information needed for documentation. Wired.com © 2011 Condé Nast Digital. All rights reserved. Image from NOAA.

36. A Home Page for a Course

> Davis, Brian. Home page. Dept. of Physics and Physical Oceanography, U of
>
>> North Carolina, Wilmington, Fall 2015, www.people.uncw.edu/davis/
>>
>> phy201.html.

37. A Podcast or a Radio Program Accessed Online

When citing a podcast or radio program online, include the full URL.

> "Teenage Skeptic Takes on Climate Scientists." *Morning Edition,* narrated by
>
>> David Kestenbaum, National Public Radio, 15 Apr. 2008, www.npr.org/
>>
>> templates/story.php?storyId=89619306.

38. An Online Video (*YouTube*)

Because videos posted to online sites can be removed at any time, you should provide as much information as possible in your citation. In the following example, a date of access in included after the full URL for the video.

> Mohr, Nicole. "How to Analyze a Poem." *YouTube,* 27 Oct. 2013. www.
>
>> youtube.com/watch?v=5lVHsfkOvV8. Accessed 22 Mar. 2016.

39. A Television Program Streamed via *Netflix* or *Amazon*

Shows that are streamed through online services are often available for a certain period of time. For this reason, you may want to include the date you accessed a program that is streamed online.

> "Episode 4." *Call the Midwife,* season 4, BBC One, 8 Feb. 2015. *Netflix,* www.
>
>> netflix.com/search/call%20the%20midwife? jbv=70245163&jbp=0&jbr=0.
>>
>> Accessed 22 Mar. 2016.

40. A Blog, Tweet, or Social Networking Post

> O'Connor, Brendan. "The Downtown Void." *The Awl,* 17 Mar. 2016, www.
>
>> theawl.com/2016/03/the-downtown-void.

For a tweet, use the full tweet as the title. Include the date and time, as well as the full tweet's URL.

> @tim_cook. "Andy Grove was one of the giants of the technology world.
>
>> He loved our country and epitomized America at its best. Rest in
>>
>> peace." *Twitter,* 21 March 2016, 10:35 p.m., twitter.com/tim_cook/
>>
>> status/712073584194105344.

41. A Comment on a Blog, Tweet, or Other Online Forum

Often commenters use screen names or pseudonyms to identify themselves. Treat the name exactly as it appears onscreen.

foxinthe_snow. Comment on "My Other Parent," by Nicole Soojung Callahan. *The Toast,* 22 Dec. 2014, www.aka-sf.org/my-other-parent-by-nicole-soojung-callahan/.

42. An App (or any Computer Software)

Paper—Stories from Facebook, version 1.2.6. *Facebook*, 11 Mar. 2016, www.facebook.com/paper.

43. A Source Accessed through an App

Dolce, Chris. "Winter Storm Selene: 2,000-Mile-Plus Snow Swath." *The Weather Channel,* version 7.3.2, 22 Mar. 2016, 8:45 a.m.

44. Email

Mauk, Karen R. "Today." Received by Stephen R. Mandell, 28 June 2015.

MLA Entries for Other Sources

45. A Photograph or Painting

For a photograph or painting viewed at a museum or other location, provide the name of the photographer or artist (last name first), followed by the title of the work in italics. Note the year in which the work was created, as well as the name of the place where it was viewed and its city. If the name of the museum contains the city name, omit the city.

Stieglitz, Alfred. *The Steerage.* 1907, Los Angeles County Museum of Art.

A photograph or painting without a title is treated the same, but in place of the italicized title, add a brief description of the work. If the work was accessed online, include the full URL where the work was viewed.

Burns, Patrick. Panoramic print of Providence, Rhode Island. 1988, Worcester Art Museum, vps343.pairvps.com:8080/emuseum/view/objects/asitem/search@/15/title-desc?t:state:flow=d8ad95ba-419f-450a-a5dc-8214e37e7e6f.

46. A Cartoon/Comic Strip

Trudeau, Gary. "Doonesbury." *The Philadelphia Inquirer*, 15 Sept. 2003, p. E13.

Stossel, Sage. "Star Wars: The Next Generation." *The Atlantic Online,* 20 May 1999, www.theatlantic.com/past/unbound/sage/ss990519.htm.

47. An Advertisement

If the source you use is not one that readers would be able to identify, include a description in your citation.

Microsoft. Advertisement. *National Review*, 8 June 2010.

48. A Map

Like the previous example, include a description in your citation if readers might not be able to identify the source.

"Philadelphia, Pennsylvania." Map. *U.S. Gazetteer,* 2016, pennsylvania.

hometownlocator.com/maps/countymap,cfips,101,c,philadelphia.cfm.

49. A Film

Include the title of the film (italicized), the distributor, and the date, along with other information that may be useful to readers, such as the name of the director, names of performers, and the screenwriter.

If you focus on the film, place it first in the citation.

Citizen Kane. Directed by Orson Welles, performances by Welles and Agnes

Moorehead, RKO, 1941.

If you focus on the contribution of a particular person, begin with the person's name.

Welles, Orson, director. *Citizen Kane.* RKO, 1941.

If you cite a film on DVD or Blu-ray, include the original release date.

Cowperthwaite, Gabriela, director. *Blackfish.* Magnolia Home Entertainment,

2013.

50. A Television Program

If the program is part of a series, begin with the episode title. Include the original air date.

"War Feels Like War." *P.O.V.,* PBS, 6 Jul. 2004.

If you accessed the program online, provide the previous information and include the season and episode number, as well as the full URL for the episode.

"The Miseducation of Susan Ross." *Scandal,* season 5, episode 6, ABC, 31 Mar.

2016, abc.go.com/shows/scandal/episode-guide/season-05/16-the-

miseducation-of-susan-ross.

51. An Audio Recording

Malloy, Dave. "No One Else." *Natasha, Pierre, and the Great Comet of 1812,*

Sh-K-Boom, 2013.

Adele. "When We Were Young." *25,* Sony, 2015. *iTunes,* itun.es/us/HIPQp.

52. An Image or Video on a Website

Einspruch, Franklin. "View Out the Window." *The Boston Globe,* 21 Feb. 2015,

www.bostonglobe.com/arts/2015/02/21-the-poetry-boston-snowfall/

maV2CoJKQfkbFAAdnh08tL/story.html.

53. A Dissertation

For a published dissertation, place the title in italics and be sure to include the full URL or DOI for the work.

> Rodriguez, Jason Anthony. *Bureaucracy and Altruism: Managing the Contradictions of Teaching*. Dissertation. U of Texas, Arlington, 2003. *ProQuest*, search.
> proquest.com.ezproxy.cul.columbia.edu/docview/305227623.

For an unpublished dissertation, place the title in quotation marks.

> Pfeffer, Miki. "An 'Enlarging Influence': Women of New Orleans, Julia Ward Howe, and the Women's Department at the Cotton Centennial Exposition, 1884-1885." Dissertation. U of New Orleans, 2011.

54. A Government Publication

For a work by a government agency, begin the citation with the name of the government, followed by a comma and the name of the organizational unit (if applicable), followed by the agency. These entities are arranged from largest to smallest, as shown in the following examples. Do not abbreviate words such as "Department" or "Government Printing Office."

> United States, Congress, Senate, Office of Consumer Affairs. *2014 Consumer's Resource Handbook,* Government Printing Office, 2014.
>
> United States, Department of Justice, Office of Justice Programs. *Violence Against Women: Estimates from the Redesigned National Crime Victimization Survey,* by Ronet Bachman and Linda E. Salzman, Aug. 1995. *Bureau of Justice Statistics,* www.bjs.gov/content/pub/pdf/ FEMVIED.PDF.

If you cite legislation of the United States Congress, include the number and session. If there is a document type (such as a report) and number, include that information, as well.

> United States, Congress, Senate, Committee on Energy and Natural Resources. *Keystone XL Pipeline*. Government Printing Office, 2015. 114th Congress, 1st session, Report 114-1.

55. A Pamphlet

Cite a pamphlet as you would a book. If no author is listed, begin with the title (italicized).

> *The Darker Side of Tanning*. American Academy of Dermatology, 2010.

56. A Lecture

If you attend a lecture or other public address, state that at the end of your citation with the word "**Lecture**" or "**Address**."

Grimm, Mary. "An Afternoon with Mary Grimm." Visiting Writers Program,

Dept. of English, Wright State U, 16 Apr. 2004. Lecture.

57. A Personal Interview or Letter

For a personal interview, begin with the interview subject and use the phrase
"**Personal Interview**," followed by the date of the interview.

Tannen, Deborah. Personal Interview. 8 June 2015.

When citing a letter, begin with the letter writer's name and use the phrase
"**Personal Letter**," followed by the date of the letter.

Tan, Amy. Personal Letter. 7 Apr. 2016.

58. A Published Interview

Include the phrase "**Interview by**" after the title of the interview. For an
interview accessed online, include the full URL for the piece.

"Bill Gates: The *Rolling Stone* Interview." Interview by Jeff Goodell, 13 Mar.

2014, *RollingStone.com,* www.rollingstone.com/culture/news/bill-gates-

the-rolling-stone-interview-20140313.

59. A Published Letter

Joyce, James. "Letter to Louis Gillet." *James Joyce,* by Richard Ellmann,

Oxford UP, 1965, p. 631.

Close-Up HOW TO CITE SOURCES NOT LISTED IN THIS CHAPTER

The examples listed in this chapter represent the sources you will most
likely encounter in your research. If you encounter a source that is not
listed here, find the model that most closely matches it, and adapt the
guidelines for your use.

For example, suppose you wanted to include **an obituary** from a print
newspaper in your list of works cited. The models that most closely resemble this type of entry *are an editorial in a newspaper* and a *letter to the
editor* (entry 9). If you used these models as your guide, your entry would
look like this:

Boucher, Geoff, and Elaine Woo. "Michael Jackson's Life Was Infused

with Fantasy and Tragedy." Obituary. *The Los Angeles Times,* 2

Jul. 2009, p. 4.

EXERCISE 17.1

Each of these notes identifies a source used in an essay about online censorship. Determine which information is required to cite each source. Then, following the guidelines and proper format for MLA documentation, create a parenthetical reference for each source, and then create a works-cited list, arranging sources in the proper order. Be sure to format source information correctly, adding quotation marks and italics as needed.

1. Page 72 in a book called Banned in the USA by Herbert N. Foerstel. The book was published in a third edition in 2006 by Greenwood Press. The author's name appears in the text of your essay.

2. A historic statement made by Esther Dyson in her keynote address at the Newspapers 1996 Conference. Her statement is quoted in an article by Jodi B. Cohen called Fighting Online Censorship. The speech has not been printed in any other source. The article is in the April 13, 1996, edition of the weekly business journal Editor & Publisher. Dyson's quotation appears on page 44. The article begins on page 44 and continues on page 60. Dyson's name is mentioned in the text of your essay.

3. An article called Trust Darknet: Control and Compromise in the Internet's Certificate Authority Model by authors Steven B. Roosa and Stephen Schultze. It appears in the online open-access collection Internet Censorship and Control, edited by Steven J. Murdoch and Hal Roberts. The article was published on April 11, 2013. It can be downloaded as a fourteen-page PDF, with numbered pages, from the site. The sponsor is Social Science Electronic Publishing. You summarize the article's findings in your essay.

4. An essay by Nat Hentoff titled Speech Should Not Be Limited on pages 22–26 in the book Censorship: Opposing Viewpoints, edited by Terry O'Neill. The book is published by Greenhaven Press. The publication year is 2005. The quotation you have used is from page 24, and the author is mentioned in the text of your essay.

5. An online essay by Gianna Palmer titled Supervising Kids Online: McAfee Survey Shows Disconnect between Parents and Tweens. The essay was posted to The Huffington Post's Huffpost Screen Sense column. The essay was posted on June 4, 2013, and updated August 4, 2013. Although the essay prints out on two pages, the pages are not numbered onscreen. In your essay, you summarize information from the second page of the document. You accessed the information from the online database Expanded Academic ASAP.

❸ Content Notes

Content notes—multiple bibliographic citations or other material that does not fit smoothly into your essay—are indicated by a **superscript** (raised numeral) in the text. Notes can appear either as footnotes at the bottom of the page or as endnotes on a separate sheet entitled **Notes**, placed after the last page of the essay and before the works-cited list. Content notes are double-spaced within and between entries. The first line is indented one-half inch, and subsequent lines are typed flush left.

For Multiple Citations

In the Essay

Many researchers emphasize the necessity of having dying patients share their experiences.[1]

In the Note

1. Kübler-Ross 27; Stinnette 43; Poston 70; Cohen and Cohen 31-34; Burke 1: 91-95.

For Other Material

In the Essay

The massacre during World War I is an event the survivors could not easily forget.[2]

In the Note

2. For a firsthand account of these events, see Bedoukian 178-81.

17b MLA-Style Manuscript Guidelines

Although MLA essays do not usually include abstracts or internal headings, this situation is changing. Be sure you know what your instructor expects.

The guidelines in the three checklists that follow are based on the *MLA Handbook* 8th edition.

17c Model MLA-Style Research Paper

The following student essay, "The Great Debate: *Wikipedia* and College-Level Research," uses MLA documentation style. It includes MLA-style in-text citations, three charts, a notes page, and a works-cited list.

CHECKLIST

Typing Your Essay

When typing your essay, use the student essay in **17c** as your model.

❑ Leave a one-inch margin at the top and bottom and on both sides of the page. Double-space your essay throughout.

❑ Capitalize all important words in your title, but not prepositions, articles, coordinating conjunctions, or the *to* in infinitives (unless they begin or end the title or subtitle). Do not italicize your title or enclose it in quotation marks. Never put a period after the title.

❑ Number all pages of your essay consecutively—including the first—in the upper right-hand corner, one-half inch from the top, flush right. Type your last name followed by a space before the page number on every page.

❑ Set off quotations of more than four lines of prose or more than three lines of poetry by indenting the whole quotation one-half inch. If you quote two or more paragraphs, indent the first line of each paragraph an additional quarter inch. (If the first sentence does not begin a paragraph, do not indent it. Indent the first line only in successive paragraphs.)

❑ Citations should follow MLA documentation style.

See 17a

CHECKLIST

Using Visuals

❑ Insert visuals into the text as close as possible to where they are discussed.

See 23d

❑ For **tables**, follow these guidelines: *Above the table*, label each table with the word **Table** followed by an arabic numeral (for instance, **Table 1**). Double-space, and type a descriptive caption, with the first line flush with the left-hand margin; indent subsequent lines one-quarter inch. Capitalize the caption as if it were a title.

  Below the table, type the word **Source**, followed by a colon and all source information. Type the first line of the source information flush with the left-hand margin; indent subsequent lines one-quarter inch.

❑ Label other types of visual material—graphs, charts, photographs, drawings, and so on—**Fig.** (Figure) followed by an arabic numeral (for example, **Fig. 2**). Directly below the visual, type the label and a title or caption on the same line, followed by source information. Type all lines flush with the left-hand margin.

❑ Do not include the source of the visual in the works-cited list unless you use other material from that source elsewhere in the essay.

See
17a3

CHECKLIST

Preparing the MLA Works-Cited List

When typing your works-cited list, follow these guidelines:

❑ Begin the works-cited list on a new page after the last page of text or content notes, numbered as the next page of the essay.

❑ Center the title **Works Cited** one inch from the top of the page. Double-space between the title and the first entry.

❑ List entries alphabetically, with last name first. Use the author's full name as it appears on the title page. If a source has no listed author, alphabetize it by the first word of the title (not counting the article).

❑ Type the first line of each entry flush with the left-hand margin; indent subsequent lines one-half inch.

❑ Double-space within and between entries.

Title Pages

Although MLA does not require a separate title page, some instructors prefer that you include one. If so, follow this format:

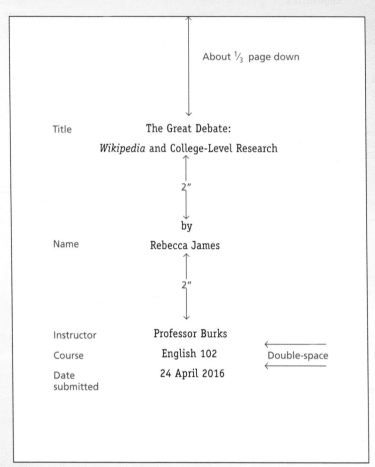

About ⅓ page down

Title

The Great Debate:

Wikipedia **and College-Level Research**

2″

by

Name

Rebecca James

2″

Instructor

Professor Burks

Course

English 102

Date submitted

24 April 2016

Double-space

½"

James 1

1"

Rebecca James

Professor Burks

English 102

24 April 2016

Center title ——→ The Great Debate: *Wikipedia*

and College-Level Research

Indent ½" ——→ When confronted with a research assignment, students

and professionals alike often turn first to *Wikipedia*, the

popular free online encyclopedia. With over 26,000,000 articles,

Double-space *Wikipedia* is a valuable resource for anyone seeking general

information on a topic. In the academic community, however,

Wikipedia has become a source of controversy. Many college

instructors say that students should not rely on *Wikipedia* as an

authoritative research source or cite it in their bibliographies;

1"   1"

they say that *Wikipedia* (like other encyclopedias) should be used

only as a starting point for in-depth research. Some academics,

troubled by the site's lack of reliability, even discourage the use

of *Wikipedia* as a source of factual information. On the other hand,

some instructors (along with some college librarians) believe that

the issue is not so clear-cut. They say that *Wikipedia* is here

to stay and that if the site has problems, it is their responsibil-

Thesis   ity to help improve it. All in all, the debate over *Wikipedia* has
statement

been a positive development because it has led the academic

community to confront the challenges of open, collaborative

software on the web.

Wikipedia is the most popular wiki, an open-source

website that allows users to edit as well as contribute content.

Derived from a Hawaiian word meaning "quick," the term *wiki*

suggests the swiftness and ease with which users can access

information on and contribute content to a site ("Wiki").

1"

Student's
last name
and page
number
on every
page
(including
the first)

Outline
point I:
Definition
of wiki and
explanation
of *Wikipedia*

James 2

In accordance with the site's policies, users can edit existing articles and add new articles using *Wikipedia*'s editing
tools, which do not require specialized programming knowledge or expertise. Since its creation in 2001 by Jimmy Wales,
Wikipedia has grown into a huge database of articles on topics
ranging from contemporary rock bands to obscure scientific
and technical concepts. Because anyone can edit or add content
to the site, however, many members of the academic community
consider *Wikipedia* unreliable.

Parenthetical
documentation
refers to
material
accessed from
a website

Student's
original
conclusions;
no docu-
mentation
necessary

Outline
point II:
Introduction
to *Wikipedia*'s
drawbacks

Without a professional editorial board to oversee its development, *Wikipedia* has several shortcomings that limit its trust-
worthiness. As *Wikipedia*'s own "Researching with *Wikipedia*"
page concedes, "not everything in *Wikipedia* is accurate,
comprehensive, or unbiased." "Reliability of *Wikipedia*," an
article on *Wikipedia*, discusses the many problems that have been
identified, presenting criticisms under categories such as "areas
of reliability," "susceptibility to bias," and "false biographical
information." Academics have similar objections. Villanova
University communication department chair Maurice L. Hall has
reservations about *Wikipedia*:

Quotations
from Internet
source,
introduced
by author's
name, are not
followed by a
paragraph or
page number
because this
information
was not
provided in the
electronic text

> As an open source that is not subjected to traditional forms
> of peer review, *Wikipedia* must be considered only as
> reliable as the credibility of the footnotes it uses. But I also
> tell students that the information can be skewed in direc-
> tions of ideology or other forms of bias, and so that is why
> it cannot be taken as a final authority. (qtd. in Burnsed)

Quotation of
more than four
lines is typed
as a block,
indented ½",
and double-
spaced, with
no quotation
marks

In fact, in 2007, *Wikipedia*'s unreliability led Middlebury
College's history department to prohibit students from citing
Wikipedia as a research source—although it does not prohibit
them from using the site for reference. Since then, however,

Qtd. in
indicates
that Hall's
comments
were quoted
in Burnsed's
article

James 3

many academics have qualified their criticisms of *Wikipedia*, arguing that although the site is not a reliable research source, it is a valuable stepping stone to more in-depth research. As retired reference librarian Joe Schallan explains, "*Wikipedia* can be useful, especially as a starting point for information on offbeat topics or niche interests that traditional encyclopedias omit." However, he believes that information from *Wikipedia* should be taken "with a very large grain of salt."

Because it is an open-source site, *Wikipedia* is not always reliable or accurate. Although many *Wikipedia* articles include citations, many others—especially those that are underdeveloped—do not. In addition, because anyone can create or edit them, *Wikipedia* articles can be inaccurate, biased, and even targets for vandalism. For example, some *Wikipedia* users tamper with the biographies of especially high-profile political or cultural figures.[1] According to the article "*Wikipedia* Vandalism Detection," seven percent of *Wikipedia*'s articles are vandalized in some way (Adler et al. 277). Although *Wikipedia* has an extensive protection policy that restricts the kinds of edits that can be made to its articles ("*Wikipedia*: Protection Policy"), there are limitations to *Wikipedia*'s control measures.

Because they can be edited by anyone, *Wikipedia* articles are often poorly written. Emory University English professor Mark Bauerlein asserts that *Wikipedia* articles are written in a "flat, featureless, factual style" (153). Even though *Wikipedia* has instituted a coding system to label the shortcomings of its less-developed articles, a warning about an article's poor writing style is likely to go unnoticed by the typical user. Bauerlein argues that the poor writing of many *Wikipedia* articles reaffirms

Outline point III: *Wikipedia's* unreliability

Superscript number identifies content note

Outline point IV: *Wikipedia's* poor writing

James 4

to students that sloppy writing and grammatical errors are acceptable in their own writing as well:

> Students relying on *Wikipedia* alone, year in and year out, absorb the prose as proper knowledge discourse, and knowledge itself seems blank and uninspiring. (153-54)

Parenthetical documentation is placed one space after end punctuation

Thus, according to Bauerlein, *Wikipedia* articles have actually lowered the standards for what constitutes acceptable college-level writing.

Despite *Wikipedia*'s drawbacks, there is no denying the popularity of the site among both college students and professionals, who turn to it first for general factual information on a variety of topics. According to Jodi L. Wilson, more than seventy percent of *Wikipedia* contributors are at least twenty-two years old, with the majority of users having higher-education degrees (885-87).[2] Figs. 1 and 2 show a breakdown of the people who most commonly consult *Wikipedia*.

Outline point V. A: *Wikipedia*'s popularity and benefits: Wilson's findings (charts)

Superscript number identifies content note

Age Distribution as Reflected in the 2011 Surveys

April 2011 Survey
(Contributors Only)

12–17
13%

40–82
28%

18–21
14%

30–39
19%

22–29
26%

Dec. 2011 Survey
(All Respondents)

12–17
11%

40–82
30%

18–21
13%

30–39
21%

22–29
25%

Figures summarize relevant data. Source information is typed directly below the figures.

Fig. 1. Jodi L. Wilson, "Proceed with Extreme Caution: Citation to *Wikipedia* in Light of Contributor Demo-graphics and Content Policies." *Vanderbilt Journal of Entertainment & Technology Law*, vol. 16, no. 4, 2014, p. 886. *Academic Search Complete*, web.a.ebscohost.com.ezproxy.cul.columbia.edu/ehost/detail/detail?vid=4&sid=14afe0c2-3351-4754-93dc-2371d2724d5d.

James 5

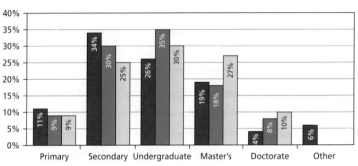

Education Level as Reflected in the 2008 & 2011 Surveys

■ 2008 Survey Contributors Only   ■ April 2011 Survey All Respondents
☐ Dec. 2011 Survey All Respondents

Fig. 2. Jodi L. Wilson, "Proceed with Extreme Caution: Citation to *Wikipedia* in Light of Contributor Demographics and Content Policies." *Vanderbilt Journal of Entertainment & Technology Law*, vol. 16, no. 4, 2014, p. 886. *Academic Search Complete*, web.a.ebscohost.com.ezproxy.cul.columbia.edu/ehost/detail/ detail?vid=4&sid=14afe0c2-3351-4754-93dc-2371d2724d5d.

Outline point V. B: *Wikipedia*'s popularity and benefits: comprehensive abstracts, links to other sources, and current and comprehensive bibliographies

There are good reasons why so many educated adults use *Wikipedia*. Longer *Wikipedia* articles often include comprehensive abstracts that summarize their content. *Wikipedia* articles also often include links to other *Wikipedia* articles, allowing users to navigate quickly through related content. In addition, many *Wikipedia* articles link to other online and print sources, including reliable peer-reviewed sources. Another benefit, noted earlier by Villanova University's Maurice L. Hall, is the inclusion of current and comprehensive bibliographies in some *Wikipedia* articles. According to Alison J. Head and Michael B. Eisenberg, "*Wikipedia* plays an important role when students are formulating and defining a topic."[3] Assuming that *Wikipedia* users make the effort to connect an article's content with more reliable, traditional research sources, *Wikipedia* can be a valuable first step for serious researchers.

Superscript number identifies content note

James 6

Wikipedia has advantages over other online encyclopedias. Because users can update articles in real time from any location, *Wikipedia* offers up-to-the-minute coverage of political and cultural events as well as timely information on popular culture topics that receive little or no attention in other reference sources. In addition, because *Wikipedia* has such a broad user base, more topics are covered in *Wikipedia* than in other online resources. For example, a student researching the history of video gaming would find *Wikipedia*'s "Wii U" article, with its numerous pages of information and nearly two hundred references, to be a valuable resource. Encyclopaedia Britannica does not contain a comparable article on this popular game console. Even when there is little information on a particular topic, *Wikipedia* allows users to create "stub" articles, which provide minimal information that users can expand over time. Thus, by offering immediate access to information on relatively obscure topics, *Wikipedia* can be a valuable first step in finding reliable research sources on such topics.

Outline point VI: Wikipedia's advantages over other online encyclopedias

In their 2014 study, Marcus Messner et al. found that *Wikipedia* has become an even more comprehensive and reliable database of information and that it is gaining increasing acceptance in the academic community. *Wikipedia*'s "About" page claims that the continual editing of articles "generally results in an upward trend of quality and a growing consensus over a neutral representation of information." In fact, *Wikipedia* has instituted control measures to help weed out inaccurate or biased information and to make its content more reliable. For example, evaluating articles on the basis of accuracy, neutrality, completeness, and style, *Wikipedia* ranks its best articles as "featured" and its second-best articles as "good."[4] Although no professional editorial board oversees the development of content

Outline point VII: Wikipedia's ongoing improvements

Superscript number identifies content note

James 7

within *Wikipedia,* experienced users may become editors, and this role allows them to monitor the process by which content is added and updated. Users may also use the "Talk" page to discuss an article's content and make suggestions for improvement. With such controls in place, some *Wikipedia* articles are comparable in scope and accuracy to articles in professionally edited online resources.

Although critics argue that the collaborative nature of the wiki format does not necessarily help improve content, the study by Messner et al. seems to suggest the opposite. In examining trends of content development in *Wikipedia* nutritional health articles, Messner et al. find that *Wikipedia*'s reliability has improved over time. They explain, "this study's goal was to close a gap in the current research and analyze the online rankings of *Wikipedia* articles on nutritional topics and the types of references they are based on" (Messner et al.).

Messner et al. summarize their findings with a positive conclusion:

> [W]hile *Wikipedia* has grown and expanded over time with reference numbers increasing, the overall quality of articles has at a minimum stayed consistently reliable and has even increased for some of the articles in recent years. This shows that as *Wikipedia* continues to grow, there has been an overall consolidation, creating a better and more reliable source for information on health and nutrition.

Fig. 3 supports this conclusion, illustrating how, in recent years, *Wikipedia* articles more consistently include references to reliable sources. In offering increasingly more consistent and well-researched coverage, *Wikipedia* is becoming a more reliable source of information than some of its critics might like to admit.

Outline point VIII: Wikipedia's content

James 8

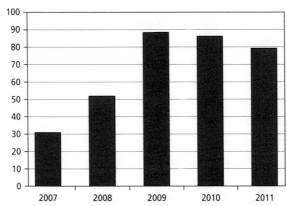

Average Number of References Over Time

Chart summarizes relevant data. Source information is typed directly below the figure.

Fig. 3. Marcus Messner, et al., "Influencing Public Opinion from Corn Syrup to Obesity: A Longitudinal Analysis of the References for Nutritional Entries on *Wikipedia*." *First Monday*, vol. 19, no. 11, 2014. *Google Scholar*, www.firstmonday.dk/ojs/index.php/fm/article/view/4823.

Some argue that the academic community's reservations about *Wikipedia* have less to do with *Wikipedia*'s shortcomings and more to do with resistance to emergent digital research technologies. Harvard Law professor Jonathan L. Zittrain suggests that academia has, in effect, fallen behind, observing that "so many projects by universities and libraries are about knowledge and information online, . . . [but academics] just couldn't get *Wikipedia* going, or anything like it" (qtd. in Foster). A recent study suggested one reason for *Wikipedia*'s bad reputation among many college instructors: "the perceived detrimental effects of the use of Web 2.0 applications not included in the university suite" (Bayliss 36). Although Jimmy Wales, cofounder of *Wikipedia*, acknowledges that

Outline point IX: Academic community's reservations about *Wikipedia*

Ellipsis indicates that the student has omitted words from the quotation

James 9

Wikipedia should serve only as a starting point for morein-depth research, he calls for the academic community to recognize *Wikipedia* as one of several new, important digital platforms that change the way people learn and disseminate knowledge. "Instead of fearing the power, complexity, and extraordinary potential of these new platforms," Wales says, "we should be asking how we can gain from their success" (qtd. in Goldstein). As many instructors and librarians argue, members of the academic community are uniquely qualified to improve *Wikipedia* by expanding stub articles and by writing new articles about their areas of expertise.

Outline point X: Instructors' and librarians' efforts to use and improve *Wikipedia*

In recent years, librarians across the country have committed their time and resources to enhancing *Wikipedia* articles that pertain to their own special collections and areas of expertise—and, in general, have become more comfortable with *Wikipedia*. In his research, Colorado Mesa University business professor Johnny Snyder found that "faculty and librarians seem to be using *Wikipedia* more than students . . ." (161). He goes on to explain, "This result was unexpected, as students in the twenty-first century are being classified as 'digital natives' and are embedded in technology and information seeking activities, while librarians and faculty are perceived to be more skeptical about this information source" (Snyder 161). June L. Power, an access service/reference librarian at the University of North Carolina at Pembroke, concedes, "Okay, I am ready for the criticism. What self-respecting librarian turns to *Wikipedia* for reference work? I admit it—this one does" (139). Power describes *Wikipedia*'s value to librarians and students alike: "While I won't complete deep research using only *Wikipedia*, being able to find quick information about a topic is something for which *Wikipedia*

James 10

is an excellent tool" (139). Snyder, Power, and others believe that
it is the responsibility of the academic community to bridge
the divide between traditional research sources and the digital
tools and technologies students are increasingly using to conduct college-level research.

Already, college instructors have found new uses and
benefits of *Wikipedia* by incorporating it into their classrooms.
In fact, *Wikipedia* has implemented an education program
as part of its outreach and collaboration initiative to help
instructors around the world build writing assignments based
on *Wikipedia*. *Wikipedia*'s "Education Program" page offers
guidelines and other resources for incorporating *Wikipedia*
into the classroom, noting that this program marks "[t]he
end of throwaway assignments and the beginning of real-
world impact for student editors." Jeff Byers, a chemistry
professor at Middlebury College (where one of the more famous
Wikipedia "bans" was instituted not long ago), has students in
his advanced organic chemistry course write *Wikipedia* entries.
Similarly, in her article "Writing for the World: *Wikipedia* as
an Introduction to Academic Writing," Christine M. Tardy, an
associate professor of writing, rhetoric, and discourse at DePaul
University, encourages instructors to use *Wikipedia* in the
classroom and outlines some sample writing assignments that
can help students "gain a real sense of audience and enjoy the
satisfaction of seeing their work published on a high-traffic
global website" (18). Instructors like Byers and Tardy emphasize the collaborative nature of *Wikipedia* writing assignments,
which offer students a unique opportunity to experience the
kinds of writing they are likely to do after college. Additionally, *Wikipedia* writing assignments encourage students to use

Outline point
XI: *Wikipedia* in
the classroom

James 11

critical thinking skills, since they require students to evaluate the articles they find on the site and to use *Wikipedia*
bibliographies as a starting place to find more suitable
research sources.

Outline point
XII: Academics'
changing view
of *Wikipedia*

With emerging research on *Wikipedia* use and with new
efforts by colleges and universities around the country to incorporate *Wikipedia* into the classroom, the debate surrounding
Wikipedia seems to be shifting. Although instructors used to
seek ways to prevent students from using *Wikipedia* as a research
source, some in the academic community are now acknowledging
the importance and usefulness of this online resource—at least
for general reference. Many former critics are acknowledging
that *Wikipedia* offers academics an opportunity to participate
in emergent digital technologies that have changed the ways
students conduct research. In other words, instructors acknowledge they need to come to terms with *Wikipedia* and develop
guidelines for its use. More and more academics are realizing that
improving *Wikipedia* actually benefits students, since the site is
often the first place students go when starting a research project. To its credit, *Wikipedia* has taken steps to improve the site's
reliability and accuracy, and *Wikipedia*'s outreach and collaboration initiative is building a comprehensive list of best practices
for continuing to enhance the quality of *Wikipedia* over time.

Conclusion
restates the
thesis and
summarizes
key points

Like any encyclopedia, *Wikipedia* is not a suitable source
for college-level research. Beyond this fact, however, it may also
not yet be as reliable as some other reference sources. Still, it is
a valuable starting point for research. As academics and others
continue to examine *Wikipedia*'s strengths and weaknesses, they
may become more open to its use and more willing to work to

James 12

improve it. In this sense, the debate over *Wikipedia* is likely to have a positive outcome. Meanwhile, however, students should exercise caution when evaluating general information they find on *Wikipedia* and refrain from citing it as a source.

James 13

Notes ← Center title

Indent ½" → 1. In one well-known example, the reputation of
journalist John Seigenthaler was tarnished when a *Wikipedia*
user edited his biography to claim inaccurately that
Seigenthaler was involved in the Kennedy assassination, a
lie that spread to other online sources.

    2. Wilson cautions that, although the majority of
Wikipedia users are educated adults, researchers should be
careful to consider the credibility of the *Wikipedia* contributors to articles they use in their research.

    3. Head and Eisenberg also note, however, that "when
students are in a deep research mode, . . . it is library
databases, such as *JSTOR* and *PsycINFO*, for instance, that
students use more frequently than *Wikipedia*."

    4. In addition, *Wikipedia*'s policies state that the
information in its articles must be verifiable and must be
based on documented, preexisting research.

James 14

Center title —————→ Works Cited

"About *Wikipedia*." *Wikipedia,* 8 Mar. 2016, 3:07, en.wikipedia.org/
wiki/Wikipedia:About.

Adler, B. Thomas, et al. "*Wikipedia* Vandalism Detection:
Combining Natural Language, Metadata, and Reputation
Features." *Lecture Notes in Computer Science*, vol. 6609,
2011, pp. 277-88. *Google Scholar,* link.springer.com/
chapter/10.1007/978-3-642-19437-5_23#page-1.

Bauerlein, Mark. *The Dumbest Generation: How the Digital Age
Stupefies Young Americans and Jeopardizes Our Future
(or, Don't Trust Anyone Under 30)*. Penguin, 2008.

Bayliss, Gemma. "Exploring the Cautionary Attitude toward
Wikipedia in Higher Education: Implications for Higher
Education Institutions." *New Review of Academic Librari-
anship*, vol. 19, no.1, 2013, pp. 36-57. *Academic Search
Complete,* doi:10.1080/13614533.2012.740439.

Burnsed, Brian. "*Wikipedia* Gradually Accepted in College
Classrooms." *USNews.com*, 20 June 2011, www.usnews.
com/education/best-colleges/articles/2011/06/20/
wikipedia-gradually-accepted-in-college-classrooms.

Foster, Andrea L. "Professor Predicts Bleak Future for the Internet."
Chronicle of Higher Education, 18 Apr. 2008, p. A29, www.
chronicle.com/article/Professor-Predicts-Bleak-Fu/31556.

Goldstein, Evan R. "The Dumbing of America?" *Chronicle of
Higher Education,* 21 Mar. 2008, p. B4. www.chronicle.
com/article/The-Dumbing-of-America-/22127.

Head, Alison J., and Michael B. Eisenberg. "How Today's College Students Use *Wikipedia* for Course-Related Research."
First Monday, vol. 15, no. 3, 2010. *Google Scholar,* papers.
ssrn.com/sol3/papers.cfm?abstract_id=2281527.

Double-space

1″

Newspaper
article
accessed
from an
online
database

Journal
article
without
pagination
accessed
from *Google
Scholar*

1″

James 15

Messner, Marcus, et al. "Influencing Public Opinion Opinion

    from Corn Syrup to Obesity: A Longitudinal Analysis of

    the References for Nutritional Entries on *Wikipedia*." *First*

    Monday, vol. 19, no. 11, 2014. *Google Scholar*, www.

    firstmonday.dk/ojs/index.php/fm/article/view/4823.

Signed letter to the editor in a monthly magazine

Power, June L. "Access the Web: Mobile Apps for Librarians."

    Journal of Access Services, vol. 10, no. 2, 2013, pp.

    138–43. *Academic Search Complete*, doi: 10.1080/

    15367967.2013.767690.

"Protection Policy." *Wikipedia*, 10 Mar. 2016, 4:23,

    en.wikipedia.org/wiki/Protection_policy.

"Reliability of *Wikipedia*." *Wikipedia*, 12 Mar. 2016, 11:02,

    en.wikipedia.org/wiki/Reliability_of_Wikipedia.

"Researching with *Wikipedia*." *Wikipedia*, 8 Mar. 2016, 3:25,

Article in an online encyclopedia

    en.wikipedia.org/wiki/Wikipedia:Researching_with_

    Wikipedia.

Schallan, Joe. "*Wikipedia* Woes." Letter. *American Libraries*,

    Apr. 2010, p. 9.

Snyder, Johnny. "*Wikipedia*: Librarians' Perspectives on Its Use

    as a Reference Source." *Reference & User Services Quar-*

Unsigned document within a website

    terly, vol. 53, no. 2, 2013, pp. 155-63. *Academic Search*

    Complete, go.galegroup.com.eduproxy.tc-library.org:8080/

    ps/i.do?id=GALE%7CA361943129.

Tardy, Christine M. "Writing for the World: *Wikipedia* as an In-

    troduction to Academic Writing." *English Teaching Forum*,

    vol. 48, no. 1, 2010, pp.12+. *ERIC*, eric.ed.gov/?q=Writing

    +for+the+World%3a+Wikipedia+%09as+an+Introduction+to

    +Academic+Writing&id=EJ914884.

"Wiki." *Encyclopaedia Britannica*, 2014, www. britannica.com/

    topic/wiki. Accessed 5 Mar. 2016.

James 16

"*Wikipedia* Education Program." *Wikipedia*, 10 Mar. 2016, 5:43,
    wikimediafoundation.org/wiki/Wikipedia_Education_
    Program.

Wilson, Jodi L. "Proceed with Extreme Caution: Citation to *Wiki-
    pedia* in Light of Contributor Demographics and Content
    Policies." *Vanderbilt Journal of Entertainment & Technology
    Law,* vol. 16, no. 4, 2014, pp. 857-908. *Academic Search
    Complete,* web.a.ebscohost.com.ezproxy.cul.columbia.edu/
    ehost/detail/detail?vid=4&sid=14afe0c2-3351-4754-93dc-
    2371d2724d5d.

Directory of APA In-Text Citations

Directory of APA Reference List Entries

PRINT SOURCES: *Entries for Articles*

Articles in Scholarly Journals

Articles in Magazines and Newspapers

PRINT SOURCES: *Entries for Books*

Authors

Editions, Multivolume Works, and Forewords

Parts of Books

Government and Technical Reports

ENTRIES FOR MISCELLANEOUS PRINT SOURCES

Letters

ENTRIES FOR OTHER SOURCES

Television Broadcasts, Films, Audio Recordings, Interviews, and Software

ELECTRONIC SOURCES: *Entries for Sources from Internet Sites*

Internet-Specific Sources

Abstracts and Newspaper Articles

CHAPTER 18

APA Documentation Style

18a Using APA Style

APA style* is used extensively in the social sciences. APA documentation has three parts: *parenthetical references in the body of the paper*, a *reference list*, and optional *content footnotes*.

1 Parenthetical References

APA documentation uses short parenthetical references in the body of the essay keyed to an alphabetical list of references at the end of the essay. A typical parenthetical reference consists of the author's last name (followed by a comma) and the year of publication.

> Many people exhibit symptoms of depression after the death of a pet (Russo, 2016).

If the author's name appears in an introductory phrase, include the year of publication there as well.

> According to Russo (2016), many people exhibit symptoms of depression after the death of a pet.

When quoting directly, include the page number, preceded by **p.** in parentheses after the quotation.

> According to Weston (2015), children from one-parent homes read at "a significantly lower level than those from two-parent homes" (p. 58).

Note: A long quotation (forty words or more) is not set in quotation marks. It is set as a block, and the entire quotation is double-spaced and indented one-half inch from the left margin. Parenthetical documentation is placed one space after the final punctuation.

---

*APA documentation format follows the guidelines set in the *Publication Manual of the American Psychological Association*, 6th ed. Washington, DC: APA, 2010.

Sample APA In-Text Citations

1. A Work by a Single Author

Many college students suffer from sleep deprivation (Anton, 2009).

2. A Work by Two Authors

There is growing concern over the use of psychological testing in elementary schools (Albright & Glennon, 2013).

3. A Work by Three to Five Authors

If a work has more than two but fewer than six authors, mention all names in the first reference; in subsequent references in the same paragraph, cite only the first author followed by **et al.** ("and others"). When the reference appears in later paragraphs, include the year.

First Reference

(Sparks, Wilson, & Hewitt, 2015)

Subsequent References in the Same Paragraph

(Sparks et al.)

References in Later Paragraphs

(Sparks et al., 2015)

4. A Work by Six or More Authors

When a work has six or more authors, cite the name of the first author followed by **et al.** and the year in all references.

(Miller et al., 2016)

Close-Up   CITING WORKS BY MULTIPLE AUTHORS

When referring to multiple authors in the text of your essay, join the last two names with **and**.

According to Rosen, Wolfe, and Ziff (2015). . . .

Parenthetical references (as well as reference list entries) require an ampersand (**&**).

(Rosen, Wolfe, & Ziff, 2015)

5. Works by Authors with the Same Last Name

If your reference list includes works by two or more authors with the same last name, use each author's initials in all in-text citations.

> Both F. Bor (2013) and S. D. Bor (2012) concluded that no further study was needed.

6. A Work by a Corporate Author

If the name of a corporate author is long, abbreviate it after the first citation.

First Reference

> (National Institute of Mental Health [NIMH], 2015)

Subsequent Reference

> (NIMH, 2015)

7. A Work with No Listed Author

If a work has no listed author, cite the first two or three words of the title (followed by a comma) and the year. Use quotation marks around titles of periodical articles and chapters of books; use italics for titles of books, periodicals, brochures, reports, and the like.

> ("New Immigration," 2014)

8. A Personal Communication

Cite letters, memos, telephone conversations, personal interviews, emails, messages from electronic bulletin boards, and so on only in the text of your essay—*not* in the reference list.

> (R. Takaki, personal communication, October 17, 2015)

9. An Indirect Source

> Cogan and Howe offer very different interpretations of the problem (cited in Swenson, 2015).

10. A Specific Part of a Source

Use abbreviations for the words *page* (**p.**), and *pages* (**pp.**), but spell out *chapter* and *section*.

> These theories have an interesting history (Lee, 2013, chapter 2).

11. An Electronic Source

For an electronic source that does not show page numbers, use the paragraph number preceded by the abbreviation **para.**

Conversation at the dinner table is an example of a family ritual (Kulp,

2015, para. 3).

In the case of an electronic source that has neither page nor paragraph numbers, cite both the heading in the source and the number of the paragraph following the heading in which the material is located.

Healthy eating is a never-ending series of free choices (Shapiro, 2016,

Introduction section, para. 2).

If the source has no headings, you may not be able to specify an exact location.

12. Two or More Works within the Same Parenthetical Reference

List works by different authors in alphabetical order, separated by semicolons.

This theory is supported by several studies (Barson & Roth, 2005; Rose,

2010; Tedesco, 2014).

List two or more works by the same author or authors in order of date of publication (separated by commas), with the earliest date first.

This theory is supported by several studies (Rhodes & Dollek, 2011, 2013, 2015).

For two or more works by the same author published in the same year, designate the work whose title comes first alphabetically *a*, the one whose title comes next *b*, and so on; repeat the year in each citation.

This theory is supported by several studies (Shapiro, 2014a, 2014b).

13. A Table

If you use a table from a source, give credit to the author in a note at the bottom of the table. Do not include this information in the reference list.

Note. From "Predictors of Employment and Earnings Among JOBS Participants,"

by P. A. Neenan and D. K. Orthner, 1996, *Social Work Research, 20*(4), p. 233.

2 **Reference List**

The **reference list** gives the publication information for all the sources you cite. It should appear at the end of your essay on a new numbered page titled **References**. Entries in the reference list should be arranged alphabetically. Double-space within and between reference list entries. The first line of each entry should start at the left margin, with the second and subsequent lines indented one-half inch. (**See 12b** for full manuscript guidelines.)

APA PRINT SOURCES Entries for Articles

Article citations include the author's name (last name first); the date of publication (in parentheses); the title of the article; the title of the periodical (italicized); the volume number (italicized); the issue number, if any (in parentheses); and the inclusive page numbers (including all digits). Figure 18.1 below shows where you can find this information.

Capitalize the first word of the article's title and subtitle as well as any proper nouns. Do not underline or italicize the title of the article or enclose it in quotation marks. Give the periodical title in full, and capitalize all words except articles, prepositions, and conjunctions of fewer than four letters. Use **p.** or **pp.** when referring to page numbers in newspapers, but omit this abbreviation when referring to page numbers in journals and popular magazines.

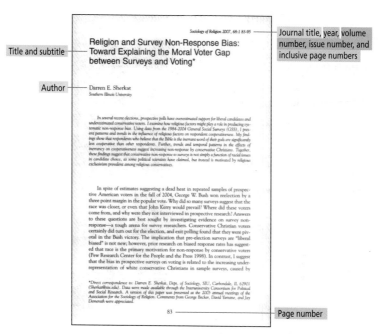

FIGURE 18.1 First page of an article showing the location of the information needed for documentation. © Association for the Sociology of Religion.

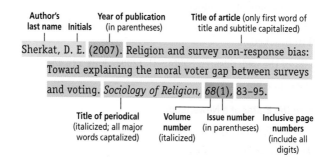

Articles in Scholarly Journals

1. **An Article in a Scholarly Journal with Continuous Pagination throughout an Annual Volume**

   Case, C. A., Hensley, R., & Anderson, A. (2014). Reflecting on heterosexual and male privilege: Interventions to raise awareness. *Journal of Social Issues, 70,* 722–740.

2. **An Article in a Scholarly Journal with Separate Pagination in Each Issue**

   Zell, E., Krizan, Z., & Teeter, S. R. (2015). Evaluating gender similarities and differences using metasynthesis. *American Psychologist, 70*(1), 10–20.

 Note: Do not leave a space between the volume and issue numbers.

3. **A Book Review in a Scholarly Journal (Unsigned)**

   A review with no author should be listed by title, followed by a description of the reviewed work in brackets.

   Coming of age and joining the cult of thinness [Review of the book *The cult of thinness,* by Sharlene Nagy Hesse-Biber]. (2008, June). *Psychology of Women Quarterly, 32*(2), 221–222.

Articles in Magazines and Newspapers

4. **A Magazine Article**

   Drevitch, G. (2014, May–June). Pop psychology. *Psychology Today, 47,* 40.

5. **A Newspaper Article**

   If an article appears on nonconsecutive pages, give all page numbers, separated by commas (for example, **A1, A14**). If the article appears on consecutive pages, indicate the full range of pages (for example, **A7–A9**).

   Jargon, J. (2010, December 27). On McDonald's menu: Variety, caution. *Wall Street Journal,* pp. A1, A14.

6. **A Newspaper Editorial (Unsigned)**

   An editorial with no author should be listed by title, followed by the label **Editorial** in brackets.

   The plight of the underinsured [Editorial]. (2008, June 12). *The New York Times,* p. A30.

7. **A Letter to the Editor of a Newspaper**

   Mania, M. (2015, February 19). Superfluous selfie sticks [Letter to the editor]. *The New York Times,* p. A24.

APA PRINT SOURCES Entries for Books

Book citations include the author's name (last name first); the year of publication (in parentheses); the book title (italicized); and publication information. Figures 18.2 below and 18.3 on page 252 show where you can find this information.

Capitalize only the first word of the title and subtitle and any proper nouns. Include any additional necessary information—edition, report number, or volume number, for example—in parentheses after the title. In the publication information, write out in full the names of associations, corporations, and university presses. Include the words **Book** and **Press**, but do not include terms such as **Publishers**, **Co.**, or **Inc.**

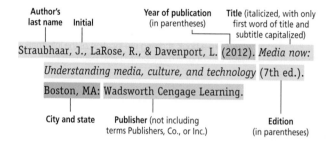

Author's last name | Initial — Year of publication (in parentheses) — Title (italicized, with only first word of title and subtitle capitalized)

Straubhaar, J., LaRose, R., & Davenport, L. (2012). *Media now: Understanding media, culture, and technology* (7th ed.). Boston, MA: Wadsworth Cengage Learning.

City and state — Publisher (not including terms Publishers, Co., or Inc.) — Edition (in parentheses)

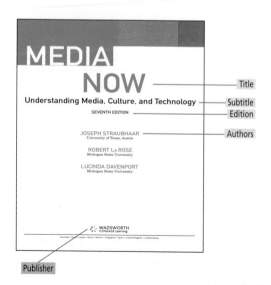

MEDIA
NOW ————— Title
Understanding Media, Culture, and Technology ——— Subtitle
SEVENTH EDITION ——— Edition

JOSEPH STRAUBHAAR
University of Texas, Austin ——— Authors

ROBERT LA ROSE
Michigan State University

LUCINDA DAVENPORT
Michigan State University

WADSWORTH
CENGAGE Learning

Publisher

FIGURE 18.2 Title page from a book showing the location of the information needed for documentation. © Cengage Learning, 2012; reprinted with permission.

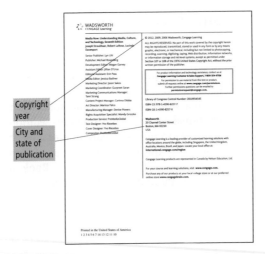

Copyright
year

City and
state of
publication

FIGURE 18.3 Copyright page from a book showing the location of the information needed for documentation. © Cengage Learning, 2012; reprinted with permission.

Authors

8. A Book with One Author

> Oatley, K. (2011). *Such stuff as dreams: The psychology of fiction*. Hoboken,
>
> NJ: Wiley.

9. A Book with More Than One Author

List up to seven authors by last name and initials, using an ampersand (&) to connect the last two names. For more than seven authors, insert an ellipsis (three spaced periods) and add the last author's name.

> Wolfinger, D., Knable, P., Richards, H. L., & Silberger, R. (2007). *The chronically*
>
> *unemployed*. New York, NY: Berman Press.

10. A Book with No Listed Author or Editor

> *Teaching in a wired classroom*. (2012). Philadelphia, PA: Drexel Press.

11. A Book with a Corporate Author

When the author and the publisher are the same, include the word **Author** at the end of the citation instead of repeating the publisher's name.

> League of Women Voters of the United States. (2008). *Local league handbook*.
>
> Washington, DC: Author.

12. An Edited Book

Wienroth, M., & Rodrigues, E. (Eds.). (2015). *Knowing new biotechnologies: Social aspects of technological convergence*. New York, NY: Routledge.

Editions, Multivolume Works, and Forewords

13. A Work in Several Volumes

O'Connor, E. E., & Garofalo, L. (2010). *Documenting Latin America*: *Gender, race, and nation*. (Vols. 1–2). New York, NY: Pearson.

14. The Foreword, Preface, or Afterword of a Book

Taylor, T. (1979). Preface. In B. B. Ferencz, *Less than slaves* (pp. ii–ix). Cambridge, MA: Harvard University Press.

Parts of Books

15. A Selection from an Anthology

Give inclusive page numbers preceded by **pp.** (in parentheses) after the title of the anthology. The title of the selection is not enclosed in quotation marks.

Lorde, A. (1984). Age, race, and class. In P. S. Rothenberg (Ed.), *Racism and sexism: An integrated study* (pp. 352–360). New York, NY: St. Martin's Press.

Note: If you cite two or more selections from the same anthology, give the full citation for the anthology in each entry.

16. An Article in a Reference Book

Edwards, P. (Ed.). (2006). Determinism. In *The encyclopedia of philosophy* (Vol. 2, pp. 359–373). New York, NY: Macmillan.

Government and Technical Reports

17. A Government Report

U.S. Department of Health and Human Services, National Institutes of Health, National Institute of Mental Health. (2007). *Motion pictures and violence: A summary report of research* (DHHS Publication No. ADM 91-22187). Washington, DC: Government Printing Office.

18. A Technical Report

Attali, Y., & Powers, D. (2008). *Effect of immediate feedback and revision on psychometric properties of open-ended GRE® subject test items* (ETS GRE Board Research Report No. 04-05). Princeton, NJ: Educational Testing Service.

APA ENTRIES FOR MISCELLANEOUS PRINT SOURCES

Letters

19. A Personal Letter

References to unpublished personal letters, like references to all other personal communications, should be included only in the text of the essay, not in the reference list.

20. A Published Letter

Joyce, J. (1931). Letter to Louis Gillet. In Richard Ellmann, *James Joyce* (p. 631). New York, NY: Oxford University Press.

APA ENTRIES FOR OTHER SOURCES

Television Broadcasts, Films, Audio Recordings, Interviews, and Software

21. A Television Broadcast

Murphy, J. (Executive Producer). (2006, March 4). *The CBS evening news* [Television broadcast]. New York, NY: Columbia Broadcasting Service.

22. A Television Series Episode

Bedard, B. (Writer). (2014). Best new girl [Television series episode]. In J. Solloway (Executive Producer), *Transparent*. Los Angeles, CA: Amazon Studios.

23. A Film

Colson, C., Winfrey, O., Gardner, D., and Kleiner, J. (Producers), & DuVernay, A. (Director). (2014). *Selma* [Motion picture]. United States: Paramount Pictures.

24. An Audio Recording

Beck. (2014). Don't let it go. On *Morning phase* [MP3]. Los Angeles, CA: Capitol Records.

Knowles, B., & Asher, J. (2013). Heaven. On *Beyoncé* [CD]. New York, NY: Columbia Records.

25. A Recorded Interview

Bartel, S. S. (1978, November 5). Interview by L. Clark [Tape recording]. Billy Graham Center, Wheaton College. BGC Archives, Wheaton, IL.

26. A Transcription of a Recorded Interview

Berry, D. W. (1986, February 14). *Interview with Donald Wesley Berry—Collection 325*. Billy Graham Center, Wheaton College. BGC Archives, Wheaton, IL.

27. Software or an App

Sharp, S. (2009). Career Selection Tests (Version 7.0) [Software]. Chico, CA: Avocation Software.

Handup. (2014). *Handup vote* (Version 2.0.1) [Mobile application software]. Retrieved from http://itunes.apple.com

APA ELECTRONIC SOURCES Entries for Sources from Internet Sites

APA guidelines for documenting electronic sources focus on web sources, which often do not include all the bibliographic information that print sources do. For example, web sources may not include page numbers or a place of publication. At a minimum, a web citation should have a title, a date (the date of publication, update, or retrieval), and a Digital Object Identifier (DOI) (when available) or an electronic address (URL). If possible, also include the author(s) of a source. Figure 18.4 shows where you can find this information.

When you need to divide a URL at the end of a line, break it after a double slash or before most other punctuation (do not add a hyphen). Do not add a period at the end of the URL.

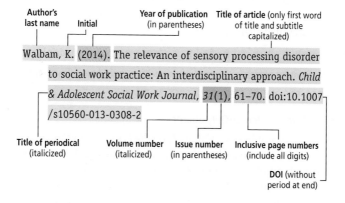

Journal title	
Year	
Volume number	
Inclusive page numbers	
DOI	
Title and subtitle	
Author	

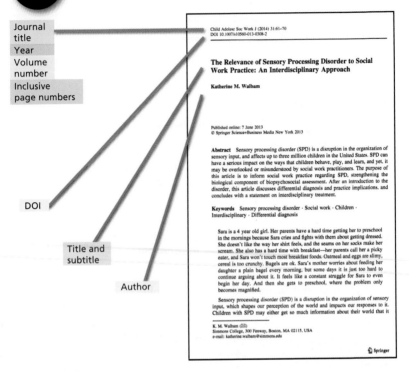

FIGURE 18.4 Part of an online article showing the location of the information needed for documentation.

Internet-Specific Sources

28. An Online Article Also Published in a Print Source

If the article has a DOI, you do not need to include the retrieval date or the URL. Always include the volume number (italicized) and the issue number (in parentheses, if available).

> Rutledge, P. C., Park, A., & Sher, K. J. (2008). 21st birthday drinking:
>
> Extremely extreme. *Journal of Consulting and Clinical Psychology, 76*(3),
>
> 511–516. doi:10.1037/0022-006X.76.3.511

29. An Article in an Internet-Only Journal

If the article does not have a DOI, include the URL. Always include the URL (when available) for the archived version of the article. If you accessed the article through an online database, include the URL for the home page of the journal. (If a single URL links to multiple articles, include the URL for the journal's home page.) No retrieval date is needed for content that is not likely to be changed or updated—for example, a journal article or a book.

Hill, S. A., & Laugharne, R. (2006). Patient choice survey in general adult
psychiatry. *Psychiatry On-Line*. Retrieved from http://www.priory.co.uk/
psych.htm

30. A Document from a University Website

Beck, S. E. (2008, April 3). *The good, the bad & the ugly: Or, why it's a good
idea to evaluate web sources.* Retrieved July 7, 2014, from New Mexico
State University Library website: http://lib.nmsu.edu/instruction
/evalcrit.html

31. An Online Document (No Author Identified, No Date)

A document with no author or date should be listed by title, followed by the
abbreviation **n.d.** (for "no date"), the retrieval date, and the URL.

The stratocaster appreciation page. (n.d.). Retrieved July 27, 2015, from
http://members.tripod.com/~AFH

32. An Email

As with all other personal communications, citations for email should be included only in the text of your essay, not in the reference list.

33. A Blog Article or Entry

List the author's name—or, if that is not available, the author's screen name.
In brackets after the title, provide information that will help readers access this
particular post. APA style recommends the term Web log post, but ask your
instructor if Blog post is an acceptable alternative.

Sullivan, A. (2015, February 15). The war [Web log post]. On *The daily
dish*. Retrieved from http://dish.andrewsullivan.com/2015/02/06
/the-war-4/

34. A Comment on a Blog or an Online Forum

Jamie. (2010, June 26). Re: Trying to lose 50 million pounds [Web log
comment]. Retrieved from http://blogs.wsj.com/numbersguy

Silva, T. (2007, March 9). Severe stress can damage a child's brain [Online
forum comment]. Retrieved from http://groups.google.com/group
/sci.psychology.psychotherapy.moderated

35. An Online Video (*YouTube*)

Learning Without Borders. (2012, February 1). The purpose of
education [Video file]. Retrieved from https://www.youtube.com
/watch?v=DdNAUJWJN08

36. A Podcast

> Koenig, S., & Snyder, J. (Producers). (2014). The alibi [Podcast episode]. In
> *Serial*. Chicago, IL: Chicago Public Media.

37. A Social Networking Post (*Facebook* post, tweet, etc.)

Provide up to the first forty words of a *Facebook, Twitter, Instagram*, or similar post. For a tweet, begin with the author's listed name, followed by the author's *Twitter* name in brackets (as in the first example below).

> Muna, D. [DemitriMuna]. (2014, February 21). Opposed to GM foods? Stop
> eating grapefruit; they are genetically modified. There was no such
> thing as a grapefruit before the 18th century [Tweet]. Retrieved from
> https://twitter.com/demitrimuna/status/569349630887985 152
> Psychology Today. (2015, February 18). Do people just not get you? This may
> be why: https://www.psychologytoday.com/articles/200909/are-you-
> misunderstood? [Facebook status update]. Retrieved from https://www
> .facebook.com/psychologytoday

38. A Searchable Database

Include the database name only if the material you are citing is obscure, out of print, or otherwise difficult to locate. No retrieval date is needed.

> Murphy, M. E. (1940, December 15). When war comes. *Vital Speeches of the
> Day, 7*(5), 139–144. Retrieved from http://www.vsotd.com

Abstracts and Newspaper Articles

39. An Abstract

> Qiong, L. (2008, July). After the quake: Psychological treatment following
> the disaster. *China Today, 57*(7), 18–21. Abstract retrieved from http://
> www.chinatoday.com.cn/ctenglish/index.htm

40. An Article in a Daily Newspaper

> Lowrey, A. (2014, February 20). Study finds greater income inequality in
> nation's thriving cities. *The New York Times*. Retrieved from http://www
> .nytimes.com

EXERCISE 18.1

Each of these notes identifies a source used in an essay about mental illness and homelessness. Determine which information is required to cite each source. Then, following the guidelines and proper format for APA documentation, create a parenthetical reference for each source, and then create a reference list, arranging sources in the proper order. Be sure to format source information correctly, adding quotation marks and italics as needed.

1. An article called A Primary Care—Public Health Partnership Addressing Homelessness, Serious Mental Illness, and Health Disparities. The authors are listed as Lara Carson Weinstein, Marianna D. LaNoue, James D. Plumb, Hannah King, Brianna Stein, and Sam Tsemberis. The article appears on pages 279–287 of a scholarly journal called Journal of the American Board of Family Medicine. The journal is specifically described as Volume 26, Issue 3, and it was published in May of 2013. You accessed the journal through PubMed, an online database. The DOI for the article is listed as doi:10.3122/jabfm.2013.03.120239.

2. Pages 60–64 of a book called Homelessness, Housing, and Mental Illness. The author is Russell K. Schutt. The book was published by Harvard University Press in Boston, Massachusetts, in March of 2011. You referred to the print version of the book.

3. The abstract of an article called Mental Illness in Homeless Families. You did not refer to the whole article. The article's author is Roxanne Amerson. It was published in a scholarly journal called The Journal for Nurse Practitioners in February 2008, in Volume 4, Issue 2, on pages 109–113. The DOI of the article is listed as doi:10.1016/j.nurpra.2008.01.001. You accessed the abstract from this website: <http://www.npjournal.org>.

4. A podcast episode titled Dr. Robert L. Okin on Silent Voices: People with Mental Disorders on the Street. The episode is part of a podcast series called The Diane Rehm Show produced by WAMU 88.5, American University Radio. The host is Diane Rehm. When you accessed this podcast, it was streaming at this URL: <http://thedianerehmshow.org/shows/2014-11-24/ dr_robert_l_okin_silent_voices_people_with_mental_disorders_on_the_street>. It was posted and last updated on November 24, 2014. You listened to it today.

5. A panel at a conference called National Healthcare for the Homeless Conference and Policy Symposium Council, given on March 14, 2013, in Washington, D.C., at the Omni Shoreham Hotel. The panel event was titled Preparing for Health Reform: Educate, Engage, and Excel. The presenters were Barbara DiPietro and Kevin Lindamood.

❸ Content Footnotes

APA format permits content notes, indicated by **superscripts** in the text. The notes are listed on a separate numbered page, titled **Footnotes**, after the reference list and before any appendices. Double-space all notes, indenting the first line of each note one-half inch and beginning subsequent lines flush left. Number the notes with superscripts that correspond to the numbers in your text.

18b APA-Style Manuscript Guidelines

Social science essays label sections with headings. Sections may include an introduction (untitled), followed by headings such as **Background, Method, Results**, and **Conclusion**. Each section of a social science essay is a complete unit with a beginning and an end so that it can be read separately and still make sense out of context. The body of the essay may include charts, graphs, maps, photographs, flowcharts, or tables.

CHECKLIST

Typing Your Essay

When you type your essay, use the student essay in **18c** as your model.

❏ Leave one-inch margins at the top and bottom and on both sides. Double-space your essay throughout.

❏ Indent the first line of every paragraph and the first line of every content footnote one-half inch from the left-hand margin.

❏ Set off a **long quotation** (more than forty words) in a block format by indenting the entire quotation one-half inch from the left-hand margin. Do not indent the first line further.

❏ Number all pages consecutively. Each page should include a **page header** (or **running head**) typed one-half inch from the top of the page. Type the page header flush left and the page number flush right.

See 23b

❏ Center major headings, and type them with uppercase and lowercase letters. Place minor headings flush left, typed with uppercase and lowercase letters. Use boldface for both major and minor headings.

See 23c

❏ Format items in a series as a numbered list.

❏ Arrange the pages of the essay in the following order:

❏ **Title page** (page 1) with a running head (in all uppercase letters), page number, title, your name, and the name of your school. (Your instructor may require additional information.)

- ❑ **Abstract and keywords** (page 2)
- ❑ **Text of essay** (beginning on page 3)
- ❑ **Reference list** (new page)
- ❑ **Content footnotes** (new page)
- ❑ **Appendices** (start each appendix on a new page)
- ❑ Citations should follow <u>APA documentation style</u>.

See
18a

CHECKLIST
Using Visuals

APA style distinguishes between two types of visuals: **tables** and **figures** (charts, graphs, photographs, and diagrams). In manuscripts not intended for publication, tables and figures are included in the text. A short table or figure should appear on the page where it is discussed; a long table or figure should be placed on a separate page just after the page where it is discussed.

Tables

Number all **tables** consecutively. Each table should have a *label* and a *title*.

- ❑ The **label** consists of the word **Table** (not in italics), along with an arabic numeral, typed flush left above the table.
- ❑ Double-space and type a brief explanatory **title** for each table (in italics) flush left below the label. Capitalize the first letters of principal words of the title.

    Table 7

    Frequency of Negative Responses of Dorm Students to Questions Concerning Alcohol Consumption

Figures

Number all **figures** consecutively. Each figure should have a *label* and a *caption*.

- ❑ The **label** consists of the word *Figure* (typed flush left below the figure) followed by the figure number (both in italics).
- ❑ The **caption** explains the figure and serves as a title. Double-space the caption, but do not italicize it. Capitalize only the first word and any proper nouns, and end the caption with a period. The caption follows the label (on the same line).

    Figure 1. Duration of responses measured in seconds.

Note: If you use a table or figure from an outside source, include full source information in a note at the bottom of the table or figure. This information does not appear in your reference list.

CHECKLIST

Preparing the APA Reference List

When typing your reference list, follow these guidelines:

❏ Begin the reference list on a new page after the last page of text, numbered as the next page of the essay.

❏ Center the title **References** at the top of the page.

❏ List the items in the reference list alphabetically (with author's last name first).

❏ Type the first line of each entry at the left margin. Indent subsequent lines one-half inch.

❏ Separate the major divisions of each entry with a period and one space.

❏ Double-space the reference list within and between entries.

Close-Up ARRANGING ENTRIES IN THE APA REFERENCE LIST

● Single-author entries precede multiple-author entries that begin with the same name.

Field, S. (2015).

Field, S., & Levitt, M. P. (2012).

● Entries by the same author or authors are arranged according to date of publication, starting with the earliest date.

Ruthenberg, H., & Rubin, R. (2013).

Ruthenberg, H., & Rubin, R. (2015).

● Entries with the same author or authors and date of publication are arranged alphabetically according to title. Lowercase letters (a, b, c, and so on) that indicate the order of publication are placed within parentheses.

Wolk, E. M. (2016a). Analysis . . .

Wolk, E. M. (2016b). Hormonal . . .

18c Model APA-Style Research Paper

The following student essay, "Sleep Deprivation in College Students," uses APA documentation style. It includes a title page, an abstract, a reference list, a table, and a bar graph. The web citations in this student essay do not have DOIs, so URLs have been provided instead.

↑ ½"

Sleep Deprivation in College Students   Title

Andrew J. Neale   Your name

University of Texas   School

Psychology 215, Section 4   Course title

Dr. Reiss   Instructor's
        name

March 12, 2015   Date

Page header on every page

1"

Abstract

Center heading

A survey was conducted of 50 first-year college students in an introductory biology class. The survey consisted of five questions regarding the causes and results of sleep deprivation and specifically addressed the students' study methods and the grades they received on the fall midterm. The study's hypothesis was that although students believe that forgoing sleep to study will yield better grades, sleep deprivation may actually cause a decrease in performance. The study concluded that while only 43% of the students who received either an A or a B on the fall midterm deprived themselves of sleep in order to cram for the test, 90% of those who received a C or a D were sleep deprived.

Keywords: sleep disorders, sleep deprivation, grade performance, grades and sleep, forgoing sleep

Abstract typed as a single paragraph in block format (not indented)

An optional list of keywords helps readers find your work in databases. Check with your instructor to see if this list is required.

SLEEP DEPRIVATION   3

Full title (centered)
Sleep Deprivation in College Students

Indent ½" → For many college students, sleep is a luxury they feel
they cannot afford. Bombarded with tests and assignments
and limited by a 24-hour day, students often attempt to make
up time by doing without sleep. Unfortunately, students may
actually hurt their academic performance by failing to get
enough sleep. According to several psychological and medical
studies, sleep deprivation can lead to memory loss and health
problems, both of which can harm a student's academic
performance.

Background

Sleep is often overlooked as an essential part of a
healthy lifestyle. Each day, millions of Americans wake up
without having gotten enough sleep. This fact indicates that
for many people, sleep is viewed as a luxury rather than a
necessity. As National Sleep Foundation Executive Director
Richard L. Gelula observes, "Some of the problems we face
as a society—from road rage to obesity—may be linked to
lack of sleep or poor sleep" (National Sleep Foundation, 2002,
para. 3). In fact, according to the National Sleep Foundation, sleep deprivation "jolts the immune system into action,
reflecting the same type of immediate response shown during
exposure to stress . . ." (2012, para. 1).

Sleep deprivation is particularly common among college
students, many of whom have busy lives and are required to
absorb a great deal of material before their exams. It is common
for college students to take a quick nap between classes or
fall asleep while studying in the library because they are sleep
deprived. Approximately 44% of young adults experience daytime
sleepiness at least a few days a month (National Sleep Foundation,

2002, para. 6). In particular, many students are sleep deprived on the day of an exam because they stayed up all night studying. These students believe that if they read and review immediately before taking a test—even though this usually means losing sleep—they will remember more information and thus get better grades. However, this is not the case.

A study conducted by professors Mary Carskadon at Brown University in Providence, Rhode Island, and Amy Wolfson at the College of the Holy Cross in Worcester, Massachusetts, showed that high school students who got adequate sleep were more likely to do well in their classes (Carpenter, 2001). According to this study, students who went to bed early on both week-nights and weekends earned mainly A's and B's. The students who received D's and F's averaged about 35 minutes less sleep per day than the high achievers (cited in Carpenter, 2001). The results of this study suggest that sleep is associated with high academic achievement.

Once students reach college, however, many believe that sleep is a luxury they can do without. For example, students believe that if they use the time they would normally sleep to study, they will do better on exams. A survey of 144 under-graduate students in introductory psychology classes disproved this assumption. According to this study, "long sleepers," those individuals who slept 9 or more hours out of a 24-hour day, had significantly higher grade point averages (GPAs) than "short sleepers," individuals who slept less than 7 hours out of a 24-hour day. Therefore, contrary to the belief of many college students, more sleep is often associated with a high GPA (Kelly, Kelly, & Clanton, 2001).

Student uses past tense when discussing other researchers' studies

Cited in indicates an indirect source

Many students believe that sleep deprivation is not the cause of their poor performance, but rather that a host of other factors is to blame. A study in the *Journal of American College Health* tested the effect that several factors have on a student's performance in school, as measured by students' GPAs. Some of the factors considered were exercise, sleep, nutritional habits, social support, time management techniques, stress management techniques, and spiritual health (Trockel, Barnes, & Egget, 2000). The most significant correlation discovered in the study was between GPA and the sleep habits of students. Sleep deprivation had a more negative impact on GPAs than any other factor (Trockel et al., 2000).

Despite these findings, many students continue to believe that they will be able to remember more material if they do not sleep before an exam. They fear that sleeping will interfere with their ability to retain information. Pilcher and Walters (1997), however, showed that sleep deprivation actually impaired learning skills. In this study, one group of students was sleep deprived, while the other got 8 hours of sleep before the exam. The students in each group estimated how well they had performed on the exam. The students who were sleep deprived believed their performance on the test was better than did those who were not sleep deprived, but actually the performance of the sleep-deprived students was significantly worse than that of those who got 8 hours of sleep prior to the test (Pilcher & Walters, 1997, cited in Bubolz, Brown, & Soper, 2001). This study supports the hypothesis that sleep deprivation harms cognitive performance.

A survey of students in an introductory biology class at the University of Texas, which demonstrated the effects of

First reference includes all three authors; *et al.* replaces second and third authors in subsequent reference in same paragraph

Student uses past tense when discussing his own research study

SLEEP DEPRIVATION   6

sleep deprivation on academic performance, also supported the

hypothesis that despite students' beliefs, forgoing sleep does

not lead to better test scores.

Method

To determine the causes and results of sleep deprivation,

a study of the relationship between sleep and test perfor-

mance was conducted. Fifty first-year college students in an

introductory biology class were surveyed, and their perfor-

mance on the fall midterm was analyzed.

Each student was asked to complete a survey consisting

of the following five questions about their sleep patterns and

their performance on the fall midterm:

1. Do you regularly deprive yourself of sleep when
   studying for an exam?

2. Did you deprive yourself of sleep when studying for
   the fall midterm?

3. What was your grade on the exam?

4. Do you feel your performance was helped or harmed
   by the amount of sleep you had?

5. Will you deprive yourself of sleep when you study for
   the final exam?

To maintain confidentiality, the students were asked not

to put their names on the survey. Also, to determine whether

the students answered question 3 truthfully, the group grade

distribution from the surveys was compared to the number of

A's, B's, C's, and D's shown in the instructor's record of the test

results. The two frequency distributions were identical.

Results

Analysis of the survey data indicated a significant

difference between the grades of students who were sleep

Numbered
list is in-
dented ½"
and set in
block
format

deprived and the grades of those who were not. The results of the survey are presented in Table 1.

> *Table 1 introduced*

The grades in the class were curved so that out of 50 students, 10 received A's, 20 received B's, 10 received C's, and 10 received D's. For the purposes of this survey, an A or B on the exam indicates that the student performed well. A grade of C or D on the exam is considered a poor grade.

Table 1

Results of Survey of Students in University of Texas Introduction to Biology Class Examining the Relationship between Sleep Deprivation and Academic Performance

> *Table placed on page where it is discussed*

Grade totals	Sleep deprived	Not sleep deprived	Usually sleep deprived	Improved	Harmed	Continue sleep deprivation?
A = 10	4	6	1	4	0	4
B = 20	9	11	8	8	1	8
C = 10	10	0	6	5	4	7
D = 10	8	2	2	1	3	2
Total	31	19	17	18	8	21

> *Table created by student; no documentation necessary*

Of the 50 students in the class, 31 (or 62%) said they deprived themselves of sleep when studying for the fall midterm. Of these students, 17 (or 34% of the class) reported that they regularly deprive themselves of sleep before an exam.

> *Statistical findings in table discussed*

Of the 31 students who said they deprived themselves of sleep when studying for the fall midterm, only 4 earned A's, and the majority of the A's in the class were received by those students who were not sleep deprived. Even more significant was the fact that of the 4 students who were sleep deprived

SLEEP DEPRIVATION   1"   10

Center
heading ————————————→   References

Indent ½" ——————→   Bubolz, W., Brown, F., & Soper, B. (2001). Sleep habits
          ——————————→
Double-space   and patterns of college students: A preliminary
          ——————————→
          | study. *Journal of American College Health, 50,*
Entries listed
in alphabetical   131–135.
order
          | Carpenter, S. (2001). Sleep deprivation may be
URL is
provided for   undermining teen health. *Monitor on Psychology,*
web citation
that does not   *32*(9). Retrieved from http://www.apa.org
have a DOI
                            /monitor/oct01/sleepteen.html

          Kelly, W. E., Kelly, K. E., & Clanton, R. C. (2001). The

                            relationship between sleep length and grade-point

                            average among college students. *College Student*

                            Journal, 35(1), 84–90.

          National Sleep Foundation. (2002, April 2). *Epidemic*

                            of daytime sleepiness linked to increased feelings

                            of anger, stress and pessimism. Retrieved from

                            http://www.sleepfoundation.org

          National Sleep Foundation. (2012, July 1). *Sleep*

                            deprivation effect on the immune system mirrors

                            physical stress. Retrieved from http://www

                            .sleepfoundation.org

          Trockel, M., Barnes, M., & Egget, D. (2000). Health-

                            related variables and academic performance among

                            first-year college students: Implications for sleep

                            and other behaviors. *Journal of American College*

                            Health, 49, 125–131.

Directory of Chicago-Style Endnotes and Bibliography Entries

PRINT SOURCES: *Entries for Articles*

Articles in Scholarly Journals

1. An article in a scholarly journal with continuous pagination throughout an annual volume (p. 277)
2. An article in a scholarly journal with separate pagination in each issue (p. 277)

Articles in Magazines and Newspapers

3. An article in a weekly magazine (signed/unsigned) (p. 277)
4. An article in a monthly magazine (signed) (p. 278)
5. An article in a monthly magazine (unsigned) (p. 278)
6. An article in a newspaper (signed) (p. 278)
7. An article in a newspaper (unsigned) (p. 278)
8. A letter to the editor of a newspaper (p. 278)
9. A book review in a newspaper (p. 279)

PRINT SOURCES: *Entries for Books*

Authors and Editors

10. A book by one author or editor (p. 279)
11. A book by two or three authors or editors (p. 279)
12. A book by more than three authors or editors (p. 280)
13. A book with no listed author or editor (p. 280)
14. A book by a corporate author (p. 280)
15. A book with an author and an editor (p. 281)
16. A book quoted in a secondary source (p. 281)

Editions and Multivolume Works

17. A subsequent edition of a book (p. 281)
18. A multivolume work (p. 281)

Parts of Books

19. A chapter in a book (p. 282)
20. An essay in an anthology (p. 282)

Religious Works

21. Sacred texts (p. 282)

ENTRIES FOR MISCELLANEOUS PRINT AND NONPRINT SOURCES

Interviews

Letters and Government Documents

DVDs and Recordings

ELECTRONIC SOURCES: *Entries for Sources from Online Publications*

Articles, Books, and Reference Works on the Internet

ELECTRONIC SOURCES: *Entries for Sources from an Online Database*

Sources from an Online Database

ELECTRONIC SOURCES: *Entries for Sources from Internet Sites*

Internet-Specific Sources

CHAPTER 19

Chicago Documentation Style

19a Using Chicago Humanities Style

The Chicago Manual of Style includes two citation methods, a notes-bibliography style used in history, in the humanities, and in some social science disciplines, and an author-date style used in the sciences and social sciences. **Chicago humanities style*** has two parts: *notes at the end of the essay* (**endnotes**) and usually a *list of bibliographic citations* (**bibliography**). (Chicago style encourages the use of endnotes, but allows the use of footnotes at the bottom of the page.)

1 Endnotes and Footnotes

The notes format calls for a **superscript** (raised numeral) in the text after source material you have either quoted or referred to. This numeral, placed after all punctuation marks except dashes, corresponds to the numeral that precedes the endnote or footnote.

Endnote and Footnote Format: Chicago Style

In the Text

> By November of 1942, the Allies had proof that the Nazis were engaged in the systematic killing of Jews.[1]

In the Note

> 1. David S. Wyman, *The Abandonment of the Jews: America and the Holocaust 1941–1945* (New York: Pantheon Books, 1984), 65.

---

*Chicago humanities style follows the guidelines set in *The Chicago Manual of Style*, 16th ed. Chicago: University of Chicago Press, 2010. The manuscript guidelines and sample research paper at the end of this chapter follow guidelines set in Kate L. Turabian's *A Manual for Writers of Research Papers, Theses, and Dissertations*, 8th ed. Chicago: University of Chicago Press, 2013. Turabian style, which is based on Chicago style, addresses formatting concerns specific to college writers.

Close-Up   SUBSEQUENT REFERENCES TO THE SAME WORK

In an essay with no bibliography, use the full citation in the first note for a work; in subsequent references to the same work, list only the author's last name, a comma, an abbreviated title, another comma, and a page number. In an essay with a bibliography, you may use the short form for all notes.

First Note on Espinoza

1. J. M. Espinoza. *The First Expedition of Vargas in New Mexico, 1692* (Albuquerque: University of New Mexico Press, 1949), 10–12.

Subsequent Note

5. Espinoza, *First Expedition,* 29.

Note: You may use the abbreviation *ibid.* ("in the same place") for subsequent references to the same work as long as there are no intervening references. *Ibid.* takes the place of the author's name, the work's title, and the page number if they are the same as those in the previous note. If the page number is different, cite *Ibid.* and the page number.

First Note on Espinoza

1. J. M. Espinoza. *The First Expedition of Vargas in New Mexico, 1692* (Albuquerque: University of New Mexico Press, 1949), 10–12.

Next Note

2. Ibid., 23.

❷ Bibliography

The **bibliography** provides complete publication information for the works consulted. Bibliography entries are arranged alphabetically by the author's last name or the first major word of the title (if there is no author). Single-space within an entry; double-space between entries.

Sample Chicago-Style Endnotes and Bibliography Entries

CHICAGO PRINT SOURCES Entries for Articles

Article citations generally include the name of the author (last name first); the title of the article (in quotation marks); the title of the periodical (in italics); the volume number, issue number, and date; and the page reference. Months are spelled out in full, not abbreviated.

Author's last name	First name and middle initial		Title of article (in quotation marks)

Strauss, David A. "Common Law, Common Ground, and Jefferson's Principle." *Yale Law Journal* 112, no. 7 (2003): 1717–55.

	Periodical title (italicized)	Volume number	Issue number	Year of publication (in parentheses)	Inclusive page numbers

Articles in Scholarly Journals

1. **An Article in a Scholarly Journal with Continuous Pagination throughout an Annual Volume**

Endnote

> 1. John Huntington, "Science Fiction and the Future," *College English* 37 (Fall 1975): 341.

Bibliography

> Huntington, John. "Science Fiction and the Future." *College English* 37 (Fall 1975): 340–58.

2. **An Article in a Scholarly Journal with Separate Pagination in Each Issue**

Endnote

> 2. R. G. Sipes, "War, Sports, and Aggression: An Empirical Test of Two Rival Theories," *American Anthropologist* 4, no. 2 (1973): 80.

Bibliography

> Sipes, R. G. "War, Sports, and Aggression: An Empirical Test of Two Rival Theories." *American Anthropologist* 4, no. 2 (1973): 65–84.

Articles in Magazines and Newspapers

3. **An Article in a Weekly Magazine (Signed/Unsigned)**

Endnote

Signed

> 3. Pico Iyer, "A Mum for All Seasons," *Time,* April 8, 2002, 51.

Unsigned

> 3. "Burst Bubble," *New Scientist,* July 27, 2002, 24.

Although both endnotes above specify page numbers, the corresponding bibliography entries include page numbers only when the pages are consecutive (as in the second example that follows).

Bibliography

Signed

> Iyer, Pico. "A Mum for All Seasons." *Time,* April 8, 2002.

Three Authors

> 11. Nathan Caplan, John K. Whitmore, and Marcella H. Choy, *The Boat People and Achievement in America: A Study of Economic and Educational Success* (Ann Arbor: University of Michigan Press, 1990), 51.

Bibliography
Two Authors

> Watson, Jack, and Grant McKerney. *A Cultural History of the Theater.* New York: Longman, 1993.

Three Authors

> Caplan, Nathan, John K. Whitmore, and Marcella H. Choy. *The Boat People and Achievement in America: A Study of Economic and Educational Success.* Ann Arbor: University of Michigan Press, 1990.

12. A Book by More Than Three Authors or Editors
Endnote

Chicago style favors **et al.** rather than **and others** after the first name in endnotes. Add a comma and **eds.** after the names of the editors in both the endnotes and the bibliography.

> 12. Robert E. Spiller et al., eds., *Literary History of the United States* (New York: Macmillan, 1953), 24.

Bibliography

List all authors' or editors' names in the bibliography.

> Spiller, Robert E., Willard Thorp, Thomas H. Johnson, and Henry Seidel Canby, eds. *Literary History of the United States.* New York: Macmillan, 1953.

13. A Book with No Listed Author or Editor
Endnote

> 13. *Merriam-Webster's Guide to Punctuation and Style,* 4th ed. (Springfield, MA: Merriam-Webster, 2008), 22.

Bibliography

> *Merriam-Webster's Guide to Punctuation and Style.* 4th ed. Springfield, MA: Merriam-Webster, 2008.

14. A Book by a Corporate Author

If a publication issued by an organization does not identify a person as the author, the organization is listed as the author even if its name is repeated in the title, in the series title, or as the publisher.

Endnote

> 14. National Geographic Society, *National Parks of the United States,* 6th ed. (Washington, DC: National Geographic Society, 2009), 77.

Bibliography

> National Geographic Society. *National Parks of the United States.* 6th ed. Washington, DC: National Geographic Society, 2009.

15. A Book with an Author and an Editor
Endnote

> 15. William Bartram, *The Travels of William Bartram,* ed. Mark Van Doren (New York: Dover Press, 1955), 85.

Bibliography

> Bartram, William. *The Travels of William Bartram*. Edited by Mark Van Doren. New York: Dover Press, 1955.

16. A Book Quoted in a Secondary Source
Endnote

> 16. Henry Adams, *Mont Saint-Michel and Chartres* (New York: Penguin Books, 1986), 296, quoted in Karen Armstrong, *A History of God: The 4000-Year Quest of Judaism, Christianity and Islam* (New York: Ballantine Books, 1993), 203–4.

Bibliography

> Adams, Henry. *Mont Saint-Michel and Chartres,* 296. New York: Penguin Books, 1986. Quoted in Armstrong, *A History of God,* 203–4.

> Armstrong, Karen. *A History of God: The 4000-Year Quest of Judaism, Christianity, and Islam.* New York: Ballantine Books, 1993.

Editions and Multivolume Works

17. A Subsequent Edition of a Book
Endnote

> 17. Laurie G. Kirszner and Stephen R. Mandell, *The Concise Cengage Handbook,* 5th ed. (Boston: Wadsworth, 2017), 52.

Bibliography

> Kirszner, Laurie G., and Stephen R. Mandell. *The Concise Cengage Handbook.* 5th ed. Boston: Wadsworth, 2017.

18. A Multivolume Work
Endnote

> 18. Kathleen Raine, *Blake and Tradition* (Princeton, NJ: Princeton University Press, 1968), 1:143.

Bibliography

> Raine, Kathleen. *Blake and Tradition*. Vol. 1. Princeton, NJ: Princeton University Press, 1968.

Parts of Books

19. A Chapter in a Book
Endnote

> 19. Roy Porter, "Health, Disease, and Cure," in *Quacks: Fakers and Charlatans in Medicine* (Stroud, UK: Tempus Publishing, 2003), 188.

Bibliography

> Porter, Roy. "Health, Disease, and Cure." In *Quacks: Fakers and Charlatans in Medicine,* 182–205. Stroud, UK: Tempus Publishing, 2003.

20. An Essay in an Anthology
Endnote

> 20. G. E. R. Lloyd, "Science and Mathematics," in *The Legacy of Greece,* ed. Moses Finley (New York: Oxford University Press, 1981), 270.

Bibliography

> Lloyd, G. E. R. "Science and Mathematics." In *The Legacy of Greece,* edited by Moses Finley, 256–300. New York: Oxford University Press, 1981.

Religious Works

21. Sacred Texts
References to religious works (such as the Bible or Qur'an) are usually limited to the text or notes and not listed in the bibliography. In citing the Bible, include the book (abbreviated), the chapter (followed by a colon), and the verse numbers. Identify the version, but do not include a page number.

Endnote

> 21. Phil. 1:9–11 (King James Version).

CHICAGO ENTRIES FOR MISCELLANEOUS PRINT AND NONPRINT SOURCES

Interviews

22. A Personal Interview
Endnote

> 22. Cornel West, interview by author, tape recording, June 8, 2013.

Personal interviews are cited in the notes or text but are usually not listed in the bibliography.

23. A Published Interview
Endnote

> 23. Gwendolyn Brooks, interview by George Stavros, *Contemporary Literature* 11, no. 1 (Winter 1970): 12.

Bibliography

> Brooks, Gwendolyn. Interview by George Stavros. *Contemporary Literature* 11, no. 1 (Winter 1970): 1–20.

Letters and Government Documents

24. A Personal Letter
Endnote

> 24. Julia Alvarez, letter to the author, April 10, 2013.

Personal letters are mentioned in the text or a note but are not listed in the bibliography.

25. A Government Document
Endnote

> 25. US Department of Transportation, *The Future of High-Speed Trains in the United States: Special Study, 2007* (Washington, DC: Government Printing Office, 2008), 203.

Bibliography

> US Department of Transportation. *The Future of High-Speed Trains in the United States: Special Study, 2007*. Washington, DC: Government Printing Office, 2008.

DVDs and Recordings

26. A DVD
Endnote

> 26. *Steve Jobs: The Lost Interview*, directed by Paul Sen (New York: Magnolia Home Entertainment, 2012), DVD, 72 min.

Bibliography

> *Steve Jobs: The Lost Interview*. Directed by Paul Sen. New York: Magnolia Home Entertainment, 2012. DVD, 72 min.

27. An Audio Recording
Endnote

> 27. Bob Marley and the Wailers, "Crisis," *Kaya*, Kava Island Records 423 095-3, 1978, compact disc.

Bibliography

> Marley, Bob, and the Wailers. "Crisis." *Kaya.* Kava Island Records 423 095-3, 1978, compact disc.

CHICAGO ELECTRONIC SOURCES · Entries for Sources from Online Publications

Citations of sources from online publications usually include the author's name; the title of the article; the title of the publication; the publication information and date; the page numbers (if applicable); and the DOI (digital object identifier), a permanent identifying number, or URL (followed by a period). If no publication date is available or if your instructor or discipline requires one, include an access date before the DOI or URL.

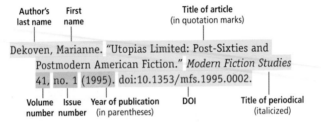

Author's last name | First name | Title of article (in quotation marks)

Dekoven, Marianne. "Utopias Limited: Post-Sixties and Postmodern American Fiction." *Modern Fiction Studies* 41, no. 1 (1995). doi:10.1353/mfs.1995.0002.

Volume number | Issue number | Year of publication (in parentheses) | DOI | Title of periodical (italicized)

You may break a DOI or URL that continues to a second line after a colon or double slash; before a comma, a period, a hyphen, a question mark, a percent symbol, a number sign, a tilde, or an underscore; or before or after an ampersand or equals sign.

Articles, Books, and Reference Works on the Internet

28. An Article in an Online Scholarly Journal

Endnote

> 28. Richard J. Schaefer, "Editing Strategies in Television Documentaries," *Journal of Communication* 47, no. 4 (1997): 80, doi:10.1111/j1460 -2446.1997.tb02726.x.

Bibliography

> Schaefer, Richard J. "Editing Strategies in Television Documentaries." *Journal of Communication* 47, no. 4 (1997): 69–89. doi:10.1111/j1460 -2446.1997.tb02726.x.

29. An Article in an Online Magazine

Endnote

> 29. Steven Levy, "I Was a Wi-Fi Freeloader," *Newsweek,* October 9, 2002, http://www.msnbc.com/news/816606.asp.

If there is no DOI for a source, cite the URL.

Bibliography

Levy, Steven. "I Was a Wi-Fi Freeloader." *Newsweek,* October 9, 2002. http://www.msnbc.com/news/816606.asp.

30. An Article in an Online Newspaper
Endnote

30. William J. Broad, "Piece by Piece, the Civil War *Monitor* Is Pulled from the Atlantic's Depths," *New York Times,* July 18, 2002, http://query .nytimes.com.

Bibliography

Broad, William J. "Piece by Piece, the Civil War *Monitor* Is Pulled from the Atlantic's Depths." *New York Times,* July 18, 2002. http://query .nytimes.com.

31. An Article in an Encyclopedia
If the reference book lists entries alphabetically, put the abbreviation **s.v.** (Latin for *sub verbo,* "under the word") before the entry name. If there is no publication or revision date for the entry, give the date of access before the DOI or URL.

Endnote

31. *Encyclopaedia Britannica Online,* s.v. "Adams, John," accessed July 5, 2015, http://www.britannica.com/EBchecked/topic/5132/John -Adams.

Dictionary and encyclopedia entries are not listed in the bibliography.

32. A Book
Endnote

32. Frederick Douglass, *My Bondage and My Freedom* (Boston, 1855), http://etext.virginia.edu/toc/modeng/public/DouMybo.html.

Bibliography

Douglass, Frederick. *My Bondage and My Freedom*. Boston, 1855. http:// etext.virginia.edu/toc/modeng/public/DouMybo.html.

Older works available online may not include all publication information. Give the DOI or URL as the last part of the citation.

33. A Government Publication
Endnote

33. US Department of Transportation, Federal Motor Carrier Safety Administration, *Safety Belt Usage by Commercial Motor Vehicle Drivers (SBUCMVD) 2007 Survey, Final Report* (Washington, DC: Government Printing Office, 2008), http://www.fmcsa.dot.gov/safety-security/safety-belt/exec-summary-2007.htm.

Bibliography

> Green, John, and CrashCourse. *Conflict in Israel and Palestine: Crash Course World History 223*. Online video, 12:52. January 28, 2015. https://www.youtube.com/watch?v=1wo2TLlMhiw.

41. A Social Networking Post (*Facebook* post, tweet, etc.)

No bibliography entry is needed. Include information about the post (such as the writer's *Twitter* name) within the text of your essay or include a note such as the following.

Endnote

> 41. Celeste Ng, Twitter post, February 18, 2015, 8:55 a.m., https://twitter.com/pronounced_ing/.

EXERCISE 19.1

Each of these notes identifies a source used in an essay comparing the 2008 and 2012 US presidential elections. Determine which information is required to cite each source. Then, following the guidelines and proper format for Chicago documentation, create a note for each source, and then create a bibliography, arranging sources in the proper order. Be sure to format source information correctly, adding quotation marks and italics as needed.

1. A scholarly journal article titled Did Obama's Ground Game Matter? The Influence of Local Field Offices during the 2008 Presidential Election. It was published in 2009 in Public Opinion Quarterly, in Volume 73, Issue 5. The article appeared on pages 1023–1039. The article was written by Seth E. Masket. You accessed the article today at this URL: <http://poq.oxfordjournals.org/content/73/5/1023.full>.

2. A map titled 2012 Presidential Election Results from The Washington Post. It appears at this URL: <http://www.washingtonpost.com/wp-srv/special/politics/election-map-2012/president/>. It was last updated on November 19, 2012. You accessed it today.

3. Pages 88–98 in a print book by Mark Halperin and John Heilemann titled Double Down: Game Change 2012. It was published by Penguin Press in New York, NY, in 2013.

4. A blog post by Andrew Sullivan posted on October 8, 2012, titled Did Obama Just Throw the Entire Election Away? It was posted on Sullivan's blog called The Daily Dish, and it appeared at this URL: <http://dish.andrewsullivan.com/2012/10/08/did-obama-just-throw-the-entire-election-away/>. You accessed it today.

5. An editorial authored and published by The New York Times on October 23, 2008. It is titled Barack Obama for President. It appears at this URL: <http://www.nytimes.com/2008/10/24/opinion/24fri1. html?pagewanted=all&_r=0>. You accessed it today.

19b Chicago Humanities Manuscript Guidelines

CHECKLIST
Typing Your Essay

When you type your essay, use the student essay in **19c** as your model.

❑ On the title page, type the full title of your essay. Also include your name, the course title, and the date.

❑ Double-space all text in your essay. Single-space block quotations, table titles, figure captions, footnotes, endnotes, and bibliography entries. Double-space between footnotes, endnotes, and bibliography entries.

❑ Leave a one-inch margin at the top, at the bottom, and on both sides of the page.

❑ Indent the first line of each paragraph one-half inch. Set off a long prose block quotation (five or more lines) from the text by indenting the quotation one-half inch from the left-hand margin. Do not use quotation marks. Double-space before and after the block quotation.

❑ Number all pages consecutively at the top of the page (centered or flush right) or centered at the bottom. Page numbers should appear at a consistent distance (at least three-fourths of an inch) from the top margin. Do not number the title page; the first full page of the essay is page 1.

❑ Use superscript numbers to indicate in-text citations. Type superscript numbers at the end of cited material (quotations, paraphrases, or summaries). Place the note number at the end of a sentence or clause (with no intervening space). The number follows any punctuation mark except a dash, which it precedes.

❑ Citations should follow Chicago humanities documentation style.

See 19a

CHECKLIST
Using Visuals

According to *The Chicago Manual of Style,* there are two types of visuals: **tables** and **figures** (or **illustrations**), including charts, graphs, photographs, maps, and diagrams.

Tables

❑ Give each **table** a label and a consecutive arabic number (**Table 1, Table 2**) followed by a period.

continued

Using Visuals *(continued)*

❑ Give each table a concise descriptive title in noun form without a period. Place the title after the table number.

❑ Place both the label and the title flush left above the table.

❑ Place source information flush left below the table, introduced by the word **Source** or **Sources**. Otherwise style the source as a complete footnote.

> *Source:* David E. Fisher and Marshall Jon Fisher, *Tube: The Invention of Television* (Washington, DC: Counterpoint Press, 1996), 185.

If you do not cite this source elsewhere in your essay, do not list it in your bibliography.

Figures

❑ Give each **figure** a label, a consecutive arabic number, and a caption.

❑ Place the label, the number, and a period flush left below the figure. Then, leave a space and add the caption.

❑ Place source information (credit line) at the end of the caption after a period.

> Figure 1. Television and its influence on young children. Photograph from ABC Photos.

CHECKLIST

Preparing the Chicago-Style Endnotes Page

When typing your endnotes page, follow these guidelines:

❑ Begin the endnotes on a new page after the last page of the text of the essay and preceding the bibliography.

❑ Type the title **Notes** and center it one inch from the top of the page. Then double-space and type the first note.

❑ Number the page on which the endnotes appear as the next page of the essay.

❑ Type and number notes in the order in which they appear in the essay, beginning with number 1. Type the note number on (not above) the line, followed by a period and one space.

❑ Indent the first line of each note one-half inch; type subsequent lines flush with the left-hand margin.

❑ Single-space lines within a note. Double-space between notes.

❑ Break DOIs and URLs after a colon or double slashes, before punctuation marks (period, single slash, comma, hyphen, and so on), or before or after the symbols = and &.

CHECKLIST

Preparing the Chicago-Style Bibliography

When typing your bibliography, follow these guidelines:

❏ Begin entries on a separate page after the endnotes.

❏ Type the title **Bibliography** and center it one inch from the top of the page. Then double-space and type the first entry.

❏ List entries alphabetically according to the author's last name.

❏ Type the first line of each entry flush with the left-hand margin. Indent subsequent lines one-half inch.

❏ Single-space within an entry; double-space between entries.

19c Model Chicago Humanities Research Paper (Excerpts)

The following pages are from a student essay, "The Flu of 1918 and the Potential for Future Pandemics," written for a history course. It uses Chicago humanities documentation and has a title page, notes page, and bibliography. The Internet citations in this student essay do not have DOIs, so URLs have been provided instead.

Title page is
not numbered

Title boldfaced
and centered

The Flu of 1918 and the Potential for

Future Pandemics

Name

Course title

Date

Rita Lin

American History 301

May 3, 2015

The Flu of 1918 and the Potential for
Future Pandemics

Indent ½" ———→ In November 2002, a mysterious new illness surfaced in China. By May 2003, what became known as SARS (Severe Acute Respiratory Syndrome) had been transported by air travelers to Europe, South America, South Africa, Australia, and North America, and the worldwide death toll had grown to 250.[1] By June 2003, there were more than 8,200 suspected cases of SARS in 30 countries and 750 deaths related to the outbreak, including 30 in Toronto. Just when SARS appeared to be waning in Asia, a second outbreak in Toronto, the hardest hit of all cities outside of Asia, reminded everyone that SARS remained a deadly threat.[2] As SARS continued to claim more victims and expand its reach, fears of a new pandemic spread throughout the world.

The belief that a pandemic could occur in the future is not a far-fetched idea. During the twentieth century, there were three, and the most deadly one, in 1918, had several significant similarities to the SARS outbreak. As David Brown points out, the 1918 influenza pandemic is in many ways a mirror reflecting the causes and symptoms, as well as the future potential, of SARS. Both are caused by a virus, lead to respiratory illness, and spread through casual contact and coughing. Outbreaks of both are often traced to one individual, quarantine is the major weapon against the spread of both, and both probably arose from mutated animal viruses. Moreover, as Brown observes, the greatest fear regarding SARS was that it would become so widespread that transmission chains would be undetectable, and health officials would be helpless to restrain outbreaks. Such was the case with the 1918 influenza, which also began mysteriously in China and was transported around the globe (at that time by

Title if required by instructor (centered and boldfaced)

Double-space the text of the essay

Introduction

Superscript numbers refer to endnotes

1"

13

Bibliography

"1918 Influenza Timeline." *Influenza 1918,* 1999. http://www
.pbs.org/wgbh/amex/influenza/timeline/index.html.

Billings, Molly. "The Influenza Pandemic of 1918." Human
Virology at Stanford: Interesting Viral Web Pages,
June 1997. http://www.stanford.edu/group/virus
/uda/index.html.

Brown, David. "A Grim Reminder in SARS Fight: In 1918,
Spanish Flu Swept the Globe, Killing Millions." MSNBC
News Online, June 4, 2003. http://www.msnbc.com
/news/921901.asp.

"Canada Waits for SARS News as Asia Under Control." *Sydney
Morning Herald,* June 2, 2003. http://www.smh.com.au
/text.

Cooke, Robert. "Drugs vs. the Bug of 1918: Virus' Deadly Code
Is Unlocked to Test Strategies to Fight It." *Newsday,*
October 1, 2002.

Crosby, Alfred W., Jr. *America's Forgotten Pandemic: The
Influenza of 1918.* New York: Cambridge University Press,
1989.

Dandurant, Daren. "Virus Changes Can Make Flu a Slippery
Foe to Combat." MSNBC News Online, January 17, 2003.
http://www.msnbc.com/local/sco/m8052.asp.

Center title
(boldfaced)
and double-
space
before first
entry

First line of
each entry
is flush with
the left-hand
margin; subse-
quent lines are
indented ½"

Single-space
within entries;
double-space
between
them

URLs are
provided for
web citations
that do not
have DOIs

Entries
are listed
alphabetically
according to
the author's
last name

Directory of CSE Reference List Entries

PRINT SOURCES: *Entries for Articles*

Articles in Scholarly Journals

1. An article in a journal paginated by issue (p. 300)
2. An article in a journal with continuous pagination (p. 300)

Articles in Magazines and Newspapers

3. A magazine article (signed) (p. 300)
4. A magazine article (unsigned) (p. 300)
5. A newspaper article (signed) (p. 300)
6. A newspaper article (unsigned) (p. 300)

PRINT SOURCES: *Entries for Books*

Authors

7. A book with one author (p. 301)
8. A book with more than one author (p. 301)
9. An edited book (p. 301)
10. An organization as author (p. 301)

Parts of Books

11. A chapter or other part of a book with a separate title but with the same author (p. 301)
12. A chapter or other part of a book with a different author (p. 301)

Professional and Technical Publications

13. Published proceedings of a conference (p. 301)
14. A technical report (p. 302)

ENTRIES FOR MISCELLANEOUS PRINT AND NONPRINT SOURCES

Films, Recordings, and Maps

15. An audio recording (p. 302)
16. A film, DVD, or Blu-ray (p. 302)
17. A map (p. 302)

ELECTRONIC SOURCES: *Entries for Sources from Internet Sites*

Internet-Specific Sources

18. An article in an online scholarly journal (p. 303)
19. An online book (p. 303)
20. An online image (p. 303)
21. A podcast (p. 303)

CHAPTER 20

CSE and Other Documentation Styles

20a Using CSE Style

CSE style,* recommended by the Council of Science Editors (CSE), is used in biology, zoology, physiology, anatomy, and genetics. CSE style has two parts—*documentation in the text* and a *reference list*.

1 Documentation in the Text

CSE style permits either of two documentation formats: *citation-sequence format* or *name-year format*.

Citation-Sequence Format The **citation-sequence format** calls for either superscripts (raised numbers) in the text of the essay (the preferred form) or numbers inserted parenthetically in the text of the essay.

> One study[1] has demonstrated the effect of low dissolved oxygen.

These numbers refer to a list of references at the end of the essay. Entries are numbered in the order in which they appear in the text of the essay. For example, if **James** is mentioned first in the text, **James** will be number 1 in the reference list. When you refer to more than one source in a single note, the numbers are separated by a hyphen if they are in sequence and by a comma if they are not.

> Some studies[2-3] dispute this claim.

> Other studies[3,6] support these findings.

Name-Year Format The **name-year format** calls for the author's name and the year of publication to be inserted parenthetically in the text. If the author's name is used to introduce the source material, only the date of publication is needed in the parenthetical citation.

---

*CSE style follows the guidelines set in the style manual of the Council of Science Editors: *Scientific Style and Format: The CSE Manual for Authors, Editors, and Publishers*, 8th ed. Chicago: University of Chicago Press, 2014.

A great deal of heat is often generated during this process (McGinness 2010).

According to McGinness (2010), a great deal of heat is often generated during this process.

When two or more works are cited in the same parentheses, the sources are arranged chronologically (from earliest to latest) and separated by semicolons.

Epidemics can be avoided by taking tissue cultures (Domb 2010) and by intervention with antibiotics (Baldwin and Rigby 2005; Martin and others 2006; Cording 2010).

Note: The citation **Baldwin and Rigby 2005** refers to a work by two authors; the citation **Martin and others 2006** refers to a work by three or more authors.

❷ Reference List

The format of the reference list depends on the documentation format you use. If you use the **name-year** documentation format, your reference list will resemble the reference list for an **APA** essay (**see Chapter 18**). If you use the **citation-sequence** documentation style (as in the essay in **20c**), your sources will be listed by number, in the order in which they appear in your essay, on a **References** page. In either case, double-space within and between entries; type each number flush left, followed by a period and one space; and align the second and subsequent lines with the first letter of the author's last name. (The following examples illustrate citation-sequence documentation style.)

CSE PRINT SOURCES Entries for Articles

List the author or authors by last name; after one space, list the initial or initials (unspaced) of the first and middle names (followed by a period); the title of the article (not in quotation marks, and with only the first word capitalized); the abbreviated name of the journal (with all major words capitalized, but not italicized or underlined); the year (followed by a semicolon); the volume number, the issue number (in parentheses), followed by a colon; and inclusive page numbers. No spaces separate the year, the volume number, and the page numbers.

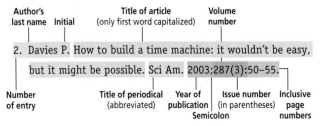

Author's last name	Initial	Title of article (only first word capitalized)	Volume number

2. Davies P. How to build a time machine: it wouldn't be easy, but it might be possible. Sci Am. 2003;287(3):50–55.

Number of entry	Title of periodical (abbreviated)	Year of publication	Semicolon	Issue number (in parentheses)	Inclusive page numbers

Articles in Scholarly Journals

1. An Article in a Journal Paginated by Issue

1. Sarmiento JL, Gruber N. Sinks for anthropogenic carbon. Phy Today. 2002;55(8):30-36.

2. An Article in a Journal with Continuous Pagination

2. Brazil K, Krueger P. Patterns of family adaptation to childhood asthma. J Pediatr Nurs. 2002;17:167-173.

Note: Omit the month (and the day for weeklies) and issue number for journals with continuous pagination through an annual volume.

Articles in Magazines and Newspapers

3. A Magazine Article (Signed)

3. Nadis S. Using lasers to detect E.T. Astronomy. 2002 Sep:44-49.

Note: Month names longer than three letters are abbreviated by their first three letters.

4. A Magazine Article (Unsigned)

4. Brown dwarf glows with radio waves. Astronomy. 2001 Jun:28.

5. A Newspaper Article (Signed)

5. Husted B. Don't wiggle out of untangling computer wires. Atlanta Journal-Constitution. 2002 Jul 21;Sect Q:1 (col 1).

6. A Newspaper Article (Unsigned)

6. Scientists find gene tied to cancer risk. New York Times (Late Ed.). 2002 Apr 22;Sect A:18 (col 6).

CSE PRINT SOURCES Entries for Books

List the author or authors (last name first); the title (not underlined, and with only the first word capitalized); the place of publication; the full name of the publisher (followed by a semicolon); the year (followed by a period); and the total number of pages (including back matter, such as the index).

Author's last name | Initials (unspaced) | Title (only first word capitalized)

1. Abbott EA. Flatland: a romance of many dimensions.

Boston (MA): Shambhala; 1999. 238 p.

Number of entry | City and state | Publisher | Year of publication | Total number of pages

Semicolon

Authors

7. A Book with One Author

7. Hawking SW. A brief history of time: from the big bang to black holes. New York (NY): Bantam; 1995. 198 p.

Note: No comma follows the author's last name, and no period separates the unspaced initials of the first and middle names.

8. A Book with More Than One Author

8. Horner JR, Gorman J. Digging dinosaurs. New York (NY): Workman; 1988. 210 p.

9. An Edited Book

9. Goldfarb TD, editor. Taking sides: clashing views on controversial environmental issues. 2nd ed. Guilford (CT): Dushkin; 1987. 323 p.

Note: The publisher's state, province, or country can be added within parentheses to clarify the location. The two-letter postal service abbreviation can be used for the state or province.

10. An Organization as Author

10. National Institutes of Health (US). Human embryonic stem-cell derived neurons treat stroke in rats. Bethesda (MD): US Dept. of Health and Human Services; 2008. 92 p.

Parts of Books

11. A Chapter or Other Part of a Book with a Separate Title but with the Same Author

11. Asimov I. Exploring the earth and cosmos: the growth and future of human knowledge. New York (NY): Crown; 1984. Part III, The horizons of matter; p. 245-294.

12. A Chapter or Other Part of a Book with a Different Author

12. Gingerich O. Hints for beginning observers. In: Mallas JH, Kreimer E, editors. The Messier album: an observer's handbook. Cambridge (GB): Cambridge Univ Pr; 1978. p. 194-195.

Professional and Technical Publications

13. Published Proceedings of a Conference

13. Al-Sherbini A. New applications of lasers in photobiology and photochemistry. Modern Trends of Physics Research, 1st International

Conference; 2004 May 12-14; Cairo, Egypt. Melville (NY): American Institute of Physics; 2005. 14 p.

14. A Technical Report

14. Forman GL. Feature selection for text classification. 2007 Feb 12. Hewlett-Packard technical reports HPL-2007-16R1. 24 p. http://www .hpl.hp.com/techreports/2007/HPL-2007-16R1.html.

 Note: See pages 302–03 for information on citing online sources.

CSE ENTRIES FOR MISCELLANEOUS PRINT AND NONPRINT SOURCES

Films, Recordings, and Maps

15. An Audio Recording

15. Nye B. Undeniable: evolution and the science of creation [CD]. New York: Macmillan Audio; 2014. 4 discs: 569 min.

16. A Film, DVD, or Blu-ray

16. Tyson ND, narrator. Cosmos: a spacetime odyssey [DVD]. Fox TV, producer. Los Angeles: 20th Century Fox; 2014. 4 discs: 572 min.

17. A Map
A Sheet Map

17. Amazonia: a world resource at risk [ecological map]. Washington (DC): National Geographic Society; 2008.
1 sheet.

A Map in an Atlas

17. Central Africa [political map]. In: Hammond citation world atlas. Maplewood (NJ): Hammond; 2008. p. 114-115. Color, scale 1:13,800,000.

CSE ELECTRONIC SOURCES Entries for Sources from Internet Sites

With Internet sources, include a description of the medium, the date of access, and the URL.

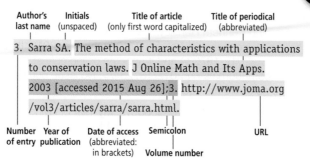

Author's last name | Initials (unspaced) | Title of article (only first word capitalized) | Title of periodical (abbreviated)

3. Sarra SA. The method of characteristics with applications to conservation laws. J Online Math and Its Apps. 2003 [accessed 2015 Aug 26];3. http://www.joma.org /vol3/articles/sarra/sarra.html.

Number of entry | Year of publication | Date of access (abbreviated: in brackets) | Semicolon / Volume number | URL

Internet-Specific Sources

18. An Article in an Online Scholarly Journal

18. Lasko P. The *Drosophila melanogaster* genome: translation factors and RNA binding proteins. J Cell Biol. 2000 [accessed 2015 Feb 15]; 150(2):F51-56. http://www.jcb.org/search.dtl.

19. An Online Book

19. Bohm D. Causality and chance in modern physics. Philadelphia: Univ of Pennsylvania Pr; c1999 [accessed 2014 Aug 17]. http://www.netlibrary .com/ebook_info.asp?product_id517169.

20. An Online Image

20. Muroe R. Atoms [cartoon]. xkcd.com. [accessed 2014 Feb 23]. http:// xkcd.com/1490/.

21. A Podcast

21. Adams R. Energy and empire by George Gonzales [podcast, episode 235]. The Atomic Show. Atomic Insights. 2015 Feb 26, 21 min. [accessed 2015 Mar 1]. http://atomicinsights.com/atomic-show-235-energy-and-empire-by-george-gonzales/.

EXERCISE 20.1

Each of these notes identifies a source used in an essay about Amyotrophic Lateral Sclerosis (ALS). Determine which information is required to cite each source. Then, following the guidelines and proper format for CSE's citation-sequence format, create a reference list entry for each source. Be sure to format source information correctly.

1. A scholarly journal article titled Progress in Therapy Development for Amyotrophic Lateral Sclerosis. It was authored by Kalina

Venkova-Hristova, Alexandar Christov, Zarine Kamaluddin, Peter Kobalka, and Kenneth Hensley. It appeared in the journal Neurology Research International, in Volume 2012 in the year 2012. Its DOI is doi:10.1155/2012/187234 and it appears online only at <http://www .hindawi.com/journals/nri/2012/187234/>. No issue number is listed. No page numbers are used. You accessed it today.

2. A print book called Until I Say Goodbye: My Year of Living with Joy by author Susan Spencer-Wendel. It was published by Harper Collins in New York, NY, in 2013.

3. A newspaper article by Katie Hafner published in The New York Times on April 8, 2013. The article is called Life as a Race against a Diagnosis. It appears at this URL: <http://www.nytimes.com/2013/04/09 /health/living-life-as-a-race-against-als.html>. A version of the article appeared in print on April 9, 2013, on page D3 of the New York edition of The New York Times. You accessed it today.

4. A page titled ALS Ice Bucket Challenge—FAQ on a website called The ALS Association. Its URL is <http://www.alsa.org/about-us /ice-bucket-challenge-faq.html>. The ALS Association is also this site's sponsor. The page was last updated in 2014. You accessed it today.

5. A scholarly journal article called Amyotrophic Lateral Sclerosis: Ethical Challenges. The article's authors are Wendy S. Johnston, Katelin Hoskins, and Leo McCluskey. It appeared in a journal called Neurology, in Volume 76, Issue 7, on pages S1–S5. It was published in February of 2011. Its DOI is doi:10.1212/WNL.0b013e31820d57ee. You accessed it through a database at this URL: <http://www.ncbi .nlm.nih.gov/pubmed/21321345>.

20b CSE-Style Manuscript Guidelines

CHECKLIST

Typing Your Essay

When you type your essay, use the student essay in **20c** as your model.

❏ Do not include a title page. Type your name, the course, and the date flush left one inch from the top of the first page.

❏ If required, include an **abstract** (a 250-word summary of the essay) on a separate numbered page.

❏ Double-space throughout.

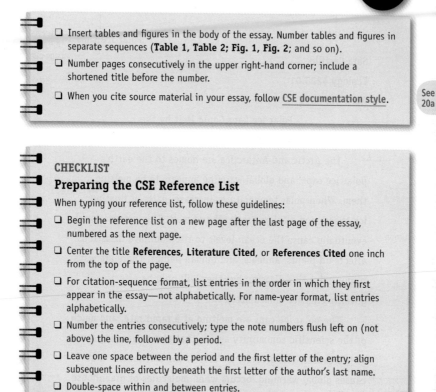

❑ Insert tables and figures in the body of the essay. Number tables and figures in separate sequences (**Table 1, Table 2; Fig. 1, Fig. 2;** and so on).

❑ Number pages consecutively in the upper right-hand corner; include a shortened title before the number.

❑ When you cite source material in your essay, follow <u>CSE documentation style</u>.

See 20a

CHECKLIST

Preparing the CSE Reference List

When typing your reference list, follow these guidelines:

❑ Begin the reference list on a new page after the last page of the essay, numbered as the next page.

❑ Center the title **References, Literature Cited**, or **References Cited** one inch from the top of the page.

❑ For citation-sequence format, list entries in the order in which they first appear in the essay—not alphabetically. For name-year format, list entries alphabetically.

❑ Number the entries consecutively; type the note numbers flush left on (not above) the line, followed by a period.

❑ Leave one space between the period and the first letter of the entry; align subsequent lines directly beneath the first letter of the author's last name.

❑ Double-space within and between entries.

20c   Model CSE-Style Research Paper (Excerpts)

The following pages are from a student essay that explores the dangers of global warming for humans and wildlife. The essay, which cites seven sources and includes a line graph, illustrates CSE citation-sequence format.

1"

Sara Castillo

Ecology 4223.01

April 10, 2015

Center title ———→ Polar Ice Caps Could Melt by the
End of This Century

Indent ½" ———→ The Arctic and Antarctica are homes to the earth's

Double-space polar ice caps, and global warming appears to be melting

them. When polar temperatures increase, parts of floating

ice sheets and glaciers break off and melt. This process could

Introduction eventually cause the ocean levels to rise and have disastrous

effects on plants, animals, and human beings. There are ways

Thesis statement to minimize this disaster, but they will only be effective if

governments act immediately.

The polar ice caps are melting at a rapid rate, and much

of the scientific community agrees that global warming is one

of the causes. The greenhouse effect, the mechanism that

1" causes global warming, occurs when molecules of greenhouse 1"

gases in the atmosphere reflect the rays of the sun back to

the earth. This mechanism enables our planet to maintain a

temperature adequate for life. However, as the concentration

of greenhouse gases in the atmosphere increases, more heat

from the sun is retained, and the temperature of the earth

Superscript numbers correspond to sources in the reference list rises.[1]

Greenhouse gases include carbon dioxide (CO_2), meth-

ane, and nitrous oxide.[2] Since the beginning of the industrial

revolution in the late 1800s, people have been burning fossil

fuels that create CO_2.[3] This CO_2 has led to an increase in the

greenhouse effect and has contributed to the global warming

Figure 1 introduced that is melting the polar ice caps. As Figure 1 shows, the sur-

face temperature of the earth has increased by about 1 degree

1"

Polar Ice Caps 2

Celsius (1.8 degrees Fahrenheit) since the 1850s. Some scientists have predicted that temperatures will increase even further.

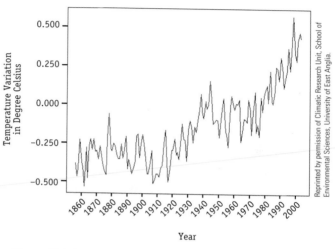

Reprinted by permission of Climatic Research Unit, School of Environmental Sciences, University of East Anglia.

Year

Fig. 1. Global temperature variation from the average during the base period 1860-2000 (adapted from Climatic research unit: data: temperature 2003). [accessed 2015 Mar 11]. http://www.cru.uea.ac.uk/cru/data/temperature.

It is easy to see the effects of global warming. For example, the Pine Island Glacier in Antarctica was depleted at a rate of 1.6 meters per year between 1992 and 1999. This type of melting is very likely to increase the fresh water that

---

Figure placed close to where it is discussed

Label, caption, and full source information

Polar Ice Caps 8

References

Book with one author
1. Edmonds A. A closer look at the greenhouse effect. Brookfield (CT): Copper Beach Books; 1997. 32 p.

Book with more than one author
2. Smith TM, Smith RL. Elements of ecology. 9th ed. San Francisco (CA): Benjamin Cummings; 2015. 704 p.

Double-space

Entries listed in order in which they first appear in the essay
3. Pringle L. Global warming: the threat of earth's changing climate. New York (NY): Sea and Star Books; 2001. 48 p.

4. Perkins S. Antarctic glacier thins and speeds up. Sci News. 2001;159(5):70.

Online journal
5. Pearce F. Arctic to lose all summer ice by 2100. NewScientist. 2002 [accessed 2015 Mar 11]; 70(2):99-133. http://www.newscientist.com.

Print journal
6. The pacific decadal oscillation. BioSci. 2000 Aug:32-39.

7. Linder C. Science on ice. Chicago (IL): University of Chicago Press; 2011. 288 p.

20d Using Other Documentation Styles

The following style manuals describe documentation formats and manuscript guidelines used in various fields.

CHEMISTRY

Coghill, Anne M., and Lorrin R. Garson, eds. *The ACS Style Guide: Effective Communication of Scientific Information.* 3rd ed. Washington: American Chemical Society, 2006. Print.

GEOLOGY

Hansen, Wallace R., ed. *Suggestions to Authors of the Reports of the United States Geological Survey.* 7th ed. Washington: GPO, 1991. Print.

GOVERNMENT DOCUMENTS

Cheney, Debora. *The Complete Guide to Citing Government Information Resources: A Manual for Social Science & Business Research.* 3rd ed. Bethesda: Congressional Information Service, 2002. Print.

United States Government Printing Office. *Style Manual*. Washington: GPO, 2009. Print.

JOURNALISM

Associated Press. *The Associated Press Stylebook and Briefing on Media Law 2015*. 46th ed. New York: Basic, 2015. Print.

LAW

The Bluebook: A Uniform System of Citation. Comp. Editors of Columbia Law Review et al. 19th ed. Cambridge: Harvard Law Review Association, 2010. Print.

MATHEMATICS

American Mathematical Society. *AMS Author Handbook*. Providence: American Mathematical Society, 2014. Web.

MEDICINE

Iverson, Cheryl. *AMA Manual of Style: A Guide for Authors and Editors*. 10th ed. Oxford: Oxford UP, 2007. Print.

MUSIC

Holoman, D. Kern. *Writing about Music: A Style Sheet*. 2nd ed. Berkeley: U of California P, 2008. Print.

PHYSICS

American Institute of Physics. *AIP Style Manual*. 5th ed. Melville: American Institute of Physics, 2000. Print.

SCIENTIFIC AND TECHNICAL WRITING

Rubens, Philip, ed. *Science and Technical Writing: A Manual of Style*. 2nd ed. New York: Routledge, 2001. Print.

Composing and Evaluating Digital Documents

PART **6**

Composing and Evaluating Digital Documents

? Frequently Asked Questions

CHAPTER 21

Understanding, Exploring, and Developing Multimodal Texts

This chapter focuses on developing multimodal texts that rely on digital communication technologies.

21a Understanding Multimodality

A **medium** of communication is the means by which a message is conveyed—for example, print, electronic, or face-to-face. A **mode** is a type of discourse or communication—for example, speech, text (print, email, instant messaging), graphic images, audio, or video. When two or more of these modes occur in a single document, the text is said to be **multimodal**. For example, a web page or a *Facebook* post may contain a short video clip or a link to other articles. An essay for a history class may contain a timeline, a chart, or photographs. Finally, presentations often make use of *PowerPoint* or *Prezi* slides or handouts.

21b Selecting a Genre

The rhetorical choices writers make when composing multimodal texts are somewhat more complicated than the ones they make when composing essays that rely on words alone. In addition to examining various aspects of the rhetorical situation, such as audience and purpose, writers of multimodal texts have to consider the characteristics of the various genres they are considering. For example, what are the advantages and disadvantages of presenting information in a blog, a wiki, or a podcast? What constraints does a particular genre impose on a writer? How does the genre expand a writer's avenues of expression? How does it limit them? (**See Chapter 22** for information on composing specific kinds of digital texts. **See Chapter 33** for information about presentations.)

See Ch. 1

21c Exploring Multimodal Texts

Businesses often use multimodal texts to reach their clients. For example, BE Furniture, a manufacturer of office furniture, uses multimedia to inform potential customers about the way kinds of furniture can affect the attitudes of employees. On its blog (Figure 21.1), BE Furniture includes pictures that emphasize the value of designing workspaces that encourage collaboration.

How to Keep Staff in the Office without Traps on the Furniture

The office can be your staff's favorite place or nightmare. Learn how your office environment and furniture can influence time spent working and having fun.

FIGURE 21.1 BE Furniture blog.

In addition to pictures, the website contains podcasts and *YouTube* videos (Figures 21.2 and 21.3).

FIGURE 21.2 Still from BE Furniture *YouTube* video.

Our Process

BE > **BE** > **BE**

Design	Furniture	Clean
We believe that innovation in a work place starts with a proper office design and layout. This is the blueprint to inspiration.	When the vision is brought to life, we uniquely consult and place furniture that supports the culture, atmosphere, and budget you need.	Maintenance and cleanliness is key to keep minds free and clear to serve you best. Keeping the investment you made to always look brand new. Clean Office, Clean Minds.

FIGURE 21.3 Still from BE Furniture *YouTube* video.

Both the company's *Facebook* page (Figure 21.4) and its website (Figure 21.5) are multimodal texts because they include words, videos, and audio to convey a message about who the company is and to make an argument about why people should buy their products. The appropriateness of the rhetorical decisions for these various texts determines how effective they will be in influencing their intended audiences.

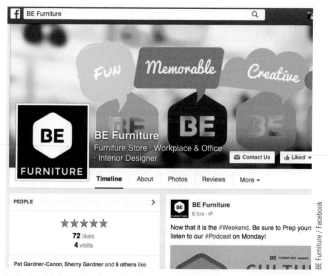

FIGURE 21.4 BE Furniture *Facebook* page.

FIGURE 21.5 BE Furniture home page.

EXERCISE 21.1

Explore BE Furniture's use of multimodal texts in more depth by visiting its website and *Facebook* page. (Note that the company's offerings will likely have changed since this textbook was published.) Identify and analyze the decisions—about purpose, audience, genre, and tone—that went into choosing and creating its images, videos, audio clips, and any other multimodal components.

21d Developing Multimodal Texts

Many college writing assignments lend themselves to a combination of print, electronic, and face-to-face texts. For example, imagine a writing situation in which you have been assigned a project to increase enrollment at your school. Before beginning, you review the content of Chapter 1. Your first step is to define your rhetorical situation.

Audience	Students at your college
Purpose	To encourage students to come to a campus located in an exciting community
Context	The need to increase enrollment at the school

Next, begin thinking about the type of text you want to develop. Do you want to send prospective students an email that contains pictures of the school? Do you want to plan a *PowerPoint* or *Prezi* presentation for prospective students who are visiting campus? Do you want to build a website that contains video clips of campus life, interviews with students, and links to the school newspaper? Spend time thinking about your options as well as the advantages (and disadvantages) of each type of text.

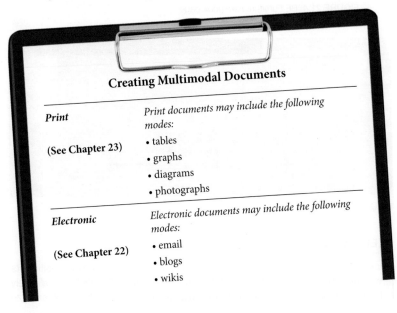

Creating Multimodal Documents

Print **(See Chapter 23)**	*Print documents may include the following modes:* • tables • graphs • diagrams • photographs
Electronic **(See Chapter 22)**	*Electronic documents may include the following modes:* • email • blogs • wikis

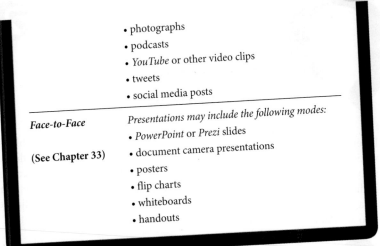

- photographs
- podcasts
- *YouTube* or other video clips
- tweets
- social media posts

Face-to-Face **(See Chapter 33)**	*Presentations may include the following modes:* • *PowerPoint* or *Prezi* slides • document camera presentations • posters • flip charts • whiteboards • handouts

---

CHECKLIST
Selecting Modes

❑ Who is the audience? What is the best medium to use to reach this audience?

❑ What modes can you use in your document? Which will best help you convey your message?

❑ What is the purpose of this project? What genres will best accomplish this purpose? How will each genre address the needs of the audience?

❑ Is there a secondary audience? If so, how will information be shared with multiple audiences?

❑ How do you think your audience will respond to the various modes?

EXERCISE 21.2

Complete the assignment outlined in **21d**: create a multimodal text (such as a website, a podcast, an email with links and photos, or a *PowerPoint* presentation) whose purpose is to help increase enrollment at your school. Use the Checklist above to guide your work. Your instructor may assign this as a group project.

CHAPTER 22

Composing in Digital Environments

In email, social-networking sites, digital classroom environments, blogs, wikis, and chat rooms, electronic communication occurs daily on a wide variety of topics. Because of the nature of the Internet, online communication is different from print communication, specifically in the ways readers interact with the text. In order to write effectively for this type of audience, you should be aware of the demands of writing in digital environments.

22a Considering Audience and Purpose

The most obvious difference between digital communication and print communication is the nature of the **audience**. Audiences for print documents are relatively passive: they read a discussion in linear fashion from beginning to end, form their own ideas about it, and then stop. Depending on the writing situation, however, audiences for electronic documents often respond differently. Although in some cases readers may be passive, in other cases they can be quite active, posting and emailing responses and directly communicating with the writer (sometimes in real time) as well as with one another.

The **purpose** of electronic communication may also be quite different from that of print communication. Unlike print documents, which appear as carefully crafted finished products in newspapers and magazines, electronic documents are frequently written in immediate response to other people's arguments or ideas. In fact, by including links to a writer's email address or to a blog, many online documents are works in progress, encouraging readers to respond—or, in the case of wikis, to add content. For this reason, in addition to trying to inform or persuade, the purpose of electronic documents may also be to support, refute, react, clarify, expand, or correct.

22b Writing in a Digital Classroom

Much of the writing you do in a digital classroom involves **collaboration**, a process in which more than one person contributes to the creation, revising, and editing of a document. In some cases, students write a draft of a document and then post it or distribute it electronically to members of a peer-editing group, who then make revision suggestions. Comments can be sent via email

Observing Netiquette

Netiquette refers to the guidelines that responsible users of the Internet should follow when they write in cyberspace. When you communicate via the Internet, keep the following guidelines in mind:

- **Don't shout.** All-uppercase letters indicate that a person is SHOUTING.
- **Watch your tone.** Make sure you send the message you actually intend to send. What might seem humorous to you may seem disrespectful to someone else.
- **Be careful what you write.** Be sure to consider carefully what you have written. Remember that digital files are permanent. Once you hit *Send*, it is often too late to call the message back.
- **Don't flame.** When you flame, you send an insulting electronic message. This tactic is not only immature, but also rude and annoying.
- **Make sure you use the correct electronic address.** Be certain that your message goes to the right person. Nothing is more embarrassing than sending an email to the wrong address.
- **Use your computer ethically and responsibly.** Don't use computer labs for personal communications or for entertainment. Not only is this a misuse of the facility but it also ties up equipment that others may be waiting to use.

or they can be inserted into the document with *Microsoft Word*'s Comment tool or with Track Changes. In other cases, students meet in groups (either electronically or face-to-face) and jointly contribute to the prewriting, drafting, and revision and editing of an entire document.

Central to this type of instruction is communication between students and between instructors and students. With **synchronous communication**, all parties involved in the communication process are online at the same time and can be involved in a real-time conversation. Chat rooms, instant messaging, and texting are examples of synchronous communication. With **asynchronous communication**, there is a delay between the time a message is sent and the time it is received. Asynchronous exchanges occur with email, blogs, wikis, web forums, and discussion forums.

Increasingly—both in online environments and in traditional class-rooms—instructors are using the Internet as well as specific web-based technology to teach writing. Some of the most popular tools that students use to create web-based content in digital writing environments are discussed in the pages that follow.

❶ Using Email

Email enables you to exchange ideas with classmates, ask questions of your instructors, and communicate with the writing center or other campus services. You can insert email links in web documents, and you can transfer files as email attachments from one computer to another. In many classes, you submit writing assignments as email attachments.

When you write email messages to your instructor, keep in mind that your communication should be fairly formal. Use the type of language that you would use to address a supervisor in a work environment. Include clear subject lines, and use appropriate salutations ("Dear Professor Jewett," never "Hi Prof") and complimentary closes.

Close-Up　EMAIL ADDRESSES

Avoid using an email address that is cute or witty or that contains puns or double entendres. Although it may be fine for your friends, this kind of address is not appropriate for the classroom or for a résumé or job application letter. Consider maintaining two separate email accounts— one for your personal use and one for school and work communication.

❷ Using Blogs

A **blog** (short for web log) is like an online personal journal. Most blogs offer commentary, news, or personal reflections and reactions—usually presented in reverse chronological order, with the most recent entry first. Blogs can also function as online diaries, communicating the personal views of the author.

Some teachers of writing encourage students to create and maintain blogs that function as online writing journals. Blogs are not limited to text; they can contain photographs, videos, music, audio, and personal artwork as well as links to websites. Most course management systems (such as *Blackboard* and *Canvas*) make it easy for instructors or students to create a blog and post comments. In addition, Web 2.0 technologies, such as *Blogger* and *WordPress*, are open-source platforms that students can use to create their own blogs. Although many blogs are open to everyone, some are password protected.

The following excerpt shows a post and two comments on a class blog for a first-year writing course. The student posted her draft on the course website and received comments from several students. These comments, along with advice in an email from her instructor, helped her to revise her essay. (As you can see, the tone in a blog is more conversational than the tone in other electronic forums used for class.)

Wednesday, September 30, 2015

The Omnivore's Dilemma by Michael Pollan

In an excerpt from his book *The Omnivore's Dilemma*, Michael Pollan discusses the drinking habits of nineteenth-century Americans and makes a connection between the cause of this "national drinking binge" and the factors behind our twenty-first-century unhealthy diets. In both cases, he blames the overproduction of grain by American farmers. He links nineteenth-century overproduction of corn and the current overproduction of grain with various social crises. Although there are certainly other causes of our current problems with obesity, particularly among young children, Pollan's analogy makes sense.

Posted by Julie at 7:14 PM

2 COMMENTS:

Alison said . . .
You did a good job of summarizing Pollan's main points in that part of the book. But I think you could give more details about the "various social crises" Pollan is writing about. I feel like I need to know what they are to understand why he's writing about them in the first place. Maybe use a quote here?

Jeremy said . . .
My response to Pollan was like yours, but at the end I gave more of an evaluation of Pollan's book, I think. Yours just ends with "Pollan's analogy makes sense," and I guess I want to know why you think it makes sense, and why it's important. I'm thinking you could just add another sentence that kind of sums things up—and explains your opinion of the book.

3 Using Wikis

Unlike a blog, which is created by an individual and does not allow visitors to edit the posted content, a **wiki** (Hawaiian for *fast* or *quick*) is a website that allows users to add, remove, or change content. The best-known wiki is *Wikipedia*, the online encyclopedia.

In the writing classroom, wikis are used for collaborative writing. They allow students to add (or delete) content while working on collaboratively produced projects. Groups of students use wikis to brainstorm and to compile class notes. Wiki sites also enable students to view the history of a revision and to compare the relative merits of various drafts of an essay. In research projects, wikis permit students to collaborate on developing research questions, to exchange hyperlinks, to share bibliographical information, to collaborate on drafts of their essays, and to get help with documentation.

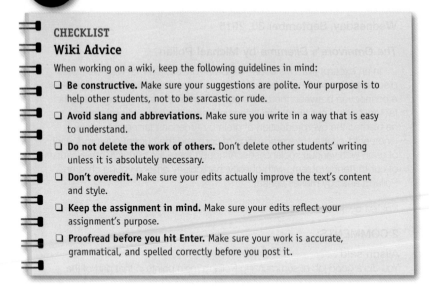

CHECKLIST
Wiki Advice

When working on a wiki, keep the following guidelines in mind:

❑ **Be constructive.** Make sure your suggestions are polite. Your purpose is to help other students, not to be sarcastic or rude.

❑ **Avoid slang and abbreviations.** Make sure you write in a way that is easy to understand.

❑ **Do not delete the work of others.** Don't delete other students' writing unless it is absolutely necessary.

❑ **Don't overedit.** Make sure your edits actually improve the text's content and style.

❑ **Keep the assignment in mind.** Make sure your edits reflect your assignment's purpose.

❑ **Proofread before you hit Enter.** Make sure your work is accurate, grammatical, and spelled correctly before you post it.

4 Using Listservs

Listservs (sometimes called **discussion lists**) are electronic mailing lists to which users must subscribe. They enable individuals to communicate with groups of people interested in particular topics. (Many schools, and even individual courses, have listservs.) Subscribers to a listserv send emails to a main email address, and these messages are routed to all members of the group. Listservs can be especially useful in composition classes, permitting students to post comments on reading assignments as well as to discuss other subjects with the entire class.

5 Using Podcasts

Originally, the term **podcast** referred to material that could be downloaded to Apple's iPod. Now, however, it refers to any audio broadcast that has been converted to an MP3 or similar format for playback on the Internet. You can access a podcast with a computer, with an iPad, or with an MP3 playback device.

Podcasting is becoming increasingly common in college classrooms. On the most basic level, instructors podcast class lectures that students can access at their leisure. Instructors also use podcasts to give feedback on students' projects, to distribute supplementary material such as audio recordings or speeches, to record student presentations, or to communicate class information or news. Students may also be asked to analyze podcasts of political speeches, radio programs, or short stories from radio programs such as National Public Radio's *Selected Shorts*. Some instructors even ask students to make their own podcasts. For example, students can read their own essays and add sound clips or visual files.

6 Using *Twitter* and *Facebook*

Twitter is a social network that enables users to send messages called *tweets* to a list of followers. Tweets can be made public, thereby giving anyone the ability to view them, or they can be restricted to friends or members of a particular group. A number of businesses use *Twitter* to keep customers informed, and political candidates use *Twitter* to keep constituents updated.

Instructors also use *Twitter* as a tool to teach writing. Because tweets have a one-hundred-and-forty character limit, they force students to be concise. As a result, in some writing classes, instructors ask students to tweet their thesis statements to the class. This exercise encourages students to state the thesis in clear, precise language. In addition, instructors can use *Twitter* as an easy way to get in touch with students (*Don't forget. Class cancelled tomorrow.*) and to reinforce important course concepts (*Your arguments must be supported by evidence. Look out for logical fallacies.*).

Some instructors form *Facebook* groups and post links to websites, documents, and other links on the group pages. Students can ask questions about class assignments and discuss topics that interest them. Joining these groups is usually optional because some students have concerns about *Facebook*'s security.

EXERCISE 22.1

Imagine that you have the flu and are too sick to go anywhere for a week. Compose each of the following digital documents:

1. **An email:** Let your instructor know why you will not be in class.
2. **A text:** Ask a classmate from that course to take notes for you.
3. **A *Facebook* post:** On the *Facebook* page of an organization you are part of, let attendees to an event you are sponsoring know that you will not be able to attend.

As you draft each document, carefully consider your audience and purpose as well as the genre you are using.

CHAPTER 23

Designing Effective Documents

Document design refers to the principles that help you determine how to design a piece of written work—print or digital—so that it communicates your ideas clearly and effectively. Although formatting conventions—for example, how tables and charts are constructed and how information is arranged on a title page—may differ from discipline to discipline, all well-designed documents share the same general characteristics: *an effective format, clear headings, useful lists,* and *helpful visuals.*

23a Creating an Effective Visual Format

An effective document contains visual cues that help readers identify, read, and interpret information on a page. For example, wide margins can give a page a balanced, uncluttered appearance; white space can set off and emphasize information; and a distinctive type size and typeface can make a word or phrase stand out on a page.

1 Margins

Margins frame a page and keep it from looking overcrowded. Because long lines of text can overwhelm readers and make a document difficult to read, every page should have margins. Different disciplines have somewhat different specifications concerning margins. For example, MLA style requires a one-inch margin at the top, bottom, and sides of a page. APA style calls for *at least* a one-inch margin on all sides of a page. CSE style, however, does not specify a style for an undergraduate essay. Because conventions vary from discipline to discipline, before you type an essay, you should be familiar with your instructor's formatting guidelines.

In general, you should **justify** (uniformly align, except for paragraph indentations) the left-hand margin. You can either leave a ragged edge on the right, or you can justify your text so all the words are aligned evenly along the right margin.

2 White Space

White space is the area of a page that is intentionally left blank. Used effectively, white space can isolate material and thus focus a reader's attention on it.

You can use white space around a block of text—a paragraph or a section, for example—or around visuals such as charts, graphs, and photographs. In documents such as flyers and brochures, you might use white space to set off blocks of text for emphasis. Used judiciously, white space can eliminate clutter, break a discussion into manageable chunks, and help readers process information more easily.

Close-Up BORDERS, HORIZONTAL RULES, AND SHADING

Your word-processing program enables you to create borders, horizontal rules, and shaded areas of text. Border and shading options are usually found under the Format menu. With these features, you can select line style, thickness, and color and adjust white space, boxed text, and the degree of shading. Keep in mind that these features should be used only when appropriate, so check with your instructor.

3 Color

Color (when used in moderation) can emphasize and clarify information while making it visually appealing. In addition to using color to emphasize information, you can use a color scheme to set off and identify different types of information. For example, titles can be one color and subheadings can be another, complementary, color. (You can also use color to differentiate the segments of a chart or the bars of a graph.) Software applications, including *Microsoft Word* and *PowerPoint*, contain templates (such as the one shown in Figure 23.1) that make it easy for you to choose a color scheme of your own. Remember, however, that too many colors can confuse readers and detract from your visual emphasis.

4 Typeface and Type Size

Your computer gives you a wide variety of typefaces and type sizes (measured in **points**) from which to choose.

Typefaces are distinctively designed sets of letters, numbers, and punctuation marks. The typeface you choose should be suitable for your purpose and audience. In your academic writing, avoid fancy or elaborate typefaces—*script* or old English, for example—that call attention to themselves and are difficult to read. Instead, select a typeface that is simple and direct—Cambria, Times New Roman, or Arial, for example. In nonacademic documents—such as web pages and flyers—decorative typefaces may be used to emphasize information or attract a reader's attention.

You also have a wide variety of **type sizes** available to you. For most of your academic essays, you will use 10- or 12-point type (headings will sometimes be larger). Documents such as advertisements, brochures, and web pages, however, may require a variety of type sizes.

5 Line Spacing

Line spacing refers to the amount of space between the lines of a document. If the lines are too far apart, the text will seem to lack cohesion; if the lines are too close together, the text will appear crowded and be difficult to read. The type of writing you do determines the line spacing. For example, the paragraphs of business letters, memos, and some reports are usually single-spaced and separated by a double space, but the paragraphs of academic essays are usually double-spaced.

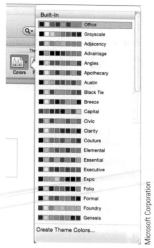

FIGURE 23.1 *Microsoft Power-Point* theme colors menu.

Microsoft Corporation

23b Using Headings

Used effectively, **headings** act as signals that help readers process information, and they also break up a text, making it inviting and easy to read. Different academic disciplines have different requirements concerning headings. For this reason, consult the appropriate style manual (or your instructor) before inserting headings in an essay.

1 Number of Headings

The number of headings you use depends on the document. A long, complicated document will need more headings than a shorter, less complicated one. Keep in mind that too few headings may not be of much use, but too many headings will make your document look like an outline.

2 Phrasing

See 38a

Headings should be brief, informative, and to the point. They can be single words—**Summary** or **Introduction**, for example—or they can be phrases (always stated in <u>parallel</u> terms): **Traditional Family Patterns, Alternative Family Patterns, Modern Family Patterns**. Finally, headings can be questions (**How Do You Choose a Major?**) or statements (**Choose Your Major Carefully**).

③ Indentation

Indenting is one way of distinguishing one level of heading from another. Keep in mind, however, that style guides for different disciplines provide different guidelines concerning the placement of headings. For example, the APA style guide makes the following recommendations: first-level headings should be centered, second-level headings should be justified left, and third-level headings should be indented one-half inch. Consult the appropriate style manual for guidelines on this issue.

④ Typographical Emphasis

You can emphasize important words in headings (and further distinguish different levels) by using **boldface**, *italics*, or ALL CAPITAL LETTERS. Used in moderation, these distinctive type styles make a text easier to read. Used excessively, however, they slow readers down.

⑤ Consistency

Headings at the same level should have the same typeface, type size, spacing, and color. Thus, if one first-level heading is boldfaced and centered, all other first-level headings must be boldfaced and centered. Using consistent patterns reinforces the connection between content and ideas and makes a document easier to understand.

Note: Never separate a heading from the text that goes with it: if a heading is at the bottom of one page and the text that goes with it is on the next page, move the heading onto the next page so that readers can see the heading and the text together.

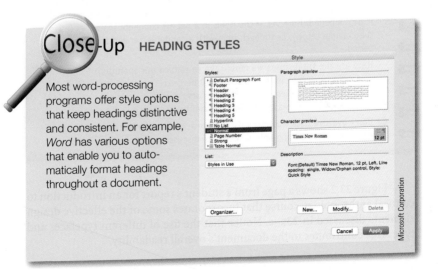

Close-Up   HEADING STYLES

Most word-processing programs offer style options that keep headings distinctive and consistent. For example, *Word* has various options that enable you to automatically format headings throughout a document.

Microsoft Corporation

23c Constructing Lists

By breaking a long discussion into a series of key ideas, a list makes information easier to understand. By isolating individual pieces of information and by providing visual cues (such as bullets or numbers), a list also directs readers to important information.

CHECKLIST
Constructing Effective Lists

When constructing lists, you should follow these guidelines:

❑ **Indent each item.** Each item in a list should be indented so that it stands out from the text around it.

❑ **Set off items with bullets or numbers.** Use **bullets** when items are not organized according to any particular sequence (the members of a club, for example). Use **numbers** when you want to indicate that items are organized according to a sequence (the steps in a process, for example).

❑ **Introduce a list with a complete sentence.** Do not simply drop a list into a document; introduce it with a complete sentence (followed by a colon) that tells readers what to look for in the list.

❑ **Use parallel structure.** Lists are easiest to read when all items are parallel and about the same length.

A decrease in several factors can cause high unemployment:
• consumer spending
• factory orders
• factory output

❑ **Capitalize and punctuate correctly.** If the items in a list are fragments (as in the example above), begin each item with a lowercase letter, and do not end it with a period. However, if the items in a list are complete sentences (as in the example below), begin each item with a capital letter and end it with a period.

Here are the three steps we must take to reduce our spending:
1. We must cut our workforce by 10 percent.
2. We must use less expensive vendors.
3. We must decrease overtime payments.

❑ **Don't overuse lists.** Too many lists will give readers the impression that you are simply enumerating points instead of discussing them.

Figure 23.2 shows a page from a student's report for an introduction to cultural anthropology course that incorporates some of the effective design elements discussed in **23a–c**. Notice that the use of different typefaces and type sizes contributes to the document's overall readability.

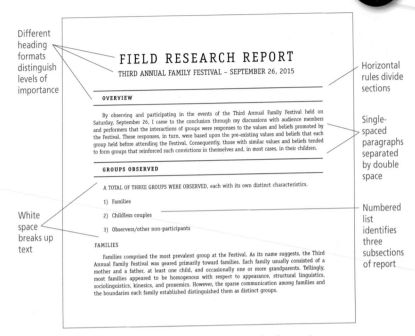

Different heading formats distinguish levels of importance

Horizontal rules divide sections

Single-spaced paragraphs separated by double space

White space breaks up text

Numbered list identifies three subsections of report

FIGURE 23.2 A well-designed page from a student's report. Created by Karen Mauk.

EXERCISE 23.1

Select two different documents—for example, a page from a procedure manual and an invitation, or a report and a flyer. Then, make a list of the design elements each document contains. Finally, evaluate the relative effectiveness of the two documents, given their intended audiences.

23d Using Visuals

Visuals, such as tables, graphs, diagrams, and photographs, can help you convey complex ideas that are difficult to communicate with words. They can also help you attract readers' attention.

Note: Use a visual in the text only if you plan to discuss it in your essay (otherwise, place the visual in an appendix).

1 Tables

Tables present data in a condensed, visual format—arranged in rows and columns. Tables may contain numerical data, text, or a combination of the two. When you plan your table, make sure you include only the data that you will need; discard information that is too detailed or difficult to understand. Keep in mind that tables interrupt the flow of your discussion, so include only those that are necessary to support your points. (The table in Figure 23.3 reports the student writer's original research and therefore needs no documentation.)

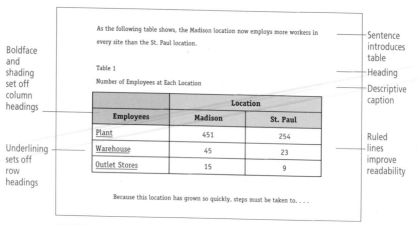

As the following table shows, the Madison location now employs more workers in every site than the St. Paul location. — Sentence introduces table

Boldface and shading set off column headings

Table 1 — Heading

Number of Employees at Each Location — Descriptive caption

Employees	Location	
	Madison	St. Paul
Plant	451	254
Warehouse	45	23
Outlet Stores	15	9

Underlining sets off row headings

Ruled lines improve readability

Because this location has grown so quickly, steps must be taken to. . . .

FIGURE 23.3 Sample table from a student essay.

2 Graphs

Like tables, **graphs** present data in visual form. Whereas tables may present specific numerical data, graphs convey the general pattern or trend that the data suggest. Because graphs tend to be more general (and therefore less accurate) than tables, they are frequently accompanied by tables. Figure 23.4 is an example of a bar graph showing data from a source.

3 Diagrams

A **diagram** calls readers' attention to specific details of a mechanism or object. Diagrams are often used in scientific and technical writing to clarify concepts that are difficult to explain in words. Figure 23.5, which illustrates the sections of an orchestra, serves a similar purpose in a music education essay.

4 Photographs

Photographs enable you to show exactly what something or someone looks like—an animal in its natural habitat, a painting, or an actor in costume, for example. Although it is easy to paste photographs directly into a text, you should do so only when they support or illustrate your points. The photograph of a wooded trail in Figure 23.6 illustrates the student writer's description.

the demographics of college students are changing. According to a 2002 US Department of Education report entitled *Nontraditional Undergraduates*, the percentage of students who could be classified as "nontraditional" has increased over the last decade (see fig. 1).

Data ———

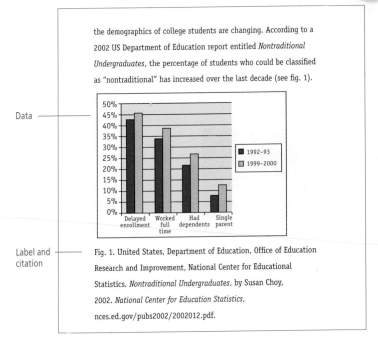

Label and citation ———

Fig. 1. United States, Department of Education, Office of Education Research and Improvement, National Center for Educational Statistics. *Nontraditional Undergraduates*, by Susan Choy, 2002. *National Center for Education Statistics*, nces.ed.gov/pubs2002/2002012.pdf.

FIGURE 23.4 Sample graph from a student essay. © US Department of Education.

The sections of an orchestra are arranged precisely to allow for a powerful and cohesive performance. Fig. 1 illustrates the placement of individual sections of an orchestra.

Label, descriptive caption, and citation ———

Fig. 1. The sections of an orchestra. *The Lyric Opera of Waco: Education Outreach*, 23 Aug. 2012, www.operabase.com/mkhouse.cgi?lang=en&house=nawc.

FIGURE 23.5 Sample diagram from a student essay. Diagram © Lyric Opera of Waco.

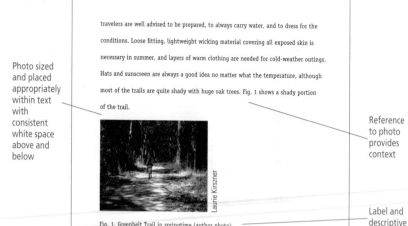

Photo sized and placed appropriately within text with consistent white space above and below

Reference to photo provides context

Label and descriptive caption

> travelers are well advised to be prepared, to always carry water, and to dress for the
> conditions. Loose fitting, lightweight wicking material covering all exposed skin is
> necessary in summer, and layers of warm clothing are needed for cold-weather outings.
> Hats and sunscreen are always a good idea no matter what the temperature, although
> most of the trails are quite shady with huge oak trees. Fig. 1 shows a shady portion
> of the trail.

Laurie Kirszner

Fig. 1. Greenbelt Trail in springtime (author photo).

FIGURE 23.6 Sample photograph from a student essay.

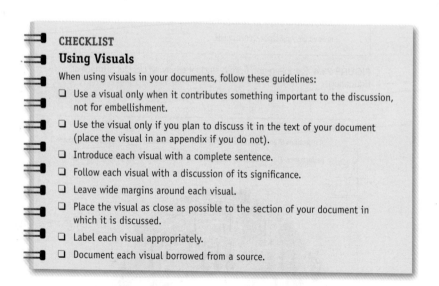

CHECKLIST

Using Visuals

When using visuals in your documents, follow these guidelines:

- ❑ Use a visual only when it contributes something important to the discussion, not for embellishment.
- ❑ Use the visual only if you plan to discuss it in the text of your document (place the visual in an appendix if you do not).
- ❑ Introduce each visual with a complete sentence.
- ❑ Follow each visual with a discussion of its significance.
- ❑ Leave wide margins around each visual.
- ❑ Place the visual as close as possible to the section of your document in which it is discussed.
- ❑ Label each visual appropriately.
- ❑ Document each visual borrowed from a source.

EXERCISE 23.2

Select three websites: one personal, one academic (such as your school's site), and one professional or organizational (such as that of the American Cancer Society). How do these sites differ in purpose, audience, and tone? How are these differences reflected in the design of each site? Be specific in your response.

PART 7

Composing in the Disciplines

Composing in the Disciplines

? Frequently Asked Questions

Composing in the Disciplines: An Overview

HUMANITIES

Disciplines	Genres	Style and Format
Languages	Response	*Style*
Literature	Rhetorical analysis	Specialized vocabulary
Philosophy	Literary analysis	Direct quotations from sources
History	Annotated bibliography	
Religion	Bibliographic essay	*Format*
Art history	Book or film review	Moderate use of internal
Music		headings or visuals

SOCIAL SCIENCES

Disciplines	Genres	Style and Format
Anthropology	Personal experience essay	*Style*
Psychology	Book review	Specialized vocabulary,
Economics	Case study	including statistical
Business	Annotated bibliography	terminology
Education	Literature review	*Format*
Sociology	Proposal	Internal headings
Political science		Visuals (graphs, maps,
Social work		flowcharts, photographs)
Criminal justice		Numerical data (in tables)
Linguistics		

NATURAL AND APPLIED SCIENCES

Disciplines	Genres	Style and Format
Natural Sciences	Laboratory report	*Style*
Biology	Observation essay	Frequent use of passive voice
Chemistry	Literature survey	Few direct quotations
Physics	Abstract	
Astronomy	Biographical essay	*Format*
Geology		Internal headings
Mathematics		Tables, graphs, and illus-
		trations (exact formats
Applied Sciences		vary)
Engineering		
Computer science		
Nursing		
Pharmacy		

(continued)

Composing in the Disciplines: An Overview *(continued)*

Documentation	Research Methods and Sources
See Ch. 17 English, languages, philosophy: MLA See Ch. 19 History, art history: Chicago	Online sources Library sources (print and electronic) Interviews Observations (museums, concerts) Oral history

Documentation	Research Methods and Sources
See Ch. 18 APA	Online sources Library sources (print and electronic) Surveys Observations (behavior of groups and individuals)

Documentation	Research Methods and Sources
See Ch. 20 Biological sciences: CSE Other scientific disciplines use a variety of different documentation styles; **see 20d**	Online sources Library sources (print and electronic) Observations Experiments Surveys

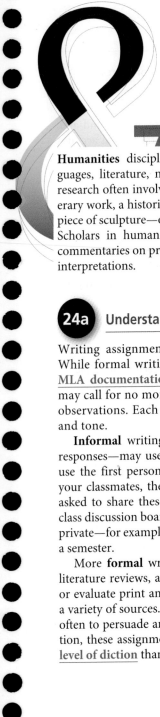

CHAPTER 24

Composing in the Humanities

Humanities disciplines include art history, drama, film, history, languages, literature, music, philosophy, and religion. In these disciplines, research often involves analyzing or interpreting a **primary source**—a literary work, a historical document, a musical composition, or a painting or piece of sculpture—or making connections between one work and another. Scholars in humanities disciplines may also cite **secondary sources**—commentaries on primary sources—to support their points or develop new interpretations.

24a Understanding the Rhetorical Situation

Writing assignments in the humanities may be formal or informal. While formal writing may require you to use academic discourse and MLA documentation style and format, informal writing assignments may call for no more than your personal responses to your reading and observations. Each of these two types of writing has a distinct purpose and tone.

See Ch. 17

Informal writing assignments—for example, journals, reflections, or responses—may use a relatively conversational, even colloquial, style and use the first person (*I*). Often, your instructor will specify an audience: your classmates, the instructor, or someone else. Sometimes you may be asked to share these writings, perhaps by posting regular responses to a class discussion board. At other times, you may keep these writings entirely private—for example, in a journal that reflects on your learning throughout a semester.

More **formal** writing assignments—literary analyses, research papers, literature reviews, and so on—often require that you summarize, analyze, or evaluate print and electronic sources and synthesize information from a variety of sources. Because the purpose of a formal writing assignment is often to persuade an audience to accept a particular point of view or position, these assignments require a more objective tone and a more formal level of diction than informal assignments do.

See Ch. 15

See 39b

24b　Genres

Assignments in the humanities call for a variety of different genres.

1　Response

In some humanities disciplines (particularly literature, music, and art), you may be asked to write a **response**, an informal first-person account of your reactions to a literary work, a painting, a dance performance, or a concert.

Assignment (World Music)

Attend one of the performances offered by the Music and Drama Department during the upcoming month. Then, write a response that expresses your reactions to the performance. What was memorable or remarkable? How did the audience react at particular moments? How did you feel as you were watching and listening, and how did you feel when the performance was over?

Sample Response (Excerpt)

When I first arrived, I saw that the people in the audience were pretty much who I expected to see at a classical music recital, including quite a few faculty. (I'm sure they were shocked to see me there.) The audience was quiet as they waited for Chu's entrance; everyone just kind of sat looking at the darkened stage, which contained a very large grand piano and a cello. When Chu came on stage, the applause was almost deafening. I hadn't realized he was so famous. The audience quieted down when he sat down and picked up his bow. The first item on the program was a solo titled *Allegretto Minimoso*. I have to admit that once Chu started to play his cello, I didn't even notice what was going on in the audience anymore. His music made me think of tall cliffs towering over the ocean under a bright sky during a storm. I was hooked from the first moment.

EXERCISE 24.1

Write a two-page response to describe your reactions to a poem, story, novel, work of art, film, play, dance or musical performance, or recorded piece of music. Remember to write your essay in the first person.

2 Book or Film Review

Instructors in the humanities may require students to write **reviews** of books, films, or art exhibits. The purpose of a review is to evaluate a work, exhibit, or performance and perhaps make recommendations to readers.

Assignment (Journalism)

Write an informal review of a film you liked when you were a child, contrasting your reactions to the film then with your reactions to it now. In choosing a film, remember that your review will be submitted to our school newspaper, where your primary audience will be students about your age.

Sample Film Review

I have always been a fan of musicals, handsome boys, and history lessons. Kenny Ortega's 1992 film *Newsies* finds a way to incorporate all these elements into one entertaining (although flawed) package.

The film begins with a narrator describing New York City in 1899 through the eyes of the poor newspaper boys who sell papers on the street. The "newsies" walk the dirty streets of New York shoeless and homeless while the rich and powerful newspaper publishers squeeze as much money as they can from the public. *Newsies* focuses on two young boys who sell newspapers for some of the most famous publishers of the time, including Joseph Pulitzer.

When Pulitzer (Robert Duvall) decides to raise the cost of the boys' newspaper purchase by a tenth of a percent, they are outraged. Jack Kelly (Christian Bale) and David Jacobs (David Moscow) set out to rally the rest of their gang, as well as the "street rats" of the other boroughs, to help fight "old man Pulitzer." At the same time, Warden Snyder (Kevin Tighe), the operator of The Refuge, a poorly run and corrupt orphanage, is trying to find Jack to bring him back to the orphanage. While trying to start a strike and evade Warden Snyder, the boys attract the attention of Bryan Denton (Bill Pullman), a reporter for the New York *Sun* who finds their troubles newsworthy.

Musicals like *Newsies* are a guilty pleasure of mine because they are films I loved when I was growing up. The first time I saw this movie, I watched it on TV with my younger brothers. They were bored, but I was swept up by the singing and dancing as well as by the glimpse into a time and place I knew nothing about. And, of course, I loved watching my former heartthrob, Christian Bale; with a handful of strappingly handsome young boys thrown into the mix, *Newsies* is basically the early 1990s version of the present-day *Twilight* films, where young girls' love is directed at Jacob and Edward.

Recently, I watched *Newsies* again, and it was not the pleasurable experience I remembered. Although the film is historically accurate and has a catchy soundtrack, I found it disappointing. Some of the young actors are not all that talented, and some of the singers and dancers are just not polished enough. And, with all the new advances in film and cinematography that have taken place since *Newsies* was made in 1992, it is startling to see backgrounds that are all too noticeably digitally imaged.

As much as I liked this movie when I first saw it, I see now that it is not as good as I thought it was. Still, there are not enough drawbacks to make me completely write it off. It may not measure up to adult standards, but it helps me remember what it was like to be young.

❸ Literature Review

See 11c2

When you are writing a research paper, your instructor may ask you to prepare an **annotated bibliography**—a list of sources (accompanied by full source information) followed by summary and evaluation. In some cases, you may also be asked to write a **literature review** that discusses these sources and their relevance to your research.

Assignment (Nineteenth-Century American History)

Write a literature review that discusses three of the sources you use in your research paper. Do not simply describe or summarize your sources; synthesize, compare, and contrast them, developing your own point of view. Be sure to include paraphrases and quotations from your sources as well as a works-cited list.

Sample Literature Review (Excerpt)

The women mill operatives of Lowell, Massachusetts, produced a variety of writings in different genres that portray the ways in which they negotiated their everyday urban experiences in their boardinghouses and on the factory production line. While their descriptions of daily life in the mill town can be read as a story of their journey to financial independence, these writings also reveal the women's collective coming of political age.

The *Lowell Offering*, first published in 1840, was a "monthly magazine, thirty pages long, priced at six and one-quarter cents an issue" (Eisler 33) that began as a corporately owned concern but later was bought, run, and edited by two women who were both former mill operatives. While the publishers of the *Offering* focused on presenting the working women's own creations, The Factory Girl's Garland, also begun in 1840 (only to fold less than a year later), was more of a "liberal reformist paper [that] spoke paternalistically in favor of the mill women, and at times even preached at them" (Vogel 791).

Jean Marie Lutes explains that some labor reformists among the operatives found the "sentimental tales, romantic stories, and poetic rhyme" of the *Offering* too "neutral," accusing it of having "neglected the operative as a working being" (8). Therefore, they chose to represent their concerns through the *Voice of Industry*, a newspaper whose "case for reform," Lutes argues, was only made possible through the preliminary cultural work performed by the less critical *Offering*: while the *Voice* explicitly called for recognition of working class women's rights, it was the *Offering* that "initiate[d] the discourse of female working-class culture" (9). These periodicals demonstrate various ways in which the operatives initiated change for white working-class women through both their physical and their literary labors.

Works Cited

Eisler, Benita. *The Lowell Offering: Writings by New England Mill Women (1840-1845)*. Norton, 1998.

Lutes, Jean Marie. "Cultivating Domesticity: Labor Reform and the Literary Culture of the Lowell Mill Girls." *Works and Days,* vol. 22, no.11, 1993, pp. 7-27.

Vogel, Lise. "Their Own Work: Two Documents from the Nineteenth-Century Labor Movement." *Signs: Journal of Women in Culture and Society*, vol. 1, no.3, 1976, pp. 787-802.

EXERCISE 24.2

Compile a working annotated bibliography or literature review for a research project you are currently developing. Be sure to provide a summary and brief analysis of each source.

④ Analysis

Instructors in various humanities disciplines often ask students to analyze texts. (For an example of a rhetorical analysis, see **25c**; for an example of a literary analysis, see **26c**.) An analysis takes apart a print or visual text, considering its various components in order to make sense of the whole.

Assignment (Mass Communications)

Research an ad campaign for a specific product, service, or cause. Select a poster, billboard, or other visual from the campaign, and write an essay analyzing the ad's purpose, target audience, and overall message. Describe how the ad's words and images work together to reach the intended audience, and explain who benefits from the ad's message, and how.

Sample Analysis (Excerpt)

The National Teen Dating Abuse Helpline, along with former Texas Attorney General Greg Abbott, launched a multimedia campaign aimed at helping to prevent teen dating abuse. The "LOVE" campaign has produced posters as well as public service announcements, songs, website images, and other materials to alert teens to the prevalence and danger of dating abuse. One poster (see fig. 1) shows the word *Love* written in a graffiti style, superimposed over a photograph of a teen couple. This ad illustrates the techniques the campaign uses to promote respectful and supportive romantic relationships to its teen audience.

Fig. 1. "LOVE" campaign poster. *loveisrespect.org,* 2009.

The "LOVE" poster uses words and images to convey the campaign's overall message: that teens can prevent and stop dating abuse when they are given the resources they need to identify warning signs and to get help. The central image of a neon pink stylized "Love" logo, framed with splattered paint and a smaller, repeated version of the logo, emphasizes the ad's positive focus on what love should be: fun, exciting, and—above all—respectful. In addition, the text beneath the logo uses an informal, conversational style (rather than formal, grammatically correct language) to appeal to its young audience. The whitewashed image behind the logo, showing the close-up embrace of a teen couple, subtly supports the ad's message that teens should trust their own instincts and ask for help when "things don't feel right."

Together, the poster's words and images work to empower teens to build healthy, loving relationships and to recognize the signs of dating abuse in time to stop it. By focusing on *love* rather than *abuse,* the ad maintains an upbeat message that supports teen dating as long as it is loving and respectful. The concluding advice to "call us or chat online," along with the Helpline's contact information, gives teens a place to go when abuse happens, enabling them not just to recognize the problem but also to do something about it.

24c Conventions of Style, Format, and Documentation

1 Style and Format

Each humanities discipline has its own specialized vocabulary. You should use the technical terms used in the field, but be careful not to overuse such terminology. You can use the first person (*I*) when you are expressing your own reactions and convictions—for example, in a response or a **reflective statement**. In other situations, however, avoid the first person.

See 29b

Although essays in the humanities do not usually include abstracts, internal headings, tables, or graphs, this situation is changing. Be sure you know what your instructor expects.

2 Documentation

Literature and modern and classical language scholars, as well as scholars in music and sometimes in art history, use **MLA documentation style**; history scholars generally use **Chicago style**.

See Ch. 17; Ch. 19

24d Using Sources Ethically

See
Ch. 16

When **plagiarism** occurs in the humanities, it is often the result of inaccurate summarizing and paraphrasing, failure to use quotation marks where they are required, and confusion between original ideas and ideas borrowed from sources.

Whenever you use sources, you must be careful to document them. In this way, you acknowledge the work of others who influenced your ideas or contributed to your conclusions. Take accurate notes; avoid cutting and pasting chunks of information from online sources directly into your essay; and whenever you quote, summarize, or paraphrase, do so honestly. Document ideas as well as words, no matter where they come from. "Borrowing" without acknowledgment is plagiarism, and the penalties for plagiarism can be severe. (You do not have to document

See
16b

common knowledge. If you have any questions about what constitutes common knowledge in a particular humanities discipline, check with your instructor.)

24e Research Sources

Each discipline within the humanities has its own methodology, so it is important to know not only the sources or tools that are used by scholars in a particular field but also the way students and scholars conduct research.

In literature, for example, scholars may analyze, explain, interpret, or evaluate the text of a poem, short story, novel, or play or the work of a particular writer. They study the text itself, the **primary** text, but often they also consult other sources for evidence that will support their conclusions. These other sources can be additional primary sources, such as letters or diaries, written at the same time as the primary text. More often, however, the other sources are **secondary sources**, such as commentaries by other scholars, often published long after the primary text was written.

Scholars use the tools of their discipline: library resources (online catalogs or discovery services, specialized databases, periodical indexes, bibliographies, and so on) as well as Internet resources to locate supporting evidence. Library databases or *Google Scholar*, in conjunction with interlibrary loan, tend to be the best ways to access secondary source material (scholarly commentary in the form of journal articles and books), while Internet sources (such as *Google Books* and other websites) can increasingly be relied upon to provide the primary source material (diaries, letters, newspapers of the day), assuming the primary source material is in the public domain (out of copyright).

Similarly, in other humanities disciplines, scholars rely upon library resources and websites to locate primary and secondary source material in their particular discipline. Across all humanities disciplines, scholars will typically examine at least one primary text, which can be a film, a philosophical treatise, a religious text, an image, a historical document, and so on. Secondary sources, usually commentary by other scholars, will be used to support the scholar's ideas about the primary text.

In the writing projects you are likely to be assigned in humanities classes, you may be asked to provide your own analysis, interpretation, or evaluation of an original text, work of art, or musical composition without reading what has already been written about it (the secondary source material). More often, however, you will be asked to use secondary sources to reinforce your conclusions, and you will need to **evaluate** the scholarly value and appropriateness of these secondary sources carefully before you use them.

See
Ch. 13

Doing library research in the humanities does not always require that you know what the latest thinking is about a particular work, writer, idea, or theory. In fact, older journal articles and books may be as valuable as (or even more valuable than) recent ones, and some topics are more time-sensitive than others. Be sure to consult with your instructor about the research specifications of the particular assignment.

You can begin your research by consulting the research guides for your discipline, authored by subject-specialist reference librarians. These guides can often be found on your library's website. From these research guides, navigate either to the recommended reference works in the discipline (to get the big picture and to identify the big questions scholars are grappling with concerning your topic) or to the core databases in your discipline (to identify the areas of interest to scholars in a given discipline).

Close-Up FINDING ADDITIONAL SOURCES

Some online databases offer citation searching, allowing you to search for any articles that cite articles you have found useful. Reading the lists of works cited at the ends of books, chapters, or journal articles may help you to identify other relevant sources. Reference works also frequently include lists of sources for further reading. Finally, annotated bibliographies can help you distinguish the useful sources from the irrelevant ones, saving you a good deal of time in the long run.

❶ Reference Works

Many humanities disciplines have preferred reference works that are valued starting places for understanding the big picture of important topics within the discipline. The best reference works will list at the bottom of each entry the most important scholarship published on a topic. You can then acquire the full text of these recommended publications through the library catalog or discovery service. Consult your library's research guides, discovery service, or catalog to see if your college has access, electronically or in print, to the following top reference works in the humanities: *Oxford Art Online* (*Grove Dictionary*), *The New Grove Dictionary of Music and Musicians, Stanford Encyclopedia of Philosophy, Encyclopedia of Latin American History & Culture, American National Biography, Oxford Dictionary of National Biography*, and *Dictionary of Literary Biography*. Finally, many reference works across multiple disciplines can be searched simultaneously in meta-reference databases, such as *Credo Reference* or *Gale Virtual Reference Library*.

❷ Core Databases in the Humanities

Specialized databases are available for each humanities discipline. These databases feature peer-reviewed journal articles, but they may incorporate citations of books and book chapters as well. The databases can be searched individually or collectively using the library's discovery service, usually located on the library home page.

Some of the most helpful databases for humanities disciplines include *Art Abstracts/Art Full Text//Art Source; MLA International Bibliography; JSTOR; ATLA Religion; Philosopher's Index; America: History and Life; Historical Abstracts; Project MUSE; International Bibliography of Theatre & Dance*; and *RILM Abstracts of Music Literature*. Consult the library website, especially the research guide appropriate to the discipline, or ask a reference librarian about the availability of these and other databases in your library.

❸ Other Sources of Information

Research in the humanities is not limited to print and electronic resources. For example, historians may do interviews and archival work; art historians visit museums and galleries; and music scholars attend concerts.

CHAPTER 25

Composing a Rhetorical Analysis

25a Using Rhetorical Analysis

When you consider how a catalog description persuaded you to take a particular course, how an advertisement convinced you to buy a specific phone, or why you cannot stop thinking about the lyrics to a certain song, you are engaging in rhetorical analysis.

In an academic context, writers use **rhetorical analysis** to break down and consider how, why, and whether a text—written or visual—works. This means considering not just what a text says but how the text achieves its purpose. In other words, you consider what rhetorical techniques the writer uses, and what logical, ethical, or emotional <u>appeals</u> he or she employs.

See
8b3

Writing a rhetorical analysis also involves examining the text's <u>rhetorical situation</u>: its purpose, author, audience, tone, genre, and medium. Some rhetorical analyses, such as film reviews, may include **evaluation**—an assessment of how well a text succeeds in achieving its goals.

See
Ch. 1

Your primary audience for a rhetorical analysis will be your instructors and your classmates. As you begin work on any analysis, it is important to consider what your audience may or may not know about the text you are analyzing. For this reason, you need to decide how much summary you will provide along with your analysis.

25b Writing to Analyze

1 Planning a Rhetorical Analysis

Once you have chosen a subject, ask the following questions to help you plan your rhetorical analysis:

- **What does the text say or show?** When planning a rhetorical analysis, your first step is to understand the text. Begin by using <u>active reading</u> strategies: preview the text, highlight key ideas, and annotate the text with your own ideas, observations, and questions. Next, consider what argument the text makes. Try summarizing the main idea of the text in your own words. Then, note your responses to it—what the text makes you think, how it makes you feel—and consider why you have these reactions.

See
Ch. 2

- **What is the text's rhetorical context?** No text exists in a vacuum, and exploring the rhetorical context of a work is central to this type of analysis. Who is the text's author, and what are his or her credentials, beliefs, affiliations, and possible motivations? To what larger debate, topic, conversation, or movement is this work related? To what or whom is it responding? Why was it written or created—and for whom? How might each of these factors determine the way the ideas are structured or expressed?
- **How does the text say what it says?** What strategies or techniques does the writer use? How are tone and voice used, and to what effect? How successfully does the writer use evidence to support the text's main idea or central claim? Consider the writer's use of appeals: are they logical, ethical, and/or emotional?—and are they effective? Is there evidence of faulty reasoning? What is the text's medium (print, electronic, face-to-face, and so on) and genre (an essay, a blog post, a speech, an animated short film, and so on)? Why did the writer choose this medium and genre, and how do these choices influence the text's message?
- **What do I want to say about the text?** Be specific in your investigation: you will use the answers to each of the above questions to help you construct your own working thesis—a statement or pointed question about how the text works. Your goal could be to prove that a writer used certain appeals for a particular purpose or to examine how a writer framed an argument in different ways for different audiences.

2 Writing and Organizing a Rhetorical Analysis

Rhetorical analyses tend to be either *thesis-driven* or *thesis-seeking*. A **thesis-driven** analysis makes a point about a text and then supports that point with specific examples from the text—for example, how a writer used a specific technique, and for what purpose. This type of analysis follows the structure of an **argumentative essay**. A **thesis-seeking** (or thematic) analysis begins by examining how a set of rhetorical elements function in a text and then draws a conclusion based on these observations. The first type of rhetorical analysis is primarily **inductive** while the second is primarily **deductive**.

See Ch. 8

See 7d–e

PLANNING GUIDE

RHETORICAL ANALYSIS

Your **assignment** will ask you to write an essay that analyzes not just what a text says but also *how* the text says it.

Your **purpose** will be to analyze the argument or the rhetorical elements within a text. For example, how was the argument put together, for what purpose was it written, and how successful is it?

Your **audience** will be anyone interested in the rhetorical dimension of the work you are analyzing; for academic assignments, this audience is your instructor and possibly other students in your class.

INTRODUCTION

- Open by briefly introducing readers to the text you will be analyzing.
- Use a specific introductory strategy (such as a description or a quotation) to generate interest in your subject.
- If your essay will be thesis-driven, include a clearly stated thesis that you will support with your analysis. If your analysis will be thesis-seeking/thematic, clarify the elements that you will analyze by asking specific questions that you will go on to answer.

Thesis statement templates:
- Analyzing the author's use of… and…in [Name of Text] reveals…
- In…[Name of Text],…[Author] uses the strategy of…to…and to appeal to…
- Using [a combination of] logical (ethical, emotional) appeals,… [Author] attempts to convince his/ her primary audience,…, that…
- …, when examined in the context of…, suggests…

BODY PARAGRAPHS

- Arrange paragraphs according to a specific pattern (or patterns) of development. If you are writing a thesis-driven analysis, introduce and support your points in order of importance, moving from least important to most important. If you are writing a thesis-seeking essay, discuss each of your points in light of the questions you asked in your introduction. Make sure that you establish the connections among them.
- If your assignment involves evaluation, integrate this into your discussion. You will need to use your analysis to support your evaluative statements.
- Begin each paragraph with a topic sentence that states the paragraph's main idea.
- In each paragraph, include material—specific references to the text, your own observations and interpretations, and possibly research sources—that supports the topic sentence.
- Include **transitional words and phrases** to connect ideas within and between paragraphs.

Topic sentence templates:
- One technique…[Author] uses to gain credibility is…
- In…[Specific Section of Text],… [Author] uses emotional (ethical, logical) appeals to…
- …proves a more successful rhetorical strategy, establishing …
- Unfortunately, what may seem at first to be…[Author's] most convincing appeal(s) is/are, when examined more closely,…(fallacious, or a specific type of fallacy).
- One (another, the final) example of…is…

Templates for introducing support:
- For example,…
- As…points out,…
- According to…,…

See 34b2

CONCLUSION

- In a thesis-driven analysis, restate the thesis, emphasizing how the evidence you present supports it. You could add an evaluative statement here, building on or responding to the thesis. In a thesis-seeking/thematic analysis, use the conclusion to state your thesis and to make a specific analytical—and possibly evaluative—statement.
- Use a specific concluding strategy (such as a recommendation for approaching the text or a carefully chosen quotation from it) to make a lasting impression.

Concluding statement templates:
- …[Name of Text or Author] draws readers in with…and uses…[Technique] compellingly through…, convincing us that… is the best course of action.
- Although…[Author's] point that …is interesting, the use of fallacies and…detract from his/her credibility.
- Together, these strategies contribute to…
- In conclusion,…[Name of Text] succeeds in appealing to its intended audience,…, through the use of…
- Ultimately, through…, [Author or Text] succeeds in…by…and…

Conventions of Writing a Rhetorical Analysis

When you write a rhetorical analysis, keep the following conventions in mind:

- Consider how much background to provide.
- To analyze an argumentative text, use the rhetorical techniques you learned when writing argumentative essays.
- Use present tense verbs to describe what techniques the writer, artist, performer, and so on uses in the work being analyzed—and how effective such techniques are.
- Use strong active verbs.
- Use summary, paraphrase, and quotation effectively.
- Clearly distinguish your rhetorical analysis of a text from the ideas of the text itself.
- Represent a source's ideas accurately, not selectively or misleadingly.
- Document sources accurately and responsibly.

See
Ch. 14

See
Pt. 5

25c Sample Rhetorical Analysis

This essay was written for a composition course. You can read the text this student is analyzing, "A Hanging," at *http://orwell.ru/library/articles/hanging/english/e_hanging*.

Dana Cho

Professor Vega

English 111

7 May 2016

Emotional Appeals, Logical Reasoning:

George Orwell's "A Hanging"

"When I saw the prisoner step aside to avoid the

puddle," George Orwell writes, "I saw the mystery, the un-

speakable wrongness, of cutting a life short when it is in full

tide." This powerful observation comes from Orwell's 1931

essay "A Hanging." Set in the 1920s in what was once Burma

(now Myanmar), the essay describes one of many executions

the writer saw while he was a member of the Indian Imperial

Police. In "A Hanging," Orwell argues against capital pun-

ishment by using vivid descriptions and a specific narrative

from his own experience to make appeals that are not only

emotional but also logical.

   Throughout the essay, Orwell appeals to readers' emotions

by using figurative language to describe a scene and to reveal

his feelings about the scene. Twice in the first few paragraphs,

he uses similes to compare the prisoners to animals: he

describes the places where condemned men are held as being

"like small animal cages" and the way guards prepare a prisoner

for the gallows as like "handling a fish which is still alive and

may jump back into the water." Although such descriptions

might make a reader pity the prisoners, they also differentiate

prisoners from the guards, who are described as "men."

   Orwell uses irony to capture the complexities of his

own complicity in the situation, and some of his most ironic

Introduction

Thesis statement

Student's analysis of emotional appeals; quotations used as support

Cho 2

language is eerily accurate. As the group walks to the gallows, a "dreadful thing" happens: a stray dog, "wild with glee at finding so many human beings together," appears and runs up to lick the prisoner's face. The dog, an actual animal (unlike the prisoners), sees no difference between the executioners and the man in shackles; the dog's treatment of all the men as equals, coupled with the "glee"-filled assumption that these men are together in a pack, makes this moment "dreadful" for all involved. Orwell's choice of the word "dreadful" forces readers to see the twisted logic of the situation. The prisoner is being treated like an animal, but he is a person. In his final moments, when the prisoner calls out a repeated prayer—"each cry another second of life"—Orwell tells us that his captors have "gone grey like bad coffee."

Student's analysis of the use of irony; quotations used as support

Through dialogue and descriptions, Orwell shows that the men responsible for carrying out executions—including him—are affected negatively by this experience. To dull their own emotional responses, the guards engage in rationalizations that distance themselves from the act itself. For instance, the army doctor rushes one man's execution because the prisoners (who are themselves doomed to die in a matter of days) "can't get their breakfast till this job's over." The dog who greets them with affection is called a "bloody brute" for interrupting not only the proceedings but the mood, for making them see the man as human. When describing a prisoner who fought off six warders to prevent his execution, the head jailer says to the condemned man, "think of all the pain and trouble you are causing to us!"

Student's analysis of the use of logic; quotations and summary used as support

One of the most powerful rhetorical moments in Orwell's narrative occurs after the condemned prisoner is dead. Orwell

Cho 3

describes the relief and even revelry, "a homely, jolly scene" shared by the survivors, "native and European alike." In this moment, being alive unites them, but it also haunts them. The men, Orwell included, find themselves overtaken by laughter, but soon this laughter gives way to anecdotes about prisoners terrified to die. Orwell may be laughing at the irony in the guard's statement—"think of all the pain and trouble you are causing to us!"—or perhaps the men are laughing at the absurdity of what they have just done. And for some, these executions may have become the norm, and these observed moments of resistance—urinating in a cell or clinging on for dear life to the bars—provide a welcome bit of amusement in an otherwise grim job. Orwell draws readers into the giddiness, and then he abruptly undercuts the mood with a powerful last line: "The dead man was a hundred yards away."

Rather than isolate readers who might question his position on capital punishment, Orwell takes his audience through his own journey, leading up to and beyond this observation: "It is curious, but till that moment I had never realized what it means to destroy a healthy, conscious man." The moment that made Orwell seriously consider the ethical implications of taking another person's life—quoted in the first lines of this essay—is deceptively simple: the writer noticed that on his way to the gallows, the prisoner side-stepped a puddle. This moment, which Orwell describes using a matter-of-fact, almost ironic tone, creates a complex response in readers. Beyond the concrete, logical description are the prisoner's humanity and the reader's emotional realization that those who participate in the execution are doing something horribly wrong:

Student's analysis of a particular scene; quotations and summary used as support

Student's analysis of the use of logic; quotations and summary used as support

Cho 4

This man was not dying, he was alive just as we were alive. All the organs of his body were working—bowels digesting food, skin renewing itself, nails growing, tissues forming—all toiling away in solemn foolery. His nails would still be growing when he stood on the drop, when he was falling through the air with a tenth of a second to live. His eyes saw the yellow gravel and the grey walls, and his brain still remembered, foresaw, reasoned—reasoned even about puddles. He and we were a party of men walking together, seeing, hearing, feeling, understanding the same world; and in two minutes, with a sudden snap, one of us would be gone—one mind less, one world less.

Conclusion

Many writers use description and narration to appeal to readers' emotions, but Orwell goes beyond this technique, using both concrete description and facts to make an emotional appeal. Orwell's point is straightforward: capital punishment undermines both our society and our humanity. Although

Strong concluding statement

Orwell's essay by itself may not be enough to persuade lawmakers, it is a valuable contribution to the argument against legally killing criminals—not just because of their humanity, but also because of our own.

Cho 5

Work Cited

Orwell, George. "A Hanging." 1931. *George Orwell's Library*,

24 Sept. 2015, www.orwell.ru/library/articles/hang-

ing/english/e_hanging.

Close-Up   ANALYZING VISUAL TEXTS

If you are assigned to write an analysis of a visual text, **see Chapter 3** for an overview of reading and interpreting visuals. For a sample analysis of a visual, **see 24b4**.

EXERCISE 25.1

Write a rhetorical analysis of an ad campaign. Refer to the Planning Guide on pages 348–49 as you work. After you complete your analysis, label it "thesis-seeking" or" thesis-driven."

CHAPTER **26**

Composing a Literary Analysis

26a Reading Literature

See Ch. 2

When you read a literary work you plan to write about, you use the same critical thinking skills and **active reading** strategies you apply to other works you read: **preview** the work and **highlight** it to identify key ideas and cues to meaning; then, **annotate** it carefully.

As you read and take notes, focus on the special concerns of literary analysis, considering elements such as a short story's plot, a poem's rhyme or meter, or a play's staging. Look for *patterns*, related groups of words, images, or ideas that run through a work. Look for *anomalies*, unusual forms, unique uses of language, unexpected actions by characters, or original treatments of topics. Finally, look for *connections*, links with other literary works, with historical events, or with biographical information.

When you read a work of literature, keep in mind that you do not read to discover the one correct meaning the writer has hidden between the lines—there *is* no "one correct meaning." The meaning of a literary work is created by the interaction between a text and its readers. Do not assume, however, that a work can mean whatever you want it to mean; ultimately, your interpretation must be consistent with the stylistic signals, thematic suggestions, and patterns of imagery in the text.

26b Writing about Literature

When you have finished your reading and annotating, you develop a topic, and then you **brainstorm** to find ideas to write about; next, you decide on a thesis and use it to help you organize your material. As you arrange related material into categories, you will begin to see a structure emerging. At this point, you are ready to start drafting your essay.

When you write about literature, your goal is to make a point and support it with appropriate references to the work under discussion or to related works or secondary sources. As you write, you observe the conventions of literary criticism, which has its own specialized vocabulary and formats. You also respond to certain discipline-specific assignments. For instance, you may be asked to **analyze** a work, to take it apart and consider one or more of its elements—perhaps the plot or characters in a story or the use of language in a poem. Or, you may be asked to **interpret** a work, to explore its possible meanings. Finally, you may be called on to **evaluate** a work, to assess its strengths and weaknesses.

More specifically, you may be asked to trace the critical or popular reactions to a work, to compare two works by a single writer (or by two different writers), or to consider the relationship between a work of literature and a literary movement or historical period. You may also be asked to analyze a character's motives or the relationship between two characters or to comment on a story's setting or tone. Whatever the case, understanding exactly what you are expected to do will make your writing task easier.

Conventions of Writing about Literature

When you write about a literary work, keep the following conventions in mind:

- Use present-tense verbs when discussing works of literature (**The character of Mrs. Mallard's husband is not developed**).

- Use past-tense verbs only when discussing historical events (**Owen's poem conveys the destructiveness of World War I, which at the time the poem was written was considered to be . . .**); when presenting historical or biographical data (**Her first novel, published in 1811 when Austen was thirty-six, . . .**); or when identifying events that occurred prior to the time of the story's main action (**Miss Emily is a recluse; since her father died she has lived alone except for a servant**).

- Support your points with specific, concrete examples from the work you are discussing, *briefly* summarizing key events, quoting dialogue or description, describing characters or setting, or paraphrasing ideas.

- Combine paraphrase, summary, and quotation with your own interpretations, weaving quotations smoothly into your essay (**see Ch. 14**).

- Be careful to acknowledge all the sources you use, including the literary work or works under discussion. Introduce the words or ideas of others with a reference to the source, and follow borrowed material with appropriate parenthetical documentation (**see 17a1**). Be sure you have quoted accurately and enclosed the words of others in quotation marks.

- Include a works-cited list in accordance with MLA documentation style.

(continued)

See 17a2

Conventions of Writing about Literature *(continued)*

- When citing a part of a short story or novel, supply the page number (**168**). For a poem, give the line numbers (**2-4**) if they are included in the text; in your first reference, include the word *line* or *lines* (**lines 2-4**). For a classic verse play, include act, scene, and line numbers (**1.4.29-31**). For other plays, supply act and/or scene numbers. (When quoting more than four lines of prose or more than three lines of poetry, follow the guidelines outlined in **52b**.)

- Avoid subjective expressions such as *I feel, I believe, it seems to me,* and *in my opinion.* These weaken your essay by suggesting that its ideas are "only" your opinion and have no validity in themselves.

- Avoid unnecessary plot summary. Your goal is to draw a conclusion about one or more works and to support that conclusion with pertinent details. If a plot development supports a point you wish to make, a *brief* summary is acceptable, but plot summary is no substitute for analysis.

- Use literary terms accurately. For example, be careful not to confuse *narrator* or *speaker* with *writer.* Feelings or opinions expressed by a narrator or character do not necessarily represent those of the writer. You should not say, **In the poem's last stanza, Frost expresses his indecision,** when you mean the poem's *speaker* is indecisive.

- Italicize titles of books and plays (**see 56a**); enclose titles of short stories and poems in quotation marks (**see 52c**). Book-length poems are treated as long works, and their titles should be italicized.

PLANNING GUIDE

LITERARY ANALYSIS

Your **assignment** will ask you to write about one or more literary works—for example, to analyze a work, compare two works, or discuss a literary element (plot, character, point of view, theme, and so on).

Your **purpose** will be to analyze, interpret, or evaluate one or more literary works.

Your **audience** will usually be your instructor or other students in your class.

INTRODUCTION

Opening statement templates:
- In the poem (story, novel, play)… [Title] by…[Author],…
- In the two stories (plays, novels, poems) to be discussed,…

- Give an overview of your subject.
- Introduce the literary work (or works) you will discuss, identifying each work by author and title.
- State your thesis, the point you will be making about the literary work or works.

BODY PARAGRAPHS

- In each body paragraph, provide support for your thesis: specific reasons, examples, and so on.
- Keep plot summary to a minimum.
- Analyze, interpret, and evaluate the literary works you discuss.
- Support your statements with summary, paraphrase, and quotations from literary texts (and from critical articles if appropriate).
- Consider adding one or more visuals to illustrate your points.
- Include **parenthetical documentation** where necessary.
- Be sure to observe the conventions of **writing about literature**.

Thesis statement templates:
- Although…and…have some basic similarities, they are very different because…
- Because of…, this literary work can be seen as…
- As these examples suggest,…

See
17a1

See
26b

Topic sentence templates:
- One incident in particular illustrates…
- An analysis of the characters' statements reveals…
- As one character states, "…"

Templates for introducing support:
- As one critic observes, "…"
- Several sources suggest that…

CONCLUSION

- Sum up the main idea you have discussed in your essay.
- Try to end with a memorable sentence, perhaps including a quotation from a work you discuss or from a critical article you read.

Concluding statement templates:
- As all these examples show,…
- As the characters' actions clearly demonstrate,…

26c Sample Literary Analysis

Margaret Chase, a student in an introductory literature course, wrote the following analysis of Alice Walker's short story "Everyday Use." The essay uses **MLA documentation style** and cites three outside sources.

See
17a

Chase 1

Margaret Chase

Professor Sierra

English 1001

6 April 2016

The Politics of "Everyday Use"

Introduction

    Alice Walker's "Everyday Use" focuses on a mother, Mrs. Johnson, and her two daughters, Maggie and Dee, and how they look at their African American heritage. The story's climax comes when Mrs. Johnson rejects Dee's request to take a hand-stitched quilt away with her so that she can hang it on her wall. Knowing that Maggie will put the quilt to "everyday use," Dee is horrified, and she tells her mother and

Thesis statement

Maggie that they do not understand their heritage. Although some literary critics see Dee's character as materialistic and shallow, a closer examination of the social and historical circumstances in which Walker wrote this 1973 story supports a different interpretation of Dee's behavior.

    At several points in the story, Walker establishes that

Dee contrasted with Maggie; quotation describes Maggie

Dee is quite different from Maggie. As the story opens, the reader learns that Dee, the college-educated daughter, is coming home to visit her mother and sister after an absence of several years. Maggie, Dee's younger, less ambitious sister, has remained at home with her mother. Unlike Dee, Maggie is shy and introverted. She is described as looking like a lame animal that has been run over by a car. According to the narrator, "She has been like this, chin in on chest, eyes on ground, feet in shuffle" (428) ever since she was burned in a fire.

Dee contrasted with Mrs. Johnson; quotations used as support

    Dee is also very different from her mother. As Mrs. Johnson waits for Dee to arrive, she thinks about a dream she had about how Dee's homecoming might look on a

Chase 2

television talk show. In her dream, Mrs. Johnson is slim and attractive, talking to the host with a "quick and witty tongue" (428). In reality, she acknowledges, she would never look "a strange white man in the eye" (428), but "Dee . . . would always look anyone in the eye. Hesitation was no part of her nature" (428). For Mrs. Johnson, looking a white man in the eye is dangerous; for Dee, it is an act of defiance and courage.

Later in the story, Mrs. Johnson says that unlike Dee, she never got an education. After second grade, she explains, the school closed down. She says, "Don't ask me why: in 1927 colored asked fewer questions than they do now" (428). Here, Mrs. Johnson concedes that she accepts the status quo even though she knows that it is unjust. This admission further establishes the difference between Mrs. Johnson and Dee. Mrs. Johnson has accepted her circumstances, while Dee has tried hard to change hers. Their differences are illustrated in the film version of the story by their contrasting dress. As shown in fig. 1, Dee and her boyfriend, Hakim, dress in the Afro-American style of the late 1960s, embracing their African roots; Mrs. Johnson and Maggie dress in plain, conservative clothing.

Although Mrs. Johnson makes several statements that hint that she admires Dee's defiant character, she also points to incidents that highlight Dee's materialism and selfish ambition. When their first house burned down, Dee watched it burn while she stood under a tree with "a look of concentration" (428) rather than remorse. Mrs. Johnson knows how much Dee hated their small, dingy house, and she knows too that Dee must have been glad it was destroyed. In fact, as Walker acknowledges in an interview with her biographer, Evelyn C. White ("Stitches in Time"), Dee might

Marginal annotations:

Contrast between Dee and others, continued; quotation analyzed to illustrate contrast

Dee's character (past); quotations from story and summary of interview blended to support student's point

Chase 3

Bruce R. Schwartz

Fig. 1. Dee and Hakim arrive at the family home. *The Wadsworth Original Film Series in Literature: "Everyday Use,"* directed by Bruce R. Schwartz, Wadsworth, 2005.

even have set the fire that destroyed the house and scarred her sister. Even now, Dee is ashamed of the tin-roofed house her family lives in, and she has said that she would never bring her friends there. Mrs. Johnson has always known that "Dee wanted nice things" (428); even as a sixteen-year-old, "she had a style of her own, and knew what style was" (428). With these observations by Mrs. Johnson, Walker indicates that Dee has always been materialistic and self-serving as well as strong willed.

Dee's character (present); student's analysis of events in story

When Dee arrives home with her new boyfriend, it is clear that her essential character is, for the most part, unchanged. As she eyes her mother's belongings and asks Mrs. Johnson if she can take the top of the butter churn home with her, it is clear that she is still materialistic. Moreover, her years away from home have also politicized her.

Chase 4

Dee now wants to be called "Wangero" because she believes (although mistakenly) that her given name comes from whites who owned her ancestors. She now wears African clothing and talks about how it is a new day for African Americans. Still selfish, she is determined to maintain her own independent identity even if doing so will estrange her from her mother and her sister.

The meaning and political importance of Dee's decision to adopt an African name and wear African clothing needs to be seen in the social and political context in which Walker's story is set. In her interview with Evelyn White, Walker explains that the late 1960s were a time of awakening for African Americans. Many turned ideologically and culturally to Africa, adopting the dress, hairstyles, and even the names of their African ancestors. Walker admits that as a young woman she too became interested in discovering her African heritage. (In fact, she herself was given the name *Wangero* during a visit to Kenya in the late 1960s.) Walker tells White that she considered keeping this new name but eventually realized that to do so would be to "dismiss" her family and her American heritage. When she researched her American family, she found that her great-great grandmother had walked from Virginia to Georgia carrying two children. "If that's not a Walker," she says in the interview, "I don't know what is." Thus, Walker realized that, over time, African Americans actually transformed the names they had originally taken from their enslavers. To respect the ancestors she knew, Walker says, she decided it was important to retain her name.

Along with adopting symbols of their African heritage, many African Americans also worked to elevate symbols of

Social and political context for Dee's behavior

Social and political context, continued

Chase 5

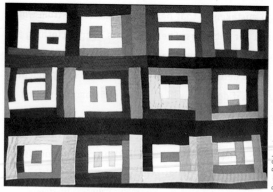

Bruce R. Schwartz

Fig. 2. Traditional hand-stitched quilt. *Evelyn C. White,* "Alice Walker: Stitches in Time," *The Wadsworth Original Film Series in Literature: "Everyday Use,"* directed by Bruce R. Schwartz, Wadsworth, 2005.

their own families' heritage, such as the quilt shown in fig. 2, to the status of high art. One way of doing this was to put these objects in museums; another was to hang them on the walls of their homes (Salaam 42). Such acts were intended to convince racist whites that African Americans were indeed cultured and civilized and consequently deserved not only basic civil rights, but also respect (Salaam 43). These gestures also helped to improve self-esteem and pride within black communities (Salaam 42).

Critics' analysis of Mrs. Johnson's decision

According to literary critics Houston Baker and Charlotte Pierce-Baker, when Mrs. Johnson chooses at the end of the story to give the quilt to Maggie, she is challenging Dee's simplistic understanding of heritage by recognizing that quilts signify "sacred generations of women who have made

Chase 6

their own special kind of beauty separate from the traditional artistic world" (qtd. in Piedmont-Marton 45). According to Baker and Peirce-Baker, Mrs. Johnson's epiphany is that her daughter Maggie, whom she has long dismissed because of her quiet nature and shyness, understands the true meaning of the quilt in a way that Dee never will (Piedmont-Marton 45). Readers can tell that Maggie, unlike Dee, has paid close attention to the traditions and skills of her mother and grandmother: she has actually learned to quilt. More important, by staying with her mother instead of going away to school, she has gotten to know her family, as she clearly shows when she tells her mother that Dee can have the quilt because she does not need it to help her remember her grandmother.

Student's analysis of Maggie's final gesture

    Although Maggie's and Mrs. Johnson's views of heritage may be more emotionally profound than Dee's, it is important not to dismiss the significance of Dee's desire to elevate the quilt to the level of high art. The political stakes of defining such an object as art in the late 1960s and early 1970s were high, and the fight for racial equality went well beyond demanding basic civil rights. Clearly, Dee is a materialistic woman who does not understand the emotional significance of her heritage. Still, her desire to hang the quilt should not be seen as a completely selfish act. At the time the story was written, displaying the quilt would have been not only a personal gesture, but a political gesture as well.

Conclusion

Defense of Dee's actions (student's opinion, based on analysis of story)

Chase 7

Works Cited

Piedmont-Marton, Elisabeth. "An Overview of 'Everyday Use.'" *Short Stories for Students,* vol. 2, 1997, pp. 42-45.

Salaam, Kalamu Ya. "A Primer of the Black Arts Movement: Excerpts from *The Magic of Juju: An Appreciation of the Black Arts Movement." Black Renaissance/Renaissance Noire,* 2002, pp. 40-59.

Walker, Alice. "Alice Walker: Stitches in Time." Interview by Evelyn C. White. *The Wadsworth Original Film Series in Literature: "Everyday Use,"* directed by Bruce R. Schwartz, Wadsworth, 2005.

---. "Everyday Use." *Compact Literature: Reading, Reacting, Writing.* 9th ed., edited by Laurie G. Kirszner and Stephen R. Mandell, Cengage, 2016, pp. 427-33.

EXERCISE 26.1

Write a literary analysis of a short story that you have not previously studied  in a course. Focus primarily on how one or two element(s) of fiction—plot, character, setting, point of view, style/tone/language, or theme—work in the story. If you have trouble choosing a story to write about, ask an instructor, librarian, or classmate for recommendations. The use of secondary sources in this essay is optional; ask your instructor what he or she prefers.

EXERCISE 26.2

Write a literary analysis of a poem that interests you. For inspiration, consult the *Academy of American Poets* website. In your essay, briefly address the poet's use of each of the following: voice, word choice/order, imagery, figures of speech, form, and rhyme and/or meter (or their absence). Use your findings to help you develop a central idea about the poem, which will serve as your thesis. Also identify a theme or themes explored in the poem. Do not consult any secondary sources; focus on your own ideas and interpretations.

CHAPTER **27**

Composing in the Social Sciences

The **social sciences** include disciplines such as anthropology, business, criminal justice, economics, education, political science, psychology, social work, and sociology. When you approach an assignment in the social sciences, your purpose is often to study the behavior of individuals or groups. You may be seeking to understand causes; predict results; define a policy, habit, or trend; or analyze a problem.

Before you can consider a problem in the social sciences, you must develop a **hypothesis**, an educated guess about what you believe your research will suggest. Then, you can gather the data that will either prove or disprove that hypothesis. Data may be quantitative or qualitative. **Quantitative data** are numerical—the "countable" results of surveys and polls. **Qualitative data** are less exact and more descriptive—the results of interviews or observations, for example.

Many assignments in the social sciences call for responses to a problem. For this reason, a clear **problem statement** at the beginning of a piece of writing, such as a proposal or a case study, is necessary to define and guide the discussion. Not only does this statement keep the reader on track, but it also helps the writer stay focused. In this sense, a problem statement establishes the structure for the piece of writing and presents the rationale for the rest of the discussion.

27a Understanding the Rhetorical Situation

Like writing assignments in the humanities, writing assignments in the social sciences can be *informal* or *formal*.

Informal writing assignments require you to examine ideas, phenomena, and data in the world around you. One example of an informal writing assignment is a personal experience essay, in which you are asked to relate your own observations of an event or an experience. Because you are being asked for your personal reactions, it is acceptable to use the first person (*I*) as well as an informal, somewhat conversational tone.

Formal writing assignments—such as case studies, research essays, and proposals—use an objective tone and a technical vocabulary. These assignments often require you to examine similarities and differences between what you have observed and what you have read or to evaluate terms and concepts from your course readings and lectures. While the purpose of writing in the social sciences is often to **inform**, it may also be to **persuade**—for example, to propose changes in an after-school tutoring center or to convince readers that binge drinking is a problem on college campuses.

Sometimes your instructor will define an audience for your assignment—your classmates, a supervisor of a social agency, or a public official, for example—but at other times you have to come up with your own or assume that you are addressing a general audience of readers in your field.

Close-Up USING THE PASSIVE VOICE

Unlike writers in the humanities, writers in the social sciences often use the passive voice, particularly in the parts of the essay that describe the research methods. Passive voice allows writers to avoid the first person and to present their research in objective terms.

See 40d

27b Genres

Assignments in the social sciences call for a variety of different genres.

❶ Personal Reaction Report

In some social science disciplines (particularly psychology, education, and sociology), you may be asked to write an informal **personal reaction report**, an account of a site visit or a visit with a professional who works in your area of study. In this kind of assignment, you record specific details about your experience.

Assignment (Anthropology: Service Learning)

Write a personal reaction report in which you describe your first visit to your service-learning field site. What expectations did you have? Record your initial impressions of the site: How did you feel as you were walking in? What were the first things you noticed? What surprises did you find?

Sample Personal Reaction Report (Excerpt)

Working with animals was my first choice for the service-learning part of this course. I have loved animals ever since I was a child. However, normally I interact with the pets in people's homes, so I was not accustomed to the behaviors of the affection-starved animals that I encountered at the Humane Society. Each animal has its own sad story. Each has its own personality traits as well. On my first day at the Humane Society, I met Barney, a dog with an engaging personality. He had a bright blue collar around his neck and was full of energy. During our 30-minute walk, he purposely walked around me and tangled me up in his leash. He repeated this "game" as often as I would allow him to, and he reacted well to affection. Because he wasn't hand-shy, I concluded that his owner probably had not abused him. Barney and I have already formed a close bond.

❷ Book Review

Instructors in the social sciences may ask you to write a book review. A **book review** should include a summary of the book's content. It should also include your evaluation of the book and your analysis of its contribution to the discipline. Be sure to include the author, date, and title of the book in your first paragraph.

Assignment (Political Science)

Write a book review summarizing the content and commenting on the usefulness to the field of Steven Kelman's *Making Public Policy: A Hopeful View of American Government*. (This book will be one of your sources for your group research project.) Reviews will be evaluated according to how well they demonstrate your understanding of the book, what insights they provide into your research topic, and how well they are written.

Sample Book Review (Excerpt)

In the next section of his book, Kelman effectively explores the relationship between the Presidency and the bureaucracy. Rather than dividing the Executive and the bureaucracy into the Senior Executive Service and the Civil Service, Kelman limits his discussion to the Executive Office of the President (EOP) and direct political appointments.

Kelman's observations concerning the importance of organizational structure, ground rules, and operating traditions are key. Particularly significant is how organizational characteristics affect the flow of debate, information, and decision making. For example, when a congressional committee debates legislation, the consequences of different organizational structures become visible and are subject to change. When a committee chair excludes an issue from debate, however, the different organizational structures never become visible. According to Kelman, political decision makers may not even be conscious of the exclusion.

❸ Case Study

Social science courses, especially psychology, sociology, and anthropology, frequently require **case studies** that focus on individuals or small groups. Case studies describe a problem and suggest solutions or treatments. In psychology, social work, and education, case studies typically focus on individuals and their interaction with peers or with agency professionals.

Assignment (Psychology of the Family)

Write a formal case study of the family you have been observing.

Sample Case Study

Family Profile

The Newberg family consists of Tom and Tina and their children David (8), Angela (6), and Cristina (4).

Problem

Tom has been laid off from his automobile production-line job. Tina is not employed outside the home. They have a mortgage on their home as well as $10,000 in credit card debt.

The loss of income when Tom was laid off from his job caused a change in the economic status of the Newberg family. Initially, Tom tried to maintain his traditional family role, wanting to be the sole provider, while Tina continued to stay at home with their children. Both Tom and Tina saw no way to alleviate their financial difficulties.

Observations

Tom spent so much time looking for a job that he had little time with his family—especially the children. Eventually, Tina borrowed money from her parents to start a door-to-door beauty products business. When this failed, she found a job driving a school bus, but it was only part time. Tom and Tina's financial situation severely strained the family. Even so, the couple made no plans for the future; they just kept hoping things would improve.

Discussion

Even when the Newbergs both managed to get full-time jobs, they could not maintain the lifestyle they were used to. Image is very important to Tom and Tina: they thought they had to look like a traditional family in order to have self-esteem. This is especially important to Tom. The prognosis for the Newberg family is not promising unless they make some changes. They have to learn to cooperate, to set goals as a family, and to share responsibilities. Both debt counseling and family counseling are strongly recommended.

④ Field Research Report

Social science instructors may ask you to write a **field research report**. **Field research** involves gathering primary information by observing people, places, or things. (It can also involve conducting an interview or carrying out a survey.) Field research reports should conform to guidelines established by your instructor.

See 12c

Assignment (Anthropology)

Groups of two or three students will engage in a firsthand observational exercise of present-day Philadelphia or its suburbs. Each group will walk along a major suburban or urban thoroughfare such as Lancaster

Avenue or Market Street. While walking, group members should observe the shifting patterns of buildings as well as the landscape configurations. Beforehand, you will be given detailed maps and survey documents that will enable you to see the buildings and the property lines as they existed over a century ago. Then, in a two- to three-page essay, you will describe what you observe and discuss the changes that have taken place over the years—and, if possible, account for these changes.

Sample Field Research Report (Excerpt)

Our group walked southwest on Buck Lane, a small street that runs perpendicular to Lancaster Avenue. As we walked away from Lancaster Avenue, The Haverford School was on our left. The school was built in 1901 on a 25-acre tract that was purchased from Howell Evans. As the years went by, the school's prestige increased, and the campus grew (see Figure 1).

On our right, the houses were small and well kept, not particularly fancy or on large lots. In 1881, almost all of the land on the right side of the road was owned by Michael Gallagher, who sold the land between 1900 and 1913 to the Kerrigan family. The Kerrigan family held the land until 1948, when it was divided into smaller subplots (in Figure 1, this tract is called the "Kerrigan Heir Plan").

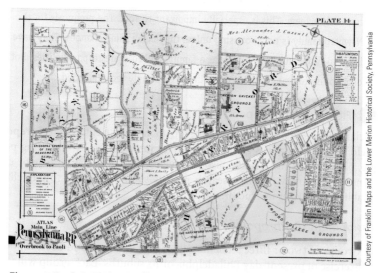

Figure 1. Buck Lane (vertical) and Lancaster Avenue (diagonal) c. 1913.

Courtesy of Franklin Maps and the Lower Merion Historical Society, Pennsylvania

At the turn of the century, many wealthy people, like the Kerrigan family, moved to the western suburbs to escape the noise and congestion of Philadelphia, which was experiencing an industrial boom. The development of the Philadelphia and Western Railroad (currently the Norristown High-Speed Line) in 1907 gave these individuals easy and inexpensive transportation into the city. They built houses on large plots of land. Eventually, these tracts were divided and developed for the middle-class families who were moving into the area. However, a few wealthy families chose not to subdivide, and even today, their houses occupy large plots of land. The major trends that affected the development of the suburbs northwest of Philadelphia were the expansion of train lines and the growth of the middle class after World War II. As the area changed, many of the older wealthy families sold their estates and moved farther from the city.

❺ Annotated Bibliography and Literature Review

Social science instructors may ask you to write an **annotated bibliography** in which you summarize and evaluate each of your research sources. You may also be asked to write a **literature review**, an essay in which you discuss the entries in your annotated bibliography and perhaps compare them. (The literature review is often part of a social science research paper.)

Assignment (Sociology)

Research an issue that interests you and that has a significant impact on particular populations in your state. Then, compile an annotated bibliography of at least six sources. Finally, write a literature review that discusses these sources.

Sample Annotated Bibliography (Excerpt)

Adams, J. R. (2010). Farm bill funding boosts FMNP. *National Association of Farmers' Market Nutrition Programs*. Retrieved from http://www.nafmnp.org. This article provides current information on the Farmers' Market Nutrition Program (FMNP), with particular emphasis on its legislative appropriation status. The author stresses the need for lobbying to keep the FMNP program alive.

Sample Literature Review (Excerpt)

J. R. Adams (2010) discusses the successful efforts farmers and lobbyists have made in securing funding for the Farmers' Market Nutrition Program.

For example, even though funding had originally been cut by half in the projected budget for 2010, this shortfall was corrected (Rosen, 2010). Farmers stand to benefit from this program and from the similar Seniors Farmers' Market Nutrition Program (SFMNP). Similarly, as S. Z. Greenberg et al. (2009) point out, these programs not only create a potential new market for farmers' products, but also may benefit from private grants to supplement government funding.

6 Proposal

A **proposal** is often the first stage of a research project. In a proposal, you define the scope and nature of the problem you will address, outline your research project, and suggest possible solutions. The purpose of the proposal is to make a convincing case for your research project.

Assignment (Psychology of Substance Abuse)

See 18a

Write a proposal to solve a problem associated with alcohol abuse. Each source you use—including websites, journal articles, monographs, and interviews—should be documented in APA style.

Sample Proposal (Excerpt)

Statement of the Problem

It is a fact that alcohol can impair coordination. The severity of this effect depends on an individual's Blood Alcohol Concentration (BAC), which is determined by the individual's weight, speed of alcohol consumption, and amount of alcohol consumed. If an individual's BAC is greater than .08, he or she can be charged with Driving Under the Influence (DUI).

As Figure 1 illustrates, the number of DUIs in Frewsdale is high, with 1067 DUI charges in the past 5 years. Of course, this number reflects only the individuals who were actually caught; the number of people driving with a BAC higher than .08 is probably much greater, as shown by our survey of Frewsdale University students, in which more than 80% of respondents—none of whom had ever received a DUI charge—indicated that they or someone they knew had driven drunk.

An alternative transportation method for people who have been drinking would greatly reduce the number of DUIs in Frewsdale. Furthermore, such a program would reduce the number of people who walk home alone late at night and potentially put themselves at risk.

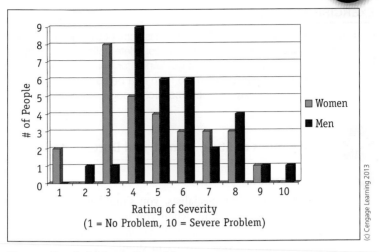

Figure 1. Drunk driving in Frewsdale.

To address this problem, we propose a safe-ride program aimed primarily at providing a free ride home on weekends (when people most frequently go out, as Figure 2 shows) for residents of Frewsdale who have been drinking.

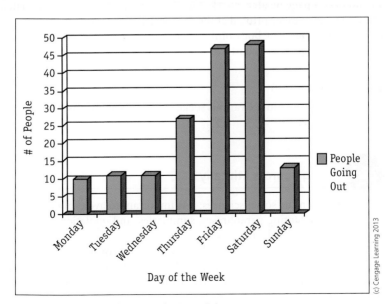

Figure 2. Nights people go out in Frewsdale.

EXERCISE 27.1

Above each writing sample in **27b** is the assignment to which its writer was responding. Choose one assignment to complete, following its specific instructions as well as the chapter's guidelines for composing in the social sciences. (Your work should take the form of a personal reaction report, a book review, a case study, or a field research report.)

27c Conventions of Style, Format, and Documentation

1 Style and Format

Because you are addressing specialists, you should use the specialized vocabulary of the discipline and, when you discuss charts and tables, you should use statistical terms, such as *mean, percentage*, and *chi square*. Keep in mind, however, that you should use clear language to explain what *percentages, means*, and *standard deviations* signify in your analysis.

See 18b

A social science research paper follows a specific format, such as that specified by the American Psychological Association (APA). APA manuscript guidelines require a title page that includes a **running head** (if the paper is being submitted for publication), a **title**, and a **byline** (your name, school, and so on). Every page of the paper, including the title page, should have a **page header** (also known as a running head), an abbreviated title and page number printed at the top. Social science papers also include **internal headings**. The body of the paper may present and discuss graphs, maps, photographs, flowcharts, or tables.

 ### 2 Documentation

See Ch. 18

Many of the journals in the various social science disciplines use APA documentation style.

27d Using Sources Ethically

See Ch. 16

When writing in the social sciences, it is important to avoid plagiarism by correctly documenting paraphrases, summaries, and quotations as well as the statistics and visuals that you use.

In addition, social scientists are bound by ethical considerations regarding the treatment of research subjects, the protection of privacy, and the granting of credit to those who have made substantial contributions to a research project.

27e Research Sources

Social scientists engage in both library and field research.

In **library research**, social scientists consult print and electronic compilations of statistics, government documents, and newspaper articles, in addition to scholarly books and articles. In **field research**, social scientists conduct <u>interviews</u> and surveys and observe individuals and groups. Because so much of their data are quantitative, social scientists must know how to generate and analyze statistics and how to read and interpret tables and graphs.

See 12c2

Social scientists may also review the literature on a topic to discover what research has already been done, or they may analyze research reports. Social scientists are particularly interested in case studies and published reports of surveys, opinion polls, interviews, experiments, and observations that may be useful in proving or disproving a theory.

Social scientists are expected to base their studies on the most current thinking surrounding a topic. Because statistics must be up to date, researchers frequently rely on electronic databases to locate the most recent scholarly journal articles and government publications.

Some excellent databases cover the literature of the social sciences. One comprehensive database is *Web of Science*. Other databases cover specific disciplines within the social sciences (**see 27e3**). In addition to databases, the <u>Internet</u> is useful for locating government information, including census data, statistics, congressional reports, laws, and reports issued by government agencies.

See 12b

1 Government Documents

Government documents are important resources for social scientists because they contain complete and up-to-date facts and figures on a wide variety of subjects.

The website *Catalog of U.S. Government Publications* (http://catalog.gpo.gov) provides access to the documents published by the Government Printing Office since July 1976 for all three branches of government. For documents published prior to July 1976, consult with a reference librarian about your library's access to the *Monthly Catalog*. In addition, *Congress.gov* (http://congress.gov), via the Library of Congress, is a good resource for federal legislative information. *Supreme Court of the United States* (http://supremecourt.gov) provides access to the Supreme Court docket, oral arguments, briefs, and opinions. Finally, *FedStats* (http://fedstats.sites.usa.gov) is a gateway for government statistics, linking to individual agencies and databases. *American FactFinder* (http://factfinder.census.gov) is the preferred source for population, housing, economic, and geographic data from the US Census Bureau.

2 Newspaper Articles

Newspaper articles are particularly good resources for research topics in political science, economics, and business. Useful newspaper databases are *NewsBank, National Newspaper Index,* and *LexisNexis Academic Universe.*

3 Core Databases in the Social Sciences

Some of the more widely used databases for social science disciplines are *General BusinessFile ASAP; JSTOR; Anthropology Plus; Communication & Mass Media Complete; Social Sciences Citation Index; Social Sciences Index; PsycINFO; ERIC; Sociological Abstracts; LISA: Library and Information Science Abstracts; PAIS International; EconLit; ABI/INFORM; Management Contents; SAGE Journals;* and *LexisNexis Academic Universe.*

4 Other Sources of Information

Interviews, surveys, and observations of the behavior of various groups and individuals are important nonlibrary sources for social science research.

CHAPTER **28**

Composing in the Natural and Applied Sciences

28a Understanding the Rhetorical Situation

The **natural and applied sciences** include biology, chemistry, geology, astronomy, physics, engineering, nursing, and computer science. Writing assignments in the sciences use a formal, objective tone and follow documentation guidelines such as those published by the Council of Science Editors (CSE).

See
Ch. 20

Most scientific writing is aimed at readers who are familiar with the technical language and writing conventions of a particular scientific discipline, but occasionally it may be aimed at general readers. Its purpose is to report **empirical data** (data that are obtained through observations and experiments).

28b Genres

Assignments in the natural and applied sciences call for a variety of different genres.

❶ Observation

Some science instructors may ask you to write about and analyze your own observations of the natural world. This is one of the few assignments in the natural and applied sciences in which you will be encouraged to use the first person (*I*). In this type of assignment, you first record your observations (using scientific terminology where necessary) and then analyze the phenomena you describe.

Assignment (Ecology)

> Write a report in which you describe a natural setting and then discuss the environmental impact of human beings on that setting.

Sample Observation (Excerpt)

> Lake Wenatchee, part of the Alpine Lakes, is in the Wenatchee National Forest, where over 700 small freshwater lakes are scattered throughout the central Cascade region. The average annual precipitation is 40 inches; this heavy rainfall accounts for the mixed conifers—Douglas firs, grand firs, and cedars—that thrive there. The rain-shadow effect also causes the soils in the region to be rich in organic materials as well as in basalt, pumice, and volcanic ash. However, human activity—clear-cutting of old-growth forest, damming of rivers, and fire suppression—is altering the area's natural ecology. These activities lead to a build-up of debris, a higher number of forest fires, severe soil erosion, and the endangerment of local species of animals and fish.
>
> While climbing one part of a barely distinguishable trail, I noticed a very large area on the side of the mountain that had no trees. This was an alarming sign. Because the terrain is sloped, clear-cutting the trees causes extreme soil erosion, including mudslides. Clear-cutting also destroys animal habitats, so many species of owl, woodpecker, and squirrel will very likely be threatened.

EXERCISE 28.1

Write an observation in which you describe a natural setting and then discuss the environmental impact of human beings on that setting. See above for an excerpted report that follows this assignment.

❷ Biographical Report

In a science or math course, an instructor may ask you to write a report about a historical figure. When writing your essay, try to relate the information you find about your subject to the work you have been doing in the course—for example, you might consider how Mendel's ideas about genetics relate to your class's work on heredity.

Assignment (Geometry)

Select a figure whose life and work we have discussed in class. Then, write a biographical essay in which you summarize his or her contributions to geometry.

Sample Biographical Report (Excerpt)

Jean-Victor Poncelet was born in Metz, northeastern France, in July 1788. He studied calculus with Gaspard Monge at the École Polytechnique and then joined the army as a lieutenant of engineers, following Napoleon to Russia. While he was a prisoner of war in Saratoff on the River Volga, he began researching projective geometry, investigating the projective properties of figures later in his great work *Traité des Propriétés Projectives des Figures*.

Projective geometry is a branch of geometry concerned with properties of geometric figures that retain their character. The basic elements of projective geometry are points, lines, and planes. The concept of parallel does not exist in projective geometry because any pair of distinct lines intersects in a point, and if these lines are parallel in the sense of Euclidean geometry, then their point of intersection is at infinity.

❸ Abstract

An **abstract**—a technical summary of a journal article—is a standard part of many assignments in the natural sciences. Abstracts are usually about two hundred words long. In the natural sciences, the purpose of an abstract is to summarize the goals, methods, and results of the research.

You begin writing an abstract after you have finished writing your essay. When writing an abstract, follow the organization of your essay, devoting a sentence or two to each of its major sections. State the purpose, the method of research, results, and conclusions in the order in which they appear in the essay, but include only essential information. Keep in mind that abstracts do not include quotations or paraphrases.

The following abstract was written as part of the assignment on page 381.

Sample Abstract

This project used Wisconsin Fast Plants to determine the effect of gibberellic acid on plants. Gibberellic acid is a growth hormone that stimulates a plant to grow taller by elongation of internode length. The research tested the hypothesis that plants that are treated with gibberellic acid will grow taller than plants that are untreated, and the internode length on treated plants will be longer than that on untreated plants. Results supported this hypothesis: the internode length on treated plants was longer than that on untreated plants. Furthermore, even the dwarf plants that were treated with gibberellic acid grew longer, reaching almost the same height as the control standard plants by the last day of measurement. Therefore, the results of this experiment indicate that gibberellic acid can stimulate the growth of plants by elongation of internode length, though not by internode number.

4 Literature Survey

Literature surveys are common in the sciences, often appearing as a section of a proposal or as part of a report or a research paper. A **literature survey** summarizes a number of studies and sometimes compares and contrasts them. By doing so, the literature survey provides the theoretical background for the paper's discussion.

Sometimes, however, a literature survey can be an essay on its own, and in this case it makes an argument about how to view the literature. In other words, a literature review essay doesn't simply survey the literature but also evaluates it.

Keep in mind that in the natural sciences *literature* means **peer-reviewed** primary sources. A literature review most often comments on **primary research literature**—articles reporting the results of original research. Typically, literature reviews do not discuss **secondary sources**, articles that comment on the work of others.

See 13a

A literature survey should have a formal tone and be aimed at readers who know the field. The purpose of a literature survey is to give these readers an overview of a range of scholarly publications about a subject. In most cases, your primary focus should be on the most current research available.

Assignment (Biology)

Research an aspect of plant biology, and present your findings in a report that contains the following sections: Abstract, Introduction, Literature Survey, Materials, Methods, Results, Discussion, Conclusions, Reference List, and Appendix (if necessary).

Sample Literature Survey (Excerpt)

The cell *Myxococcus xanthus* responds to starvation by initiating a cycle that culminates with the cell forming spore-filled fruiting bodies. This developmental cycle, which is dependent upon changes in gene expression, ensures cell sporulation at the appropriate time and place. Thousands of cells are affected by this process. Recent studies strongly suggest that NtrC-like activators are a crucial component of the complex regulatory controls of *M. xanthus'* developmental program. Twelve NtrC activators were found to be most important in the process. [1] These findings led to further research that examined the specific developmental moments at which NtrC proteins activate specific sets of genes throughout the process. [2] In addition, Garza and others [3] identified two inductive components of the early part of the developmental process.

References

1. Gorski L, Kaiser D. Targeted mutagenesis of σ^{54} activator proteins in *Myxococcus xanthus*. J Bacteriol. 2010;180:5896-5905.
2. Keseler IM, Kaiser D. An early A-signal-dependent gene in *Myxococcus xanthus* has a σ^{54}-like promoter. J Bacteriol. 2007;177:4638-4644.
3. Garza AG, Pollack JS, Harris BZ, Lee A, Keseler IM, Licking EF, Singer M. SdeK is required for early fruiting body development in *Myxococcus xanthus*. J Bacteriol. 2010;180:4628-4637.

5 Lab Report

The **lab report** is one of the most frequently assigned writing tasks in the natural sciences. Lab reports typically contain the following sections: *Purpose, Apparatus, Method, Procedure, Data, Results,* and *Conclusion.* However, not every section will be necessary for every experiment, and some experiments may require additional components, such as an abstract or a reference list. In addition, lab reports may include tables, charts, graphs, and diagrams. The format for a lab report is usually defined by a course's lab manual.

EXERCISE 28.2

Use what you have learned in this chapter to revise a lab report, abstract, or literature survey that you wrote for a science course. Submit the original and the revision, along with a paragraph explaining how you have improved your work.

28c Conventions of Style, Format, and Documentation

1 Style and Format

Because writing in the sciences focuses on the results of experiments, not on those conducting the experiments, writers often use the passive voice.

Another stylistic convention concerns verb tense: a conclusion or a statement of generally accepted fact should be in the present tense ("Objects in motion *tend* to stay in motion"); a summary of a study, however, should be in the past tense ("Watson and Crick *discovered* the structure of DNA"). Finally, note that direct quotations are seldom used in scientific papers.

Keep in mind that each scientific discipline prescribes its own formats for **tables** and other visuals and the way they are to be presented.

See 23d1

Remember that different scientific journals may specify different formatting guidelines. For example, the *Journal of Immunology* might have a format different from that of the *Journal of Parasitology*. Your instructor may ask you to prepare your essay according to the style sheet of a particular journal to which you could submit your work. Although publication may seem a remote possibility to you, following a style sheet reminds you that writing in the sciences involves writing for a specific audience.

2 Documentation

Citation systems (documentation styles) within the sciences vary from one scientific discipline to another; even within a given discipline, the citation system may vary from one journal to another. For this reason, ask your instructor which system is required.

28d Using Sources Ethically

In the sciences, it is especially important to acknowledge the work of others who contributed to your research results. If many people contribute to a research project, the work of each one must be properly cited. Falsifying data or using the experimental results, computer codes, chemical formulas, graphs, images, ideas, or words of others without proper acknowledgment undermines the integrity of your work.

If you need more information about what constitutes **plagiarism** in the sciences or how to cite the work of individual collaborators in a research project, check with your instructor.

See Ch. 16

28e Research Sources

Although much scientific research takes place in the laboratory or in the natural world, it is also important that scientists know how to do library research. Literature surveys allow scientists to discover what research has already been done. Building on this research, they can conduct meaningful experiments that prove or disprove a theory or solve a problem. Much of this research is collaborative. It is not uncommon for several people to work on different aspects of a research problem in the laboratory or in online databases and then jointly report on the results.

Scientists must use the most current information. Although books may provide background material, scholarly journal articles, conference proceedings, technical reports, and research reports provide the most up-to-date information.

1 Core Databases in the Natural and Applied Sciences

Numerous comprehensive databases cover the sciences. *Web of Science: Science Citation Index Expanded, ScienceDirect,* and *Google Scholar* cover all the natural and applied sciences. (Proceed with caution in using *Google Scholar,* as not all articles indexed there have been formally published or have undergone peer review. Consult with a reference librarian or your instructor about the scholarly value of a publication.)

Other databases cover specific disciplines: *PubMed* (medicine), *BioOne* (biology), *arXiv* (physics), and *SciFinder* (*Chemical Abstracts Service*) (chemistry) are examples of specialized databases.

Other helpful databases for research in the sciences include *American Chemical Society Publications; Analytical Abstracts; APS Journals; BioMed Central; CINAHL; Environment Complete; GeoRef; Health Source;* and *SpringerLink.* Check with a reference librarian about the availability of these and other databases in your library.

2 Other Sources of Information

Opportunities for research outside the library vary widely because of the many ways in which scientists can gather information. In agronomy, for example, researchers collect soil samples; in toxicology, they test air or water quality; and in chemistry, they conduct experiments to identify unknown substances. Scientists also conduct surveys. And, of course, the Internet is an important source of up-to-date scientific information.

Composing in Other Genres

PART **8**

Composing in Other Genres

❓ Frequently Asked Questions

CHAPTER 29

Creating a Writing Portfolio

A **writing portfolio**, a collection of written work in print or electronic form, offers a unique opportunity for you to present your intellectual track record, showing how you have developed as a writer in response to the **learning outcomes** (what you are expected to learn) set by your instructor or your school. Increasingly, colleges have been using portfolios as a way not only to assess individual students' performance but also to see if the student body as a whole is meeting the school's standards.

The purpose of a writing portfolio is to demonstrate a writer's skill sets, knowledge, and achievements. Portfolios allow writers to collect a body of writing in one place and to organize and present it in an effective, attractive format, offering a view of a student's writing that focuses more on the complete body of work than on individual assignments. While compiling individual items (sometimes called **artifacts**) to include in their portfolios, students reflect on their work and measure their progress; as they do so, they may improve their ability to evaluate their own work.

There are two kinds of portfolios:

1. **Growth** or **process portfolios**, typically used to assess your learning in a course or program, are designed to show a writer's improvement over time. They may include multiple essay drafts with instructor comments (and sometimes peer reviewers' comments) in addition to other work completed in and out of class for each assignment.
2. **Best-works** or **presentation portfolios** are designed to highlight a writer's notable achievements. They contain only finished products, such as the final drafts of essays or reports. This type of portfolio is often used when you are applying for a job or for graduate school, to show that you have the required skills and knowledge.

Portfolios may be assembled in print or electronic form. A **print portfolio** collects and presents hard copy in a file folder. In contrast, an **electronic portfolio** compiles material in electronic files, which may be stored on a USB flash drive but are most commonly housed online. Some portfolios combine print and electronic formats—for example, posting finished material on a website and collecting hard copies of early essay drafts with handwritten instructor comments in a folder. Many academic disciplines are moving toward electronic portfolios because, when available online, they are immediately accessible to peers, instructors, and prospective employers. However, not all material lends itself to an electronic format. You may need to supplement your electronic portfolio with print documents if they cannot be easily scanned.

29a Assembling Your Portfolio

The material you include in a growth or process portfolio depends on individual course or program requirements. If you are developing a best-works portfolio, consider your specific goals and how you want to showcase your strengths. An electronic format allows for a wide range of possible content, including multimedia content—for example, video or audio clips, *PowerPoint* presentations, and web pages.

Many academic disciplines are moving toward electronic portfolios because when posted on the Internet, they are immediately accessible to peers, instructors, and prospective employers. However, not all material

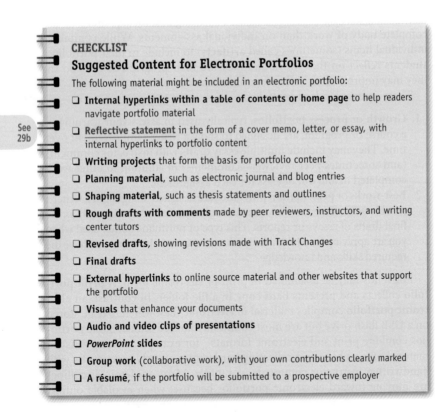

CHECKLIST

Suggested Content for Electronic Portfolios

The following material might be included in an electronic portfolio:

❑ **Internal hyperlinks within a table of contents or home page** to help readers navigate portfolio material

See 29b

❑ **Reflective statement** in the form of a cover memo, letter, or essay, with internal hyperlinks to portfolio content

❑ **Writing projects** that form the basis for portfolio content

❑ **Planning material**, such as electronic journal and blog entries

❑ **Shaping material**, such as thesis statements and outlines

❑ **Rough drafts with comments** made by peer reviewers, instructors, and writing center tutors

❑ **Revised drafts**, showing revisions made with Track Changes

❑ **Final drafts**

❑ **External hyperlinks** to online source material and other websites that support the portfolio

❑ **Visuals** that enhance your documents

❑ **Audio and video clips of presentations**

❑ *PowerPoint* **slides**

❑ **Group work** (collaborative work), with your own contributions clearly marked

❑ **A résumé**, if the portfolio will be submitted to a prospective employer lends itself to an electronic format. You may need to supplement your electronic portfolio with print documents if they cannot be easily scanned.

Once you are sure you understand your purpose and your instructor's requirements, you can assemble your portfolio, using the following checklist as a guide.

CHECKLIST

Assembling an Electronic Portfolio

As you assemble your electronic portfolio, keep the following guidelines in mind:

❑ If you are preparing the portfolio for a course, **select material** that corresponds to your instructor's guidelines. (This material may include content from the Checklist on page 388.) If you are developing a best-works portfolio, consider your audience and purpose when selecting content to include. Keep in mind that a best-works portfolio should showcase your skills for the particular job or program for which you are applying.

❑ **Revise your material**, using comments made by peer reviewers and by your instructor.

❑ **Compile your material** in electronic files and save your files on a storage device or post them to a website. For a best-works portfolio, it is recommended that you post your content online, even if you need to use a password-protected site, so that potential employers can view your content. Consider including the link to your portfolio on your résumé and in your letter of application.

❑ **Format your material**, following principles of effective web design to help you present your work.

❑ **Arrange your material** in a logical order, which your instructor's guidelines may specify. Include a home page to help the audience navigate your portfolio.

❑ **Write a reflective statement** that demonstrates your thoughtful analysis of your portfolio and of the individual artifacts within it.

❑ **Collect additional materials** as hard copy in a folder (if necessary) or convert hard copy to PDF format.

❑ **Submit your portfolio**, following your school's guidelines for electronic submission.

Figure 29.1 on page 390 shows the home page for a student's electronic writing portfolio, which supplies evidence from her major projects to illustrate how she met the course's learning outcomes. Notice how effective web design elements highlight and distinguish key information on the page.

Unlike the course portfolio shown in Figure 29.1, Figure 29.2 on page 391 shows the home page of a graduate student's teaching portfolio, which accompanied her application for a doctoral program. This is a presentation portfolio that showcases the student's best work in her master's program.

Close-Up FREE VERSUS PROPRIETARY ELECTRONIC PORTFOLIO TOOLS

Electronic portfolio tools available through free or **open-source** software, such as *Drupal, Weebly*, and *WordPress*, allow users to edit the software's source code and customize their online portfolio experience. Because open-source software is free, users are granted unlimited access.

Proprietary or **closed-source** software, such as *Sakai* and *Blackboard*, restricts users from editing its code but may still allow various customization options. Proprietary software requires a paid subscription that expires unless renewed. If you consider using an electronic portfolio tool, be sure to find out what its restrictions are before using it to assemble your portfolio. There are many Web 2.0 open-source platforms that can be used for portfolio development. These platforms allow you to choose an interface and upload content much the way you do with *PowerPoint*.

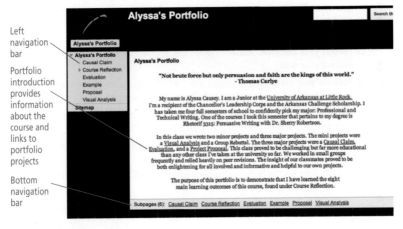

FIGURE 29.1 Home page for student's writing portfolio posted online. © Alyssa Causey

Across the top is the navigation, where the student includes her teaching materials, in addition to her curriculum vitae (résumé in academia) and some of her best writing to show her skills not only as a teacher but also as a scholar.

Visual
highlights
student's name

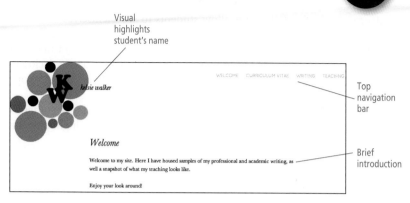

Top
navigation
bar

Brief
introduction

FIGURE 29.2 Home page for a graduate student's teaching portfolio posted online.
© Kelsie Walker

29b Writing a Reflective Statement

Instructors usually require students to introduce their portfolios with a
reflective statement—a memo, letter, or essay in which students assess their
writing improvement and achievements over a period of time. An instructor
often wants you to respond in this statement to the course learning outcomes
and provide evidence, or an artifact, to show you understand each particular

---

CHECKLIST

Writing a Reflective Statement

As you write your reflective statement, consider the following questions:

❑ What skills or knowledge does each item in your portfolio demonstrate? How do
these skills and knowledge relate to your instructor's goals? How do they relate
to your own academic or professional goals?

❑ How are the individual items in your portfolio related? What have you learned
about each project in the context of your entire portfolio? How do the projects
illustrate your skills and knowledge?

❑ How have comments made by peer reviewers and by your instructor helped you
revise your work? Keep in mind that you may choose to refer to or even include
written feedback from your instructor; however, you are not required to include
graded work, which is confidential under the Family Educational Rights and
Privacy Act (FERPA).

❑ How, specifically, has your writing changed throughout the course (if the portfolio
is for a course), or how does the portfolio best showcase your strengths if the
portfolio is a best-works portfolio? What skills will you continue to work on?

❑ Which items in your portfolio best represent your development as a writer? Now
that you have some distance from this work, do you have new insights about
your writing that you didn't have before?

outcome. Reflective statements allow students to see themselves as writers and to discover their strengths as well as the areas in which there is still room for improvement. Keep in mind that a reflective statement is not merely a summary of your completed work; it is an opportunity for you to look closely and analytically at your writing and thus to gain insights about your development as a writer.

Following is an excerpt from the reflective statement for a student's writing portfolio. Notice how both content and design highlight the achievements and improvement demonstrated by her portfolio.

Sample Reflective Statement (Excerpt)

Purpose statement

This memo summarizes the knowledge and skills demostrated by my English Composition I Portfolio.

Color-coded headings can be used to emphasize and distinguish skill categories

Drafting and Revising

What scares me even more than staring at a blank computer screen is working hard on an essay only to have it returned full of red comments. The relationship essay assignment made me confront my fear of revision and realize that revision is essential to my success as a writer—both in college and after I graduate.

Body of memo describes each assignment, how each project responds to the assignment, and what the writer learned

This assignment asked us to explore the deep layers of a relationship. In my essay, "Moments of Silence," I wrote about the relationship I have with my hair and what it says about the relationships I have with my mother, my history, and my identity. While the topic was personal and interesting to me, I was unsure how to present it to my readers so that it would interest them. I ended up writing my first draft in a standard five-paragraph format, stating my main idea in a thesis statement and then discussing supporting points in the body paragraphs.

Explanation of how peer and instructor feedback helped student writer to revise

However, comments I received from peers and from you during our one-on-one conferences made me realize that my structure and general approach to my topic needed work. One peer reviewer told me that my essay's traditional organization made him feel distanced from a story that should have been both personal and unique. I worked through another draft before realizing that my essay needed to show my readers why this particular relationship is so important to me. At that point, I changed the entire structure of the essay into a personal narrative to better convey the emotional impact of the relationship I was describing.

This assignment showed me that it is not enough to have a compelling topic; I also need to present that topic to readers in a compelling way.

As I realized again and again throughout the semester, considering my audience and incorporating suggestions from my readers will help me to achieve my purpose for writing. This assignment made me see early in the semester how important revision is to my development as a college writer and (as I explain later) as an aspiring journalist.

Discussion of how revision relates to course goals as well as to student writer's academic and professional goals

29c Evaluating Writing Portfolios

Evaluation criteria for portfolios may differ from discipline to discipline, but all effective writing portfolios should be *comprehensive, well-organized, attractively presented*, and *consistent with your instructor's style and format guidelines*. Before you begin developing your portfolio, be sure you understand your instructor's expectations.

Comprehensive   A **comprehensive** portfolio includes a varied collection of coursework and demonstrates your ability to respond to various writing situations. Be sure to include all the material requested by your instructor.

Well-Organized   A **well-organized** portfolio follows a consistent, logical organization that smoothly guides readers through your work.

Portfolio content may be organized in various ways. For example, portfolios may be arranged chronologically, or they may be arranged by assignment, format, skill, level of improvement, or applicability to your major. Regardless of the method you use, be sure to label each item in your portfolio with a title and any other information your instructor requires. To show readers the portfolio's content and organization at a glance, include a table of contents (for print portfolios) or a home page (for electronic portfolios) to guide readers through the portfolio's content and to provide a context for the material included.

Attractively Presented   An **attractively presented** portfolio presents your work in the best possible light. You should use the principles of effective document design and web design to enhance the readability and accessibility of your work. Remember, however, that design elements should never be superfluous or obtrusive; rather, they should always identify and emphasize important information on a page.

Close-Up   PORTFOLIOS IN OTHER DISCIPLINES

Portfolios are not limited to writing courses; in fact, instructors in disciplines other than writing often require portfolios that collect and assess students' work. For example, a math portfolio might indicate a student's progress during a particular unit of study or over an entire semester, and a portfolio for a web design course might demonstrate mastery of a particular set of skills.

Consistent with Your Instructor's Style and Format Guidelines A portfolio that is **consistent with your instructor's style and format guidelines** fulfills expectations established by the instructor and by his or her academic discipline. Carefully follow the documentation style and format guidelines your instructor requires for each assignment.

EXERCISE 29.1

List the items you might include in a portfolio for one of your classes, and think about how you could arrange this material. Write a paragraph outlining the specific content and format of your portfolio.

CHAPTER **30**

Writing Essay Exams

See Ch. 7

To write an essay exam (or even a paragraph-length response to an exam question), you must do more than memorize facts; you must see the relationships among them. In other words, you must **think critically** about your subject.

Be sure you know beforehand the scope and format of the exam. How much of your textbook content and class notes will be covered—the entire semester's work or only the material presented since the last exam? Will you have to answer every question, or will you be able to choose among alternatives? Will the exam be composed entirely of fill-in, multiple-choice, or true/false questions, or will it call for sentence-, paragraph-, or essay-length answers? Will the exam test your ability to recall specific facts, or will it require you to demonstrate your understanding of the course material by drawing conclusions?

Different kinds of exams require different strategies. When you prepare for a short-answer exam, you may memorize facts without analyzing their relationship to one another or their relationship to a body of knowledge as a whole. When you prepare for an essay exam, however, you must do more than remember bits of information; you must also make connections among ideas.

When you are sure you know what to expect, see if you can anticipate the essay questions your instructor might ask. Try out likely questions on classmates in a **study group**, and see whether you can do some collaborative brainstorming to outline answers to possible questions. (If you have time, you might even practice answering one or two in writing.)

30a Planning an Essay Exam Answer

Because you are under time pressure during an exam, you may be tempted to skip the planning and revision stages of the writing process. However, if you write in a frenzy and hand in your exam without a second glance, you are likely to produce a disorganized or even incoherent answer. With careful planning and editing, you can write an answer that demonstrates your understanding of the material.

1 Read through the Entire Exam

Before you begin to write, read the questions carefully to determine your priorities and your strategy. First, be sure that your copy of the test is complete and that you understand exactly what each question requires. If you need clarification, ask your instructor or proctor for help. Then, plan carefully, deciding how much time you should devote to answering each question. Often, the point value of each question or the number of questions on the exam indicates how much time you should spend on each answer. If an essay question is worth fifty out of one hundred points, for example, you should spend at least half (and perhaps more) of your time planning, writing, and proofreading your answer to that particular question.

Next, decide where to start. Responding first to questions whose answers you are sure of is usually a good strategy. This tactic ensures that you will not become bogged down in a question that baffles you and left with too little time to write a strong answer to a question that you understand well. Moreover, starting with the questions that you are sure of can help build your confidence.

2 Read Each Question Carefully

To write an effective answer, you need to understand the question. As you read any essay question, you may find it helpful to underline keywords and important terms.

> **Sociology:** Distinguish among Social Darwinism, instinct theory, and sociobiology, giving examples of each.

> **Music:** Explain how Milton Babbitt used the computer to expand Schoenberg's twelve-tone method.

> **Philosophy:** Define existentialism and identify three influential existentialist works, explaining why they are important.

Look carefully at the wording of each question. If the question calls for a comparison and contrast of two styles of management, an analysis of *one* style, no matter how comprehensive, will not be acceptable; if the question asks for causes and effects, a discussion of causes alone will not do.

Close-Up   KEY WORDS IN EXAM QUESTIONS

Pay careful attention to the words used in exam questions:

- explain
- compare
- contrast
- trace
- evaluate
- discuss

- clarify
- relate
- justify
- analyze
- interpret
- describe

- classify
- identify
- illustrate
- define
- support
- summarize

The wording of the exam question suggests what you should emphasize. For instance, an American history instructor would expect very different responses to the following two exam questions:

- Give a detailed explanation of the major <u>causes</u> of the Great Depression, noting briefly some of the effects of the economic collapse on the United States.
- Give a detailed summary of the <u>effects</u> of the Great Depression on the United States, briefly discussing the major causes of the economic collapse.

Although these two questions look alike, the first calls for an essay that stresses *causes*, whereas the second calls for one that stresses *effects*.

❸ Brainstorm to Find Ideas

Once you think you understand the question, you need to find something to say. Begin by brainstorming, quickly listing all the relevant ideas you can remember. Then, identify the most important points on your list, and delete the others. A quick review of the exam question and your supporting ideas should lead you toward a workable thesis for your essay answer.

30b   Shaping an Essay Exam Answer

See 5a–c

Like an essay, an effective exam answer has a **thesis-and-support** structure.

❶ Stating a Thesis

Often, you can rephrase the exam question in the form of a **thesis statement**. For example, the American history exam question "Give a detailed summary of the effects of the Great Depression on the United States, briefly discussing the major causes of the economic collapse" suggests the following thesis statement:

Effective Thesis Statement: The Great Depression, caused by the American government's economic policies, had major political, economic, and social effects on the United States.

This effective thesis statement addresses all aspects of the question but highlights only relevant concerns.

The following thesis statements are not effective:

Vague Thesis Statement: The Great Depression, caused largely by irresponsible spending, had a number of very important results.

Incomplete Thesis Statement: The Great Depression caused major upheaval in the United States.

Irrelevant Thesis Statement: The Great Depression, caused largely by America's poor response to the 1929 stock market crash, had more important consequences than World War II did.

2 Constructing a Scratch Outline

Because time is limited, you should plan your answer before you write it. Therefore, once you have decided on a suitable thesis, you should make a scratch outline that lists your major points. Once you have completed your outline, check it against the exam question to make certain it covers everything the question calls for—and *only* what the question calls for. Then, you can consult your outline as you draft your essay.

See 5d

30c Writing and Revising an Essay Exam Answer

PLANNING GUIDE

ESSAY EXAM

Your **assignment** will be to write an essay that answers a specific question.
Your **purpose** will be to demonstrate that you understand the course material and can use this information to answer the exam question.
Your **audience** will be your instructor.

INTRODUCTION

- Begin by providing background to establish the context for your discussion.
- State your thesis (in the form of an answer to the exam question).

Opening statement templates:
- In class this semester,...
- To give an overview of the situation,...
- Some background information can put things in perspective; for example,...

continued

PLANNING GUIDE: Essay Exam (continued)

BODY PARAGRAPHS

Thesis statement templates:
- Although some sources suggest that…, it makes more sense to conclude that…
- Because of…, it is obvious that…

Topic sentence templates:
- One (another, the most important) reason is…
- The first (second, another) example is…
- One (the next, a final) cause (or effect) is…

Templates for introducing support:
- For example,…
- As our textbook makes clear,…
- Several of the readings support the idea that…

- Provide specific support for your thesis, referring to your reading and the course materials.
- Arrange material in each paragraph according to the specific pattern (or patterns) of development suggested by the exam question.
- Include as many specific examples and details as possible.
- Include clear topic sentences and transitions.
- Use parallel sentence structure and repeat key words and terms.
- Refer to the exam question to keep yourself (and your reader) on track.

CONCLUSION

Concluding statement templates:
- For all these reasons,…
- As these examples show,…

- Restate your thesis (in different words).
- Summarize your key points.
- End with a strong concluding statement.

MULTILINGUAL TIP

Because of time pressure, it is difficult to write in-class essay exam answers that are as polished as your out-of-class writing. Even so, you should do your best to convey your ideas as clearly as you can, but keep in mind that instructors are usually more concerned with the accuracy of the content of your answers than with your writing style. Therefore, instead of wasting time searching for the "perfect" words or phrases, use words and grammatical constructions that are familiar to you. You can use any remaining time to check your grammar and mechanics. Finally, don't waste time recopying your work unless what you have written is illegible.

Although essay answers should be complete and detailed, they should not contain irrelevant material. Every unnecessary fact or opinion increases your chance of error, so don't repeat yourself or volunteer unrequested information, and don't express your own feelings or opinions unless you are asked to do so. In addition, be sure to support all your general statements with specific examples.

Finally, be sure to leave enough time to revise what you have written. If you remember something you want to add, you can insert a few additional words with a caret (∧). Neatly insert a longer addition at the end of your answer, box it, and label it so your instructor will know where it belongs.

In the following essay exam answer, notice how the student restates the question in her thesis statement and keeps the question in focus by repeating key words such as *cause, effect, result,* and *impact.*

Effective Essay Exam Answer

Question: Give a detailed summary of the effects of the Great Depression on the United States, briefly discussing the major causes of the economic collapse.

The Great Depression, caused by the American government's economic policies, had major political, economic, and social effects on the United States.

Introduction—thesis statement rephrases exam question

The Depression was precipitated by the stock market crash of October 1929, but its actual causes were more subtle: they lay in the US government's economic policies. First, personal income was not well distributed. Although production rose during the 1920s, the farmers and other workers got too little

Policies leading to Depression (¶ 2 summarizes causes)

of the profits; instead, a disproportionate amount of income went to the richest 5 percent of the population. The tax policies at this time made inequalities in income even worse. A good deal of income also went into development of new manufacturing plants. This expansion stimulated the economy but encouraged the production of more goods than consumers could purchase. Finally, during the economic boom of the 1920s, the government did not attempt to limit speculation or impose regulations on the securities market; it also did little to help build up farmers' buying power. Even after the crash began, the government made mistakes: instead of trying to address the country's deflationary economy, the government focused on keeping the budget balanced and making sure the United States adhered to the gold standard.

The Depression, devastating to millions of individuals, had a tremendous impact on the nation as a whole. Its political, economic, and social consequences were great.

Transition from causes to effects

Between October 1929 and Roosevelt's inauguration on March 4, 1933, the economic situation grew worse. Businesses were going bankrupt, banks were failing, and stock prices were falling. Farm prices fell drastically, and hungry farmers were forced to burn their

Early effects (¶s 4–8 summarize important results in chronological order)

corn to heat their homes. There was massive unemployment, with millions of workers jobless and humiliated, losing skills and self-respect. President Hoover's Reconstruction Finance Corporation made loans available to banks, railroads, and businesses, but Hoover thought state and local funds (not the federal government) should finance public works programs and relief. Confidence in the president declined as the country's economic situation worsened.

Additional effects: Roosevelt's emergency measures

One result of the Depression was the election of Franklin Delano Roosevelt. By the time of his inauguration, most American banks had closed, thirteen million workers were unemployed, and millions of farmers were threatened by foreclosure. Roosevelt's response was immediate: two days after he took office, he closed all the remaining banks and took steps to support the stronger ones with loans and to prevent the weaker ones from reopening. During the first hundred days of his administration, he kept Congress in special session. Under his leadership, Congress enacted emergency measures designed to provide "Relief, Recovery, and Reform."

Additional effects: Roosevelt's reform measures

In response to the problems caused by the Depression, Roosevelt set up agencies to reform some of the conditions that had helped to cause the Depression in the first place. The Tennessee Valley Authority, created in May 1933, was one of these. Its purposes were to control floods by building new dams and improving old ones and to provide cheap, plentiful electricity. The TVA improved the standard of living of area farmers and drove down the price of power all over the country. The Agricultural Adjustment Administration, created the same month as the TVA, provided for taxes on basic commodities, with the tax revenues used to subsidize farmers to produce less. This reform measure caused prices to rise.

Additional effects: NIRA, other laws, and so on

Another response to the problems of the Depression was the National Industrial Recovery Act. This act established the National Recovery Administration, an agency that set minimum wages and maximum hours for workers and set limits on production and prices. Other laws passed by Congress between 1935 and 1940 strengthened federal regulation of power, interstate commerce, and air traffic. Roosevelt also changed the federal tax structure to redistribute American income.

One of the most important results of the Depression was the Social Security Act of 1935, which established unemployment insurance and provided financial aid for the blind and disabled and for dependent children and their mothers. The Works Progress Administration (WPA) gave jobs to over two million workers, who built public buildings, roads, streets, bridges, and sewers. The WPA also employed artists, musicians, actors, and writers. The Public Works Administration (PWA) cleared slums and created public housing. In the National Labor Relations Act (1935), workers received a guarantee of government protection for their unions against unfair labor practices by management.

Additional effects: Social Security, WPA, and so on

As a result of the economic collapse known as the Great Depression, Americans saw their government take responsibility for providing immediate relief, for helping the economy recover, and for taking steps to ensure that the situation would not be repeated. The economic, political, and social impact of the laws passed during the 1930s is still with us, helping to keep our government and our economy stable.

Conclusion— restatement of thesis

Strong concluding statement

Notice that in her answer the student does not include any irrelevant material: she does not, for example, describe the conditions of people's lives in detail, blame anyone in particular, discuss the president's friends and enemies, or consider parallel events in other countries. She covers only what the question asks for. Notice, too, how topic sentences (**"One result of the Depression . . ."**; **"In response to the problems caused by the Depression . . ."**; **"One of the most important results of the Depression . . ."**) keep the primary purpose of the discussion in focus and guide her instructor through the essay.

EXERCISE 30.1

Treat the following as an essay exam question. Give yourself ninety minutes to write; set a timer. Try outlining your response before writing it.

Identify your biggest challenge in taking in-class essay exams. Using what you have learned in this chapter, describe how you will address this challenge in future exams. In your response, demonstrate knowledge of what makes an effective essay exam answer.

CHAPTER 31

Writing for the Public

Some of the writing you do—such as diaries and journals—is strictly private, written just for yourself. Other writing—such as research papers and essay exams—is directed at an academic audience. At times, you may also be called upon to do **public writing**, producing documents directed to individuals and groups in the community both inside and outside your school.

In a composition course, a work-study job, a service-learning course, a co-op placement, or an internship (and, later, in the workplace), you may be required to write letters, proposals, flyers, brochures, media releases, and newsletters as well as web pages, blog posts, and email messages directed at an audience beyond the classroom.

Many courses in various academic disciplines also include public-writing components. Depending on the discipline, you might be assigned to produce a variety of documents—for example, an op-ed piece for a criminal justice or political science course, a brochure for a public health course, book or film reviews for a literature class, or popular "translations" of scientific or technical material for a science or engineering course.

Through public writing, you learn more about how to identify an audience and accommodate its needs as well as how to write for a variety of purposes. You also have an opportunity to practice the principles of good document design. And, of course, the skills you develop in public writing projects can help you succeed in the workplace. For example, you can develop rhetorical skills you might use in writing business reports, memos, and proposals or in developing a marketing campaign. More generally, working on public-writing projects can help you learn to write concise prose, to work as a member of a team, and to communicate with nonexpert audiences in business-to-business contexts.

See 22b
1–2

See
Pt. 7

See
Ch. 23

31a Writing Media Releases

One common kind of public writing is the **media release**, a document designed to provide information about a project or event to media outlets (newspapers, magazines, online publications, and so on). Media releases can announce events at a business or on a college campus, and they can also be used to announce a change in leadership or a new appointment or program. The information provided in a media release can be used to help publications develop articles informing their readers about the subject.

The media release that follows was written by a student in an advanced composition course. It was sent to various local media outlets to advertise an upcoming conference on her university's campus. Note that the media release includes an attention-getting headline set in boldface and large type and a standard heading that provides contact information. (Sometimes a media release is accompanied by a cover letter. See **32a** for information on business letter format.)

Sample Media Release

For Immediate Release:

Contact:

Carol Hulse

Instructor of English, University of West Florida

(850) 474-2933

chulse@uwf.edu

Linda Moore

Instructor of English, University of West Florida

(850) 857-6074

lmoore@uwf.edu

HIGH SCHOOL ARTICULATION CONFERENCE TO BE HELD AT UWF ON MARCH 8, 2016

UWF English Department Will Host Event for Escambia and Santa Rosa High Schools

University of West Florida—On March 8, 2016, a high school articulation conference will be held for high school teachers in Escambia and Santa Rosa County from 8:00 a.m. to 3:00 p.m. The UWF English Department and students of composition are sponsoring this event, which will be held in Building 51. Students, teachers, and administrators are all invited to attend. The purpose of the conference is to establish better communication with local high schools in order to improve high school graduates' preparation for college-level coursework.

This year's keynote speaker will be Dr. David Jolliffe, the former Advanced Placement Exam Chief Reader and current Brown Chair in English Literacy at the University of Arkansas. Other speakers will include Dr. Peggy Jolly, Professor and Director of Freshman English and Developmental Studies at the University of Alabama at Birmingham; Bruce Swain, Chairperson of Communication Arts at UWF; and the winner of the "Call for Papers" abstract contest. The main topic of the conference will be "The Severity of Plagiarism."

A tour of the UWF Writing Lab will be available from 11:00 a.m. to 12:00 p.m., and lunch will be provided. Please contact Carol Hulse or Linda Moore for more information.

The UWF English Department and students of composition are sponsoring this event in order to promote better college readiness and success.

###

EXERCISE 31.1

Choose a new program or service that has been recently implemented at your school—or invent one that you wish were offered. Write a media release to announce this program to the general public as well as current and prospective students.

31b Writing Proposals

In public writing, **proposals** are often written to identify a specific problem in a community and propose a detailed, concrete plan for solving it. **See Chapter 9** for information on writing proposals; a sample proposal also appears there.

31c Designing Brochures

A **brochure** is a short pamphlet or booklet that provides information about a service, program, or event.

The following student brochure, directed at the campus community (students, faculty, and staff) was designed to promote a book drive on a university campus in support of the school's efforts to fight illiteracy in the community.

Sample Brochure

The following people are coordinating this project:

Sara Holcomb
Christian Cabral
Justin Ellis
Carl Shouppe
Sarah Neuland

For more information, please contact

Student Government Association
University of West Florida
11000 University Parkway
Commons Bldg. 22, Room 227
Pensacola, FL 32514
Phone: (850) 474-2393
Fax: (850) 474-2390
www.uwf.edu/sga/

November 7-21

Front and back cover of brochure. © Cengage Learning 2013.

Why have a book drive?

- To promote the importance of literacy throughout our community
- To provide books for people who cannot afford to buy them
- To supply books to residents of shelters for homeless families
- To encourage families to read together
- To improve literacy for future generations of children

Why should you help to promote literacy?

- 771 million people in the world are illiterate
- In the US alone, 42 million people cannot read
- Nonreaders lack the skills they need to succeed in the workplace

How can you help make this book drive successful?

- Look for bright green boxes around campus, and donate new or gently used books for children and adults
- Volunteer to help sort through and distribute the books that are collected
- SPREAD THE WORD!

Inside pages of brochure. © Cengage Learning 2013.

31d Designing Flyers

A **flyer** is a one-page document that uses text and graphics to advertise an upcoming event. (**See 23a** for information on creating an effective visual format.)

Students in a composition course created the flyer below to promote a benefit concert on their campus.

? *Sample Flyer*

Mayland Community College

Benefit Concert
Featuring six local bands and appetizers
donated by the State Street Grill

Art Building, Main Campus   **March 21ˢᵗ – 7pm**   **$10**

Proceeds from this event go to the Herter-O'Neal Scholarship fund
sponsored by the Young Professionals student association.

Created by Karen Mauk.

EXERCISE 31.2

Design a flyer or brochure to share information about the new program or service announced in Exercise 31.1. This time, consider only your fellow students and members of the campus community to be your audience.

CHAPTER **32**

Writing in the Workplace

Employers value good writing skills. In fact, to ensure that job applicants can communicate effectively, some businesses now include a writing assess-ment as part of the hiring process. Employers know that a good part of each workday is spent writing. They also know that the higher up people go in a company, the more they write. Poorly written memos, letters, and reports can cost businesses millions of dollars each year. Because good writing skills are so important in the business world, the writing skills you learn in the academic environment can give you a definite advantage in the workplace.

32a Writing Business Letters

Business letters should be brief and to the point, with important information placed early in the letter. Be concise, avoid digressions, and try to sound as natural as possible.

The first paragraph of your letter should introduce your subject and mention any pertinent previous correspondence. The body of your letter should present the information readers need to understand your points. (If your ideas are complicated, present your points in a bulleted or numbered list.)

See 23c

Your conclusion should reinforce your message.

Most often, business letters use a **block format**, with all parts of the letter aligned with the left-hand margin. Single-space within paragraphs, and double-space between paragraphs. (Note that, in block format, paragraphs are not indented.) Proofread carefully to make sure there are no errors in spelling or punctuation.

32b Writing Letters of Application

A **letter of application** (also called a **cover letter**) summarizes your qualifications for a specific job. Letters of application (electronic or print) should be short and focused. Your primary objective in writing this letter is to obtain an interview.

Begin your letter of application by identifying the job you are applying for and stating where you heard about it—in a newspaper, in a professional journal, on a website, or from your school's job placement service, for example. Be sure to include the date of the advertisement and the exact title of the position. End your introduction with a statement that expresses your confidence in your ability to do the job.

Sample Letter of Application

Heading

246 Hillside Drive
Urbana, IL 61801
Kr237@metropolis.105.com
(217) 283-3017

March 21, 2015

Inside
address

Mr. Maurice Snyder, Personnel Director
Guilford, Fox, and Morris
22 Hamilton Street
Urbana, IL 61822

Salutation
(followed
by a colon)

Dear Mr. Snyder:

My college advisor, Dr. Raymond Walsh, has told me that you are interested in hiring a part-time intern. I believe that my academic background and my work experience qualify me for this position.

Body

I am presently a junior accounting major at the University of Illinois. During the past year, I have taken courses in taxation, trusts, and busi-ness law. I am also proficient in *Sage 50* and *QuickBooks Pro*. Last spring, I gained practical accounting experience by working in our department's tax clinic.

Double- ---→
space

After I graduate, I hope to earn a master's degree in taxation and then return to the Urbana area. I believe that my experience in taxation as well as my familiarity with the local business community would enable

Single- ---→
space

me to contribute to your firm.

I have enclosed a résumé for your examination. I will be available for an interview any time after March 25. I look forward to hearing from you.

Complimentary
close

Sincerely,

Written
signature

Sandra Kraft

Typed
signature

Sandra Kraft

Additional
data

Enc: Résumé

In the body of your letter of application, provide the information that will convince readers that you are qualified—for example, relevant courses you have taken and pertinent employment experience. Be sure to address the specific points mentioned in the advertisement. You want to show the employer how closely your knowledge and skills match those needed by the company. Above all, emphasize your strengths, and explain how they relate to the job for which you are applying.

Conclude by saying that you have enclosed your résumé and that you are available for an interview. Be sure to include both your phone number and your email address in your letter.

Before you send your letter, proofread carefully. At this stage of the application process, errors in spelling or grammar could easily disqualify you.

32c Writing Follow-Up Emails

After you have been interviewed, be sure to send a **follow-up email** to the person (or persons) who interviewed you. First, thank your interviewer for taking the time to see you. Then, briefly summarize your qualifications and reinforce your interest in the position. Because many applicants do not write follow-up emails, this kind of message can make a very positive impression.

Sample Follow-Up Email

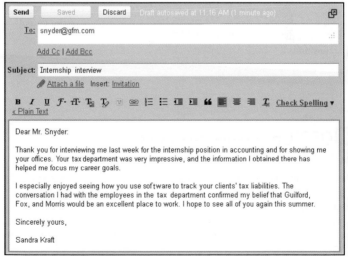

32d Designing Print Résumés

A **résumé** lists relevant information about your education, your job experience, your goals, and your personal interests.

The majority of résumés are submitted on paper or as email attachments. Either way, the guidelines are the same.

There is no single correct format for a résumé. You will most likely arrange your résumé in **chronological order** (see page 411), listing your education and work experience in sequence (beginning with the most recent). Your résumé should be brief—one page is usually sufficient for an undergraduate—easy to read, clear and emphatic, logically organized, and free of errors. Emphasize important information with italics, bullets, boldface, or different fonts.

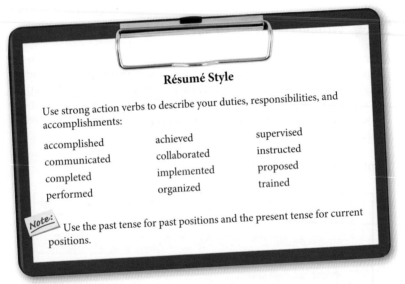

Résumé Style

Use strong action verbs to describe your duties, responsibilities, and accomplishments:

accomplished	achieved	supervised
communicated	collaborated	instructed
completed	implemented	proposed
performed	organized	trained

Note: Use the past tense for past positions and the present tense for current positions.

Close-Up RÉSUMÉ TEMPLATES

Although **résumé templates**, such as those contained in *Microsoft Word*, can help you design a résumé, you should not simply plug information into them. Many recruiters and employers will dismiss résumés that closely follow one of these standardized formats. For this reason, take the time to create your own résumé, one that clearly demonstrates both your initiative and creativity.

Sample Résumé: Chronological Order

KAREN L. OLSON

	SCHOOL	HOME
	3812 Hamilton St. Apt. 18	110 Ascot Ct.
	Philadelphia, PA 19104	Harmony, PA 16037
	215-382-0831	412-452-2944
	olsont@dunm.ocs.drexel.edu	

EDUCATION

DREXEL UNIVERSITY, Philadelphia, PA 19104
Bachelor of Science in Graphic Design
Anticipated Graduation: May 2016
Cumulative Grade Point Average: 3.2 on a 4.0 scale

COMPUTER SKILLS AND COURSEWORK

HARDWARE
Familiar with both Macintosh and PC systems

SOFTWARE
Adobe Creative Cloud, QuarkXPress 2015, CorelDRAW Graphics Suite X7

COURSES
Corporate Identity, Environmental Graphics, Typography, Photography, Painting and Print-making, Sculpture, Computer Imaging, Art History

EMPLOYMENT EXPERIENCE

THE TRIANGLE, Drexel University, Philadelphia, PA 19104
January 2013–present
Graphics Editor. Design all display advertisements submitted to Drexel's student newspaper.

UNISYS CORPORATION, Blue Bell, PA 19124
June–September 2013, Cooperative Education
Graphic Designer. Designed interior pages as well as covers for target marketing brochures. Created various logos and spot art designed for use on interoffice memos and departmental publications.

CHARMING SHOPPES, INC, Bensalem, PA 19020
June–December 2012, Cooperative Education
Graphic Designer/Fashion Illustrator. Created graphics for future placement on garments. Did various textile designing. Drew flat illustrations of garments to scale in computer. Prepared presentation boards.

DESIGN AND IMAGING STUDIO, Drexel University, Philadelphia, PA 19104
October 2011–June 2012
Monitor. Supervised computer activity in studio. Answered telephone. Assisted other graphic design students in using computer programs.

ACTIVITIES AND AWARDS

The Triangle, Graphics Editor: 2012–present
Kappa Omicron Nu Honor Society, vice president: 2012–present
Graphics Group, vice president: 2011–present
Dean's List: spring 2011, fall and winter 2012

REFERENCES AND PORTFOLIO

Available upon request.

32e Designing Electronic Résumés

Two types of electronic résumés—scannable and web-based—are gaining in popularity.

❶ Scannable Résumés

Many employers request scannable résumés that they can store in a database for future reference. When preparing such a résumé, keep in mind that scanners will not pick up columns, bullets, or italics and that shaded or colored paper will make your résumé difficult to scan.

Whereas in a print résumé you use specific action verbs (**edited**) to describe your accomplishments, in a scannable résumé you also use key nouns (**editor**) that can be entered into a company database. These words will help employers find your résumé when they carry out a keyword search for applicants with certain skills.

> **MULTILINGUAL TIP**
> In some countries, job applicants list information about their age and marital status in their job application materials. However, in the United States, this is usually not done.

To facilitate a keyword search, applicants often include a Skills section on their résumé. For example, if you wanted to emphasize your computer skills, you would include keywords such as *Microsoft Suite, Adobe Creative Cloud*, and *C++*.

Sample Résumé: Scannable

Deborah Keller
2000 Clover Lane
Fort Worth, TX 76107

Phone: (817) 735-9120
Email: kell5@aol.com

Employment Objective: Entry-level position in an organization that will enable me to use my academic knowledge and the skills that I learned in my work experience.

Education:

University of Texas at Arlington, Bachelor of Science in Civil Engineering, May 2015. Major: Structural Engineering. Graduated Magna Cum Laude. Overall GPA: 3.754 on a 4.0 base.

Scholastic Honors and Awards:

Member of Phi Eta Sigma First-Year Academic Honor Society, Chi Epsilon Civil Engineering Academic Society, Tau Beta Pi Engineering Academic Society, Golden Key National Honor Society.

Jack Woolf Memorial Scholarship for Outstanding Academic Performance.

Grant from the Society of Women Engineers.

Cooperative Employment Experience:

Johnson County Electric Cooperative, Clebume, TX, Jan. 2015 to June 2015. Junior Engineer in Plant Dept. of Maintenance and Construction Division. Inspected and supervised in-plant construction. Devised solutions to construction problems. Estimated costs of materials for small construction projects. Presented historical data relating to the function of the department.

Dallas-Fort Worth International Airport, Tarrant County, TX, Dec. 2013 to June 2014. Assistant Engineer. Supervised and inspected airfield paving, drainage, and utility projects as well as terminal building renovations. Performed on-site and laboratory soil tests. Prepared concrete samples for load testing.

Dallas-Fort Worth International Airport, Tarrant County, TX, Jan. 2013 to June 2013. Draftsperson in Design Office. Prepared contract drawings and updated base plans as well as designed and estimated costs for small construction projects.

Skills:

Organizational and leadership skills. Written and oral communication skills, C++, PC, Macintosh, Windows 10, Mac OS X, Microsoft Suite, Adobe Creative Cloud, and Internet client software. Computer model development. Technical editor.

2 Web-Based Résumés

It is becoming common to have a version of your résumé posted on a website such as *Monster.com* (Figure 32.1) or *CareerBuilder.com*. Usually, a web-based résumé is an alternative to a print résumé that you have mailed or a scannable version that you have submitted to a database or as an email attachment.

FIGURE 32.1 *Monster.com*, a popular website for posting résumés.

32f Writing Memos

Memos communicate information within an organization. Begin your memo with a purpose statement, followed by a background section. In the body of your memo, support your main point. If your memo is short, use bulleted or numbered lists to emphasize information. If it is more than two or three paragraphs, use headings to designate individual sections. End your memo by stating your conclusions and recommendations.

Sample Memo

<table>
<tr><td>Opening component</td><td>

TO: Ina Ellen, Senior Counselor
FROM: Kim Williams, Student Tutor Supervisor
SUBJECT: Construction of a Tutoring Center
DATE: November 10, 2015
</td></tr>
</table>

Opening component

TO: Ina Ellen, Senior Counselor
FROM: Kim Williams, Student Tutor Supervisor
SUBJECT: Construction of a Tutoring Center
DATE: November 10, 2015

Purpose statement

This memo proposes the establishment of a tutoring center in the Office of Student Affairs.

BACKGROUND
Under the present system, tutors must work with students at a number of facilities scattered across the university campus. As a result, tutors waste a lot of time running from one facility to another and are often late for appointments.

Body

NEW FACILITY
I propose that we establish a tutoring facility adjacent to the Office of Student Affairs. The two empty classrooms next to the office, presently used for storage of office furniture, would be ideal for this use. We could furnish these offices with the desks and file cabinets already stored in these rooms.

BENEFITS
The benefits of this facility would be the centralizing of the tutoring services and the proximity of the facility to the Office of Student Affairs. The tutoring facility could also use the secretarial services of the Office of Student Affairs.

RECOMMENDATIONS

Conclusion

To implement this project we would need to do the following:
1. Clean up and paint rooms 331 and 333
2. Use folding partitions to divide each room into five single-desk offices
3. Use stored office equipment to furnish the center

These changes would do much to improve the tutoring service. I look forward to discussing this matter with you in more detail.

EXERCISE 32.1

Working in a group of three students, write a memo to your school's administration that proposes an on-campus job fair. Explain what purpose the job fair would serve and support your main point with specific examples and facts that pertain to the student body at your school.

32g Using Email

In many workplaces, virtually all internal (and many external) communications are transmitted as email. Although personal email tends to be informal, business email should observe the conventions of standard written communication. In addition, email should follow certain guidelines that can help you communicate effectively in digital environments. (See **22b1** for a list of those guidelines.)

Close-Up WRITING EMAILS

The following rules can help you communicate effectively in digital business environments.

- Write in complete sentences. Avoid slang, imprecise diction, and abbreviations.
- Use an appropriate tone. Address readers with respect, just as you would in a standard business letter.
- Include a subject line that clearly identifies your content.
- Make your message as short as possible. Because most emails are read on the screen, long discussions are difficult to follow.
- Use short paragraphs, leaving an extra space between paragraphs.
- Use lists and internal headings to focus your discussion and to break it into manageable parts.
- Reread and edit your email after you have written it.
- Proofread carefully before sending your email.
- Make sure that your list of recipients is accurate and that you do not send your email to unintended recipients.
- Do not send your email until you are absolutely certain that your message says exactly what you want it to say.
- Do not forward an email you receive unless you have the permission of the sender.
- Watch what you write. Keep in mind that email written at work is the property of the employer, who has the legal right to access it—even without your permission.

Close-Up WORKPLACE PRIVACY

In almost all cases, business emails are not considered private. Courts have held that an employer has the right to monitor all email sent over its system. (The same is true for voice mail as well as texts and instant messages.) For this reason, you should not assume that any message you send at work is private.

Some companies have policies that limit what an employee can post on social networking sites. Policies vary from company to company and are subject to state law, but derogatory comments about an employer or about the company (or any comments that could possibly damage the company) may be prohibited. You should check with your employer to find out if the company has a policy concerning social media.

CHAPTER **33**

Developing and Delivering Presentations

At school and on the job, you may be called on to make **presentations**. Although many people cringe at the thought of giving presentations, the following guidelines can make the experience much less stressful.

33a Getting Started

Just as with writing an essay, the preparation stage of a presentation is extremely important. The time you spend on this stage of the process will make your task easier later on.

Identify Your Topic   The first step in planning a presentation is to identify your topic. Sometimes you are given a topic; at other times, you will choose your own. Once you have a topic, you will be able to decide how much information, as well as what kind of information, you will need.

Consider Your Audience The easiest way to determine how much and what kind of information you will need is to consider the nature of your audience. Is your audience made up of experts or of people who know little about your topic? How much background information will you have to provide? Can you use technical terms, or should you avoid them? Do you think your audience will be interested in your topic, or will you have to create interest?

MULTILINGUAL TIP

When making presentations, some multilingual students choose topics related to their cultural backgrounds or home countries. This is a good idea because they are often able to provide insightful information on these topics that is new to their instructor and classmates. If you choose such a topic, try to determine beforehand how much background your audience has by speaking with your instructor and classmates.

Consider Your Purpose Your speech should have a specific purpose that you can sum up concisely. To help you zero in on your purpose, ask yourself what you are trying to accomplish with your presentation. It is a good idea to write down this purpose and to keep it in front of you as you plan your speech.

Purpose: to convince an audience that college athletes should be paid a salary

Consider Your Constraints How much time do you have for your presentation? (Obviously, a ten-minute presentation requires more information and preparation than a three-minute presentation.) Do you already know enough about your topic, or will you have to do research?

Close-Up GROUP PRESENTATIONS

Group presentations require a great deal of coordination. Before you begin to plan your speech, you should take these steps:

- Choose a leader who will coordinate the group's efforts.
- Determine who is responsible for each part of the presentation.
- Determine who will prepare and display visuals.
- Agree on a schedule for both work and rehearsal.
- Agree on acceptable team behavior—for example, how to dress and how to behave during the presentation.

33b Planning Your Speech

In the planning phase, you develop a thesis; then, you decide what specific points you will discuss and divide your speech into a few manageable sections.

PLANNING GUIDE

PRESENTATION

Your **assignment** will ask you to deliver a presentation on a particular topic.
Your **purpose** will be to inform, persuade, or entertain listeners.
Your **audience** could be people who know a lot about your topic or people who
know very little about it.

INTRODUCTION

- If you think your listeners know little about your topic, begin by creating interest—possibly by identifying common ground.
- If you think your listeners know a lot about your topic, begin with some general opening remarks.
- State your thesis.

Thesis statement templates:
- As my speech will show,...
- Many people think..., but...
- Instead of..., we should...

BODY

- Establish your credibility, demonstrating why your audience should listen to you.
- Present your points one at a time.
- Support your points with specific examples and facts.
- Be sure to acknowledge and identify information from outside sources.
- Use visuals to reinforce your points and to add interest.
- Maintain eye contact with your listeners.
- Speak slowly and distinctly, and pay attention to your body language.

Topic sentence templates:
- My first (second, third) point is...
- First (second, third), I will discuss...
- One (another) reason is...

Templates for introducing support:
- According to...
- In his/her article,...
- As the following chart shows,...

CONCLUSION

- Restate your thesis, possibly listing your points.
- End with a strong closing statement.
- Remember to ask listeners if they have questions.

Closing statement templates:
- Remember, the next time you...
- For these reasons,...
- In summary,...

Note: Be sure to plan your introduction and your conclusion *in advance.* Because these sections are what your audience hears first and last, they play a large part in determining the impression your speech makes. Don't make the mistake of thinking that you can make up an introduction or conclusion as you deliver your speech.

33c Preparing Your Presentation Notes

Most people use some form of presentation notes when they give a speech. Each system of notes has advantages and disadvantages.

Full Text   Some people like to type out the full text of their speech and refer to it during their presentation. If the type is large enough, and if you triple-space, this strategy can be useful. The main disadvantage of using the full text of your speech is that it is easy to lose your place and become disoriented; another is that you may end up reading your speech.

Index Cards   Some people write key points on index cards. Cards are portable, so they can be flipped through easily. They are also small, so they can be placed inconspicuously on a podium or a table. With some practice, you can learn to use note cards effectively. You have to be careful, however, not to become so dependent on the cards that you lose eye contact with your audience or begin fidgeting with the cards as you speak. Also, be sure to number the cards so that you can easily put them in order in case they get mixed up.

Outlines   Some people like to refer to an outline when they give a speech. As they speak, they can glance down at the outline to get their bearings or to remind themselves of a point they have to make. Because an outline does not contain the full text of a speech, the temptation to read is eliminated. However, if for some reason you draw a blank, an outline gives you very little to fall back on.

Note: *PowerPoint* enables users to add presentation notes to each slide. The speaker is able to see these notes during the presentation, but they are invisible to the audience (**see 33d2**).

33d Preparing Visual Aids

❶ Using Visuals

Visual aids can reinforce important information and make your speech easier to understand. For a short speech, a visual aid may be no more than a few key terms, definitions, or names written on the board. For a longer, more complicated presentation you might need charts, graphs, diagrams, photographs, or objects.

If you are using equipment, such as an overhead projector or a document camera, make sure you know how to operate it—and have a contingency plan just in case the equipment does not work (for example, have printouts that you can distribute if the need arises). If possible, visit the room in which you will be giving your speech ahead of time, and see whether it has the equipment you need (and whether the equipment works).

❷ Using Presentation Software

Microsoft PowerPoint, the most widely used presentation software package, enables you to organize a presentation and prepare professional-looking slides. Effective slides are open and easy to read, and they reinforce

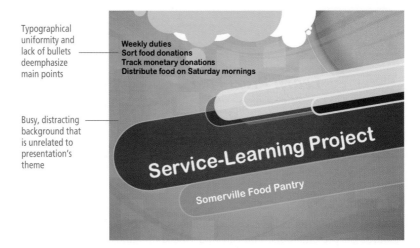

Clear, logical color schemes help improve legibility

Clean, simple background

Bulleted points presented clearly and prominently

Effective use of clip art to illustrate presentation's theme

FIGURE 33.1 Effective *PowerPoint* slide. © Cengage Learning 2017.

important information (see Figure 33.1). Ineffective slides have the opposite effect and can undercut an otherwise effective presentation (see Figure 33.2).

PowerPoint's more advanced features enable you to create multimedia presentations that combine images, video, audio, and animation. You can also use the Insert menu to insert various items—for example, clip art, word art, and image files you have created with a digital camera or scanner—into

Typographical uniformity and lack of bullets deemphasize main points

Busy, distracting background that is unrelated to presentation's theme

FIGURE 33.2 Ineffective *PowerPoint* slide. © Cengage Learning 2017.

your slide templates. You can even import charts and tables from *Microsoft Word* and *Excel* and download images from Internet sites directly into your slide templates.

Note: Increasingly, people are using tablets and smartphones to make presentations. Applications, such as *Keynote* for the iPad and iPhone, enable users to create and share slides.

Prezi, available free on the Internet at *prezi.com*, is a presentation tool that is gaining in popularity. Many people think that *Prezi* presentations are more interesting and engaging than *PowerPoint* presentations. With *Prezi*, images and text are pasted on a large screen or "stage" instead of on individual slides (see Figure 33.3). Users can move around the stage (much the way a Skycam at a football game does) and zoom in and out, depending on what they want to emphasize. In addition, videos, such as those available on *YouTube*, can easily be pasted into *Prezi*.

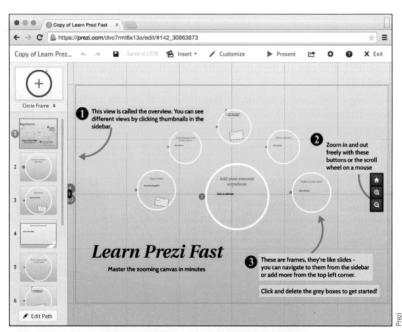

FIGURE 33.3 *Prezi* presentation stage.

3 Using *YouTube*

Because *YouTube* provides access to millions of videos, it is an excellent resource for presentations. You can find videos on almost any subject—for example, how to change the oil in a car, how to create a web page, or even how

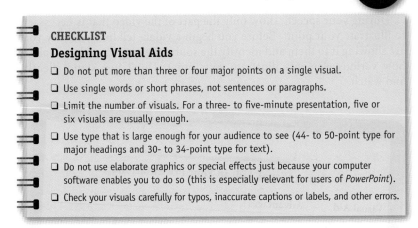

CHECKLIST

Designing Visual Aids

❑ Do not put more than three or four major points on a single visual.

❑ Use single words or short phrases, not sentences or paragraphs.

❑ Limit the number of visuals. For a three- to five-minute presentation, five or six visuals are usually enough.

❑ Use type that is large enough for your audience to see (44- to 50-point type for major headings and 30- to 34-point type for text).

❑ Do not use elaborate graphics or special effects just because your computer software enables you to do so (this is especially relevant for users of *PowerPoint*).

❑ Check your visuals carefully for typos, inaccurate captions or labels, and other errors.

to land a plane. You can also find videos showing current events, speeches, and television news shows. Figure 33.4 shows the *YouTube* home page.

Note: All versions of *PowerPoint* since 2010 enable users to insert a video link directly into their presentations. However, it is a good idea to have a backup plan in case a computer problem prevents you from connecting to the Internet or using videos in your presentation.

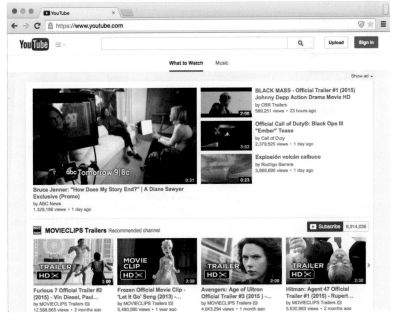

FIGURE 33.4 *YouTube* home page. © YouTube/Google, Inc.

During your speech, show only the part of the video that is necessary to illustrate your point. Before you begin a video, tell listeners why you are showing it to them and identify the source. During the video, explain how various elements illustrate your point. Don't just stand silently and watch.

Using Visual Aids in Your Presentations

Visual Aid	Advantages	Disadvatages
Computer presentations Bob Daemmrich/PhotoEdit	Clear Easy to read Professional Graphics, video, sound, and animated effects Portable (USB flash drive)	Special equipment needed Expertise needed Special software needed Software might not be compatible with all computer systems
Overhead projectors iStockphoto.com/ Clickstock	Transparencies are inexpensive Transparencies are easily prepared with computer or copier Transparencies are portable Transparencies can be written on during presentation Projector is easy to operate	Transparencies can stick together Transparencies can be accidentally placed upside down Transparencies must be placed on projector by hand Some projectors are noisy Speaker must avoid tripping over power cord during presentation
Document cameras (digital visualizers) Business Wire/Handout/ Getty Images Publicity/ Getty Images	Captures visual images in real time Projects images from a sheet of paper or projects 3D objects Zooms in on small text, pictures, or objects Interfaces with a whiteboard or a computer Has a high-definition display	Much more expensive than an overhead projector Must connect to another device to display an image Not yet widely available

Visual Aid	Advantages	Disadvatages
Slide projector Andy Crawford/Dorling Kindersley/Getty Images	Slides are colorful Slides look professional Projector is easy to use Order of slides can be rearranged during presentation Portable (slide carousel)	Slides are expensive to produce Special equipment needed for lettering and graphics Dark room needed for presentation Slides can jam in projector
Posters or flip charts iStockphoto.com/Mbbirdy	Low-tech and personal Good for small-group presentations Portable	May not be large enough to be seen in some rooms Artistic ability needed May be expensive if prepared professionally Must be secured to an easel
Chalkboards or whiteboards Jeffrey Coolidge/Stone/ Getty Images	Available in most rooms Easy to use Easy to erase or change information during presentation	Difficult to draw complicated graphics Handwriting must be legible Must catch errors while writing Cannot face audience when writing or drawing Very informal

33e Rehearsing Your Speech

Practice your speech often—at least five times—and make sure you practice with your visuals. Do not try to memorize your entire speech, but be sure you know it well enough so you can move from point to point without constantly looking at your notes. Finally, time yourself. Make certain your three-minute speech actually takes three minutes to deliver.

33f Delivering Your Speech

The most important part of your speech is your delivery. Keep in mind that a certain amount of nervousness is normal, so try not to focus on it too much. Channel the nervous energy into your speech, and let it work for you. Once you get to the front of the room, don't start right away; wait until your audience settles down.

CHECKLIST

Delivering Your Speech

As you deliver your speech, keep in mind the following tips on body language, eye contact, and pacing:

- ❑ Turn off your cell phone to ensure that it will not ring during your presentation.
- ❑ Position yourself effectively.
- ❑ Stand straight.
- ❑ Speak slowly and clearly.
- ❑ Maintain eye contact with the audience.
- ❑ Use natural gestures.
- ❑ Face the audience at all times.
- ❑ Do not block your visuals.
- ❑ If you forget something, don't let your audience know. Work the information in later.
- ❑ Leave time for questions.
- ❑ Distribute any handouts before or after the speech, not during it.

33g Answering Audience Questions

Most speeches will end with audience members asking questions, and this question-and-answer session is as much a part of your presentation as your prepared remarks are. The impression you make here will play a large part in how they judge your speech. For this reason, when you prepare your speech, you should take time to anticipate possible questions.

As you review your presentation notes, think of the most obvious questions listeners could ask—and the most difficult or perplexing questions listeners could ask. Then, write down and rehearse your answers. If necessary, prepare a note card with any specific information—statistics or facts—that you will need.

CHECKLIST

Answering Audience Questions

Once the question-and-answer part of your presentation begins, keep the following guidelines in mind:

❏ **Control the situation.** Try to call on people in the order in which they raise their hands. Don't let audience members ask questions at will.

❏ **Listen carefully.** Give your questioners your full attention, and don't interrupt them. Wait until they are finished asking their questions before you begin your answer.

❏ **Repeat questions.** By repeating questions, you make sure that everyone can hear them. You also give yourself time to put together an answer.

❏ **Answer questions concisely.** Keep your answers concise, direct, and focused. If a question is complicated and will require a long answer, summarize your response, and ask the questioner to see you after the presentation.

❏ **Be polite.** Don't indicate that you think a question is silly or misguided. Answer all questions respectfully.

❏ **Don't fake an answer.** If you don't know the answer to a question, say so. Then, tell the person that you will research the answer and email it to him or her.

EXERCISE 33.1

Follow the strategies outlined in this chapter to develop (and deliver) a ten- minute presentation focusing on a major you are interested in pursuing. (This could be a group project.) Consider your fellow students and your instructor to be your audience. Focus on why you think your major could be valuable: What skills will it help you build? How will it prepare you for a job after you graduate? What are the other—less tangible—benefits of such a major? For example, will it expand your worldview? Will it help you develop better critical thinking skills?

Use at least two of the following in your presentation:

- Hard-copy visual aids (such as handouts)
- Presentation software (such as *Prezi, Keynote,* or *PowerPoint*)
- A flip chart or whiteboard
- A short *YouTube* video

PART **9**

Developing Paragraph and Sentence Style

P A R T **9**

Developing Paragraph and Sentence Style

❓ Frequently Asked Questions

CHAPTER 34

Writing Effective Paragraphs

A **paragraph** is a group of related sentences. It may be complete in itself or part of a longer piece of writing.

CHECKLIST

When to Begin a New Paragraph

❏ Begin a new paragraph whenever you move from one major point to another.

❏ Begin a new paragraph whenever you move from one time period or location to another.

❏ Begin a new paragraph whenever you introduce a new step in a process.

❏ Begin a new paragraph when you want to emphasize an important idea.

❏ Begin a new paragraph every time a new person speaks.

❏ Begin a new paragraph to signal the end of your introduction and the beginning of your conclusion.

34a Writing Unified Paragraphs

A paragraph is **unified** when it develops a single main idea. The **topic sentence** states the main idea of the paragraph, and the other sentences in the paragraph support that idea.

1 Using Topic Sentences

A topic sentence often comes at the beginning of a paragraph. Occasionally, however, a topic sentence may occur at the end of a paragraph, particularly if a writer wants to lead up to an unexpected conclusion.

Topic Sentence at the Beginning A topic sentence at the beginning of a paragraph tells readers what to expect and helps them to understand your paragraph's main idea immediately.

> I was a listening child, careful to hear the very different sounds of Spanish and English. Wide-eyed with hearing, I'd listen to sounds more than words. First, there were English (*gringo*) sounds. So many words were still unknown that when the butcher or the lady at the drugstore said something to me,

exotic polysyllabic sounds would bloom in the midst of their sentences. Often the speech of people in public seemed to me very loud, booming with confidence. The man behind the counter would literally ask, "What can I do for you?" But by being so firm and so clear, the sound of his voice said that he was a *gringo*; he belonged in public society. (Richard Rodriguez, *Aria: Memoir of a Bilingual Childhood*)

Topic Sentence at the End   A topic sentence at the end of a paragraph is useful if you are presenting an unusual or hard-to-accept idea. By presenting a logical chain of reasoning before you state your main idea in your topic sentence, you are more likely to convince readers that your paragraph's main idea is reasonable.

These sprays, dusts and aerosols are now applied almost universally to farms, gardens, forests, and homes—nonselective chemicals that have the power to kill every insect, the "good" and the "bad," to still the song of birds and the leaping of fish in the streams, to coat the leaves with a deadly film, and to linger on in soil—all this though the intended target may be only a few weeds or insects. Can anyone believe it is possible to lay down such a barrage of poisons on the surface without making it unfit for life? They should not be called "insecticides," but "biocides." (Rachel Carson, "The Obligation to Endure," *Silent Spring*)

Note: In some paragraphs—especially narrative and descriptive paragraphs—a topic sentence may seem forced or unnatural. In these cases, the topic sentence may be implied rather than explicitly stated.

② Testing for Unity

Each sentence in a paragraph should support the main idea that is stated in the topic sentence. The following paragraph is not unified because it includes sentences that do not support the main idea.

Paragraph Not Unified

One of the first problems I had as a college student was improving my computer skills. All students were required to buy a computer before school started. Throughout the first semester, we took a special course to teach us to use a computer. My laptop has a lot of memory and can do graphics and spreadsheets. It has a large retina display screen and a wireless keyboard and trackpad. My parents were happy that I had a computer, but they were concerned about the price. Tuition was high, and when they added in the price of the computer, it was almost out of reach. To offset expenses, I got a part-time job in the school library. (student writer)

[Sentences do not support main idea]

When he revised, the writer deleted the sentences about his parents' financial situation and the computer's characteristics and added details related to the main idea.

Revised Paragraph

> One of the first problems I had as a college student was improving my computer skills. All first-year students were required to buy a computer before school started. Throughout the first semester, we took a special course to teach us to use the computer. In theory this system sounded fine, but in my case it was a disaster. Most of the students in my computer orientation course already knew how to work with spreadsheets, presentation software, and wikis. They were also familiar with the course management software that my college uses. They could navigate the discussion boards and use the chat function that was part of my composition course. The high school that I attended didn't have this (or any) system, so I felt that I was at a great disadvantage. By the end of the first week, I was convinced that I would never be able to keep up with the rest of the class.

Sentences now support main idea

EXERCISE 34.1

The following paragraph is unified by one main idea, but that idea is not explicitly stated. Identify the paragraph's main idea, write a topic sentence that expresses it, and decide where in the paragraph to place it.

> The narrator in Ellison's novel leaves an all-black college in the South to seek his fortune—and his identity—in the North. Throughout the story, he experiences bigotry in all forms. Blacks as well as whites, friends as well as enemies, treat him according to their preconceived notions of what he should be or how he can help to advance their causes. Clearly, this is a book about racial prejudice. However, on another level, *Invisible Man* is more than the account of a young African American's initiation into the harsh realities of life in the United States before the civil rights movement. The narrator calls himself invisible because others refuse to see him. He becomes so alienated from society—black and white—that he chooses to live in isolation. But, when he has learned to see himself clearly, he will emerge demanding that others see him too.

34b Writing Coherent Paragraphs

A paragraph is **coherent** when all its sentences clearly relate to one another. You can create coherence by arranging details or ideas according to an organizing principle, by using transitional words and phrases, by using parallel structure, and by repeating key words and phrases.

1 Arranging Details

Even if all its sentences are about the same subject, a paragraph lacks coherence if the sentences are not arranged according to a general organizing principle—that is, if they are not arranged *spatially, chronologically,* or *logically.*

See 34d2
- **Spatial order** establishes the perspective from which readers will view details. For example, an object or scene can be viewed from top to bottom or from near to far. Spatial order is central to **descriptive paragraphs**.

See 34d1, 4
- **Chronological order** presents events in sequence, using transitional words and phrases to establish the time order of events—*at first, yesterday, later, in 1930,* and so on. Chronological order is central to **narrative paragraphs** and **process paragraphs**.

See 34d3, 6
- **Logical order** presents details or ideas in terms of their logical relationships to one another. For example, the ideas in a paragraph may move from *least important to most important.* Transitional words and phrases such as *the most important* and *the least important* or *first, second,* and *finally* establish these relationships and lead readers through the paragraph. Logical order is central to **exemplification paragraphs** and **comparison-and-contrast paragraphs**.

2 Using Transitional Words and Phrases

Transitional words and phrases create coherence by emphasizing the spatial, chronological, and logical organizing principles discussed above. The following paragraph, which has no transitional words and phrases, illustrates just how important these words and phrases are.

Paragraph without Transitional Words and Phrases

Napoleon certainly made a change for the worse by leaving his small kingdom of Elba. He went back to Paris, and he abdicated for a second time. He fled to Rochefort in hope of escaping to America. He gave himself up to the English captain of the ship *Bellerophon.* He suggested that the Prince Regent grant him asylum, and he was refused. All he saw of England was the Devon coast and Plymouth Sound as he passed on to the remote island of St. Helena. He died on May 5, 1821, at the age of fifty-two.

In the narrative paragraph above, the topic sentence states the main idea of the paragraph, and the rest of the sentences support this idea. Because of the absence of transitional words and phrases, however, readers cannot tell exactly how one event in the paragraph relates to another in time. Notice how much clearer this passage is once transitional words and phrases (such as *after, finally, once again,* and *in the end*) have been added.

Paragraph with Transitional Words and Phrases

Napoleon certainly made a change for the worse by leaving his small kingdom of Elba. After Waterloo, he went back to Paris, and he abdicated for a second time. A hundred days after his return from Elba, he fled to Rochefort in hope of escaping to America. Finally, he gave himself up to the English captain of the ship *Bellerophon*. Once again, he suggested that the Prince Regent grant him asylum, and once again, he was refused. In the end, all he saw of England was the Devon coast and Plymouth Sound as he passed on to the remote island of St. Helena. After six years of exile, he died on May 5, 1821, at the age of fifty-two. (Norman Mackenzie, *The Escape from Elba*)

Frequently Used Transitional Words and Phrases

To Signal Sequence or Addition

again
also
besides
first . . . second . . . third
furthermore

in addition
moreover
one . . . another
too

To Signal Time

afterward
as soon as
at first
at the same time
before
earlier
finally
in the meantime

later
meanwhile
next
now
soon
subsequently
then
until

To Signal Comparison

also
in comparison
in the same way

likewise
moreover
similarly

To Signal Contrast

although
but
despite
instead
meanwhile

even though
however
in contrast
on the one hand . . . on the other hand

(continued)

Frequently Used Transitional Words and Phrases (*continued*)

nevertheless

nonetheless

on the contrary

still

whereas

yet

To Introduce Examples

for example

for instance

namely

in other words

thus

To Signal Narrowing of Focus

after all

indeed

in fact

in other words

in particular

specifically

that is

To Introduce Conclusions or Summaries

as a result

consequently

in conclusion

in other words

in summary

therefore

thus

to conclude

To Signal Concession

admittedly

certainly

granted

naturally

of course

To Introduce Causes or Effects

accordingly

as a result

because

consequently

hence

since

so

then

therefore

3 Using Parallel Structure

See
36c, 38a

Parallelism—the use of matching words, phrases, clauses, or sentence structures to emphasize similar ideas—can increase coherence in a paragraph. Note in the following paragraph how parallel constructions beginning with *He was* link (and emphasize) Thomas Jefferson's accomplishments.

Thomas Jefferson was born in 1743 and died at Monticello, Virginia, on July 4, 1826. During his eighty-four years, he accomplished a number of things. Although best known for his draft of the Declaration of Independence, Jefferson was a man of many talents who had a wide intellectual range. He was a patriot who was one of the revolutionary founders of the United States. He was a reformer who, when he was governor of Virginia, drafted the Statute for Religious Freedom. He was an innovator who drafted an ordinance for governing the West and devised the first decimal monetary system. He was a president who abolished internal taxes, reduced the national debt, and made the Louisiana Purchase. And, finally, he was an architect who designed Monticello and the University of Virginia. (student writer)

4 Repeating Key Words and Phrases

Repeating **key words and phrases** throughout a paragraph connects the sentences to one another and to the paragraph's main idea. The following paragraph repeats the key word *mercury* to keep readers focused on the subject.

Mercury poisoning is a problem that has long been recognized. "Mad as a hatter" refers to the condition prevalent among nineteenth-century workers who were exposed to mercury during the manufacturing of felt hats. Workers in many other industries, such as mining, chemicals, and dentistry, were similarly affected. In the 1950s and 1960s, there were cases of mercury poisoning in Minamata, Japan. Research showed that there were high levels of mercury pollution in streams and lakes surrounding the village. In the United States, this problem came to light in 1969, when a New Mexico family got sick from eating food tainted with mercury. Since then, pesticides containing mercury have been withdrawn from the market, and chemical wastes can no longer be dumped into the ocean. (student writer)

Note: The same methods you use to link sentences within paragraphs may also be used to link the paragraphs in an essay.

EXERCISE 34.2

Revise the following paragraph to make it more coherent.

The theory of continental drift was first put forward by Alfred Wegener in 1912. The continents fit together like a gigantic jigsaw puzzle. The opposing Atlantic coasts, especially South America and Africa, seem to have been attached. He believed that at one time, probably 225 million years ago, there was one supercontinent.

This continent broke into parts that drifted into their present positions. The theory stirred controversy during the 1920s and eventually was ridiculed by the scientific community. In 1954, the theory was revived. The theory of continental drift is accepted as a reasonable geological explanation of the continental system.

34c   Writing Well-Developed Paragraphs

A paragraph is **well developed** when it includes the **support**—examples, statistics, expert opinion, and so on—that readers need to understand its main idea. Keep in mind that length alone does not determine whether a paragraph is well developed. To determine the amount and kind of support you need, consider your audience, your purpose, and the scope of your paragraph's main idea.

The following paragraph is not adequately developed because it does not include enough support to convince readers that children and parents are "bombarded by ads for violent toys."

Underdeveloped Paragraph

> From Thanksgiving until Christmas, children and their parents are bombarded by ads for violent toys and games. Toy manufacturers persist in thinking that only toys that appeal to children's aggressiveness will sell. Despite claims that they (unlike action toys) have educational value, video games have escalated the level of violence. The real question is why parents continue to buy these violent toys and games for their children. (student writer)

When the student writer revised her paragraph, she added specific examples to support her topic sentence.

Revised Paragraph (Examples Added)

> From Thanksgiving until Christmas, children and their parents are bombarded by ads for violent toys and games. Toy manufacturers persist in thinking that only toys that appeal to children's aggressiveness will
>
> Examples   sell. One television commercial praises the merits of a commando team that attacks and captures a miniature enemy base. Toy soldiers wear realistic uniforms and carry automatic rifles, pistols, knives, grenades, and ammunition. Another commercial shows children playing with cars that turn into robots that shoot missiles and have projectile-launching wings. Despite claims that they (unlike action toys) have educational value,
>
> Examples   video games have escalated the level of violence. The most popular video games—such as *Grand Theft Auto V* and *Resident Evil 6*—depict graphic violence, criminal behavior, nudity, and other objectionable material. One game allows players to hack up zombies with a variety of weapons, such as

ice picks, swords, and chain saws as well as guns and grenades. Other best-selling games graphically simulate hand-to-hand combat on city streets and feature dismembered bodies and the sound of breaking bones. The real question is why parents continue to buy these violent toys and games for their children.

EXERCISE 34.3

Write a paragraph for two of the following topic sentences. Be sure to include all the examples and other support necessary to develop the paragraph adequately. Assume that you are writing your paragraph for the students in your composition class.

1. First-year students can take specific steps to make sure that they are successful in college.
2. Setting up a first apartment can be quite a challenge.
3. Whenever I get depressed, I think of _____, and I feel better.
4. The person I admire most is _____.
5. If I won the lottery, I would do three things.

34d Using Patterns of Development

Patterns of paragraph development—*narration, exemplification*, and so on—reflect the way a writer arranges material to express ideas most effectively.

1 Narration

A **narrative** paragraph tells a story by presenting events in chronological (time) order. Most narratives move in a logical, orderly sequence from beginning to end, from first event to last. Clear transitional words and phrases (*later, after that*) and time markers (*in 1990, two years earlier, the next day*) establish the chronological sequence.

My academic career almost ended as soon as it began when, three weeks after I arrived at college, I decided to pledge a fraternity. By midterms, I was wearing a pledge cap and saying "Yes, sir" to every fraternity brother I met. When classes were over, I ran errands for the fraternity members, and after dinner I socialized and worked on projects with the other people in my pledge class. In between these activities, I tried to study. Somehow I managed to write essays, take tests, and attend lectures. By the end of the semester, though,

Topic sentence identifies subject of narrative

Sequence of events

Philip Gould/Corbis

FIGURE 34.1 Student in pledge cap; one event in narrative sequence.

my grades had slipped, and I was exhausted. It was then that I began to ask myself some important questions. I realized that I wanted to be popular, but not at the expense of my grades and my future career. At the beginning of my second semester, I dropped out of the fraternity and got a job in the biology lab. Looking back, I realize that it was then that I actually began to grow up. (student writer)

2 Description

A **descriptive** paragraph communicates how something looks, sounds, smells, tastes, or feels. The most natural arrangement of details in a description reflects the way you actually look at a person, scene, or object: near to far, top to bottom, side to side, or front to back. This arrangement of details is made clear by transitions that identify precise spatial relationships: *next to, near, beside, under, above,* and so on.

Note: Sometimes a descriptive paragraph does not have a topic sentence. In such cases, it is unified by a **dominant impression**—the effect created by all the details in the description.

Details convey dominant impression

When you are inside the jungle, away from the river, the trees vault out of sight. It is hard to remember to look up the long trunks and see the fans, strips, fronds, and sprays of glossy leaves. Inside the jungle you are more likely to notice the snarl of climbers and creepers round the trees' boles, the flowering bromeliads and epiphytes in every bough's crook, and the fantastic silk-cotton tree trunks thirty or forty feet across, trunks buttressed in flanges of wood whose curves can make three high walls of a room—a shady, loamy-aired room where you would gladly live, or die. Butterflies, iridescent blue, striped, or clear-winged, thread the jungle paths at eye level. And at your feet is a swath of ants bearing triangular bits of green leaf. The ants with their leaves look like a wide fleet of sailing dinghies—but they don't quit. In either direction they wobble over the jungle floor as far as the eye can see. I followed them off the path as far as I dared, and never saw an end to ants or to those luffing chips of green they bore. (Annie Dillard, "In the Jungle")

Buddy Mays/Corbis

FIGURE 34.2 Vividly detailed close-up of Blue Morpho butterfly in Costa Rican rainforest.

3 Exemplification

An **exemplification** paragraph supports a topic sentence with a series of examples (or, sometimes, with a single extended example). These examples can be drawn from personal observation, experience, or research.

Topic sentence identifies paragraph's main idea

Illiterates cannot travel freely. When they attempt to do so, they encounter risks that few of us can dream of. They cannot read traffic signs and, while they often learn to recognize and to decipher symbols, they cannot manage street names which they haven't seen before. The same is true for bus and subway stops. While ingenuity can sometimes help a man or woman to discern directions from familiar landmarks, buildings, cemeteries, churches, and the like, most illiterates are virtually immobilized. They seldom wander past the streets and neighborhoods they know. Geographical paralysis becomes a bitter metaphor for their entire existence. They are immobilized in almost every sense we can imagine. They can't move up.

Series of examples

They can't move out. They cannot see beyond. Illiterates may take an oral test for drivers' permits in most sections of America. It is a questionable concession. Where will they go? How will they get there? How will they get home? Could it be that some of us might like it better if they stayed where they belong? (Jonathan Kozol, *Illiterate America*)

FIGURE 34.3 Street signs illustrate one area of confusion for illiterates.

4 Process

Process paragraphs describe how something works, presenting a series of steps in strict chronological order. The topic sentence identifies the process, and the rest of the paragraph presents the steps. Transitional words such as *first, then, next, after this,* and *finally* link steps in the process.

Members of the court have disclosed, however, the general way the conference is conducted. It begins at ten A.M. and usually runs on until late afternoon. At the start each justice, when he enters the room, shakes hands with all others there (thirty-six handshakes altogether). The custom, dating back generations, is evidently designed to begin the meeting at a friendly level, no matter how heated the intellectual differences may be. The conference takes up, first, the applications for review—a few appeals, many more petitions for certiorari. Those on the Appellate Docket, the regular paid cases, are considered first, then the pauper's applications on the Miscellaneous Docket. (If

Topic sentence identifies process

Steps in process

any of these are granted, they are then transferred to the Appellate Docket.) After this the justices consider, and vote on, all the cases argued during the preceding Monday through Thursday. These are tentative votes, which may be and quite often are changed as the opinion is written and the problem thought through more deeply. There may be further discussion at later conferences before the opinion is handed down. (Anthony Lewis, *Gideon's Trumpet*)

FIGURE 34.4 US Supreme Court justices after final step in process (handing down opinion in *Gideon v. Wainwright*, November 1962).

Close-Up INSTRUCTIONS

When a process paragraph presents **instructions** to enable readers to actually perform the process, it is written in the present tense and in the imperative mood—"*Remove* the cover . . . and *check* the valve."

5 Cause and Effect

A **cause-and-effect** paragraph explores causes or predicts or describes results; sometimes a single cause-and-effect paragraph does both. Clear, specific transitional words and phrases such as *one cause, another cause, a more important result, because*, and *as a result* convey the cause-and-effect relationships.

Paragraphs that examine **causes** explain why something happens or happened.

Topic sentence establishes major cause

The main reason that a young baby sucks his thumb seems to be that he hasn't had enough sucking at the breast or bottle to satisfy his sucking needs. Dr. David Levy pointed out that babies who are fed every 3 hours don't suck their thumbs as much as babies fed every 4 hours, and that babies who have cut down on nursing time from 20 minutes to 10 minutes...are more likely

FIGURE 34.5 Baby sucking thumb.

Atthapol Saita/Shutterstock.com

Cause explored in detail

to suck their thumbs than babies who still have to work for 20 minutes. Dr. Levy fed a litter of puppies with a medicine dropper so that they had no chance to suck during their feedings. They acted just the same as babies who don't get enough chance to suck at feeding time. They sucked their own and each other's paws and skin so hard that the fur came off. (Benjamin Spock, *Baby and Child Care*)

Paragraphs that focus on **effects** explain how a change is or was the result of a specific set of causes or actions.

Topic sentence establishes major effect

On December 8, 1941, the day after the Japanese attack on Pearl Harbor in Hawaii, my grandfather barricaded himself with his family—my grandmother, my teenage mother, her two sisters and two brothers—inside of his home in La'ie, a sugar plantation village on Oahu's North Shore. This was my maternal grandfather, a man most villagers called by his last name, Kubota. It could mean either "Wayside Field" or else "Broken Dreams," depending on

Discussion of other effects

which ideograms he used. Kubota ran La'ie's general store, and the previous night, after a long day of bad news on the radio, some locals had come by, pounded on the front door, and made threats. One was said to have brandished a machete. They were angry and shocked, as the whole nation was

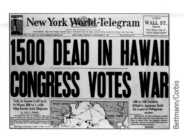

New York World-Telegram WALL ST.

1500 DEAD IN HAWAII
CONGRESS VOTES WAR

Bettmann/Corbis

FIGURE 34.6 Headline announcing attack on Pearl Harbor.

in the aftermath of the surprise attack. Kubota was one of the few Japanese Americans in the village and president of the local Japanese language school. He had become a target for their rage and suspicion. A wise man, he locked all his doors and windows and did not open his store the next day, but stayed closed and waited for news from some official. (Garrett Hongo, "Kubota")

6 Comparison and Contrast

Comparison-and-contrast paragraphs examine the similarities and differences between two subjects. **Comparison** focuses on similarities; **contrast** emphasizes differences. Comparison-and-contrast paragraphs can be organized in one of two ways: **point-by-point** or **subject-by-subject**.

Point-by-point comparisons discuss two subjects together, alternating points about one subject with comparable points about the other.

> There are two Americas. One is the America of Lincoln and Adlai Stevenson; the other is the America of Teddy Roosevelt and the modern superpatriots. One is generous and humane, the other narrowly egotistical; one is self-critical, the other self-righteous; one is sensible, the other romantic; one is good-humored, the other solemn; one is inquiring, the other pontificating; one is moderate, the other filled with passionate intensity; one is judicious and the other arrogant in the use of great power. (J. William Fulbright, *The Arrogance of Power*)

Topic sentence establishes comparison

Alternating points about the two subjects

Mathew B. Brady/Corbis   Bettmann/Corbis

FIGURE 34.7 Abraham Lincoln (left) and Theodore Roosevelt (right) symbolize the contrast between the two Americas.

Subject-by-subject comparisons treat one subject completely and then move on to the other subject. In the following paragraph, notice how the writer shifts from one subject to the other with the transitional word *however*.

Topic sentence establishes comparison

First subject discussed

Second subject introduced

First, it is important to note that men and women regard conversation quite differently. For women it is a passion, a sport, an activity even more important to life than eating because it doesn't involve weight gain. The first sign of closeness among women is when they find themselves engaging in endless, secretless rounds of conversation with one another. And as soon as a woman begins to relax and feel comfortable in a relationship with a man, she tries to have that type of conversation with him as well. However, the first sign that a man is feeling close to a woman is when he admits that he'd rather she please quiet down so he can hear the TV. A man who feels truly intimate with a woman often reserves for her and her alone the precious gift of one-word answers. Everyone knows that the surest way to spot a successful long-term relationship is to look around a restaurant for the table where no one is talking. Ah . . . now that's real love. (Merrill Markoe, "Men, Women, and Conversation")

FIGURE 34.8 Man watching TV to halt conversation (illustrates contrast between conversation styles of men and women).

Paula Connelly/Getty Images

7 Division and Classification

Division paragraphs take a single item and break it into its component parts.

Topic sentence identifies categories

Categories discussed

The blood can be divided into four distinct components: plasma, red cells, white cells, and platelets. One component, plasma, is ninety percent water and holds a great number of substances in suspension. It contains proteins, sugars, fat, and inorganic salts. Plasma also contains urea and other by-products from the breaking down of proteins, hormones, enzymes, and dissolved gases. The red cells, another component of blood, give blood its distinctive color. The red cells are most numerous; they get oxygen from the lungs and release it in the tissues. The less numerous white cells are a component of blood that defends the body against invading organisms. Finally, the platelets, which occur in almost the same number as white cells, are responsible for clotting. (student writer)

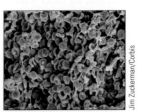

FIGURE 34.9 Components of blood—blood cells and platelets—in vein.

Jim Zuckerman/Corbis

Classification paragraphs take many separate items and group them into categories according to qualities or characteristics they share.

Topic sentence establishes categories

Charles Babbage, an English mathematician, reflecting in 1830 on what he saw as the decline of science at the time, distinguished among three major kinds of scientific fraud. He called the first "forging," by which he meant complete fabrication—the recording of observations that were never made. The second category he called "trimming"; this consists of manipulating the data to make

FIGURE 34.10 The FeJee mermaid illustrates "forging," one of three categories of scientific fraud.

Gift of the Heirs of David Kimball © President and Fellows of Harvard College, Peabody Museum of Archaeology and Ethnology, PM# 97-39-70/72853 (digital file# 60743308).

them look better, or, as Babbage wrote, "clipping off little bits here and there from those observations which differ most in excess from the mean and in sticking them on to those which are too small." His third category was data selection, which he called "cooking"— the choosing of those data that fitted the researcher's hypoth- esis and the discarding of those that did not. To this day, the serious discussion of scientific fraud has not improved on Babbage's typology. (Morton Hunt, *New York Times Magazine*)

Categories discussed

8 Definition

Definition paragraphs develop a definition by means of other patterns—for instance, defining *happiness* by telling a story (narration) or defining a diesel engine by telling how it works (process).

The following definition paragraph is developed by means of exemplification: it begins with a straightforward definition of *gadget* and then cites an example.

FIGURE 34.11 Rural mailbox with semaphore (term defined by exemplification).

Alain Schein Photography/Corbis

A gadget is nearly always novel in design or concept and it often has no proper name. For example, the semaphore which signals the arrival of the mail in our rural mailbox certainly has no proper name. It is a contrivance consisting of a piece of shingle. Call it what you like, it saves us frequent frustrating trips to the mailbox in winter when you have to dress up and wade through snow to get there. That's a gadget! (*Smithsonian*)

Topic sentence gives general definition

Definition expanded with an example

EXERCISE 34.4

Determine one possible pattern of development for a paragraph on each of these topics. Then, write a paragraph on one of the topics.

1. What success is (or is not)
2. How to prepare for a job interview
3. The kinds of people who appear on reality TV shows
4. My worst experience
5. Two fast-food restaurants
6. The benefits (or dangers) of social media sites
7. Budgeting money wisely
8. The dangers of texting while driving

34e Writing Special Kinds of Paragraphs

So far, this chapter has focused on **body paragraphs**, the paragraphs that carry the weight of your essay's discussion. Other kinds of paragraphs—*transitional paragraphs, introductory paragraphs*, and *concluding paragraphs*—have special functions in an essay.

1 Transitional Paragraphs

A **transitional paragraph** connects one section of the essay to another. At their simplest, transitional paragraphs can be single sentences that move readers from one point to another.

> What is true for ants is also true for people.

More often, however, writers use transitional paragraphs to summarize what they have already said before they move on to a new point.

The following transitional paragraph uses a series of questions to sum up some of the ideas the writer has been discussing. In the next part of his essay, he goes on to answer these questions.

> Can we bleed off the mass of humanity to other worlds? Right now the number of human beings on Earth is increasing by 80 million per year, and each year that number goes up by 1 and a fraction percent. Can we really suppose that we can send 80 million people per year to the Moon, Mars, and elsewhere, and engineer those worlds to support those people? And even so, nearly remain in the same place ourselves? (Isaac Asimov, "The Case against Man")

2 Introductory Paragraphs

An **introductory paragraph** prepares readers for the essay to follow. It typically introduces the subject, narrows it, and then states the essay's thesis.

> Christine was just a girl in one of my classes. I never knew much about her except that she was strange. She didn't talk much. Her hair was dyed black and purple, and she wore heavy black boots and a black turtle-neck sweater, even in the summer. She was attractive—in spite of the ring she wore through her left eyebrow—but she never seemed to care what the rest of us thought about her. Like the rest of my classmates, I didn't really want to get close to her. It was only when we were assigned to do our chemistry project together that I began to understand why Christine dressed the way she did. (student writer)

To arouse their audience's interest, writers may vary this direct approach by using one of the following introductory strategies.

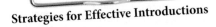

Strategies for Effective Introductions

Quotation or Series of Quotations

When Mary Cassatt's father was told of her decision to become a painter, he said: "I would rather see you dead." When Edgar Degas saw a show of Cassatt's etchings, his response was: "I am not willing to admit that a woman can draw that well." When she returned to Philadelphia after twenty-eight years abroad, having achieved renown as an Impressionist painter and the esteem of Degas, Huysmans, Pissarro, and Berthe Morisot, the *Philadelphia Ledger* reported: "Mary Cassatt, sister of Mr. Cassatt, president of the Pennsylvania Railroad, returned from Europe yesterday. She has been studying painting in France and owns the smallest Pekingese dog in the world." (Mary Gordon, "Mary Cassatt")

Question or Series of Questions

Of all the disputes agitating the American campus, the one that seems to me especially significant is that over "the canon." What should be taught in the humanities and social sciences, especially in introductory courses? What is the place of the classics? How shall we respond to those professors who attack "Eurocentrism" and advocate "multiculturalism"? This is not the sort of tedious quarrel that now and then flutters through the academy; it involves matters of public urgency. I propose to see this dispute, at first, through a narrow, even sectarian lens, with the hope that you will come to accept my reasons for doing so. (Irving Howe, "The Value of the Canon")

Definition

Moles are collections of cells that can appear on any part of the body. With occasional exceptions, moles are absent at birth. They first appear in the early years of life, between ages two and six. Frequently, moles appear at puberty. New moles, however, can continue to appear throughout life. During pregnancy, new moles may appear and old ones darken. There are three major designations of moles, each with its own unique distinguishing characteristics. (student writer)

Controversial Statement

Many Americans would probably be surprised to learn that Head Start has not been an unqualified success. Founded in 1965, the Head Start program provides early childhood education, social services, and medical check-ups to poor children across the US. In recent years, it has also focused on the children of migrant workers and on children who are homeless. For the most part, Americans view Head Start not just as a success but also as a model for other social programs.

(continued)

Strategies for Effective Introductions (*continued*)

What many people do not know, however, is that although Head Start is a short-term success for many children, the ambitious long-term goals of the program have not been met. For example, studies have shown that children who participate in Head Start do not see long-term increases in IQ or in academic achievement. For this reason, it may be time to consider making significant changes in the way Head Start is run. (student writer)

Close-Up   INTRODUCTORY PARAGRAPHS

- Avoid introductions that begin by announcing your subject ("In my essay, I will talk about Lady Macbeth").
- Avoid introductions that undercut your credibility ("I don't know much about alternative energy sources, but I would like to present my opinion about the subject").
- Avoid introductions that discuss the difficulty of the topic ("I had trouble deciding what to write about, but I finally . . .").

CHECKLIST
Writing Effective Introductions

After you draft your introduction, check its effectiveness by asking the following questions:

- ❏ Does your introductory paragraph include a thesis statement?
- ❏ Does it lead naturally into the body of your essay?
- ❏ Does it create interest?
- ❏ Does it avoid statements that undercut your credibility?

3 Concluding Paragraphs

A **concluding paragraph** typically begins by reinforcing the essay's thesis and then moves to more general comments. Whenever possible, it should end with a sentence that readers will remember.

Keep in mind that an effective conclusion does not simply restate what was said in the introduction. It presents information in the context of what you have said in the body of your essay. Because your conclusion brings your essay to a close, it should never introduce new points or pursue new lines of thought.

> As an Arab-American, I feel I have the best of two worlds. I'm proud to be part of the melting pot, proud to contribute to the tremendous diversity of cultures, customs and traditions that makes this country unique. But Arab-bashing—public acceptance of hatred and bigotry—is something no American can be proud of. (Ellen Mansoor Collier, "I Am Not a Terrorist")

Writers may use any of the following concluding strategies to sum up their essay's ideas.

Strategies for Effective Conclusions

Prediction

   Looking ahead, [we see that] prospects may not be quite as dismal as they seem. As a matter of fact, we are not doing so badly. It is something of a miracle that creatures who evolved as nomads in an intimate, small-band, wide-open-spaces context manage to get along at all as villagers or surrounded by strangers in cubicle apartments. Considering that our genius as a species is adaptability, we may yet learn to live closer and closer to one another, if not in utter peace, then far more peacefully than we do today. (John Pheiffer, "Seeking Peace, Making War")

Warning

   The Internet is the twenty-first century's talking drum, the very kind of grassroots communication tool that has been such a powerful source of education and culture for our people since slavery. But this talking drum we have not yet learned to play. Unless we master the new information technology to build and deepen the forms of social connection that a tragic history has eroded, African-Americans will face a form of cybersegregation in the next century as devastating to our aspirations as Jim Crow segregation was to those of our ancestors. But this time, the fault will be our own. (Henry Louis Gates Jr., "One Internet, Two Nations")

Recommendation for Action

   Computers have revolutionized learning in ways that we have barely begun to appreciate. We have experienced enough, however, to recognize the need to change our thinking about our purposes, methods, and outcome of higher education. Rather than resisting or postponing

(continued)

Strategies for Effective Conclusions (*continued*)

change, we need to anticipate and learn from it. We must harness the technology and use it to educate our students more effectively than we have been doing. Otherwise, we will surrender our authority to those who can. (Peshe Kuriloff, "If John Dewey Were Alive Today, He'd Be a Webhead")

Quotation

Apart from what any critic had to say about my writing, I knew I had succeeded where it counted when my mother finished reading my book and gave me her verdict: "So easy to read." (Amy Tan, "Mother Tongue")

Close-Up CONCLUDING PARAGRAPHS

- Don't waste time repeating sentences from your introduction in different words.
- Don't apologize or undercut your credibility ("Of course, I am not an expert" or "At least, this is my opinion").
- Don't introduce any new points or go off in new directions.

CHECKLIST
Writing Effective Conclusions

After you draft your conclusion, check its effectiveness by asking the following questions:

❏ Does your concluding paragraph sum up your essay, perhaps by reinforcing the essay's main points?

❏ Does it do more than just repeat the introduction's wording?

❏ Does it avoid introducing new points?

❏ Does it avoid apologies?

❏ Does it end memorably?

CHAPTER 35

Writing Varied Sentences

Varied sentences can make your writing livelier and more interesting. In addition, varying sentence structure, length, and openings can help you emphasize the most important ideas in your sentences.

35a Varying Sentence Structure

Paragraphs that mix simple, compound, and complex sentences are more varied—and therefore more interesting—than those that do not.

1 Using Compound Sentences

A **compound sentence** consists of two or more independent clauses joined with *coordinating conjunctions, transitional words and phrases, correlative conjunctions, semicolons,* or *colons.*

Coordinating Conjunctions

The pianist made some mistakes, <u>but</u> the concert was a success.

Note: Use a comma before a coordinating conjunction—*and, or, nor, but, for, so,* and *yet*—that joins two <u>independent clauses</u>.

See B3.2

Transitional Words and Phrases

Frequently used <u>transitional words and phrases</u> include conjunctive adverbs such as *consequently, finally, still,* and *thus* as well as expressions such as *for example, in fact,* and *for instance.*

See 34b2

Exercise can help lower blood pressure; <u>however</u>, those with high blood pressure should still limit salt intake.

The saxophone does not belong to the brass family; <u>in fact</u>, it is a member of the woodwind family.

Note: Use a semicolon—not a comma—before a transitional word or phrase that joins two independent clauses.

Correlative Conjunctions

Diana <u>not only</u> passed the exam, <u>but</u> she <u>also</u> received the highest grade in the class.

<u>Either</u> he left his coat in his locker, <u>or</u> he left it on the bus.

Semicolons

Alaska is the largest state; Rhode Island is the smallest.

Colons

He got his orders; he was to leave for Fort Drum on Sunday.

Close-Up USING COMPOUND SENTENCES

When you join independent clauses to create compound sentences, you help readers to see the relationships between your ideas. Compound sentences can indicate the following relationships:

- Addition (*and, in addition, not only . . . but also*)
- Contrast (*but, however*)
- Causal relationships (*so, therefore, consequently*)
- Alternatives (*or, either . . . or*)

EXERCISE 35.1

Revise the compound sentences in this passage so the sentence structure is varied. Be sure that the writer's emphasis and the relationships between ideas are clear.

> Dr. Alice I. Baumgartner and her colleagues at the Institute for Equality in Education at the University of Colorado surveyed two thousand Colorado schoolchildren, and they found some startling results. They asked, "If you woke up tomorrow and discovered that you were a (boy) (girl), how would your life be different?" and the answers were sad and shocking. The researchers assumed they would find that boys and girls would see advantages in being either male or female, but instead they found that both boys and girls had a fundamental contempt for females. Many elementary school boys titled their answers "The Disaster" or "Doomsday," and they described the terrible lives they would lead as girls, but the girls seemed to feel they would be better off as boys, and they expressed feelings that they would be able to do more and have easier lives. (Adapted from *Redbook*)

2 Using Complex Sentences

A **complex sentence** consists of one independent clause and at least one dependent clause.

A **dependent clause** cannot stand alone; it must be combined with an independent clause to form a sentence. In a complex sentence, a **subordinating conjunction** or **relative pronoun** links the independent and dependent clauses and indicates the relationship between them.

dependent clause   independent clause
[<u>After</u> the town was evacuated], [the hurricane began].

independent clause   dependent clause
[Officials watched the storm] [<u>that</u> threatened the town].

Sometimes a dependent clause may be embedded within an independent clause.

dependent clause
Town officials, [<u>who</u> were very concerned], watched the storm.

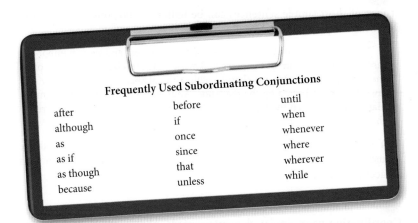

Frequently Used Subordinating Conjunctions

after	before	until
although	if	when
as	once	whenever
as if	since	where
as though	that	wherever
because	unless	while

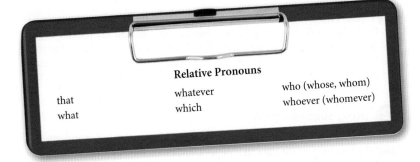

Relative Pronouns

that	whatever	who (whose, whom)
what	which	whoever (whomever)

Close-Up   USING COMPLEX SENTENCES

When you join clauses to create complex sentences, you help readers to see the relationships between your ideas. Complex sentences can indicate the following relationships:

- Time relationships (*before, after, until, when, since*)
- Contrast (*however, although*)
- Causal relationships (*therefore, because, so that*)
- Conditional relationships (*if, unless*)
- Location (*where, wherever*)
- Identity (*who, which, that*)

35b   Varying Sentence Length

Strings of short simple sentences can be tedious—and sometimes hard to follow, as the paragraph below illustrates.

> John Peter Zenger was a newspaper editor. He waged and won an important battle for freedom of the press in America. He criticized the policies of the British governor. He was charged with criminal libel as a result. Zenger's lawyers were disbarred by the governor. Andrew Hamilton defended him. Hamilton convinced the jury that Zenger's criticisms were true. Therefore, the statements were not libelous.

You can revise choppy sentences like the ones in the paragraph above by using *coordination, subordination,* or *embedding* to combine them with adjacent sentences.

1 Using Coordination

Coordination pairs similar elements—words, phrases, or clauses—giving equal weight to each.

Two choppy sentences linked with *and,* creating a compound sentence

> John Peter Zenger was a newspaper editor. He waged and won an important battle for freedom of the press in America. He criticized the policies of the British governor, and he was charged with criminal libel as a result. Zenger's lawyers were disbarred by the governor. Andrew Hamilton defended him. Hamilton convinced the jury that Zenger's criticisms were true. Therefore, the statements were not libelous.

2 Using Subordination

Subordination places the more important idea in an independent clause and the less important idea in a dependent clause.

John Peter Zenger was a newspaper editor who waged and won an important battle for freedom of the press in America. He criticized the policies of the British governor, and he was charged with criminal libel as a result. When Zenger's lawyers were disbarred by the governor, Andrew Hamilton defended him. Hamilton convinced the jury that Zenger's criticisms were true. Therefore, the statements were not libelous.

Complex
sentence

Complex
sentence

3 Using Embedding

Embedding is the working of additional words and phrases into sentences.

John Peter Zenger was a newspaper editor who waged and won an important battle for freedom of the press in America. He criticized the policies of the British governor, and he was charged with criminal libel as a result. When Zenger's lawyers were disbarred by the governor, Andrew Hamilton defended him, convincing the jury that Zenger's criticisms were true. Therefore, the statements were not libelous.

The sentence
*Hamilton
convinced
the jury…*
becomes
the phrase
*convincing
the jury*

This final revision of the original string of choppy sentences is interesting and readable because it is composed of varied and logically linked sentences. (The short simple sentence at the end has been retained for emphasis.)

MULTILINGUAL TIP

Some multilingual students rely on simple sentences and coordination in their writing because they are afraid of making sentence structure errors. The result is a monotonous style. To add variety, try using **subordination** and **embedding** (as illustrated above) in your sentences.

EXERCISE 35.2

Combine each of the following sentence groups into one long sentence. Next, compose a relatively short sentence to follow each long one. Finally, combine all the sentences into a paragraph, adding a topic sentence and any transitions necessary for coherence. Proofread your paragraph to be sure the sentences are varied in length.

1. Chocolate is composed of more than 300 compounds. Phenylethylamine is one such compound. Its presence in the brain may be linked to the emotion of falling in love.

2. Americans now consume a good deal of chocolate. On average, they eat more than nine pounds of chocolate per person per year. The typical Belgian, however, consumes almost fifteen pounds per year.

3. In recent years, Americans have begun a serious love affair with chocolate. Elegant chocolate boutiques sell exquisite bonbons by the piece. At least one hotel offers a "chocolate binge" vacation. The bimonthly *Chocolate News* for connoisseurs is flourishing.

(Adapted from *Newsweek*)

35c Varying Sentence Openings

Rather than beginning every sentence with the subject (*I* or *It*, for example), try beginning with a modifying *word, phrase,* or *clause.*

Words

Proud and relieved, Henry's parents watched him receive his diploma. (adjectives)

Hungrily, he devoured his lunch. (adverb)

Phrases

For better or for worse, credit cards are now widely available to college students. (prepositional phrase)

Located on the west coast of Great Britain, Wales is part of the United Kingdom. (participial phrase)

His artistic interests expanding, Picasso designed ballet sets and illustrated books. (absolute phrase)

Clauses

After President Woodrow Wilson was incapacitated by a stroke, his wife Edith unofficially performed many presidential duties. (adverb clause)

CHAPTER **36**

Writing Emphatic Sentences

In speaking, we emphasize certain ideas and deemphasize others with intonation and gestures; in writing, we convey **emphasis**—the relative importance of ideas—through the selection and arrangement of words.

36a Conveying Emphasis through Word Order

Because readers tend to focus on the beginning and end of a sentence, you should place the most important information there.

1 Begin with Important Ideas

Placing key ideas at the beginning of a sentence stresses their importance. The unedited version of the following sentence emphasizes the study, not those who conducted it. Editing can shift this focus to place the emphasis on the researcher, not the study.

> ~~In a landmark study of alcoholism,~~ Dr. George Vaillant ^, in a landmark study of alcoholism,^ followed two hundred Harvard graduates and four hundred inner-city, working-class men from the Boston area.

Close-Up *THERE IS* AND *THERE ARE*

Beginning a sentence with an empty phrase such as *there is* or *there are* generally weakens the sentence.

> ^MIT places^ ~~There is~~ heavy emphasis ~~placed~~ on the development of computational
>
> skills ^.^ ~~at MIT.~~

Situations that call for straightforward presentations—reports, memos, technical papers, business correspondence, and the like—require sentences that present vital information first and qualifiers later.

> New targeted therapies for treating cancer have been the subject of a good deal of research. (emphasizes the treatment, not the research)

> Dividends will be paid if the stockholders agree. (emphasizes the dividends, not the stockholders)

2 End with Important Ideas

Placing key elements at the end of a sentence is another way to convey their importance.

Use a Colon or a Dash A colon or a dash can emphasize an important word or phrase by isolating it at the end of a sentence.

> Beth had always dreamed of owning one special car: a 1953 Corvette.

> The elderly need a good deal of special attention—but they do not always get that attention.

> ## Close-Up PLACING TRANSITIONAL WORDS AND PHRASES
>
> When they are placed at the end of a sentence, conjunctive adverbs or other transitional expressions lose their power to indicate the relationship between ideas. Placed earlier in the sentence, transitional words and phrases can link ideas and add emphasis.
>
> *however,*
> Smokers do have rights; ^they should not try to impose their habit on
>
> others ^ however.

Use Climactic Word Order **Climactic word order**, the arrangement of a series of items from the least to the most important, places emphasis on the last item in the series.

> Binge drinking can lead to sexual abuse, traffic accidents, and even death. (*Death* is the most serious consequence.)

3 Experiment with Word Order

In English sentences, the most common <u>word order</u> is subject-verb-object (or subject-verb-complement). When you depart from this expected word order, you call attention to the word, phrase, or clause you have relocated.

> More modest and less inventive than Turner's paintings are John Constable's landscapes.

Here the writer calls special attention to the modifying phrase *more modest and less inventive than Turner's paintings* by inverting word order, placing the complement and the verb before the subject (*John Constable's landscapes*).

EXERCISE 36.1

Revise the following sentences to make them more emphatic. For each, decide which ideas should be highlighted, and place these key ideas at sentence beginnings or endings. Use climactic order or depart from conventional word order where appropriate.

1. Some police departments want to upgrade their firepower because criminals are better armed than ever before.
2. Previously, felons used so-called Saturday night specials, small-caliber six-shot revolvers.
3. Now, semiautomatic pistols capable of firing fifteen to twenty rounds, along with paramilitary weapons such as the AK-47, have replaced these weapons.

4. Police departments are adopting weapons such as new fast-firing shotguns and 9mm automatic pistols in order to gain an equal footing with their adversaries.
5. Faster reloading and a hair trigger are two of the numerous advantages that automatic pistols, the weapons of choice among law-enforcement officers, have over the traditional .38-caliber police revolver.

36b Conveying Emphasis through Sentence Structure

As you construct sentences, try to emphasize more important ideas and deemphasize less important ones.

1 Use Cumulative Sentences

A **cumulative sentence** begins with an independent clause, followed by the additional words, phrases, or clauses that expand or develop it.

> She holds me in strong arms, arms that have chopped cotton, dismembered trees, scattered corn for chickens, cradled infants, shaken the daylights out of half-grown upstart teenagers. (Rebecca Hill, *Blue Rise*)

Because it presents its main idea first, a cumulative sentence tends to be clear and straightforward. (Most English sentences are cumulative.)

2 Use Periodic Sentences

A periodic sentence moves from supporting details, expressed in modifying phrases and dependent clauses, to the sentence's key idea, which is placed in the independent clause at the end of the sentence.

> Unlike World Wars I and II, which ended decisively with an unconditional surrender, the war in Vietnam did not have a clear-cut resolution.

Note: In some periodic sentences, the modifying phrase or dependent clause comes between the subject and predicate: *Columbus, after several discouraging and unsuccessful voyages, finally reached America.*

36c Conveying Emphasis through Parallelism and Balance

By reinforcing the similarity between grammatical elements, parallelism can help you emphasize information.

See 38a

> We seek an individual who is a self-starter, who owns a car, and who is willing to work evenings.
> Do not pass go; do not collect $200.

The Faust legend is central in Benét's *The Devil and Daniel Webster,* in Goethe's *Faust,* and in Marlowe's *Dr. Faustus.*

A **balanced sentence** is neatly divided between two parallel structures—for example, two independent clauses in a compound sentence. The symmetrical structure of a balanced sentence adds emphasis by highlighting similarities or differences between the ideas in the two clauses.

In the 1950s, the electronic miracle was the television, but in the 1980s, the electronic miracle was the computer.

Alive, the elephant was worth at least a hundred pounds; dead, he would only be worth the value of his tusks, five pounds, possibly. (George Orwell, "Shooting an Elephant")

36d Conveying Emphasis through Repetition

See 37b Unnecessary repetition makes sentences dull and monotonous as well as wordy.

He had a good arm and also could field well, and he was also a fast runner.

Effective repetition, however, can emphasize key words or ideas.

They decided to begin again: to begin hoping, to begin trying to change, to begin working toward a goal.

During those years when I was just learning to speak, my mother and father addressed me only in Spanish; in Spanish I learned to reply. (Richard Rodriguez, *Aria: Memoir of a Bilingual Childhood*)

36e Conveying Emphasis through Active Voice

See 40d

ml 61a6 The active voice is generally more emphatic than the passive voice.

Passive: The prediction that oil prices will rise is being made by economists.

Active: Economists are predicting that oil prices will rise.

Notice that the passive voice sentence above does not specify who is performing the action. In a passive voice sentence, the subject is the recipient of the action, so the actor fades into the background (*by economists*)—or may even be omitted entirely (*the prediction . . . is being made*). In contrast, active voice places the emphasis where it belongs: on the actor or actors (*Economists*).

Sometimes, of course, you *want* to stress the action rather than the actor; if this is the case, use the passive voice.

Passive: The West was explored by Lewis and Clark. (stresses the exploration of the West, not who explored it)

Active: Lewis and Clark explored the West. (stresses the contribution of the explorers)

Note: Passive voice is also used when the identity of the person performing the action is irrelevant or unknown (*The course was canceled*). For this reason, the passive voice is frequently used in scientific and technical writing: *The beaker was filled with a saline solution.*

EXERCISE 36.2

Revise this paragraph to eliminate awkward or excessive use of passive constructions.

Jack Dempsey, the heavyweight champion between 1919 and 1926, had an interesting but uneven career. He was considered one of the greatest boxers of all time. Dempsey began fighting as "Kid Blackie," but his career did not take off until 1919, when Jack "Doc" Kearns became his manager. Dempsey won the championship when Jess Willard was defeated by him in Toledo, Ohio, in 1919. Dempsey immediately became a popular sports figure; President Franklin D. Roosevelt was one of his biggest fans. Influential friends were made by Jack Dempsey. Boxing lessons were given by him to the actor Rudolph Valentino. He made friends with Douglas Fairbanks Sr., Damon Runyon, and J. Paul Getty. Hollywood serials were made by Dempsey, but the title was lost by him to Gene Tunney, and Dempsey failed to regain it the following year. After his boxing career declined, a restaurant was opened by Dempsey, and many major sporting events were attended by him. This exposure kept him in the public eye until he lost his restaurant. Jack Dempsey died in 1983.

CHAPTER 37

Writing Concise Sentences

A sentence is not concise simply because it is short; a concise sentence contains only the words necessary to make its point.

Close-Up TEXT MESSAGES

If you send texts, which are limited to 160 characters, you have already learned how to be concise. In text messages, you omit articles and other nonessential words, and you use nonstandard spellings (*nite*), abbreviations, and shorthand (*ru home?*). This kind of language is not acceptable in college writing. In college writing, you need to find other strategies (such as those discussed in this chapter) to make your writing concise.

37a Eliminating Wordiness

A good way to find out which words are essential in a sentence is to underline the key words. Look carefully at the remaining words to see which are unnecessary, and then eliminate wordiness by deleting them.

It seems to me that it does not make sense to allow any <u>bail</u> to be <u>granted</u> to <u>anyone</u> who has ever been <u>convicted</u> of a <u>violent crime</u>.

The underlining shows you immediately that none of the words in the long introductory phrase are essential. The following revised sentence includes just the words necessary to convey the key ideas:

Bail should not be granted to anyone who has ever been convicted of a violent crime.

Whenever possible, delete nonessential words—*deadwood, utility words,* and *circumlocution*—from your writing.

1 Eliminate Deadwood

The term **deadwood** refers to unnecessary phrases that take up space and add nothing to meaning.

Many
~~There were many~~ factors ~~that~~ influenced his decision to become a priest.

The two plots are ~~both~~ similar in ~~the way~~ that they trace the characters' increasing rage.

Shoppers ~~who are~~ looking for bargains often go to outlets.

an exhausting
They played a racquetball game ~~that was exhausting~~.

This
~~In this~~ article ~~it~~ discusses lead poisoning.

is
The most tragic character in *Hamlet* ~~would have to be~~ Ophelia.

Deadwood also includes unnecessary statements of opinion, such as *I feel, it seems to me,* and *in my opinion.*

The
~~I think the~~ characters seem undeveloped.

This
~~As far as I'm concerned, this~~ course should not be required.

2 Eliminate Utility Words

Utility words function as filler and have no real meaning in a sentence. Utility words include nouns with imprecise meanings (*factor, situation, type, aspect,* and so on); adjectives so general that they are almost meaningless (*good, bad, important*); and common adverbs denoting degree (*basically, actually, quite, very, definitely*). Often, you can just delete the utility word; if you cannot, replace it with a more precise word.

Registration
~~The registration situation~~ was disorganized.

an
The scholarship ~~basically~~ offered Fran ~~a good~~ opportunity to study Spanish.

It was ~~actually~~ a worthwhile book, but I didn't ~~really~~ finish it.

3 Avoid Circumlocution

Circumlocution is taking a roundabout way to say something (using ten words when five will do). Instead of complicated constructions, use specific words and concise phrases that come right to the point.

             The

~~It is not unlikely that the~~ trend toward lower consumer spending
    probably
will continue.

              while

Joe was in the army ~~during the same time that~~ I was in college.

Close-Up REVISING WORDY PHRASES

A wordy phrase can almost always be replaced by a more concise, more direct term.

Wordy	Concise
at the present time	now
at this point in time	now
for the purpose of	for
due to the fact that	because
on account of the fact that	because
until such time as	until
in the event that	if
by means of	by
in the vicinity of	near
have the ability to	be able to

EXERCISE 37.1

Revise the following paragraph to eliminate deadwood, utility words, and circumlocution. Whenever possible, delete wordy phrases or replace them with more concise expressions.

    For all intents and purposes, the shopping mall is no longer an important factor on the American cultural scene. In the 1980s, malls became gathering places where teenagers met, walkers came to get in a few miles, and shoppers who were looking for a wide selection and were not concerned about value went to shop. There are several factors that have worked to undermine the mall's popularity. First, due to the fact that today's shoppers are more likely to be interested in value, many of them have headed to the discount stores. Today's shopper is now more likely to shop in discount stores or bulk-buying warehouse stores than in the small, expensive specialty shops in the large malls. Add to this a resurgence of the values of community, and we can see how mall shopping would have to be less attractive than shopping at local stores.

Many malls actually have up to 20 percent empty storefronts, and some have had to close down altogether. Others have met the challenge by expanding their roles from shopping centers into community centers. They have added playgrounds for the children and more amusements and restaurants for the adults. They have also appealed to the growing sense of value shopping by giving gift certificates and discounts to shoppers who spend money in their stores. For a while, it seemed as if the huge shopping malls that had become familiar cultural icons were dying out, replaced by online shopping. Now, however, it looks as if some of those icons just might make it and survive by reinventing themselves as more than just places to shop.

37b Eliminating Unnecessary Repetition

Repetition can make your writing more **emphatic**, but unnecessary repetition and **redundant** word groups (repeated words or phrases that say the same thing, such as *intentionally choose, combine together,* and *unanticipated surprise*) can obscure your meaning. Correct unnecessary repetition by using one of the following strategies.

See 36d

1 Delete Redundancy

People's clothing ~~attire~~ can reveal a good deal about their personalities.

These stories hint at ~~a suggestion of~~ the supernatural.

The two candidates share several positions ~~in common.~~

2 Substitute a Pronoun

Agatha Christie's fictional detective Miss Marple solved many crimes.
The Murder at the Vicarage was one of ~~Miss Marple's~~ *her* most challenging cases.

3 Create an Appositive

Red Barber ~~was~~, a sportscaster, ~~He was~~ known for his colorful expressions.

4 Create a Compound

John F. Kennedy was the youngest man ever elected president ~~/~~ *and* ~~He was~~ the first Catholic to hold this office.

5 Create a Complex Sentence

Americans value freedom of speech/~~Freedom of speech~~ is guaranteed *, which* by the First Amendment.

EXERCISE 37.2

Eliminate any unnecessary repetition of words or ideas in this paragraph. Also, revise to eliminate deadwood, utility words, and circumlocution.

For a wide variety of different reasons, more and more people today are choosing a vegetarian diet. There are three kinds of vegetarians: strict vegetarians eat no animal foods at all; lactovegetarians eat dairy products, but they do not eat meat, fish, poultry, or eggs; and ovolactovegetarians eat eggs and dairy products, but they do not eat meat, fish, or poultry. Famous vegetarians include such well-known people as George Bernard Shaw, Leonardo da Vinci, Ralph Waldo Emerson, Henry David Thoreau, and Mahatma Gandhi. Like these well-known vegetarians, the vegetarians of today have good reasons for becoming vegetarians. For instance, some religions recommend a vegetarian diet. Some of these religions are Buddhism, Brahmanism, and Hinduism. Other people turn to vegetarianism for reasons of health or for reasons of hygiene. These people believe that meat is a source of potentially harmful chemicals, and they believe meat contains infectious organisms. Some people feel meat may cause digestive problems and may lead to other difficulties as well. Other vegetarians adhere to a vegetarian diet because they feel it is ecologically wasteful to kill animals after we feed plants to them. These vegetarians believe we should eat the plants. Finally, there are facts and evidence to suggest that a vegetarian diet may possibly help people live longer lives. A vegetarian diet may do this by reducing the incidence of heart disease and lessening the incidence of some cancers. (Adapted from *Jane Brody's Nutrition Book.*)

37c Tightening Rambling Sentences

The combination of nonessential words, unnecessary repetition, and complicated syntax creates **rambling sentences**. Revising such sentences frequently requires extensive editing.

1 Eliminate Excessive Coordination

When you string a series of clauses together with coordinating conjunctions, you create a rambling, unfocused compound sentence. To revise such sentences, first identify the main idea, and then add the supporting details.

Wordy: Puerto Rico is a large island and it is very mountainous, and it has steep slopes, and they fall to gentle plains along the coast.

Concise: A large island, Puerto Rico is very mountainous, with steep slopes falling to gentle plains along the coast. (Puerto Rico's mountainous terrain is the sentence's main idea.)

2 Eliminate Adjective Clauses

A series of adjective clauses is also likely to produce a rambling sentence. To revise, substitute concise modifying words or phrases for the adjective clauses.

See B3.2

Wordy: *Moby-Dick*, which is a novel about a white whale, was written by Herman Melville, who was friendly with Nathaniel Hawthorne, who urged him to revise the first draft.

Concise: *Moby-Dick*, a novel about a white whale, was written by Herman Melville, who revised the first draft at the urging of his friend Nathaniel Hawthorne.

3 Eliminate Passive Constructions

Unnecessary use of the passive voice can also create a rambling sentence. Correct this problem by changing passive to active voice.

See 40d

~~Water rights are being fought for in court by~~ Indian tribes such as
are fighting in court for water rights.
the Papago in Arizona and the Pyramid Lake Paiute in Nevada/.

ml 61a6

4 Eliminate Wordy Prepositional Phrases

When you revise, substitute adjectives or adverbs for wordy prepositional phrases.

See B3.1

dangerous   *exciting.*
The trip was ~~one of danger~~ but also ~~one of excitement.~~

confidently   *authoritatively.*
He spoke ~~in a confident manner~~ and ~~with a lot of authority.~~

5 Eliminate Wordy Noun Constructions

Substitute strong verbs for wordy noun phrases.

See B3.1

decided
We have ~~made the decision~~ to postpone the meeting until ~~the~~

appear
~~appearance of~~ all the board members.

EXERCISE 37.3

Revise the rambling sentences in these paragraphs by eliminating excessive coordination; unnecessary use of the passive voice; and overuse of adjective clauses, prepositional phrases, and noun constructions. As you revise, make your sentences more concise by deleting nonessential words and unnecessary repetition.

Some colleges that have been in support of fraternities and sororities for a number of years are at this time in the process of conducting a reevaluation of the position of those Greek organizations on campus. In opposition to the fraternities and sororities are a fair number of students, faculty members, and administrators who claim these groups are inherently sexist, which they say makes it impossible for the groups to exist in a coeducational institution, which is supposed to offer equal opportunities for members of both sexes. More and more members of the college community also see these groups as elitist as well as sexist and favor their abolition. In addition, many point out that fraternities are associated with dangerous practices, such as hazing and alcohol abuse.

However, some students, faculty, and administrators remain wholeheartedly in support of traditional fraternities and sororities, which they believe are responsible for helping students make the acquaintance of people and learn the leadership skills that they believe will be of assistance to them in their future lives as adults. Supporters of fraternities and sororities believe that students should retain the right to make their own social decisions, and they think that joining a Greek organization is one of those decisions, and they also believe fraternities and sororities are responsible for providing valuable services. Some of these are tutoring, raising money for charity, and running campus safe-ride services. Therefore, these individuals are not of the opinion that the abolition of traditional fraternities and sororities makes sense.

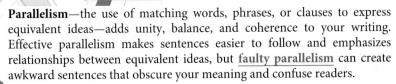

Using Parallelism

Parallelism—the use of matching words, phrases, or clauses to express equivalent ideas—adds unity, balance, and coherence to your writing. Effective parallelism makes sentences easier to follow and emphasizes relationships between equivalent ideas, but <u>faulty parallelism</u> can create awkward sentences that obscure your meaning and confuse readers.

See 38b

38a Using Parallelism Effectively

Parallelism highlights the correspondence between *items in a series, paired items*, and elements in *lists and outlines*.

1 With Items in a Series

Items in a series should be presented in parallel terms.

<u>Eat</u>, <u>drink</u>, and <u>be</u> merry.

<u>Baby food consumption</u>, <u>toy production</u>, and <u>school construction</u> are likely to decline as the US population ages.

Three factors influenced his decision to seek new employment: <u>his desire to relocate</u>, <u>his need for greater responsibility</u>, and <u>his dissatisfaction with his current job</u>.

 For information on punctuating items in a series, **see 49b** and **50b**.

2 With Paired Items

Paired words, phrases, or clauses should be presented in parallel terms.

The thank-you note was <u>short</u> but <u>sweet</u>.

<u>Roosevelt represented the United States</u>, and <u>Churchill represented Great Britain</u>.

<u>Ask not what your country can do for you</u>; <u>ask what you can do for your country</u>. (John F. Kennedy)

Paired elements linked by **correlative conjunctions** (such as *not only/ but also, both/and, either/or, neither/nor,* and *whether/or*) should always be parallel.

The design team paid close attention not only <u>to color</u> but also <u>to texture</u>.

Either <u>repeat physics</u> or <u>take calculus</u>.

Parallelism is also used with paired elements linked by *than* or *as.*

Richard Wright and James Baldwin chose <u>to live in Paris</u> rather than <u>to remain in the United States</u>.

Success is as much <u>a matter of hard work</u> as <u>a matter of luck</u>.

③ In Lists and Outlines

See 23c Elements in a <u>list</u> should be parallel.

The Irish potato famine had four major causes:
1. The establishment of the landlord-tenant system
2. The failure of the potato crop
3. The reluctance of England to offer adequate financial assistance
4. The passage of the Corn Laws

See 11i Elements in an <u>outline</u> should also be parallel.

EXERCISE 38.1

Combine each of the following sentence pairs or sentence groups into one sentence that uses parallel structure. Be sure all paired items and items in a series (words, phrases, or clauses) are expressed in parallel terms.

1. Originally, there were five performing Marx Brothers. One was nicknamed Groucho. The others were called Chico, Harpo, Gummo, and Zeppo.
2. Groucho was very well known. So were Chico and Harpo. Gummo soon dropped out of the act. And later Zeppo did too.
3. They began in vaudeville. That was before World War I. Their first show was called *I'll Say She Is*. It opened in New York in 1924.
4. The Marx Brothers' first movie was *The Cocoanuts*. The next was *Animal Crackers*. And this was followed by *Monkey Business, Horse Feathers*, and *Duck Soup*. Then came *A Night at the Opera*.
5. In each of these movies, the Marx Brothers make people laugh. They also exhibit a unique, zany comic style.
6. In their movies, each brother has a set of familiar trademarks. Groucho has a mustache and a long coat. He wiggles his eyebrows and smokes a cigar. There is a funny hat that Chico always wears. And he affects a phony Italian accent. Harpo never speaks.
7. Groucho is always cast as a sly operator. He always tries to cheat people out of their money. He always tries to charm women.

8. In *The Cocoanuts*, Groucho plays Mr. Hammer, proprietor of the run-down Coconut Manor, a Florida hotel. In *Horse Feathers*, his character is named Professor Quincy Adams Wagstaff. Wagstaff is president of Huxley College. Huxley also has financial problems.

9. In *Duck Soup*, Groucho plays Rufus T. Firefly, president of the country of Fredonia. Fredonia was formerly ruled by the late husband of a Mrs. Teasdale. Fredonia is now at war with the country of Sylvania.

10. Margaret Dumont is often Groucho's leading lady. She plays Mrs. Teasdale in *Duck Soup*. In *A Night at the Opera*, she plays Mrs. Claypool. Her character in *The Cocoanuts* is named Mrs. Potter.

38b Revising Faulty Parallelism

Faulty parallelism occurs when elements in a sentence that express equivalent ideas are not presented in parallel terms.

Many residents of developing countries lack adequate housing,
adequate
adequate food, and ~~their~~ health-care facilities ~~are also inadequate.~~

To correct faulty parallelism, match nouns with nouns, verbs with verbs, and phrases or clauses with similarly constructed phrases or clauses.

weight training,
Popular exercises for men and women include spinning, ~~weights,~~ and jogging.

having
I look forward to hearing from you and to ~~have~~ an opportunity to tell you more about myself.

Close-Up   REPEATING KEY WORDS

Although the use of similar grammatical structures may be enough to convey parallelism, sometimes sentences are even clearer if certain key words (for example, articles, prepositions, and the *to* in infinitives) are also repeated in each element of a pair or series. In the following sentence, repeating the preposition *by* makes it clear that *not* applies only to the first phrase.

Computerization has helped industry by not allowing labor costs to
by   *by*
skyrocket, increasing the speed of production, and improving efficiency.

EXERCISE 38.2

Identify and correct faulty parallelism in these sentences. Then, underline the parallel elements—words, phrases, and clauses—in your corrected sentences. If a sentence is already correct, mark it with a *C*, and underline the parallel elements.

Example: Alfred Hitchcock's films include *North by Northwest*, *Vertigo*,

Psycho, ~~and he also directed~~ *Notorious* ,and *Saboteur*.

1. The world is divided between those with boots on and those who discover continents.
2. World leaders, members of Congress, and religious groups are all concerned about global climate change.
3. A national task force on education recommended improving public education by making the school day longer, higher teachers' salaries, and integrating more technology into the curriculum.
4. The fast food industry has expanded to include many kinds of restaurants: those that serve pizza, fried chicken chains, some offering Mexican-style menus, and hamburger franchises.
5. The consumption of Scotch in the United States is declining because of high prices, tastes are changing, and increased health awareness has led many whiskey drinkers to switch to wine or beer.

CHAPTER **39**

Choosing Words

39a Choosing an Appropriate Level of Diction

Diction, which comes from the Latin word for *say*, refers to the choice and use of words. Different audiences and situations call for different levels of diction.

1 Formal Diction

Formal diction is grammatically correct and uses words familiar to an educated audience. A writer who uses formal diction often maintains emotional distance from the audience by avoiding *I* and *you*. In addition, the tone of the writing—as determined by word choice, sentence structure, and choice of subject—is dignified and objective.

2 Informal Diction

Informal diction is the language that people use in conversation and in personal emails. You should use informal diction in your college writing only to reproduce speech or dialect or to give an essay a conversational tone.

Colloquial Diction **Colloquial diction** is the language of everyday speech. Contractions—*isn't, I'm*—are typical, as are **clipped forms**—*phone* for *telephone, TV* for *television, dorm* for *dormitory.* Other colloquialisms include placeholders such as *kind of* and utility words such as *nice* for *acceptable, funny* for *odd,* and *great* for almost anything. Colloquial English also includes expressions such as *get across* for *communicate, come up with* for *find,* and *check out* for *investigate.*

> **MULTILINGUAL TIP**
> Some of the spoken expressions you learn from other students or from television are not appropriate for use in college writing. When you hear new expressions, pay attention to the contexts in which they are used.

Slang **Slang,** language that calls attention to itself, is used to establish or reinforce identity within a group—urban teenagers, rock musicians, or computer users, for example. One characteristic of slang is that it is usually short-lived, coming into existence and fading out much more quickly than other words do. Because slang terms can emerge and disappear so quickly, no dictionary—even a dictionary of slang—can list all or even most of the slang terms currently in use.

In personal email and instant messages, writers commonly use **emoticons**—emojis that indicate emotions or feelings—and **Internet slang** (or **text shorthand**), such as BTW (by the way) or 2 Day. Although these typographical devices are common in informal electronic communication, they are inappropriate in academic essays or emails to professors or supervisors.

Regionalisms **Regionalisms** are words, expressions, and idiomatic forms that are used in particular geographical areas but may not be understood by a general audience. In eastern Tennessee, for example, a paper bag is a *poke,* and empty soda bottles are *dope bottles.* And New Yorkers stand *on line* for a movie, whereas people in most other parts of the country stand *in line.*

Nonstandard Diction **Nonstandard diction** refers to words and expressions not generally considered a part of standard English—words such as *ain't, nohow, anywheres, nowheres, hisself,* and *theirselves.*

No absolute rules distinguish standard from nonstandard usage. In fact, some linguists reject the idea of nonstandard usage altogether, arguing that this designation relegates both the language and those who use it to second-class status.

Note: Remember, colloquial expressions, slang, regionalisms, and nonstandard diction are almost always inappropriate in your college writing.

3 College Writing

The level of diction appropriate for college writing depends on your assignment and your audience. A personal-experience essay calls for a somewhat informal style, but a research paper, an exam, or a report requires a more formal level of diction. Most college writing falls somewhere between formal and informal English, using a conversational tone but maintaining grammatical correctness and using a specialized vocabulary when the situation requires it. (This is the level of diction that is used in this book.)

Close-Up EMAILS TO INSTRUCTORS

Different instructors have different opinions about how students should address them. Unless you are told otherwise, however, think of emails to your instructors as business communications. Avoid highly informal salutations, such as "Hi prof"; instead, use a more formal salutation, such as "Dr. Sweeny."

EXERCISE 39.1

After reading the following paragraph, underline the words and phrases that identify it as formal diction. Then, rewrite the paragraph using the level of diction that you would use in your college writing. Consult a dictionary if necessary.

> In looking at many small points of difference between species, which, as far as our ignorance permits us to judge, seem quite unimportant, we must not forget that climate, food, etc., have no doubt produced some direct effect. It is also necessary to bear in mind that owing to the law of correlation, when one part varies and the variations are accumulated through natural selection, other modifications, often of the most unexpected nature, will ensue. (Charles Darwin, *The Origin of Species*)

39b Choosing the Right Word

Choosing the right word to use in a particular context is very important. If you use the wrong word—or even *almost* the right one—you run the risk of misrepresenting your ideas.

1 Denotation and Connotation

A word's **denotation** is its basic dictionary meaning, what it stands for without any emotional associations. A word's **connotations** are the emotional, social, and political associations it has in addition to its denotative meaning.

Word	Denotation	Connotation
politician	someone who holds a political office	opportunist; wheeler-dealer

Selecting a word with the appropriate connotation can be challenging. For example, the word *skinny* has negative connotations, whereas *thin* is neutral, and *slender* is positive. And words and expressions such as *mentally ill, insane, neurotic, crazy, psychopathic,* and *emotionally disturbed,* although similar in meaning, have different emotional, social, and political connotations. If you use terms without considering their connotations, you run the risk of undercutting your credibility, to say nothing of confusing and possibly angering readers.

Close-Up USING A THESAURUS

Synonyms are words that have similar meanings, such as *well* and *healthy.* **Antonyms** are words that have opposite meanings, such as *courage* and *cowardice.*

When you consult a **thesaurus**, a book or website that lists synonyms and antonyms, remember that no two words have exactly the same meanings. Use synonyms carefully, checking a dictionary to make sure the connotation of the synonym is close to that of the original word.

EXERCISE 39.2

The following words have negative connotations. For each, list one word with a similar meaning whose connotation is neutral and another whose connotation is positive.

Example: Negative: skinny / Neutral: thin / Positive: slender

1. deceive	6. blunder
2. antiquated	7. weird
3. pushy	8. rhetoric
4. pathetic	9. shack
5. cheap	10. stench

2 Euphemisms

A **euphemism** is a mild or polite term used in place of a blunt or harsh term to describe something unpleasant or embarrassing. College writing is no place for euphemisms. Say what you mean—*pregnant*, not *expecting*; *died*, not *passed away*; and *strike*, not *work stoppage*.

3 Specific and General Words

Specific words refer to particular persons, items, or events; **general** words denote entire classes or groups. *Queen Elizabeth II*, for example, is more specific than *monarch*; *jeans* is more specific than *clothing*; and *hybrid* is more specific than *vehicle*. Although you can use general words to describe entire classes of items, you should use specific words to clarify such generalizations.

Take particular care to avoid general words such as *nice, great,* and *terrific* that say nothing and could be used in almost any sentence. These utility words convey only enthusiasm, not precise meanings. Replace them with more specific words.

See
37a2

4 Abstract and Concrete Words

Abstract words—*beauty, truth, justice,* and so on—refer to ideas, qualities, or conditions that cannot be perceived by the senses. **Concrete** words name things that readers can see, hear, taste, smell, or touch. The more concrete your words and phrases, the more vivid the image you evoke in the reader's mind.

EXERCISE 39.3

Revise the following paragraph from a job application letter by substituting specific, concrete language for general or abstract words and phrases. Exchange your revision with a classmate.

> I have had several part-time jobs lately. Some of them would qualify me for the position you advertised. In my most recent job, I sold products in a store. My supervisor said I was a good worker who had a number of valuable qualities. I am used to dealing with different types of people in different settings. I feel that my qualifications would make me a good candidate for your job opening.

39c Using Figures of Speech

Writers often use **figures of speech** (such as *similes* and *metaphors*) to go beyond the literal meanings of words. By doing so, they make their writing more vivid or emphatic.

Commonly Used Figures of Speech

A **simile** is a comparison between two unlike things on the basis of a shared quality. A simile is introduced by *like* or *as*.

> Like travelers with exotic destinations on their minds, the graduates were remarkably forgetful. (Maya Angelou, *I Know Why the Caged Bird Sings*)

A **metaphor** also compares two dissimilar things, but instead of saying that one thing is like another, it equates them.

> All the world's a stage,
> And all the men and women
> merely players; . . .
> (William Shakespeare, *As You Like It*)

An **analogy** explains an unfamiliar item or concept by comparing it to a more familiar one.

> According to Robert Frost, writing free verse is like playing tennis without a net.

Personification gives an idea or inanimate object human attributes, feelings, or powers.

> Truth strikes us from behind, and in the dark, as well as from before in broad daylight. (Henry David Thoreau, *Journals*)

A **hyperbole** (or overstatement) is an intentional exaggeration for emphasis. For example, Jonathan Swift uses hyperbole in his essay "A Modest Proposal" when he suggests that eating Irish babies would help the English solve their food shortage.

Understatement intentionally makes something seem less important than it actually is.

> According to Mao Tse-tung, a revolution is not a tea party.

EXERCISE 39.4

Rewrite the following sentences by adding a figure of speech to each sentence to make the ideas more vivid and exciting. Identify each figure of speech you use.

like the inside of a cathedral (simile)

Example: The room was cool and still ∧.

1. The last of the marathon runners limped toward the finish line.
2. The breeze gently stirred the wind chimes.
3. Jeremy has shoulder-length hair and a high forehead, and he wears small, red glasses.
4. The chemistry lab was quiet.
5. The demolition crew worked slowly but efficiently.
6. Interstate highways often make for tedious driving.
7. Diego found calculus easy.
8. Music is essentially mathematical.
9. Katrina claims her dog is far more intelligent than her brother is.
10. Emotions are curious things.

39d Avoiding Inappropriate Language

1 Jargon

Jargon is the specialized or technical vocabulary of a trade, profession, or academic discipline. Although it is useful for communicating in the field for which it was developed, outside that field it is often imprecise and confusing. For example, business executives may want departments to *interface* effectively, and sociologists may identify the need for *perspectivistic thinking* to achieve organizational goals. If they are addressing other professionals in their respective fields, these terms can facilitate communication. If, however, they are addressing a general audience, these terms are often confusing.

2 Neologisms

Neologisms are newly coined words that are not part of standard English. New situations call for new words, however, and frequently a neologism will become an accepted part of the language—*app, locavore, phishing, blog,* and *outsource,* for example. Other coined words are never fully accepted—for example, the neologisms created when the suffix -*wise* is added to existing words, creating nonstandard words such as *weatherwise, sportswise, time-wise,* and *productwise.*

3 Pretentious Diction

Good writing is clear and direct, not pompous or flowery. Revise to eliminate **pretentious diction**, inappropriately elevated and wordy language.

               asleep   *thought*   *hiking*

As I fell ∧ ~~into slumber,~~ I ~~cogitated~~ about my day ∧ ~~ambling~~ through ~~the~~ ~~splendor of~~ the Appalachian Mountains.

Frequently, pretentious diction is formal diction used in a relatively informal situation. In such a context, it is out of place. For every pretentious word, there is a clear and direct alternative.

Pretentious	Clear	Pretentious	Clear
ascertain	discover	reside	live
commence	start	terminate	end
implement	carry out	utilize	use
minuscule	small	individual	person

4 Clichés

Clichés are tired expressions that have lost their impact because they have been used so often. At one time, expressions such as the following might have called up vivid images in a reader's mind, but because of overuse, they have become clichés—pat, meaningless phrases.

> **MULTILINGUAL TIP**
>
> Many multilingual students have learned a long list of English idioms. Some of these, however, have become clichés. Although becoming familiar with these idioms can help you understand them when you encounter them, university instructors discourage students from using clichés in their writing, preferring language that is more original and more precise.

back in the day

the bottom line

it is what it is

face the music

game plan

give 110 percent

smoking gun

a level playing field

a perfect storm

wake up and smell the coffee

old school

what goes around comes around

Writers sometimes resort to clichés when they run out of ideas. To capture your readers' attention, take the time to think of original expressions.

EXERCISE 39.5

> Rewrite the following passage, eliminating jargon, neologisms, pretentious diction, and clichés. Feel free to add words and phrases and to reorganize sentences to make their meanings clear. If you are not certain about the meaning or status of a word, consult a dictionary.
>
> At a given point in time, there coexisted a hare and a tortoise. The aforementioned rabbit was overheard by the tortoise to be blowing his horn about the degree of speed he could attain. The latter

quadruped thereupon put forth a challenge to the former by advancing the suggestion that they interact in a running competition. The hare acquiesced, laughing to himself. The animals concurred in the decision to acquire the services of a certain fox to act in the capacity of judicial referee. This particular fox was in agreement, and, consequently, implementation of the plan was facilitated. In a relatively small amount of time, the hare had considerably outdistanced the tortoise and, after ascertaining that he himself was in a more optimized position distance-wise than the tortoise, he arrived at the unilateral decision to avail himself of a respite. He made the implicit assumption in so doing that he would anticipate no difficulty in overtaking the tortoise when his suspension of activity ceased. An unfortunate development race-wise occurred when the hare's somnolent state endured for a longer-than-anticipated time frame, facilitating the tortoise's victory in the contest and affirming the concepts of unhurriedness and firmness triumphing in competitive situations. Thus, the hare was unable to snatch victory out of the jaws of defeat.

39e Avoiding Offensive Language

Most of us want to live in a society where everyone—regardless of background, gender, race, sexual orientation, age, or physical condition—is able to realize his or her full potential. Language that undercuts this goal has no place in civil discourse and should be avoided—in the workplace, in the classroom, and in our daily lives. Although people certainly have the right to express themselves, they should be aware of the potentially negative consequences—moral, ethical, and practical—of their words. Because the language we use not only expresses our ideas but also shapes our thinking, it is in everyone's best interest to avoid using words that could insult, degrade, or otherwise harm others.

1 Stereotypes

Race and Ethnicity   When referring to any racial, ethnic, or religious group, use words with neutral connotations or words that the group itself uses in formal speech or writing—for example, *African American, Latino* or *Latina, Native American, Chinese American*, and so on.

 It is acceptable to use *black* in second references to *African Americans.*

Age   Avoid potentially offensive labels relating to age. Many older people do not like to be called *senior citizens* or *seniors*. Perhaps the best strategy is to avoid any reference to age unless it is relevant to the discussion. In that case, be specific—for example, "The former president went skydiving on his ninetieth birthday." Also, avoid comments that may seem patronizing—for example, "For an older person, she really is funny."

Class Do not demean certain jobs because they are low-paying or praise others because they have impressive titles. Similarly, do not use words—*hick, cracker, redneck,* or *trailer trash,* for example—that denigrate people based on their social class.

Physical Disability Use respectful language when referring to people with physical or mental disabilities. Refer to a person's disability only when it is relevant to the discussion. Also, avoid outdated terms such as *retarded* and *crippled.* Instead use terms such as *mentally challenged individual* and *person with a disability.*

Sexual Orientation Always use neutral terms (such as *gay, lesbian,* and *transgendered*), but do not mention a person's sexual orientation unless it is relevant to your discussion.

2 Sexist Language

Avoid **sexist language** that promotes and reinforces gender stereotypes. Sexist language entails much more than the use of derogatory words, however. Assuming that some professions are exclusive to one gender—for instance, that *nurse* denotes only women and that *engineer* denotes only men—is also sexist. So is the use of outdated job titles, such as *postman* for *letter carrier, fireman* for *firefighter,* and *stewardess* for *flight attendant.*

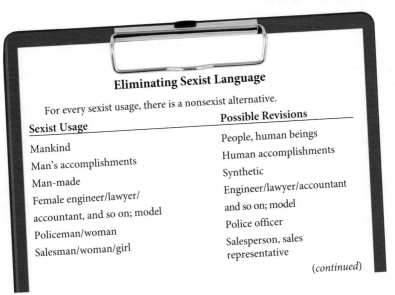

Eliminating Sexist Language

For every sexist usage, there is a nonsexist alternative.

Sexist Usage	Possible Revisions
Mankind	People, human beings
Man's accomplishments	Human accomplishments
Man-made	Synthetic
Female engineer/lawyer/accountant, and so on; model	Engineer/lawyer/accountant and so on; model
Policeman/woman	Police officer
Salesman/woman/girl	Salesperson, sales representative

(continued)

Eliminating Sexist Language (*continued*)

Businessman/woman

Everyone should complete <u>his</u>
application by Tuesday.

Businessperson, executive

Everyone should complete
<u>his or her</u> application by
Tuesday.

All students should complete
<u>their</u> applications by Tuesday.

Note: When trying to avoid sexist use of *he* and *him* in your writing, be careful not to use the plural pronoun *they* or *their* to refer to a singular antecedent.

Drivers
~~Any driver~~ caught speeding should have their driving privileges suspended.

Sexist language occurs when a writer fails to apply the same terminology to both men and women. For example, refer to two scientists with PhDs not as Dr. Sagan and Mrs. Yallow, but as Dr. Sagan and Dr. Yallow. Refer to two writers as James and Wharton, or Henry James and Edith Wharton, not James and Mrs. Wharton.

In your writing, always use *women* when referring to adult females. Use *Ms.* as the form of address when a woman's marital status is unknown or irrelevant (for example, in business correspondence). Finally, avoid using the generic *he* or *him* when your subject could be either male or female. Use the third-person plural (*they*) or the phrase *he or she* (not *he/she*).

Sexist: Before boarding, each passenger should make certain that <u>he</u> has <u>his</u> ticket.

Revised: Before boarding, <u>passengers</u> should make certain that they have <u>their</u> tickets.

Revised: Before boarding, each <u>passenger</u> should make certain that <u>he or she</u> has a ticket.

Note: Remember not to use words to refer to a woman that you would not use to describe a man. For example, do not describe a woman as *pushy* or *bossy* if you would not use the same term to describe a man.

EXERCISE 39.6

Suggest at least one alternative form for each of the following words or phrases. In each case, comment on the advantages and disadvantages of the alternative you recommend. If you feel that a particular term is not sexist, explain why.

forefathers	manpower
man-eating	everyman
point man	(to) man the battle stations
draftsman	man overboard
workmen's compensation	fisherman
men at work	foreman
waitress	manned space program
first baseman	gentleman's agreement
congressman	no man's land
manhunt	spinster
longshoreman	old maid
committeeman	old wives' tale

PART **10**

Sentence Grammar

Understanding Sentence Grammar

Understanding Sentence Grammar

❓ Frequently Asked Questions

CHAPTER 40

Using Verbs

40a Understanding Verb Forms

Every verb has four **principal parts**: a **base form** (the present tense form of the verb used with *I*), a **present participle** (the *-ing* form of the verb), a **past tense form**, and a **past participle**.

Note: The verb *be* is so irregular that it is the one exception to this definition; its base form is *be*.

1 Regular Verbs

A **regular verb** forms both its past tense and its past participle by adding *-d* or *-ed* to the base form of the verb.

Principal Parts of Regular Verbs

Base Form	Past Tense Form	Past Participle
smile	smiled	smiled
talk	talked	talked
jump	jumped	jumped

2 Irregular Verbs

Irregular verbs do not follow the pattern discussed above. The chart that follows lists the principal parts of the most frequently used irregular verbs.

Frequently Used Irregular Verbs

Base Form	Past Tense Form	Past Participle
arise	arose	arisen
awake	awoke, awaked	awoke, awaked
be	was/were	been
beat	beat	beaten
begin	began	begun
bend	bent	bent
bet	bet, betted	bet
bite	bit	bitten
blow	blew	blown
break	broke	broken
bring	brought	brought
build	built	built
burst	burst	burst
buy	bought	bought
catch	caught	caught
choose	chose	chosen
cling	clung	clung
come	came	come
cost	cost	cost
deal	dealt	dealt
dig	dug	dug
dive	dived, dove	dived
do	did	done
drag	dragged	dragged
draw	drew	drawn
drink	drank	drunk
drive	drove	driven
eat	ate	eaten
fall	fell	fallen
fight	fought	fought
find	found	found
fly	flew	flown
forget	forgot	forgotten, forgot

Base Form	Past Tense Form	Past Participle
freeze	froze	frozen
get	got	gotten
give	gave	given
go	went	gone
grow	grew	grown
hang (execute)	hanged	hanged
hang (suspend)	hung	hung
have	had	had
hear	heard	heard
keep	kept	kept
know	knew	known
lay	laid	laid
lead	led	led
lend	lent	lent
let	let	let
lie (recline)	lay	lain
lie (tell an untruth)	lied	lied
make	made	made
prove	proved	proved, proven
read	read	read
ride	rode	ridden
ring	rang	rung
rise	rose	risen
run	ran	run
say	said	said
see	saw	seen
set (place)	set	set
shake	shook	shaken
shrink	shrank, shrunk	shrunk, shrunken
sing	sang	sung
sink	sank	sunk
sit	sat	sat
sneak	sneaked, snuck	sneaked, snuck
speak	spoke	spoken
speed	sped, speeded	sped, speeded
spin	spun	spun
spring	sprang	sprung

(continued)

Frequently Used Irregular Verbs *(continued)*

Base Form	Past Tense Form	Past Participle
stand	stood	stood
steal	stole	stolen
strike	struck	struck, stricken
swear	swore	sworn
swim	swam	swum
swing	swung	swung
take	took	taken
teach	taught	taught
throw	threw	thrown
wake	woke, waked	waked, woken
wear	wore	worn
wring	wrung	wrung
write	wrote	written

Close-Up *LIE/LAY* AND *SIT/SET*

Lie means "to recline" and does not take an object ("He likes to *lie* on the floor"); *lay* means "to place" or "to put" and does take an object ("He wants to *lay* a rug on the floor").

Base Form	Past Tense Form	Past Participle
lie	lay	lain
lay	laid	laid

Sit means "to assume a seated position" and does not take an object ("She wants to *sit* on the table"); *set* means "to place" or "to put" and usually takes an object ("She wants to *set* a vase on the table").

Base Form	Past Tense Form	Past Participle
sit	sat	sat
set	set	set

EXERCISE 40.1

Complete each of the sentences in the following paragraph with an appropriate form of the verb in parentheses.

Example: An air of mystery surrounds many of those who have ___sung___ (sing) and played the blues.

The legendary blues musician Robert Johnson supposedly _____ (sell) his soul to the devil in order to become a guitar virtuoso. Myth has it that the young Johnson could barely play his instrument and annoyed other musicians by trying to sit in at clubs, where he _____ (sneak) onto the bandstand to play every chance he got. He disappeared for a short time, the story goes, and when he returned he was a phenomenal guitarist, having _____ (swear) a Faustian oath to Satan. Johnson's song "Crossroads Blues"—rearranged and recorded by the sixties band Cream as simply "Crossroads"— supposedly recounts this exchange, telling how Johnson _____ (deal) with the devil. Some of his other songs, such as "Hellhound on My Trail," are allegedly about the torment he suffered as he _____ (fight) for his soul.

40b Understanding Tense

ml
61a2

<u>Tense</u> is the form a verb takes to indicate when an action occurred or when a condition existed.

English Verb Tenses

Simple Tenses
Present (I *finish*, she or he *finishes*)
Past (I *finished*)
Future (I *will finish*)

Perfect Tenses
Present perfect (I *have finished*, she or he *has finished*)
Past perfect (I *had finished*)
Future perfect (I *will have finished*)

Progressive Tenses
Present progressive (I *am finishing*, she or he *is finishing*)
Past progressive (I *was finishing*)
Future progressive (I *will be finishing*)
Present perfect progressive (I *have been finishing*)
Past perfect progressive (I *had been finishing*)
Future perfect progressive (I *will have been finishing*)

1 Using the Simple Tenses

The **simple tenses** include *present, past,* and *future.*

- The **present tense** usually indicates an action that is taking place at the time it is expressed. It can also indicate an action that occurs regularly.

  I <u>see</u> your point. (an action taking place when it is expressed)

  We <u>wear</u> wool in the winter. (an action that occurs regularly)

Close-Up SPECIAL USES OF THE PRESENT TENSE

The present tense has four special uses:

1. **To indicate future time:** The grades <u>arrive</u> next Thursday.
2. **To state a generally held belief:** Studying <u>pays</u> off.
3. **To state a scientific truth:** An object at rest <u>tends</u> to stay at rest.
4. **To discuss a literary work:** *Family Installments* <u>tells</u> the story of a Puerto Rican family.

- The **past tense** indicates that an action has already taken place.

  John Glenn <u>orbited</u> the earth three times on February 20, 1962. (an action completed in the past)

  As a young man, Mark Twain <u>traveled</u> through the Southwest. (an action that occurred once or many times in the past but did not extend into the present)

- The **future tense** indicates that an action will or is likely to take place.

  Halley's Comet <u>will reappear</u> in 2061. (a future action that will definitely occur)

  The growth of community colleges <u>will</u> probably <u>continue</u>. (a future action that is likely to occur)

2 Using the Perfect Tenses

The **perfect tenses** indicate actions that were or will be completed before other actions or conditions. The perfect tenses are formed with the appropriate tense form of the auxiliary verb *have* plus the past participle.

- The **present perfect** tense can indicate two types of continuing action beginning in the past.

Dr. Kim has finished studying the effects of BHA on rats. (an action that began in the past and is finished at the present time)

My mother has invested her money wisely. (an action that began in the past and extends into the present)

- The **past perfect** tense indicates an action occurring before a certain time in the past.

By 1946, engineers had built the first electronic digital computer.

- The **future perfect** tense indicates that an action will be finished by a certain future time.

By Tuesday, the transit authority will have run out of money.

Close-Up COULD HAVE, SHOULD HAVE, AND WOULD HAVE

Do not use the preposition *of* after *would, should, could,* and *might.* Use the auxiliary verb *have* after these words.

have
I should̲ of left for class earlier.

---

3 Using the Progressive Tenses

The **progressive tenses** indicate continuing action. They are formed with the appropriate tense of the verb *be* plus the present participle.

- The **present progressive** tense indicates that something is happening at the time it is expressed.

The volcano is erupting, and lava is flowing toward the town.

- The **past progressive** tense indicates two kinds of past action.

Roderick Usher's actions were becoming increasingly bizarre. (a continuing action in the past)

The French revolutionary Marat was stabbed to death while he was bathing. (an action occurring at the same time in the past as another action)

- The **future progressive** tense indicates a continuing action in the future.

The treasury secretary will be monitoring the money supply regularly.

- The **present perfect progressive** tense indicates action continuing from the past into the present and possibly into the future.

Rescuers <u>have been working</u> around the clock.

- The **past perfect progressive** tense indicates that a past action went on until another one occurred.

Before President Kennedy was assassinated, he <u>had been working</u> on civil rights legislation.

- The **future perfect progressive** tense indicates that an action will continue until a certain future time.

By eleven o'clock we <u>will have been driving</u> for seven hours.

4 Using Verb Tenses in a Sentence

Within a sentence, you may need to use different tenses to indicate that actions are taking place at different times. By choosing tenses that accurately express these times, you enable readers to follow the sequence of actions.

- *When a **verb** appears in a dependent clause, its tense depends on the tense of the main verb in the independent clause.* When the main verb in the independent clause is in the past tense, the verb in the dependent clause is usually in the past or past perfect tense. When the main verb in the independent clause is in the past perfect tense, the verb in the dependent clause is usually in the past tense. (When the main verb in the independent clause is in any tense except the past or past perfect, the verb in the dependent clause may be in any tense needed for meaning.)

Main Verb	**Verb in Dependent Clause**
George Hepplewhite <u>was</u> (past) an English cabinetmaker	who <u>designed</u> (past) distinctive chair backs.
The battle <u>had ended</u> (past perfect)	by the time reinforcements <u>arrived</u>. (past)

- *When an **infinitive** appears in a verbal phrase, the tense it expresses depends on the tense of the sentence's main verb.* The ***present infinitive*** (the *to* form of the verb) indicates an action happening at the same time as or later than the main verb. The ***perfect infinitive*** (*to have* plus the past participle) indicates action happening earlier than the main verb.

Main Verb	**Infinitive**
I <u>went</u>	<u>to see</u> the Eagles play last week. (Present infinitive indicates that the going and seeing occurred at the same time.)

I want   to see the Eagles play tomorrow. (Present infinitive indicates that wanting occurs in the present and seeing will occur in the future.)

I would like   to have seen the Eagles play. (Perfect infinitive indicates that liking occurs in the present and seeing would have occurred in the past.)

- *When a **participle** appears in a verbal phrase, its tense depends on the tense of the sentence's main verb.* The *present participle* indicates action happening at the same time as the action of the main verb. The *past participle* or the *present perfect participle* indicates action occurring before the action of the main verb.

Participle	Main Verb
<u>Addressing</u> the 1896 Democratic Convention,	William Jennings Bryan <u>delivered</u> his Cross of Gold speech. (The addressing and the delivery occurred at the same time.)
<u>Having written</u> her research paper,	Sophia <u>studied</u> for her history final. (The writing occurred before the studying.)

EXERCISE 40.2

A verb is missing from each of the following sentences. Fill in the form of the verb indicated in parentheses.

Example: The Outer Banks *stretch* (stretch: present) along the North Carolina coast for more than 175 miles.

1. Many portions of the Outer Banks of North Carolina _____ (give: present) the visitor a sense of history and timelessness.
2. Many students of history _____ (read: present perfect) about the Outer Banks and its mysteries.
3. It was on Roanoke Island in the 1580s that English colonists _____ (establish: past) the first settlement in the New World.
4. That colony vanished soon after it was settled, _____ (become: present participle) known as the famous "lost colony."
5. By 1718, the pirate Blackbeard _____ (made: past perfect) the Outer Banks a hiding place for his treasures.
6. It was at Ocracoke, in fact, that Blackbeard _____ (meet: past) his death.
7. Even today, people _____ (search: present progressive) the Outer Banks for Blackbeard's hidden treasures.
8. The Outer Banks are also famous for Kitty Hawk; even as technology has advanced into the space age, the number of tourists flocking to

the site of the Wright brothers' epic flight _____ (grow: present perfect progressive).

9. Long before that famous flight occurred, however, the Outer Banks _____ (claim: past perfect) countless ships along its ever-shifting shores, resulting in its nickname—the "Graveyard of the Atlantic."

10. If the Outer Banks continue to be protected from the ravages of overdevelopment and commercialization, visitors _____ (enjoy: future progressive) the mysteries of this tiny finger of land for years to come.

40c Understanding Mood

Mood is the form a verb takes to indicate whether a writer is making a statement, asking a question, giving a command, or expressing a wish or a contrary-to-fact statement. There are three moods in English:

- The **indicative** mood expresses an opinion, states a fact, or asks a question: *Jackie Robinson had a great impact on professional baseball.* (The indicative is the mood used in most English sentences.)

- The **imperative** mood is used in commands and direct requests. Usually, the imperative includes only the base form of the verb without a subject: *Use a dictionary.*

- The **subjunctive** mood is not as common as it once was, but it is still used to express wishes, contrary-to-fact statements, and requests or recommendations.

1 Forming the Subjunctive Mood

The **present subjunctive** uses the base form of the verb, regardless of the subject. The **past subjunctive** has the same form as the past tense of the verb. (However, when *be* is used as an auxiliary verb, it takes the form *were* regardless of the number or person of the subject.)

> Dr. Gorman suggested that I study the Cambrian Period. (present subjunctive)

> I wish I were going to Europe. (past subjunctive)

2 Using the Subjunctive Mood

The **present subjunctive** is used in *that* clauses after words such as *ask, suggest, require, recommend,* and *demand.*

> The report recommended that juveniles be given mandatory counseling.

> Captain Ahab insisted that his crew hunt the white whale.

The **past subjunctive** is used in **conditional statements** (statements beginning with *if* that are contrary to fact, including statements that express a wish).

If John <u>were</u> here, he could see Marsha. (John is not here.)

The father acted as if he <u>were</u> having the baby. (The father couldn't be having the baby.)

I wish I <u>were</u> more organized. (expresses a wish)

Note: In many situations, the subjunctive mood can sound stiff or formal. Alternative expressions can often eliminate the need for subjunctive constructions.

The group asked ~~that~~ the city council ^to^ ban smoking in public places.

EXERCISE 40.3

Complete the sentences in the following paragraph by inserting the appropriate form (indicative, imperative, or subjunctive) of the verb in parentheses. Compare your choices with those of a classmate.

Harry Houdini was a famous escape artist. He _____ (perform) escapes from every type of bond imaginable: handcuffs, locks, straitjackets, ropes, sacks, and sealed chests underwater. In Germany, workers _____ (challenge) Houdini to escape from a packing box. If he _____ (be) to escape, they would admit that he _____ (be) the best escape artist in the world. Houdini accepted. Before getting into the box, he asked that the observers _____ (give) it a thorough examination. He then asked that a worker _____ (nail) him into the box. "_____ (place) a screen around the box," he ordered after he had been sealed inside. In a few minutes, Houdini _____ (step) from behind the screen. When the workers demanded that they _____ (see) the box, Houdini pulled down the screen. To their surprise, they saw the box with the lid still nailed tightly in place.

40d Understanding Voice

Voice is the form a verb takes to indicate whether the subject of the verb acts or is acted upon.

When the subject of a verb does something—that is, acts—the verb is in the **active voice**. When the subject of a verb receives the action—that is, is acted upon—the verb is in the **passive voice**.

Active Voice: Hart Crane <u>wrote</u> *The Bridge*.

Passive Voice: *The Bridge* <u>was written</u> by Hart Crane.

Close-Up VOICE

Because the active voice emphasizes the person or thing performing an action, it is usually briefer, clearer, and more emphatic than the passive voice. For this reason, you should usually use the active voice in your college writing.

Some scientific disciplines, however, encourage the use of the passive voice. The purpose is to convey objectivity—to shift the focus away from the scientists and to emphasize the experimental results.

DDT <u>was found</u> in soil samples. (Passive voice emphasizes the discovery of DDT; who found it is not important.)

Grits <u>are eaten</u> throughout the South. (Passive voice emphasizes the fact that grits are eaten, not who eats them.)

1 Changing Verbs from Passive to Active Voice

You can change a verb from passive to active voice by making the subject of the passive verb the object of the active verb. The person or thing performing the action then becomes the subject of the new sentence.

Passive: The novel *Frankenstein* <u>was written</u> by Mary Shelley.

Active: Mary Shelley <u>wrote</u> the novel *Frankenstein*.

EXERCISE 40.4

Determine which passive voice sentences in the following paragraph should be in the active voice, and rewrite those sentences.

Rockets were invented by the Chinese about AD 1000. Gunpowder was packed into bamboo tubes and ignited by means of a fuse. These rockets were fired by soldiers at enemy armies and usually caused panic. In thirteenth-century England, an improved form of gunpowder was introduced by Roger Bacon. As a result, rockets were used in battles and were a common—although unreliable— weapon. In the early eighteenth century, a twenty-pound rocket that traveled almost two miles was constructed by William Congreve, an English artillery expert. By the late nineteenth century, thought was given to supersonic speeds by the physicist Ernst Mach, and the sonic boom was predicted by him. The first liquid-fuel rocket was launched by the American Robert Goddard in 1926. A pamphlet written by him anticipated almost all future rocket developments. As a result of his pioneering work, he is known as the father of modern rocketry.

2 Changing Verbs from Active to Passive Voice

You can change a verb from active to passive voice by making the object of the active verb the subject of the passive verb. The person or thing performing the action then becomes the object of the passive verb.

Active: Sir James Murray <u>compiled</u> *The Oxford English Dictionary.*

Passive: *The Oxford English Dictionary* <u>was compiled</u> by Sir James Murray.

CHAPTER 41

Using Pronouns

41a Understanding Pronoun Case

Case is the form a noun or pronoun takes to indicate its function in a sentence. **Nouns** change form only in the possessive case: the *cat's* eyes, *Molly's* book. **Pronouns**, however, have three cases: *subjective, objective,* and *possessive.*

Pronoun Case Forms

Subjective						
I	he, she	it	we	you	they	who
						whoever

Objective						
me	him, her	it	us	you	them	whom
						whomever

Possessive						
my	his, her	its	our	your	their	whose
mine	hers		ours	yours	theirs	

1 Subjective Case

A pronoun takes the **subjective case** in the following situations.

Subject of a Verb: I bought a new cell phone.

Subject Complement: It was <u>he</u> who volunteered at the shelter.

2 Objective Case

A pronoun takes the **objective case** in the following situations.

Direct Object: The boss asked Adam and <u>me</u> to work late.

Indirect Object: The plumber's bill gave <u>them</u> quite a shock.

Object of a Preposition: We own ten shares of stock between <u>us</u>.

Close-Up *I* VERSUS *ME*

I is not always more appropriate than *me*. In the following example, *me* is correct.

Just between you and <u>me</u> [not *I*], I think the data are inconclusive.
(*Me* is the object of the preposition *between*.)

---

3 Possessive Case

A pronoun takes the **possessive case** when it indicates ownership. The possessive case is also used before a **gerund**.

Napoleon gave <u>his</u> approval to <u>their</u> ruling Naples. (*His* indicates ownership; *ruling* is a gerund.)

EXERCISE 41.1

Underline the correct form of the pronoun within the parentheses. Compare your choices with those of a classmate.

Example: Toni Morrison, Alice Walker, and (<u>she</u>, her) are perhaps the most widely recognized African American women writing today.

1. Both Walt Whitman and (he, him) wrote a great deal of poetry about nature.
2. Our instructor gave Matthew and (me, I) an excellent idea for our project.
3. The sales clerk objected to (me, my) returning the sweater.
4. I understand (you, your) being unavailable to work tonight.
5. The waiter asked Michael and (me, I) to move to another table.

41b Determining Pronoun Case in Special Situations

1 In Comparisons with *Than* or *As*

When a comparison ends with a pronoun, the pronoun's function in the sentence determines your choice of pronoun case. If the pronoun functions as a subject, use the subjective case; if it functions as an object, use the objective case. You can determine the function of the pronoun by completing the comparison.

> Darcy likes John more than I. (... *more than I like John: I* is the subject.)

> Darcy likes John more than me. (... *more than she likes me: me* is the object.)

2 With *Who* and *Whom*

The case of the pronouns *who* and *whom* depends on their function *within their own clause*. When a pronoun serves as the subject of its clause, use *who* or *whoever;* when it functions as an object, use *whom* or *whomever.*

> The Salvation Army gives food and shelter to whoever is in need. (*Whoever* is the subject of the dependent clause *whoever is in need.*)

> I wonder whom jazz musician Miles Davis influenced. (*Whom* is the object of *influenced* in the dependent clause *whom jazz musician Miles Davis influenced.*)

Close-Up PRONOUN CASE IN QUESTIONS

To determine whether to use the subjective case (*who*) or the objective case (*whom*) in a question, use a personal pronoun to answer the question. If the pronoun in your answer is the subject, use *who*; if the pronoun is the object, use *whom*.

> Who wrote *The Age of Innocence*? She wrote it. (subject)

> Whom do you support for mayor? I support him. (object)

EXERCISE 41.2

Using the word in parentheses, combine each pair of sentences into a single sentence. You may change word order and add or delete words.

Example: After he left the band The Police, bass player Sting continued as a solo artist. He once taught middle-school English. (who)

Revised: After he left the band The Police, bass player Sting, who once taught middle-school English, continued as a solo artist.

1. Herb Ritts has photographed world leaders, leading artistic figures in dance and drama, and a vanishing African tribe. He got his start by taking photographs of Hollywood stars. (who)
2. Tim Green has written several novels about a fictional football team. He played for the Atlanta Hawks and has a law degree. (who)
3. Some say Carl Sagan did more to further science education in America than any other person. He wrote many books on science and narrated many popular television shows. (who)
4. Jodie Foster has won two Academy Awards for her acting. She was a child star. (who)
5. Sylvia Plath met fellow poet Ted Hughes at Cambridge University in England. She later married him. (whom)

③ With Appositives

ml
61c4

An **appositive** is a noun or noun phrase that identifies or renames an adjacent noun or pronoun. The case of a pronoun in an appositive depends on the function of the word the appositive identifies or renames.

Two recording artists, he and Smokey Robinson, had contracts with Motown Records. (*Artists* is the subject of the sentence, so the pronoun in the appositive *he and Smokey Robinson* takes the subjective case.)

We heard two Motown recording artists, Smokey Robinson and him. (*Artists* is the object of the verb *heard*, so the pronoun in the appositive *Smokey Robinson and him* takes the objective case.)

④ With *We* and *Us* before a Noun

When a first-person plural pronoun directly precedes a noun, the case of the pronoun depends on how the noun functions in the sentence.

We women must stick together. (*Women* is the subject of the sentence, so the pronoun *we* takes the subjective case.)

Teachers make learning easy for us students. (*Students* is the object of the preposition *for*, so the pronoun *us* must be in the objective case.)

41c   Revising Pronoun Reference Errors

❓ An **antecedent** is the word or word group to which a pronoun refers. The connection between a pronoun and its antecedent should always be clear. If the <u>pronoun reference</u> is not clear, revise the sentence.

ml
61c1

Alicia forgot her cell phone.

The students missed their train.

1 Ambiguous Antecedent

Sometimes it is not clear to which antecedent a pronoun—for example, *this, that, which,* or *it*—refers. In such cases, eliminate the ambiguity by substituting a noun for the pronoun.

> The accountant took out his calculator and added up the list of
> *the calculator*
> numbers. Then, he put it back in his briefcase. (The pronoun *it* can refer either to *calculator* or to *list of numbers.*)

2 Remote Antecedent

The farther a pronoun is from its antecedent, the more difficult it is for readers to make a connection between them. If a pronoun and its antecedent are far apart, replace the pronoun with a noun.

> During the mid-1800s, many Czechs began to immigrate to America.
>
> By 1860, about 23,000 had left their country; by 1900, 13,000 Czechs
> *America's*
> were coming to its shores each year.

3 Nonexistent Antecedent

Sometimes a pronoun—for example, *this*—refers to an antecedent that does not appear in the sentence. In such cases, add the missing antecedent.

> Some one-celled organisms contain chlorophyll yet are considered
> *paradox*
> animals. This illustrates the difficulty of classifying single-celled
>
> organisms. (What does *this* refer to?)

Note: Expressions such as "*It* says online" and "*He* said on the news," which refer to unidentified antecedents, are not acceptable in college writing. When you revise, substitute an appropriate noun for the unclear pronoun: "*The online article* says . . ." and "In his commentary, *Chuck Todd* observes. . . ."

4 Who, Which, and That

In general, *who* refers to people or to animals that have names. *Which* and *that* refer to things or to unnamed animals. When referring to an antecedent, be sure to choose the appropriate pronoun (*who, which,* or *that*).

David Henry Hwang, <u>who</u> wrote the Tony Award-winning play *M. Butterfly*, also wrote *Chinglish*.

The spotted owl, <u>which</u> lives in old-growth forests, is in danger of extinction.

Houses <u>that</u> are built today are usually more energy efficient than those built years ago.

Never use *that* to refer to a person.

who
The man ~~that~~ holds the world record for eating hot dogs is my neighbor.

See 49d1 *Note:* Use *which* to introduce <u>**nonrestrictive clauses**</u>, which are always set off with commas. Use *that* to introduce <u>**restrictive clauses**</u>, which are not set off with commas. (*Who* can introduce either restrictive or nonrestrictive clauses.)

EXERCISE 41.3

Analyze the pronoun reference errors in each of the following sentences. After doing so, revise each sentence by substituting an appropriate noun or noun phrase for the underlined pronoun.

Example: Jefferson asked Lewis to head the expedition, and Lewis selected

Clark
~~him~~ as his associate. (*Him* refers to a nonexistent antecedent.)

1. The purpose of the expedition was to search out a land route to the Pacific and to gather information about the West. The Louisiana Purchase increased the need for <u>it</u>.
2. The expedition was going to be difficult. <u>They</u> trained the men in Illinois, the starting point.
3. Clark and most of the men who descended the Yellowstone River camped on the bank. <u>It</u> was beautiful and wild.
4. Both Jefferson and Lewis had faith that <u>he</u> would be successful in this transcontinental journey.
5. The expedition was efficient, and only one man was lost. <u>This</u> was extraordinary.

CHAPTER **42**

Using Adjectives and Adverbs

Adjectives modify nouns and pronouns. **Adverbs** modify verbs, adjectives, or other adverbs—or entire phrases, clauses, or sentences.

The function of a word in a sentence, not its form, determines whether it is an adjective or an adverb. Although many adverbs (such as *immediately* and *hopelessly*) end in *-ly*, others (such as *almost* and *very*) do not. Moreover, some words that end in *-ly* (such as *lively*) are adjectives.

> MULTILINGUAL TIP
>
> For information on correct placement of adjectives and adverbs in a sentence, **see 61d1**. For information on correct order of adjectives in a series, **see 61d2**.

42a Using Adjectives

Use an **adjective**, not an adverb, to modify a noun or a pronoun. Also use an adjective as a subject complement. A **subject complement** is a word that follows a linking verb and modifies the sentence's subject, not its verb. A **linking verb** does not show physical or emotional action. *Seem, appear, believe, become, grow, turn, remain, prove, look, sound, smell, taste, feel,* and the forms of the verb *be* are (or can be used as) linking verbs.

> Michelle seemed <u>brave</u>. (*Seemed* shows no action, so it is a linking verb. Because *brave* is a subject complement that modifies the noun *Michelle*, it takes the adjective form.)
>
> Michelle smiled <u>bravely</u>. (*Smiled* shows action, so it is not a linking verb. Because *bravely* modifies *smiled*, it takes the adverb form.)

Note: Sometimes the same verb can function as either a linking verb or an action verb: *He remained <u>stubborn</u>.* (He was still stubborn.) *He remained <u>stubbornly</u>.* (He remained, in a stubborn manner.)

42b Using Adverbs

Use an **adverb**, not an adjective, to modify a verb, an adjective, or another adverb—or an entire phrase, clause, or sentence.

505

very well
Most students did ~~great~~ on the midterm. (*Very* modifies *well*; *well* modifies *did*.)

ly
My parents dress a lot more conservative~~^~~ than I do. (*More* modifies *conservatively*; *conservatively* modifies *dress*.)

Close-Up USING ADJECTIVES AND ADVERBS

In informal speech, adjective forms such as *good, bad, sure, real, slow, quick,* and *loud* are often used to modify verbs, adjectives, and adverbs. Avoid these informal modifiers in college writing.

really well
The program ran ~~real good~~ the first time we tried it, but the new
badly
system performed ~~bad~~.

EXERCISE 42.1

Revise each of the incorrect sentences in the following paragraph so that only adjectives modify nouns and pronouns and only adverbs modify verbs, adjectives, or other adverbs.

A popular self-help trend in the United States today is motivational podcasts. These podcasts, with titles like *How to Attract Love, Freedom from Acne,* and *I Am a Genius,* are intended to address every problem known to modern society—and to solve these problems quick and easy. The podcasts are said to work because they contain "hidden messages" that bypass conscious defense mechanisms. The listener hears only music or relaxing sounds, like waves rolling slow and steady. At decibel levels perceived only subconsciously, positive words and phrases are embedded, usually by someone who speaks deep and rhythmic. The top-selling podcasts are those that help listeners lose weight or quit smoking real fast. The popularity of such material is not hard to understand. They promise easy solutions to complex problems.

42c Using Comparative and Superlative Forms

Most adjectives and adverbs have **comparative** and **superlative** forms.

Comparative and Superlative Forms		
Form	Function	Example
Positive	Describes a quality; indicates no comparison	big, easily
Comparative	Indicates comparison between two qualities (greater or lesser)	bigger, more easily
Superlative	Indicates comparison among three or more qualities (greatest or least)	biggest, most easily

1 Regular Comparative Forms

To form the comparative, all one-syllable adjectives and many two-syllable adjectives (particularly those that end in *-y, -ly, -le, -er,* and *-ow*) add *-er: slower, funnier.* (Note that a final *y* becomes *i* before *-er* is added.)

Other two-syllable adjectives and all long adjectives form the comparative with *more: more famous, more incredible.*

Adverbs ending in *-ly* also form the comparative with *more: more slowly.* Other adverbs use the *-er* ending to form the comparative: *sooner.*

All adjectives and adverbs form the comparative with *less: less lovely, less slowly.*

2 Regular Superlative Forms

Adjectives that form the comparative with *-er* add *-est* to form the superlative: *nicest, funniest.* Adjectives that indicate the comparative with *more* use *most* to indicate the superlative: *most famous, most challenging.*

The majority of adverbs use *most* to indicate the superlative: *most quickly.* Others use the *-est* ending: *soonest.*

All adjectives and adverbs form the superlative with *least: least interesting, least willingly.*

Close-Up USING COMPARATIVES AND SUPERLATIVES

- Never use both *more* and *-er* to form the comparative or both *most* and *-est* to form the superlative.

(continued)

USING COMPARATIVES AND SUPERLATIVES *(continued)*

Nothing could have been ~~more~~ easier.

Jack is the ~~most~~ meanest person in town.

● Never use the superlative when comparing only two things.

> *older*
> Stacy is the ~~oldest~~ of the two sisters.
>   ^

● Never use the comparative when comparing more than two things.

> *earliest*
> We chose the ~~earlier~~ of the four appointments.
>   ^

3 Irregular Comparative and Superlative Forms

Some adjectives and adverbs have irregular comparative and superlative forms.

Irregular Comparative and Superlative Forms

	Positive	Comparative	Superlative
Adjectives:	good	better	best
	bad	worse	worst
	a little	less	least
	many, some, much	more	most
Adverbs:	well	better	best
	badly	worse	worst

42d Avoiding Illogical Comparatives and Superlatives

❓ Many adjectives—for example, *perfect, unique, excellent, impossible, parallel, empty,* and *dead*—are **absolutes** and therefore have no comparative or superlative forms.

> *better*
> "The Cask of Amontillado" is a ~~more excellent~~ story than "The Tell-Tale Heart."
>   ^

> *a*
> I saw ~~the most~~ unique vase in the museum.
>   ^

These adjectives can, however, be modified by words that suggest approaching the absolute state—*nearly* or *almost,* for example.

He revised until his draft was <u>almost perfect</u>.

Note: Some adverbs, particularly those indicating time, place, and degree (*almost, very, here, immediately*), do not have comparative or superlative forms.

EXERCISE 42.2

Supply the correct comparative and superlative forms for each of the following adjectives or adverbs. Then, use each form in a sentence.

Example: strange/stranger/strangest

> The story had a *strange* ending.
>
> The explanation sounded *stranger* each time I heard it.
>
> This is the *strangest* gadget I have ever seen.

1. difficult
2. eccentric
3. confusing
4. bad
5. mysterious

6. softly
7. embarrassing
8. well
9. often
10. tiny

CHAPTER **43**

Revising Fragments

43a Recognizing Fragments

A **fragment** is an incomplete sentence—a phrase or clause that is punctuated as if it were a complete sentence. A sentence may be incomplete for any of the following reasons:

- **It has no subject.**

Many astrophysicists now believe that galaxies are distributed in clusters. <u>And even form supercluster complexes.</u>

- **It has no verb.**

  Every generation has its defining events. <u>Usually the events with the most news coverage</u>.

- **It has neither a subject nor a verb.**

  Researchers are engaged in a variety of studies. <u>Suggesting a link between alcoholism and heredity</u>. (*Suggesting* is a **verbal**, which cannot serve as a sentence's main verb.)

See
49c1
- **It is a <u>dependent clause</u>.**

  Bishop Desmond Tutu was awarded the Nobel Peace Prize. <u>Because he fought to end apartheid</u>.

  The pH meter and the spectrophotometer are two scientific instruments. <u>That changed the chemistry laboratory dramatically</u>.

Note: A sentence cannot consist of a single clause that begins with a subordinating conjunction (such as *because*) or a relative pronoun (such as *that*); moreover, unless it is a question, a sentence cannot consist of a single clause beginning with *when, where, who, which, what, why,* or *how*.

EXERCISE 43.1

Identify each of the following word groups as either a fragment or a complete sentence. Be prepared to explain why each fragment is not a complete sentence. When you have finished, run a grammar check on each in your word-processing program.

1. Consisting of shortness of breath, a high fever, and a racing pulse.
2. Held in contempt of court by the presiding judge.
3. Walking to the end of the road and back is good exercise.
4. On her own at last, after many years of struggle for independence.
5. Because he felt torn between two cultures.
6. With boundaries extending from the ocean to the bay.
7. Although language study can be challenging.

43b Correcting Fragments

If you identify a fragment in your writing, use one of the following three strategies to correct it.

1 Attach the Fragment to an Independent Clause

In most cases, the simplest way to correct a fragment is by attaching it to an adjacent **independent clause** that contains the missing words.

President Lyndon Johnson did not seek a second term/~For~ *for* a number of reasons. (prepositional phrase fragment)

Students sometimes take a leave of absence/~To~ *to* decide on definite career goals. (verbal phrase fragment)

The pilot changed course/~Realizing~ *, realizing* that the weather was worsening. (verbal phrase fragment)

Brian was the star forward of the Blue Devils/~The~ *, the* team with the most wins. (appositive fragment)

Fairy tales are full of damsels in distress/~Such~ *, such* as Rapunzel. (appositive fragment)

People with dyslexia have trouble reading/~And~ *, and* may also find it difficult to write. (part of compound predicate)

They took only a compass and a canteen/~And~ *, and* some trail mix. (part of compound object)

Property taxes rose sharply/~Although~ *although* city services declined. (dependent clause fragment)

The battery is dead/~Which~ *, which* means the car won't start. (dependent clause fragment)

② Delete the Subordinating Conjunction or Relative Pronoun

When a fragment consists of a dependent clause that is punctuated as though it were a complete sentence, you can correct it by attaching it to an adjacent independent clause, as illustrated in **43b1**. Alternatively, you can simply delete the subordinating conjunction or relative pronoun.

Property taxes rose sharply. ~Although~ *City* city services declined. (subordinating conjunction *although* deleted)

The battery is dead. ~Which~ *This* means the car won't start. (relative pronoun *which* replaced by *this*, a word that can serve as the sentence's subject)

Note: Simply deleting the subordinating conjunction or relative pronoun is usually the least desirable way to revise because it is likely to create two choppy sentences and obscure the connection between them.

Close-Up LISTS

When a fragment takes the form of a list, add a colon to connect the list to the independent clause that introduces it.

See
23c

> :
> Tourists often outnumber residents in four European cities/Venice,
> Florence, Canterbury, and Bath.

③ Supply the Missing Subject or Verb

Another way to correct a fragment is to add the missing words (a subject or a verb or both) that are needed to make the fragment a sentence.

It was divided
In 1948, India became independent. ~~Divided~~ into the nations of India and Pakistan. (verbal phrase fragment)

It reminds
A familiar trademark can increase a product's sales. ~~Reminding~~ shoppers that the product has a longstanding reputation. (verbal phrase fragment)

Close-Up FRAGMENTS INTRODUCED BY TRANSITIONS

See
34b2

Many fragments are word groups that are introduced by transitional words and phrases, such as *also, finally, in addition*, and *now*, but are missing subjects and verbs. To correct such a fragment, add the missing subject and verb.

he found
Finally, a new home for the family.

we need
In addition, three new keyboards for the computer lab.

EXERCISE 43.2

Identify the fragments in the following paragraph. Then, correct each fragment either by attaching the fragment to an independent clause or by deleting or replacing the subordinating conjunction or relative pronoun to create a sentence that can stand alone. (In some cases, you will have to replace a relative pronoun with another word that can serve as the subject.)

The drive-in movie came into being just after World War II. When both movies and cars were central to the lives of many Americans. Drive-ins were especially popular with teenagers and young families during the 1950s. When cars and gas were relatively inexpensive. Theaters charged by the carload. Which meant that a group of teenagers or a family with several children could spend an evening at the movies for a few dollars. In 1958, when the fad peaked, there were over four thousand drive-ins in the United States. While today there are just a few hundred. Many of these are in the Sunbelt, especially in California. Although many Sunbelt drive-ins continue to thrive because of the year-round warm weather. Many northern drive-ins are in financial trouble. Because land is so expensive. Some drive-in owners break even only by operating flea markets or swap meets in daylight hours. While others, unable to attract customers, are selling their theaters to land developers. Soon, drive-ins may be a part of our nostalgic past. Which will be a great loss for many who enjoy them.

43c Using Fragments Intentionally

Fragments are often used in speech as well as in personal email, text messages, and other informal writing—as well as in journalism, political slogans, creative writing, and advertising (see Figure 43.1). In professional and academic writing, however, sentence fragments are generally not acceptable.

Close-Up USING FRAGMENTS INTENTIONALLY

In college writing, it is permissible to use fragments in the following special situations:

- In lists
- In captions that accompany visuals
- In topic outlines
- In quoted dialogue
- In *PowerPoint* presentations
- In titles and subtitles of essays and reports

FIGURE 43.1 Intentional fragments used in advertising. Images courtesy of The Advertising Archives.

EXERCISE 43.3

Select several online or print advertisements. Identify word groups that you think are fragments. Then, run a grammar check on each in your word-processing program. Keep in mind that some word groups may look like fragments but may in fact be imperative sentences (commands) that have an implied subject (*you*) and will therefore be recognized as grammatically correct sentences.

Revise each fragment you identify so that it is a complete sentence. Then, decide which version—the fragment or your corrected sentence—is more effective for each advertisement's rhetorical situation.

CHAPTER **44**

Revising Run-Ons

44a **Recognizing Comma Splices and Fused Sentences**

A **run-on** is an error that occurs when two independent clauses are joined incorrectly. There are two kinds of run-ons: *comma splices* and *fused sentences*.

A **comma splice** is a run-on that occurs when two independent clauses are joined with just a comma. A **fused sentence** is a run-on that occurs when two independent clauses are joined with no punctuation.

> **Comma Splice:** Charles Dickens created the character of Mr. Micawber, he also created Uriah Heep.

> **Fused Sentence:** Charles Dickens created the character of Mr. Micawber he also created Uriah Heep.

44b Correcting Comma Splices and Fused Sentences

To correct a comma splice or fused sentence, use one of the following four strategies:

1. Add a period between the clauses, creating two separate sentences.
2. Add a semicolon between the clauses, creating a compound sentence.
3. Add an appropriate coordinating conjunction between the clauses, creating a compound sentence.
4. Subordinate one clause to the other, creating a complex sentence.

1 Add a Period

You can add a period between the independent clauses, creating two separate sentences. This is a good strategy to use when the clauses are long or when they are not closely related.

> In 1894, Frenchman Alfred Dreyfus was falsely convicted of
>   . His
> treason/~~his~~ struggle for justice made his case famous.

Close-Up COMMA SPLICES AND FUSED SENTENCES

Do not use a comma to punctuate an interrupted quotation that consists of two complete sentences; this creates a comma splice. Instead, use a period.

> ."In
> "This is a good course," Eric said/,"~~in~~ fact, I wish I'd taken it sooner."

---

2 Add a Semicolon

You can add a <u>semicolon</u> between two closely related clauses that convey parallel or contrasting information. The result will be a **compound sentence**.

See
50a

Before World War II, very few Europeans had access to a university

education$\overset{;}{/}$however, this situation changed dramatically after the war.
                    $\land$

See
34b2 **Note:** When you use a **transitional word or phrase** (such as *however, there-fore,* or *for example*) to connect two independent clauses, the transitional element must be preceded by a semicolon and followed by a comma. If you use a comma alone, you create a comma splice. If you omit punctuation entirely, you create a fused sentence.

3 Add a Coordinating Conjunction

You can use a coordinating conjunction (*and, or, but, nor, for, so, yet*) to join two closely related clauses of equal importance into one **compound sentence**. The coordinating conjunction you choose indicates the relation-ship between the clauses: addition (*and*), contrast (*but, yet*), causality (*for, so*), or a choice of alternatives (*or, nor*). Be sure to add a comma before the coordinating conjunction.

and
Elias Howe invented the sewing machine,$_\land$Julia Ward Howe was a poet and social reformer.

4 Create a Complex Sentence

When the ideas in two independent clauses are not of equal importance, you can use an appropriate subordinating conjunction or a relative pro-noun to join the clauses into one **complex sentence**, placing the less impor-tant idea in the dependent clause.

because
Stravinsky's 1913 ballet *The Rite of Spring* shocked Parisians$\overset{}{/}$ the dancing seemed erotic.
            $\land$

, who
Lady Mary Wortley Montagu$_\land$had suffered from smallpox

herself$'$ ~~she~~ helped spread the practice of inoculation in the eighteenth
       $\land$
century.

EXERCISE 44.1

Identify the comma splices and fused sentences in the following paragraph. Correct each in two of the four possible ways discussed above. If a sen-tence is correct, leave it alone.

Example: The fans rose in their seats, the game was almost over.
Revised: The fans rose in their seats; the game was almost over.
The fans rose in their seats because the game was almost over.

Entrepreneurship is the study of small businesses, college students are embracing it enthusiastically. Many schools offer one or more courses in entrepreneurship these courses teach the theory and practice of starting a small business. Students are signing up for courses, moreover, they are starting their own businesses. One student started with a car-waxing business, now he sells condominiums. Other students are setting up catering services they supply everything from waiters to bartenders. One student has a thriving cake-decorating business, in fact, she employs fifteen students to deliver the cakes. All over the country, student businesses are selling everything from tennis balls to bagels, the student owners are making impressive profits. Formal courses at the graduate as well as undergraduate level are attracting more business students than ever, several schools (such as Baylor University, the University of Southern California, and Babson College) even offer degree programs in entrepreneurship. Many business school students are no longer planning to be corporate executives instead, they plan to become entrepreneurs.

CHAPTER **45**

Revising Agreement Errors

Agreement is the correspondence between words in number, gender, or person. Subjects and verbs <u>agree</u> in **number** (singular or plural) and **person** (first, second, or third); pronouns and their antecedents agree in number, person, and **gender** (masculine, feminine, or neuter).

ml
61a1

45a Making Subjects and Verbs Agree

Singular subjects take singular verbs, and plural subjects take plural verbs.

Singular: <u>Hydrogen peroxide</u> <u><u>is</u></u> an unstable compound.

Plural: <u>Characters</u> <u><u>are</u></u> not well developed in O. Henry's short stories.

<u>Present tense</u> verbs, except *be* and *have*, add *-s* or *-es* when the subject is third-person singular. (Third-person singular subjects include nouns; the personal pronouns *he, she, it,* and *one*; and many **indefinite pronouns**, such as *everyone* and *anyone*.)

ml
61a2

The <u>president</u> <u>has</u> the power to veto congressional legislation.

<u>She</u> frequently <u>cites</u> statistics to support her points.

In every group, <u>somebody</u> <u>emerges</u> as a natural leader.

Present tense verbs do not add *-s* or *-es* when the subject is a plural noun, a first-person or second-person pronoun (*I, we, you*), or a third-person plural pronoun (*they*).

<u>Experts</u> <u>recommend</u> that dieters avoid processed meat.

At this stratum, <u>we</u> <u>see</u> rocks dating back ten million years.

<u>They</u> <u>say</u> that even some wealthy people default on their student loans.

In the following situations, making subjects and verbs agree can be challenging for writers.

❶ When Words Come between Subject and Verb

If a modifying phrase comes between subject and verb, the verb should agree with the subject, not with the last word in the modifying phrase.

The <u>sound</u> of the drumbeats <u>builds</u> in intensity in Eugene O'Neill's play *The Emperor Jones.*

The <u>games</u> won by the intramural team <u>are</u> few and far between.

<u>Communication</u> among family members <u>is</u> strained.

Note: This rule also applies to phrases introduced by *along with, as well as, in addition to, including,* and *together with*: *Heavy <u>rain,</u> along with high winds, <u>causes</u> hazardous driving conditions.*

❷ When Compound Subjects Are Joined by *And*

Compound subjects joined by *and* usually take plural verbs.

<u>Air bags and antilock brakes</u> <u>are</u> standard on all new models.

There are, however, two exceptions to this rule:

- Compound subjects joined by *and* that stand for a single idea or person are treated as a unit and take singular verbs.

<u>Rhythm and blues</u> <u>is</u> a forerunner of rock and roll.

- When *each* or *every* precedes a compound subject joined by *and*, the subject takes a singular verb.

<u>Every desk and file cabinet</u> <u>was</u> searched before the letter was found.

3 When Compound Subjects Are Joined by *Or*

Compound subjects joined by *or* (or by *either . . . or* or *neither . . . nor*) may take either a singular or a plural verb.

If both subjects are singular, use a singular verb; if both subjects are plural, use a plural verb. If one subject is singular and the other is plural, the verb agrees with the subject that is nearer to it.

Either radiation treatments or chemotherapy is combined with surgery for the most effective results. (Singular verb agrees with *chemotherapy*.)

Either chemotherapy or radiation treatments are combined with surgery for effective results. (Plural verb agrees with *treatments*.)

4 With Indefinite Pronoun Subjects

Most **indefinite pronouns**—*another, anyone, everyone, one, each, either, neither, anything, everything, something, nothing, nobody,* and *somebody*—are singular and take singular verbs.

ml
61c3

Anyone is welcome to apply for this grant.

Some indefinite pronouns—*both, many, few, several, others*—are plural and take plural verbs.

Several of the articles are useful.

A few indefinite pronouns—*some, all, any, more, most,* and *none*—can be singular or plural, depending on the noun they refer to.

Some of this trouble is to be expected. (*Some* refers to *trouble*.)

Some of the spectators are getting restless. (*Some* refers to *spectators*.)

5 With Collective Noun Subjects

A **collective noun** names a group of persons or things—for instance, *navy, union, association, band.* When it refers to the group as a unit (as it usually does), a collective noun takes a singular verb; when it refers to the individuals or items that make up the group, it takes a plural verb.

To many people, the royal family symbolizes Great Britain. (The family, as a unit, is the symbol.)

The family all eat at different times. (Each family member eats separately.)

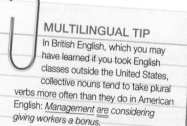

MULTILINGUAL TIP

In British English, which you may have learned if you took English classes outside the United States, collective nouns tend to take plural verbs more often than they do in American English: *Management are considering giving workers a bonus.*

Note: If a plural verb sounds awkward with a collective noun, reword the sentence: *Family members* all eat *at different times.*

Phrases that name fixed amounts—*three-quarters, twenty dollars, the majority*—are treated like collective nouns. When the amount denotes a unit, it takes a singular verb; when it denotes part of the whole, it takes a plural verb.

Three-quarters of his usual salary is not enough to live on.

Three-quarters of the patients improve after treatment.

Note: *The number* is always singular, and *a number* is always plural: *The number* of voters has declined. *A number* of students have missed preregistration.

6 When Singular Subjects Have Plural Forms

A singular subject takes a singular verb even if the form of the subject is plural.

Statistics deals with the collection and analysis of data.

When such a word has a plural meaning, however, use a plural verb.

The statistics prove him wrong.

Note: Some nouns retain their Latin plural forms, which do not look like English plural forms. Be particularly careful to use the correct verbs with such words: *criterion* is, *criteria* are; *medium* is, *media* are; *bacterium* is, *bacteria* are.

7 When Subject-Verb Order Is Inverted

ml
61f

Even when word order is inverted and the verb comes before the subject (as it does in questions and in sentences beginning with *there is* or *there are*), the subject and verb must agree.

Is either answer correct?

There are currently thirteen US courts of appeals.

8 With Linking Verbs

See
42a

A linking verb should agree with its subject, not with the subject complement.

The problem was termites.

Termites were the problem.

9 With Relative Pronouns

When you use a **relative pronoun** (*who, which, that,* and so on) to introduce a dependent clause, the verb in that clause agrees with the pronoun's **antecedent**, the word to which the pronoun refers.

The farmer is among the ones who suffer during a grain embargo.

The farmer is the only one who suffers during a grain embargo.

45b Making Pronouns and Antecedents Agree

A pronoun must agree with its **antecedent**—the word or word group to which the pronoun refers.

Singular pronouns—such as *he, him, she, her, it, me, myself,* and *oneself*—should refer to singular antecedents. Plural pronouns—such as *we, us, they, them,* and *their*—should refer to plural antecedents.

In the following special situations, pronoun-antecedent agreement can present challenges for writers.

1 With Compound Antecedents

In most cases, use a plural pronoun to refer to a **compound antecedent** (two or more antecedents connected by *and* or *or*).

Mormonism and Christian Science were similar in their beginnings.

However, this general rule has several exceptions:

- If a compound antecedent denotes a single unit—one person or thing or idea—use a singular pronoun to refer to the compound antecedent.

  In 1904, the husband and father brought his family from Russia to the United States.

- Use a singular pronoun when a compound antecedent is preceded by *each* or *every*.

  Every programming language and software package has its limitations.

- Use a singular pronoun to refer to two or more singular antecedents linked by *or* or *nor*.

  Neither Thoreau nor Whitman lived to see his work read widely.

- When one part of a compound antecedent is singular and one part is plural, the pronoun agrees in person and number with the antecedent that is nearer to it.

Neither the boy nor his parents had fastened their seat belts.

2 With Collective Noun Antecedents

If the meaning of a collective noun antecedent is singular (as it will be in most cases), use a singular pronoun. If the meaning is plural, use a plural pronoun.

The teachers' union announced its plan to strike. (The members acted as a unit.)

The team ran onto the field and took their positions. (Each member acted individually.)

3 With Indefinite Pronoun Antecedents

ml
61c3

Most **indefinite pronouns**—*each, either, neither, one, anyone,* and the like—are singular and take singular pronouns.

Neither of the men had his proposal ready by the deadline.

Each of these neighborhoods has its own traditions and values.

A few indefinite pronouns are plural; some others can be singular or plural.

Close-Up   PRONOUN-ANTECEDENT AGREEMENT

In speech and in informal writing, many people use the plural pronouns *they* or *their* with singular indefinite pronouns that refer to people, such as *someone, everyone,* and *nobody.*

Everyone can present their own viewpoint.

In college writing, however, you should avoid using a plural pronoun with a singular indefinite pronoun subject. Instead, you can use both masculine and feminine pronouns.

Everyone can present his or her own viewpoint.

Or, you can make the sentence's subject plural.

All participants can present their own viewpoints.

See
39e2

The use of *his* alone to refer to a singular indefinite pronoun (*Everyone can present his* own viewpoint) is considered sexist language.

EXERCISE 45.1

The sentences below illustrate correct subject-verb and pronoun-antecedent agreement. Following the instructions in parentheses after each sentence, revise each so its verbs and pronouns agree with the newly created subject.

Example: One child in twenty suffers from a learning disability. (Change *One child in twenty* to *Five percent of all children*.)

Revised: Five percent of all children suffer from a learning disability.

1. The governess is seemingly pursued by evil as she tries to protect Miles and Flora from those she feels seek to possess the children's souls. (Change *The governess* to *The governess and the cook*.)
2. Insulin-dependent diabetics are now able to take advantage of new technology that can help alleviate their symptoms. (Change *diabetics* to the *diabetic*.)
3. All homeowners in coastal regions worry about the possible effects of a hurricane on their property. (Change *All homeowners* to *Every homeowner*.)
4. Federally funded job-training programs offer unskilled workers an opportunity to acquire skills they can use to secure employment. (Change *workers* to *the worker*.)
5. Foreign imports pose a major challenge to the American textile market. (Change *Foreign imports* to *The foreign import*.)
6. *Brideshead Revisited* tells how one family and its devotion to its Catholic faith influence Charles Ryder. (Delete *and its devotion to its Catholic faith*.)
7. *Writer's Digest* and *The Writer* are designed to aid writers as they seek markets for their work. (Change *writers* to *the writer*.)
8. Most Americans have cell phones; in fact, many are dropping their landline service. (Change *Most Americans* to *Almost every American*.)
9. In Montana, it seems as though every town's elevation is higher than its population. (Change *every town's elevation* to *all the towns' elevations*.)
10. A woman without a man is like a fish without a bicycle. (Change *A woman/a man* to *Women/men*.)

"Are you   *?"*

My mother asked, ~~was I~~ ever going to get a job/ (neither indirect nor direct discourse)

EXERCISE 46.1

Read the following sentences, and eliminate any unnecessary shifts. Some sentences may be correct, and others may be revised in more than one way.

           you

Example: When ~~one~~ examines the history of the women's movement, you

        see that it had many different beginnings.

1. Some historians see World War II and women's work in the factories as the beginning of the push toward equal rights for women.
2. Women went to work in the textile mills of Lowell, Massachusetts, in the late 1800s, and her efforts at reforming the workplace are seen by many as the beginning of the equal rights movement.
3. The factories promised the girls decent wages, and parents were promised by them that their daughters would live in a safe, wholesome environment.
4. Dormitories were built by the factory owners; they are supposed to ensure a safe environment for the girls.
5. When you look at the lives of the loom girls, one can see that their work laid part of the foundation for women's later demands for equal rights.

46b Revising Mixed Constructions

A **mixed construction** is an error created when a dependent clause, prepositional phrase, or independent clause is incorrectly used as the subject of a sentence.

                                      ,

Because she studies every day ~~explains why~~ she gets good grades. (dependent clause incorrectly used as subject)

                           you can

By calling for information ~~is the way to~~ learn more about the benefits of ROTC. (prepositional phrase incorrectly used as subject)

Being

He was late ~~was what~~ made him miss the first act. (independent clause incorrectly used as subject)

EXERCISE 46.2

Revise the following mixed constructions so their parts fit together both grammatically and logically.

Investing
Example: ~~By investing~~ in commodities made her rich.

1. In implementing the "motor voter" bill has made it easier for people to register to vote.
2. She sank the basket was the reason they won the game.
3. Just because situations change, does not change the characters' hopes and dreams.
4. By dropping the course would be his only chance to avoid a low GPA.
5. Because she works for a tobacco company explains why she is against laws prohibiting smoking in restaurants.

46c Revising Faulty Predication

Faulty predication occurs when a sentence's subject and predicate do not logically go together.

1 Incorrect Use of *Be*

Faulty predication is especially common in sentences that contain a **linking verb**—a form of the verb *be*, for example—and a subject complement.

caused
Mounting costs and decreasing revenues ~~were~~ the downfall of the hospital.

This sentence incorrectly states that mounting costs and decreasing revenues were the downfall of the hospital when, in fact, they were the reasons for its downfall.

2 *Is When* or *Is Where*

Faulty predication also occurs when a one-sentence definition includes the construction *is where* or *is when*. (In a definition, *is* must be preceded and followed by a noun or noun phrase.)

the construction of
Taxidermy is ~~where you construct~~ a lifelike representation of an animal from its preserved skin.

3 *The Reason . . . Is Because*

Finally, faulty predication occurs when the phrase *the reason is* precedes *because*. In this situation, *because* (which means "for the reason that") is redundant and should be deleted.

that
The reason we drive is ~~because~~ we are afraid to fly.

The life that everyone thought would fulfill her totally bored her.

To correct a squinting modifier, place the modifier so that it is clear which word it modifies.

The life that everyone thought would totally fulfill her bored her.
(Everyone expected her to be totally fulfilled.)

The life that everyone thought would fulfill her bored her totally.
(She was totally bored.)

2 Relocate Misplaced Phrases

Placing a modifying phrase incorrectly can change the meaning of a sentence or create an unclear or confusing (or even unintentionally humorous) construction.

To avoid ambiguity, place phrases as close as possible to the words they modify.

- Place **verbal phrase** modifiers directly before or directly after the words they modify.

  Roller-skating along the shore,
  Jane watched the boats roller skating along the shore.

- Place **prepositional phrase** modifiers immediately after the words they modify.

  with no arms
  Venus de Milo is a statue created by a famous artist with no arms.

3 Relocate Misplaced Dependent Clauses

A dependent clause that serves as a modifier must be clearly related to the word it modifies.

- An **adjective clause** appears immediately *after* the word it modifies.

  During the Civil War, Lincoln was the president who governed the United States.

- An **adverb clause** can appear in various positions, as long as its relationship to the word it modifies is clear.

  When Lincoln was president, the Civil War raged.

  The Civil War raged when Lincoln was president.

EXERCISE 47.1

Relocate the misplaced verbal phrases, prepositional phrases, or dependent clauses so that they clearly point to the words or word groups they modify.

Example: *Silent Running* is a film ˄about a scientist left alone in space ˄~~with Bruce Dern.~~
 with Bruce Dern

1. She realized that she had married the wrong man after the wedding.
2. *The Prince and the Pauper* is a novel about an exchange of identities by Mark Twain.
3. The energy was used up in the ten-kilometer race that he was saving for the marathon.
4. He loaded the bottles and cans into his new car, which he planned to leave at the recycling center.
5. The manager explained the sales figures to the board members using a graph.

47b Revising Intrusive Modifiers

An **intrusive modifier** awkwardly interrupts a sentence, making it difficult to understand.

- Revise when a long modifier comes between an auxiliary verb and the main verb.

 Without
 ˄She had, ~~without~~ giving it a second thought or considering the
 she had
 consequences,˄planned to reenlist.

- Revise when a modifier creates an awkward **split infinitive**—that is, when a modifier comes between ("splits") the word *to* and the base form of the verb.

 beat his previous record
 He hoped to ˄in a matter of months, if not days,/~~beat his previous record.~~

 Note: A split infinitive is acceptable when the intervening modifier is short, especially if the alternative would be awkward or ambiguous: *She expected to almost beat her previous record.*

47c Revising Dangling Modifiers

A **dangling modifier** is a word or phrase that cannot logically modify any word in the sentence.

Dangling: Using this drug, many undesirable side effects are experienced. (Who is using this drug?)

- One way to correct this dangling modifier is to **create a new subject** by adding a word that the modifier (*using this drug*) can logically modify.

Revised: Using this drug, <u>patients</u> experience many undesirable side effects.

- Another way to correct the dangling modifier is to **create a dependent clause.**

Revised: <u>When they use this drug</u>, patients experience many undesirable side effects.

Close-Up **DANGLING MODIFIERS AND THE PASSIVE VOICE**

See
40d

Most sentences that include dangling modifiers are in the passive voice. Changing the <u>passive voice</u> to <u>active voice</u> often corrects the dangling modifier.

ml
61a6

EXERCISE 47.2

Eliminate the dangling modifier from each of the following sentences. Either supply a word that the dangling modifier can logically modify or change the dangling modifier into a dependent clause.

Example: Skiing down the mountain, my hat flew off. (dangling modifier)

Revised: Skiing down the mountain, I lost my hat. (new subject added)

<u>As I skied down the mountain</u>, my hat flew off. (dependent clause)

1. Writing for eight hours every day, her lengthy books are published every year or so.
2. As an out-of-state student without a car, it was difficult to get to off-campus cultural events.
3. To build a campfire, kindling is necessary.
4. With every step upward, the trees became sparser.
5. Being an amateur tennis player, my backhand is weaker than my forehand.
6. When exiting the train, the station will be on your right.
7. Driving through the Mojave, the bleak landscape was oppressive.
8. By requiring auto manufacturers to further improve emission-control devices, the air quality will get better.
9. Using a piece of filter paper, the ball of sodium is dried as much as possible and placed in a test tube.
10. Surrounded by acres of farmland, my nearest neighbor was far away.

Understanding Punctuation

Understanding Punctuation

❓ Frequently Asked Questions

Overview of Sentence Punctuation: Commas, Semicolons, Colons, Dashes, Parentheses

(Further explanations and examples are located in the sections listed in parentheses after each example.)

SEPARATING INDEPENDENT CLAUSES

With a Comma and a Coordinating Conjunction
The House approved the bill, but the Senate rejected it. (**49a**)

With a Semicolon
Paul Revere's *The Boston Massacre* is traditional American protest art; Edward Hicks's paintings are socially conscious art with a religious strain. (**50a**)

With a Semicolon and a Transitional Word or Phrase
Thomas Jefferson brought two hundred vanilla beans and a recipe for vanilla ice cream back from France; thus, he gave America its all-time favorite ice-cream flavor. (**50a**)

With a Colon
The survey presents an interesting finding: Americans do not trust the news media. (**53a2**)

SEPARATING ITEMS IN A SERIES

With Commas
Chipmunk, raccoon, and *Mugwump* are Native American words. (**49b**)

With Semicolons
Laramie, Wyoming; Wyoming, Delaware; and Delaware, Ohio were three of the places they visited. (**50b**)

SETTING OFF EXAMPLES, EXPLANATIONS, OR SUMMARIES

With a Colon
She had one dream: to play professional basketball. (**53a2**)

With a Dash
"Study hard," "Respect your elders," "Don't talk with your mouth full"—Sharon had often heard her parents say these things. (**53b2**)

SETTING OFF NONESSENTIAL MATERIAL

With a Single Comma
His fear increasing, he waited to enter the haunted house. (**49d4**)

With a Pair of Commas
Jonas Salk, not Albert Sabin, developed the first polio vaccine. (**49d3**)

With Dashes
Neither of the boys—both nine-year-olds—had any history of violence. (**53b1**)

With Parentheses
In some European countries (notably Sweden and France), high-quality day care is offered at little or no cost to parents. (**53c1**)

CHAPTER 48

Using End Punctuation

48a Using Periods

1 Ending a Sentence

Use a period to signal the end of a statement, a mild command or polite request, or an indirect question.

Something is rotten in Denmark. (statement)

Be sure to have the oil checked before you start out. (mild command)

When the bell rings, please exit in an orderly fashion. (polite request)

They wondered whether the water was safe to drink. (indirect question)

2 Marking an Abbreviation

Use periods in most abbreviations.

Mr. Spock	9 p.m.	Aug.
etc.	Dr. Dolittle	1600 Pennsylvania Ave.

If an abbreviation ends the sentence, do not add another period.

He promised to be there at 6 a.m./

However, do add a question mark if the sentence is a question.

Did he arrive at 6 p.m.?

If the abbreviation falls *within* a sentence, use normal punctuation after the period.

He promised to be there at 6 p.m. , but he forgot.

Close-Up ABBREVIATIONS WITHOUT PERIODS

Abbreviations composed of all capital letters do not usually require periods unless they stand for initials of people's names (E. B. White).

Familiar abbreviations of names of corporations or government agencies and abbreviations of scientific and technical terms do not require periods.

TMZ   CD-ROM   DNA   EPA   HBO   NFL   NYPD

Acronyms—new words formed from the initial letters or first few letters of a series of words—do not include periods.

modem   op-ed   scuba   radar
OSHA   AIDS   NAFTA   C-SPAN

Clipped forms (commonly accepted shortened forms of words, such as *gym, dorm, math,* and *fax*) do not use periods.

Postal abbreviations do not include periods.

TX   CA   MS   PA   FL   NY

3 Marking Divisions in Dramatic, Poetic, and Biblical References

Use periods to separate act, scene, and line numbers in plays; book and line numbers in long poems; and chapter and verse numbers in biblical references. (Do not space between the periods and the elements they separate.)

Dramatic Reference: *Hamlet* 2.2.1–5

Poetic Reference: *Paradise Lost* 7.163–67

Biblical Reference: Judges 4.14

Note: In <u>MLA parenthetical references</u>, titles of classic literary works and books of the Bible are often abbreviated: (*Ham.* **2.2.1-5**); (**Judg. 4.14**).

See 17a1

4 Marking Divisions in Electronic Addresses

Periods, along with other punctuation marks (such as slashes and colons), are also used in electronic addresses (URLs).

http://academic.cengage.com

Note: When you type a URL, do not end it with a period, and do not add spaces after periods within the address.

EXERCISE 48.1

Correct these sentences by adding missing periods and deleting unnecessary ones. If a sentence is correct, mark it with a *C*.

Example: Their mission changed the war.

1. Julius Caesar was killed in 44 B.C.
2. Dr. McLaughlin worked hard to earn his Ph.D..
3. Carmen was supposed to be at A.F.L.-C.I.O. headquarters by 2 p.m.; however, she didn't get there until 10 p.m.
4. After she studied the fall lineup proposed by N.B.C., she decided to work for C.B.S.
5. Representatives from the U.M.W. began collective bargaining after an unsuccessful meeting with Mr Pritchard, the coal company's representative.

48b Using Question Marks

1 Marking the End of a Direct Question

Use a question mark to signal the end of a direct question.

Who was at the door?

2 Marking Questionable Dates and Numbers

Use a question mark in parentheses to indicate uncertainty about a date or number.

Aristophanes, the Greek playwright, was born in 448 (?) BC and died in 380 (?) BC.

3 Editing Misused Question Marks

Use a period, not a question mark, with an **indirect question** (a question that is not quoted directly).

The personnel officer asked whether he knew how to type?

Do not use a question mark to convey sarcasm. Instead, suggest your attitude through your choice of words.

not very
I refused his generous (?) offer.

Do not use question marks along with other punctuation marks (except for closing quotation marks).

"Can it be true?/" he asked.

 Never use more than one question mark to end a sentence.

48c Using Exclamation Points

An exclamation point is used to signal the end of an emotional or emphatic statement, an emphatic interjection, or a forceful command.

Remember the *Maine*!

"No! Don't leave!" he cried.

 Except for recording dialogue, exclamation points are almost never appropriate in college writing. Even in informal writing, use exclamation points sparingly—and never use two or more in a row.

EXERCISE 48.2

Correct the use of question marks and other punctuation in the following sentences.

Example: She asked whether Freud's theories were accepted during his

lifetime?/

1. He wondered whether he should take a nine o'clock class?
2. The instructor asked, "Was the Spanish-American War a victory for America."
3. Are they really going to China??!!
4. He took a modest (?) portion of dessert—half a pie!
5. "Is *data* the plural of *datum*?," he inquired.

CHAPTER **49**

Using Commas

49a Setting Off Independent Clauses

Use a comma when you form a compound sentence by linking two independent clauses with a **coordinating conjunction** or with a pair of **correlative conjunctions**.

The House approved the bill , but the Senate rejected it.

Either the hard drive is full , or the modem is too slow.

Note: You may omit the comma if the two independent clauses are very short: *Love it or leave it.*

EXERCISE 49.1

Combine each of the following sentence pairs into one compound sentence, adding commas where necessary.

Example: Emergency medicine became an approved medial specialty in

1979, ~~Now~~ *, and now* pediatric emergency medicine is becoming

increasingly important. (and)

1. Pope Benedict did not hesitate to encourage talks between the United States and Cuba. He did not hesitate to broker a deal for the release of Alan Gross. (nor)
2. Agents place brand-name products in prominent positions in films. The products are seen and recognized by large audiences. (and)
3. Unisex insurance rates may have some drawbacks for women. These rates may be very beneficial. (or)
4. Cigarette advertising no longer appears on television. It does appear in print media. (but)
5. Dorothy Day founded the Catholic Worker movement in the 1930s. Her followers still dispense free food, medical care, and legal advice to the needy. (and)

49b Setting Off Items in a Series

1 Coordinate Elements

Use commas between items in a series of three or more **coordinate elements** (words, phrases, or clauses joined by a coordinating conjunction).

Chipmunk, *raccoon*, and *Mugwump* are Native American words.

You may pay by check, with a credit or debit card, or in cash.

Brazilians speak Portuguese, Colombians speak Spanish, and Haitians speak French and Creole.

> *Note:* To avoid ambiguity, use a comma before the *and* (or other coordinating conjunction) that separates the last two items in a series of three or more items: *He was inspired by his parents, the Dalai Lama, and Mother Teresa.*

> *Note:* If phrases or clauses in a **series** already contain commas, separate the items with semicolons.

See 50b

EXERCISE 49.2

Correct the use of commas in the following sentences, adding or deleting commas and words where necessary. If a sentence is punctuated correctly, mark it with a *C*.

Example: Neither dogs, snakes, bees, nor dragons frighten her.

1. Seals, whales, dogs, lions and horses all are mammals.
2. Mammals are warm-blooded vertebrates that bear live young, nurse them, and usually have fur.
3. Seals are mammals, but lizards, and snakes, and iguanas are reptiles, and salamanders are amphibians.
4. Amphibians also include frogs, and toads and newts.
5. Eagles geese ostriches turkeys chickens and ducks are classified as birds.

2 Coordinate Adjectives

Use a comma between items in a series of two or more **coordinate adjectives**—adjectives that modify the same word or word group—unless they are joined by a conjunction.

> **MULTILINGUAL TIP**
> For more information on the correct order of adjectives in a series, see **61d2**.

She brushed her long, shining hair.

The baby was tired and cranky and wet. (no commas required)

CHECKLIST

Punctuating Adjectives in a Series

☐ If you can reverse the order of the adjectives or insert *and* between the adjectives without changing the meaning, the adjectives are coordinate, and you should use a comma.

> She brushed her <u>long</u>, <u>shining</u> hair.
>
> She brushed her <u>shining</u>, <u>long</u> hair.
>
> She brushed her <u>long</u> [and] <u>shining</u> hair.

☐ If you cannot reverse the order of the adjectives or insert *and*, the adjectives are not coordinate, and you should not use a comma.

> <u>Ten red</u> balloons fell from the ceiling.
>
> <u>Red ten</u> balloons fell from the ceiling.
>
> <u>Ten</u> [and] <u>red</u> balloons fell from the ceiling.

Note: Numbers—such as *ten*—are not coordinate with other adjectives.

49c Setting Off Introductory Elements

1 Dependent Clauses

An introductory **dependent clause** is generally set off from the rest of the sentence by a comma.

> <u>When war came to Baghdad</u>, many victims were children.

If an introductory dependent clause is short and designates time, you may omit the comma—provided the sentence will be clear without it.

> <u>When I exercise</u> I drink plenty of water.

Note: Do not use a comma to set off a dependent clause at the *end* of a sentence: *I drink plenty of water, when I exercise.*

2 Verbal and Prepositional Phrases

An introductory **verbal phrase** is generally set off by a comma.

> <u>Thinking that this might be his last chance</u>, Peary struggled toward the North Pole. (participial phrase)
>
> <u>To write well</u>, one must read a lot. (infinitive phrase)

However, a verbal phrase that serves as a subject is *not* set off by a comma.

<u>Laughing out loud</u> can release tension. (gerund phrase)

<u>To know him</u> is to love him. (infinitive phrase)

An introductory **prepositional phrase** is also usually set off by a comma.

<u>During the Depression</u>, movie attendance rose.

However, if an introductory prepositional phrase is short and no ambiguity is possible, you may omit the comma.

<u>After lunch</u> I took a four-hour nap.

3 Transitional Words and Phrases

When a **transitional word or phrase** begins a sentence, it is usually set off with a comma.

<u>However</u>, any plan that is enacted must be fair.

<u>In other words</u>, we cannot act hastily.

EXERCISE 49.3

Add commas in the following paragraph where necessary to set off an introductory element from the rest of a sentence.

> While childhood is shrinking adolescence is expanding. Whatever the reason girls are maturing earlier, beginning puberty at increasingly younger ages. What's more both boys and girls are staying in the nest longer. At present, it is not unusual for children to stay in their parents' home through their twenties or early thirties, delaying adulthood and extending adolescence. To some who study the culture this increase in adolescence portends dire consequences. With teenage hormones running amuck for longer the problems of teenage pregnancy and sexually transmitted diseases loom large. Young boys' spending long periods of their lives without responsibilities is also a recipe for disaster. However others see this "youthing" of American culture in a more positive light. Without a doubt adolescents are creative, lively, and more willing to take risks. If we channel their energies carefully they can contribute, even in their extended adolescence, to American culture and technology.

49d Setting Off Nonessential Material

Sometimes words, phrases, or clauses *contribute* to the meaning of a sentence but are not *essential* for conveying the sentence's main point. Use commas to set off such **nonessential** material whether it appears at the beginning, in the middle, or at the end of a sentence.

1 Nonrestrictive Modifiers

Use commas to set off **nonrestrictive modifiers**, which supply information that is not essential to the meaning of the words they modify. (Do *not* use commas to set off **restrictive modifiers**, which supply information that *is* essential to the meaning of the words they modify.)

> **Nonrestrictive** (commas required): Actors, <u>who have inflated egos,</u> are often insecure. (*All* actors—not just those with inflated egos—are insecure.)
>
> **Restrictive** (no commas): Actors <u>who have inflated egos</u> are often insecure. (Only those actors with inflated egos—not all actors—are insecure.)

In the following examples, commas set off only nonrestrictive modifiers—those that supply nonessential information. Commas do not set off restrictive modifiers, which supply essential information.

Adjective Clauses

> **Nonrestrictive:** He ran for the bus, <u>which was late as usual.</u>
>
> **Restrictive:** He ran for the bus <u>that was pulling away from the bus stop.</u>

Prepositional Phrases

> **Nonrestrictive:** The clerk, <u>with a nod,</u> dismissed me.
>
> **Restrictive:** The man <u>with the gun</u> demanded their money.

Verbal Phrases

> **Nonrestrictive:** The marathoner, <u>running his fastest,</u> beat his previous record.
>
> **Restrictive:** The candidates <u>running for mayor</u> have agreed to a debate.

Appositives

> **Nonrestrictive:** *Citizen Kane,* <u>Orson Welles's first film,</u> made him famous.
>
> **Restrictive:** The film *Citizen Kane* made Orson Welles famous.

CHECKLIST

Restrictive and Nonrestrictive Modifiers

To determine whether a modifier is restrictive or nonrestrictive, ask yourself these questions:

❑ Is the modifier essential to the meaning of the word it modifies (*The man <u>with the gun</u>*, not just any man)? If so, it is restrictive.

❑ Is the modifier introduced by *that* (*something that most people fear*)? If so, it is restrictive. *That* cannot introduce a nonrestrictive clause.

❑ Can you delete the relative pronoun without causing ambiguity or confusion (*something [that] most people fear*)? If so, the clause is restrictive.

❑ Is the appositive more specific than the noun that precedes it (*the film* Citizen Kane)? If so, it is restrictive.

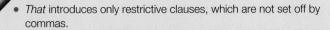

Close-Up   USING COMMAS WITH *THAT* AND *WHICH*

- *That* introduces only restrictive clauses, which are not set off by commas.

  I bought a used car that cost $2,000.

- *Which* generally introduces only nonrestrictive clauses, which are set off by commas.

  The used car I bought, which cost $2,000, broke down after a week.

2 Transitional Words and Phrases

Transitional words and phrases—which include conjunctive adverbs such as *however, therefore, thus,* and *nevertheless* as well as expressions such as *for example* and *on the other hand*—qualify, clarify, and make connections. However, they are not essential to a sentence's meaning. For this reason, they are always set off by commas when they interrupt a clause or when they begin or end a sentence.

The Outward Bound program, for example, is extremely safe.

In fact, Outward Bound has an excellent reputation.

Other programs are not so safe, however.

Note: When a transitional word or phrase joins two independent clauses, it must be preceded by a semicolon and followed by a comma: *Laughter is the best medicine; of course, penicillin also comes in handy sometimes.*

3 Contradictory Phrases

A phrase that expresses a **contradiction** is usually set off by commas.

This medicine is taken after meals, never on an empty stomach.

Jonas Salk, not Albert Sabin, developed the first polio vaccine.

4 Absolute Phrases

An **absolute phrase**, which includes a noun or pronoun and a participle and modifies an entire independent clause, is always set off by a comma from the clause it modifies.

His fear increasing, he waited to enter the haunted house.

Many soldiers were lost in Southeast Asia, their bodies never recovered.

5 Miscellaneous Nonessential Elements

Other nonessential elements usually set off by commas include tag questions, names in direct address, mild interjections, and *yes* and *no*.

This is your first day on the job, isn't it?

I wonder, Mr.Honeywell, whether Mr. Albright deserves a raise.

Well, it's about time.

Yes, that's what I thought.

EXERCISE 49.4

Set off the nonessential material in these sentences with commas. If a sentence is correct, mark it with a *C*.

Example: Piranhas, like sharks, will attack and eat almost anything if the opportunity arises.

1. Kermit the Frog is a Muppet a cross between a marionette and a puppet.
2. The common cold a virus is frequently spread by hand contact not by mouth.
3. Many US welfare recipients, such as children, the aged, and the severely disabled, are unable to work.
4. The submarine *Nautilus* was the first to cross under the North Pole wasn't it?
5. A firefly is a beetle not a fly and a prairie dog is a rodent not a dog.

49e Using Commas in Other Conventional Contexts

1 With Direct Quotations

In most cases, use commas to set off a direct quotation from the **identifying tag**—the phrase that identifies the speaker (*he said, she answered,* and so on).

Emerson said, "I greet you at the beginning of a great career."

"I greet you at the beginning of a great career," Emerson said.

"I greet you," Emerson said, "at the beginning of a great career."

When the identifying tag comes between two complete sentences, however, the tag is introduced by a comma but followed by a period.

"Winning isn't everything," Coach Vince Lombardi once said. "It's the only thing."

If the first sentence of an interrupted quotation ends with a question mark or an exclamation point, do not use commas.

"Should we hold the front page?" she asked. "It's a slow news day."

"Hold the front page!" he cried. "There's breaking news!"

② With Titles or Degrees Following a Name

Hamlet, Prince of Denmark, is Shakespeare's most famous character.

Michael Crichton, MD, wrote *Jurassic Park*.

③ In Addresses and Dates

When a date or an address falls within a sentence, use a comma after the last element.

On August 30, 1983, the space shuttle *Challenger* exploded.

Her address is 600 West End Avenue, New York, NY 10024.

Note: When only the month and year are given, do not use a comma to separate the month from the year: *August 1983*. Do not use a comma to separate the street number from the street or the state name from the ZIP code.

EXERCISE 49.5

Add commas where necessary to set off quotations, names, dates, and addresses.

1. Nikita Khrushchev, former Soviet premier, once said "We will bury you!"
2. Mount St. Helens, northeast of Portland Oregon, began erupting on March 27 1980 and eventually killed at least thirty people.
3. Located at 1600 Pennsylvania Avenue Washington DC, the White House is a popular tourist attraction.
4. Lewis Thomas MD was born in Flushing New York and attended Harvard Medical School in Cambridge Massachusetts.
5. "The reports of my death" Mark Twain remarked "have been greatly exaggerated."

49f Using Commas to Prevent Misreading

In some cases, you need a comma to avoid ambiguity. For example, consider the following sentence.

> Those who can, sprint the final lap.

Without the comma, *can* appears to be an auxiliary verb ("Those who <u>can</u> <u>sprint</u>. . . ."), and the sentence seems incomplete. The comma tells readers to pause and thus prevents confusion.

Also use a comma to acknowledge the omission of a repeated word, usually a verb, and to separate words repeated consecutively.

> Pam carried the box; Tim, the suitcase.

> Everything bad that could have happened, happened.

EXERCISE 49.6

Add commas where necessary to prevent misreading.

Example: Whatever will be, will be.

1. According to Maria Frank's phone is obsolete.
2. Da Gama explored Florida; Pizarro Peru.
3. By Monday evening students must begin preregistration for fall classes.
4. When batting practice carefully.
5. Technology has made what once seemed not possible possible.

49g Editing Misused Commas

Do not use commas in the following situations.

1 To Join Two Independent Clauses

A comma alone cannot join two independent clauses; it must be followed by a coordinating conjunction. Using just a comma to connect two independent clauses creates a **comma splice**.

> The season was unusually cool, *but* the orange crop was not seriously harmed.

2 To Set Off Restrictive Modifiers

Commas are not used to set off restrictive modifiers. (Commas are only used to set off nonrestrictive modifiers.)

The film⫻ *Malcolm X⫻* was directed by Spike Lee.

They planned a picnic⫻ in the park.

③ Between Inseparable Grammatical Constructions

Do not place a comma between grammatical elements that cannot be logically separated: a subject and its predicate, a verb and its complement or direct object, a preposition and its object, or an adjective and the word or phrase it modifies.

A woman with dark red hair⫻ opened the door. (comma incorrectly placed between subject and predicate)

Louis Braille developed⫻ an alphabet of raised dots for the blind. (comma incorrectly placed between verb and object)

They relaxed somewhat during⫻ the last part of the obstacle course. (comma incorrectly placed between preposition and object)

Wind-dispersed weeds include the well-known and plentiful⫻ dandelions, milkweed, and thistle. (comma incorrectly placed between adjective and words it modifies)

④ Between a Verb and an Indirect Quotation or Indirect Question

Do not use a comma between a verb and an indirect quotation or between a verb and an indirect question.

General Douglas MacArthur vowed⫻ that he would return. (comma incorrectly placed between verb and indirect quotation)

The landlord asked⫻ if we would sign a two-year lease. (comma incorrectly placed between verb and indirect question)

⑤ In Compounds That Are Not Composed of Independent Clauses

Do not use a comma before a coordinating conjunction, such as *and* or *but*, when it joins two elements of a compound subject, predicate, object, or complement.

During the 1400s plagues⫻ and pestilence were common. (compound subject)

Many nontraditional students are returning to college⫻ and tend to do well there. (compound predicate)

Mattel has marketed a lab coat⫻ and an astronaut suit for its Barbie doll. (compound object)

glasses, *Bwana Devil* and *The Creature from the Black Lagoon* were two early 3-D ventures. *The Robe* was the first picture filmed in Cinemascope in this technique a shrunken image was projected on a screen twice as wide as it was tall. Smell-O-Vision (or Aroma-rama) enabled audiences to smell the scenes, it was impossible to get one odor out of the theater in time for the next smell to be introduced. William Castle's *Thirteen Ghosts* introduced special glasses for cowardly viewers, the red part of the glasses was the "ghost viewer," and the green part was the "ghost remover." Perhaps the ultimate in movie gimmicks accompanied the film *The Tingler* seats in the theater were wired to generate mild electric shocks. w chain reaction that led to hysteria in the theater. During the 1960s, such gimmicks all but disappeared, viewers were able once again to simply sit back and enjoy a movie. In 1997, *Mr. Payback*, a short interactive film, introduced a new gimmick, it allowed viewers to vote on how they wanted the plot to unfold.

50b Separating Items in a Series

Use semicolons between items in a series when one or more of the items already include commas.

I have visited Laramie, Wyoming; Wyoming, Delaware; and Delaware, Ohio.

EXERCISE 50.2

Replace commas with semicolons where necessary to separate internally punctuated items in a series.

Example: Luxury automobiles have some strong selling points: they are

status symbols**;** some, such as the Corvette, appreciate in value**;**

and they are usually comfortable and well appointed.

1. The history of modern art seems at times to be a collection of "isms": Impressionism, a term that applies to painters who attempted to depict contemporary life by reproducing an "impression" of what the eye sees, Abstract Expressionism, which applies to artists who stress emotion and the unconscious in their nonrepresentational works, and, more recently, Minimalism, which applies to painters and sculptors whose work reasserts the physical reality of the object.
2. Some of the most commonly confused words in English are *aggravate*, which means "to worsen," and *irritate*, which means "to annoy," *continual*, which means "recurring at intervals," and *continuous*, which means "an action occurring without interruption," *imply*, which means

"to hint, suggest," and *infer*, which means "to conclude from," and *compliment*, which means "to praise," and *complement*, which means "to complete or add to."

3. Tennessee Williams wrote *The Glass Menagerie*, which is about Laura Wingfield, a disabled young woman, and her family, *A Streetcar Named Desire*, which starred Marlon Brando, and *Cat on a Hot Tin Roof*, which won a Pulitzer Prize.

50c Editing Misused Semicolons

Do not use semicolons in the following situations.

1 Between a Phrase and a Clause

Use a comma, not a semicolon, between a phrase and a clause.

Increasing rapidly; computer crime poses a challenge for business and government.

2 Between a Dependent and an Independent Clause

Use a comma, not a semicolon, between a dependent and an independent clause.

Because drugs can now suppress the body's immune reaction; fewer organ transplants are rejected.

3 To Introduce a List

Use a colon, not a semicolon, to introduce a <u>list</u>.

See 23c

Millions of people spend time every day on four of the most popular social

networking sites; Twitter, Facebook, LinkedIn, and Pinterest.

Note: Always introduce a list with a complete sentence followed by a <u>colon</u>.

See 53a

4 To Introduce a Quotation

Do not use a semicolon to introduce <u>quoted speech or writing</u>.

See 52a

Marie Antoinette may not have said; "Let them eat cake."

EXERCISE 50.3

Read the following paragraph carefully. Then, add semicolons where necessary, and delete incorrectly used ones, substituting other punctuation where necessary.

Barnstormers were aviators; who toured the country after World War I, giving people short airplane rides and exhibitions of stunt flying, in fact, the name *barnstormer* was derived from the use of barns as airplane hangars. Americans' interest in airplanes had all but disappeared after the war. The barnstormers helped popularize flying; especially in rural areas. Some were pilots who had flown in the war; others were just young men with a thirst for adventure. They gave people rides in airplanes; sometimes charging a dollar a minute. For most passengers, this was their first ride in an airplane, in fact, sometimes it was their first sight of one. After Lindbergh's 1927 flight across the Atlantic; Americans suddenly needed no encouragement to embrace aviation. The barnstormers had outlived their usefulness; and an era ended. (Adapted from William Goldman, *Adventures in the Screen Trade*)

CHAPTER **51**

Using Apostrophes

Use an apostrophe to form the possessive case, to indicate omissions in contractions, and to form certain plurals.

51a Forming the Possessive Case

The possessive case indicates ownership. In English, the possessive case of nouns and indefinite pronouns is indicated either with a phrase that includes the word *of* (the hands *of* the clock) or with an apostrophe and, in most cases, an *s* (the clock's hands).

1 Singular Nouns and Indefinite Pronouns

To form the possessive case of **singular nouns** and **indefinite pronouns**, add *-'s*.

"The Monk's Tale" is one of Chaucer's *Canterbury Tales*.

When we would arrive was anyone's guess.

2 Singular Nouns Ending in -s

To form the possessive case of **singular nouns that end in** *-s*, add -'s in most cases.

> Chris's goal was to become a surgeon.
>
> Reading Henry James's *The Ambassadors* was not Maris's idea of fun.
>
> The class's time was changed to 8 a.m.

Note: With some singular nouns that end in *-s*, pronouncing the possessive ending as a separate syllable can sound awkward. In such cases, it is acceptable to use just an apostrophe: *Crispus Attucks' death, Aristophanes' Lysistrata, Achilles' left heel.*

3 Plural Nouns

To form the possessive case of **regular plural nouns** (those that end in *-s* or *-es*), add only an apostrophe.

> Laid-off employees received two weeks' severance pay and three months' medical benefits.
>
> The Lopezes' three children are triplets.

To form the possessive case of nouns that have **irregular plurals**, add -'s.

> *The Children's Hour* is a play by Lillian Hellman.

4 Compound Nouns or Groups of Words

To form the possessive case of **compound nouns** (nouns formed from two or more words) or of word groups, add -'s to the last word.

> The President accepted the Secretary of State's resignation.
>
> This is someone else's responsibility.

5 Two or More Items

To indicate **individual ownership** of two or more items, add -'s to each item.

> Ernest Hemingway's and Gertrude Stein's writing styles have some similarities.

To indicate **joint ownership**, add -'s only to the last item.

> We studied Lewis and Clark's expedition.

EXERCISE 51.1

Change each word or phrase in parentheses to its possessive form. In some cases, you may have to use a phrase to indicate the possessive.

Example: The (children) toys were scattered all over their (parents) bedroom. The children's toys were scattered all over their parents' bedroom.

1. Jane (Addams) settlement house was called Hull House.
2. (*A Room of One's Own*) popularity increased with the rise of feminism.
3. The (chief petty officer) responsibilities are varied.
4. Vietnamese (restaurants) numbers have grown dramatically in ten (years) time.
5. (Charles Dickens) and (Mark Twain) works have sold millions of copies.

51b Indicating Omissions in Contractions

1 Omitted Letters

Apostrophes replace omitted letters in **contractions** that combine a pronoun and a verb (*he + will = he'll*) or the elements of a verb phrase (*do + not = don't*).

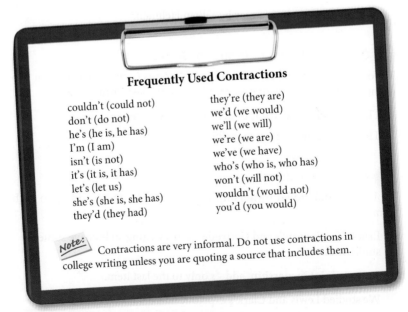

Frequently Used Contractions

couldn't (could not)
don't (do not)
he's (he is, he has)
I'm (I am)
isn't (is not)
it's (it is, it has)
let's (let us)
she's (she is, she has)
they'd (they had)

they're (they are)
we'd (we would)
we'll (we will)
we're (we are)
we've (we have)
who's (who is, who has)
won't (will not)
wouldn't (would not)
you'd (you would)

Note: Contractions are very informal. Do not use contractions in college writing unless you are quoting a source that includes them.

Close-Up USING APOSTROPHES

Be careful not to confuse contractions (which always include apostrophes) with the possessive forms of personal pronouns (which never include apostrophes).

Contractions	**Possessive Forms**
Who's on first?	Whose book is this?
They're playing our song.	Their team is winning.
It's raining.	Its paws were muddy.
You're a real pal.	Your résumé is impressive.

EXERCISE 51.2

In the following sentences, correct any errors in the use of apostrophes. (Remember, apostrophes are used in contractions but not in possessive pronouns.) If a sentence is correct, mark it with a *C*.

Example: ~~Who's~~ *Whose* troops were sent to Afghanistan?

1. Its never easy to choose a major; whatever you decide, your bound to have second thoughts.
2. Your correct in assuming its a challenging course.
3. Their watching too much television; in fact, they're eyes are glazed.
4. Whose coming along on the backpacking trip?
5. The horse had been badly treated; it's spirit was broken.

2 Omitted Numbers

In informal writing, an apostrophe may also be used to replace the century in a year: Class of '03, the '60s. In college writing, however, write out the number in full: 2003, 1960s.

51c Forming Plurals

In a few special situations, add -'s to form plurals.

Plurals of Letters
The Italian language has no *j*'s, *k*'s, or *w*'s.

Plurals of Words Referred to as Words
The supervisor would accept no *if*'s, *and*'s, or *but*'s.

See
56c

Note: **Elements spoken of as themselves** (letters, numerals, or words) are set in italic type; the plural ending, however, is not.

Note: Apostrophes are not used in plurals of abbreviations (including acronyms) or numbers.

DVDs   PACs   1960s

51d   Editing Misused Apostrophes

Do not use apostrophes with plural nouns that are not possessive.

The Thompson's are not at home.

Down vest's are very warm.

The Philadelphia 76er's have had good years and bad.

Do not use apostrophes to form the possessive case of personal pronouns.

This ticket must be your's or her's.

The next turn is their's.

Her doll had lost it's right eye.

The next great moment in history is our's.

EXERCISE 51.3

In the following sentences, correct all errors in the use of apostrophes to form noun plurals or the possessive case of personal pronouns.

Example: Dr. Sampson's lecture-s were more interesting than her-s.

1. The Schaefer's seats are right next to our's.
2. Most of the college's in the area offer courses open to outsider's as well as to their own students.
3. Romantic poets are his favorite's.
4. Debbie returned the books to the library, forgetting they were her's.
5. Cultural revolution's do not occur very often, but when they do they bring sweeping change's.

CHAPTER 52

Using Quotation Marks

Use quotation marks to set off brief passages of quoted speech or writing, to set off titles, and to set off words used in special ways. Do not use quotation marks when quoting long passages of prose or poetry.

52a Setting Off Quoted Speech or Writing

When you quote a word, phrase, or brief passage of someone's speech or writing, enclose the quoted material in a pair of quotation marks.

> Gloria Steinem said, "We are becoming the men we once hoped to marry."

> Galsworthy writes that Aunt Juley is "prostrated by the blow" (329). (Note that in this example from a student essay, the end punctuation follows the parenthetical documentation.)

Close-Up USING QUOTATION MARKS WITH DIALOGUE

When you record **dialogue** (conversation between two or more people), enclose the quoted words in quotation marks. Begin a new paragraph each time a new speaker is introduced.

When you are quoting several paragraphs of dialogue by one speaker, begin each new paragraph with quotation marks. However, use closing quotation marks only at the end of the *entire quoted passage*, not at the end of each paragraph.

Special rules govern the punctuation of a quotation when it is used with an **identifying tag**, a phrase (such as *he said*) that identifies the speaker or writer.

1 Identifying Tag in the Middle of a Quoted Passage

Use a pair of commas to set off an identifying tag that interrupts a quoted passage.

> "In the future," pop artist Andy Warhol once said, "everyone will be world famous for fifteen minutes."

If the identifying tag follows a complete sentence but the quoted passage continues, use a period after the tag. Begin the new sentence with a capital letter, and enclose it in quotation marks.

> "Be careful," Erin warned. "Reptiles can be tricky."

2 Identifying Tag at the Beginning of a Quoted Passage

Use a comma after an identifying tag that introduces quoted speech or writing.

> The Raven repeated, "Nevermore."

Use a colon instead of a comma before a quotation if the identifying tag is a complete sentence.

> She gave her final answer: "No."

3 Identifying Tag at the End of a Quoted Passage

Use a comma to set off a quotation from an identifying tag that follows it.

> "Be careful out there," the sergeant warned.

If the quotation ends with a question mark or an exclamation point, use that punctuation mark instead of the comma. (In this situation, the identifying tag begins with a lowercase letter even though it follows end punctuation.)

> "Is Ankara the capital of Turkey?" she asked.
> "Oh, boy!" he cried.

Note: For information on placement of punctuation marks with quotation marks, **see 52e**.

EXERCISE 52.1

Add quotation marks and other punctuation to these sentences where necessary to set off quotations from identifying tags.

Example: Wordsworth's phrase "splendor in the grass" was used as the title of a movie about young lovers.

1. Few people can explain what Descartes's words I think, therefore I am actually mean.
2. Gertrude Stein said, You are all a lost generation.
3. Freedom of speech does not guarantee anyone the right to yell fire in a crowded theater, she explained.
4. There's no place like home, Dorothy insisted.
5. If everyone will sit down the teacher announced the exam will begin.

52b Setting Off Long Prose Passages and Poetry

1 Long Prose Passages

Do not enclose a **long prose passage** (a passage of more than four lines) in quotation marks. Instead, set it off by indenting the entire passage one-half inch from the left-hand margin. Treat the quoted passage like regular text: double-space above and below it, and double-space between lines within it. Introduce the passage with a colon, and place parenthetical documentation one space *after* the end punctuation.

> The following portrait of Aunt Juley illustrates several of the devices Galsworthy uses throughout *The Forsyte Saga*, such as a journalistic detachment that is almost cruel in its scrutiny, a subtle sense of the grotesque, and an ironic stance:
>
> > Aunt Juley stayed in her room, prostrated by the blow. Her face, discoloured by tears, was divided into compartments by the little ridges of pouting flesh which had swollen with emotion. . . . At fixed inter-vals she went to her drawer, and took from beneath the lavender bags a fresh pocket-handkerchief. Her warm heart could not bear the thought that Ann was lying there so cold. (329)
>
> Many similar portraits of characters appear throughout the novel.

Close-Up QUOTING LONG PROSE PASSAGES

When you quote a long prose passage that is a single paragraph, do not indent the first line. When quoting two or more paragraphs, however, indent the first line of each paragraph (including the first) an additional one-quarter inch. If the first sentence of the quoted passage does not

(continued)

> **QUOTING LONG PROSE PASSAGES** *(continued)*
>
> begin a paragraph in the source, do not indent it—but do indent the first line of each subsequent paragraph. If the passage you are quoting includes material set in quotation marks, keep those quotation marks.

See 18b *Note:* **APA guidelines** differ from those summarized here, which conform to MLA style.

2 Poetry

Treat one line of poetry like a short prose passage: enclose it in quotation marks, and run it into the text.

> One of John Donne's best-known poems begins with the line "Go and catch a falling star."

If you quote two or three lines of poetry, separate the lines with **slashes**, and run the quotation into the text. (Leave one space before and one space after the slash.)

> Alexander Pope writes, "True Ease in Writing comes from Art, not Chance, / As those move easiest who have learned to dance."

See 52b1 If you quote more than three lines of poetry, set them off like a <u>long prose passage</u>. (For special emphasis, you may set off fewer lines in this manner.) Be sure to reproduce punctuation, spelling, capitalization, and indentation of the quoted lines *exactly* as they appear in the poem.

> Wilfred Owen, a poet who was killed in action in World War I, expressed the horrors of war with vivid imagery:
>
>> Bent double, like old beggars under sacks.
>>
>> Knock-kneed, coughing like hags, we cursed through sludge.
>>
>> Till on the haunting flares we turned our backs
>>
>> And towards our distant rest began to trudge. (lines 1–4)

52c Setting Off Titles

Titles of short works and titles of parts of long works are enclosed in quotation marks. Other titles are italicized.

Titles Requiring Quotation Marks

Articles in Magazines, Newspapers, and Professional Journals
"Why Johnny Can't Write"

Essays, Short Stories, Short Poems, and Songs
"Fenimore Cooper's Literary Offenses"
"Flying Home"
"The Road Not Taken"
"The Star-Spangled Banner"

Chapters or Sections of Books
"Miss Sharp Begins to Make Friends" (Chapter 10 of *Vanity Fair*)

Episodes of Radio or Television Series
"Lucy Goes to the Hospital" (*I Love Lucy*)

See 56a for a list of titles that require italics.

EXERCISE 52.2

Add quotation marks to the following sentences where necessary to set off titles. If italics are incorrectly used, substitute quotation marks. Place commas and periods inside quotation marks. If a sentence is correct, mark it with a *C*.

Example: Margaret Atwood has written stories, such as ~~Happy Endings~~, "*Happy Endings,*"

and poems, such as You Fit into Me.

1. One of the essays from her new book *Good Bones and Simple Murder* was originally published in *Harper's* magazine.
2. Her collection of poems, *Morning in the Burned House*, contains the moving poem *In the Secular Night*.
3. You may have seen the movie *The Handmaid's Tale*, starring Robert Duvall, based on her bestselling novel.
4. *Surfacing* was the first book of hers I read, but my favorite work of hers is the short story Hair Ball.
5. I wasn't surprised to find her poems The Animals in the Country and This Is a Photograph of Me in our English textbook last year.

52d Setting Off Words Used in Special Ways

Enclose a word used in a special or unusual way in quotation marks. (If you use *so-called* before the word, do not use quotation marks as well.)

It was clear that adults approved of children who were "readers," but it was not at all clear why this was so. (Annie Dillard)

52e Using Quotation Marks with Other Punctuation

At the end of a quotation, punctuation is sometimes placed before the quotation marks and sometimes placed after the quotation marks.

● Place a comma or period *before* the closing quotation marks.

Many, like the poet Robert Frost, think about "the road not taken," but not many have taken "the one less traveled by."

● Place a semicolon or colon *after* the closing quotation marks.

Students who do not pass the test receive "certificates of completion"; those who pass are awarded diplomas.

Taxpayers were pleased with the first of the candidate's promised "sweeping new reforms": a balanced budget.

● If a question mark, exclamation point, or dash is part of the quotation, place the punctuation mark *before* the closing quotation marks.

"Who's there?" she demanded.

"Stop!" he cried.

"Should we leave now, or—" Vicki paused, unable to continue.

● If a question mark, exclamation point, or dash is *not* part of the quotation, place the punctuation mark *after* the closing quotation marks.

Did you finish reading "The Black Cat"?

Whatever you do, don't yell "Uncle"!

The first story—Updike's "A&P"—provoked discussion.

Close-Up QUOTATIONS WITHIN QUOTATIONS

Use *single* quotation marks to enclose a quotation within a quotation.

> Claire noted, "Liberace always said, 'I cried all the way to the bank.'"

Also use single quotation marks within a quotation to indicate a title that would normally be enclosed in double quotation marks.

> I think what she said was, "Play it, Sam. Play 'As Time Goes By.'"

Use *double* quotation marks around quotations or titles within a <u>long prose passage</u>.

See
52b1

EXERCISE 52.3

In the following paragraph, correct the use of single and double quotation marks to set off direct quotations, titles, and words used in special ways. Supply quotation marks where they are required, and delete those that are not required, substituting italics where necessary.

> In her essay 'The Obligation to Endure' from the book "Silent Spring," Rachel Carson writes: As Albert Schweitzer has said, 'Man can hardly even recognize the devils of his own creation.' Carson goes on to point out that many chemicals have been used to kill insects and other organisms, which, she writes, are "described in the modern vernacular as pests." Carson believes such "advanced" chemicals, by contaminating our environment, do more harm than good. In addition to "Silent Spring," Carson is also the author of the book "The Sea Around Us." This work, divided into three sections (Mother Sea, The Restless Sea, and Man and the Sea About Him), was published in 1951.

52f Editing Misused Quotation Marks

Do not use quotation marks in the following situations.

1 To Set Off Indirect Quotations

Do not use quotation marks to set off **indirect quotations** (someone else's written or spoken words that are not quoted exactly).

> Freud wondered ʌwhat women wanted.⸖

2 To Set Off Slang or Technical Terms

Do not use quotation marks to set off slang or technical terms. (Note that slang is not appropriate in college writing.)

Dawn is ⁻into⁻ running.

⁻Biofeedback⁻ is sometimes used to treat migraine headaches.

Note: Do not use quotation marks (or italics) to set off the titles of your own essays.

CHAPTER **53**

Using Other Punctuation Marks

53a Using Colons

The **colon** is a strong punctuation mark that points readers ahead to the material that follows it. When a colon introduces a list or series, explanatory material, or a quotation, *it must be preceded by a complete sentence.*

1 Introducing Lists or Series

Use colons to set off lists or series, including those introduced by phrases such as *the following* or *as follows.*

Waiting tables requires three skillls: memory, speed, and balance.

2 Introducing Explanatory Material

Use a colon to introduce material that explains, exemplifies, or summarizes. Frequently, such material is presented as an **appositive**, a word group that identifies or renames an adjacent noun or pronoun.

Painter Diego Rivera was well known for a controversial mural: the one commissioned for Rockefeller Center in the 1930s.

She had one dream: to play professional basketball.

Sometimes a colon separates two independent clauses, with the second illustrating or clarifying the first.

The survey presents an interesting finding: Americans do not trust the news media.

Note: When a complete sentence follows a colon, the sentence may begin with either a capital or a lowercase letter. However, if the sentence is a quotation, the first word is always capitalized (unless it was not capitalized in the source).

3 Introducing Quotations

When you quote a long prose passage, always introduce it with a colon. Also use a colon before a short quotation when it is introduced by a complete sentence.

See 52b1

With dignity, Bartleby repeated the familiar words: "I prefer not to."

Colons are also used in the following situations:

● **To Separate Titles from Subtitles**

Family Installments: Memories of Growing Up Hispanic

● **To Separate Minutes from Hours**

6:15 a.m.

● **After Salutations in Business Letters**

Dear Dr. Evans:

4 Editing Misused Colons

Do not use colons after *namely, for example, such as,* or *that is.*

The Eye Institute treats patients with a wide variety of conditions, such as: myopia, glaucoma, and cataracts.

Do not place colons between verbs and their objects or complements or between prepositions and their objects.

James Michener wrote: *Hawaii, Centennial, Space,* and *Poland.*

Hitler's armies marched through: the Netherlands, Belgium, and France.

EXERCISE 53.1

Add colons where appropriate in the following sentences, and delete any misused colons.

Example: There was one thing he really hated getting up at 7:00 every

morning.

1. Books about the late John F. Kennedy include the following *A Hero for Our Time*; *Johnny, We Hardly Knew Ye*; *One Brief Shining Moment*; and *JFK: Reckless Youth*.
2. Only one task remained to tell his boss he was quitting.
3. The story closed with a familiar phrase "And they all lived happily ever after."
4. The sergeant requested: reinforcements, medical supplies, and more ammunition.
5. She kept only four souvenirs a photograph, a matchbook, a theater program, and a daisy pressed between the pages of *William Shake-speare The Complete Works*.

53b Using Dashes

1 Setting Off Nonessential Material

Like commas, **dashes** can set off nonessential material. Unlike commas, however, dashes call attention to the material they set off. Indicate a dash with two unspaced hyphens (which your word-processing program will automatically convert to a dash).

For emphasis, you may use dashes to set off explanations, qualifications, examples, definitions, and appositives.

Neither of the boys—both nine-year-olds—had any history of violence.

Too many parents learn the dangers of swimming pools the hard way—after a toddler has drowned.

2 Introducing a Summary

Use a dash to introduce a statement that summarizes a list or series before it.

"Study hard," "Respect your elders," "Don't talk with your mouth full"—Sharon had often heard her parents say these things.

3 Indicating an Interruption

In dialogue, a dash may indicate a hesitation or an unfinished thought.

"I think—no, I know—that this is the worst day of my life," Julie sighed.

4 Editing Overused Dashes

Too many dashes can make your writing seem disorganized and out of control, so be careful not to overuse them.

. *Most*

Registration was a nightmare—̶m̶o̶s̶t̶ of the courses I wanted to take—
geology and conversational Spanish, for instance—met at inconvenient
times—̶or were closed by the time I tried to sign up for them.

EXERCISE 53.2

Add dashes and other punctuation where needed in the following sentences. If a sentence is correct, mark it with a *C*.

Example: World War I called "the war to end all wars" was, unfortunately no
such thing.

1. Tulips, daffodils, hyacinths, lilies all these flowers grow from bulbs.
2. India a country with a rich cultural history gained independence after
   two hundred years of British rule.
3. "But it's not" She paused and thought about her next words.
4. He considered several different majors history, English, political
   science, and business before deciding on journalism.
5. The two words added to the Pledge of Allegiance in the 1950s "under
   God" remain part of the Pledge today.

53c Using Parentheses

1 Setting Off Nonessential Material

Use **parentheses** to enclose material that expands, clarifies, illustrates, or
supplements. (Note that unlike dashes, parentheses tend to de-emphasize
the words they enclose.)

In some European countries (notably Sweden and France), high-quality
day care is offered at little or no cost to parents.

When a complete sentence enclosed in parentheses falls within another
sentence, it should not begin with a capital letter or end with a period.

The area is so cold (temperatures average in the low twenties) that it is
virtually uninhabitable.

However, if the parenthetical sentence does *not* fall within another sentence, it must begin with a capital letter and end with appropriate punctuation.

The region is very cold. (Temperatures average in the low twenties.)

2 Using Parentheses in Other Situations

Use parentheses around letters and numbers that identify points on a list, dates, cross-references, and documentation.

All reports must include the following components: (1) an opening summary, (2) a background statement, and (3) a list of conclusions.

Russia defeated Sweden in the Great Northern War (1700–1721).

Other scholars also make this point (see p. 54).

One critic has called the novel "puerile" (Arvin 72).

Note: Never use a comma before an opening parenthesis. A comma may follow the closing parenthesis, however.

EXERCISE 53.3

Add parentheses where appropriate in the following sentences. If a sentence is correct, mark it with a *C*.

Example: The greatest battle of the War of 1812 (the Battle of New Orleans)
was fought after the war was declared over.

1. During the Great War 1914–1918, Britain censored letters written from the front lines.
2. Those who lived in towns on the southern coast such as Dover could often hear the mortar shells across the channel in France.
3. Wilfred Owen wrote his most famous poem "Dulce et Decorum Est" in the trenches in France.
4. The British uniforms with bright red tabs right at the neck were responsible for many British deaths.
5. It was difficult for the War Poets as they are now called to return to writing about subjects other than the horrors of war.

53d Using Brackets

1 Setting Off Comments within Quotations

Brackets within quotations tell readers that the enclosed words are yours and not those of your source. You can bracket an explanation, a clarification, a correction, or an opinion.

"Even at Princeton he [F. Scott Fitzgerald] felt like an outsider."

If a quotation contains an error, indicate that the error is not yours by following the error with the Latin word *sic* ("thus") in brackets.

As the website notes, "The octopuss [sic] is a cephalopod mollusk with eight arms."

Note: Use brackets to indicate changes that you make in order to fit a <u>quotation</u> smoothly into your sentence.

See 14d1

2 Replacing Parentheses within Parentheses

When one set of parentheses falls within another, use brackets in place of the inner set.

In her classic study of American education (*The Troubled Crusade* [New York: Basic, 1963]), Diane Ravitch addresses issues such as educational reforms and campus unrest.

53e   Using Slashes

1 Separating One Option from Another

The either/or fallacy is a common error in logic.

Writer/director M. Night Shyamalan spoke at the film festival.

In this situation, do not leave a space before or after the slash.

2 Separating Lines of Poetry Run into the Text

The poet James Schevill writes, "I study my defects / And learn how to perfect them."

In this situation, leave one space before and one space after the slash.

EXERCISE 53.4

Add appropriate punctuation—colons, dashes, parentheses, brackets, or slashes—to the following sentences. If a sentence is correct, mark it with a *C.*

Example: There was one thing she was sure of : if she did well at the interview,

the job would be hers.

1. Mark Twain Samuel L. Clemens made the following statement "I can live for two months on a good compliment."

2. Liza Minnelli, the actress singer who starred in several films, is the daughter of legendary singer Judy Garland.
3. John Adams 1735–1826 was the second president of the United States; John Quincy Adams 1767–1848 was the sixth.
4. The sign said, "No tresspassing sic."
5. Before the introduction of the potato in Europe, the parsnip was a major source of carbohydrates in fact, it was a dietary staple.

53f Using Ellipses

Use ellipses in the following situations.

1 Indicating an Omission in Quoted Prose

Use an **ellipsis**—three *spaced* periods—to indicate that you have omitted words from a prose quotation. (Note that an ellipsis in the middle of a quoted passage can indicate the omission of a word, a sentence or two, or even a whole paragraph or more.) When deleting material from a quotation, be very careful not to change the meaning of the original passage.

> **Original:** "When I was a young man, being anxious to distinguish myself, I was perpetually starting new propositions." (Samuel Johnson)

> **With Omission:** "When I was a young man, . . . I was perpetually starting new propositions."

Note that when you delete words immediately after a punctuation mark (such as the comma in the above example), you retain the punctuation mark before the ellipsis.

When you delete material at the end of a sentence, place the ellipsis *after* the sentence's period or other end punctuation.

> According to humorist Dave Barry, "from outer space Europe appears to be shaped like a large ketchup stain. . . . " (period followed by ellipsis)

 Never begin a quoted passage with an ellipsis.

When you delete material between sentences, place the ellipsis *after* any punctuation that appeared in the original passage.

> **Deletion from Middle of One Sentence to End of Another:** According to Donald Hall, "Everywhere one meets the idea that reading is an activity desirable in itself. . . . People surround the idea of reading with piety and do not take into account the purpose of reading." (period followed by ellipsis)

Deletion from Middle of One Sentence to Middle of Another: "When I was a young man, . . . I found that generally what was new was false." (Samuel Johnson) (comma followed by ellipsis)

Note: If a quoted passage already contains an ellipsis, MLA recommends that you enclose any ellipses of your own in brackets to distinguish them from those that appear in the original quotation.

Close-Up USING ELLIPSES

If a quotation ending with an ellipsis is followed by parenthetical documentation, the final punctuation *follows* the documentation.

As Jarman argues, "Compromise was impossible . . ." (161).

---

2 Indicating an Omission in Quoted Poetry

Use an ellipsis when you omit a word or phrase from a line of poetry. When you omit one or more lines of poetry, use a line of spaced periods. (The length may be equal either to the line above it or to the missing line—but it should not be longer than the longest line of the poem.)

Original:

> Stitch! Stitch! Stitch!
> In poverty, hunger, and dirt,
> And still with a voice of dolorous pitch,
> Would that its tone could reach the Rich,
> She sang this "Song of the Shirt!"
>
> > (Thomas Hood)

With Omission:

> Stitch! Stitch! Stitch!
> In poverty, hunger, and dirt,
> . . . .
> She sang this "Song of the Shirt!"

PART **12**

Understanding Spelling and Mechanics

PART 12

Understanding Spelling and Mechanics

? Frequently Asked Questions

CHAPTER 54

Improving Spelling

Like most students, you probably use a spell checker when you write and revise essays, but this does not eliminate your need to know how to spell. For one thing, a spell checker will only check words that are in its dictionary. In addition, a spell checker will not tell you if you have confused two homophones, such as *principal* and *principle*, and it will not catch typos that create new words, such as *form* for *from* or *its* for *it's*. For these reasons, you still have to be a competent speller.

54a Understanding Spelling and Pronunciation

Because pronunciation in English often provides few clues to spelling, you must memorize the spellings of many words and use a dictionary or a spell checker regularly.

1 Vowels in Unstressed Positions

Many unstressed vowels sound exactly alike. For instance, it is hard to tell from pronunciation alone that the *i* in *terrible* is not an *a*. In addition, the unstressed vowels *a*, *e*, and *i* are impossible to distinguish in the suffixes *-able* and *-ible*, *-ance* and *-ence*, and *-ant* and *-ent*.

comfortable	brilliance	servant
compatible	excellence	independent

2 Silent Letters

Some English words contain silent letters, such as the *b* in *climb* and the *t* in *mortgage*.

aisle	depot	pneumonia
climb	knight	silhouette
condemn	mortgage	sovereign

3 Words That Are Often Pronounced Carelessly

Most of us pronounce words rather carelessly in everyday speech. Consequently, people tend to leave out, add, or transpose letters when they spell them.

candidate	library	recognize
environment	lightning	specific
February	nuclear	supposed to
government	perform	surprise
hundred	quantity	used to

4 American and British Spellings

Some words are spelled one way in the United States and another way in Great Britain.

American	British
color	colour
defense	defence
judgment	judgement
theater	theatre
toward	towards
traveled	travelled

5 Homophones

Homophones are words—such as *accept* and *except*—that are pronounced alike but spelled differently.

accept	to receive
except	other than
affect	to have an influence on (*verb*)
effect	result (*noun*); to cause (*verb*)
its	possessive of *it*
it's	contraction of *it is*
principal	most important (*adjective*); head of a school (*noun*)
principle	a basic truth; rule of conduct

For a full list of these and other homophones, along with their meanings and sentences illustrating their use, **see Appendix C, Glossary of Usage.**

Close-Up ONE WORD OR TWO?

Some words may be written as one word or two, depending on their meaning.

any way vs. anyway
The early pioneers made the trip west *any way* they could.
It began to rain, but the game continued *anyway*.

every day vs. everyday
Every day brings new opportunities.
John thought of his birthday as an *everyday* event.

Other words are frequently misspelled because people are not sure whether they are one word or two.

One Word	Two Words
already	a lot
cannot	all right
classroom	even though
overweight	no one

Consult a dictionary if you have any doubts about whether a word is written as one word or two.

54b Learning Spelling Rules

Memorizing a few simple rules (and their exceptions) can help you identify and correct words that you have misspelled.

1 The *ie/ei* Combinations

Use *i* before *e* except after *c* or when pronounced *ay*, as in *neighbor*.

i before *e*: belief, chief, niece, friend

ei after *c*: ceiling, deceit, receive

ei pronounced *ay*: weigh, freight, eight

Exceptions: *either, neither, foreign, leisure, weird,* and *seize*. In addition, if the *ie* combination is not pronounced as a unit, the rule does not apply: *atheist, science*.

EXERCISE 54.1

Fill in the blanks with the proper *ie* or *ei* combination. After completing the exercise, use a dictionary or spell checker to check your answers.

Example: conc__*ei*__ve

1. rec_____pt
2. var_____ty
3. caff_____ne
4. ach_____ve
5. kal_____doscope

6. misch_____f
7. effic_____nt
8. v_____n
9. spec_____s
10. suffic_____nt

2 Doubling Final Consonants

The only words that double their consonants before a suffix that begins with a vowel (*-ed* or *-ing*) are those that pass the following three tests:

1. They have one syllable or are stressed on the last syllable.
2. They have only one vowel in the last syllable.
3. They end in a single consonant.

The word *tap* satisfies all three conditions: it has only one syllable, it has only one vowel (*a*), and it ends in a single consonant (*p*). Therefore, the final consonant doubles before a suffix beginning with a vowel (*tapped, tapping*).

The word *relent*, however, meets only two of the three conditions: it is stressed on the last syllable, and it has one vowel in the last syllable, but it does not end in a single consonant. Therefore, its final consonant is not doubled (*relented, relenting*).

3 Prefixes

The addition of a prefix never affects the spelling of the root (*mis + spell = misspell*). Some prefixes can cause spelling problems, however, because they are pronounced alike although they are not spelled alike: *ante-/anti-, en-/in-, per-/pre-*, and *de-/di-*.

ante̲bellum	anti̲aircraft
en̲circle	in̲tegrate
per̲ceive	pre̲scribe
de̲duct	di̲rect

4 Silent e before a Suffix

When a suffix that begins with a consonant is added to a word ending in a silent *e*, the *e* is generally kept: *hope/hopeful; lame/lamely; bore/boredom*. **Exceptions:** *argument, truly, ninth, judgment*, and *acknowledgment*.

When a suffix that begins with a vowel is added to a word ending in a silent *e*, the *e* is generally dropped: *hope/hoping; trace/traced; grieve/grievance; love/lovable*. **Exceptions:** *changeable, noticeable*, and *courageous*.

EXERCISE 54.2

Combine the following words with the suffixes in parentheses. Keep or drop the silent *e* as you see fit. Then, compare your choices with those of a classmate.

Example: fate (al)
fatal

1. surprise (ing)
2. sure (ly)
3. force (ible)
4. manage (able)

5. due (ly)
6. outrage (ous)
7. service (able)

8. awe (ful)
9. shame (ing)
10. shame (less)

5 *y* before a Suffix

When a word ends in a consonant plus *y*, the *y* generally changes to an *i* when a suffix is added (*beauty + ful = beautiful*). The *y* is kept, however, when the suffix *-ing* is added (*tally + ing = tallying*) and in some one-syllable words (*dry + ness = dryness*).

When a word ends in a vowel plus *y*, the *y* is kept (*joy + ful = joyful; employ + er = employer*). **Exception:** *day + ly = daily.*

EXERCISE 54.3

Add the endings in parentheses to the following words. Change or keep the final *y* as you see fit. Then, compare your choices with those of a classmate.

Example: party (ing)
partying

1. journey (ing)
2. study (ed)
3. carry (ing)
4. shy (ly)
5. study (ing)

6. sturdy (ness)
7. merry (ment)
8. likely (hood)
9. plenty (ful)
10. supply (er)

6 *seed* Endings

Endings with the sound *seed* are nearly always spelled *cede*, as in *precede, intercede, concede,* and so on. **Exceptions:** *supersede, exceed, proceed,* and *succeed.*

7 -able, -ible

If the root of a word is itself a word, the suffix *-able* is most commonly used. If the root of a word is not a word, the suffix *-ible* is most often used.

agree<u>able</u>
comfort<u>able</u>
dry<u>able</u>

compat<u>ible</u>
incred<u>ible</u>
plaus<u>ible</u>

8 Plurals

Most nouns form plurals by adding *-s: savage/savages, tortilla/tortillas, boat/boats.* There are, however, a number of exceptions.

Words Ending in -f *or* -fe   Some words ending in *-f* or *-fe* form plurals by changing the *f* to *v* and adding *-es* or *-s: life/lives, self/selves.* Others add just -*s*: *belief/beliefs, safe/safes*. Words ending in -*ff* take -*s* to form plurals: *tariff/tariffs*.

Words Ending in -**y** Most words that end in a consonant followed by *y* form plurals by changing the *y* to *i* and adding -*es*: *baby/babies*. **Exceptions:** proper nouns such as *Kennedys* (never *Kennedies*).

Words that end in a vowel followed by a *y* form plurals by adding -*s*: *monkey/monkeys*.

Words Ending in -**o** Words that end in a vowel followed by *o* form the plural by adding -*s*: *radio/radios, stereo/stereos, zoo/zoos*. Most words that end in a consonant followed by *o* add -*es* to form the plural: *tomato/tomatoes, hero/heroes*. **Exceptions:** *silo/silos, piano/pianos, memo/memos, soprano/sopranos*.

Words Ending in -**s**, -**ss**, -**sh**, -**ch**, -**x**, *and* -**z** These words form plurals by adding -*es*: *Jones/Joneses, mass/masses, rash/rashes, lunch/lunches, box/boxes, buzz/buzzes*. **Exceptions:** Some one-syllable words that end in -*s* or -*z* double their final consonants when forming plurals: *quiz/quizzes*.

Compound Nouns **Compound nouns**—nouns formed from two or more words—usually form the plural with the last word in the compound construction: *welfare state/welfare states; snowball/snowballs*. However, compound nouns whose first element is more important than the others form the plural with the first element: *sister-in-law/sisters-in-law, attorney general/attorneys general, hole in one/holes in one*.

Foreign Plurals Some words, especially those borrowed from Latin or Greek, keep their foreign plurals.

Singular	Plural
criterion	criteria
datum	data
larva	larvae
medium	media
memorandum	memoranda
stimulus	stimuli

Note: Some linguists find Latin and Greek plural endings pretentious and encourage the use of English plural forms—for example, *condominiums* rather than *condominia*, *stadiums* rather than *stadia*, and *octopuses* rather than *octopi*.

Knowing When to Capitalize

55a Capitalizing the First Word of a Sentence

Capitalize the first word of a sentence, including a sentence of quoted speech or writing.

 As Shakespeare wrote, "Who steals my purse steals trash."

Do not capitalize a sentence set off within another sentence by dashes or parentheses.

 Finding the store closed—it was a holiday—they went home.

 The candidates are Frank Lester and Jane Lester (they are not related).

55b Capitalizing Proper Nouns

Proper nouns—the names of specific persons, places, animals, or things—are capitalized, and so are adjectives formed from proper nouns.

1 Specific People's Names

Always capitalize people's names: Kirsten Gillibrand, Barack Obama.

Capitalize a title when it precedes a person's name (Senator Kirsten Gillibrand) or is used instead of the name (Dad). Do not capitalize titles that *follow* names (Kirsten Gillibrand, the senator from New York) or those that refer to the general position, not the particular person who holds it (a stay-at-home dad).

> **MULTILINGUAL TIP**
> Do not capitalize a word simply because you want to emphasize its importance. If you are not sure whether a noun should be capitalized, look it up in a dictionary.

You may, however, capitalize titles that indicate very high-ranking positions even when they are used alone or when they follow a name: the Pope; Barack Obama, President of the United States. Never capitalize a title denoting a family relationship when it follows an article or a possessive pronoun (an uncle, his mom).

Capitalize titles that represent academic degrees or abbreviations of those degrees even when they follow a name: Dr. Sanjay Gupta; Sanjay Gupta, MD.

2 Names of Particular Structures, Special Events, Monuments, and So On

the *Titanic*	the World Series	the Taj Mahal
the Brooklyn Bridge	Mount Rushmore	the Great Wall

3 Places and Geographical Regions

Saturn	the Straits of Magellan
Budapest	the Western Hemisphere

Note: Capitalize a common noun, such as *bridge, river, lake,* or *county,* when it is part of a proper noun: Lake Erie, Kings County.

Capitalize *north, east, south,* and *west* when they denote particular geographical regions, but not when they designate directions.

There are more tornadoes in Kansas than in the East. (*East* refers to a specific region.)

Turn west at Broad Street and continue north to Market. (*West* and *north* refer to directions, not specific regions.)

4 Days of the Week, Months, and Holidays

Saturday   Diwali

January   Cinco de Mayo

5 Historical Periods, Documents, and Names of Legal Cases

the Reformation   the Treaty of Versailles

the Battle of Gettysburg *Brown v. Board of Education*

Note: Names of court cases are italicized in the text of essays but not in works-cited entries.

6 Philosophic, Literary, and Artistic Movements

Naturalism   Dadaism

Romanticism   Expressionism

7 Races, Ethnic Groups, Nationalities, and Languages

African American   Korean

Latino/Latina   Farsi

Note: When the words *black* and *white* refer to races, they have tradition-ally not been capitalized. Current opinion is divided on whether or not to capitalize *black*.

8 Religions and Their Followers; Sacred Books and Figures

Jews   the Talmud   Buddha

Islam   God   the Bible

9 Specific Organizations

the New York Yankees   the National Rifle Association

the Democratic Party   the Rolling Stones

10 Businesses, Government Agencies, and Other Institutions

General Electric

the Environmental Protection Agency

Lincoln High School

the University of Maryland

11 Brand Names and Words Formed from Them

Coke   Astroturf   Rollerblades   Post-it   Velcro

Note: In general, use generic references, not brand names, in college writing—*photocopy*, not *Xerox*, for example. These generic names are not capitalized.

12 **Specific Academic Courses**

Sociology 201   English 101

Note: Do not capitalize a general subject area (sociology, zoology) unless it is the name of a language (French).

13 **Adjectives Formed from Proper Nouns**

Keynesian economics   Elizabethan era
Freudian slip   Shakespearean sonnet

Note: When words derived from proper nouns have lost their specialized meanings, do not capitalize them: *china bowl, french fries.*

55c Capitalizing Important Words in Titles

In general, capitalize all words in titles with the exception of articles (*a, an,* and *the*), prepositions, coordinating conjunctions, and the *to* in infinitives. If an article, preposition, or coordinating conjunction is the *first* or *last* word in the title or subtitle, however, do capitalize it.

"Dover Beach"   *On the Waterfront*
The Declaration of Independence   *Madame Curie: A Biography*
Across the River and into the Trees   "What Friends Are For"

55d Capitalizing the Pronoun *I*, the Interjection *O*, and Other Single Letters in Special Constructions

Always capitalize the pronoun *I*, even if it is part of a contraction (*I'm, I'll, I've*).

Always capitalize the interjection *O*.

Give us peace in our time, O Lord.

However, do not capitalize the interjection *oh* unless it begins a sentence.

Note: Many other single letters are capitalized in certain usages: *an A in history, vitamin B, C major.* Check a dictionary to determine whether or not to use a capital letter.

55e Editing Misused Capitals

Do not use capital letters for emphasis or as an attention-getting strategy. If you are not certain whether a word should be capitalized, consult a dictionary.

1 Seasons

Do not capitalize the names of the seasons—summer, fall, winter, spring—unless they are personified, as in *Old Man Winter*.

2 Centuries and Loosely Defined Historical Periods

Do not capitalize the names of centuries or of general historical periods.

seventeenth-century poetry
the automobile age

Do, however, capitalize the names of specific historical, anthropological, and geological periods.

the Renaissance   Iron Age   Paleozoic Era

3 Diseases and Other Medical Terms

Do not capitalize names of diseases or medical tests or conditions unless a proper noun is part of the name or unless the disease is an **acronym**.

smallpox   Apgar test   AIDS
Lyme disease   autism   Ebola

EXERCISE 55.1

Capitalize words where necessary in these sentences.

>   *P*   *P*   *P*
> ***Example:*** John F. Kennedy won the pulitzer prize for his book *profiles*
>   *C*
>   *in eourage.*

1. Two of the brontë sisters wrote *jane eyre* and *wuthering heights*, nineteenth-century novels that are required reading in many English classes that focus on victorian literature.
2. It was a beautiful day in the spring—it was april 15, to be exact—but all Ted could think about was the check he had to write to the internal revenue service and the bills he had to pay by friday.
3. Traveling north, they hiked through british columbia, planning a leisurely return on the cruise ship *canadian princess*.
4. Alice liked her mom's apple pie better than aunt nellie's rhubarb pie, but she liked grandpa's punch best of all.
5. A new elective, political science 30, covers the vietnam war from the gulf of tonkin to the fall of saigon, including the roles of ho chi minh, the viet cong, and the buddhist monks; the positions of presidents johnson and nixon; and the influence of groups such as the student mobilization committee and vietnam veterans against the war.
6. When the central high school drama club put on a production of shaw's *pygmalion*, the director xeroxed extra copies of the parts for

eliza doolittle and professor henry higgins so he could give them to the understudies.

7. Shaking all over, Bill admitted, "driving on the los angeles freeway is a frightening experience for a kid from brooklyn, even in a bmw."

8. The new united federation of teachers contract guarantees teachers many paid holidays, including columbus day, veterans day, and washington's birthday; a week each at christmas and easter; and two full months (july and august) in the summer.

9. The sociology syllabus included the books *beyond the best interests of the child, regulating the poor: the functions of public welfare*, and *a welfare mother*; in anthropology, we were to begin by studying the stone age; and in geology, we were to focus on the Mesozoic era.

10. Winners of the nobel peace prize include lech walesa, former leader of the polish trade union solidarity; the reverend dr. martin luther king jr., founder of the southern christian leadership conference; and archbishop desmond tutu of south africa.

CHAPTER **56**

Using Italics

56a Setting Off Titles and Names

See
52c

Use italics for the categories of titles and names listed in the box below. All other titles are set off with **quotation marks**.

Titles and Names Set in Italics

Books: *Twilight, Harry Potter and the Deathly Hallows*
Newspapers: *The Washington Post, The Philadelphia Inquirer*
Magazines and Journals: *Rolling Stone, Scientific American*
Online Magazines and Journals: *salon.com, theonion.com*

Websites or Home Pages: *urbanlegends.com, movie-mistakes.com*

Pamphlets: *Common Sense*

Films: *Citizen Kane, The Hunger Games*

Television Programs: *Glee, American Idol, The Biggest Loser*

Radio Programs: *All Things Considered, A Prairie Home Companion*

Long Poems: *John Brown's Body, The Faerie Queen*

Plays: *Macbeth, A Raisin in the Sun*

Long Musical Works: *Rigoletto, Eroica*

Software Programs: *Microsoft Word, PowerPoint*

Search Engines and Web Browsers: *Google Chrome, Internet Explorer, Safari*

Databases: *Academic Search Premier, Expanded Academic ASAP Plus*

Paintings and Sculpture: *Guernica, Pietà*

Ships: *Lusitania,* U.S.S. *Saratoga* (S.S. and U.S.S. are not italicized.)

Trains: *City of New Orleans,* the *Orient Express*

Aircraft: the *Hindenburg, Enola Gay* (Only particular aircraft, not makes or types such as Piper Cub or Airbus, are italicized.)

Spacecraft: *Challenger, Enterprise*

 Names of sacred books, such as the Bible and the Qur'an, and well-known documents, such as the Constitution and the Declaration of Independence, are neither italicized nor placed within quotation marks.

56b Setting Off Foreign Words and Phrases

Italics are often used to set off foreign words and phrases that have not become part of the English language.

"C'est la vie," Madeleine said when she saw the long line for the concert.

Spirochaeta plicatilis is a corkscrew-like bacterium.

If you are not sure if a foreign word has been assimilated into English, consult a dictionary.

56c Setting Off Elements Spoken of as Themselves and Terms Being Defined

Use italics to set off letters, numerals, and words that refer to the letters, numerals, and words themselves.

Is that a *p* or a *g*?

I forget the exact address, but I know it has a *3* in it.

Why doesn't *though* rhyme with *cough*?

Also use italics to set off words and phrases that you go on to define.

A *closet drama* is a play meant to be read, not performed.

Note: When you quote a dictionary definition, put the word you are defining in italics and the definition itself in quotation marks.

Infer means "to draw a conclusion"; *imply* means "to suggest."

56d Using Italics for Emphasis

Italics can occasionally be used for emphasis.

Initially, poetry might be defined as a kind of language that says *more* and says it *more intensely* than does ordinary language. (Lawrence Perrine, *Sound and Sense*)

However, overuse of italics is distracting. Instead of italicizing, try to indicate emphasis through word choice and sentence structure.

EXERCISE 56.1

Underline to indicate italics where necessary, and delete any italics that are incorrectly used. If a sentence is correct, mark it with a *C*.

Example: However is a conjunctive adverb, not a coordinating conjunction.

1. I said Carol, not Darryl.
2. A *deus ex machina*, an improbable device used to resolve the plot of a fictional work, is used in Charles Dickens's novel Oliver Twist.
3. He dotted every i and crossed every t.
4. The Metropolitan Opera's production of Carmen was a tour de force for the principal performers.
5. *Laissez-faire* is a doctrine holding that government should not interfere with trade.
6. Antidote and anecdote are often confused because their pronunciations are similar.
7. Hawthorne's novels include Fanshawe, The House of the Seven Gables, The Blithedale Romance, and The Scarlet Letter.
8. Words such as mailman, policeman, and fireman have been replaced by nonsexist terms such as letter carrier, police officer, and firefighter.
9. A classic black tuxedo was considered de rigueur at the charity ball, but Jason preferred to wear his *dashiki*.
10. Thomas Mann's novel Buddenbrooks is a bildungsroman.

CHAPTER 57

Using Hyphens

Hyphens have two conventional uses: to break a word at the end of a line and to link words in certain compounds.

57a Breaking a Word at the End of a Line

Sometimes you may want to break a word with a hyphen—for example, to fill in excessive space at the end of a line when you want to enhance a document's visual appeal. When you break a word at the end of a line, divide it only between syllables, consulting a dictionary if necessary. Never divide a word at the end of a page, and never hyphenate a one-syllable word. In addition, never leave a single letter at the end of a line or carry only one or two letters to the next line.

See
57b

If you divide a <u>compound word</u> at the end of a line, put the hyphen between the elements of the compound (*snow-mobile*, not *snowmo-bile*).

Close-Up DIVIDING ELECTRONIC ADDRESSES (URLS)

MLA style recommends that you break the URL after a mark of punctuation (such as a slash, period, or hyphen). In addition, omit *http://* or *https://* when noting the URL.

57b Dividing Compound Words

A **compound word** is composed of two or more words. Some familiar compound words are always hyphenated: *no-hitter, helter-skelter*. Other compounds are written as one word (*peacetime, fireplace*) or as two separate words (*labor relations, bunk bed*). Many formerly hyphenated compound nouns (for example, *daycare* and *healthcare*) are now often written as one word. Consult a dictionary to determine whether a particular compound requires a hyphen.

591

Hyphens are generally used in the following compounds.

1 In Compound Adjectives

A **compound adjective** is made up of two or more words that function together as an adjective.

- When a compound adjective *precedes* the noun it modifies, use hyphens to join its elements.

  The research team tried to use nineteenth-century technology to design a space-age project.

- When a compound adjective *follows* the noun it modifies, do not use hyphens to join its elements.

  The three government-operated programs were run smoothly, but the one that was not government operated was short of funds.

Note: A compound adjective formed with an adverb ending in *-ly* is not hyphenated even when it precedes the noun: *Many upwardly mobile families are on tight budgets.*

Use **suspended hyphens**—hyphens followed by a space or by appropriate punctuation and a space—in a pair or series of compounds that have the same principal elements.

Graduates of two- and four-year colleges were eligible for the grants.

The exam called for sentence-, paragraph-, and essay-length answers.

2 With Certain Prefixes or Suffixes

Use a hyphen between a prefix and a proper noun or proper adjective.

mid-July   pre-Columbian

Use a hyphen to connect the prefixes *all-*, *ex-*, *half-*, *quarter-*, *quasi-*, and *self-* and the suffix *-elect* to a noun.

ex-senator	self-centered	quasi-legal
quarter-moon	president-elect	all-inclusive

Note: The words *selfhood*, *selfish*, and *selfless* do not include hyphens because in these cases, *self* is the root, not a prefix.

3 In Compound Numerals and Fractions

Hyphenate compounds that represent numbers below one hundred (even if they are part of a larger number).

the twenty-first century
three hundred sixty-five days

Also hyphenate the written form of a fraction when it modifies a noun.

a two-thirds share of the business

4 For Clarity

Hyphenate to prevent readers from misreading one word for another.

In order to reform criminals, we must re-form our ideas about prisons.

Hyphenate to avoid certain hard-to-read combinations, such as two *i*'s (*semi-illiterate*) or more than two of the same consonant (*skill-less*).

In most cases, hyphenate between a capital initial and a word when the two combine to form a compound: *A-frame, T-shirt, D-day.*

5 In Coined Compounds

A **coined compound,** one that uses a new combination of words as a unit, requires hyphens.

He looked up with a who-do-you-think-you-are expression.

EXERCISE 57.1

Add hyphens to the compounds in these sentences wherever they are required. Consult a dictionary if necessary.

Example: Alaska was the forty-ninth state to join the United States.

1. One of the restaurant's blue plate specials is chicken fried steak.
2. Virginia and Texas are both right to work states.
3. He stood on tiptoe to see the near perfect statue, which was well hidden by the security fence.
4. The dollar store had a self service makeup counter and stocked many up to the minute gadgets.
5. The so called Saturday night special is opposed by pro gun control groups.
6. He ordered two all beef patties with special sauce, lettuce, cheese, pickles, and onions on a sesame seed bun.
7. The material was extremely thought provoking, but it hardly presented any earth shattering conclusions.
8. The Red Sox Orioles game was rained out, so the long suffering fans left for home.
9. Bone marrow transplants carry the risk of what is known as a graft versus host reaction.
10. The state funded child care program was considered a highly desirable alternative to family day care.

CHAPTER 58

Using Abbreviations

Generally speaking, **abbreviations** are not appropriate in college writing except in tables, charts, and works-cited lists. Some abbreviations are acceptable in scientific, technical, or business writing, or only in a particular academic <u>discipline</u>. If you have questions about the appropriateness of a particular abbreviation, consult a style manual for the appropriate field.

See Pt. 7

Close-Up ABBREVIATIONS IN ELECTRONIC COMMUNICATIONS

Like emoticons, which are popular in personal email and instant messages, shorthand abbreviations and symbols—such as GR8 and 2NITE—are common in text messages. Although acceptable in informal electronic communication, such abbreviations are not appropriate in college writing or in business communications.

58a Abbreviating Titles

Titles before and after proper names are usually abbreviated.

Mr. Homer Simpson   Rep. Carolyn McCarthy
Henry Kissinger, PhD   Dr. Martin Luther King Jr.

Do not, however, use an abbreviated title without a name.

doctor
The ~~Dr.~~ diagnosed hepatitis.

58b Abbreviating Organization Names and Technical Terms

Well-known businesses and government, social, and civic organizations are frequently referred to by capitalized initials. These abbreviations fall into two categories: those in which the initials are pronounced as separate units (EPA, MTV) and **acronyms**, in which the initials are pronounced as words (UNICEF, NATO).

To save space, you may also use accepted abbreviations for complex technical terms that are not well known, but be sure to spell out the full term the first time you mention it, followed by the abbreviation in parentheses.

> Citrus farmers have been using ethylene dibromide (EDB), a chemical pesticide, for more than twenty years. Now, however, EDB has contaminated water supplies.

Close-Up ABBREVIATIONS IN MLA DOCUMENTATION

MLA documentation style requires abbreviations of publishers' company names—for example, **Columbia UP** for *Columbia University Press*—in the works-cited list. Do not, however, use such abbreviations in the text of an essay.

See 17a

MLA style permits the use of abbreviations that designate parts of written works (**ch. 3, sec. 7**)—but only in the works-cited list and parenthetical documentation.

Finally, MLA recommends abbreviating literary works and books of the Bible in parenthetical references: **(*Oth.*)** for *Othello*, **(Exod.)** for Exodus. These words should not be abbreviated in the text of an essay.

58c Abbreviating Dates, Times of Day, and Temperatures

Dates, times of day, and temperatures are often abbreviated.

50 BC (*BC* follows the date)	AD 432 (*AD* precedes the date)
3:03 p.m.	180° F (Fahrenheit)

Always capitalize *BC* and *AD*. (The alternatives *BCE*, for "before the Common Era," and *CE*, for "Common Era," are also capitalized.) Use lowercase letters for *a.m.* and *p.m.*, but use these abbreviations only when they are accompanied by numbers.

> *morning.*
> I'll see you in the ~~a.m.~~

Note: Avoid the abbreviation *no.* (written either *no.* or *No.*), except in technical writing, and then use it only before a specific number: *The unidentified substance was labeled no. 52.*

58d Editing Misused Abbreviations

In college writing, the following are not abbreviated.

1 Names of Days, Months, or Holidays

Do not abbreviate days of the week, months, or holidays.

On ~~Sat., Dec.~~ 23, I started my ~~Xmas~~ shopping.
     Saturday, December   *Christmas*

2 Names of Streets and Places

In general, do not abbreviate names of streets and places.

He lives on Riverside ~~Dr.~~ in ~~NYC.~~
     Drive   *New York City.*

Exceptions: The abbreviation *US* is often acceptable (*US Coast Guard*), as is *DC* in *Washington, DC*. Also permissible are *Mt.* before the name of a mountain (*Mt. Etna*) and *St.* in a place name (*St. Albans*).

3 Names of Academic Subjects

Do not abbreviate names of academic subjects.

~~Psych.~~ and English ~~lit.~~ are required courses.
     Psychology   *literature*

4 Names of Businesses

Write company names exactly as the firms themselves write them: *AT&T, Charles Schwab & Co., Inc.* Abbreviations for *company, corporation*, and the like are used only along with a company name.

The ~~corp.~~ merged with a ~~co.~~ in Ohio.
     corporation   *company*

5 Latin Expressions

Abbreviations of the common Latin phrases *i.e.* ("that is"), *e.g.* ("for example"), and *etc.* ("and so forth") are not appropriate in college writing.

Other musicians (~~e.g.~~ Bruce Springsteen) have also been influenced by Bob Dylan.
     for example,

Poe wrote "The Raven," "Annabel Lee," ~~etc.~~
     and other poems.

6 Units of Measurement

In technical and business writing, some units of measurement are abbreviated when they are preceded by a numeral.

The hurricane had winds of more than 35 mph.

One new hybrid car gets over 50 mpg.

MLA style, however, requirses that you write out units of measurement and spell out words such as *inches, feet, years, miles, pints, quarts,* and *gallons.*

7 Symbols

The symbols +, =, and # are acceptable in technical and scientific writing but not in nontechnical college writing. The symbols % and $ are acceptable only when used with <u>numerals</u> (15%, $15,000), not with spelled-out numbers.

See 59b4, 7

EXERCISE 58.1

Correct any incorrectly used abbreviations in the following sentences, assuming that all are intended for a college audience. If a sentence is correct, mark it with a *C*.

                           and
Example: *Romeo* & *Juliet* is a play by Shakespeare.
                      ^

1. The committee meeting, attended by representatives from Action for Children's Television (ACT) and NOW, Sen. Putnam, & the pres. of ABC, convened at 8 A.M. on Mon. Feb. 24 at the YWCA on Germantown Ave.
2. An econ. prof. was suspended after he encouraged his students to speculate on securities issued by a corp. under investigation by the SEC.
3. Benjamin Spock, who wrote *Baby and Child Care*, was a respected dr. known throughout the USA.
4. The FDA banned the use of Red Dye no. 2 in food in 1976, but other food additives are still in use.
5. The Rev. Dr. Martin Luther King Jr., leader of the SCLC, led the famous Selma, Ala., march.
6. William Golding, a novelist from the U.K., won the Nobel Prize in lit.
7. The adult education center, financed by a major technology corp., offers courses in basic subjects such as introductory bio. and tech. writing as well as teaching HTML and XML.
8. All the fraternity brothers agreed to write to Pres. Dexter appealing their disciplinary probation under Ch. 4, Sec. 3, of the IFC constitution.
9. A 4 qt. (i.e., 1 gal.) container is needed to hold the salt solution.
10. According to Prof. Morrison, all those taking the exam should bring two sharpened no. 2 pencils to the St. Joseph's University auditorium on Sat.

CHAPTER 59

Using Numbers

Convention determines when to use a **numeral** (22) and when to spell out a number (twenty-two). Numerals are commonly used in scientific and technical writing and in journalism, but they are used less often in academic or literary writing.

Note: The guidelines in this chapter are based on the *MLA Handbook*, 8th ed. (2016). APA style, however, requires that all numbers below ten be spelled out if they do not represent specific measurements and that numbers ten and above be expressed in numerals.

See Ch. 18

59a Spelled-Out Numbers versus Numerals

Unless a number falls into one of the categories listed in **59b**, spell it out *if you can do so in one or two words.*

The Hawaiian alphabet has only <u>twelve</u> letters.

Class size stabilized at <u>twenty-eight</u> students.

The subsidies are expected to total about <u>two</u> million dollars.

Numbers *more than two words* long are expressed in figures.

The dietitian prepared <u>125</u> sample menus.

The developer of the community purchased <u>300,000</u> doorknobs and <u>153,000</u> faucets.

Never begin a sentence with a numeral. If necessary, reword the sentence.

~~250 students are currently enrolled~~ in World History 106.

Current enrollment ^ *is 250 students.*

Note: When one number immediately precedes another in a sentence, spell out the first, and use a numeral for the second: *five 3-quart containers.*

59b Conventional Uses of Numerals

1 Addresses

1920 Walnut Street, Philadelphia, PA 19103

2 Dates

January 15, 1929   1914–1919

3 Exact Times

9:16   10 a.m. (or 10:00 a.m.)

Exceptions: Spell out times of day when they are used with *o'clock*: *eleven o'clock*, not *11 o'clock*. Also spell out times expressed as round numbers: *They were in bed by ten*.

4 Exact Sums of Money

$25.11 $6,752.00

Note: Always use a numeral (not a spelled-out number) with a $ symbol. You may spell out a round sum of money if you use sums infrequently in an essay, provided you can do so in two or three words: *five dollars; two thousand dollars*.

5 Divisions of Written Works

Use arabic (not roman) numerals for page, chapter, and volume numbers; for acts, scenes, and lines of plays; for chapters and verses of the Bible; and for line numbers of long poems.

6 Measurements before an Abbreviation or Symbol

12"   55 mph
32°   15 cc

7 Percentages and Decimals

80%   3.14

Note: You may spell out a percentage (*eighty percent*) if you use percentages infrequently in an essay, provided the percentage can be expressed in two or three words. However, always use a numeral (not a spelled-out number) with a % symbol.

8 Ratios, Scores, and Statistics

See
Ch. 18

In an essay that follows **APA** style, use numerals for numbers presented as a comparison.

> Children preferred Fun Flakes over Graino by a ratio of 20 to 1.
>
> The Orioles defeated the Phillies 6–0.
>
> The median age of the voters was 42; the mean age was 40.

9 Identification Numbers

> Route 66   Track 8   Channel 12

When writing out large numbers, insert a comma every three digits from the right, beginning after the third digit.

> 3,000   25,000   6,751,098

Do not, however, use commas in four-digit page and line numbers, addresses, or year numbers.

> page 1202   3741 Laurel Ave.   1968

EXERCISE 59.1

Following MLA guidelines, revise the use of numbers in these sentences, making sure usage is correct and consistent. If a sentence uses numbers correctly, mark it with a C.

Example: The Empire State Building is ~~one hundred and two~~ stories high.
(102)

1. *1984*, a novel by George Orwell, is set in a totalitarian society.
2. The English placement examination included a 30-minute personal experience essay, a 45-minute expository essay, and a 150-item objective test of grammar and usage.
3. In a control group of two hundred forty-seven patients, almost three out of four suffered serious adverse reactions to the new drug.
4. Before the Thirteenth Amendment to the Constitution, slaves were counted as 3/5 of a person.
5. The intensive membership drive netted 2,608 new members and additional dues of over 5 thousand dollars.
6. They had only 2 choices: either they could take the yacht at Pier Fourteen, or they could return home to the penthouse at Twenty-seven Harbor View Drive.
7. The atomic number of lithium is three.
8. Approximately 3 hundred thousand schoolchildren in District 6 were given hearing and vision examinations between May third and June 26.
9. The United States was drawn into the war by the Japanese attack on Pearl Harbor on December seventh, 1941.
10. An upper-middle-class family can spend more than 450,000 dollars to raise each child up to age 18.

P A R T **13**

Composing for Multilingual Writers

Composing for Multilingual Writers

❓ Frequently Asked Questions

CHAPTER **60**

Adjusting to the US Classroom

If you went to school outside of the United States, you may not be familiar with the way writing is taught in US composition classes.

Characteristics of US Classrooms

Here are some aspects of US classrooms that may be unfamiliar to you:

- **Punctuality** Students are expected to be in their seats and ready to begin class at the scheduled time. If you are repeatedly late, your grade may be lowered.
- **Student–Instructor Relationships** The relationship between students and instructors may be more casual or friendly than you are used to. However, instructors still expect students to abide by the rules they set.
- **Class Discussion** Instructors typically expect students to volunteer ideas in class and may even enjoy it when students disagree with their opinions (as long as the students can make good arguments for their positions). Rather than being a sign of disrespect, this is usually considered to be evidence of interest and involvement in the topic under discussion.

60a Understanding the Writing Process

Typically, US composition instructors teach writing as a <u>process</u>. This process usually includes the following components:

See
Chs. 4–6

- **Planning and shaping your writing** Your instructor will probably help you get ideas for your writing by assigning relevant readings, conducting class discussions, and asking you to keep a journal or engage in <u>freewriting</u> and <u>brainstorming</u>.

See
4e

- **Writing multiple drafts** After you draft your essay for the first time, you will probably get feedback from your instructor or your classmates so that you can **revise** (improve) your work before receiving a grade

603

on it. Instructors expect students to use the suggestions they receive to make significant improvements to their work. (For more information on the drafting process, **see Chapter 6.**)

- **Looking at sample essays** Your instructor may provide the class with sample essays of the type that he or she has assigned. Such samples can help you understand how to complete the assigned work. Sometimes the samples are strong essays that can serve as good examples of what to do. However, most samples will have both strengths and weaknesses, so be sure you understand your instructor's opinion of the samples he or she provides.

See
6c2

- **Engaging in** <u>peer review</u> (sometimes called peer editing) Your instructor may ask the class to work in small groups or in pairs to exchange ideas about an assigned essay. You will be expected to provide other students with feedback on the strengths and weaknesses of their work. Afterward, you should think carefully about your classmates' comments about your essay and make changes to improve it.

- **Attending conferences** Your instructor may schedule one or more appointments with you to discuss your writing and may ask you to bring a draft of the essay you are working on. Your instructor may also be available to help you with your essay without an appointment during his or her office hours. In addition, many educational institutions have **writing centers** where tutors help students get started on their essays or improve their drafts. When you meet with your instructor or writing center tutor, bring a list of specific questions about your essay, and be sure to make careful notes about what you discuss. You can refer to these notes when you revise your work.

Close-Up USING YOUR NATIVE LANGUAGE

Depending on your language background and skills, you may find it helpful to use your native language in some stages of your writing.

When you are making notes about the content of your essay, you may be able to generate more ideas and record them more quickly if you do some of the work in your native language. Additionally, when you are drafting your essay and cannot think of a particular word in English, it may be better simply to write the word in your native language (and come back to it later) so you do not lose your train of thought.

However, if you use another language a great deal as you draft your writing and then try to translate your work into English, the English may sound awkward or be hard for readers to understand. The best strategy when you draft your essays is to write in English as much as you can, using the vocabulary and structures that you already know.

60b Understanding English Language Basics

Getting used to writing and editing your work in English will be easier if you understand a few basic principles:

- **In English, words may change their form according to their function.** For example, <u>verbs</u> change form to communicate whether an action is taking place in the past, present, or future. **ml 61a**
- **In English, context is extremely important to understanding function.** In the following sentences, for instance, the very same words can perform different functions according to their relationships to other words.

    Juan and I are taking a <u>walk</u>. (*Walk* is a noun, a direct object of the verb *taking*, with an article, *a*, attached to it.)

    If you <u>walk</u> instead of driving, you will help conserve the Earth's resources. (*Walk* is a verb, the predicate of the subject *you*.)

- **Spelling in English is not always phonetic and sometimes may seem illogical.** <u>Spelling</u> in English may be related more to the history of the word and to its origins in other languages than to the way the word is pronounced. Therefore, learning to spell correctly is often a matter of memorization, not sounding out the word phonetically. For example, "ough" is pronounced differently in *tough*, *though*, and *thought*. **See Ch. 54**
- <u>Word order</u> **is extremely important in English sentences.** In English sentences, word order may indicate which word is the subject of the sentence and which is the object, whether the sentence is a question or a statement, and so on. **ml 61f**

60c Learning to Edit Your Work

<u>Editing</u> your work involves focusing on grammar, spelling, punctuation, and mechanics. The approach you take to editing for grammar errors should depend on your strengths and weaknesses in English. **See 6d1**

If you learned English mostly by speaking it, if you have strong oral skills, and if you instinctively make correct judgments about English, the best approach for you may be reading your essay aloud and listening for mistakes, correcting them by deciding what sounds right. You may even find that as you read aloud, you automatically correct your written mistakes. (Be sure to transfer those corrections to your essay.) In addition to proofreading your essay from beginning to end, you might find it helpful to start from the end of the essay, reading and proofreading sentence by sentence. This strategy can keep you from being distracted by your ideas, allowing you to focus on grammar alone.

If you learned English mostly by reading, studying grammar rules, and/ or translating between your native language and English, you may not feel that you have good instincts about what sounds right in English. If this is the case, you should take a different approach to editing your work. First, identify the errors you make most frequently by looking at earlier work your instructor has marked or by asking your instructor for help. Once you have identified your most common errors, read through your essay, checking each sentence for these errors. Try to apply the grammar and mechanics rules you already know, or check the relevant grammar explanations in **Chapter 61** for help.

After you check your work for grammar errors, you should check again to make sure that you have used proper punctuation, capitalization, and spelling. If you have difficulty with spelling, you can use a spell checker to help you, but remember that spell checkers cannot catch every error. After you have made grammar and mechanics corrections on your own, you can seek outside help in identifying errors you might have missed. You should also keep a notebook with a list of your most frequent grammatical errors and review it often.

EXERCISE 60.1

US writing classrooms may require different approaches and practices than those in other countries. In the following list, place a checkmark next to each item that correctly describes the way writing is taught in most US composition classes. Correct any statements that are incorrect or misleading by rewriting them.

1. Student–instructor relationships are always strictly formal.
2. Writing multiple drafts is an important part of revising and improving writing skills.
3. Voicing different points of view in class discussion is encouraged.
4. Peer review is usually discouraged, but conferences with instructors are often an important part of revision.
5. Class participation is often an important part of showing engagement in the class.
6. Using proper grammar and mechanics (punctuation, capitalization, and so on) in essays is important for clarity as well as correctness.
7. In English, the order in which words are used is often important to their meaning.
8. Unlike in other languages, the context and function of English words are rarely related.
9. Planning techniques, such as brainstorming and journal writing, are encouraged.
10. Writing is usually taught as a series of skills, not as a process.

CHAPTER 61

Grammar and Style for Multilingual Writers

For multilingual writers (as for many native English writers), grammar can be a persistent problem. Grammatical knowledge in a second language usually develops slowly, with time and practice, and much about English is idiomatic and not subject to easy-to-learn rules. This chapter is designed to provide you with the tools you will need to address some of the most common grammatical problems multilingual writers face.

61a Using Verbs

❶ Subject-Verb Agreement

English **verbs** change their form according to person, number, and tense. The verb in a sentence must **agree** with the subject in both person and number. **Person** refers to *who* or *what* is performing the action of the verb (for example, *I, you,* or someone else), and **number** refers to *how many* people or things are performing the action (one or more than one).

See A3

In English, the rules for **subject-verb agreement** are very important. Unless you use the correct person and number in the verbs in your sentences, you will confuse your English-speaking audience by communicating meanings you do not intend.

See 45a

Close-Up SUBJECT-VERB AGREEMENT

Follow these basic guidelines when selecting verbs for your sentences:

- If the subject consists of only one noun or pronoun, use a singular verb.

  He is at the park.

- If the subject consists of two or more nouns or pronouns connected with the word *and*, use a plural verb.

  Bob and Carol are at the park.

  (continued)

SUBJECT-VERB AGREEMENT *(continued)*

• If the subject contains both a singular and a plural noun or pronoun connected with the word *or*, the verb should agree with the noun that is nearer to it.

Either <u>Bob</u> or <u>the boys</u> <u>are</u> at the park.

Either <u>the boys</u> or <u>Bob</u> <u>is</u> at the park.

Note: Don't be confused by phrases that come between the subject and the verb. The verb should agree with the subject of the sentence, not with a noun that appears within an intervening phrase.

<u>The woman</u> with all of the children <u>is</u> at the park.

<u>The coach</u>, as well as the players, <u>is</u> nervous.

For information on subject-verb agreement with **indefinite pronouns**, such as *each, everyone*, and *nobody*, **see 45a4**.

---

② **Verb Tense**

See 40b

In English, the form of the verb changes to indicate **tense**—when the action of the verb takes place (in the past, present, or future). One problem that many nonnative speakers of English have with English verb tenses results

See 40a2

from the large number of **irregular verbs** in English. For example, the first-person singular present tense of *be* is not "I be" but "I am," and the past tense is not "I beed" but "I was."

Note: Multilingual writers whose first language is Chinese, Japanese, Korean, Russian, Thai, or Vietnamese are especially likely to have difficulty with verb tenses.

Close-Up CHOOSING THE SIMPLEST VERB FORMS

Some nonnative English speakers use verb forms that are more complicated than they need to be. They may do this because their native language uses more complicated verb forms than English does or because they "overcorrect" their verbs into complicated forms. Specifically, nonnative speakers tend to use progressive and perfect verb forms instead of simple verb forms. To communicate your ideas clearly to an English-speaking audience, choose the simplest possible verb form.

3 Auxiliary Verbs

The **auxiliary verbs** (also known as **helping verbs**) *be, have,* and *do* are used to create some present, past, and future forms of verbs in English: "Julio is taking a vacation"; "I have been tired lately"; "He does not need a license." The auxiliary verbs *be, have,* and *do* change form to reflect the time frame of the action or situation and to agree with the subject.

Note: Multilingual writers whose first language is Arabic, Chinese, Creole, Haitian, or Russian are likely to have more difficulty with auxiliary verbs because their first language sometimes omits the *be* verb.

Close-Up AUXILIARY VERBS

Only auxiliary verbs, not the verbs they "help," change form to indicate person, number, and tense.

Present: We have to eat.

Past: We had to eat. (*not* "We had to ate.")

Modal auxiliaries (such as *can* and *should*) do not change form to indicate tense, person, or number.

See A3

EXERCISE 61.1

A student wrote the following two paragraphs as part of an essay for his composition class. He was asked to write about several interviews he conducted with people in his future profession, hotel management. The paragraphs contain errors in subject-verb agreement and verb tense, which the student's instructor underlined. Correct the underlined verbs by changing their form: begin by considering when the action took place, and then choose the simplest appropriate verb form to express that time. (Be sure to pay attention to the meaning and context of the sentences to determine which verb form is appropriate.)

In the past, when someone (1) ask me why I was interested in the hotel business, I always (2) have a hard time answering that question. I do not know exactly when and why I (3) decide to be a hotel manager. The only reason I can think of is my father. In his current job, he (4) travel a lot, and I have had a few chances to follow him and see other cities. Every time I went with him on a business trip, we (5) spended the night in a hotel, and I was surprised at how much hotels (6) does to satisfy their customers. All the employees are always friendly and polite. This gave me a positive image of hotels that made me (7) <u>decided</u> that the hotel business would be right for me.

For this essay, I (8) <u>spended</u> almost two weeks interviewing department heads at a local Hilton Hotel. Mr. Andrew Plain, the person who (9) <u>spend</u> the most time with me, (10) <u>share</u> an experience related to when he first got into the business. One of his first jobs was to plan a wedding, and he (11) <u>feel</u> a lot of responsibility because he (12) <u>believe</u> that a wedding is a one-time life experience for most people. So he wanted to take care of everything and make sure that everything was on track. To prepare for the wedding, he (13) <u>need</u> to work almost every Sunday, and one night he even (14) <u>have</u> to sleep in his office to attend the early wedding ceremony the next morning. From my experience with this interview, I realized that the people who are interested in the hotel business (15) <u>needs</u> great dedication to their career.

4 Negative Verbs

The meaning of a verb may be made negative in English in a variety of ways, chiefly by adding the words *not* or *does not* to the verb (is, is *not*; can ski, *can't* ski; drives a car, *does not* drive a car).

Close-Up CORRECTING DOUBLE NEGATIVES

A **double negative** is an error that occurs when the meaning of a verb is made negative not just once but twice in a single sentence.

any   has

Henry doesn't have ~~no~~ friends. (*or* Henry ~~doesn't have~~ no friends.)

I looked for relevant articles, but there weren~~'t~~ none. (*or* I looked for
any
relevant articles, but there weren't ~~none~~.)

Note: Multilingual writers whose first language is Spanish may tend to use double negatives.

---

5 Phrasal Verbs

Many verbs in English are composed of two or more words that are combined to create a new idiomatic expression—for example, *check up on, run for, turn into,* and *wait on.* These verbs are called **phrasal verbs**. It is important to become familiar with phrasal verbs and their definitions so you will recognize these verbs as phrasal verbs instead of as verbs that are followed by prepositions.

Separable Phrasal Verbs Often, the words that make up a phrasal verb can be separated by a direct object. In these **separable phrasal verbs**, the object can come either before or after the preposition. For example, "Ellen turned down the job offer" and "Ellen turned the job offer down" are both correct. However, when the object is a pronoun, the pronoun must come before the preposition. Therefore, "Ellen turned it down" is correct, but "Ellen turned down it" is incorrect.

Close-Up SEPARABLE PHRASAL VERBS

Verb	Definition
call off	cancel
carry on	continue
cheer up	make happy
clean out	clean the inside of
cut down	reduce
figure out	solve
fill in	substitute
find out	discover
give back	return something
give up	stop doing something or stop trying
leave out	omit
pass on	transmit
put away	place something in its proper place
put back	place something in its original place
put off	postpone
start over	start again
talk over	discuss
throw away/out	discard
touch up	repair

Inseparable Phrasal Verbs Some phrasal verbs—such as *look into, make up for*, and *break into*—consist of words that can never be separated. With these **inseparable phrasal verbs**, you do not have a choice about where to place the object; the object must always directly follow the preposition. For example, "Anna cared for her niece" is correct, but "Anna cared her niece for" is incorrect.

Close-Up   INSEPARABLE PHRASAL VERBS

Verb	Definition
come down with	develop an illness
come up with	produce
do away with	abolish
fall behind in	lag
get along with	be congenial with
get away with	avoid punishment
keep up with	maintain the same achievement or speed
look up to	admire
make up for	compensate
put up with	tolerate
run into	meet by chance
see to	arrange
show up	arrive
stand by	wait or remain loyal to
stand up for	support
watch out for	beware of or protect

6 Voice

See
40d
Verbs may be in either active or passive <u>voice</u>. When the subject of a sentence performs the action of the verb, the verb is in **active voice**. When the action of the verb is performed on the subject, the verb is in **passive voice**.

Karla and Miguel <u>purchased</u> the tickets. (active voice)

The tickets <u>were purchased</u> by Karla and Miguel. (passive voice)

Because your writing will usually be clearer and more concise if you use the active voice, you should use the passive voice only when you have a good reason to do so. For example, in scientific writing, it is common for writers to use the passive voice in order to convey scientific objectivity (lack of bias).

When deciding whether to use the passive or active voice, you need to consider what you want to focus on. In the first example above, the focus is on Karla and Miguel. However, the second example above, which uses the passive voice, puts the focus on the fact that the tickets were purchased rather than on who purchased them.

Note: Multilingual writers whose first language is Creole, Japanese, Korean, Russian, Thai, or Vietnamese encounter unique challenges with voice when writing in English.

⑦ Transitive and Intransitive Verbs

Many nonnative English speakers find it difficult to decide whether or not a verb needs an object and in what order direct and indirect objects should appear in a sentence. Learning the difference between transitive verbs and intransitive verbs can help you with such problems.

A **transitive verb** is a verb that has a direct object: "My father asked a question" (subject + verb + direct object). In this example, *asked* is a transitive verb; it needs an object to complete its meaning.

An **intransitive verb** is a verb that does not take an object: "The doctor smiled" (subject + verb). In this example, *smiled* is an intransitive verb; it does not need an object to complete its meaning.

A transitive verb may be followed by a direct object or by both an indirect object and a direct object. (An indirect object answers the question "To whom?" or "For whom?") The indirect object may come before or after the direct object. If the indirect object follows the direct object, the preposition *to* or *for* must precede the indirect object.

> s   v   do
> Keith wrote a letter. (subject + verb + direct object)

> s   v   io   do
> Keith wrote his friend a letter. (subject + verb + indirect object + direct object)

> s   v   do   io
> Keith wrote a letter to his friend. (subject + verb + direct object + *to/for* + indirect object)

Some verbs in English look similar and have similar meanings, except that one is transitive and the other is intransitive. For example, *lie* is intransitive, *lay* is transitive; *sit* is intransitive, *set* is transitive; *rise* is intransitive, *raise* is transitive. Knowing whether a verb is transitive or intransitive will help you with troublesome verb pairs such as these and will help you place words in the correct order. (**See Appendix C** for more on these verb pairs.)

Note: It is also important to know whether a verb is transitive or intransitive because only transitive verbs can be used in the **passive voice**. To determine whether a verb is transitive or intransitive—that is, to determine whether or not it needs an object—consult the example phrases in a dictionary.

See 40d

8 Infinitives and Gerunds

In English, two verb forms may be used as nouns: **infinitives**, which always begin with *to* (as in *to work, to sleep, to eat*), and **gerunds**, which always end in *-ing* (as in *working, sleeping, eating*).

> To bite into this steak requires better teeth than mine. (infinitive used as a noun)

> Cooking is one of my favorite hobbies. (gerund used as a noun)

Sometimes the gerund and the infinitive form of the same verb can be used interchangeably. For example, "He continued *to sleep*" and "He continued *sleeping*" convey the same meaning. However, this is not always the case. Saying, "Marco and Lisa stopped *to eat* at Julio's Café" is not the same as saying, "Marco and Lisa stopped *eating* at Julio's Café." In this example, the meaning of the sentence changes depending on whether a gerund or infinitive is used.

Note: Multilingual writers whose first language is Arabic, Chinese, Farsi, French, Greek, Korean, Portuguese, Spanish, or Vietnamese may have difficulty with gerunds.

9 Participles

In English, verb forms called **present participles** and **past participles** are frequently used as adjectives. Present participles end in *-ing*, as in *working, sleeping*, and *eating*, and past participles usually end in *-ed, -t,* or *-en*, as in *worked, slept*, and *eaten*.

> She had a burning desire to be president. (present participle used as an adjective)

> Some people think raw fish is healthier than cooked fish. (past participle used as an adjective)

A **participial phrase** is a group of words consisting of the participle plus the noun phrase that functions as the object or complement of the action being expressed by the participle. To avoid confusion, the participial phrase must be placed as close as possible to the noun it modifies.

> Having visited San Francisco last week, Jim and Lynn showed us pictures from their vacation. (The participial phrase is used as an adjective that modifies *Jim and Lynn*.)

10 Verbs Formed from Nouns

In English, nouns can sometimes be used as verbs, with no change in form (other than the addition of an *-s* for agreement with third-person singular subjects or the addition of past tense endings). For example, the nouns *chair, book, frame,* and *father* can all be used as verbs.

She <u>chairs</u> a committee on neighborhood safety.

We <u>booked</u> a flight to New York for next week.

I will <u>frame</u> my daughter's diploma after she graduates.

He <u>fathered</u> seventeen children.

61b Using Nouns

<u>Nouns</u> name things: people, animals, objects, places, feelings, ideas. If a noun names one thing, it is singular; if a noun names more than one thing, it is plural.

See A1

1 Recognizing Noncount Nouns

Some English nouns do not have a plural form. These are called **noncount nouns** because what they name cannot be counted. (**Count nouns** name items that *can* be counted, such as *cat* or *desk*.)

Note: Multilingual writers whose first language is Chinese or Japanese are likely to have trouble with noncount nouns.

Close-Up   NONCOUNT NOUNS

The following commonly used nouns are noncount nouns. These words have no plural forms. Therefore, you should never add *-s* to them.

advice	homework
clothing	information
education	knowledge
equipment	luggage
evidence	merchandise
furniture	revenge

EXERCISE 61.2

A student wrote the following paragraph on page 616 as part of an essay about her experiences learning English. Read the paragraph, and decide which of the underlined words need to be made plural and which should remain unchanged. If a word should be made plural, make the necessary correction. If a word is correct as is, mark it with a *C*.

Visiting Ireland for three (1) <u>month</u> expanded my (2) <u>knowledge</u> of English. I took a part-time English (3) <u>course</u>, which was the key to improving my writing. The (4) <u>course</u> helped me understand the essential (5) <u>rule</u> of English, and I learned a lot of new (6) <u>vocabulary</u> and expressions. In the first three (7) <u>lecture</u>, the teacher, Mr. Nelson, explained the fundamentals of writing in English. My (8) <u>enthusiasm</u> for the English language increased because I realized the importance of this (9) <u>language</u> for my (10) <u>future</u>. Mr. Nelson recommended that I read more English (11) <u>book</u>. I took his advice, and my English got better.

❷ Using Articles with Nouns

English has two kinds of **articles**, *indefinite* and *definite*.

Use an **indefinite article** (*a* or *an*) with a noun when readers are not familiar with the noun you are naming—for example, when you are introducing the noun for the first time. To say, "James entered *a* building," signals to the audience that you are introducing the idea of the building for the first time. The building is indefinite, or not specific, until it has been identified.

The indefinite article *a* is used when the word following it (which may be a noun or an adjective) begins with a consonant or with a consonant sound: *a tree, a onetime offer*. The indefinite article *an* is used if the word following it begins with a vowel (*a, e, i, o*, or *u*) or with a vowel sound: *an apple, an honor*.

Use the **definite article** (*the*) when the noun you are naming has already been introduced, when the noun is already familiar to readers, or when the noun to which you refer is specific. To say, "James entered *the* building," signals to readers that you are referring to the same building you mentioned earlier. The building has now become specific and may be referred to by the definite article.

Note: Multilingual writers whose first language is Chinese, Farsi, Japanese, Russian, or Swahili will have difficulty with articles.

Close-Up   USING ARTICLES WITH NOUNS

There are two exceptions to the rules governing the use of articles with nouns:

1. **Plural** nouns do not require indefinite articles: "I love horses," not "I love <u>a</u> horses." (However, plural nouns do require definite articles if you have already introduced the noun or if you are referring to a specific noun: "I love <u>the</u> horses on the carousel in the park near my house.")

2. **Noncount nouns** may not require articles: "Love conquers all," not "<u>A</u> love conquers all" or "<u>The</u> love conquers all."

EXERCISE 61.3

The following introductory paragraph of an essay about renewable energy power sources was written for a composition course. Read the paragraph, and decide whether or not each of the underlined nouns or noun phrases requires an article. If a noun or noun phrase is correct as is, mark it with a *C*. If a noun or noun phrase needs an article, indicate whether that article should be *a, an,* or *the*.

(1) Use of electrical power has increased dramatically over (2) last thirty years and continues to rise. (3) Most ordinary sources of (4) electricity require (5) oil, (6) gas, or (7) uranium, which are not (8) renewable resources. Living without (9) electrical power is not feasible as long as everything in our lives depends on (10) electricity, but (11) entire world will be in (12) big crisis if (13) ignorance regarding renewable energy continues. (14) Renewable energy, including (15) solar energy, (16) wind energy, (17) hydro energy, and (18) biomass energy, needs (19) more attention from (20) scientists.

❸ Using Other Determiners with Nouns

Determiners are words that function as adjectives to limit or qualify the meaning of nouns. In addition to articles, **demonstrative pronouns, possessive nouns and pronouns, numbers** (both **cardinal** and **ordinal**), and other words indicating number and order can function in this way.

Close-Up   USING OTHER DETERMINERS WITH NOUNS

- **Demonstrative pronouns** (*this, that, these, those*) communicate the following:

  1. the relative distance of the noun from the speaker's position (*this* and *these* for things that are *near, that* and *those* for things that are *far*): *this* book on my desk, *that* book on your desk; *these* shoes on my feet, *those* shoes in my closet.

  2. the number of things indicated (*this* and *that* for *singular* nouns, *these* and *those* for *plural* nouns): *this* (or *that*) flower in the vase, *these* (or *those*) flowers in the garden.

- **Possessive nouns and possessive pronouns** (*Ashraf's, his, their*) show who or what the noun belongs to: *Maria's* courage, *everybody's* fears, the *country's* natural resources, *my* personality, *our* groceries.

(continued)

USING OTHER DETERMINERS WITH NOUNS *(continued)*

- **Cardinal** numbers (*three, fifty, a thousand*) indicate how many of the noun you mean: *seven* continents. **Ordinal** numbers (*first, tenth, thirtieth*) indicate in what order the noun appears among other items: *third* planet.
- Words other than numbers may indicate **amount** (*many, few*) and **order** (*next, last*) and function in the same ways as cardinal and ordinal numbers: *few* opportunities, *last* chance.

61c Using Pronouns

See A2

Any English noun may be replaced by a <u>pronoun</u>. For example, *doctor* may be replaced by *he* or *she*, *books* by *them*, and *computer* by *it*.

❶ Pronoun Reference

See 41c

<u>Pronoun reference</u> is very important in English sentences, where the noun the pronoun replaces (the **antecedent**) must be easily identified. In general, you should place the pronoun as close as possible to the noun it replaces so the noun to which the pronoun refers is clear. If this is impossible, use the noun itself instead of replacing it with a pronoun.

Unclear: When Tara met Emily, she was nervous. (Does *she* refer to Tara or to Emily?)

Clear: When Tara met Emily, <u>Tara</u> was nervous.

Unclear: Stefano and Victor love his sneaker collection. (Whose sneaker collection—Stefano's, Victor's, or someone else's?)

Clear: Stefano and Victor love <u>Emilio's</u> sneaker collection.

Note: Multilingual writers whose first language is Spanish or Thai will likely have difficulty with pronoun reference.

❷ Pronoun Placement

Never use a pronoun immediately after the noun it replaces. For example, do not say, "Most of my classmates *they* are smart"; instead, say, "Most of my classmates are smart."

The only exception to this rule occurs with an **intensive pronoun**, which ends in *-self* and emphasizes the preceding noun or pronoun: *Marta <u>herself</u> was eager to hear the results.*

❸ Indefinite Pronouns

Unlike **personal pronouns** (*I, you, he, she, it, we, they, me, him, her, us, them*, and so on), **indefinite pronouns** do not refer to a particular person, place, or thing. Therefore, an indefinite pronoun does not require an antecedent. **Indefinite pronoun subjects** (*anybody, nobody, each, either, someone, something, all, some*), like personal pronouns, must <u>agree</u> in number with the sentence's verb.

See 45a

> *has*
> Nobody ̭have failed the exam. (*Nobody* is a singular subject and requires a singular verb.)

❹ Appositives

Appositives are nouns or noun phrases that identify or rename an adjacent noun or pronoun. An appositive usually follows the word it explains or modifies but can sometimes precede it.

> My parents, Mary and John, live in Louisiana. (*Mary and John* identifies *parents.*)

Note: The <u>case</u> of a pronoun in an appositive depends on the case of the word it identifies.

See 41a

If an appositive is *not* essential to the meaning of the sentence, use commas to set off the appositive from the rest of the sentence. If an appositive *is* essential to the meaning of the sentence, do not use commas.

> His aunt Trang is in the hospital. (*Trang* is necessary to the meaning of the sentence because it identifies which aunt is in the hospital.)

> Akta's car, a 1994 Jeep Cherokee, broke down last night, so she had to walk home. (*a 1994 Jeep Cherokee* is not essential to the meaning of the sentence.)

❺ Pronouns and Gender

A pronoun must agree in **gender** with the noun to which it refers.

> My *sister* sold *her* old car.

> Your *uncle* is walking *his* dog.

Keep in mind that in English, most nonhuman nouns are referred to as *it* because they do not have grammatical gender. However, exceptions are sometimes made for pets, ships, and countries. Pets are often referred to as *he* or *she*, depending on their sex, and ships and countries are sometimes referred to as *she*.

Note: Multilingual writers whose first language is Bengali, Farsi, Gujarati, or Thai are likely to have problems with pronouns and gender.

EXERCISE 61.4

There are no pronouns in the following passage. The repetition of the nouns again and again would seem strange to a native English speaker. Rewrite the passage, replacing as many of the nouns as possible with appropriate pronouns. Be sure that the connection between the pronouns and the nouns they replace is clear.

The young couple seated across from Daniel at dinner the night before were newlyweds from Tokyo. The young couple and Daniel ate together with other guests of the inn at long, low tables in a large dining room with straw mat flooring. The man introduced himself immediately in English, shook Daniel's hand firmly, and, after learning that Daniel was not a tourist but a resident working in Osaka, gave Daniel a business card. The man had just finished college and was working at the man's first real job, clerking in a bank. Even in a sweatsuit, the man looked ready for the office: chin closely shaven, bristly hair neatly clipped, nails clean and buffed. After a while the man and Daniel exhausted the man's store of English and drifted into Japanese. The man's wife, shy up until then, took over as the man fell silent. The woman and Daniel talked about the new popularity of hot springs spas in the countryside around the inn, the difficulty of finding good schools for the children the woman hoped to have soon, the differences between food in Tokyo and Osaka. The woman's husband ate busily. From time to time the woman refilled the man's beer glass or served the man radish pickles from a china bowl in the middle of the table, and then returned to the conversation.

61d Using Adjectives and Adverbs

See Ch. 42, A4–5

<u>Adjectives and adverbs</u> are words that **modify** (describe, limit, or qualify) other words.

❶ Position of Adjectives and Adverbs

Adjectives in English usually appear *before* the nouns they modify. A native speaker of English would not say, "*Cars red and black* are involved in more accidents than *cars blue or green*" but would say instead, "*Red and black cars* are involved in more accidents than *blue or green cars.*"

However, adjectives may appear *after* linking verbs ("The name seemed *familiar*"), *after* direct objects ("The coach was *tired* but *happy*"), and *after* indefinite pronouns ("Anything *sad* makes me cry").

Adverbs may appear before or after the verbs they describe, but they should be placed as close to the verb as possible: not "I *told* John that I couldn't meet him for lunch *politely*," but "I *politely told* John that I couldn't meet him for lunch" or "I *told* John *politely* that I couldn't meet him for lunch." When an adverb describes an adjective or another adverb, it usually comes *before* that adjective or adverb: "The essay has *basically* sound logic"; "You must express yourself *absolutely* clearly."

Never place an adverb between the verb and the direct object.

Incorrect: Rolf drank *quickly* the water.

Correct: Rolf drank the water *quickly* (or, Rolf *quickly* drank the water).

Incorrect: Suong took *quietly* the test.

Correct: Suong *quietly* took the test (or, Suong took the test *quietly*).

Note: Multilingual writers whose first language is Creole, French, or Haitian are likely to have problems with adverbs.

❷ Order of Adjectives

A single noun may be modified by more than one adjective, perhaps even by a whole list of adjectives. Given a list of three or four adjectives, most native speakers would arrange them in a sentence in the same order. If, for example, shoes are to be described as *green* and *big*, numbering *two*, and of the type worn for playing *tennis*, a native speaker would say "two big green tennis shoes." Generally, the adjectives that are most important in completing the meaning of the noun are placed closest to the noun.

Close-Up ORDER OF ADJECTIVES

1. Articles (*a, the*), demonstratives (*this, those*), and possessives (*his, our, Maria's, everybody's*)
2. Amounts (*one, five, many, few*), order (*first, next, last*)
3. Personal opinions (*nice, ugly, crowded, pitiful*)
4. Sizes and shapes (*small, tall, straight, crooked*)
5. Age (*young, old, modern, ancient*)
6. Colors (*black, white, red, blue, dark, light*)
7. Nouns functioning as adjectives to form a unit with the noun (*soccer* ball, *cardboard* box, *history* class)

EXERCISE 61.5

Write five original sentences in which two or three adjectives describe a noun. Be sure that the adjectives are in the correct order.

 61e **Using Prepositions**

See
A6

In English, **prepositions** (such as *to, from, at, with, among, between*) give meaning to nouns by linking them with other words and other parts of the sentence. Prepositions convey various kinds of information:

- Relations to **time** (*at* nine o'clock, *in* five minutes, *for* a month)
- Relations of **place** (*in* the classroom, *at* the library, *beside* the chair) and **direction** (*to* the market, *onto* the stage, *toward* the freeway)
- Relations of **association** (go *with* someone, the tip *of* the iceberg)
- Relations of **purpose** (working *for* money, dieting *to* lose weight)

❶ Commonly Used Prepositional Phrases

In English, the use of prepositions is often **idiomatic** rather than governed by grammatical rules. In many cases, therefore, learners of English as a second language need to memorize which prepositions are used in which phrases.

In English, some prepositions that relate to time have specific uses with certain nouns, such as days, months, and seasons:

- *On* is used with days and specific dates: *on* Tuesday, *on* September 11, 2001.
- *In* is used with months, seasons, and years: *in* November, *in* the spring, *in* 1999.
- *In* is also used when referring to some parts of the day: *in* the morning, *in* the afternoon, *in* the evening.
- *At* is used to refer to other parts of the day: *at* noon, *at* night, *at* seven o'clock.

Close-Up DIFFICULT PREPOSITIONAL PHRASES

The following phrases (accompanied by their correct prepositions) sometimes cause difficulties for multilingual writers:

according *to*	appeal *to*	*at* least
apologize *to*	different *from*	*at* most

(continued)

DIFFICULT PREPOSITIONAL PHRASES *(continued)*

refer *to*   similar *to*   subscribe *to*
relevant *to*

❷ Commonly Confused Prepositions

The prepositions *to, in, on, into,* and *onto* are very similar to one another
and are therefore easily confused.

Close-Up USING COMMON PREPOSITIONS

When deciding whether to use *to, in, on, into,* or *onto*, follow these guidelines:

- *To* is the basic preposition of direction. It indicates movement toward a
  physical place: "She went *to* the restaurant"; "He went *to* the meeting."
  To is also used to form the infinitive of a verb: "He wanted *to deposit*
  his paycheck before noon"; "Irene offered *to drive* Maria to the baseball
  game."

- *In* indicates that something is within the boundaries of a particular space
  or period of time: "My son is *in* the garden"; "I like to ski *in* the winter";
  "The map is *in* the car."

- *On* indicates position above or the state of being supported by something: "The toys are *on* the porch"; "The baby sat *on* my lap"; "The
  book is *on* top of the magazine."

- *Into* indicates movement to the inside or interior of something: "She
  walked *into* the room"; "I threw the stone *into* the lake"; "He put the
  photos *into* the box." Although *into* and *in* are sometimes interchangeable,
  note that usage depends on whether the subject is stationary or moving. *Into* usually indicates movement, as in "I jumped *into* the water." *In*
  usually indicates a stationary position relative to the object of the preposition, as in "Mary is swimming *in* the water."

- *Onto* indicates movement to a position on top of something: "The cat
  jumped *onto* the chair"; "Crumbs are falling *onto* the floor." Both *on* and
  onto can be used to indicate a position on top of something (and therefore they can sometimes be used interchangeably), but *onto* specifies
  that the subject is moving to a place from a different place or from an
  outside position.

Close-Up PREPOSITIONS IN IDIOMATIC EXPRESSIONS

Common Nonnative Speaker Usage	Native Speaker Usage
according *with*	according *to*
apologize *at*	apologize *to*
appeal *at*	appeal *to*
believe *at*	believe *in*
different *to*	different *from*
for least, *for* most	*at* least, *at* most
refer *at*	refer *to*
relevant *with*	relevant *to*
similar *with*	similar *to*
subscribe *with*	subscribe *to*

EXERCISE 61.6

A student in a composition class wrote the following paragraphs as part of an essay about her experiences learning to write in English. In several cases, she chose the wrong prepositions. The student's instructor has underlined the misused prepositions. Your task is to replace each underlined preposition with a correct preposition. (In some cases, there may be more than one possible correct answer.)

My first experience writing (1) of English took place (2) at my early youth. I don't remember what the experience was like, but I do know that I have improved my writing skills since then. The improvement stems from various reasons. One major impact (3) to my writing was the fact that I attended an American school (4) of my country. This helped a lot because the first language (5) to the school was English. Being surrounded (6) in English helped me improve both my verbal skills and my writing skills. Another major factor that helped me develop my English writing skills, especially my grammar and vocabulary, was reading novels.

(7) At the future, I plan to improve my writing skills in English by participating (8) to several activities. I plan to read more novels so I can further develop the grammar and vocabulary skills that will help me earn my degree. I also plan to communicate verbally with native speakers and to listen (9) at public speeches (such as the president's state of the union address), which usually contain rich vocabulary. But my main plan is to keep writing more essays and discussing my writing (10) to my instructor. The more I write, the more confident I will become and the more my writing will improve. And there is always room for improvement.

61f Understanding Word Order

Word order is extremely important in English sentences. For example, word order may indicate which word is the subject of a sentence and which is the object, or it may indicate whether a sentence is a question or a statement.

1 Standard Word Order

Like Chinese, English is an "SVO" language, or one in which the most typical sentence pattern is "subject-verb-object." (Arabic, by contrast, is an example of a "VSO" language.)

2 Word Order in Questions

Word order in questions can be particularly troublesome for speakers of languages other than English, partly because there are so many different ways to form questions in English.

Close-Up WORD ORDER IN QUESTIONS

1. To **create a yes/no question** from a statement whose verb is a form of *be* (*am, is, are, was, were*), move the verb so it precedes the subject.

   Rasheem <u>is</u> in his laboratory.

   <u>Is</u> Rasheem in his laboratory?

   When the statement is *not* a form of *be*, change the verb to include a form of *do* as a helping verb, and then move that helping verb so it precedes the subject.

   Rasheem <u>researched</u> the depletion of the ozone level.

   <u>Did</u> Rasheem <u>research</u> the depletion of the ozone level?

2. To **create a yes/no question** from a statement that includes one or more helping verbs, move the first helping verb so it precedes the subject.

   Rasheem <u>is researching</u> the depletion of the ozone layer.

   <u>Is</u> Rasheem <u>researching</u> the depletion of the ozone layer?

3. To **create a question asking for information**, replace the information being asked for with an interrogative word (*who, what, where, why, when, how*) at the beginning of the question, and invert the order of the subject and verb as with a yes/no question.

   (continued)

WORD ORDER IN QUESTIONS *(continued)*

Rasheem <u>is</u> in his laboratory.

Where <u>is</u> Rasheem?

Rasheem <u>is researching</u> the depletion of the ozone layer.

What <u>is</u> Rasheem <u>researching</u>?

Rasheem <u>researched</u> the depletion of the ozone level.

What <u>did</u> Rasheem <u>research</u>?

If the interrogative word is the subject of the question, however, do *not* invert the subject and verb.

Who <u>is researching</u> the depletion of the ozone level?

4. You can also form a question by adding a **tag question** (such as *won't he?* or *didn't I?*) to the end of a statement. If the verb of the main statement is *positive*, then the verb of the tag question is *negative*; if the verb of the main statement is *negative*, then the verb of the tag question is *positive*.

Rasheem <u>is</u> researching the depletion of the ozone layer, <u>isn't</u> he?

Rasheem <u>doesn't</u> intend to write his dissertation about the depletion of the ozone layer, <u>does</u> he?

3 **Word Order in Imperative Sentences**

Imperative sentences state commands. It is common for the subject of an imperative sentence to be left out because the word *you* is understood to be the subject: "Go to school"; "Eat your dinner." Therefore, the word order pattern in an imperative sentence is usually "verb-object," or "VO."

61g **Distinguishing Commonly Confused Words**

A number of word pairs in English have similar meanings. These word pairs can be confusing to nonnative English speakers because the ways in which the expressions are used in sentences are different although their meanings may be similar. (For additional examples of commonly confused words, **see Appendix C**.)

NO **AND** *NOT*

No is an adjective; *not* is an adverb. Therefore, use *no* with nouns, and use *not* with verbs, adjectives, and other adverbs.

She has <u>no</u> desire to go to the football game.

Sergio's sisters are <u>not</u> friendly.

TOO AND VERY

Too is an intensifier. It is used to add emphasis and to indicate excess.

It is <u>too</u> cold outside to go swimming.

Very is also an intensifier. It means "greatly" or "intensely," but not to excess.

It was <u>very</u> cold outside, but not cold enough to keep us from playing in the backyard.

EVEN, EVEN IF, AND EVEN THOUGH

As an adverb, *even* is used to intensify or to indicate surprise.

Greta felt <u>even</u> worse than she looked.

<u>Even</u> my little brother knows how to figure that out!

Even if is used where there is a condition that may or may not occur.

<u>Even if</u> it rains tomorrow, I'm going to the park.

Even though is similar in meaning to *although*.

<u>Even though</u> Christopher is a very fast runner, he did not make the national track team.

A FEW/A LITTLE AND FEW/LITTLE

A few and *a little* mean "not much," but "some" or "enough." *A few* is used with count nouns. *A little* is used with noncount nouns.

We have <u>a few screws</u> remaining from the project.

There is <u>a little paint</u> left in the can.

Few and *little* mean "a small number"—there are some, but perhaps not as much as one would like.

<u>Few singers</u> are as talented as Kelly.

I have <u>little hope</u> that this situation will change.

MUCH AND MANY

Both *much* and *many* mean "a great quantity" or "to a great degree." Use *much* to modify noncount nouns: *much experience*; *much money*. Use *many* to modify count nouns: *many people*; *many incidents*.

MOST OF, MOST, AND THE MOST

Most and *most of* have similar meanings. *Most of* means "nearly all of something." Use *most of* when the noun that follows is a specific plural noun. When you use *most of*, be sure to use the definite article *the* before the noun.

<u>Most of the children</u> had cookies for dessert.

Most is used for more general observations and means "nearly all."

Most houses in the United States have electricity.

The most is used for comparing more than two of something.

Thomas has the most jellybeans.

Pedro is the most experienced of the engineers.

SOME AND ANY

Some denotes an unspecified amount or quantity that may be part of a larger amount. It can modify both count and noncount nouns: *some water*; *some melons*. *Any* indicates an unspecified amount, which may be none, some, or all. It can modify both count and noncount nouns: *any person*; *any luggage*.

Parts of Speech

The eight basic **parts of speech**—the building blocks for all English sentences—are *nouns, pronouns, verbs, adjectives, adverbs, prepositions, conjunctions*, and *interjections*. How a word is classified depends on its function in a sentence.

A1 Nouns

<u>Nouns</u> name people, animals, places, things, ideas, actions, or qualities.

ml 61b

A **common noun** names any of a class of people, places, or things: *artist, judge, building, event, city.*

A **proper noun,** always capitalized, refers to a particular person, place, or thing: *Mary Cassatt, Crimean War.*

A **count noun** names something that can be counted: *five dogs, two dozen grapes.*

A **noncount noun** names a quantity that is not countable: *time, dust, work, gold.* Noncount nouns generally have only a singular form.

A **collective noun** designates a group thought of as a unit: *committee, class, family.* Collective nouns are generally singular unless the members of the group are referred to as individuals.

An **abstract noun** refers to an intangible idea or quality: *love, hate, justice, anger, fear, prejudice.*

A2 Pronouns

<u>Pronouns</u> are words used in place of nouns or other pronouns. The word for which a pronoun stands is its **antecedent**.

ml 61c

If you use a <u>quotation</u> in your essay, you must document <u>it</u>. (Pronoun *it* refers to antecedent *quotation*.)

Note: Although different types of pronouns may have exactly the same form, they are distinguished from one another by their function in a sentence.

A **personal pronoun** stands for a person or thing: *I, me, we, us, my, mine, our, ours, you, your, yours, he, she, it, its, him, his, her, hers, they, them, their, theirs.*

The firm made Debbie an offer, and she couldn't refuse it.

An **indefinite pronoun** does not refer to any particular person or thing, so it does not require an antecedent. Indefinite pronouns include *another, any, each, few, many, some, nothing, one, anyone, everyone, everybody, everything, someone, something, either,* and *neither.*

Many are called, but few are chosen.

A **reflexive pronoun** ends with *-self* and refers to a recipient of the action that is the same as the actor: *myself, yourself, himself, herself, itself, oneself, themselves, ourselves, yourselves.*

They found themselves in downtown Pittsburgh.

An **intensive pronoun** emphasizes a noun or pronoun that directly precedes it. Intensive pronouns have the same form as reflexive pronouns.

Darrow himself was sure his client was innocent.

A **relative pronoun** introduces an adjective or noun clause in a sentence. Relative pronouns include *which, who, whom, that, what, whose, whatever, whoever, whomever,* and *whichever.*

Gandhi was the man who led India to independence. (introduces adjective clause)

Whatever happens will be a surprise. (introduces noun clause)

An **interrogative pronoun** introduces a question. Interrogative pronouns include *who, which, what, whom, whose, whoever, whatever,* and *whichever.*

Who is at the door?

A **demonstrative pronoun** points to a particular thing or group of things. *This, that, these,* and *those* are demonstrative pronouns.

This is one of Shakespeare's early plays.

A **reciprocal pronoun** denotes a mutual relationship. The reciprocal pronouns are *each other* and *one another. Each other* indicates a relationship between two individuals; *one another* denotes a relationship among more than two.

Cathy and I respect each other despite our differences.

Many of our friends do not respect one another.

EXERCISE A.1

In each of the following sentences, circle the type of noun or pronoun (from the options in parentheses) that describes the underlined word in this context.

1. In 2015, NASA's Curiosity rover uncovered possible signs of life on Mars. (common noun, proper noun)
2. These signs of life are formations in a former lake; long ago, Mars had water on its surface. (count noun, noncount noun)
3. The formations resemble similar patterns on Earth that were caused by microorganisms. (demonstrative pronoun, reflexive pronoun, relative pronoun)
4. However, they could have been caused by erosion. (personal pronoun, relative pronoun, intensive pronoun)
5. Thinking about life on other planets inspires wonder in many people. (collective noun, abstract noun)

A3 Verbs

A verb may express either action or a state of being.

> He ran for the train. (physical action)
>
> He thought about taking the bus. (mental action)
>
> Jen became ill after dinner. (state of being)

ml
61a

Verbs can be classified into two groups: *main verbs* and *auxiliary verbs*.

Main Verbs **Main verbs** carry most of the meaning in a sentence or clause. Some main verbs are action verbs.

> Emily Dickinson wrote poetry. (physical action)
>
> He wanted a new laptop. (emotional action)

Other main verbs are linking verbs. A **linking verb** does not show any physical or emotional action. Its function is to link the subject to a **subject complement**, a word or phrase that renames or describes the subject. Linking verbs include *be, become,* and *seem* and verbs that describe sensations—*look, appear, feel, taste, smell,* and so on.

> Carbon disulfide smells bad.

Auxiliary Verbs **Auxiliary verbs** (also called **helping verbs**), such as *be* and *have*, combine with main verbs to form **verb phrases**. Auxiliary verbs indicate tense, voice, or mood.

[auxiliary] [main verb]   [auxiliary] [main verb]

The train has started. We are leaving soon.

[verb phrase]   [verb phrase]

Certain auxiliary verbs, known as **modal auxiliaries**, indicate necessity, possibility, willingness, obligation, or ability.

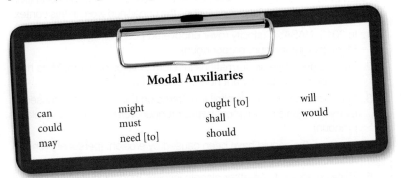

Modal Auxiliaries

can	might	ought [to]	will
could	must	shall	would
may	need [to]	should	

Verbals   **Verbals**, such as *known* or *running* or *to go*, are verb forms that act as adjectives, adverbs, or nouns. A verbal can never serve as a sentence's main verb unless it is used with one or more auxiliary verbs (*He is running*). Verbals include *participles, infinitives,* and *gerunds.*

PARTICIPLES

Virtually every verb has a **present participle**, which ends in *-ing* (*loving, learning*), and a **past participle**, which usually ends in *-d* or *-ed* (*agreed, learned*). Some verbs have irregular past participles (*gone, begun, written*). Participles may function in a sentence as adjectives or as nouns.

> Twenty brands of <u>running</u> shoes were on display. (Present participle serves as adjective modifying *shoes.*)

> The <u>wounded</u> were given emergency first aid. (Past participle serves as subject.)

INFINITIVES

An **infinitive** is made up of *to* and the base form of the verb (*to defeat*). An infinitive may function as an adjective, as an adverb, or as a noun.

> Ann Arbor was clearly the place <u>to be</u>. (Infinitive serves as adjective modifying *place.*)

> Carla went outside <u>to think</u>. (Infinitive serves as adverb modifying *went.*)

> <u>To win</u> was everything. (Infinitive serves as subject.)

GERUNDS

Gerunds, which like present participles end in *-ing*, always function as nouns.

> <u>Seeing</u> is <u>believing</u>. (Gerunds serve as subject and subject complement.)

> Andrew loves <u>skiing</u>. (Gerund is direct object of verb *loves.*)

EXERCISE A.2

In each of the following sentences, underline all full verb phrases, labeling the main verbs (MV) and, where they appear, any auxiliary verbs (AV).

1. The conductor raises his baton, and the lights begin dimming.
2. The show has begun.
3. The orchestra is playing the overture.
4. The music fills the concert hall.
5. The curtain opens, and soon the dancers are spinning around the stage.

EXERCISE A.3

Underline the verbal(s) in each of the following sentences. Then, identify it as a participle (P), infinitive (I), or gerund (G).

1. She put on her swimming cap before diving into the pool.
2. Swimming had always been her favorite sport.
3. In her freshman year, she'd also enjoyed running track, but a bad knee forced her to stop running.
4. She hoped to apply for swimming scholarships.
5. The coaching sessions she attended were helpful; she also attended a series of breathing workshops.

A4 Adjectives

Adjectives describe, limit, qualify, or in some other way modify nouns or pronouns.

ml 61d

Descriptive adjectives name a quality of the noun or pronoun they modify.

After the game, they were exhausted.

They ordered a chocolate soda and a butterscotch sundae.

When articles, pronouns, numbers, and the like function as adjectives, limiting or qualifying nouns or pronouns, they are referred to as **determiners**.

A5 Adverbs

Adverbs describe the action of verbs or modify adjectives or other adverbs (or complete phrases, clauses, or sentences). They answer the questions "How?" "Why?" "Where?" "When?" "Under what conditions?" and "To what extent?"

ml 61d1

He walked rather hesitantly toward the front of the room. (walked *how?*)

Let's meet tomorrow for coffee. (meet *when?*)

Adverbs that modify adjectives or other adverbs limit or qualify the words they modify.

He pitched an <u>almost</u> perfect game yesterday.

Interrogative Adverbs　The **interrogative adverbs** (*how, when, why,* and *where*) introduce questions.

<u>Why</u> did the compound darken?

Conjunctive Adverbs　**Conjunctive adverbs** act as transitional words, joining and relating independent clauses.

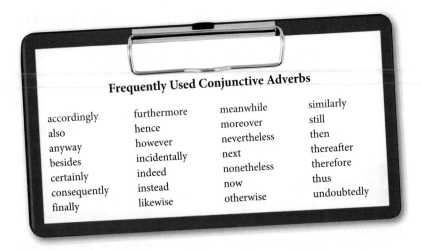

Frequently Used Conjunctive Adverbs

accordingly	furthermore	meanwhile	similarly
also	hence	moreover	still
anyway	however	nevertheless	then
besides	incidentally	next	thereafter
certainly	indeed	nonetheless	therefore
consequently	instead	now	thus
finally	likewise	otherwise	undoubtedly

EXERCISE A.4

In the following sentences, underline any adjectives, and circle the adverbs.

1. When the ruggedly handsome man arrived, the crowd cheered enthusiastically.
2. His modest bow only made everyone scream louder.
3. Gently motioning with his arms, he urged his ardent fans to settle down.
4. "I'm honored to be the next Bachelor," he said, raising a single red rose.
5. My friend turned off the television and said, "Let's spend today outside; the weather is too beautiful for reality TV."

A6　Prepositions

ml
61e

A <u>preposition</u> introduces a noun or pronoun (or a phrase or clause) that functions in the sentence as a noun, linking it to other words in the sentence. The word or word group that the preposition introduces is its **object**.

prep   obj   prep   obj

They received a postcard <u>from</u> Bobby telling <u>about</u> his trip.

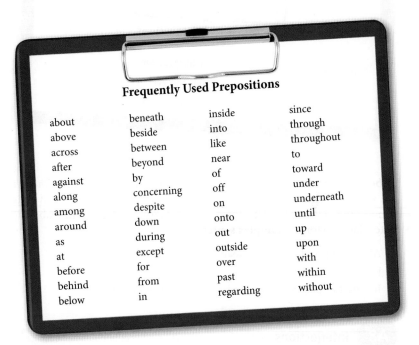

Frequently Used Prepositions

about	beneath	inside	since
above	beside	into	through
across	between	like	throughout
after	beyond	near	to
against	by	of	toward
along	concerning	off	under
among	despite	on	underneath
around	down	onto	until
as	during	out	up
at	except	outside	upon
before	for	over	with
behind	from	past	within
below	in	regarding	without

A7   Conjunctions

Conjunctions connect words, phrases, clauses, or sentences.

Coordinating Conjunctions **Coordinating conjunctions** (*and, or, but, nor, for, so, yet*) connect words, phrases, or clauses of equal weight.

Should I order chicken <u>or</u> fish? (*Or* links two nouns.)

Thoreau wrote *Walden* in 1854, <u>and</u> he died in 1862. (*And* links two independent clauses.)

Correlative Conjunctions Always used in pairs, **correlative conjunctions** also link items of equal weight.

<u>Both</u> Hancock <u>and</u> Jefferson signed the Declaration of Independence. (Correlative conjunctions link nouns.)

<u>Either</u> I will renew my lease, <u>or</u> I will move. (Correlative conjunctions link independent clauses.)

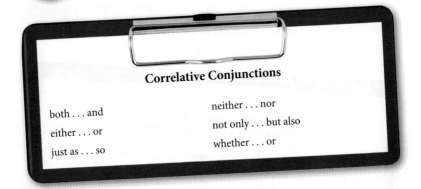

Correlative Conjunctions

both . . . and

either . . . or

just as . . . so

neither . . . nor

not only . . . but also

whether . . . or

Subordinating Conjunctions Words such as *since, because,* and *although* are **subordinating conjunctions**. They introduce adverb clauses and thus connect the sentence's independent (main) clause to a dependent (subordinate) clause to form a **complex sentence**.

> <u>Although</u> people may feel healthy, they can still have medical problems.

> It is best to diagram your garden <u>before</u> you start to plant.

A8 Interjections

Interjections are words used as exclamations to express emotion: *Oh! Ouch! Wow! Alas! Hey!* They may be set off in a sentence by commas, or (for greater emphasis) they may be followed by an exclamation point.

EXERCISE A.5

Each of the following items is followed by a part of speech in parentheses. Identify and underline that part of speech wherever it appears in that sentence.

1. Hey! Can you help me catch that dog? (interjection)
2. The yard was filled with trash after the big party. (preposition)
3. Although it was February 19, the Christmas tree in front of the bank was still decorated. (subordinating conjunction)
4. The student realized he should neither steal from published work nor copy his peers' papers. (correlative conjunction)
5. She looked under the bed, behind the dresser, and in all the drawers, but she could not find the earring. (preposition)

6. The nurse recommended drinking lots of fluids and resting. (coordinating conjunction)
7. It was the first day of her new job. (preposition)
8. When a man called to say he'd found my dog, I was overcome with joy until he said he lived more than a day's drive away. I took the day off and drove without stopping. (subordinating conjunction)
9. I wanted to move to California, but my parents hoped I would stay in the Midwest. (coordinating conjunction)
10. It had been a year since we'd visited our friends in Gulf Shores, Alabama. (subordinating conjunction)

Sentence Review

B1 Basic Sentence Elements

A **sentence** is an independent grammatical unit that contains a subject and a predicate (a verb or verb phrase) and expresses a complete thought.

The quick brown fox jumped over the lazy dog.

It came from outer space.

A **simple subject** is a noun or pronoun (*fox, it*) that tells who or what the sentence is about. A **simple predicate** is a verb or verb phrase (*jumped, came*) that tells or asks something about the subject. The **complete subject** of a sentence includes the simple subject plus all its modifiers (*the quick brown fox*). The **complete predicate** includes the verb or verb phrase and all the words associated with it—such as modifiers, objects, and complements (*jumped over the lazy dog, came from outer space*).

B2 Basic Sentence Patterns

A **simple sentence** consists of at least one subject and one predicate. Simple sentences conform to one of five patterns.

Subject + Intransitive Verb (s + v)

     s   v

The price of gold rose.

     s   v

Stock prices may fall.

In the sentences above, the verbs *rose* and *may fall* are **intransitive**—that is, they do not need an object to complete their meaning.

Subject + Transitive Verb + Direct Object (s + v + do)

     s   v   do

Van Gogh created *The Starry Night*.

     s   v   do

Caroline saved Jake.

In the preceding sentences, the verbs *created* and *saved* are **transitive**—they require an object to complete their meaning. In each case, a **direct object** indicates where the verb's action is directed and who or what is affected by it.

Subject + Transitive Verb + Direct Object + Object Complement (s + v + do + oc)

This pattern includes an object complement that describes or renames the direct object.

> s   v   do   oc
> I found the exam easy. (Object complement *easy* describes direct object *exam*.)

> s   v   do   oc
> The class elected Bridget treasurer. (Object complement *treasurer* renames direct object *Bridget*.)

Subject + Linking Verb + Subject Complement (s + v + sc)

> s   v   sc
> The injection was painless.

> s   v   sc
> David Cameron became prime minister.

In the sentences above, a **linking verb** (*was, became*) connects a subject to a **subject complement** (*painless, prime minister*), a word or phrase that describes or renames the subject. In the first sentence, the complement is a **predicate adjective** that describes the subject; in the second, the complement is a **predicate nominative** that renames the subject. The linking verb is like an equals sign, equating the subject with its complement (*David Cameron = prime minister*).

See A3

Subject + Transitive Verb + Indirect Object + Direct Object (s + v + io + do)

The **indirect object** tells to whom or for whom the verb's action was done.

> s   v   io   do
> Cyrano wrote Roxanne a poem. (Cyrano wrote a poem for Roxanne.)

> s   v   io do
> Hester gave Pearl a kiss. (Hester gave a kiss to Pearl.)

EXERCISE B.1

In each of the following sentences, underline the subject once and the predicate twice. Then, label direct objects (DO), indirect objects (IO), subject complements (SC), and object complements (OC).

>   sc
> *Example:* Isaac Asimov was a science fiction writer.

1. Isaac Asimov first saw science fiction stories in his parents' Brooklyn store.
2. He practiced writing by telling his schoolmates stories.
3. Asimov published his first story in *Astounding Science Fiction*.
4. The magazine's editor, John W. Campbell, encouraged Asimov to continue writing.
5. The young writer researched scientific principles to make his stories more accurate.
6. Asimov's "Foundation" series of novels is a "future history."
7. The World Science Fiction Convention gave the series a Hugo Award.
8. Sometimes Asimov used "Paul French" as a pseudonym.
9. *Biochemistry and Human Metabolism* was Asimov's first nonfiction book.
10. Asimov coined the term *robotics*.

B3 Phrases and Clauses

1 Phrases

A **phrase** is a group of related words that lacks a subject or predicate or both and functions as a single part of speech. It cannot stand alone as a sentence.

- A **verb phrase** consists of a **main verb** and all its auxiliary verbs. (Time *is flying*.) A **noun phrase** includes a noun or pronoun plus all related modifiers. (I'll climb *the highest mountain*.)

See A6
- A **prepositional phrase** consists of a <u>preposition</u>, its object, and any modifiers of that object.

They discussed the ethical implications <u>of the animal studies</u>.

He was last seen heading <u>into the sunset</u>.

See A3
- A **verbal phrase** consists of a <u>verbal</u> and its related objects, modifiers, or complements. A verbal phrase may be a **participial phrase**, a **gerund phrase**, or an **infinitive phrase**.

<u>Encouraged by the voter turnout</u>, the candidate predicted a victory. (participial phrase)

<u>Taking it easy</u> always makes sense. (gerund phrase)

The jury recessed <u>to evaluate the evidence</u>. (infinitive phrase)

- An **absolute phrase** usually consists of a noun and a participle, accompanied by modifiers. It modifies an entire independent clause rather than a particular word or phrase.

<u>Their toes tapping</u>, they watched the auditions.

② Clauses

A **clause** is a group of related words that includes a subject and a predicate. An **independent** (main) **clause** may stand alone as a sentence, but a **dependent** (subordinate) **clause** cannot. It must always be joined to an independent clause to form a complex sentence.

[Lucretia Mott was an abolitionist]. [She was also a pioneer for women's rights]. (two independent clauses)

[Lucretia Mott was an abolitionist] [who was also a pioneer for women's rights]. (independent clause, dependent clause)

[Although Lucretia Mott was known for her support of women's rights], [she was also a prominent abolitionist]. (dependent clause, independent clause)

Dependent clauses may be *adjective, adverb,* or *noun* clauses.

- **Adjective clauses,** sometimes called **relative clauses,** modify nouns or pronouns and always follow the nouns or pronouns they modify. They are introduced by relative pronouns—*that, what, which, who,* and so forth—or by the adverbs *where* and *when.*

  Celeste's grandparents, who were born in Romania, speak little English. (Adjective clause modifies the noun *grandparents.*)

  The Pulitzer Prizes are prestigious awards that are presented for excellence in journalism. (Adjective clause modifies the noun *awards.*)

  Sophie's Choice is a novel set in Brooklyn, where the narrator lives in a pink house. (Adjective clause modifies the noun *Brooklyn.*)

- **Adverb clauses** modify verbs, adjectives, adverbs, entire phrases, or independent clauses. They are always introduced by subordinating conjunctions.

  Mark will go wherever there's a party. (Adverb clause modifies *will go,* telling *where* Mark will go.)

  Because 75 percent of its exports are fish products, Iceland's economy is heavily dependent on the fishing industry. (Adverb clause modifies independent clause, telling *why* the fishing industry is so important.)

- **Noun clauses** function as subjects, objects, or complements. A noun clause may be introduced by a relative pronoun or by *whether, when, where, why,* or *how.*

What you see is what you get. (Noun clauses are subject and subject complement.)

They wondered why it was so quiet. (Noun clause is direct object.)

To whom it may concern: (Noun clause is object of preposition.)

EXERCISE B.2

Which of the following groups of words are independent clauses? Which are dependent clauses? Which are phrases? Label each word group *IC, DC,* or *P.*

Example: Coming through the rye. (P)

1. Beauty is truth.
2. When knights were bold.
3. In a galaxy far away.
4. He saw stars.
5. I hear a symphony.
6. Whenever you're near.
7. The clock struck ten.
8. The red planet.
9. Slowly I turned.
10. For the longest time.

B4 Types of Sentences

1 Simple, Compound, Complex, and Compound-Complex Sentences

A **simple sentence** is a single independent clause. A simple sentence may consist of just a subject and a predicate.

Jessica fell.

Or, a simple sentence can be expanded with different kinds of modifying words and phrases.

On Halloween, Jessica fell hopelessly in love with the mysterious Henry Goodyear.

A **compound sentence** consists of two or more simple sentences (independent clauses) linked by a coordinating conjunction (preceded by a comma), by a semicolon (alone or with a transitional word or phrase), by correlative conjunctions, or by a colon.

       independent clause   independent clause
[The moon rose in the sky], and [the stars shone brightly].

           independent clause
[José planned to spend a quiet afternoon reading]; however,

       independent clause
[his friends dropped by unexpectedly].

A **complex sentence** consists of an independent clause along with one or more dependent clauses.

independent clause   depen dent clause
[It was hard for us to believe] [that anyone could be so cruel].

dependent clause
[Because the program had been so poorly attended in the past],
independent clause   dependent clause
[the committee wondered] [whether it should be funded this year].

A **compound-complex sentence** is a compound sentence—made up of at least two independent clauses—that also includes at least one dependent clause.

dependent clause   independent
[Because driving a cab can be so dangerous], [my mother always
clause   dependent clause   independent
worried] [when my father had to work late], and [she could rarely
clause
sleep more than a few minutes at a time].

EXERCISE B.3

After reading the following paragraph, edit it to create as many compound sentences as you think your readers need to understand the relationships between ideas. When you have finished, bracket the independent clauses and underline the coordinating conjunctions, transitional words or phrases, correlative conjunctions, and punctuation marks that link clauses.

Paolo Soleri came to the United States from Italy. He came as an apprentice to Frank Lloyd Wright. Frank Lloyd Wright's designs celebrate the suburban lifestyle, with standalone homes meant for single families. Soleri's Utopian designs celebrate the city. Soleri believed that suburban lifestyles separate people from true nature. He also believed that our lifestyle separates us from the energy of the city. His first theoretical design was called Mesa City. It proposed to house two million people. Soleri built one of his dream cities, Arcosanti, in the desert outside of Scottsdale, Arizona. This project was funded privately by Soleri. He taught design and building classes to students who helped build the city. The students' tuition helped pay for construction. He also made wind bells and chimes. He sold these all over the world. The profits further financed Arcosanti. The design for Arcosanti evokes images of colonies erected on space stations. It also resembles the hillside towns in Soleri's home country, Italy. The problems with our current city structures grow each year. People are looking for ways to revitalize the city. Some are looking at Soleri's Arcosanti as a model for sustainable urban development and renewal.

② Declarative, Interrogative, Imperative, and Exclamatory Sentences

Sentences can also be classified according to their function.

Declarative sentences, the most common type, make statements: *World War II ended in 1945.*

Interrogative sentences pose questions, usually by inverting standard subject-verb order (often with an interrogative word) or adding a form of *do: Is Maggie at home? Where is Maggie? Does Maggie live here?*

Imperative sentences express commands or requests, using the second-person singular of the verb and generally omitting the pronoun subject *you: Go to your room. Please believe me. Stop that.*

Exclamatory sentences express strong emotion and end with an exclamation point: *The genocide in Darfur must stop now!*

Glossary of Usage

This glossary of usage lists words and phrases that writers often find troublesome and explains how they are used.

a, an Use *a* before words that begin with consonants and words with initial vowels that sound like consonants: *a* person, *a* historical document, *a* one-horse carriage, *a* uniform. Use *an* before words that begin with vowels and words that begin with a silent *h*: *an* artist, *an* honest person.

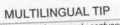

MULTILINGUAL TIP

For a list of commonly confused words that present particular challenges for multilingual writers, see **61g**.

accept, except *Accept* is a verb that means "to receive"; *except* as a preposition or conjunction means "other than" and as a verb means "to leave out": The auditors will *accept* all your claims *except* the last two. Some businesses are *excepted* from the regulation.

advice, advise *Advice* is a noun meaning "opinion or information offered"; *advise* is a verb that means "to offer advice to": The broker *advised* her client to take his attorney's *advice*.

affect, effect *Affect* is a verb meaning "to influence"; *effect* can be a verb or a noun—as a verb it means "to bring about," and as a noun it means "result": We know how the drug *affects* patients immediately, but little is known of its long-term *effects*. The arbitrator tried to *effect* a settlement between the parties.

all ready, already *All ready* means "completely prepared"; *already* means "by or before this or that time": I was *all ready* to help, but it was *already* too late.

all right, alright Although the use of *alright* is increasing, current usage calls for *all right*.

allusion, illusion An *allusion* is a reference or hint; an *illusion* is something that is not what it seems: The poem makes an *allusion* to the Pandora myth. The shadow created an optical *illusion*.

a lot *A lot* is always two words.

among, between *Among* refers to groups of more than two things; *between* refers to just two things: The three parties agreed *among* themselves to settle the case. There will be a brief intermission *between* the two acts. (Note that *amongst* is British, not American, usage.)

amount, number *Amount* refers to a quantity that cannot be counted; *number* refers to things that can be counted: Even a small *amount* of caffeine can be harmful. Seeing their commander fall, a large *number* of troops ran to his aid.

an, a See **a, an**.

and/or In business or technical writing, use *and/or* when either or both of the items it connects can apply. In college writing, however, avoid the use of *and/or*.

as, like *As* can be used as a conjunction (to introduce a complete clause) or as a preposition; *like* should be used as a preposition only: In *The Scarlet Letter*, Hawthorne uses imagery *as* (not *like*) he does in his other works. After classes, Fred works *as* a manager of a fast food restaurant. Writers *like* Carl Sandburg appear once in a generation.

at, to Many people use the prepositions *at* and *to* after *where* in conversation: *Where* are you working *at*? Where are you going *to*? This usage is redundant and should not appear in college writing.

awhile, a while *Awhile* is an adverb; *a while*, which consists of an article and a noun, is used as the object of a preposition: Before we continue, we will rest *awhile* (modifies the verb *rest*). Before we continue, we will rest for *a while* (object of the preposition *for*).

bad, badly *Bad* is an adjective, and *badly* is an adverb: The school board decided that *Adventures of Huckleberry Finn* was a *bad* book. American automobile makers did not do *badly* this year. After verbs that refer to any of the senses or after any other linking verb, use the adjective form: He looked *bad*. He felt *bad*. It seemed *bad*.

being as, being that These awkward phrases add unnecessary words, thereby weakening your writing. Use *because* instead.

beside, besides *Beside* is a preposition meaning "next to"; *besides* can be either a preposition meaning "except" or "other than" or an adverb meaning "as well": *Beside* the tower was a wall that ran the length of the city. *Besides* its industrial uses, laser technology has many other applications. Edison invented not only the lightbulb but the phonograph *besides*.

between, among See **among, between**.

bring, take *Bring* means "to transport from a farther place to a nearer place"; *take* means "to carry or convey from a nearer place to a farther place": *Bring* me a souvenir from your trip. *Take* this message to the general, and wait for a reply.

can, may *Can* denotes ability; *may* indicates permission: If you *can* play, you *may* use my piano.

cite, site *Cite* is a verb meaning "to quote as an authority or example"; *site* is a noun meaning "a place or setting"; it is also a shortened form of *website*: Jeff *cited* five sources in his research paper. The builder cleared the *site* for the new bank. Marisa uploaded her *site* to the web.

climactic, climatic *Climactic* means "of or related to a climax"; *climatic* means "of or related to climate": The *climactic* moment of the movie occurred unexpectedly. If scientists are correct, the *climatic* conditions of Earth are changing.

complement, compliment *Complement* means "to complete or add to"; *compliment* means "to give praise": A double-blind study would *complement* their preliminary research. My instructor *complimented* me on my improvement.

conscious, conscience *Conscious* is an adjective meaning "having one's mental faculties awake"; *conscience* is a noun that means the moral sense of right and wrong: The patient will remain *conscious* during the procedure. His *conscience* would not allow him to lie.

continual, continuous *Continual* means "recurring at intervals"; *continuous* refers to an action that occurs without interruption: A pulsar is a star that emits a *continual* stream of electromagnetic radiation. (It emits radiation at regular intervals.) A small battery allows the watch to run *continuously* for five years. (It runs without stopping.)

could of, should of, would of The contractions *could've*, *should've*, and *would've* are often misspelled as the nonstandard constructions *could of, should of,* and *would of.* Use *could have, should have,* and *would have* in college writing.

couple, couple of *Couple* means "a pair," but *couple of* is often used colloquially to mean "several" or "a few." In your college writing, specify "four points" or "two examples" rather than using "a couple of."

criterion, criteria *Criteria*, from the Greek, is the plural of *criterion*, meaning "standard for judgment": Of all the *criteria* for hiring graduating seniors, class rank is the most important *criterion*.

data *Data* is the plural of the Latin *datum*, meaning "fact." In colloquial speech and writing, *data* is often used as the singular as well as the plural form. In college writing, use *data* only for the plural: The *data* discussed in this section *are* summarized in Appendix A.

different from, different than *Different than* is widely used in American speech. In college writing, use *different from.*

disinterested, uninterested *Disinterested* means "objective" or "capable of making an impartial judgment"; *uninterested* means "indifferent or unconcerned": The American judicial system depends on *disinterested* jurors. Finding no treasure, Hernando de Soto was *uninterested* in going farther.

don't, doesn't *Don't* is the contraction of *do not; doesn't* is the contraction of *does not.* Do not confuse the two: My dog *doesn't* (not *don't*) like to walk in the rain. (Note that contractions are generally not acceptable in college writing.)

economic, economical *Economic* refers to the economy—to the production, distribution, and consumption of goods. *Economical* means "avoiding waste" or "careful use of resources": There was strong *economic* growth this quarter. It is *economical* to have roommates in this city.

effect, affect   See **affect, effect**.

e.g.   *E.g.* is an abbreviation for the Latin *exempli gratia*, meaning "for example" or "for instance." In college writing, do not use *e.g.* Instead, use *for example* or *for instance.*

emigrate from, immigrate to   To *emigrate* is "to leave one's country and settle in another"; to *immigrate* is "to come to another country and reside there." The noun forms of these words are *emigrant* and *immigrant*: My great-grandfather *emigrated from* Warsaw along with many other *emigrants* from Poland. Many people *immigrate to* the United States for economic reasons, but *immigrants* still face great challenges.

eminent, imminent   *Eminent* is an adjective meaning "standing above others" or "prominent"; *imminent* means "about to occur": Oliver Wendell Holmes Jr. was an *eminent* jurist. In ancient times, a comet signaled *imminent* disaster.

enthused   *Enthused*, a colloquial form of *enthusiastic*, should not be used in college writing.

etc.   *Etc.*, the abbreviation of *et cetera*, means "and the rest." Do not use it in your college writing. Instead, use *and so on*—or, better yet, specify what *etc.* stands for.

everyday, every day   *Everyday* is an adjective that means "ordinary" or "commonplace"; *every day* means "occurring daily": In the Gettysburg Address, Lincoln used *everyday* language. She exercises almost *every day.*

everyone, every one   *Everyone* is an indefinite pronoun meaning "every person"; *every one* means "every individual or thing in a particular group": *Everyone* seems happier in the spring. *Every one* of the packages had been opened.

except, accept   See **accept, except**.

explicit, implicit   *Explicit* means "expressed or stated directly"; *implicit* means "implied" or "expressed or stated indirectly": The director *explicitly* warned the actors to be on time for rehearsals. Her *implicit* message was that lateness would not be tolerated.

farther, further   *Farther* designates distance; *further* designates degree: I have traveled *farther* from home than any of my relatives. Critics charge that welfare subsidies encourage *further* dependence.

fewer, less   Use *fewer* with nouns that can be counted: *fewer* books, *fewer* people, *fewer* dollars. Use *less* with quantities that cannot be counted: *less* pain, *less* power, *less* enthusiasm.

firstly (secondly, thirdly, . . .)   Archaic forms meaning "in the first place," "in the second place," "in the third place," and so on. Use *first, second, third*, and so on instead.

further, farther   See **farther, further**.

good, well   *Good* is an adjective, never an adverb: She is a *good* swimmer. *Well* can function as an adverb or as an adjective. As an adverb, it means "in a good manner": She swam *well* (not *good*) in the meet. *Well* is used as an adjective meaning "in good health" with verbs that denote a state of being or feeling: I feel *well*.

got to   *Got to* is not acceptable in college writing. To indicate obligation, use *have to, has to,* or *must.*

hanged, hung   Both *hanged* and *hung* are past participles of *hang. Hanged* is used to refer to executions; *hung* is used to mean "suspended": Billy Budd was *hanged* for killing the master-at-arms. The stockings were *hung* by the chimney with care.

he, she   Traditionally, *he* has been used in the generic sense to refer to both males and females. To acknowledge the equality of the sexes, however, avoid the generic *he.* Use plural pronouns whenever possible. **See 39e2.**

historic, historical   *Historic* means "important" or "momentous"; *historical* means "relating to the past" or "based on or inspired by history": The end of World War II was a *historic* occasion. *Historical* records show that Quakers played an important part in the abolition of slavery.

hopefully   The adverb *hopefully,* meaning "in a hopeful manner," should modify a verb, an adjective, or another adverb. Do not use *hopefully* as a sentence modifier meaning "it is hoped." Rather than "*Hopefully,* scientists will soon discover a cure for AIDS," write "*People hope* scientists will soon discover a cure for AIDS."

i.e.   *I.e.* is an abbreviation for the Latin *id est,* meaning "that is." In college writing, do not use *i.e.* Instead, use its English equivalent.

if, whether   When asking indirect questions or expressing doubt, use *whether*: He asked *whether* (not *if*) the flight would be delayed. The flight attendant was not sure *whether* (not *if*) it would be delayed.

illusion, allusion   See **allusion, illusion.**

immigrate to, emigrate from   See **emigrate from, immigrate to.**

implicit, explicit   See **explicit, implicit.**

imply, infer   *Imply* means "to hint" or "to suggest"; *infer* means "to conclude from": Mark Antony *implied* that the conspirators had murdered Caesar. The crowd *inferred* his meaning and called for justice.

infer, imply   See **imply, infer.**

irregardless, regardless   *Irregardless* is a nonstandard version of *regardless.* Use *regardless* or *irrespective* instead.

is when, is where   These constructions are faulty when they appear in definitions: A playoff is (not *is when* or *is where*) an additional game played to establish the winner of a tie.

its, it's   *Its* is a possessive pronoun; *it's* is a contraction of *it is*: *It's* no secret that the bank is out to protect *its* assets.

kind of, sort of   The use of *kind of* and *sort of* to mean "rather" or "somewhat" is colloquial. These expressions should not appear in college writing: It is well known that Napoleon was rather (not *kind of*) short.

lay, lie   See **lie, lay**.

leave, let   *Leave* means "to go away from" or "to let remain"; *let* means "to allow" or "to permit": *Let* (not *leave*) me give you a hand.

less, fewer   See **fewer, less**.

let, leave   See **leave, let**.

lie, lay   *Lie* is an intransitive verb (one that does not take an object) meaning "to recline." Its principal forms are *lie, lay, lain, lying*: Each afternoon she would *lie* in the sun and listen to the surf. *As I Lay Dying* is a novel by William Faulkner. By 1871, Troy had *lain* undisturbed for two thousand years. The painting shows a nude *lying* on a couch.

   Lay is a transitive verb (one that takes an object) meaning "to put" or "to place." Its principal forms are *lay, laid, laid, laying*: The Federalist Papers *lay* the foundation for American conservatism. In October 1781, the British *laid* down their arms and surrendered. He had *laid* his money on the counter before leaving. We watched the stonemasons *laying* a wall.

life, lifestyle   *Life* is the span of time that a living thing exists; *lifestyle* is a way of living that reflects a person's values or attitudes: Before he was hanged, Nathan Hale said, "I only regret that I have but one *life* to lose for my country." The writer Virginia Woolf was known for her unconventional *lifestyle*.

like, as   See **as, like**.

loose, lose   *Loose* is an adjective meaning "not rigidly fastened or securely attached"; *lose* is a verb meaning "to misplace": The marble facing of the building became *loose* and fell to the sidewalk. After only two drinks, most people *lose* their ability to judge distance.

lots, lots of, a lot of   These words are colloquial substitutes for *many, much*, or *a great deal of*. Avoid their use in college writing: The students had *many* (not *lots of* or *a lot of*) options for essay topics.

man   Like the generic pronoun *he, man* has been used in English to denote members of both sexes. This usage is being replaced by *human beings, people*, and similar terms that do not specify gender. **See 39e2**.

may, can   See **can, may**.

may be, maybe   *May be* is a verb phrase; *maybe* is an adverb meaning "perhaps": She *may be* the smartest student in the class. *Maybe* her experience has given her an advantage.

media, medium   *Medium*, meaning "a means of conveying or broadcasting something," is singular; *media* is the plural form and requires a plural verb: The *media have* distorted the issue.

might have, might of   *Might of* is a nonstandard spelling of the contraction of *might have* (*might've*). Use *might have* in college writing.

number, amount   See **amount, number.**

OK, O.K., okay   All three spellings are acceptable, but this term should be avoided in college writing. Replace it with a more specific word or words: The lecture was *adequate* (not *okay*), if uninspiring.

passed, past   *Passed* is the past tense of the verb *pass*; *past* means "belonging to a former time" or "no longer current": The car must have been going eighty miles per hour when it *passed* us. In the envelope was a bill marked *past* due.

percent, percentage   *Percent* indicates a part of a hundred when a specific number is referred to: "*10 percent* of his salary." *Percentage* is used when no specific number is referred to: "a *percentage* of next year's receipts." In technical and business writing, it is permissible to use the % sign after percentages you are comparing. Write out the word *percent* in college writing.

plus   As a preposition, *plus* means "in addition to." Avoid using *plus* as a substitute for *and*: Include the principal, *plus* the interest, in your calculations. Your quote was too high; *moreover* (not *plus*), it was inaccurate.

precede, proceed   *Precede* means "to go or come before"; *proceed* means "to go forward in an orderly way": Robert Frost's *North of Boston* was *preceded* by an earlier volume. In 1532, Francisco Pizarro landed at Tumbes and *proceeded* south.

principal, principle   As a noun, *principal* means "a sum of money (minus interest) invested or lent" or "a person in the leading position"; as an adjective, it means "most important"; a *principle* is a noun meaning a rule of conduct or a basic truth: He wanted to reduce the *principal* of the loan. The *principal* of the high school is a talented administrator. Women are the *principal* wage earners in many American households. The Constitution embodies certain fundamental *principles*.

quote, quotation   *Quote* is a verb. *Quotation* is a noun. In college writing, do not use *quote* as a shortened form of *quotation*: Scholars attribute these *quotations* (not *quotes*) to Shakespeare.

raise, rise   *Raise* is a transitive verb, and *rise* is an intransitive verb—that is, *raise* takes an object, and *rise* does not: My grandparents *raised* a large family. The sun will *rise* at 6:12 tomorrow morning.

real, really   *Real* means "genuine" or "authentic"; *really* means "actually." In college writing, do not use *real* as an adjective meaning "very."

reason is that, reason is because   *Reason* should be used with *that* and not with *because*, which is redundant: The *reason* he left is *that* (not *because*) you insulted him.

regardless, irregardless   See **irregardless, regardless.**

rise, raise   See **raise, rise.**

set, sit *Set* means "to put down" or "to lay." Its principal forms are *set*, and *setting*: After rocking the baby to sleep, he *set* her down carefully in her crib. After *setting* her down, he took a nap.

Sit means "to assume a sitting position." Its principal forms are *sit, sat*, and *sitting*: Many children *sit* in front of the television five to six hours a day. The dog *sat* by the fire. We were *sitting* in the airport when the flight was canceled.

shall, will *Will* has all but replaced *shall* to express all future action.

should of See **could of, should of, would of**.

simple, simplistic *Simple* means "plain, ordinary, or uncomplicated"; *simplistic* means "overly or misleadingly simplified": Because she had studied, Tanya thought the test was *simple*. His explanation of how the Internet works is *simplistic*.

since Do not use *since* for *because* if there is any chance of confusion. In the sentence "*Since* President Nixon traveled to China, trade between China and the United States has increased," *since* could mean either "from the time that" or "because." To be clear, use *because*.

sit, set See **set, sit**.

so Avoid using *so* as a vague intensifier meaning "very" or "extremely." Follow *so* with *that* and a clause that describes the result: She was *so* pleased with their work *that* she took them out to lunch.

sometime, sometimes, some time *Sometime* means "at some time in the future"; *sometimes* means "now and then"; *some time* means "a period of time": The president will address Congress *sometime* next week. All automobiles, no matter how reliable, *sometimes* need repairs. It has been *some time* since I read that book.

sort of, kind of See **kind of, sort of**.

supposed to, used to *Supposed to* and *used to* are often misspelled. Both verbs require the final *d* to indicate past tense.

take, bring See **bring, take**.

than, then *Than* is a conjunction used to indicate a comparison; *then* is an adverb indicating time: The new shopping center is bigger *than* the old one. He did his research; *then*, he wrote a report.

that, which, who Use *that* or *which* when referring to a thing; use *who* when referring to a person: It was a speech *that* inspired many. The movie, *which* was a huge success, failed to impress her. Anyone *who* (not *that*) takes the course will benefit.

their, there, they're *Their* is a possessive pronoun; *there* indicates place and is also used in the expressions *there is* and *there are*; *they're* is a contraction of *they are*: Watson and Crick did *their* DNA work at Cambridge University. I love Los Angeles, but I wouldn't want to live *there*. *There* is nothing we can do to resurrect an extinct species. When *they're* well treated, rabbits make excellent pets.

themselves, theirselves, theirself   *Theirselves* and *theirself* are nonstandard variants of *themselves.*

then, than   See **than, then.**

till, until, 'til   *Till* and *until* have the same meaning, and both are acceptable. *Until* is preferred in college writing. *'Til,* a contraction of *until,* should be avoided.

to, at   See **at, to.**

to, too, two   *To* is a preposition that indicates direction; *too* is an adverb that means "also" or "more than is needed"; *two* expresses the number 2: Last year we flew from New York *to* California. "Tippecanoe and Tyler, *too*" was William Henry Harrison's campaign slogan. The plot was *too* complicated for the average reader. Just north of *Two* Rivers, Wisconsin, is a petrified forest.

try to, try and   *Try and* is the colloquial equivalent of the more formal *try to*: He decided to *try to* (not *try and*) do better. In college writing, use *try to.*

-type   Deleting this empty suffix eliminates clutter and clarifies meaning: Found in the wreckage was an incendiary (not *incendiary-type*) device.

uninterested, disinterested   See **disinterested, uninterested.**

unique   Because *unique* means "the only one," not "remarkable" or "unusual," never use constructions such as *the most unique* or *very unique.*

until   See **till, until, 'til.**

used to   See **supposed to, used to.**

utilize   In most cases, replace *utilize* with *use* (*utilize* often sounds pretentious).

wait for, wait on   To *wait for* means "to defer action until something occurs." To *wait on* means "to act as a waiter": I am *waiting for* (not *on*) dinner.

weather, whether   *Weather* is a noun meaning "the state of the atmosphere"; *whether* is a conjunction used to introduce an alternative: The *weather* will improve this weekend. It is doubtful *whether* we will be able to ski tomorrow.

well, good   See **good, well.**

were, we're   *Were* is a verb; *we're* is the contraction of *we are*: The Trojans *were* asleep when the Greeks attacked. We must act now if *we're* going to succeed.

whether, if   See **if, whether.**

which, who, that   See **that, which, who.**

who, whom   When a pronoun serves as the subject of its clause, use *who* or *whoever*; when it functions in a clause as an object, use *whom* or *whomever*: Sarah, *who* is studying ancient civilizations, would like to visit Greece. Sarah, *whom* I met in France, wants me to travel to Greece with her. **See 41b2.**

who's, whose   *Who's* means "who is" or "who has"; *whose* indicates possession: *Who's* going to take calculus? *Who's* already left for the concert? The writer *whose* book was in the window was autographing copies.

will, shall   See **shall, will**.

would of   See **could of, should of, would of**.

your, you're   *Your* indicates possession; *you're* is the contraction of *you are*: You can improve *your* stamina by jogging two miles a day. *You're* certain to be the winner.

Text

p. 3–4: ARIA: MEMOIRS OF A BILINGUAL CHILDHOOD by Richard Rodriguez. Copyright (c) 1980 by Richard Rodriguez. Originally appeared in *The American Scholar*. Reprinted by permission of Georges Borchardt, Inc., on behalf of the author.

p. 5: Alexander Petrunkevitch, "The Spider and the Wasp."

p. 5: Richard D. Lamm, "English Comes First," The *New York Times*, July 1, 1986.

p. 19: Bar graph from student paper.

p. 19: Table from student paper.

p. 90, 91: Landrum, Hood, and McAdams, (744).

p. 103: Texas A&M Transportation Institute (Dec. 2012): 6

p. 108: Salary chart 1 from the CPIT Maths2Go online tutorial.

p. 108: Salary chart 2 from the CPIT Maths2Go online tutorial.

p. 119: http://firstmonday.org/ojs/index.php/fm/article/view/4823/4162.

p. 120: *Vanderbilt Journal of Entertainment & Technology Law* 16.4 (2014): 857

p. 166: From "Freedom of Hate Speech?" by Phil Sudo. Published in SCHOLASTIC UPDATE, June 3, 1992. Copyright © 1992 by Scholastic Inc. Reprinted by permission.

p. 168–69: Turkle, Sherry. *The Second Self: Computers and the Human Spirit.*

p. 184: Conkling, John A. "Pyrotechnics."

p. 185: Howe, Irving. "The Value of the Canon."

p. 205: © College Composition and Communication/National Council of Teachers of English.

p. 215: Source: https://ebscohost.com.

p. 229: *Vanderbilt Journal of Entertainment & Technology Law* 16.4 (2014): 886

p. 230: *Vanderbilt Journal of Entertainment & Technology Law* 16.4 (2014): 887

p. 307: [cited 2011 Mar 11]. Available from: http://www.cru.uea.ac.uk/cru/data/temperature.

p. 329: Created by Karen Mauk.

p. 331: (c) US Department of Education.

p. 331: Diagram (c) Lyric Opera of Waco.

p. 406: Created by Karen Mauk.

p. 421: © Cengage Learning.

p. 431–32: ARIA: MEMOIRS OF A BILINGUAL CHILDHOOD by Richard Rodriguez. Copyright (c) 1980 by Richard Rodriguez. Originally appeared in *The American Scholar*. Reprinted by permission of Georges Borchardt, Inc., on behalf of the author.

p. 432: Rachel Carson, "The Obligation to Endure," *Silent Spring*.

p. 434–35: Norman Mackenzie, *The Escape from Elba*.

p. 440: Annie Dillard, "In the Jungle."

p. 440–41: Jonathan Kozol, *Illiterate America*.

p. 441: Anthony Lewis, *Gideon's Trumpet*.

p. 442: Benjamin Spock, *Baby and Child Care*.

p. 442–43: Garrett Hongo, "Kubota."

p. 443: J. William Fulbright, *The Arrogance of Power*.

p. 444: Merrill Markoe, "Men, Women, and Conversation."

p. 444–45: Morton Hunt, *New York Times Magazine*.

p. 445: *Smithsonian*.

p. 446: Isaac Asimov, "The Case against Man."

p. 447: Mary Gordon, "Mary Cassatt."

p. 447: Irving Howe, "The Value of the Canon."

p. 447: (student writer)

p. 449: Ellen Mansoor Collier, "I Am Not a Terrorist."

p. 449: John Pheiffer, "Seeking Peace, Making War"

p. 449: From the *New York Times*, October 31, 1999. Reprinted by permission of Janklow & Nesbit, on behalf of the author.

p. 449–50: Peshe Kuriloff, "If John Dewey Were Alive Today, He'd Be a Webhead."

p. 459: Rebecca Hill, *Blue Rise*.

p. 460: George Orwell, "Shooting an Elephant."

p. 460: ARIA: MEMOIRS OF A BILINGUAL CHILDHOOD by Richard Rodriguez. Copyright (c) 1980 by Richard Rodriguez. Originally appeared in *The American Scholar*. Reprinted by permission of Georges Borchardt, Inc., on behalf of the author.

Index

Note: Page numbers in blue type indicate definitions.

Contents